Child Development

The Library of Essays in Child Welfare and Development
Series Editor: Michael Little

Titles in the Series:

1. Child Development
Barbara Maughan and Michael Little

2. Defining and Classifying Children in Need
Nick Axford

3. The Law and Child Development
Emily Buss and Mavis Maclean

4. Children in State Care
Mark Courtney and June Thoburn

5. Effective Interventions for Children in Need
Michael Little and Barbara Maughan

6. Children's Services in the Developing World
Dwan Kaoukji and Najat M'Jid

7 DAY

Child Development

Edited by

Barbara Maughan

University of London, UK

and

Michael Little

Social Research Unit, Dartington, UK

University of Chicago, USA

ASHGATE

Published by
Ashgate Publishing Limited
Wey Court East
Union Road
Farnham
Surrey GU9 7PT
England

Ashgate Publishing Company
Suite 420
101 Cherry Street
Burlington, VT 05401-4405
USA

Ashgate website: http://www.ashgate.com

British Library Cataloguing in Publication Data
Child development.– (The library of essays in child
  welfare and development)
  1. Child development.
  I. Series II. Maughan, Barbara, 1946– III. Little, Michael,
  1958–
  305.2'31–dc22

Library of Congress Control Number: 2009925015

ISBN: 978-07546-2883-5

Mixed Sources
Product group from well-managed
forests and other controlled sources
www.fsc.org Cert no. SGS-COC-2482
© 1996 Forest Stewardship Council
FSC

Printed and bound in Great Britain by
TJ International Ltd, Padstow, Cornwall

Contents

Acknowledgements   vi
Series Preface   ix
Introduction   xi

PART I   KEY CONCEPTS IN DEVELOPMENTAL RESEARCH

  1 Mary D. Salter Ainsworth and John Bowlby (1991), 'An Ethological Approach to
     Personality Development', *American Psychologist*, **46**, pp. 333–41.   5
  2 Michael Rutter, Thomas G. O'Connor and the English and Romanian Adoptees
     (ERA) Study Team (2004) 'Are There Biological Programming Effects for
     Psychological Development? Findings From a Study of Romanian Adoptees',
     Developmental Psychology, **40**, pp. 81–94.   17
  3 George C. Patton and Russell Viner (2007), 'Pubertal Transitions in Health',
     The Lancet, **369**, pp. 1130–39.   33
  4 Glen H. Elder, Jr. (1998), 'The Life Course as Developmental Theory', *Child
     Development*, **69**, pp. 1–12.   45
  5 Michael Rutter (2006), 'Implications of Resilience Concepts for Scientific
     Understanding', *Annals of the New York Academy of Sciences*, **1094**, pp. 1–12.   59

PART II   INFLUENCES ON DEVELOPMENT

  6 Michael Rutter (2007), 'Gene–Environment Interdependence', *Developmental
     Science*, **10**, pp. 12–18.   73
  7 Sandra Scarr and Kathleen McCartney (1983), 'How People Make Their Own
     Environments: a Theory of Genotype → Environment Effects', *Child Development*,
     54, pp. 424–35.   81
  8 Kenneth S. Kendler and Jessica H. Baker (2007), 'Genetic Influences on Measures
     of the Environment: A Systematic Review', *Psychological Medicine*, **37**, pp. 615–26.   93
  9 Frances A. Champagne and James P. Curley (2005), 'How Social Experiences
     Influence the Brain', *Current Opinion in Neurobiology*, **15**, pp. 704–709.   105
 10 Laurence Steinberg (2005), 'Cognitive and Affective Development in
     Adolescence', *Trends in Cognitive Sciences*, **9**, pp. 69–74.   111
 11 J. Douglas Bremner (1999), 'Does Stress Damage the Brain?', *Biological
     Psychiatry*, **45**, pp. 797–805.   117
 12 Barbara Maughan (2009), 'The Influence of Family, School, and the Environment',
     in M. Gelder (ed.), *New Oxford Textbook of Psychiatry*, Oxford: Oxford University
     Press, pp. 1724–28.   127
 13 Ann S. Masten and Anne Shaffer (2006), 'How Families Matter in Child
     Development: Reflections from Research on Risk and Resilience', in
     A. Clarke-Stewart and J. Dunn (eds), *Families Count: Effects on Child and
     Adolescent Development*, Cambridge: Cambridge University Press, pp. 5–26.   133

14   Robert H. Bradley and Robert F. Corwyn (2002), 'Socioeconomic Status and Child
     Development', *Annual Review of Psychology*, **53**, pp. 371–99.   155
15   Karl L. Alexander, Doris R. Entwisle and Linda Steffel Olson (2007), 'Lasting
     Consequences of the Summer Learning Gap', *American Sociological Review*, **72**,
     pp. 167–80.   185
16   Rebecca Shiner and Avshalom Caspi (2003), 'Personality Differences in Childhood
     and Adulthood: Measurement, Development, and Consequences', *Journal of Child
     Psychology and Psychiatry*, **44**, pp 2–32.   199

PART III IMPAIRMENT AND DISORDER

17   E. Jane Costello, Helen Egger and Adrian Angold (2005), '10-year Research
     Update Review: The Epidemiology of Child and Adolescent Psychiatric Disorders:
     I. Methods and Public Health Burden', *Journal of the American Academy of Child
     and Adolescent Psychiatry*, **44**, pp. 972–86.   233
18   E. Jane Costello, Debra L. Foley and Adrian Angold (2006), '10-year Research
     Update Review: The Epidemiology of Child and Adolescent Psychiatric Disorders:
     II. Developmental Epidemiology', *Journal of the American Academy of Child and
     Adolescent Psychiatry*, **45**, pp. 8–25.   249
19   Andrew Pickles and Adrian Angold (2003), 'Natural Categories or Fundamental
     Dimensions: On Carving Nature at the Joints and the Rearticulation of
     Psychopathology', *Development and Psychopathology*, **15**, pp. 529–51.   267
20   Tamsin Ford, Robert Goodman and Howard Meltzer (2003), 'The British Child
     and Adolescent Mental Health Survey 1999: The Prevalence of *DSM-IV* Disorders',
     Journal of the American Academy of Child and Adolescent Psychiatry, **42**,
     pp. 1203–11.   291
21   Tamsin Ford, Panos Vostanis, Howard Meltzer and Robert Goodman (2007),
     'Psychiatric Disorder among British Children Looked after by Local Authorities:
     Comparison with Children Living in Private Households, *British Journal of
     Psychiatry*, **190**, pp. 319–25.   301
22   Adrian Angold, E. Jane Costello and Alaattin Erkanli (1999) 'Comorbidity',
     Journal of Child Psychology and Psychiatry and Allied Disciplines, **40**, pp. 57–8.   309
23   Stephan Collishaw, Barbara Maughan, Robert Goodman and Andrew Pickles
     (2004), 'Time Trends in Adolescent Mental Health', *Journal of Child Psychology
     and Psychiatry*, **45**, pp. 1350–62.   341
24   Nouchka T. Tick, Jan van der Ende and Frank C. Verhulst (2007), 'Twenty-Year
     Trends in Emotional and Behavioral Problems in Dutch Children in a Changing
     Society', *Acta Psychiatrica Scandinavica*, **116**, pp. 473–82.   355
25   Thomas M. Achenbach, Levent Dumenci and Leslie A. Rescorla (2003), 'Are
     American Children's Problems Still Getting Worse? A 23-year Comparison',
     Journal of Abnormal Child Psychology, **31**, pp. 1–11.   365

Index   377

Acknowledgements

The editor and publishers wish to thank the following for permission to use copyright material.

American Psychological Association for the essays: Mary D. Salter Ainsworth and John Bowlby (1991), 'An Ethological Approach to Personality Development', *American Psychologist*, **46**, pp. 333–41. Copyright © 1991 American Psychological Association; Michael Rutter, Thomas G. O'Connor and the English and Romanian Adoptees (ERA) Study Team (2004) 'Are There Biological Programming Effects for Psychological Development? Findings From a Study of Romanian Adoptees', *Developmental Psychology*, **40**, pp. 81–94. Copyright © 2004 American Psychological Association.

American Sociological Association for the essay: Karl L. Alexander, Doris R. Entwisle and Linda Steffel Olson (2007), 'Lasting Consequences of the Summer Learning Gap', *American Sociological Review*, **72**, pp. 167–80. Copyright © 2007 American Sociological Association.

Annual Reviews for the essay: Robert H. Bradley and Robert F. Corwyn (2002), 'Socioeconomic Status and Child Development', *Annual Review of Psychology*, **53**, pp. 371–99. Copyright © 2002 Annual Reviews.

Cambridge University Press for the essays: Kenneth S. Kendler and Jessica H. Baker (2007), 'Genetic Influences on Measures of the Environment: A Systematic Review', *Psychological Medicine*, **37**, pp. 615–26. Copyright © 2007 Cambridge University Press; Ann S. Masten and Anne Shaffer (2006), 'How Families Matter in Child Development: Reflections from Research on Risk and Resilience', in A. Clarke-Stewart and J. Dunn (eds), *Families Count: Effects on Child and Adolescent Development*, Cambridge: Cambridge University Press, pp. 5–26. Copyright © 2006 Cambridge University Press; Andrew Pickles and Adrian Angold (2003), 'Natural Categories or Fundamental Dimensions: On Carving Nature at the Joints and the Rearticulation of Psychopathology', *Development and Psychopathology*, **15**, pp. 529–51. Copyright © 2003 Cambridge University Press.

Elsevier for the essays: George C. Patton and Russell Viner (2007), 'Pubertal Transitions in Health', *The Lancet*, **369**, pp. 1130–39. Copyright © 2007 Elsevier; Frances A. Champagne and James P. Curley (2005), 'How Social Experiences Influence the Brain', *Current Opinion in Neurobiology*, **15**, pp. 704–709. Copyright 2005 Elsevier; Laurence Steinberg (2005), 'Cognitive and Affective Development in Adolescence', *Trends in Cognitive Sciences*, **9**, pp. 69–74. Copyright © 2005 Elsevier; J. Douglas Bremner (1999), 'Does Stress Damage the Brain?', *Biological Psychiatry*, **45**, pp. 797–805. Copyright © 1999 Elsevier.

John Wiley and Sons for the essays: Glen H. Elder, Jr. (1998), 'The Life Course as Developmental Theory', *Child Development*, **69**, pp. 1–12. Copyright © John Wiley and Sons;

Series Preface

This series of books crosses rarely traversed academic and disciplinary boundaries. There are many experts in child development, but few who understand the law or the provision of effective interventions. Few leading thinkers on the law bother much with questions of child development, or the way the law is put into practice by children's services. Those that pioneer prevention generally know little about safety nets to catch the impoverished whose impairments are so significant that the state becomes the parent. Most of the writing and thinking on these subjects comes from Europe, North America and Australasia, ignoring the development of the majority of children who live in what is now called the economic South.

This series of books brings together thinking from across these fields of interest. In so doing, it provides an ecology of evidence on how the state responds to children, effectively and ineffectively.

The starting point is the volume by Barbara Maughan and Michael Little, *Child Development*. In the last quarter of a century understanding about the causes and consequences of impairments to children's health and development has transformed. More is known about the relative contribution of genetics and the environment. The way in which the brain re-wires itself at critical points in a child's development is now clearer. The interplay of environmental influences such as poverty, neighbourhood and family with the individual characteristics of the child is beginning to come into view.

There is a considerable distance, however, between knowing why problems occur and doing something about them. There are other influences on society's response such as the relative merits of children's and parents' rights, the relationship between state and parent in deciding what should be done, as well as questions of resource and priority. Nick Axford's volume *Defining and Classifying Children in Need* explains the benefits of a single theoretical framework for dealing with these and other questions.

This theme is taken forward by Emily Buss and Mavis Maclean in their volume *The Law and Child Development*. They helpfully contrast the situation in the US and the UK explaining how the former has placed greater emphasis on the parents' and children's rights to autonomy, while the latter has made more progress in articulating and protecting children's needs.

The hinterland between these worlds is state care for extremely poor children suffering significant impairments to their health and development. Here the state has to decide who is in need, and why and how to intervene. Mark Courtney and June Thoburn's volume *Children in State Care* shows how, when it is responsible, the state struggles to get right even the basic elements of child development, for example, the stability of living situations.

Michael Little and Barbara Maughan take a much more expansive and optimistic view of children's services in their volume *Effective Interventions for Children in Need*. But very little of what is known about what works, for whom, when and why – a reasonable proportion of which is summarised in their volume – is put into mainstream practice.

Is it worse still in poorer parts of the planet? As Dwan Kaoukji and Najat M'Jid demonstrate in their volume *Children's Services in the Developing World*, fortunes are mixed. Catastrophe, war and poverty produce risks that children in the economically developed world can hardly contemplate. Yet most children do not succumb to these risks, and the ability of civil society to respond to those that do often puts children's services in the economic North to shame.

As well as providing a sound body of evidence for students of child development and children's services, it is hoped this *Library of Essays in Child Welfare and Development* series will encourage the inquiring mind to exploit the potential for understanding what follows from straying across academic and disciplinary borders.

MICHAEL LITTLE
Series Editor
Chapin Hall Center for Research at the University of Chicago, USA
and Social Research Unit at Dartington, UK

Introduction

This volume forms the first in a series of readers that are each, from different perspectives, designed with one shared purpose: to highlight issues relevant to those who provide, design and evaluate services for children in need. Later volumes focus on the definition and classification of children in need, on effective strategies for intervention and on the legislative framework for service provision. Special attention is given to the needs of children in state care, and a further volume is given over to what can be learnt from attempts to better support children in what is now called the economic South, previously known as the developing world.

It is no accident that the series should start with a focus on child development. As the volume in the series by Nick Axford clearly demonstrates, the most effective classifications of children's needs depend on an understanding of children's development. Legal frameworks increasingly acknowledge children's changing capabilities and understandings, as Emily Buss and Mavis Maclean's contribution to the series shows. The most disadvantaged children taken into substitute care settings are still children whose problems generally reflect a greater combination and intensity of risks that can threaten the well-being of all children, as amply demonstrated in the volume by Mark Courtney and June Thoburn. And children in the economic South develop in exactly the same way as children in the relatively prosperous North, but they are exposed to different combinations of risks – the subject of Dwan Kaoukji and Najat M'Jid's book.

Understanding child development is, to use an often over-used and unjustified word, crucial to so many aspects of children's services. We see this argument most strongly in the volume we prepared on effective interventions where we use evidence about the potential causes of impairments to children's health and development to explain the best design and implementation of education, health, social care and youth justice services. Knowledge about the processes underlying children's health and development, and the factors that support, impede or impair it, is more often than not the bedrock of other explorations of children's lives and efforts to improve them.

Recent years have seen major transformations in our understanding of children's health and development. At one time, for example, it was assumed that very early experiences held the key to much later development, so that the study of 'child development' in effect meant the study of the first few years of life. Today, we have a much better appreciation of the ways in which development unfolds throughout the life course and the challenges and opportunities that each phase of that process presents. Though there are still huge gaps in understanding, we now know much more than in the very recent past about the ways in which genetic endowments combine with life experiences to influence children's outcomes, and how the changing architecture of the brain impacts on children's feelings and thoughts. And we have begun – though again there is still a long way to go – to accumulate systematic knowledge about the types of impairments most common at different stages in development, the factors that underlie them and the extent to which they are likely to remit or persist.

Any one of these themes could, of course, be the subject of a volume in its own right. Research in child development is a wide and rapidly expanding field, and we cannot hope to provide comprehensive or in-depth coverage of all its facets in a short collection of this kind. Instead, our aim has been to select contributions that reflect at least some of the richness of the history of the field, and of current thinking and findings, in the hope that these will act as a spur to enquiring readers to find out more. To that end, though some of the articles we have chosen are reports of individual studies, many more are overviews and commentaries that themselves bring together evidence and thinking and point the way to promising future lines of enquiry.

The volume as a whole is organized into three main parts. Part I sets the scene by highlighting some of the core concepts, frameworks and questions that have informed research on children's development across the years. Part II takes up these themes in more detail, exploring evidence on a range of more specific influences on development, both individual and environmental. And finally, in Part III, we present key findings from epidemiological studies of the levels and types of impairments to development that many children in our societies face – and that our services are designed to alleviate or prevent.

Key Concepts in Developmental Research

We begin in Chapter 1 with an historical account of the partnership between two major figures in the child development field – John Bowlby and Mary Ainsworth – that led to the development of attachment theory and research. For those involved with services for children, attachment theory is often one of the most familiar contributions of developmental research. The original impetus for the theory lay in Bowlby's concern to understand the roots of the problems displayed by 'maladjusted' children, and his sense that the theoretical models dominant when he began his career (in the 1930s and 1940s) paid too little attention to the quality of children's early experiences. Through a series of research investigations, and informed by a wide range of theoretical approaches, Bowlby developed the key tenets of attachment theory, and Mary Ainsworth developed a research paradigm that elegantly highlights the differing patterns of attachment security displayed by infants in stressful situations. As their essay reproduced here as Chapter 1 underlines, attachment theory did not – as is sometimes assumed – aim to address all aspects of personality development, and neither did it argue that all aspects of the parent–child relationship are pertinent to attachment. What it has provided, however, is an extraordinarily rich set of propositions about the effects of early attachment relationships on psychological development. These continue to be influential to the present day.

Chapter 2, by Michael Rutter and colleagues, continues on the theme of early experience, this time through the lens of a specific research study. In the early 1990s, after the fall of the Ceaușescu regime, families in many parts of the world adopted children who had spent their early lives in profoundly depriving institutions in Romania. In the UK, many of those families agreed to take part in a research study designed to explore how those early experiences, and the dramatic change in the children's environments that took place when they were adopted, influenced the pattern of their development.

As Rutter and his colleagues outline, this 'natural experiment' made it possible to investigate many issues central to developmental theory: are there sensitive periods in development and, if early adversities do carry long-term implications, how might they come about? The researchers explore three equally plausible possibilities here. First, for many children, adversity persists across development, making it difficult if not impossible to separate current impairments from their early roots. Second, early adversity might influence the ways in which individuals process experiences, influencing their subsequent expectations and behaviour. Or third, adverse early experiences might result in lasting changes in biological systems, affecting aspects of brain development and mechanisms associated with the organism's response to stress.

As we shall see, many of these themes recur in later chapters in this volume. This study of the children raised in Romanian orphanages demonstrates how research data can be used to pit contrasting but tenable accounts against one another to find not only the best explanation but also new answers. Possibly against accepted wisdom, later studies of the same sample of Romanian young people placed for adoption in the UK have highlighted both the major gains that have followed from their changed environments and also the persisting effects of some aspects of their early experience.

The next two chapters in this sequence take us forward in developmental time, first to adolescence, and second to a broad overview of development from a life course perspective. In Chapter 3 George Patton and Russell Viner focus on the effects of the major changes that puberty brings for young people's mental and physical health. As they note, puberty is marked not only by physical changes but also by psychological and emotional change.

Adolescence also sees further key changes in brain development. Evidence is accumulating that greater neural plasticity in the teenage years may make young people especially sensitive to their environments. Animal studies suggest, for example, that enrichment of the social and learning environment in adolescence may allow for the reversal of some effects of adverse early experience; conversely, however, there are also pointers that the adolescent brain may be at heightened vulnerability to the effects of stress. Though the mechanisms involved are unclear, we now know that many types of psychological difficulties and disorders become more common as young people enter their teens. The social context in which young people grow up also plays its part. As Patton and Viner argue, the social context of modern adolescence is vastly different from that at any past period of human evolutionary history. In many Western societies young people now reach biological maturity many years before they take on adult social roles; this disjunction, along with the emergence of youth culture and the associated pressures of consumerism, has had a profound effect on youth lifestyles.

The intersection of individual development and historical context is one of the key themes of Glen Elder's discussion of the life course as developmental theory in Chapter 4. Many of the insights underlying this approach derived from pioneering long-term longitudinal studies of individuals not only across childhood, but also into adulthood and older age. As Elder sets out, findings from these studies have made it abundantly clear that development varies with historical and social context, and also with the timing of key events and transitions in individuals' lives. Development continues across the life course, and we all, through the choices and the actions that we take, play an active role in constructing the shape and course of that development.

The final chapter in the opening section of the book raises issues of central concern for all those who work with children at risk: why are some children resilient in the face of adversity, while all too many succumb to its effects? In discussing the concepts of risk and resilience, Michael Rutter, in Chapter 5, highlights the differing mechanisms that may be implicated in these varying patterns of response. Some may rest within the individual, in the form of physiological or psychological coping processes; some may arise from controlled exposure to adversities that can have the effect of strengthening, rather than reducing, resistance to later stress; and some may lie in later adult experiences that offer 'turning points' out of adverse early trajectories. In discussing these issues Rutter highlights the need to explore biological as well as psychological mechanisms that contribute to risk and resilience, and the ways in which individual characteristics work together with life experiences to influence the course of development.

Influences on Development

These themes are taken up in more detail in the chapters selected to illustrate potential influences on the course of children's health and development. Decades of research have confirmed that children's well-being varies systematically not only with their own characteristics – their temperament, personality and behavioural styles – but also with the quality of their day-to-day experiences. When those experiences are good, outcomes are likely to be positive; when they are adverse, the risk of poor outcomes is greatly increased.

From a research perspective, these observations raise two central questions: first, which types of experience are most important in influencing children's development and, second, how and why do these effects occur? How, as it were, do negative experiences 'get under the skin', affecting development in sometimes quite enduring ways?

In the early years of developmental research, work on these themes was primarily devoted to the important task of identifying the *types* of experiences and contexts most strongly associated with variations in children's outcomes. Studies of this kind pointed to a series of influences, varying in terms of their 'proximity' to the child. Figure 1 (broadly styled on models proposed by the eminent developmentalist Urie Bronfenbrenner (1979)) shows a schematic version of the types of findings that emerged. With the child at its centre, the model highlights some of the key domains now known to show systematic links with aspects of children's development. At its heart is the family, including relationships with parents and styles of parenting, and – increasingly important as children grow older – the influence of friends and peers. Each of these 'proximal' influences is embedded within, and itself likely to be influenced by, a range of wider contexts: schools and neighbourhoods, communities and the broader culture, and families' social position and access to material resources.

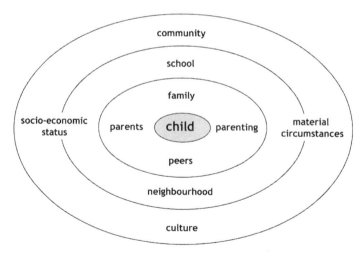

Figure 1 Ecological model of influences on development

How might these differing domains of influences have their effects? As developmental research has progressed, approaches to this question have become increasingly complex. First, researchers began to appreciate that simple one-way models of causation were inadequate. Most of us acknowledge that children will be influenced by their families – but we are apt to overlook the fact that, from the first days and months of life, children themselves also influence those around them. The fretful baby is more demanding to care for than her more placid sibling, and may evoke quite different responses from parents; the outgoing child will settle more easily in school than her shy counterpart, and may find learning easier as a result; and the rebellious teenager will seek out – and in turn be influenced by – a quite different peer group from that of his more studious contemporaries. The environments that children experience cannot simply be viewed as independent, extraneous influences on their development; to an extent, we are all agents of our own destiny.

Nature and Nurture

Insights of this kind have informed developmental thinking for many years. More recently, however, they have taken on an added impetus as genetic studies have made increasingly important contributions to developmental research. Initially concerned with demonstrating that individual characteristics show heritable influences, genetic studies have since come to cast major new light on our understanding of the environment and the ways in which nature and nurture combine to influence development. More recently still, exciting new developments in neuroscience mean that we can now begin to examine, much more directly than has ever been possible in the past, the ways in which experience impacts on the developing brain. Taken together, it is little exaggeration to say that work in these and related areas promises to revolutionize our understanding of influences on development.

Against that backdrop, the chapters in the second section of this volume have been selected to offer a brief introduction to these differing areas of research. They include now 'classic' contributions – such as Sandra Scarr and Kathleen McCartney's exposition of the ways in which genotypic differences function to 'select' individuals into different environments – alongside more recent reviews and overviews. The rapid pace of research in many of these areas means, of course, that new findings are constantly emerging. The reports we include here reflected the state of the art at the time they were written; we hope that they will encourage readers to explore more recent findings in each of these important domains.

Beginning with the question of genetic influences, recent research has clearly demonstrated that we need to move on from any simple 'nature *versus* nurture' debate; both genetic and environmental influences are important for children's development – and often they go hand in hand. Michael Rutter provides a broad road map in Chapter 6, outlining four different types of gene–environment interplays that are now well supported by empirical research. Subsequent chapters in this section discuss these in more detail.

In Chapter 7 Sandra Scarr and Kathleen McCartney focus on gene–environment correlations, highlighting the differing ways in which children's environments can come to reflect aspects of their own or their parents' genes. At first blush, the notion that environments are influenced by genes might seem implausible; Scarr and McCartney highlight a variety of ways in which this could, however, come about. The first concerns the effects of parental genes, and arises when genetically-influenced traits in parents affect the styles of parenting or the nature of the home environments they provide for their children. The broader developmental literature gives ample support for processes of this kind. We know all too well, for example, that depression can make mothers less responsive to their infants, and that anti-social parents often show harsh or erratic parenting. Because both depression and anti-social behaviour are to some extent heritable, children in such families may face a 'double whammy', inheriting genetic vulnerabilities from their parents at the same time as experiencing less than optimal rearing environments.

For service providers, findings of this kind – though they may ring true – can also at times seem dispiriting, suggesting that problematic aspects of parenting may be difficult to change. This is not, of course, in any sense an inevitable conclusion. As Kenneth Kendler and Jessica Baker demonstrate in Chapter 8, although genetic influences on the environment are pervasive, their effects are at most modest to moderate. Not only are genetic influences far from deterministic, they can be amenable to alteration by the environment. As we illustrate in our volume in this series on effective interventions, programmes to improve the parenting of adults with many different types of background difficulties can, if properly carried through, have good impact.

Among the many other issues discussed in these chapters, we highlight just one other form of gene–environment interplay here – that of interactions between children's genetic inheritance and the effects of environmental exposures. Findings in this area have begun to cast light on a puzzling conclusion that has emerged consistently from much developmental research. Even in the face of apparently severe adversities, there are marked individual differences in children's response: some children are seriously affected, while others emerge relatively unscathed. Here, insights from molecular genetic studies that focus on the effects of particular measured genes are beginning to show that genetic variations between individuals may moderate environmental effects. The first example of this kind in the behavioural field showed how the effects of exposure to adverse family circumstances on risk for anti-social outcomes varied systematically with an individual's genotype. Numerous subsequent examples have since confirmed effects of this kind: by virtue of aspects of their genetic inheritance, some children are relatively protected from the effects of adverse experiences while others are rendered more vulnerable. In the medical arena, findings of this kind are already giving clinicians the capacity to tailor the treatments they provide to the particular genetic background of their patients. Although it is only a distant promise as yet, such findings nonetheless hint that at some point in the future social interventions might also be able to be tailored to be maximally effective in similar ways.

Insights from Neuroscience

Findings from neuroscience are beginning to trace further pivotal steps in our understanding of the effects of experience on child development – in this case, effects on the structure and function of the brain. In Chapter 9 Frances Champagne and James Curley summarize findings from an elegant series of studies in animals showing how variations in early maternal care can influence offspring behaviour in ways that – through processes that affect the expression of genes – can be passed on across generations. Here, then, we see evidence that early experience impacts on gene expression in potentially profoundly important ways. As Champagne and Curley emphasize, we cannot be certain at this stage that similar processes operate in human development; in addition, effects in animal studies have been focused at particular and possibly especially sensitive early stages in development. It remains to be seen whether similar processes operate at later developmental phases.

In Chapter 10 Laurence Steinberg discusses how research about the re-wiring of the brain that is now known to occur in adolescence is beginning to cast new light on our understanding of the major behavioural changes that occur in the teenage years. Although much of the detail of his argument remains to be confirmed, Steinberg makes a persuasive case for viewing adolescence as a period of heightened vulnerability to experience because the behavioural and cognitive systems within the brain are developing at different rates. As Steinberg stresses, the key brain changes of adolescence – changes that affect in particular the development of executive and regulatory mechanisms – are now known to progress over a quite lengthy period, often extending late into the adolescent years. Yet many young people face challenging and emotionally-laden life experiences much earlier in the teens, when other biological changes associated with puberty are already well underway. As research in each of these areas progresses, and becomes increasingly integrated, it promises important further insights into the ways in which disjunctions among these differing developmental systems may increase vulnerability to environmental stress.

Chapter 11, by Douglas Bremner, provides further evidence – and raises further questions – about the ways in which exposure to stress experiences may have long-term effects on specific systems in the brain. Drawing on research on post-traumatic stress disorder in both war veterans and individuals exposed to abusive experiences in childhood, Bremner outlines findings of studies pointing to effects on both the function and the structure of brain systems central to a cascade of other stress response mechanisms. While direct evidence on brain functioning is of course complex and difficult to accumulate, key indicators of some of these downstream mechanisms – in particular, variations in cortisol levels – are relatively easy to collect, and are increasingly being incorporated into behavioural studies of development. As research in this area progresses it promises to provide increasingly specific evidence of the ways in which adverse experiences influence children's functioning.

Key Settings for Children's Development

Whatever the genetic and neurobiological influences on children's development, the environmental forces outlined in the diagram (p. xiv this volume) will also continue to play their part. There is of course an extensive literature on each element in this model, covering the child, the family, the neighbourhood, school and society. Barbara Maughan (Chapter 12) provides an overview of these influences, and Chapters 13-15 focus on specific contextual effects associated with the family, socio-economic disadvantage and the impact of schooling.

Ann Masten and Anne Shaffer, in Chapter 13, set their discussion of family influences in a risk/resilience framework, beginning with a series of models of the ways in which families could 'matter'. These models provide a valuable way of thinking about the effects of many different types of influences on children's outcomes: are they direct; are they mediated or moderated by wider influences, or perhaps by characteristics of the child; or are they transactional, influenced by, as well as influencing, the child's stage of development and typical ways of functioning? To explicate these models, Masten and Shaffer go on to outline the differing ways in which families function as adaptive contexts for development, and also as sources of risk and threat. As they argue, understanding of each of these types of family influences, both positive and negative, is crucial for the development of interventions to promote child well-being and offset potential sources of risk.

In Chapter 14 Robert Bradley and Robert Corwyn provide an authoritative review of evidence on a closely related topic: associations between child outcomes and a family's socioeconomic status (SES). As they document, such links are pervasive, evident in measures of children's physical health, their academic achievements and their socioemotional well-being.

How might these widespread associations come about? As Bradley and Corwyn emphasize, we know far more about the size of the effect than why the effect occurs. Pathways vary for different aspects of development, and many outcomes are multiply determined. Some pathways are not difficult to seek: poor families are less likely than their more affluent counterparts to have adequate access to good nutrition and health-care, to the resources needed to provide children with cognitively stimulating experiences, and to the health-related behaviours and lifestyles likely to promote optimal development. Other models – at this stage more speculative, at least in relation to children – centre on the likely effects of stress on biological systems, outlined in earlier chapters.

Karl Alexander and colleagues (Chapter 15) focus on one central pathway for the effects of low SES: its impact on children's school achievements. We have extensive evidence, gleaned from research in many Western societies, that children from less advantaged backgrounds achieve less well in school than their more advantaged peers. Over a sequence of seminal publications Alexander and his colleagues have made elegant use of a simple natural experiment – the long summer recess, when children are out of school – to demonstrate that achievement gains over the early years of schooling mainly reflect school-year learning, whereas the high SES-low SES achievement gap largely reflects differential 'summer learning' for children from different social backgrounds. Here, they extend that picture to show that these summer learning variations persist, affecting young people's progress in high school and beyond. Though schooling cannot entirely 'compensate for society', these findings offer a powerful reminder that it can do much to offset the effects of social background – and suggest that additional provision for disadvantaged groups may reap rich rewards.

The final chapter in this section both returns us to the starting point of this volume and points us in the direction of later contributions. Rebecca Shiner and Avshalom Caspi, in Chapter 16, examine current thinking on individual differences in temperament and personality and the roles that these play in shaping adaptation throughout life. As they argue, though research has for many years highlighted consistencies in personality styles across development, we still know relatively little of how they come about or how variations in personality might contribute – as many developmentalists have speculated – to vulnerability to more serious difficulties in mental health. Shiner and Caspi set out a conceptual model of possible associations here, highlighting a series of ways in which individual characteristics may contribute to vulnerability or resilience. In some instances, for example, personality features may put children at increased risk for disorder, as when social inhibition contributes to risk for clinically significant anxiety or depression, or low self-control increases vulnerability for disruptive disorders. Equally important, some temperamental features appear to be protective for children facing very challenging environmental circumstances. Werner and Smith's (1992) classic follow-up showed, for example, that young people with positive adult outcomes who had grown up against a background of perinatal risk, poverty and family difficulties had shown particular temperamental profiles in infancy, being active, easy-going and affectionate even in their very early years. And finally, effects can of course go the other way, with severe mental health problems leaving scars on personality functioning long after overt disorder has been resolved.

Impairment and Disorder

The final section of the volume focuses more directly on children who face impairments to their development, and so may be in need of interventions or services. In the main, it does so through the lens of one particular discipline: epidemiology. As Jane Costello and her colleagues outline in Chapters 17 and 18, epidemiology – formally, the study of the distribution of diseases and disorders in time and space – provides the scientific underpinnings for the prevention and control of disease. Broadly, it can be thought of as having two main arms: a public health arm, monitoring the burden of disease in different populations, and a scientific arm, tracing links between disorders and the factors that put individuals at risk. The demonstration of a link between smoking and lung cancer – built on evidence patiently accumulated over many years – is one of the best-known achievements of an epidemiological approach in the medical field.

How have epidemiological studies contributed to our understanding of emotional and behavioural disorders in childhood? As the final chapters in this volume show, one of their main achievements has been to document the huge burden that such problems present for young people, their families and society as a whole. Public awareness of child mental health problems is much greater today than it was just a few years ago – and concern for child mental health figures much more prominently on the public policy agenda. Both of those changes have come about because researchers and lobbyists have made major efforts to encourage epidemiological research, and then to publicize its findings.

As these chapters also demonstrate, simply documenting the extent of child mental health problems is a far from straightforward task. How can we tell how many children are impaired, and may need help? In Chapter 19, Andrew Pickles and Adrian Angold discuss one of the central debates in this field: is psychopathology best seen as categorical or dimensional? For the clinician, faced daily with decisions over whether a particular child will benefit from available treatments, a categorical approach often seems natural. Other evidence, however, presses for a dimensional view. Pickles and Angold review the arguments and the evidence, and conclude that there is unlikely to be one best solution: each approach has its advantages, depending on the particular questions being addressed.

Although the great majority of children with severe, pervasive disorders will be in touch with services, many others with less severe but nonetheless incapacitating difficulties are not. As a result, the only way to get reliable estimates of the full extent of the problem is to undertake community surveys. Inevitably, these are expensive: large samples of children and families need to be contacted for us to feel confident that the estimates they provide are correct. In addition, there have been huge challenges in devising reliable ways of assessing children's difficulties and finding reliable measures to be included in community surveys of this kind. Costello and her colleagues sketch in some of the background here, outlining the different types of interviews and questionnaires that have been developed over the years and the efforts that have been made to refine them. They conclude that, even though agreement between instruments is still far from perfect, we have now reached a point where we have a range of assessment tools that work well in community surveys and are capable of generating adequately reliable conclusions.

What do such studies show? The two contributions by Tamsin Ford and colleagues highlight some of the key findings. Chapter 20 reports on what is in many ways a landmark study: the first nationally representative survey of levels of mental health problems among children and adolescents in the UK. Carried out in 1999 by the Office for National Statistics, and supported by government funding, this survey charted rates of all of the main types of disorders in a sample of over 10,000 children and families. The results are striking. Applying quite conservative criteria, the researchers concluded that at any one time almost one in ten children aged from 5 to 15 years can be expected to be facing problems severe enough to impair their functioning or to cause them major distress.

A second survey in 2004 confirmed a similar figure, and a follow-up of members of the 1999 sample three years after they were first contacted showed that many of their problems persisted. The follow-up study also included questions on service use. Of children with psychiatric disorders, 58 per cent had been in touch with some services (including social services, special educational needs resources and the youth justice system) during the follow-up period; only 23 per cent, however, had seen specialist child and adolescent mental health professionals. In practice, this figure is higher than the rate of specialist mental health contacts reported in studies from many other countries – but it still clearly falls massively short of what would be ideal.

The second chapter by Ford and colleagues (Chapter 21) focuses on a more specific at-risk group: children in public care, the subject of Courtney and Thoburn's volume in this series of books. Although these children have long been known to be especially vulnerable, they (along with others, such as young offenders and homeless young people) are often excluded from prevalence surveys because they are mobile or because of difficulties in ensuring parental consent. The Ford study broke new ground here by examining a large, representative sample of 'looked after' children in the full range of placement types. Though not unexpected, the findings still make distressing reading: overall, rates of disorder were more than three times higher than among even the most socially disadvantaged children living in private households, and for children in some placement types (most notably those in residential care) rates were exceptionally high. The authors note the heavy burden that this inevitably imposes on care staff – and the strong need for all of those working with these vulnerable groups of young people to have adequate training in recognizing and responding appropriately to their mental health needs.

These two chapters give just a flavour of the key policy-related insights that can be gleaned from well-conducted epidemiological research. Costello and colleagues, in their overview chapters, highlight a number of other important themes. Epidemiological studies have identified a series of important developmental issues, charting the ages at which different disorders usually appear and key features of their long-term course. In terms of age at onset, for example, it is now clear that we can distinguish two main groups of disorders: one, typically starting very early in childhood, includes what are now thought of as neurodevelopmental disorders, including autism spectrum disorders, specific language impairments, dyslexia and attention-deficit hyperactivity disorder. All of these types of difficulty are more common in boys than in girls.

The second group – this time more common in girls – generally emerges in adolescence and centres on 'emotional' problems: depression, eating disorders and some types of anxiety. Conduct problems are the exception to the rule: some children show major behavioural difficulties from early in childhood, while a second group only starts to show problems in the early teens. Current theory suggests that these two groups differ in important ways: they have different early risk factors and they also differ in long-term outcomes. In general, the outlook for early onset difficulties is poor, with a high risk of persistence in anti-social behaviour into adult life; by contrast, 'adolescent onset' conduct problems may be more time-limited and show a more benign long-term course.

Epidemiological studies also show that in community samples as well as in the clinic, many of these apparently separate disorders overlap. Possible reasons for these patterns of comorbidity are taken up by Adrian Angold and colleagues in Chapter 22. As they argue, it is highly unlikely that the striking patterns of overlap found between disorders are simply artefacts: instead, they raise important issues for developmental theory as well as for practice. Do overlaps between apparently differing disorders mean, for example, that they each share common risks, that some difficulties vary in the form of their expression with development or that experiencing one type of disorder may, in some circumstances or at particular developmental periods, put children at increased risk for other difficulties? The answers to these scientific questions continue to present challenges today. The implications of comorbidity for service provision are equally profound: if children face multiple threats to their development, can treatments for one aspect of their difficulties serve to offset other risks or does each set of vulnerabilities require specific treatments?

We conclude the volume with a set of three chapters that highlight a relatively new theme in child psychiatry research, but one clearly pre-figured in other contributions to this volume. As we have seen, developmentalists have long argued that the pattern of children's development may vary not only across social contexts but also with historical time. For many years, epidemiological researchers were – somewhat ironically – hampered in their attempts to investigate these issues by the very methodological developments they were keen to promote: constantly improving methods made it difficult if not impossible to compare levels of problems today with those documented in the past. More recently, however, investigators have begun to identify sources of evidence that can allow for such historical comparisons. The final three chapters in this volume illustrate findings of this kind from the UK (Stephan Collishaw and colleagues, Chapter 23), the Netherlands (Nouchka Tick and colleagues, Chapter 24) and the United States (Thomas Achenbach and colleagues, Chapter 25). What they have found varies in specifics from country to country but suggests that, in some Western societies at least, levels of problems can change to quite a marked extent over relatively short historical periods. As the authors of these studies underline, variations of this kind must reflect some aspect of environmental influences, of the changing features of our societies and the contexts they provide for children's development that allow or even encourage such vulnerabilities to be expressed. The challenges this presents for children's services are all too readily apparent.

Conclusions

Within a relatively short period of time much of the empirical evidence presented in this volume will be out of date. As has been indicated, knowledge about the relative impact of genes, environment and interactions of genes and environment is shifting so rapidly it is hard for most developmental scientists to keep up. The discovery of the role of the MAOA genetic variant in the lives of children exposed to maltreatment (Caspi *et al.*, 2002) heralds the first of many important breakthroughs in our understanding of the place of nature and nurture in child development. Perversely, knowledge about genes is demanding that those interested in the environment are able to measure it and its effects more precisely than in the past. Advances in the measurement of neurological functioning have been huge but the science remains in its infancy. As it grows up, the contribution to the sum of our knowledge will likely mirror that of changes in our appreciation of the role of genes and environment.

But this book should still serve as a good foundation for understanding influences on children's health and development. Why should this be so? There are at least three reasons. First, the basic concepts described in these pages will remain the same. It is hard to imagine that in half a decade from now there will be no explorations of the role of children's early attachments in their subsequent development. The focus of the science may have altered and the tools of investigation may no doubt have transformed, but people will still be interested in attachment, and they will still be reading Bowlby and Ainsworth.

Second, the broad structure of influences on children's development will change little. We hope there will be a better understanding of the relative contribution of society, neighbourhood, school, family and individual factors to child well-being. We will know more about the genetic influences within the individual and how these shape the environments in which an individual participates. But we will still be talking about society, environment, neighbourhoods, schools and families, and we will still be reading Bronfenbrenner to help us think about these ideas.

Third, science builds on the empirical findings of the past. Rutter and colleagues in their exploration of the impact of extreme deprivation among Romanian orphans began to uncover variations of childhood disorders not evident in previous studies. The next generation of research will clarify this issue, either proving Rutter and colleagues wrong or better defining the variations and their potential causes. Angold has led the way in explaining the overlap between childhood disorders, but he would be the first to welcome the new generation of studies that will help us to understand whether these comorbidities are the product of weaknesses in the taxanomies currently available, or of poor measurement, or of as yet uncharted causal pathways. Many more illustrations could be given.

So while readers should always be mindful of the need to check relevant journals for the latest empirical results for any particular component of this book, they should find that the illustrations offered in the pages that follow to be as good a starting point as any, and that the structure for thinking about those examples will endure.

As we said at the outset, this volume in the series acts as a good underpinning for the other five. These other volumes will also inform readers' appreciation of child development. In closing, we illustrate this point with respect to our volume on effective interventions for children in need.

In that volume we make the argument for evidence on the incidence and potential causes of impairments to children's health and development as the primary underpinning for interventions to improve child outcomes. This argument is far from accepted in any jurisdiction, even in the United States which leads the way in its scientific contribution.

But let us look at the argument in reverse. What can we learn from evaluations of interventions that can help us better comprehend child development? There are so many possibilities that we will restrict ourselves to three. First, knowing what does not work is as important as knowing what does. The repeated discovery that placing anti-social young people in groups increases anti-social behaviour, or that telling young people about the negative effects of drug use increases drug use, has the potential to tell us much about possible causal pathways. Second, each experiment based on good epidemiological research offers an opportunity to confirm or deny findings. We know from epidemiology that poverty increases the risk of impairments to development. Costello and colleagues' report of a natural experiment that reduced poverty in the Great Smoky Mountains in the United States (Costello *et al*, 2003) showed that taking people out of poverty has greater effects on children's conduct than on their emotional difficulties. Future epidemiological studies can explore this further with more fine-grained estimates. Findings from these studies can in turn be tested in future policy experiments. Third, epidemiology depends on multivariate analysis to estimate the differential contribution of competing influences on a child's development. Experiments have the potential to reduce greatly or even turn off the impact of a single influence, and to demonstrate how other variables interact in that context, as when the negative effects of poor parenting are diminished in families still coping with the stressor of low income or a dangerous neighbourhood.

We could go on with numerous examples. In closing this introduction we would just remind readers that the findings presented in this opening volume of the series will inform future learning in areas covered by the other five volumes. Similarly, what we learn about effective interventions, the classification of need, the health and development of children in the economic South or in child welfare systems will in time inform our understanding of children's health and development.

References

Bronfenbrenner, U. (1979), *The Ecology of Human Development: Experiments by Nature and Design*, Cambridge, MA: Harvard University Press.

Caspi, A., McClay, J., Moffitt, T.E., Mill, J., Martin, J., Craig, I.W., Taylor, A. and Poulton, R. (2002), 'Role of Genotype in the Cycle of Violence in Maltreated Children', *Science*, **297**, pp. 851–54.

Costello E.J., Compton, S.N., Keeler G. and Angold, A. (2003), 'Relationships between Poverty and Psychopathology – A Natural Experiment', *JAMA-Journal of the American Medical Association*, **290**, pp. 2023–29.

Werner, E.E., and Smith, R.S. (1992), *Overcoming the Odds: High Risk Children from Birth to Adulthood*, Ithaca, NY: Cornell University Press.

Part I
Key Concepts In
Developmental Research

Attachment

[1]

An Ethological Approach to Personality Development

Mary D. Salter Ainsworth   *University of Virginia*
John Bowlby   *Tavistock Clinic, London, England*

This is a historical account of the partnership in which Bowlby and Ainsworth participated to develop attachment theory and research. Beginning with their separate approaches to understanding personality development before Ainsworth joined Bowlby's research team at the Tavistock Clinic in London for 4 years, it describes the origins of the ethological approach that they adopted. After Ainsworth left London, her research in Uganda and in Baltimore lent empirical support to Bowlby's theoretical constructions. The article shows how their contributions to attachment theory and research interdigitated in a partnership that endured for 40 years across time and distance.

The distinguishing characteristic of the theory of attachment that we have jointly developed is that it is an ethological approach to personality development. We have had a long and happy partnership in pursuing this approach. In this article we wish to give a brief historical account of the initially separate but compatible approaches that eventually merged in the partnership, and how our contributions have intertwined in the course of developing an ethologically oriented theory of attachment and a body of research that has both stemmed from the theory and served to extend and elaborate it.

Before 1950

Even before beginning graduate training, each of us became keenly interested in personality development and the key role played in it by the early interaction between children and parents. In Bowlby's case this was kindled by volunteer work in a residential school for maladjusted children, which followed his undergraduate studies in medicine at Cambridge University. Two children especially impressed him. One was an isolated, affectionless adolescent who had never experienced a stable relationship with a mother figure, and the other was an anxious child who followed Bowlby around like a shadow. Largely because of these two children, Bowlby resolved to continue his medical studies toward a specialty in child psychiatry and psychotherapy, and was accepted as a student for psychoanalytic training. From early in his training he believed that analysts, in their preoccupation with a child's fantasy life, were paying too little attention to actual events in the child's real life. His experience at the

London Child Guidance Clinic convinced him of the significant role played by interaction with parents in the development of a child's personality, and of the ways in which this interaction had been influenced by a parent's early experiences with his or her own parents. His first systematic research was begun also at the London Child Guidance Clinic, where he compared 44 juvenile thieves with a matched control group and found that prolonged experiences of mother–child separation or deprivation of maternal care were much more common among the thieves than in the control group, and that such experiences were especially linked to children diagnosed as affectionless (Bowlby, 1944).

The outbreak of war in 1939 interrupted Bowlby's career as a child psychiatrist but brought him useful research experience in connection with officer selection and with a new group of congenial associates, some of whom at the end of the war joined together to reorganize the Tavistock Clinic. Soon afterward the clinic became part of the National Health Service, and Bowlby served as full-time consultant psychiatrist and director of the Department for Children and Parents. There he also picked up the threads of his clinical and research interests.

Unfortunately, the Kleinian orientation of several members of the staff made it difficult to use clinic cases for the kind of research Bowlby wanted to undertake. He established a research unit of his own, which began operations in 1948. Convinced of the significance of real-life events on the course of child development, he chose to focus on the effects of early separation from the mother because separation was an event on record, unlike dis-

Editor's note. Articles based on APA award addresses that appear in the *American Psychologist* are scholarly articles by distinguished contributors to the field. As such, they are given special consideration in the *American Psychologist's* editorial selection process.

This article was originally presented as a Distinguished Scientific Contributions award address at the 98th Annual Convention of the American Psychological Association in Boston in August 1990.

Author's note. John Bowlby's death on September 2, 1990, at his summer home on the Isle of Skye in Scotland, prevented him from completing all that he intended to do in preparing this article for publication. As his coauthor I am greatly saddened by his death, but am secure in the knowledge that he would have wished me to complete the task.

Correspondence concerning this article should be addressed to Mary D. Salter Ainsworth, 920 Rosser Lane, Charlottesville, VA 22903.

turbed family interaction, of which, in those days, there were no adequate records.

Members of the research team began two research projects, one retrospective, the other prospective. The retrospective project was a follow-up study of 66 school-age children who had experienced separation from their families in a tuberculosis sanatorium at some time between the ages of one and four years, and who had subsequently returned home. The prospective project was undertaken single-handedly by James Robertson, then a social worker, who had had experience in Anna Freud's wartime nursery. Robertson observed young children's behavior as they underwent separation in three different institutional settings. Where possible, he observed the children's behavior in interaction with parents at home, both prior to the separation and after they were reunited with them. Bowlby himself undertook a third project, in response to a request by the World Health Organization (WHO) to prepare a report on what was known of the fate of children without families. This request led him to read all the available literature on separation and maternal deprivation, and to travel widely to find out what was being done elsewhere about the care of motherless children. The report was published both by WHO as a monograph entitled *Maternal Care and Mental Health* (Bowlby, 1951) and subsequently in a popular Penguin edition with the title *Child Care and the Growth of Love* (Bowlby & Ainsworth, 1965).

Let us turn now to the beginnings of Ainsworth's career. She entered the honor course in psychology as an undergraduate at the University of Toronto, hoping (as many do) to understand how she had come to be the person she was, and what her parents had to do with it. She was interested in the whole wide range of courses available to her, but in two particularly. One was run as a class experiment by S. N. F. Chant, in which she learned that research is a fascinating pursuit. The other, taught by William E. Blatz, focused on Blatz's newly formulated theory of security as an approach to understanding personality development. After graduation Ainsworth continued on at the University of Toronto as a graduate student, and was delighted when Blatz proposed that she base her dissertation research on his security theory.

Because she carried some highlights of security theory with her into attachment theory, it is appropriate here to say something about it (Blatz, 1966).[1] *Security*, as its Latin root—*sine cura*—would suggest, means "without care" or "without anxiety." According to Blatz, there are several kinds of security, of which the first to develop is what he called *immature dependent security*. Infants, and to a decreasing extent young children, can feel secure only if they can rely on parent figures to take care of them and take responsibility for the consequences of their behavior. Children's appetite for change leads them to be curious about the world around them and to explore it and learn about it. But learning itself involves insecurity. If and when children become uneasy or frightened while exploring, they are nevertheless secure if they can retreat to a parent figure, confident that they will receive comfort and reassurance. Thus the parent's availability provides the child with a secure base from which to explore and learn.

As children gradually gain knowledge about the world and learn skills to cope with it, they can increasingly rely on themselves and thus acquire a gradually increasing basis for *independent security*. By the time of reaching maturity, according to Blatz, a person should be fully emancipated from parents. Blatz viewed any substantial continuation of dependence on them to be undesirable. But one cannot be secure solely on the basis of one's independent knowledge and skills. To be secure, a person needs to supplement with *mature dependent security* whatever degree of independent security he or she has managed to achieve. Blatz thought of this as occurring in a mutually contributing, give-and-take relationship with another of one's own generation—a relationship in which each partner, on the basis of his or her knowledge and skills, can provide a secure base to the other. Blatz also acknowledged that defense mechanisms (he called them *deputy agents*) could provide a temporary kind of security, but did not themselves deal with the source of the insecurity—like treating a toothache with an analgesic.

For her dissertation, Ainsworth (then Salter, 1940) constructed two self-report, paper–pencil scales intended to assess the degree to which a person was secure rather than insecure. The first scale concerned relations with parents, and the second relations with friends. Together these scales were intended to indicate the extent to which the person's security rested on immature dependence on parents, independence, mature dependent relations with age peers, or the pseudosecurity of defense mechanisms. Individual differences were identified in terms of patterns of scores—a classificatory type of assessment for which she found much later use. The subjects were third-year university students, for each of whom an autobiography was available as a validity check.

To anticipate her later evaluation in the light of further experience, Ainsworth came to believe that Blatz's security theory did not deal adequately with defensive processes. Rejecting Freud's theory of unconscious processes, Blatz held that only conscious processes were of any significance in personality development. This was one aspect of his theory that Ainsworth did not carry forward. Furthermore, it became clear to her that with the self-report paper–pencil method of appraisal it is well-nigh impossible to assess accurately how much defensive maneuvers have inflated security scores. However, the general trends in her dissertation findings gave support to security theory as formulated at the time, and sustained her enthusiasm for it.

Upon completing her degree in 1939, Ainsworth hoped to continue security research with Blatz, and sought

---

[1] Blatz's security theory was largely embedded in an oral tradition, from which those who listened drew different meanings. Ainsworth has dwelt on those aspects that particularly influenced her at the time. Blatz's own 1966 account contained much that is at variance with what Ainsworth carried into attachment theory.

and obtained an appointment to the faculty. Their research plan was interrupted by the outbreak of war three months later. Blatz and most of the other faculty of the department soon departed for war-related jobs. Ainsworth continued teaching until 1942, but then joined the newly established Canadian Women's Army Corps, where she was assigned to personnel selection. After V-E Day, she spent a year as Superintendent of Women's Rehabilitation in the Department of Veterans' Affairs. In 1946 she happily returned to the University of Toronto as an assistant professor of psychology.

Through her war work she had developed an interest in clinical assessment, and she chose this as her area of academic specialization. She focused on projective techniques, especially the Rorschach, which she learned through workshops directed by Bruno Klopfer. This led to coauthorship of a book on the Rorschach technique (Klopfer, Ainsworth, Klopfer, & Holt, 1954). She gained practical experience in clinical assessment as a volunteer in a veterans' hospital, and as planned earlier, she codirected research with Blatz into further assessments of security.

In 1950 she left the University of Toronto, having married Leonard Ainsworth, a member of the security research team who had been admitted for PhD training at the University of London. Jobless, she was guided by Edith Mercer, a friend she had met during the war years, to an advertisement in the *Times Educational Supplement*. This sought a developmental researcher, proficient in projective techniques, for a project at the Tavistock Clinic investigating the effect on personality development of separation from the mother in early childhood. She got the job—and it transformed her research career, while at the same time incorporating some of its earlier threads.

1950 to 1954

Bowlby had just completed his report for the WHO when Ainsworth joined his research team. She was put to work reading the literature he had incorporated into the report and, like Bowlby, was impressed by the evidence of the adverse effects on development attributable to the lack of interaction with a mother figure when infants and young children spent prolonged periods in impersonal institutional care. She also joined in the team's analysis of the data yielded by the other two projects. It was clear that the richer yield came from the prospective study. Direct observation in the child's real-life environment showed how a young child passed from initial distressed protest upon being separated from his mother, to despair, and then finally to detachment, especially if the separation exceeded a week or so. Upon reunion it was clear that the child's tie to its mother had not disappeared, but that it had become anxious. In cases in which detachment lasted beyond separation and initial reunion a continuation of the bond could be inferred, even though it was masked by defensive processes (Bowlby, 1953; Robertson & Bowlby, 1952). A classificatory analysis of the social worker's interviews of the sanatorium follow-up cases confirmed that persistent insecurity of child–mother attachment endured for some years after long, institutional separation, with very few having regained a secure attachment—but indeed few having continued in a condition of affectionless detachment (Bowlby, Ainsworth, Boston, & Rosenbluth, 1956).

During this period Jimmy Robertson (1952) made his film *A Two-Year-Old Goes to Hospital*, as an illustration of the distress caused even by a short separation of several days. This film had immediate impact and Jimmy increasingly turned from research activities toward impressing the public with the urgent need for improvements in the way that young children were cared for while separated from their families. Although Bowlby strongly supported the reforms that followed Jimmy's efforts, he refused to be drawn away from an emphasis on research and theory. He and Ainsworth were both concerned with the multiplicity of the variables that influence the effect of separation, and published a monograph discussing how they need to be considered in planning strategies in separation research (Ainsworth & Bowlby, 1953).

Bowlby, meanwhile, had begun a search for an adequate explanation of the empirical findings, having found none in current psychoanalytic theories to account for young children's responses to separation and reunion, or indeed how the tie to the mother develops. At this point Konrad Lorenz's work on imprinting became available in translation. Sensing its possible relevance to his problem and encouraged by Julian Huxley, Bowlby began delving into the ethological literature. He found the descriptions of separation distress and proximity seeking of precocial birds, who had become imprinted on the mother, strikingly similar to those of young children. He was also struck by the evidence that a strong social bond can be formed that is not based on oral gratification. Furthermore he was impressed with the fact that ethological research began with field observations of the animal in its natural environment, a starting point analogous to that of a clinician. His ethological reading led him to evolutionary biology, and also to systems theory.

During the early 1950s Bowlby was also deeply influenced by his membership in an international and interdisciplinary study group on the psychobiology of the child convened by the World Health Organization, which met annually. Among the members were Piaget, Lorenz, and Margaret Mead, and among guest speakers were Julian Huxley, von Bertalanffy, and Erik Erikson. Bowlby reported on these meetings and the plethora of new ideas he was entertaining at meetings of the research team, but no one took time then to dig into these fields themselves.

In the autumn of 1953 Ainsworth's time at the Tavistock Clinic was drawing to a close, her husband having completed his doctoral work. She had become fascinated with the issues Bowlby's research team had been exploring. She resolved that wherever she went next she would undertake research into what goes on between an infant and its mother that accounts for the formation of its strong bond to her, and the absence or the interruption of which can have such an adverse effect on personality development. She also resolved to base her study on direct observations of infants and mothers in the context of home and family. The first opportunity came at the East African Institute of Social Research in Kampala, Uganda, where her husband obtained a research appointment beginning early in 1954.

Her link with Bowlby and his research team continued for a while after arriving in Kampala. In particular, she remembers a document that he circulated that resulted from his theoretical explorations and foreshadowed a series of publications of his new ethologically based theory of attachment. She read it with great interest, but suggested that his new theory needed to be tested empirically. And, in effect, that is what she has spent the rest of her research career attempting to provide—beginning with a project observing Ganda babies and their mothers in their village homes, with the support of the East African Institute of Social Research.

1954 to 1963

Meanwhile, Bowlby continued his theory-oriented explorations of the relevant literature in ethology, evolution theory, systems theory, and cognitive psychology, as well as rereading psychoanalytic literature pertinent to his theme. His guide to ethology was Robert Hinde, who began to attend seminars at the Tavistock Institute in 1954. They had a profound influence on each other. Bowlby was drawn further into the animal research literature, notably including Harlow's work with infant monkeys, which supported his conviction that it is proximity to and close bodily contact with a mother figure that cements the infant's attachment rather than the provision of food. On the other hand, the connection with Bowlby led Hinde to study both the interaction of infant rhesus monkeys with their mothers and the effects of mother–infant separation; his findings lent experimental support to Bowlby's position. Although much influenced by the ethologists' observations of other species, Bowlby remained a clinician, continuing to see children and families and to practice individual and family psychotherapy. Moreover, for 20 years he ran a mother's group in a well-baby clinic, learning much from his informal observations of mother–child interaction there, and from the reports of mothers about their children's behavior.

Several classic papers emerged from this theoretical ferment, in each of which his new ethological approach was contrasted with then current psychoanalytic theories: first, "The Nature of the Child's Tie to His Mother" (Bowlby, 1958), then in rapid succession two papers on separation anxiety (Bowlby, 1960b, 1961b), and three on grief and mourning (Bowlby, 1960a, 1961a, 1963). In the first paper he proposed that a baby's attachment came about through a repertoire of genetically based behaviors that matured at various times from birth to several months of age, and became focused on the principal caregiver, usually the mother. This repertoire included crying, sucking, smiling, clinging, and following—of which he considered the latter two the most central. He also discussed how these behaviors were activated and terminated, at first independently before an attachment was formed, but afterward as organized together toward the attachment figure. Finally, he emphasized the active nature of attachment behavior, contrasting it with the passive conception of dependence. Whereas in traditional theory, dependence is considered inevitable in infancy, regressive and undesirable in later years, and having no biological value, he conceived of attachment behavior as a major component of human behavioral equipment, on a par with eating and sexual behavior, and as having protection as its biological function, not only in childhood but throughout life. Its presence in humans, as in many other species, could be understood in terms of evolution theory.

The papers on separation anxiety were based partly on research by a new member of the team, Christoph Heinicke (e.g., Heinicke, 1956; Heinicke & Westheimer, 1966), but chiefly on Robertson's observations, which were discussed earlier. Bowlby reviewed six psychoanalytic explanations of separation anxiety, but rejected them in favor of his own hypothesis. He believed that separation anxiety occurs when attachment behavior is activated by the absence of the attachment figure, but cannot be terminated. It differs from fright, which is aroused by some alarming or noxious feature of the environment and activates escape responses. However, fright also activates attachment behavior, so that the baby not only tries to escape from the frightening stimulus but also tries to reach a haven of safety—the attachment figure. Later in infancy, the baby is capable of expectant anxiety in situations that seem likely to be noxious or in which the attachment figure is likely to become unavailable. He emphasized that only a specific figure, usually the mother figure, could terminate attachment behavior completely once it had been intensely activated. He went on to point out that hostility toward the mother is likely to occur when attachment behavior is frustrated, as it is when the child is separated from her, rejected by her, or when she gives major attention to someone else. When such circumstances are frequent or prolonged, primitive defensive processes may be activated, with the result that the child may appear to be indifferent to its mother (as in the detachment attributable to separation) or may be erroneously viewed as healthily independent.

Whereas separation anxiety dominates the protest phase of response to separation, with its heightened but frustrated attachment behavior mingled with anger, grief and mourning dominate the despair phase, as the frustration of separation is prolonged. Bowlby disagreed with the psychoanalytic theorists who held that infants and young children are incapable of mourning and experiencing grief, and also with those who, like Melanie Klein, believed that the loss of the breast at weaning is the greatest loss in infancy. In his papers on grief and mourning he pointed to the similarities between adults and young children in their responses to loss of a loved one: thoughts and behavior expressing longing for the loved one, hostility, appeals for help, despair, and finally reorganization. Many fellow psychoanalysts have vigorously rejected his views on grief and mourning, as indeed they have protested his ethological approach to the child's tie to the mother and his interpretation of separation anxiety. Having been trained in another theoretical paradigm, they have found it difficult to break out of it enough to entertain a new way of viewing old problems.

Meanwhile, in Uganda, Ainsworth had begun her study of Ganda babies. She assembled a sample of 28 unweaned babies and their mothers from several villages near Kampala and, with a splendid interpreter–assistant, visited their homes every two weeks over a period of nine months. They interviewed the mother about her infant-care practices and about the infant's development, and observed their behavior in interaction, and that of the rest of the household. What she saw did not support the Freudian notion of a passive, recipient, narcissistic infant in the oral phase. Rather, she was impressed by the babies' active search for contact with the mother when they were alarmed or hurt, when she moved away or left even briefly, and when they were hungry—and even then she was struck by their initiative in seeking the breast and managing the feeding. There was impressive evidence of the use of the mother as a secure base from which to explore the world and as a haven of safety. She observed the very beginnings of the infant's formation of attachment to the mother in differential termination of crying, and differential smiling and vocalization. Indications that an attachment had clearly been formed were distress and following when separation occurred or threatened, and forms of greeting when mother returned from an absence.

She divided the babies into three groups: securely attached, insecurely attached, and nonattached. Insecurely attached babies cried a lot even when the mother was present, whereas securely attached babies cried little unless mothers were absent or seemed about to leave. Nonattached babies were left alone for long periods by unresponsive mothers but, because they were the youngest in the sample, Ainsworth now believes that they may merely have been delayed in developing attachment. She devised several rather crude scales for rating maternal behavior, of which three significantly differentiated the mothers of secure babies from the others. In retrospect she sees how all three reflected some facet of mother's accessibility and responsiveness to infant behavioral signals. At the time she was pleased that her data meshed with what she had learned about Bowlby's new attachment theory, and also with aspects of Blatz's security theory. However, it was not for some years, after having both begun a second longitudinal study and followed later developments of Bowlby's attachment theory, that the full findings of the Ganda study were published (Ainsworth, 1967).

The Ainsworths left Uganda late in the summer of 1955 and went to Baltimore, where Leonard had found a position. Early in 1956, Mary asked Wendell Garner, then chairman of the Department of Psychology at Johns Hopkins University, about job possibilities in Baltimore. To her surprise and delight he patched together a job for her there as a clinical psychologist, although there was no official vacancy in the department. She was expected to teach the scheduled courses on personality and assessment in this experimental department, and to give to interested students a taste of clinical experience at the Sheppard and Enoch Pratt Hospital, where a part-time appointment for her had been arranged. To supplement her low salary, she began a part-time private practice in diagnostic assessment, mostly with children, aided enormously by her research experience at the Tavistock Clinic.

Ainsworth's desire to begin another longitudinal study of the development of attachment had to be put on hold, but her subsequent work greatly benefited from the clinical experience she obtained meanwhile. She did, however, publish some review papers on maternal deprivation and separation (e.g., Ainsworth, 1962), coauthor with her husband a book on security measurement (Ainsworth & Ainsworth, 1958), and begin work on the data collected in Uganda. In the spring of 1959 John Bowlby visited Baltimore, and she had an opportunity to fill him in on the details of what she was finding in the Ganda data. This served to revive their association, which had lapsed somewhat, and he included her in the Tavistock Mother–Infant Interaction Study Group that had just begun to meet biennially. At the second meeting she gave a preliminary report of her Ganda study (Ainsworth, 1963). The meetings of this interdisciplinary, international group reignited her eagerness to pursue developmental research, and provided a stimulating scientific support network. In 1961 she sought successfully to be released from her clinical role at Johns Hopkins, and to focus on developmental research and teaching. In 1962 she obtained a grant to begin the second longitudinal study that she had so long wanted to do, and in 1963 she was promoted to full professor with tenure.

1963 to 1980

Having hired Barbara Wittig as a research assistant, Ainsworth located a sample of 15 infant–mother pairs through pediatricians in private practice, usually before the baby's birth. Data collection proceeded during 1963 and 1964. Visits were made to the families every 3 weeks from 3 to 54 weeks after the baby's birth. Each visit lasted for approximately 4 hours, resulting in about 72 hours of observation altogether for each dyad. In 1966–1967, with two new assistants (Robert Marvin and George Allyn), 11 more dyads were added to the sample. Direct observation of behavior was supplemented by information yielded in informal conversations with the mother. Notes made during the visit were later dictated in a narrative account, and then transcribed; these raw data took up two full drawers in a filing cabinet. (Needless to say the data took years to analyze, even with the help of many valued research associates and student assistants.)

The home visitor had been alerted to note infant behaviors that had been earlier identified as attachment behaviors by both Bowlby and Ainsworth, and to pay particular attention to situations in which they were most likely to occur, and to the mother's response to them. Data reduction procedures included event coding, rating, and classification. The data analysis yielded information about both normative development and how individual differences in the security or insecurity of the infants' attachment to their mothers were related to the mothers' behavior.

At the end of the baby's first year, baby and mother were introduced to a 20-minute laboratory situation—the strange situation—a preliminary report of which was made by Ainsworth and Wittig (1969). Although this situation was originally designed for a normative exploration, it turned out to provide a relatively quick method of assessment of infant–mother attachment. This procedure soon became widely used, if not always wisely and well, and has quite overshadowed the findings of the research project that gave rise to it and on which its validity depended. However, the longitudinal home visit data, (which include information about how mother's behavior is linked to the course of infant development) and the strange situation together have yielded important information about the development of attachment in infancy.

The findings of the data analyses of both the strange situation and the home visits were published in a series of articles beginning in 1969 as each analysis was completed. The original research reports were coauthored by the research associate or assistant who was chiefly involved in each piece of data analysis. Ainsworth is deeply indebted to their dedicated and creative contributions.

Highlights of the findings are as follows. Mothers who fairly consistently responded promptly to infant crying early-on had infants who by the end of the first year cried relatively little and were securely attached. Indeed, mothers who were sensitively and appropriately responsive to infant signals in general, including feeding signals, fostered secure infant–mother attachment (Ainsworth & Bell, 1969; Ainsworth, Blehar, Waters, & Wall, 1978; Bell & Ainsworth, 1972). As Bowlby implied from the beginning, close bodily contact with the mother terminates attachment behavior that has been intensely activated. Full-blown crying indicates such intense activation, and indeed our mothers' most usual response to such crying was to pick the baby up (Bell & Ainsworth, 1972). It was not the total amount of time that the baby was held by the mother that promoted secure attachment so much as the contingency of the pick-up with infant signals of desire for contact, and the manner in which the mother then held and handled the baby. Babies who were securely attached not only responded positively to being picked up, being readily comforted if they had been upset, but also they responded positively to being put down, and were likely to turn toward exploration. Timely and appropriate close bodily contact does not "spoil" babies, making them fussy and clingy (Ainsworth, 1979).

About the middle of the first year the babies had clearly become attached, and one of the signs of this was that they began to show distress when mother left the room (separation anxiety). However, babies whose attachment was secure seemed to build up a working model of mother as being available even though out of sight, and thus came to protest little everyday departures at home less often than did infants who were insecurely attached. On the other hand, they were more likely than

insecure babies to greet the mother positively upon reunion, and less likely to greet her grumpily or with a cry (Stayton & Ainsworth, 1973; Stayton, Ainsworth, & Main, 1973). However, if the mother left when the baby was mildly stressed by an unfamiliar situation, as in the strange situation, even a secure child was likely to protest her departure. A useful paradox that emerged was that some infants who were clearly insecure at home, showing frequent separation protest or crying a lot in general, were apparently indifferent to their mothers' departure in the strange situation and avoided them upon reunion. Our interpretation was that under the increased stress of the unfamiliar situation a defensive process is activated, akin to the detachment that develops in young children undergoing major separations (Ainsworth & Bell, 1970; Ainsworth et al., 1978). Although the avoidant infants had themselves experienced no major separations, their mothers had tended to be rejecting at home during the first year, especially when their babies sought contact, as well as being generally insensitive to infant signals.

In regard to socialization, the findings suggest that infants have a natural behavioral disposition to comply with the wishes of the principal attachment figure. This disposition emerges most clearly if the attachment figure is sensitively responsive to infant signals, whereas efforts to train and discipline the infant, instead of fostering the wished-for compliance, tend to work against it (Ainsworth, Bell, & Stayton, 1974; Stayton, Hogan, & Ainsworth, 1971).

All of these findings tend to be supportive of attachment theory, but one in particular supports our emphasis on the interaction of behavioral systems. Bretherton and Ainsworth (1974), in an analysis of the responses of 106 one-year-olds to a stranger in a strange situation, showed how such responses involve the interactions between the fear–wariness system and the affiliative (sociable) system activated by the stranger, and also affect attachment behavior directed toward the mother and exploration of the toys. For example, nearly all babies manifested both sociability to the stranger and some degree of fear or wariness—the more of one, the less of the other. Few displayed only fear with no sociability, and very few displayed only sociability and no fear. Publication of these and other findings was interspersed with theoretical expositions (e.g., Ainsworth, 1969, 1972, 1977, 1979).

Finally, the strange situation procedure highlighted the distinction between secure and insecure infants, and between two groups of insecure infants—avoidant and ambivalent–resistant. Much evidence emerged in our studies relating these differences to maternal caregiving behavior, but these are most comprehensively dealt with by Ainsworth, Bell, and Stayton (1971) and Ainsworth et al. (1978).

In the meantime John Bowlby, whose research group had received generous support from the Ford Foundation, and who from 1963 was himself supported by the United Kingdom Medical Research Council, was working on his *Attachment and Loss* volumes. This trilogy brought to fruition the themes introduced in his earlier papers. It was planned with the whole in mind, and is best viewed as a whole. The first volume, *Attachment,* was published in 1969. From the early 1960s he and Ainsworth were exchanging drafts of all major publications, making comments and suggestions, and were continually taking each other's work into account. Ainsworth's work, including the Ganda study and the early findings of the strange situation, were drawn on in Bowlby's first volume, which included her major contribution of the concept of a secure base and variations in the security of attachment shown by different children. At the same time, this volume had profound influence on her work. In it, Bowlby elaborated the ethological and evolutionary underpinnings of attachment theory, discarded drive theory, and in its place, developed the concept of behavioral systems as control systems designed to achieve a specified end, activated in certain conditions and terminated in others. Postulating a plurality of behavioral systems, Bowlby described interactions among them, for example the dovetailing of the infant's attachment system and the caregiving system of the adult, and the way the activation of attachment behavior often alternates with that of exploratory behavior. The control systems approach to attachment behavior emphasizes inner organization and the development of working models of attachment figures and the self, which permit the development of the goal-corrected partnership between child and mother during the preschool years.

The second volume of the trilogy dealt with separation (Bowlby, 1973). The first half expanded Bowlby's earlier papers about separation anxiety, and presented a theory of fear that was merely suggested earlier. Of particular interest is the proposal that a child is genetically disposed to respond with fear to certain stimuli, such as sudden movement and sharp changes in the level of light and sound that, although not being dangerous in themselves, are statistically associated with dangerous situations. These natural clues to potential danger, of which one is being alone, activate either escape behavior or attachment behavior, and usually both, and thus promote the individual's survival. In the second half of the volume, Bowlby dealt with anxious attachment, conditions that promote it, and the intimate relationship of anger to attachment-related anxiety. As clinical examples of anxious attachment he considered both "school phobias" of children and the agoraphobia of adults, and stressed cross-generational effects in the etiology of each.

Two very important chapters have too often been overlooked. One dealt with the essential link between secure attachment and the development of healthy self-reliance—of particular interest to Ainsworth because of its roots in the *secure base* concept. The other, entitled "Pathways for the Growth of Personality," based on Waddington's theory of epigenesis, emphasized the constant interaction between genetic and environmental influences in personality development.

The third volume of the trilogy was concerned with loss (Bowlby, 1980). Near the beginning of it he included one of the most basic chapters of the trilogy—entitled "An Information Processing Approach to Defence"—

that is as pertinent to the earlier two volumes as it is to the third. Drawing on cognitive psychological concepts and research, he pointed out that much sensory input normally is evaluated quickly and unconsciously in terms of stored knowledge, and then excluded from the highest, conscious level of cognitive processing as a matter of sheer efficiency. Under other circumstances, when accessing stored experience to evaluate current input would occasion significant anxiety, there may be *defensive* exclusion of input before it can proceed to conscious processing. Attachment behavior and associated feelings are especially vulnerable to such exclusion. When the attachment system is intensely activated and is often or for an extended period not terminated, defensive exclusion is likely to occur. This results in the defence manifested by avoidant children and in the detachment attributable to severe separation experiences. Such exclusion may well occur in adults as a response to loss, and accounts for some of the pathological variants of mourning. In addition to defensive processes, this chapter includes a valuable discussion of internal working models of attachment figures and of the self, pointing out that there may be more than one model of each figure and that these may conflict.

In the second section of the volume, which dealt with the mourning of adults, Bowlby drew heavily on the works of Colin Murray Parkes (e.g., Parkes, 1972), who joined the research team in 1962. It described four phases of mourning: (a) numbing; (b) yearning for the lost figure, and anger; (c) disorganization and despair; and (d) finally, if all goes well, reorganization. Bowlby considered disorders of mourning together with conditions contributing to them. Finally, he examined the connection between loss and depression, with particular attention to the work of Brown and Harris (1978). The last section, which dealt with children's mourning, emphasized both the similarity of the processes involved in children's and adults' responses to loss, and the reasons why children may have particular difficulty in resolving their mourning by successful reorganization of their lives.

1980 to 1990

Bowlby intended his contribution as an up-to-date version of psychoanalytic object-relations theory, compatible with contemporary ethology and evolution theory, supported by research, and helpful to clinicians in understanding and treating child and adult patients. Nevertheless, it was developmental psychologists rather than clinicians who first adopted attachment theory, having found both traditional psychoanalytic and social learning theory to provide inadequate theoretical and methodological guidelines for research into personality development. Psychotherapists at that time were relatively content with one or another existing version of psychoanalytic theory as a guide, perhaps relying more on technique than theory for their therapeutic successes.

In several articles Bowlby suggested explicit guidelines for treatment that had been implicit in attachment theory (e.g., Bowlby, 1988b). The therapist begins with an understanding of the patient's current difficulties, especially difficulties in interpersonal relations. He or she then tries to serve as a secure base, helping the patient build up trust enough to be able to explore current relationships, including relations with the therapist. The therapist recognizes that a patient's difficulties are likely to have their origin in real-life experiences, rather than in fantasies. The therapist thus seeks to guide the patient's explorations toward earlier experiences—especially, painful ones with parents—and to expectations about current relationships derived from the internal working models of self and attachment figure that have resulted, and so to consider how these models, perhaps appropriate to the earlier situation, may be giving rise to feelings and actions inappropriate in the present. This review of past experiences is likely to lead to a reevaluation of them, a revision of working models, and gradually, to improved interpersonal relations in the here and now.

A second aspect of Bowlby's effort to draw attachment theory to the attention of clinicians was his acceptance of many invitations to speak at professional meetings throughout the world. A number of the addresses were subsequently published in professional journals or drawn together in collections (e.g., Bowlby, 1979, 1988a). Now, consequently, the clinical group that he originally wanted to reach undoubtedly outnumbers his devoted group of developmental researchers.

Finally, Bowlby's most recent contribution was a new biography of Charles Darwin (Bowlby, 1990). Long an admirer of Darwin, who esteemed his theory of evolution as a keystone in an ethological approach to personality development, Bowlby turned to applying attachment theory to an understanding of the chronic ill health that plagued Darwin. Darwin's mother had become seriously ill when he was very young, and died when he was eight years old. Bowlby cited evidence to show that Darwin never had been able fully to mourn her death. Bowlby maintained that this left him as an adult sensitized to real or threatened losses of family members, and accounted for his psychological symptoms in terms of attachment theory (Bowlby, 1990).

Ainsworth in 1975–1976, nearing the completion of the publication of the findings of her Baltimore study, accepted an appointment at the University of Virginia and began work with a new generation of students, and continued her interest (sometimes participation) in the work of former students and colleagues. This subsequent research has substantially extended the field, inspired by the larger vistas opened by the latter two volumes of Bowlby's trilogy. Attachment research, which usually used infant attachment classification as a base line, has been moving increasingly into the preschool years, adolescence, and adulthood. Two sets of researchers should be mentioned especially. Alan Sroufe of the University of Minnesota and his students and colleagues have been undertaking long-term longitudinal follow-ups to ascertain the effect of the security or insecurity of infant–mother attachment on children's performance of later developmental tasks, and to identify conditions that alter expected

performance. Mary Main of the University of California at Berkeley and her students and colleagues have focused on devising new procedures for assessing attachment at later ages—specifically at age six and in adulthood. Her Adult Attachment Interview has proved to be useful with adolescents as well as adults, and promises to be very useful in clinical research. Another extension of attachment research of special interest to clinicians is the application of current techniques to understand the ways in which attachment develops in various at-risk populations.

Thus, current attachment research has made progress in elucidating conditions that affect the extent to which an individual remains on an initial developmental pathway or shifts direction at one or more points in development. It also is yielding support to Bowlby's emphasis on cross-generational effects. Ainsworth's own chief original contribution in recent years has been to extend ethologically oriented attachment theory to cover attachments and affectional bonds other than those between parents and their offspring, in the hope that this can be a theoretical guideline for future research into other interpersonal aspects important in personality development (e.g., Ainsworth, 1989; in press).

In conclusion, we feel fortunate indeed in the outcome of our partnership in an ethological approach to personality development. At first rejected by theoreticians, clinicians, and researchers alike, the intertwining of an open-ended theory and research both guided by it and enriching it has come to be viewed by many as fruitful. Focusing on intimate interpersonal relations, attachment theory does not aspire to address all aspects of personality development. However, it is an open-ended theory and, we hope, open enough to be able to comprehend new findings that result from other approaches. From its outset it has been eclectic, drawing on a number of scientific disciplines, including developmental, cognitive, social, and personality psychology, systems theory, and various branches of biological science, including genetics. Although, at present, attachment theory leaves open many questions, both theoretical and practical, we are confident that attachment theorists will continue to be alert to new developments, in these and other areas, that will help to provide answers to problems still outstanding.

REFERENCES

Ainsworth, M. D. (1962). The effects of maternal deprivation: A review of findings and controversy in the context of research strategy. In *Deprivation of maternal care: A reassessment of its effects* (Public Health Papers, No. 15, pp. 87–195). Geneva, Switzerland: World Health Organization.

Ainsworth, M. D. (1963). The development of mother–infant interaction among the Ganda. In B. M. Foss (Ed.), *Determinants of infant behaviour* (Vol. 2, pp. 67–112). London: Methuen.

Ainsworth, M. D. S. (1967). *Infancy in Uganda: Infant care and the growth of love*. Baltimore: Johns Hopkins University Press.

Ainsworth, M. D. S. (1969). Object relations, dependency and attachment: A theoretical review of the infant–mother relationship. *Child Development, 40*, 969–1025.

Ainsworth, M. D. S. (1972). Attachment and dependency: A comparison.

In J. L. Gewirtz (Ed.), *Attachment and dependency* (pp. 97–137). Washington, DC: Winston.

Ainsworth, M. D. S. (1977). Attachment theory and its utility in cross-cultural research. In P. H. Leiderman, S. R. Tulkin, & A. Rosenfeld (Eds.), *Culture and infancy: Variations in the human experience* (pp. 49–67). San Diego, CA: Academic Press.

Ainsworth, M. D. S. (1979). Attachment as related to mother–child interaction. In J. S. Rosenblatt, R. A. Hinde, C. Beer, & M. Busnel (Eds.), *Advances in the study of behavior* (Vol. 9, pp. 1–51). San Diego, CA: Academic Press.

Ainsworth, M. D. S. (1989). Attachments beyond infancy. *American Psychologist, 44,* 709–716.

Ainsworth, M. D. S. (in press). Attachments and other affectional bonds across the life cycle. In C. M. Parkes, J. Stevenson-Hinde, & P. Marris (Eds.), *Attachment across the life cycle.* New York: Routledge.

Ainsworth, M. D., & Ainsworth, L. H. (1958). *Measuring security in personal adjustment.* Toronto, Canada: University of Toronto Press.

Ainsworth, M. D. S., & Bell, S. M. (1969). Some contemporary patterns of mother–infant interaction in the feeding situation. In A. Ambrose (Ed.), *Stimulation in early infancy* (pp. 133–170). San Diego, CA: Academic Press.

Ainsworth, M. D. S., & Bell, S. M. (1970). Attachment, exploration, and separation: Individual differences in strange-situation behavior of one-year-olds. *Child Development, 41,* 49–67.

Ainsworth, M. D. S., Bell, S. M., & Stayton, D. J. (1971). Individual differences in the strange-situation behavior of one-year-olds. In H. R. Schaffer (Ed.), *The origins of human social relations* (pp. 17–58). San Diego, CA: Academic Press.

Ainsworth, M. D. S., Bell, S. M., & Stayton, D. J. (1974). Infant–mother attachment and social development: Socialisation as a product of reciprocal responsiveness to signals. In M. J. M. Richards (Ed.), *The integration of a child into a social world* (pp. 99–135). London: Cambridge University Press.

Ainsworth, M. D. S., Blehar, M. C., Waters, E., & Wall, S. (1978). *Patterns of attachment: A psychological study of the strange situation.* Hillsdale, NJ: Erlbaum.

Ainsworth, M. D., & Bowlby, J. (1953). *Research strategy in the study of mother–child separation.* Paris: Courrier de la Centre International de l'Enfance.

Ainsworth, M. D. S., & Wittig, B. A. (1969). Attachment and exploratory behaviour of one-year-olds in a strange situation. In B. M. Foss (Ed.), *Determinants of infant behaviour* (Vol. 4, pp. 111–136). London: Methuen.

Bell, S. M., & Ainsworth, M. D. S. (1972). Infant crying and maternal responsiveness. *Child Development, 43,* 1171–1190.

Blatz, W. E. (1966). *Human security: Some reflections.* Toronto, Canada: University of Toronto Press.

Bowlby, J. (1944). Forty-four juvenile thieves: Their characters and their home life. *International Journal of Psycho-Analysis, 25,* 19–52, 107–127.

Bowlby, J. (1951). *Maternal care and mental health.* Geneva, Switzerland: World Health Organization.

Bowlby, J. (1953). Some pathological processes set in train by early mother–child separation. *Journal of Mental Science, 2,* 265–272.

Bowlby, J. (1958). The nature of a child's tie to his mother. *International Journal of Psycho-Analysis, 39,* 350–373.

Bowlby, J. (1960a). Grief and mourning in infancy and early childhood. *Psychoanalytic Study of the Child, 15,* 9–52.

Bowlby, J. (1960b). Separation anxiety. *International Journal of Psycho-Analysis, 41,* 89–113.

Bowlby, J. (1961a). Processes of mourning. *International Journal of Psycho-Analysis, 42,* 317–340.

Bowlby, J. (1961b). Separation anxiety: A critical review of the literature. *Journal of Child Psychology and Psychiatry, 1,* 251–269.

Bowlby, J. (1963). Pathological mourning and childhood mourning. *Journal of the American Psychoanalytic Association, 11,* 500–541.

Bowlby, J. (1969). *Attachment and loss: Vol. 1. Attachment.* New York: Basic Books.

Bowlby, J. (1973). *Attachment and loss: Vol. 2. Separation: Anxiety and anger.* New York: Basic Books.

Bowlby, J. (1979). *The making and breaking of affectional bonds.* London: Tavistock.

Bowlby, J. (1980). *Attachment and loss: Vol. 3. Loss: Sadness and depression.* New York: Basic Books.

Bowlby, J. (1988a). *A secure base.* New York: Basic Books.

Bowlby, J. (1988b). Attachment, communication, and the therapeutic process. In J. Bowlby, *A secure base* (pp. 137–157). New York: Basic Books.

Bowlby, J. (1990). *Charles Darwin: A new biography.* London: Hutchinson.

Bowlby, J., & Ainsworth, M. D. S. (1965). *Child care and the growth of love* (2nd ed.). Harmondsworth, England: Penguin Books.

Bowlby, J., Ainsworth, M. D., Boston, M., & Rosenbluth, D. (1956). Effects of mother–child separation. *British Journal of Medical Psychology, 29,* 169–201.

Bretherton, I., & Ainsworth, M. D. S. (1974). Responses of one-year-olds to a stranger in a strange situation. In M. Lewis & L. A. Rosenblum (Eds.), *The origin of fear* (pp. 131–164). New York: Wiley.

Brown, G. W., & Harris, T. (1978). *The social origins of depression: A study of psychiatric disorder in women.* London: Tavistock.

Heinicke, C. (1956). Some effects of separating two-year-old children from their parents. *Human Relations, 9,* 105–176.

Heinicke, C., & Westheimer, I. (1966). *Brief separations.* New York: International Universities Press.

Klopfer, B., Ainsworth, M. D., Klopfer, W. G., & Holt, R. R. (1954). *Developments in the Rorschach technique* (Vol. 1). Yonkers-on-Hudson, NY: World Book.

Parkes, C. M. (1972). *Studies of grief in adult life.* New York: International Universities Press.

Robertson, J. (1952). *A two-year-old goes to hospital* [Film]. New York: New York University Film Library.

Robertson, J., & Bowlby, J. (1952). Responses of young children to separation from their mothers. *Courrier de la Centre International de l'Enfance, 2,* 131–142.

Salter, M. D. (1940). *An evaluation of adjustment based on the concept of security* (University of Toronto Studies, Child Development Series, No. 18). Toronto, Canada: University of Toronto Press.

Stayton, D. J., & Ainsworth, M. D. S. (1973). Individual differences in infant responses to brief, everyday separations as related to other infant and maternal behavior. *Developmental Psychology, 9,* 226–235.

Stayton, D. J., Ainsworth, M. D. S., & Main, M. (1973). The development of separation behavior in the first year of life: Protest, following, and greeting. *Developmental Psychology, 9,* 213–225.

Stayton, D. J., Hogan, R., & Ainsworth, M. D. S. (1971). Infant obedience and maternal behavior: The origins of socialization reconsidered. *Child Development, 42,* 1057–1069.

Sensitive Periods in Development

[2]

Are There Biological Programming Effects for Psychological Development? Findings From a Study of Romanian Adoptees

Michael Rutter, Thomas G. O'Connor, and the English and Romanian Adoptees (ERA) Study Team
Institute of Psychiatry

Associations between experiences and outcomes could be due to (a) continuation of adversity or (b) organismic changes, including experience-expectant and experience-adaptive developmental programming. The adoption into British families of children who had been reared in profoundly depriving institutions in Romania presented an opportunity to test mechanisms. Romanian children reared from infancy in very depriving institutions for periods up to 42 months were compared with 52 nondeprived UK-born children placed into adoptive families before the age of 6 months. The results at 6 years of age showed substantial normal cognitive and social functioning after the provision of family rearing but also major persistent deficits in a substantial minority. The pattern of findings suggests some form of early biological programming or neural damage stemming from institutional deprivation, but the heterogeneity in outcome indicates that the effects are not deterministic.

During the 1950s to 1970s, strong claims were made regarding the supposed permanent effects of early adverse experiences and also about the importance of critical periods in development that required particular experiences to occur during a narrow time frame for normal development to proceed (Bowlby, 1951; Klaus & Kennell, 1976; Pilling & Kellmer-Pringle, 1978; World Health Organization Expert Committee on Mental Health, 1951). Both claims failed to be supported by empirical research findings, at least with respect to their strong form (Bateson, 1966; Bornstein, 1987; Rutter, 1981; Sluckin, 1973), and the concepts went out of fashion. It came to be accepted that experiences at all ages could be influential and that the extent to which the effects of adverse experiences did or did not persist depended in large part on whether the early disadvantage or deprivation was followed by later disadvantage or deprivation (Clarke & Clarke, 1976, 2000). During the 1990s, there was a reemergence of these earlier claims in a slightly different form, supposedly supported by neuroscience findings on early brain development and on the ways in which such development is sculpted and shaped by early experiences (see Bruer, 1999, for a critique).

In this article, we seek first to clarify the relevant theoretical notions and then to use our data set on children reared in extremely depriving Romanian orphanages, who were subsequently adopted into United Kingdom (UK) families at ages ranging from infancy

to 3½ years and then followed up at the ages of 4 and 6 years (they have recently been reassessed at 11–12 years), in order to test alternative causative models. The sample provided a particularly striking example of a "natural experiment" (see Rutter, Pickles, Murray, & Eaves, 2001) in which there was a sharp discontinuity between early and later rearing environments and in which the change was extremely sudden (and thus easy to time exactly) and also involved an unusually radical shift from a profound and pervasive institutional deprivation to somewhat above-average rearing circumstances in a low-risk family setting. The key question is whether, given the high quality of the later environment, there were any persisting sequelae and, if there were, to what they might be due.

Possible Mediators of Persisting Effects of Psychosocial Adversity

The starting point is the evidence from previous research that, in certain circumstances, there may be long-term sequelae of adverse early experiences; the question to be addressed concerns the possible mechanisms underlying such effects (Rutter, 1989, 2000, 2002a). Three main types of possibility need to be considered. First, the persistence of effects might be brought about by continuities in psychosocial adversity, the main influence deriving from the current (rather than the past) environment (Clarke & Clarke, 1976, 2000). This view builds on the evidence that early adverse experiences frequently lead people to behave in ways, or put themselves in circumstances, that predispose them to a recurrence of psychosocial adversities, not necessarily of the same kind. For example, studies of institution-reared children have shown that many feel that they have a lack of control over their lives and, for that reason, tend to respond impulsively to difficulties, leaping out of one stressful situation into another that may be even more damaging (Pawlby, Mills & Quinton, 1997; Pawlby, Mills, Taylor & Quinton, 1997; Quinton, Pickles, Maughan, & Rutter, 1993; Quinton & Rutter, 1988; Rutter & Robins, 1990).

A second alternative is that the persistence or otherwise of the psychological effects of psychosocial adversity is determined by

Michael Rutter, Thomas G. O'Connor, and the English and Romanian Adoptees (ERA) Study Team, Social, Genetic and Developmental Psychiatry Research Centre, Institute of Psychiatry, London, United Kingdom.

This research was supported by generous grants from the United Kingdom Department of Health and the Helmut Horten Foundation.

We are extremely grateful to the families who generously gave us so much of their time to help us with our research and to the professionals who, with parental permission, gave us access to their findings.

Correspondence concerning this article should be addressed to Michael Rutter, Box PO 80, Social, Genetic and Developmental Psychiatry Research Centre, Institute of Psychiatry, De Crespigny Park, Denmark Hill, London SE5 8AF, United Kingdom. E-mail: j.wickham@iop.kcl.ac.uk the individual's cognitive/affective processing of the experiences. According to this view, the main lasting influence derives from the person's interpretation of, or thoughts about, the experiences. There is no doubt that even quite young children do actively process their experiences, and the notion that the mental sets that they develop about themselves and their experiences could constitute the key mediating influence for later effects is a plausible one (Main, Kaplan, & Cassidy, 1985). On this basis, Kagan (1980) hypothesized that the main reason why, on the whole, very early experiences so rarely had enduring effects was a consequence of infants' much more restricted ability, compared with the abilities of older children and adults, to engage in active processing. Moreover, although there is evidence that even young infants can and do remember events over periods of months, it is uncommon for older children and adults to have memories of discrete events in the first 2 years (Bruce, Dolan, & Phillips-Grant, 2000). It seems that this lack of early memories (so-called infantile amnesia) probably arises, at least in part, because retrieval is hampered by the major differences between cognitive concepts in infancy and those in middle childhood and beyond (Howe & Courage, 1993; Rutter, Maughan, Pickles, & Simonoff, 1998). It has proved difficult to put cognitive/affective processing notions to the test in a rigorous fashion, even in the postinfancy period. Nevertheless, there is good evidence that young people themselves develop internal working models of their experiences and of their interactions with others (Bretherton & Mulholland, 1999; Teasdale & Barnard, 1993). Moreover, there are modest pointers that cognitive/affective processing may play some part in the transduction of adverse experiences into maladaptive behavior (Dodge, Pettit, Bates, & Valente, 1995).

The third alternative is that early adverse experiences bring about a lasting change in the organism, with the main influence deriving from an enduring effect on somatic structure and function. That this can occur is clearly shown by the animal evidence on the effects of early stress experiences on the structure and function of the neuroendocrine system (Bakshi & Kalin, 2000; Barbazanges et al., 1996; Francis, Diorio, Liu, & Meaney, 1999; Hennessey & Levine, 1979; Schneider & Moore, 2000). In recent years, the concept has increasingly been applied to the effects of experiences on the brain.

Implications of Alternative Hypotheses on Mediators

Each of these postulates has a rather different set of predicted consequences, which help in determining how the alternatives may be pitted against one another in a research design.

Continuation of Adversity

The first possibility, that the effects derive from the continuation of adversity, implies that the sequelae should be largely reversible if there is a sufficiently radical change in the relevant environmental circumstances and if the later environment provides persistent high quality. It also follows that later functioning should vary systematically according to differences in the quality of the later environment. There are no particular implications for predicted age-specific effects, although cumulative effects may be anticipated. At the time when this study was first planned, more than a decade ago, this was our favored hypothesis (Rutter, 1981).

Cognitive/Affective Processing

The second alternative gives rise to a quite different set of predictions. The implication is that the sequelae should be much less marked if the adverse experiences were restricted to an age period when an individual had a rather limited capacity to process experiences and when later amnesia for early events is to be expected. Clearly, the cognitive/affective processing skills are likely to function dimensionally rather than categorically. Because of the evidence suggesting that early established attachment qualities together with their mental sets or internal working models are modified by later experiences if these are very different (Kobak, 1999; Thompson, 1998), it may also be anticipated that there will be limited persistence, and continuing change, if the children's later experiences are good and are relevant to the sequelae being considered. In view of our findings on the role of a cognitive style of planning (Quinton & Rutter, 1988), we hypothesized initially that cognitive sets might play a key role in psychological outcomes.

Lasting Changes in the Organism

The hypothesis that effects derive from lasting changes in the organism implies a quite different set of expectations. Because persistence is postulated to derive from changes in somatic structure, it may be anticipated that only a limited recovery is likely to be possible (although, of course, some effects of some sorts of stress can be reversed—see Maccari et al., 1995). Also, the extent of the sequelae should be more strongly associated with the duration of adverse experiences in early life than with the length of time in the compensatory good environment later. Later functioning should *not* vary greatly according to differences in the qualities of the later environment. If the organismic changes affected brain growth, the sequelae might be associated with head size, because this constitutes an index of brain growth.

Possible Types of Changes in the Organism

First, there must be a neural substrate for all forms of learning. This carries with it no particular implications for persistence because the effects of early learning can be altered by later learning—what Greenough, Black, and Wallace (1987) have termed *experience-dependent effects*. Thus, memories and acquired knowledge are laid down, can be retrieved later, and can be modified by new learning or new experiences. Our understanding of the precise brain processes that are involved remains quite limited, particularly with respect to functioning in humans, but there is no doubt that there is a neural substrate for learning (see Rutter, 2002b).

Second, there is animal evidence that severe stress experiences may damage the brain (McEwen, 1999). Thus, for example, this has been shown in relation to changes in the hippocampus (Bremner, 1999). The implication in this case is that there are likely to be some persisting consequences for mental functioning. To date, uncertainties remain about the extent to which the animal findings can be extrapolated to humans, and there is even more uncertainty about the links between brain structure and the functioning of the mind. Nevertheless, this mechanism certainly seems to have validity.

The third possible type of change in the organism concerns the operation of developmental programming during a sensitive period of development. This implies a lasting alteration of the soma that takes place during a maturational phase in which the organismic structure is being laid down and in which the establishment of that structure is shaped by experiences. The implication is that the changes brought about during this sensitive period of development involve influences on later function and on adaptation to later environments.

Different Concepts of Developmental Programming

There are at least two different concepts of developmental programming: experience-expectant and experience-adaptive, the implications of which are rather different.

Experience-Expectant Developmental Programming

The first concept implies that normal somatic development *requires* particular experiences during the relevant sensitive phase of development if the appropriate somatic structure is to be laid down (Greenough et al., 1987). The best-established model here is that provided by the role of visual input in the development of the visual cortex. This was first shown by Hubel and Wiesel (1965; Hubel, Wiesel, & Le Vay, 1977) and has since been confirmed by numerous other investigators (Blakemore, 1991). Normal visual functioning in later life is dependent on adequate visual input in infancy (Le Grand, Mondloch, Maurer, & Brent, 2001). In humans, this is evident, for example, in the finding that unless strabismus (a visual squint) is corrected in the first few years, normal binocular vision later is unlikely. Animal studies have shown that, to a very limited extent, there may be later modification of these effects, but the modifications are rather marginal in most circumstances.

The implication of this concept of experience-expectant development is that the required experiences cover a very broad range of expectable environments and *not* variations within the normal range. It is also to be expected that a lack of such experiences will interfere with normal somatic structural and functional development irrespective of the nature of later environments. These effects, however, operate only within the sensitive period of development in which the somatic structure is being established. Insofar as the experiences (albeit within a broad range) are regarded as essential for normal somatic development, marked individual differences that include normal functioning are not to be expected.

Experience-Adaptive Developmental Programming

The concept of experience-adaptive development is quite different. It implies that the particular form of somatic development, both structural and functional, is shaped by the specifics of experiences during a relatively sensitive phase of development in such a way that there is optimal adaptation to the specifics of that environment (see Bateson & Martin, 1999; Caldji, Diorio, & Meaney, 2000; Sackett, 1965). This concept has been written about most extensively in relation to the findings with respect to the role of early subnutrition in bringing about a much-increased risk for later coronary artery disease, hypertension, and diabetes because the programming has been for low nutrition and not the richer diets

encountered in adulthood (Barker, 1997; O'Brien, Wheeler, & Barker, 1999). The finding is particularly interesting from a developmental point of view because the correlates are the opposite of those found in later life. That is, although early subnutrition is associated with an increased risk of later coronary artery disease, in midlife the risk comes from overnutrition. So far, the physiological basis of these findings remains ill-understood, but the theoretical notion is that the organism is programmed to deal with poor nutrition and that it is thereby maladapted to deal with later overnutrition, if that is what is encountered in the later years. There are similar sorts of effects in relation to immunity and infection (Bock & Whelan, 1991).

The most obvious likely parallel within the field of psychological development is provided by phonological development. Infants in all countries show broadly comparable skills in phonological discrimination, but from the second half of the 1st year onward, phonological discrimination skills are increasingly shaped by the language of the rearing environment (Kuhl, 1994; Kuhl et al., 1997). Thus, it has often been observed that Japanese people find great difficulty discriminating *r* from *l*, a discrimination that is taken for granted by those who have been English speakers from infancy onward.

The implications of this form of developmental programming are the same as those for experience-expectant development only with respect to the postulate that the effects will operate exclusively within the sensitive period of development when the somatic structure is being established. The two key differences are, first, that the relevant experiences and outcomes include variations within (as well as outside) the normal range and, second, that the nature of such experiences will foster somatic development that is well adapted for the environment experienced during the sensitive phase. Whether such development will be well adapted for later environments will depend on whether they are similar to, or different from, those provided by early experiences. In other words, the development that has been shaped by the early experiences cannot be regarded as normal in an absolute sense; rather, it is adapted to a particular type of environment.

Hypotheses

The research design with respect to data analysis was determined by the need to test competing hypotheses about the effects of profound early deprivation. Five main alternatives were considered:

1. The effects are entirely due to subnutrition rather than to psychological deprivation. The expectation in this case is that there should be a major effect on outcome of nutritional level (as indexed by weight) at the time of leaving Romania and that duration of institutional care should no longer relate to psychological outcomes after nutrition is taken into account.

2. Psychological outcome is primarily determined by the qualities of the environments prevailing at outcome. The expectation in this case is that there should be complete recovery if the later environments are of high quality, and insofar as there are any deficits, these should be a function of later environmental limitations and not of the earlier adversities.

3. Psychological outcome is primarily determined by the cognitive/affective mental sets or internal working models that the children develop about their experiences and about the implica-

tions for their concepts of themselves as individuals. The expectation in this case is that the sequelae should be least marked when children's ability to process experiences is most limited and when their later memories of such experiences will be weakest. On this basis, the prediction is that psychological sequelae (in relation to social outcome) should be least severe for children whose developmental level at the time of entry into the UK was below 1 year.

4. Psychological outcome is primarily determined by experience-adaptive biological programming. The expectation that follows is that psychological deficits at follow-up should be a function of the pervasiveness of the early institutional deprivation, as indexed by the duration of institutional care, and not of the qualities of the later environment. Because this form of programming concerns adaptations within the normal range, no effect on brain growth is expected.

5. Psychological outcome is primarily determined by either experience-expectant biological programming or by neural damage (we saw no clear way of differentiating between these two alternatives with the measures available to us). The predictions are similar to those for Hypothesis 4 except that there might be associations with head growth, on the grounds that if the experiences are required for normal brain development, some impairment of brain growth (resulting in diminished head growth) might be expected.

Psychological Outcomes

In this article, we focus on just two contrasting psychological outcomes: (a) cognitive impairment and (b) disinhibited attachment. The rationale was that we wished to compare two outcomes for which the evidence suggested that somewhat different psychosocial influences might be operative (Rutter, 1985a, 1985b, 2002a) and hence that, possibly, different mediating mechanisms might be relevant.

Method

Sample

The sample of adoptees from Romanian institutions was drawn from the 324 children adopted into UK families between February 1990 and September 1992 who were processed through the Department of Health and/or the Home Office. A stratified random sampling design, based on the child's age at the time of coming to the UK, was used. Overall, 81% of the parents of Romanian adoptees who were approached agreed to participate. The study sample as a whole ($N = 165$) included a few children who were adopted from a home setting, but in this article we confine attention to the 144 who were reared from infancy in very depriving institutions and who were adopted into UK families at various ages up to 42 months. There were 45 children placed at under 6 months, 54 placed between 6 and 24 months, and 45 placed between 24 and 42 months. The last group was too old at the start of the study to be assessed at 4 years of age, but these children were evaluated at age 6 in exactly the same fashion as the other groups. The findings in this article are confined to the assessments at age 6 and therefore cover the whole sample of 144 institution-reared children.

The comparison sample comprised 52 UK-born children who were placed into adoptive families before the age of 6 months. The choice of this sample was dictated by our wish to equate the groups with respect to the experience of adoption but to seek a contrast with respect to early experiences. Social Service records indicated that none of the comparison sample had been removed from parents because of abuse or neglect and

none had experienced an institutional rearing. The decision to focus on a group adopted before 6 months of age was predicated on the wish to have a "best case" adoption sample. The interest in the duration of deprivation was relevant only within the Romanian sample and not within the comparison group, who had not experienced severe deprivation. Accordingly, there were no late-adopted UK-born children. Intracountry adoptees were obtained through adoption agencies and social services departments. It was not possible to determine the rate of participation among the intracountry adoptees because a name was provided to the project by the adoption agency only after the family consented to participate. Available information suggests that approximately 50% of the families who were contacted agreed to participate.

The adoptive families of both UK and Romanian children were generally middle class and slightly better educated than the general UK population but did not differ in these respects from one another (Rutter & the ERA Research Team, 1998). Differences that did exist between parents adopting from the UK and from Romania were a direct consequence of UK adoption policies (e.g., with respect to the presence of biological children in the family); these demographic variables were not associated with outcomes and were therefore dropped from the analyses. Among the families adopting from Romania, no association was found between family characteristics and the child's age at entry into the UK. Also, children who entered the UK at a relatively young age were similar to those who entered later in terms of the age when they were placed in the institution and in terms of subnutrition at entry into the UK (O'Connor, Rutter, Beckett, et al., 2000). In the great majority of cases, the Romanian children entered the institution in early infancy (85% within the 1st month of life), and it is evident that institutionalized children were not placed there because of developmental delay or handicap. Children adopted from Romania had experienced unusually severe and pervasive deprivation (Castle et al., 1999), as reflected in their marked physical and developmental delay evident at the time of UK entry (Rutter et al., 1998).

Measures

A wide range of measures was obtained similarly on all children at the ages of 4 and 6 years (see Kreppner, O'Connor, Dunn, Anderson-Wood, & the ERA Study Team, 1999; Kreppner, O'Connor, Rutter, & the E.R.A. Study Team, 2001; O'Connor, Bredenkamp, Rutter, & the English and Romanian Adoptees (ERA) Study Team, 1999; O'Connor, Rutter, Beckett, et al., 2000; O'Connor, Rutter, & the English and Romanian Adoptees Study Team, 2000; Rutter, Kreppner, O'Connor, & the ERA Study Team, 2001; Rutter et al., 1998, 1999). Details are given here only of the physical, cognitive, and social measures used in the present set of analyses.

Measures concerning the child's state at the time of UK entry. Weight at the time of the child's entry to the UK, which indexed nutritional deprivation, and head circumference, which indexed brain growth, were assessed in terms of standard deviation units with respect to population norms. Thus, a score of -1.5 indicated a score 1.5 standard deviations below average (Boyce & Cole, 1993, based on the work of Buckler, 1990). Developmental assessment was available on the Romanian children and was based on retrospective parental reports on the Revised Denver Prescreening Developmental Questionnaire (R–PDQ; Frankenburg, van Doorninck, Liddell, & Dick, 1986). Previous analyses (showing the concurrent and predictive correlations with the children's scores on the McCarthy Scales of Children's Abilities) supported the validity of these retrospective measures (Rutter et al., 1998).

Measures at age 6 years. At both 4 years and 6 years of age, the families were visited at home by a trained interviewer for a tape-recorded intensive interview with the primary caregiver and the administration of a set of behavioral and family-related questionnaires. Approximately 3 months later, an extensive assessment of the child was conducted by different research workers, using standard cognitive and developmental measures and observations. For the present purposes, attention is confined to the general cognitive index (GCI) of the McCarthy Scales of Children's Abilities (McCarthy, 1972)—a widely used measure of intellectual functioning that comprises four subscales: Verbal, Quantitative, Perceptual, and Memory. A small subset of 5 late-placed children did not attain a basal score on the GCI at age 6: The Merrill-Palmer Scale was administered to those children, and a GCI score was imputed on the basis of the Merrill-Palmer Scale results.

Evidence for disinhibited attachment disturbance was derived from a semistructured interview designed to assess the child's behavior toward the parent and other adults in both novel and familiar situations. Three items indexed disinhibited behavior: a definite lack of differentiation among adults; a clear indication that the child would readily go off with a stranger; and a definite lack of checking back with the parent in anxiety-provoking situations. For each of these items, a score of 0 was given if there was no evidence of the specified behavior; a score of 1 was given if there was some or mild evidence; and a score of 2 was given if the behavior was marked or pervasive. The scores for each of the three items were then summed. For the current sample, internal consistency was .77. Interrater reliability on each of the items from the interviews was determined, using a weighted kappa statistic, for 20 interview protocols from 3 interviewers. Kappas ranged from .86 to 1.00. In order to identify children with severe social disinhibition, we used a cutoff score of 4 or more on the 6-point scale, which identified about 1 in 9 of the sample. Previous analyses had indicated that this measure was closely associated with the presence and duration of deprivation (O'Connor et al., 1999). The attachment classification findings based on the modified separation–reunion procedure, used at age 4, were used to validate the parents' descriptions of disinhibited behavior (O'Connor et al., 2003). Compared with the remainder of the sample of Romanian adoptees, the children with disinhibited attachment patterns were significantly less likely to show secure attachment (13% vs. 45%) and much more likely to show an "other" nonnormative pattern (81% vs. 39%). This pattern was based more on the response to the stranger than on the response to the mother, either before separation or after reunion. An unusually friendly initial approach to the stranger was common, but this was sometimes followed by later wariness. However, probably what was most characteristic was coy, silly, overexuberant, or overexcited behavior. The validation provided a rigorous test in that the videotaped child observations were rated by raters blind to group. It may be concluded that parents were describing a quite unusual pattern of behavior of a distinctive kind.

Of the original sample of 144, all were followed up at 6 years of age with parental interviews. In 8 cases, parents declined permission for the children to be interviewed and tested, so direct child measures were available for 136 (94%) of the sample. The main sources of missing data were the weight at the time of UK entry (13 missing) and head circumference at entry (11 missing). Parent estimates on child nutrition were available for missing cases, and the findings were analyzed using these in the place of missing data, with almost identical results. However, data are reported here strictly in terms of actual quantified measures obtained at the time. Follow-up parental interviews when the children were 6 years old were obtained for all of the 52 within-UK adoptees, and direct child measures were available for 50 (96%).

Analytic Strategy

A multistage analytic strategy was followed. First, as already established in published analyses (Rutter, Kreppner, et al., 2001), the hypothesis of a specific effect of institutional deprivation on cognitive impairment and on disinhibited attachment had been tested by determining whether these variables showed both a between-groups difference (between Romanian adoptees and within-UK adoptees) and a within-group difference according to the duration of institutional deprivation. Second, again as already published, although subnutrition had a significant effect on cognitive outcome at the age of 6 years, a large effect of duration of deprivation remained after

nutrition was taken into account (O'Connor, Rutter, and the English and Romanian Adoptees Study Team, 2000). There was no effect of subnutrition on disinhibited attachment (O'Connor, Rutter, Beckett, et al., 2000). Nevertheless, because subnutrition constituted a potentially important confound, it was included in the new analyses reported here. Third, developmental catch-up was considered with respect to weight because previous research had shown that weight catch-up was usually complete or nearly complete (i.e., there was no developmental programming). Fourth, catch-up for head circumference (which is strongly related to brain growth) was assessed to determine whether or not it followed the pattern for weight. Fifth, cognitive catch-up was assessed at age 6 through comparison of cognitive levels with those of the within-UK adoptee group. Sixth, the competing hypotheses on mechanisms were tested through examination of the correlates of cognitive level at age 6, with particular attention given to head circumference (as an index of biological underpinning) and adoptive parental educational level (as an index of the home rearing environment). Seventh, a parallel examination of competing hypotheses was undertaken with respect to disinhibited attachment, with the same attention paid to head circumference but also to the children's developmental level at the time of UK entry (as an index of cognitive processing abilities at that time). Eighth, the temporal stability of deficits between 4 years and 6 years was examined to determine whether there was persistence of the effects of the early adverse environment. Finally, there was an examination of the heterogeneity in outcome. Because our hypotheses included the possibility of effects only on subgroups, and because prior analyses had shown no effects for children who left institutional care at younger than 6 months, we used categorical, as well as dimensional, approaches (see Farrington & Loeber, 2000). In all cases, we checked whether the findings using dimensional measures were similar and found that they were.

Results

Patterns Associated and Not Associated With Institutional Deprivation

The first step in the analytic strategy—namely, testing for the associations between each of the two outcome variables and institutional deprivation—had already been taken in previously published studies (O'Connor, Rutter, Beckett, et al., 2000; O'Connor, Rutter, and the English and Romanian Adoptees Study Team, 2000). In brief, cognitive impairment (defined here as a McCarthy test GCI of less than 80) occurred in 15.4% of the institution-reared adoptees from Romania, compared with 2.0% of within-UK adoptees ($p = .01$ on two-sided Fisher's exact test). There was a linear association with duration of institutional care, with 2.3% cognitive impairment in those experiencing 6 months or less of institutional deprivation, 12.0% cognitive impairment in those experiencing greater than 6 but not more than 24 months, and 32.6% in those experiencing greater than 24 but not more than 42 months, $\chi^2(1, N = 136)$ for trends $= 15.12$, $p < .01$. The comparable figures for disinhibited attachment behavior were 22.4% versus 3.8% ($p = .002$) for Romanian and UK adoptees, respectively, and 8.9% versus 24.5% versus 33.3% for ≤ 6 months, > 6 but ≤ 24 months, and >24 but ≤ 42 months, respectively, $\chi^2(1, N = 143)$ for trends $= 7.69$, $p < .01$. In most of the remainder of the article, attention is confined to the 99 children who left Romanian institutions after the age of 6 months, because no significant deficits were found in those who entered the UK below that age.

Developmental Catch-Up and Deficits for Weight and Head Circumference

Previous research had shown that severely malnourished children usually showed a catch-up in growth once normal nutritional intake was provided (e.g., Lien, Meyer, & Winick, 1977). The next step, therefore, was to determine whether that was so in our sample. Table 1 shows the catch-up in weight for the 58 children whose weight at the time of entry into the UK was at least 1.5 standard deviations below the UK population mean for their age group and sex (i.e., the sample used here includes only those children showing severe subnutrition). Those whose weight at entry was higher than that were excluded because the question of catch-up could not apply in the same way. Despite the fact that half the total group of Romanian adoptees had a weight below the third percentile, the catch-up in weight for those who left the institution between the ages of 6 and 24 months was virtually complete by the age of 6 years. There was a similarly dramatic catch-up in those who remained in the institution until after age 2, but the catch-up was not quite complete by age 6.

The next analytic step was to determine whether the catch-up in head growth followed the same pattern as that found for weight. Table 2 shows the findings for head circumference in the Romanian adoptees with and without severe subnutrition. Strikingly, although there was very substantial, and highly significant, catch-up for both those with and those without severe subnutrition, the catch-up in head circumference was far from complete. For those without severe subnutrition at the time of UK entry, head circumference at age 6 was still about 1½ standard deviations below the general population mean. For those with between 6 and 24 months of institutional deprivation, the findings at 6 years differed significantly from those for weight (as shown by the lack of overlap between the confidence intervals). In short, significant head-circumference deficits persisted even when weight catch-up was largely complete. A multivariate, using a within-subject, repeated measures analysis (with time, head circumference, and weight as within-subject measures), revealed a significant interaction between measure and time, $F(1, 47) = 32.24, p < .01$, as well as a main effect of time. That is, the catch-up for weight was significantly greater than the catch-up for head circumference. The finding that the pattern for head circumference differed from that for weight means that the continuing impaired head growth found in some children could not be accounted for solely in terms of the effects of malnutrition on overall body growth.

Cognitive Catch-Up and Deficit

Cognitive progress was assessed by using the initial R–PDQ developmental quotient at the time of UK entry as the starting point and the McCarthy GCI at age 6 as the outcome. In the group of Romanian adoptees as a whole, over half were initially functioning in the severely retarded range, and by age 6 their cognitive functioning had almost caught up to the UK population mean (O'Connor, Rutter, Beckett, et al., 2000). This was so for both those with and those without severe subnutrition initially, although the catch-up was less complete in those who remained in the institution longest and who were severely subnourished.

The further question, however, was whether, despite the dramatic catch-up, there was a persistent cognitive deficit at age 6 in those who remained longest in the profoundly depriving institutional care (see Table 3). No deficit was found in the Romanian adoptees from institutions who entered the UK before the age of 6 months ($M = 114.2$; 95% confidence interval [CI] = 108.8–119.7; $n = 44$), their GCI scores not being significantly different from those of the within-UK adoptees ($M = 116.7$; 95% CI = 111.6–121.7; $n = 50$). This was so for both those with ($M = 108.8$; 95% CI = 102.3–115.3) and those without ($M = 122.9$; 95% CI = 113.7–132.2) severe subnutrition. By sharp contrast, deficits were apparent in those whose institutional care continued for more than 6 but less than 24 months and for those for whom it continued for more than 24 but less than 42 months. This was apparent in both those with and those without severe subnutrition. The greatest deficit, however, was found in those who remained in the institutions longest and who had severe subnutrition. Moreover, the deficit in the mean scores of those who came to the UK after 6 months compared with those adopted within the UK in infancy was quite substantial—some 18–25 points in those who were not malnourished and 18–35 points in those who were malnourished.

Because, with very few exceptions, the children moved without any appreciable time gap from institutional care to the adoptive home in the UK, cross-sectional data did not allow differentiation between the effects of duration of institutional privation and the effects of the length of time in the adoptive home. However, this contrast could be made through use of longitudinal data (by making use of the continuities between the scores at 4 years and 6 years). In order to make this contrast, we confined attention to Romanian adoptees, all of whom had been in their adoptive homes for 2½ to 4 years but who varied in their duration of exposure to institutional rearing. Because the findings on the dose–response

Table 1

Weight (in Standard Deviation Units) Catch-Up by Age at UK Entry in Romanian Adoptees With Severe Subnutrition

	Weight at entry			Weight at 6 years		
Age at UK entry	M	95% CI	n	M	95% CI	n
>6 but ≤24 months	−3.21	−3.67 to −2.77	35	−0.35	−.70 to −.01	32
>24 but ≤42 months	−4.10	−5.42 to −2.77	23	−1.16	−1.55 to −.77	23

Note. Severe subnutrition was defined as weight 1.5 *SD*s below United Kingdom (UK) population norms at the time of entry into the UK. A repeated measures analysis of variance indicated a significant effect of time, $F(1, 53) = 94.08, p < .01$, and group, $F(1, 53) = 5.57, p < .05$, but no interaction, $F(1, 53) = 0.02$ (i.e., the extent of catch-up was the same across groups). The means at entry were not significantly different, but those at age 6 were, $F(1, 53) = 9.68, p < .01$. CI = confidence interval.

Table 2

Head Circumference (in Standard Deviation Units) Catch-Up According to Age at UK Entry in Romanian Adoptees With and Without Severe Subnutrition

	Head circumference at entry			Head circumference at 6 years		
Age at UK entry	M	95% CI	n	M	95% CI	n
>6 but ≤24 months						
Without severe subnutrition	−2.27	−2.83 to −1.69	17	−1.60	−2.00 to −1.19	16
With severe subnutrition	−2.77	−3.28 to −2.26	32	−1.63	−1.98 to −1.29	32
>24 but ≤42 months						
Without severe subnutrition	−2.23	−3.09 to −1.38	11	−1.32	−1.77 to −0.87	12
With severe subnutrition	−3.37	−4.09 to −2.66	21	−2.52	−3.00 to −2.03	22

Note. Severe subnutrition was defined as weight 1.5 SDs below United Kingdom (UK) population norms at the time of entry into the UK. A repeated measures analysis of variance indicated a significant effect of time, $F(1, 71) = 33.87, p < .01$, and group, $F(3, 71) = 5.25, p < .01$, but no interaction, $F(3, 71) = 0.18$. CI = confidence interval.

effect of duration of institutional care were derived from the total sample, this analysis was also undertaken with the total sample (i.e., including those with less than 6 months in institutions). The subgroup of 84 children (79 of whom had cognitive data available) whose institutional care had lasted for no more than 18 months had a mean GCI of 108.2 (95% CI = 104.1–112.3). By sharp contrast, those whose institutional care had lasted between 24 and 42 months ($n = 60$, 57 with available cognitive scores) had a mean score of 88.1 (95% CI = 82.0–94.1). There was only limited further cognitive catch-up between 4 and 6 years of age, and the catch-up that was observed was unrelated to duration of deprivation but was instead associated with lower cognitive scores at the earlier assessment (see O'Connor, Rutter, Beckett, et al., 2000). It is evident that the effect of duration of institutional care was extremely strong, even after the period of time in the adoptive home was taken into account. The deficit on this comparison amounted to some 20 IQ points.

Correlates for Cognitive Functioning and Cognitive Impairment

Apart from the effects of duration of institutional care, the only major correlate with cognitive functioning was the head circum-

ference both at the time of UK entry and at age 6. The 21 children with a GCI score below 80 at age 6 had a head circumference that was approximately 1 standard deviation lower than that of those without cognitive impairment, the differences at both time points being statistically significant. At the time of UK entry, the means (and 95% CIs) were −2.38 (−2.70 to −2.07) for the 115 children with a cognitive score above 80 at age 6 and −3.39 (−4.01 to −2.78) for the 20 children with a cognitive score of less than 80 at age 6. At 6 years, the comparable figures were −1.52 (−1.71 to −1.32) and −2.22 (−2.78 to −1.65). There were significant main effects on cognitive level for time, cognitive impairment, and nutritional deprivation, but no significant interactions of any kind in a repeated measures analysis.

These differences in cognitive scores were not just a function of subnutrition. Indeed, in the group without subnutrition, there was still a significant effect of head circumference at the time of UK entry on cognitive impairment at age 6 (for those without impairment, $M = −1.59$, 95% CI = −2.08 to −1.1; for those with cognitive impairment, $M = −3.01$, 95% CI = −4.49 to −1.55), $F(1, 40) = 4.91, p < .05$. The difference for head circumference at age 6 was in the same direction ($Ms = 1.16$ vs. 1.43), but it fell well short of statistical significance, $F(1, 42) = 0.45$. The corre-

Table 3

Cognitive Catch-Up by Age at UK Entry in Romanian Adoptees With and Without Severe Subnutrition

	R–PDQ score at UK entry			GCI at 6 years		
Age at UK entry	M	95% CI	n	M	95% CI	n
>6 but ≤24 months						
Without severe subnutrition	44.55	32.10 to 57.00	17	91.94	80.91 to 102.87	16
With severe subnutrition	44.87	37.25 to 52.49	30	98.56	92.52 to 104.61	32
>24 but ≤42 months						
Without severe subnutrition	40.06	32.27 to 47.86	11	98.08	80.86 to 115.31	12
With severe subnutrition	38.73	32.83 to 44.62	23	82.04	72.39 to 91.70	23

Note. Severe subnutrition was defined as weight 1.5 SDs below United Kingdom (UK) population norms at the time of entry into the UK. A repeated measures analysis of variance indicated a significant effect of time, $F(1, 73) = 384.75, p < .001$. There were nonsignificant trends for group, $F(3, 73) = 2.17, p = .10$, and for the interaction, $F(3, 73) = 2.29, p = .09$. The possible interaction reflected a significant difference among groups at age 6 but not at entry. R–PDQ = Revised Denver Prescreening Developmental Questionnaire; GCI = general cognitive index of the McCarthy Scales of Children's Abilities; CI = confidence interval.

lations between the GCI at age 6 and head circumference at UK entry and at age 6 were almost identical (.27 and .31, respectively, for those without subnutrition and .26 and .31, respectively, for those with subnutrition).

Although the group of adopting parents as a whole (both of Romanian children and within-UK children) had educational and occupational levels above those for general population norms, there was a meaningful spread. In order to determine the effects of parental educational level on children's cognitive functioning, we subdivided the parents' educational backgrounds into four groups: (a) a university degree or equivalent professional qualification; (b) superior scholastic achievement as reflected in successful exam performance at age 18 (advanced levels) or at least 5 good passes at age 16; (c) lower levels of exam performance at age 16; and (d) leaving school without scholastic credentials. Table 4 shows the mean GCI score of the children at age 6 across these four groups in relation to the father's educational level and, separately, the mother's educational level. There was no significant association either when assessed categorically (as shown in Table 4) or in terms of correlations when treating educational attainment in dimensional terms.

Gender differences were examined for all of the dependent variables considered in this article. No statistically significant main effects or interactions were found.

Disinhibited Attachment Patterns at Age 6

As already noted, the pattern of disinhibited attachment not only was much commoner in the adoptees from Romanian institutions but was also strongly associated with the duration of institutional deprivation. There was, however, the same issue as for cognitive impairment of needing to check whether this association could have been an artifact of the period of time in the adoptive home. Findings showed that it was not. The proportion of children showing disinhibited attachment was examined within the Romanian adoptees, all of whom had spent 2½ to 4 years in the adoptive home but who varied in the duration of their exposure to institutional rearing. Of those whose institutional care lasted less than 18 months, the rate of disinhibited attachment was 16% (13/84), compared with 33% (15/45) in those whose institutional care lasted between 24 and 42 months, $\chi^2(1, N = 129) = 5.50, p < .02$.

In contrast to the findings for cognitive impairment, there was no association between disinhibited attachment and head circumference either at the time of entry into the UK or at age 6 in the total sample of 144 institutionalized children. Head circumference, both at the time of UK entry and at age 6, did not differ substantially or significantly for those with versus those without disinhibited attachment: at UK entry, $M = -2.85$, 95% CI $= -3.38$ to -2.32, $n = 28$ versus $M = -2.50$, 95% CI $= -2.84$ to -2.15, $n = 28$, respectively, $F(1, 130) = 0.98, p = .33$; at age 6, $M = -1.75$, 95% CI $= -2.10$ to -1.39, $n = 31$ versus $M = -1.61$, 95% CI $= -1.83$ to -1.39, $n = 104$, respectively, $F(1, 133) = 0.38, p = .54$. Unlike the situation with cognition, there was no effect of subnutrition on disinhibited attachment. Weight at the time of UK entry and at 6 years did not differ significantly for those with versus those without disinhibited attachment at age 6: at UK entry, $M = -3.05$, 95% CI $= -4.17$ to -1.93, $n = 27$ versus $M = -2.28$, 95% CI $= -2.65$ to -1.91, $n = 103$, respectively, $F(1, 128) = 2.81, p = .10$; at age 6, $M = -0.61$, 95% CI $= -0.99$ to -0.22, $n = 31$ versus $M = -0.34$, 95% CI $= -0.52$ to -0.16, $n = 105$, respectively, $F(1, 134) = 1.80, p = .18$.

In order to test the hypothesis that attachment disinhibition might be a function of cognitive/affective processing, we compared children whose mental age, as assessed on the R–PDQ, was below 12 months at the time of UK entry with children whose mental age was higher. In almost all cases, even in the higher mental age group, the mental age was below 2 years, there being only 2 children whose levels were slightly above that. No significant association was found between mental age and attachment disinhibition; the proportions with disinhibition were 29.5% (23/78) for those with a mental age under 12 months at UK entry and 28.6% (4/14) for those with a higher mental age. The lack of difference still applied when comparisons were made among those with more than 6 but less than 24 months of institutional care (23.9% [11/46] vs. 25% [1/4]) or among those with more than 24 months of institutional care (37.5% [12/32] vs. 30.0% [3/10]). The lack of association between mental age and attachment disinhibition applied similarly when mental age was treated as a dimension and when cutoffs below or above 12 months were used.

Gender differences were also examined. Again, no statistically significant main effects or interactions were found.

Table 4

Educational Level of Adoptive Fathers and Mothers and General Cognitive Index at 6 Years of Romanian Adoptees

General Cognitive Index at age 6	Educational level of adoptive parents			
	Low	Moderate	High	Very high
	Fathers			
M	103.6	97.9	103.5	99.5
95% CI	95.1–112.1	87.2–108.7	96.7–110.3	95.7–103.4
	Mothers			
M	105.2	92.9	99.6	102.2
95% CI	96.9–113.6	83.9–101.8	92.6–106.6	94.6–109.7

Comparison of Correlates With Cognitive Impairment and With Disinhibited Attachment

As already stated, whereas both head circumference and subnutrition correlated with cognitive impairment, neither correlated with disinhibited attachment. Treated dimensionally, the Pearson correlations for the GCI were .29 and .24 for head circumference and weight at entry, respectively, compared with −.09 and −.16 in relation to the disinhibited attachment scores at age 6. In both cases, the correlations for the two outcome measures differed significantly when Steiger's (1980) method for comparing dependent correlations was used: $t(110) = 2.66$, $p < .05$ for correlations with head circumference, and $t(110) = 2.33$, $p < .05$ for correlations with weight ($n = 113$ in both instances).

Stability of Patterns Between 4 and 6 Years of Age

The hypothesis involving programming predicts at least moderate stability in adverse sequelae between ages 4 and 6. The findings are summarized in Table 5. With respect to both cognitive impairment and disinhibited behavior, there was substantial stability. The proportion of children showing these patterns remained much the same, individual differences across this 2-year time span were moderately stable, and the association with duration of deprivation was just about as strong at age 6 as it had been at age 4. Thus, the correlation between the GCI and the duration of institutional care was −.54 at 4 years and −.48 ($n = 91$) at 6 years (in both cases, $p < .01$). The Pearson correlation between attachment disinhibition and duration of institutional care was .22 ($p < .05$) at age 4 and .25 ($p < .05$) at age 6.

Heterogeneity in Outcome

As is implicit in the findings already reported here, there was substantial heterogeneity in outcome even for the children who had spent at least 2 years in profoundly depriving Romanian institutions. Even with this relatively late-adopted group, the IQ levels spanned the range from mental retardation to superior, with most children having GCI scores at 6 years somewhere in the range

Table 5
Stability of Effects on Cognitive Impairment and Attachment Disinhibition

Measure of stability	Cognitive impairment	Attachment disinhibition
Showing impairment at age 6 given impairment at age 4		
M	6/14	11/18
%	43	61
Odds ratio	67.00*	16.16*
Agreement on categorical distinctions between ages 4 and 6 (phi)	.56*	.57*

Note. Because children over the age of 2 years at the time of United Kingdom (UK) entry were already too old to be assessed at age 4, this table is based on children who came to the UK when they were younger than 2 years of age. The denominators in the first row concern only those showing impairment at age 4 years; accordingly, the numbers are much lower than those for the total sample of children experiencing institutional care.
* $p < .01$.

between the two extremes. Figure 1 shows the scattergram for the GCI scores at age 6 for the total sample of 144 institutional children (data were available on 136). There was no narrowing of the spread even in those with the longest duration of institutional deprivation. Exactly the same pattern was found with respect to disinhibited attachment although the rate was relatively high in the late-adopted children, two thirds of whom did *not* show this pattern (see O'Connor, Rutter, & the English and Romanian Adoptees Study Team, 2000).

Discussion

Differentiating Among Available Models of Early Experience Effects

The findings on cognitive impairment were reasonably clear-cut. There was a strong association with institutional deprivation and, within the group of adoptees from Romanian institutions, there was a strong association with the length of institutional deprivation. With respect to outcome, two findings stand out. First, there was a remarkable degree of recovery after restoration of normal family rearing. Second, however, substantial deficits persisted after the children were placed in generally well-functioning adoptive families. Moreover, the deficits were quite marked. Thus, the mean GCI at age 6 was some 25–26 points lower in the children leaving institutions after the age of 2 years than in those who entered the UK before the age of 6 months. It is noteworthy that this effect was found to a similar degree even within the group who did not suffer substantial subnutrition. The developmental catch-up in head circumference was less than that found for weight, and cognitive impairment was particularly likely in those whose head circumferences remained substantially below population norms. It is also noteworthy that the duration of institutional deprivation was by far the strongest predictive factor for cognitive outcome, but, particularly in those who spent the longest time in depriving institutions, there was some effect from subnutrition.

By sharp contrast, cognitive functioning was unassociated with the length of time in the adoptive home after the first 2 to 2½ years, during which time the major developmental catch-up occurred. Also, the children's level of cognitive functioning at age 6 was completely unassociated with the educational level of either the adoptive mother or the adoptive father. This negative finding is particularly striking in view of the strong effect of educational attainment of adoptive parents in the Duyme, Dumaret, and Tomkiewicz (1999) study of a less seriously deprived sample.

The lack of any association between the GCI score at 6 years and the educational level of the adoptive parents, together with the strong association with duration of depriving institutional rearing even after taking into account the span of time in the adoptive home, makes any continuing psychosocial adversity explanation for the cognitive deficits found in some children implausible. Of course, it is possible that more detailed measures of parent–child interaction and communication might show an effect, but our findings do not support that suggestion (Croft et al., 2001). Specifically, observational measures of parent–child interactions at ages 4 and 6 indicated that an increase in the child's cognitive index predicted a positive change over time in the parents' interactional style, but there was no evidence of a reverse effect (Croft et al., 2001). That is, parent–child interaction at age 4 did not

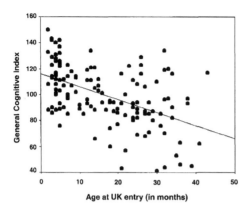

Figure 1. Scattergram and regression line for the association between cognitive level and age at entry into the United Kingdom (UK).

predict a positive change in the child's cognitive level between 4 and 6 years. Thus, none of the three available indices of the adoptive home environment (time in the adoptive home, parental educational level, or observational pattern of parent–child interaction) was predictive of the wide variation in children's cognitive scores at age 6.

In summary, the lack of association with conditions of rearing in the adoptive home, and the stability of the duration-of-deprivation effect across the age period from 4 to 6 years, suggests some form of programming effect or neural damage. The moderate association with head circumference (which was not dependent on general physical development, as indexed by weight gain) makes either experience-expectant programming or neural damage the most plausible of the available models.

The patterns of findings on disinhibited attachment were both very similar in some respects and rather different in others. They were the same in showing a substantial association with institutional deprivation and, within the institutionally deprived group, with duration of deprivation. There was considerable recovery of normal social functioning after provision of normal family rearing, and the majority of the relatively late-adopted children did not show disinhibited attachment. Nevertheless, the pattern of disinhibited attachment did persist after restoration of normal family rearing in a significant minority of the children. What was different from the findings with cognitive impairment was that there was no association with small head circumference and no association with subnutrition. It was also noteworthy that although the disinhibited attachment pattern was clearly highly discrepant from that normally found in well-functioning children, it did not show the usual features of insecure attachment. Rather, the details, both as observed and as reported by parents, suggested a relative failure to develop selective attachments rather than the acquisition of attachments that were insecure in quality.

As with cognitive impairment, the findings run counter to a continuing psychosocial adversity explanation. The association between duration of institutional care and disinhibited attachment

at 6 years was as strong as that at 4 years; there was no association with any occupational or educational measure of the adoptive parents; and there was moderately strong stability in the behavioral pattern between 4 and 6 years of age. Little is known about the family qualities that predispose children to disinhibited attachment (other than early institutional care). Accordingly, it is possible that unmeasured aspects of family interaction could have had an effect, but there was no indication that this might be so. Although not reported here, the observational measures of parent–child interaction used by Croft et al. (2001) showed no association with disinhibited attachment.

The lack of association between disinhibited attachment and the children's mental age at the time of UK entry also casts doubt on a cognitive processing explanation. It is implausible that children with a mental age of less than 12 months could remember specific experiences in infancy several years later, and it is also unlikely that any cognitive set established at that age would still be operative at age 6, especially after a major change in the rearing environment (see Kobak, 1999; Thompson, 1998). However, given that it is not known how cognitive sets or models are either established or retrieved, it is not possible to rule out their operation completely. Neural damage, too, does not seem a likely cause in view of the lack of association between disinhibited attachment and head circumference and in view of the lack of any effect of subnutrition. Rather, some form of developmental programming seems the most plausible explanation.

With both cognitive impairment and disinhibited attachment, there was a significant degree of stability in level between the ages of 4 and 6 years, as well as moderate consistency in individual differences. The findings clearly do not imply that there cannot be later recovery (the follow-up at ages 11–12 that is currently under way should cast light on that issue), but they do suggest that the patterns persist for at least 2 years after children leave the depriving institutional environment.

Limitations of Existing Models

The starting point for any discussion of models for the causal mechanisms involved in the sequelae of severe early institutional deprivation is the combination of three features: marked recovery following removal from the depriving environment, major deficits in a substantial minority that persist for at least 2½ years after rearing in a good family environment, and considerable individual differences in outcome. The implications for notions of developmental biological programming are provocative because the results both confirm and challenge the postulates of programming as put forward in a hard form. That is because programming concepts (whether experience-expectant or experience-adaptive) suppose that the effects will be universal, even if they vary in degree, and persistent even after good rearing conditions are provided if such provision occurs only after the end of the relevant sensitive period. The concepts also require the existence of a sensitive period during which biological development is shaped by relevant experiences.

The major degree of recovery found in children suffering profound institutional deprivation for 2 to 3½ years shows that the effects were far from fixed and irreversible. To the contrary, there was a remarkable degree of recovery following removal from the institutional environment, and the outcomes were surprisingly heterogeneous. Even within the subgroup of children whose institutional deprivation lasted until after 2 years of age, the majority did *not* show substantial cognitive impairment (a few even showed superior cognitive functioning), and most did *not* show disinhibited attachment. Accordingly, the findings run counter to any programming concept that presupposes universal and irreversible effects. Either the limited variations within the severe institutional deprivation range mean that some individuals received sufficient relevant experiences for normal or near-normal brain development to take place, or neural plasticity after the age of 2 years is enough to allow functional recovery to take place.

On the other hand, the major persisting deficits in many children also indicate that there were lasting changes in the organism that continued long after normal high-quality family rearing was provided. We thought perhaps that significant deficits would be found only if the deprivation continued for at least 2–3 years. Our results, however, contradict that expectation. To the contrary, the deficits began to be evident after institutional deprivation lasting for a period as short as 1 year (that is to say, they were evident in the group whose deprivation extended from 6 months up to 24 months). Detailed examination of the trends showed no indication of a threshold effect either during this age period or later. In short, the persistence of deficits requires some mechanism for the carry-forward of the effects of severe early institutional deprivation despite the radical change to a generally good rearing environment in a family context. Also, however, the occurrence of deficits in children who entered adoptive families well before 2 years of age implies that, if there is a sensitive period, it must begin to tail off by that age. On the other hand, the recovery findings imply that even if the tail-off begins early, it must continue for much longer.

With respect to cognitive impairment, the associations with subnutrition (albeit weaker than those with duration of institutional deprivation) and with a small head circumference both point to the likelihood of abnormal brain development (because it is brain growth that largely determines head size). The main alternatives, therefore, are positive neural damage (such as that found in rodents from high levels of stress on the hippocampus) or negative effects of a lack of experiences on normal brain development. In both cases, there is a neural basis; the difference lies between the active effects of noxious stimuli and the passive effects of a lack of experiences. The latter alternative definitely requires a sensitive period, whereas the former may or may not. Both imply, however, a mechanism that is distinct from the effects of variations in cognitive experiences on function at any age. There is, so far as is known, no sensitive period for the effects of experiences on cognitive function, but there may be one for those neural effects of experiences outside the normal range. Our data do not allow us to differentiate between active and passive mechanisms. However, experience-adaptive programming seems implausible because there is no reason to expect that this would be associated with impaired brain growth and because it seems unlikely that poor cognitive functioning would be adaptive even in a depriving institutional environment. Moreover, other research shows that the consequences do not derive from institutional rearing per se. Neither of the two British studies of children in residential group care (Hodges & Tizard, 1989a; Roy, Rutter, & Pickles, 2000) showed a significant effect on cognitive functioning. It may be concluded that institutional rearing as such has no necessary adverse effects on cognitive development. Rather, the ill effects seem to derive from the combination of institutional rearing and unusu-ally severe and pervasive restriction of human interactions, play, conversation, and experiences. This gross pervasive deprivation seems to fall outside the range of expectable environments required for normal development.

The inferences with respect to disinhibited attachment are rather different. The lack of associations with head circumference and subnutrition suggest that there are no grounds for implicating active neural damage. Although the evidential base is weak, there is more reason than with cognitive development to infer a possible sensitive period. It is well established that young children ordinarily develop their first selective attachments between about 6 and 12 months of age, and clearly this has to be based on social interactions (Cassidy & Shaver, 1999). From the outset (Bowlby, 1969), attachment theory has postulated that there is a sensitive period for this development and that institutional care by rotating caregivers provides a poor source for the necessary experiences. Roy, Rutter, and Pickles (in press) found that impaired selective attachments were a feature of children reared in institutions and not of children from similarly deprived backgrounds who were reared in foster families. Wolkind (1974) showed that indiscriminate friendliness (a behavior related to disinhibited attachment) was evident in children admitted to institutions in infancy but not in those whose institutional care only began in middle childhood. Hodges and Tizard (1989b) found that the social deficits associated with early residential care persisted into adolescence even after years of rearing in a family environment.

The alternative explanations lie between the two forms of programming and some quite different mechanism that could account for the degree of persistence despite a radical change in environment. Some sort of sensitive period seems likely to be operative, but studies of selective attachments in children who experience institutional care only in middle childhood or later are much needed to test the possibility. Unlike the situation with cognitive impairment, disinhibited attachment seems to derive from some aspect of institutional care as such, without the need for gross pervasive experiential deprivation. That is because impaired social relationships (measured in rather diverse ways) have been found in children in relatively well-functioning residential group homes. What stood out as distinctive in these group homes was the lack of personalized caregiving, and it may well be that that is the key feature that puts children's social development at risk.

Experience-expectant programming carries the implication that an institutional environment, even one not associated with gross experiential restriction, falls outside the range of expectable environments required for normal brain development with respect to the neural systems underlying selective social relationships. That is quite possibly the case, but if the analogy with binocular vision is at all appropriate, there would seem to be an expectation that later compensatory social experiences might be of little benefit. Also, insofar as such experiences could be remedial, they probably need to be of a kind similar to those thought to shape early selective attachments and the brain systems that underpin them.

Experience-adaptive programming carries the very different implication that, in some sense, disinhibited attachment may be adaptive in an institutional environment even if it is clearly maladaptive in an adoptive home. At first sight, that seems implausible because the essential feature of early attachments concerns their selectivity and the sense of security that they provide. Possibly, in an institutional environment with a lack of personalized caregiving and a very large number of rotating caregivers, it could be adaptive to seek interactions in a nonselective way in order to make some sort of relationship with the caregivers who come and go. The possibility warrants further study because, if valid, it implies that, rather than moving swiftly into selective intimate relationships in the adoptive family, a more gradual transition may be preferable.

If both forms of programming are rejected as explanations, some alternative mechanism for the carryforward of effects must be postulated. If it is not to involve some type of persisting neural change that is resistant to the effects of later environments (the hallmark of the programming concept), it is most likely to involve the effects on other people of the young children's behavior. There is no doubt that children do indeed have effects on those with whom they interact (Bell, 1968; Bell & Chapman, 1986; Rutter et al., 1997; Rutter & Silberg, 2002), and this could lead to persistence of sequelae. However, neither our quantitative findings nor our qualitative observations suggested that these effects (though clearly they were present) accounted for the persistence of disinhibited attachment. On the other hand, this explanation could not be ruled out.

Individual Differences and Implications for Resilience

Individual differences in both cognitive and social functioning were great even in those who had experienced the longest periods of institutional deprivation. In itself, the occurrence of wide individual variations is unremarkable. After all, there is every reason to suppose that the children differed in their genetic backgrounds and that this is likely to have had effects on their cognition and social relationships. It is unlikely that their experiences before admission to the institutions would have had much impact because, in almost all cases, these lasted only a very few weeks. On the other hand, there is likely to have been some variation in the children's experiences within the institutions (but within a range of very poor quality) and some variation in experiences within their adoptive homes (although, in this case, within a range of generally above-average environments). The surprising aspects of the individual differences were three: (a) the extent of the variations given the extraordinarily severe deprivation in the institutions, which might have been expected to wipe out other influences; (b) the substantial minority of children who experienced the most prolonged deprivation but yet showed no measurable deficits; and (c) the relative frequency of normality (or near-normality) given the expectations of the programming concepts.

Do these findings mean that we should reject the programming concept in relation to our findings? Not necessarily given the other indications of its possible relevance—but, if accepted, it does imply that programming effects may be less absolute and less fixed than commonly supposed. However, if that is accepted, it leaves open the question of what influences brought about the individual differences. Do they stem from influences (perhaps genetic) unconnected with the institutional deprivation? Or do they reflect variations in the degree of institutional deprivation or differences in the ways in which the children responded to their experiences (possibly as a result of gene–environment interactions)? Alternatively, do they derive from variations in the adoptive home environments? Clearly, our present data set provides no answers on these important questions, but the just-completed follow-up at age 11 may be informative.

Research Implications

A range of different research strategies are required to answer the questions we have raised. Structural brain imaging could be informative with respect to the variations in head circumference. Functional brain imaging should be helpful in determining whether the brain systems underlying social processing in these children are at all unusual. Follow-up data in adolescence will provide better leverage on the extent to which deficits persist, revert, or change and on the environmental factors operating in middle childhood that influence these features. Intervention studies will be needed to provide systematic information on the factors that influence persistence and desistance in behavioral patterns.

Limitations of the Data Set

Our findings are based on a group of children who suffered a degree of institutional deprivation far beyond that ordinarily seen in modern industrialized societies. Inevitably, therefore, there must be considerable caution in extrapolating the findings to less extreme conditions of deprivation. Nevertheless, the findings raise important questions about the effects of early experiences on later development, effects that would seem likely to be mediated by some sort of effect on brain structure and function, although just what those are remains uncertain. Our findings cannot differentiate between the two broad forms of developmental programming that have been postulated, and we cannot rule out the possibility that there has been brain damage (rather than programming). Finally, it is important to emphasize that nothing is known about the neural substrate of developmental programming as it affects the brain—either with respect to cognitive impairment or disinhibited attachment.

Conclusion

Our research findings as a whole indicate that the effects of institutional rearing on IQ apply only when such rearing involves profound general deprivation. The association between IQ, subnutrition, and head circumference suggests that it is unlikely that the effects involve experience-adaptive programming; rather, experience-expectant programming or biological damage seems probable. By contrast, the effects of institutional rearing on attachment disinhibition seem to apply to institutional rearing even when profound deprivation is not involved. The lack of association with either subnutrition or head circumference makes brain damage a less plausible explanation. Either experience-expectant or experience-adaptive programming seems to be the most plausible explanation. The research challenge for the future is to determine what these effects mean in terms of their neural basis, and if that challenge is to be taken up successfully, it will certainly be necessary that the relevant psychosocial and developmental research be integrated with biology and with biological studies.

References

Bakshi, V. P., & Kalin, N. H. (2000). Corticotropin-releasing hormone and animal models of anxiety: Gene–environment interactions. *Biological Psychiatry, 48,* 1164–1174.

Barbazanges, A., Vallée, M., Mayo, W., Day, J., Simon, H., Le Moal, M., & Maccari, S. (1996). Early and later adoptions have different long-term effects on male rat offspring. *The Journal of Neuroscience, 16*, 7783–7790.

Barker, D. J. (1997). Fetal nutrition and cardiovascular disease in later life. *British Medical Bulletin, 53*, 96–108.

Bateson, P. P. (1966). The characteristics and context of imprinting. *Biological Review, 41*, 177–211.

Bateson, P., & Martin, P. (1999). *Design for a life: How behaviour develops*. London: Jonathan Cape.

Bell, R. Q. (1968). A reinterpretation of the direction of effects in studies of socialization. *Psychological Review, 75*, 81–95.

Bell, R. Q., & Chapman, M. (1986). Child effects in studies using experimental or brief longitudinal approaches to socialization. *Developmental Psychology, 22*, 595–603.

Blakemore, C. (1991). Sensitive and vulnerable periods in the development of the visual system. In G. R. Bock & J. Whelan (Eds.), *The childhood environment and adult disease: Ciba Foundation Symposium 156* (pp. 129–146). Chichester, England: Wiley.

Bock, G. R., & Whelan, J. (Eds.). (1991). *The childhood environment and adult disease: Ciba Foundation Symposium 156*. Chichester, England: Wiley.

Bornstein, M. (1987). *Sensitive periods and development*. Hillsdale, NJ: Erlbaum.

Bowlby, J. (1951). *Maternal care and mental health*. Geneva: World Health Organization.

Bowlby, J. (1969). *Attachment and loss: Vol. 1. Attachment*. London: Hogarth Press.

Boyce, L., & Cole, T. (1993). Growth Programme (Version 1 & 2) [Computer software]. Ware, England: Castlemead.

Bremner, J. D. (1999). Does stress damage the brain? *Biological Psychiatry, 45*, 797–805.

Bretherton, I., & Mulholland, K. A. (1999). Internal working models in attachment relationships: A construct revisited. In J. Cassidy & P. R. Shaver (Eds.), *Handbook of attachment: Theory, research and critical applications* (pp. 89–111). New York: Guilford Press.

Bruce, D., Dolan, A., & Phillips-Grant, K. (2000). On the transition from childhood amnesia to the recall of personal memories. *Psychological Science, 11*, 360–364.

Bruer, J. T. (1999). *The myth of the first three years*. New York: Free Press.

Buckler, J. (1990). *A longitudinal study of adolescent growth*. London: Springer-Verlag.

Caldji, C., Diorio, J., & Meaney, M. J. (2000). Variations in maternal care in infancy regulate the development of stress reactivity. *Biological Psychiatry, 48*, 1164–1174.

Cassidy, J., & Shaver, P. R. (1999). *Handbook of attachment: Theory, research and clinical applications*. New York: Guilford Press.

Castle, J., Groothues, C., Bredenkamp, D., Beckett, C., O'Connor, T. G., Rutter, M., & the E.R.A. Study Team (1999). Effects of qualities of early institutional care on cognitive attainment. *American Journal of Orthopsychiatry, 69*, 424–437.

Clarke, A. M., & Clarke, A. D. B. (1976). *Early experience: Myth and evidence*. London: Open Books.

Clarke, A. M., & Clarke, A. D. B. (2000). *Early experience and the life path*. London: Jessica Kingsley.

Croft, C., O'Connor, T., Keaveney, L., Groothues, C., Rutter, M., & the English and Romanian Adoption Study Team. (2001). Longitudinal change in parenting associated with developmental delay and catch-up. *Journal of Child Psychology and Psychiatry, 42*, 649–659.

Dodge, K. A., Pettit, G. S., Bates, J. E., & Valente, E. (1995). Social information-processing patterns partially mediate the effects of early physical abuse on later conduct problems. *Journal of Abnormal Psychology, 104*, 632–643.

Duyme, M., Dumaret, A.-C., & Tomkiewicz, S. (1999). How can we boost IQs of "dull children"? A late adoption study. *Proceedings of the National Academy of Sciences, USA, 96*, 8790–8794.

Farrington, D. P., & Loeber, R. (2000). Some benefits of dichotomization in psychiatric and criminological research. *Criminal Behaviour and Mental Health, 10*, 100–122.

Francis, D., Diorio, J., Liu, D., & Meaney, M. J. (1999). Nongenomic transmission across generations of maternal behavior and stress response in the rat. *Science, 286*, 1155–1158.

Frankenburg, W. K., van Doorninck, W. J., Liddell, T. N., & Dick, N. P. (1986). *Revised Denver Prescreening Developmental Questionnaire (R-PDQ)*. High Wycombe, England: DDM Inc./The Test Agency Ltd.

Greenough, W. T., Black, J. E., & Wallace, C. S. (1987). Experience and brain development. *Child Development, 58*, 539–559.

Hennessey, J. W., & Levine, S. (1979). Stress, arousal, and the pituitary-adrenal system: A psychoendocrine hypothesis. In J. M. Sprague & A. N. Epstein (Eds.), *Progress in psychobiology and physiological psychology* (pp. 133–178). New York: Academic Press.

Hodges, J., & Tizard, B. (1989a). IQ and behavioural adjustment of ex-institutional adolescents. *Journal of Child Psychology and Psychiatry and Allied Disciplines, 30*, 53–75.

Hodges, J., & Tizard, B. (1989b). Social and family relationships of ex-institutional adolescents. *Journal of Child Psychology and Psychiatry and Allied Disciplines, 30*, 77–97.

Howe, M. L., & Courage, M. L. (1993). On resolving the enigma of infantile amnesia. *Psychological Bulletin, 113*, 305–326.

Hubel, D. H., & Wiesel, T. N. (1965). Binocular interaction in striate cortex of kittens reared with artificial squint. *Journal of Neurophysiology, 28*, 1041–1049.

Hubel, D. H., Wiesel, T. N., & Le Vay, S. (1977). Plasticity of ocular dominance columns in monkey striate cortex. *Philosophical Transactions of the Royal Society of London—Series B: Biological Sciences, 278*, 377–409.

Kagan, J. (1980). Perspectives on continuity. In O. G. Brim & J. Kagan (Eds.), *Constancy and change in human development* (pp. 26–74). Cambridge, MA: Harvard University Press.

Klaus, M. H., & Kennell, J. H. (1976). *Maternal–infant bonding: The impact of early separation or loss on family development*. St. Louis, MO: C. V. Mosby.

Kobak, R. (1999). The emotional dynamics of disruptions in attachment relationships: Implications for theory, research and clinical intervention. In J. Cassidy & P. R. Shaver (Eds.), *Handbook of attachment: Theory, research and clinical applications* (pp. 21–43). New York: Guilford Press.

Kreppner, J., O'Connor, T. G., Dunn, J., Anderson-Wood, L., & the ERA Study Team (1999). The pretend and social role play of children exposed to severe early deprivation. *British Journal of Developmental Psychology, 17*, 319–332.

Kreppner, J., O'Connor, T. G., Rutter, M., & the E. R. A. Study Team (2001). Can inattention/overactivity be an institutional deprivation disorder? *Journal of Abnormal Child Psychology, 29*, 513–528.

Kuhl, P. K. (1994). Learning and representation in speech and language. *Current Opinion in Neurobiology, 4*, 812–822.

Kuhl, P. K., Andruski, J. E., Chistovich, I. A., Chistovich, L. A., Kozhevnikova, E. V., Ryskina, V. L., et al. (1997). Cross-language analysis of phonetic units in language addressed to infants. *Science, 277*, 684–686.

Le Grand, R., Mondloch, C., Maurer, D., & Brent, H. P. (2001). Neuroperception: Early visual experience and face processing. *Nature, 410*, 890.

Lien, N. M., Meyer, K. K., & Winick, M. (1977). Early malnutrition and "late" adoption: A study of their effects on development of Korean orphans adopted into American families. *American Journal of Clinical Nutrition, 30*, 1734–1739.

Maccari, S., Piazza, P. V., Kabbaj, M., Barbazanges, A., Simon, H., & Le Moal, M. (1995). Adoption reverses the long-term impairment in glucocorticoid feedback induced by prenatal stress. *Journal of Neuroscience, 15*, 110–116.

Main, M., Kaplan, N., & Cassidy, J. (1985). Security in infancy, childhood and adulthood: A move to the level of representation. In I. Bretherton & E. Waters (Eds.), Growing points in attachment theory and research (pp. 66–106). *Monographs of the Society for Research in Child Development, 50*(1–2, Serial No. 209).

McCarthy, D. (1972). *The McCarthy Scales of Children's Abilities.* New York: Psychological Corporation/Harcourt Brace Jovanovich.

McEwen, B. S. (1999). The effects of stress on structural and functional plasticity in the hippocampus. In D. S. Charney, E. J. Nestler, & B. S. Bunney (Eds.), *Neurobiology of mental illness* (pp. 475–493). New York: Oxford University Press.

O'Brien, P. M. S., Wheeler, T., & Barker, D. J. P. (Eds.). (1999). *Fetal programming: Influences on development and disease in later life.* London: RCOG Press.

O'Connor, T. G., Bredenkamp, D., Rutter, M., and the English and Romanian Adoptees (ERA) Study Team. (1999). Attachment disturbances and disorders in children exposed to early severe deprivation. *Infant Mental Health Journal, 20,* 10–29.

O'Connor, T. G., Marvin, R. S., Rutter, M., Olrick, J., Britner, P. A., & the E. R. A. Study Team. (2003). Child–parent attachment following severe early institutional deprivation. *Development and Psychopathology, 15,* 19–38.

O'Connor, T. G., Rutter, M., Beckett, C., Keaveney, L., Kreppner, J. M., & the English and Romanian Adoptees (ERA) Study Team. (2000). The effects of global severe privation on cognitive competence: Extension and longitudinal follow-up. *Child Development, 71,* 376–390.

O'Connor, T. G., Rutter, M., & the English and Romanian Adoptees Study Team. (2000). Attachment disorder behaviour following early severe deprivation: Extension and longitudinal follow-up. *Journal of the American Academy of Child and Adolescent Psychiatry, 39,* 703–712.

Pawlby, S. J., Mills, A., & Quinton, D. (1997). Vulnerable adolescent girls: Opposite sex relationships. *Journal of Child Psychology and Psychiatry and Allied Disciplines, 38,* 909–920.

Pawlby, S. J., Mills, A., Taylor, A., & Quinton, D. (1997). Adolescent friendships mediating childhood adversity and adult outcome. *Journal of Adolescence, 20,* 633–644.

Pilling, D., & Kellmer-Pringle, M. (1978). *Controversial issues in child development.* London: Elek Books.

Quinton, D., Pickles, A., Maughan, B., & Rutter, M. (1993). Partners, peers, and pathways: Assortative pairing and continuities in conduct disorder. *Development and Psychopathology 5,* 763–783.

Quinton, D., & Rutter, M. (1988). *Parenting breakdown: The making and breaking of intergenerational links.* Aldershot, England: Avebury.

Roy, P., Rutter, M., & Pickles, A. (2000). Institutional care: Risk from family background or pattern of rearing? *Journal of Child Psychology and Psychiatry and Allied Disciplines, 41,* 139–149.

Roy, P., Rutter, M., & Pickles, A. (in press). Institutional care: Associations between overactivity and a lack of selectivity in attachment relationships. *Journal of Child Psychology and Psychiatry and Allied Disciplines.*

Rutter, M. (1981). *Maternal deprivation reassessed* (2nd ed.). Harmondsworth, Middlesex, England: Penguin Books.

Rutter, M. (1985a). Family and school influences on behavioural development. *Journal of Child Psychology and Psychiatry and Allied Disciplines, 26,* 349–368.

Rutter, M. (1985b). Family and school influences on cognitive development. *Journal of Child Psychology and Psychiatry and Allied Disciplines, 26,* 683–704.

Rutter, M. (1989). Pathways from childhood to adult life. *Journal of Child Psychology and Psychiatry and Allied Disciplines, 30,* 23–51.

Rutter, M. (2000). Psychosocial influences: Critiques, findings, and research needs. *Development and Psychopathology, 12,* 375–405.

Rutter, M. (2002a). Maternal deprivation. In M. Bornstein (Ed.), *Handbook of parenting* (2nd ed., pp. 181–202). Mahwah, NJ: Erlbaum.

Rutter, M. (2002b). Nature, nurture and development: From evangelism through science towards policy and practice. *Child Development, 73,* 1–21.

Rutter, M., Anderson-Wood, L., Beckett, C., Bredenkamp, D., Castle, J., Groothues, C., Kreppner, J., Keaveney, L., Lord, C., O'Connor, T. G., & the E. R. A. Study Team. (1999). Quasi-autistic patterns following severe early global privation. *Journal of Child Psychology and Psychiatry and Allied Disciplines, 40,* 537–549.

Rutter, M., Dunn, J., Plomin, R., Simonoff, E., Pickles, A., Maughan, B., et al. (1997). Integrating nature and nurture: Implications of person–environment correlations and interactions for developmental psychopathology. *Development and Psychopathology, 9,* 335–366.

Rutter, M., & the ERA Research Team. (1998). Developmental catch-up and deficit following adoption after severe global early privation. *Journal of Child Psychology and Psychiatry and Allied Disciplines, 39,* 465–476.

Rutter, M., Kreppner, J. K., O'Connor, T. G., & the ERA Study Team. (2001). Specificity and heterogeneity in children's responses to profound privation. *British Journal of Psychiatry, 179,* 97–103.

Rutter, M., Maughan, B., Pickles, A., & Simonoff, E. (1998). Retrospective recall recalled. In R. B. Cairns, L. R. Bergman, & J. Kagan (Eds.), *Methods and models for studying the individual* (pp. 219–242). Thousand Oaks, CA: Sage.

Rutter, M., Pickles, A., Murray, R., & Eaves, L. (2001). Testing hypotheses on specific environmental causal effects on behavior. *Psychological Bulletin, 127,* 291–324.

Rutter, M., & Robins, L. (Eds.). (1990). *Straight and devious pathways from childhood to adulthood.* New York: Cambridge University Press.

Rutter, M., & Silberg, J. (2002). Gene–environment interplay in relation to emotional and behavioral disturbance. *Annual Review of Psychology, 53,* 463–490.

Sackett, G. P. (1965). Effects of rearing conditions upon the behavior of rhesus monkeys (*Macaca Mulatta*). *Child Development, 36,* 855–868.

Schneider, M. L., & Moore, C. F. (2000). Effect of prenatal stress on development: A nonhuman primate model. In C. A. Nelson (Ed.), *Minnesota Symposium on Child Psychology: Vol. 31. The effects of early adversity on behavioural development* (pp. 201–244). Mahwah, NJ: Erlbaum.

Sluckin, W. (1973). *Imprinting and early learning* (2nd ed.). Chicago: Aldine.

Steiger, J. H. (1980). Tests for comparing elements of a correlation matrix. *Psychological Bulletin, 87,* 245–251.

Teasdale, J. D., & Barnard, P. J. (1993). *Affect, cognition, and change: Re-modelling depressive thought.* Hove, England: Erlbaum.

Thompson, R. A. (1998). Early sociopersonality development. In W. Damon (Series Ed.) & N. Eisenberg (Vol. Ed.), *Handbook of child psychology: Vol. 3. Social, emotional, and personality development* (5th ed., pp. 25–104). New York: Wiley.

Wolkind, S. N. (1974). The components of "affectionless psychopathology" in institutionalized children. *Journal of Child Psychology and Psychiatry and Allied Disciplines, 15,* 215–220.

World Health Organization Expert Committee on Mental Health. (1951). *Report on the second session, 1951.* Geneva: World Health Organization.

Received November 5, 2001
Revision received August 26, 2003
Accepted September 15, 2003 ∎

Adolescence

[3]

Pubertal transitions in health

George C Patton, Russell Viner

Puberty is accompanied by physical, psychological, and emotional changes adapted to ensure reproductive and parenting success. Human puberty stands out in the animal world for its association with brain maturation and physical growth. Its effects on health and wellbeing are profound and paradoxical. On the one hand, physical maturation propels an individual into adolescence with peaks in strength, speed, and fitness. Clinicians have viewed puberty as a point of maturing out of childhood-onset conditions. However, puberty's relevance for health has shifted with a modern rise in psychosocial disorders of young people. It marks a transition in risks for depression and other mental disorders, psychosomatic syndromes, substance misuse, and antisocial behaviours. Recent secular trends in these psychosocial disorders coincide with a growing mismatch between biological and social maturation, and the emergence of more dominant youth cultures.

Puberty is initiated in late childhood through a cascade of endocrine changes that lead to sexual maturation and reproductive capability. Human puberty is accompanied by major physical growth and substantial brain maturational changes, features that are unique in the animal world.[1] Its consequences for health and wellbeing are profound and paradoxical. On the one hand, physical maturation propels an individual into adolescence with peaks in strength, speed, and fitness. Yet puberty also triggers emotional, cognitive, and behavioural changes. Aristotle's comment that "Youth are heated by nature as drunken men by wine" has been echoed through the ages. Today, these changes lie behind the increased mortality and morbidity from accidental and intentional injuries, suicide and mental disorders, substance abuse, and eating disorders in young people.

Puberty

Puberty begins with the poorly understood activation of a complex neuroendocrine network, quiescent since neonatal life.[2] Sexual maturation (gonadarche) is initiated with the pulsatile nocturnal release of gonadotrophin

Search strategy

The aims in this review were to consider the role of puberty and pubertal timing on the course of pre-existing childhood health problems, the initiation of adolescent health problems, and risk for illness later in life. We searched the MEDLINE, PsychLit, and Embase databases (1996 to December, 2005 for each). We used the terms "puberty", "menarche", and "age factors" in combination with: "depression", "mental disorders", "substance-related disorders", "child behavior disorders", "obesity", "anorexia nervosa", "bulimia nervosa", "attention deficit with hyperactivity", "headache", "migraine", "asthma", "constipation", "enuresis", "asthma", and "chronic illness". We selected publications from the past 10 years but also included commonly cited and seminal papers published earlier.

releasing hormone from a small number of specialised hypothalamic neurones that in turn leads to the pituitary release of follicle-stimulating hormone and lutenising hormone. The resulting gonadal growth and production of gonadal sex steroids bring about the development of secondary sexual characteristics.[2]

Preceding and independent of the hypothalamo-pituitary-gonadal axis, the production of adrenal androgens increases from around age 6–8 years in a process known as adrenarche, unknown in species other than human beings and chimpanzees.[3] These androgens have a role in the development of axillary and pubic hair and contribute to the emergence of acne. The evolutionary significance of adrenarche is unclear, but evidence suggests that its timing might affect risk of physical and mental health problems.[4]

In this paper we will use the term puberty to encompass the changes following gonadarche and adrenarche, as well as less well-characterised biological changes. These include the maturation of the growth hormone-insulin like growth factor and thyroid axes that lead to the pubertal growth spurt and achievement of adult height, maturation of many organ systems, and changes in blood lipids, haematological indices, and enzyme systems, including liver cytochrome P-450 systems. Changes in the regulation of oxytocin and vasopressin are associated with altered patterns of social interaction and attachment.

Puberty can therefore be considered as an interconnected suite of changes with wide individual variations in the sequence and timing of its components.[5] A system of reliable staging of the external signs of puberty was developed by Marshall and Tanner in the 1960s.[6,7] The earliest external changes—breast buds in girls and enlargement of testicular volume to greater than 4 mL in boys—appear at the mean ages of 11·0 years and 11·1 years, respectively, in the UK (figure 1). Despite the similar age of gonadarche in both sexes, these early changes have greater visibility in girls than in boys, coupled with an earlier onset of the growth spurt.

Menarche, often seen as the defining element of female puberty, occurs in late puberty, about 2·0–2·5 years after breast budding. In boys, no such easy signifier exists, although spermaturia and first ejaculation occur from about age 13–14 years. Puberty is generally complete over the 2–4 years after gonadarche, but other changes induced by sex steroids, including sexually dimorphic patterning of fat and muscle, continue throughout adolescence. For boys, puberty-initiated physical changes, such as androgenic patterns of hair growth and loss, continue well into old age.

Pubertal timing

The 4–5 year variation in age of onset of puberty among healthy individuals is a physiological peculiarity of man and is observed even where living conditions are similar for all members of a group.[8] This variation reflects a strong genetic component, with nutrition, psychological status, and socioeconomic conditions having additional effects.[8–10] Pathological pubertal delay is most commonly associated with chronic illness, stress, and undernutrition. Precocity is more commonly reported in females and is generally a consequence of premature activation of the hypothalamo-pituitary-gonadal axis, sometimes secondary to neoplasia.[8] It can also arise from autonomous gonadal hormone production. Premature adrenarche in girls can be a forerunner of the polycystic ovary syndrome and its associated metabolic consequences.[11]

Change in pubertal timing, as indicated by a falling mean age of menarche during the twentieth century in most developed and developing countries, has attracted much attention.[8,12] The mean menarcheal age is now 12–13 years in most developed countries, with minor variations.[8] This secular trend ceased in most developed countries after the 1960s, but concerns were re-ignited in the late 1990s with the publication of American studies[13,14] that suggested a sudden fall in the age of onset of puberty in girls and boys. A possibility loomed of ever-younger children entering puberty, exacerbating the modern pattern of young people developing biological reproductive capability well before psychosocial maturity.[10] However, little evidence exists to support claims of a recommencement of the secular trend outside the USA in developed countries.[2,8,15,16] Indeed, studies done after 1960 show a modest increase in menarcheal age in northern European countries including the UK, Sweden, and Belgium (0·14, 0·05, and 0·03 years per decade, respectively).[8] Well-observed studies of large Dutch[17] and Danish[12] cohorts show no change in the age of puberty or menarche from the 1960s to 1990s, despite a substantial increment in height over this period. The published US findings might well reflect selection and misclassification bias in studies not specifically designed to assess trends in pubertal timing.[2,15] In short, the mean age of menarche seems to have stabilised at around 12–13 years in well-nourished populations, an age that evolutionary theorists suggest is biologically appropriate, because it is about the

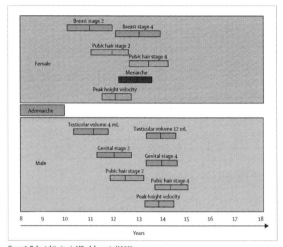

Figure 1: Pubertal timing in UK adolescents (1990)
Bars show 75th and 25th centiles for entry into pubertal stages.

same as that estimated for that of early hunter-gatherer *Homo sapiens* (figure 2).[10] The much later menarche seen in the more recent past may be an artifact of poor nutrition as a result of population growth that followed agricultural settlement.

Puberty and adolescent development

Early adolescent theorists built on Haeckel's view that individual development (ontogeny) recapitulates evolutionary development (phylogeny). Puberty was typically considered as the trigger to a biologically driven phase of inevitable emotional turmoil[18] with biology driving psychological and social development.[19,20] It is now clear that broader social processes define adolescence, not least because its form varies so widely across societies and cultures. In pre-industrial societies the adolescent transition from puberty to adult roles, as defined by the onset of sexual activity, marriage, and parenthood, ranged from around 2 years in girls to 4 years in boys.[10] In today's developed economies, longer periods in education, increased affluence, and the availability of effective contraception means that adolescence commonly persists for well over a decade.[10]

Current concepts of adolescence typically encompass a biological onset at puberty and highly variable social transitions that mark its completion. The biological processes initiated at puberty interact with the social context to affect an individual's emotional and social development.[21–23] The modern pattern for mature reproductive capacity, as well as sexual activity, to precede role transitions into parenthood and marriage by more than a decade is exceptional in human history (figure 2).[24,25] An accompanying rise in number of sexual partners prior to marriage has been linked to changing patterns of sexually transmitted diseases. So, too, the delay in taking on mature social roles and responsibilities in marriage, parenthood, and employment, tied with earlier initiation of substance use, has been linked to rises in mental disorders and substance abuse in young people.[26]

Although emotional turmoil is a far from inevitable consequence of puberty, there is evidence that puberty affects early psychosocial development.[27] Male individuals who reach puberty later than their peers are often less assertive and popular.[28,29] and late in engaging in sexual activity.[30] By contrast, early puberty in females is associated with emotional and behavioural problems and early sexual activity.[31]

The effects of puberty on behaviour are evident in findings from animal studies, particularly in primates. They include altered social interactions with peers, sometimes accompanied by conflicts with parents as well as behaviours characterised by sensation-seeking and risk taking.[32,33] Pubertal changes in the regulation of oxytocin in females and vasopressin in males have been linked to social attachment, pair-bonding, and parental behaviour across species.[34] Such cross-species conservation of adolescent typical behaviours[35] suggests their relevance for reproductive success, perhaps by facilitating migration away from genetically related adults and building a social network to support offspring.[36] However, no other species shows the complexity of changes in brain seen in humans nor the repertoire of behavioural changes. These behavioural changes are in turn greatly affected by the socio-cultural and economic milieu in which humans mature.[1] For these reasons findings from the study of rodents and even non-human primates may be less applicable to humans.

Brain changes

Many brain changes take place during adolescence. Some precede and initiate puberty. Others continue for around a decade beyond. Yet gonadal hormones affect a wide range of neuronal processes: neurogenesis, dendritic growth, synapse formation and elimination, apoptosis, neuropeptide expression, and sensitivity of neurotransmitter receptors.[37] Sex differences in brain development during puberty might reflect the different effects of male and female gonadal hormones. Frontal lobes, which are involved in planning, organising, and executive functions, reach a peak thickness at 11·0 years in girls and 12·1 years in boys.[38] These changes result from increased dendritic branching rather than increasing neuronal numbers. Similarly, parietal lobe grey matter reaches a peak at 10·2 years in girls and 11·8 years in boys.

Early studies of the effects of gonadal hormones on brain function focused on the hypothalamus and other regions directly involved in reproduction. Later studies, however, also showed effects on the hippocampus, striatum, cerebellum amygdala, and cerebral cortex. Three known oestrogen receptors mediate effects on cholinergic, noradrenergic, serotinergic, and dopaminergic neurotransmitter systems. The functions affected include cognitive abilities, aggression, affect regulation, learning, and memory.[37,39]

Gonadal hormones affect many pubertal changes in social interaction, sexual drive, attachment, and responses to stressors.[39] Animals show an increased response of adrenocorticotropic hormone to stress in females in early adolescence, a process that is partly mediated by ovarian hormones.[40] In human beings there is also some evidence for pubertal changes in sex-specific responses to stressors, with men showing greater hypothalamic-pituitary-adrenal reactivity to achievement challenges and women to social rejection.[41]

A range of factors beyond gonadal hormones—genetic effects, nutrition, and sensory inputs—also seem to be involved in pubertal brain changes. Stress during puberty and early adolescence may affect brain development and vulnerability to psychopathologies of different kinds.[39] Conversely, enrichment of the social and learning environment in peripubertal rats can reverse many of the adverse effects of early maternal separation.[42] This evidence of greater neural plasticity around puberty and persisting changes in neural function as a result of early adolescent experiences has major implications for health promotion.[43]

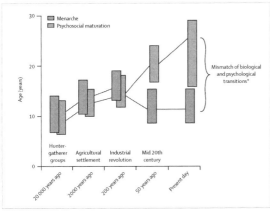

Figure 2: Changing relation between probable range of menarcheal age and psychosocial transitions into adulthood
Adapted from Gluckman and Hanson.[10] *Psychosocial transitions range from first sexual activity through to marriage and parenthood

A possibility that behavioural problems arise because of a mismatch between the emotional reactions and cognitive capacities of young adolescents has long interested clinicians. Early studies of so-called off-time puberty commonly cited emotional immaturity, perhaps compounded by peer rejection, as the basis of the increased emotional and behavioural problems of early developers.[44,45] The more recent understanding that neurodevelopment continues into early adulthood, especially in regions linked to regulation of behaviour and emotion, has again heightened interest in an idea that difficulties in emotional and impulse control in younger adolescents are the result of brain immaturity. A reduction in grey matter in the pre-frontal cortex and expansion of cortico-cortical communication continues into the third decade of life.[46-48] These changes correlate with the development of self-control and mature judgement, yet continue for more than a decade after puberty brings profound emotional and behavioural shifts. The importance of this biological gap might now be accentuated by later marriage and parenthood, social transitions that have historically been linked to maturing out of problem behaviours. The clinical relevance is evident in the early adolescent rise in deliberate self-harm, which peaks at around age 15 years in girls. Pubertal changes in depressive symptoms, substance misuse, and sexual activity are linked to the early adolescent increase in self-harm, but advancing age, a possible marker of brain maturation, is associated with a reduced risk of this problem.[49]

Chronic physical illness

General paediatric wisdom has maintained that many of the commonest childhood conditions, such as asthma and other atopic conditions, chronic constipation, and primary nocturnal enuresis, remit in early adolescence. Children were thought to outgrow these conditions due to maturation of the autonomic and central nervous systems under the effect of sex steroids during puberty.[50,51] However, data to support these clinical assumptions are scant. Puberty does not predict remission of asthma, and nearly two-thirds of children with chronic asthma have persistent symptoms throughout puberty.[52] Chronic constipation persists into young adulthood in at least a third of individuals.[53] The prevalence of enuresis declines from 10% at age 7 years to 1% at 15 years, but no published studies have formally assessed the association between enuresis and puberty.[54]

However, evidence suggests that early puberty is an independent risk factor for the persistence of asthma into adolescence and severity of asthma in adulthood.[55] The mechanism is unclear, and might reflect hormonal effects on reactivity of airways or common environmental risk factors for both asthma and early puberty.[56] Such evidence is not available for enuresis or constipation; the only longitudinal study to examine puberty in relation to constipation suggests that remission or successful treatment was related to neither pubertal timing nor status.[53]

Sex differences in chronic physical illnesses alter during puberty. The peak age of onset of type 1 diabetes is in the early pubertal years in both sexes, possibly due to the metabolic demands of growth and to heightened insulin resistance during puberty. However, this peak is about 2 years earlier in girls than in boys.[57] In many other autoimmune conditions, such as systemic lupus erythematosis, autoimmune thyroid conditions, and juvenile rheumatoid arthritis, puberty coincides with a rise in prevalence and a marked shift in sex ratio towards female.[58] A similar shift to female predominance at puberty is seen in atopic conditions. These differences between the sexes might arise from the different effects of oestrogen and testosterone on the initiation or course of underlying autoimmune processes.[59-61]

Attention deficit hyperactivity disorder, antisocial behaviour, and substance misuse

Until two decades ago, a dominant clinical view was that attention deficit hyperactivity disorder (ADHD) remitted during the transition to adolescence. Findings of recent studies of children with ADHD at puberty have challenged this view. Antisocial behaviour, substance misuse, and academic failure become more prominent during adolescence in individuals with ADHD, and psychostimulants remain useful in the treatment of adolescents with childhood-onset ADHD.[62-64] A decrease in the proportion of individuals meeting diagnostic criteria for ADHD does occur in adolescence as the mean levels of hyperactive, impulsive, and inattentive behaviours drop, but whether this fall reflects a fundamental change in the underlying disorder is unclear.[65] No studies have examined the effect of puberty compared with age on symptoms of ADHD.

Evidence is more consistent that puberty is linked to antisocial behaviour and delinquency, with boys who mature early having increased rates of antisocial behaviour.[66,67] More recent findings have emphasised the effects of pubertal status rather than age on risk for violent crimes, property damage, and precocious sexual behaviour.[68] This effect seems to be more prominent in boys with delinquent and antisocial friends, suggesting that advancing pubertal stage brings either a change in peer group or a greater susceptibility to peer influence.

Substance use and misuse rarely occur before puberty. With downwards secular trends in the age of initiation for many substances, the early teens now commonly herald the onset of substance use and misuse.[69-71] Substance misuse is associated with risky sexual behaviour and injuries in teenagers, and strongly predicts substance misuse and dependence in adulthood.[72] Puberty was first implicated by the finding that girls who matured early had increased use of tobacco and alcohol.[31,70,73] Conversely, late maturation was associated with persisting abstinence, a difference that continues into young adulthood.[74,75] More recent findings indicate that pubertal stage holds an association with use of tobacco, alcohol, and cannabis that is independent of age.[69] Links with substance misuse seem to be even stronger, with late puberty associated with a three-fold increase in rate of such problems.[76] The most widely accepted explanations for the association of pubertal stage and substance use concern altered patterns of sensation-seeking or differential peer affiliation with substance users, or both, in individuals who reach puberty early.[75-77] This pattern might be equivalent to the increases in novelty seeking, orientation to adult stimuli, and sensitivity to social status found in peri-adolescent animals.[78-80] Since early puberty is not associated with increased substance use in adult life, it is possible that the association of early puberty with substance use does not persist beyond adolescence.[81]

Depression and anxiety

Differences between the sexes in internalising emotional disorders characterised by depression and anxiety appear in early adolescence.[82] Such disorders commonly persist into adulthood, so that the early adolescent rise in female depression largely accounts for the persisting higher rates of depression in women than in men throughout the reproductive years.[83] Evidence of increases in overall prevalence in recent decades suggests that sociocultural influences have a role in development of these disorders in adolescence.[84]

The study of depression in adolescence and any link with puberty was overlooked in early epidemiological research, partly because adolescent emotional disturbances were seen as transient and universal, and depression as a distinct disorder of adulthood. In fact, depressive symptoms in girls shift markedly in early adolescence so that by the mid-teens, rates of depressive disorder are over two-fold higher in girls than in boys.[85,86] Panic attacks are also rare before puberty, but increase markedly in girls with pubertal development.[87] Early explanations emphasised the different consequences of puberty with more negative psychological reactions to bodily changes or more difficult transitions in social and sexual roles in girls than in boys.[88] Altered responses of post-pubertal girls to adversity, including a propensity to ruminate and adopt self-blaming coping styles were further possible factors.[89-92] Certainly conflict and an absence of closeness with parents, as well as difficulties in adjustment to secondary school and peer victimisation, seemed to be linked to depression in girls.[93,94]

Earlier findings showed inconsistent associations between gonadal and adrenocortical hormones and internalising symptoms in girls, but study power was limited in many instances.[23,95] With convincing evidence that advancing pubertal stage rather than chronological age accounts for the early adolescent rise in female depressive symptoms, the role of pubertal biological changes again came into focus.[83,96,97] Changing concentrations of gonadal hormones parallel the change in depression across pubertal stage independent of altered body morphology, timing of pubertal change, or levels of stress.[97,98] However, an absence of association between depressive symptoms and menarche in African-American and Hispanic or Latino young people suggests that sociocultural context might be an important moderator of the association.[99]

A recent finding that peak dehydroepiandrosterone concentrations predict later major depression in a group at high risk because of life events and temperament has raised a question about whether pubertal changes in the hypothalamic-pituitary-adrenal axis are also implicated in the altered risks for depression in early adolescence.[100] Pubertal changes in the regulation of oxytocin and vasopressin might also be relevant through promotion of heightened need for affiliation in girls compared with boys.[101] These physiologically driven processes might then interact with genetic, social, and psychological vulnerabilities to give rise to depressive symptoms. Pubertal changes in affective arousal might interact with neurobiological development and the loss of social controls traditionally associated with earlier marriage and parenthood to explain the upsurge in early adolescent depression. This early adolescent gap in emotional regulation is likely to be particularly acute in social contexts characterised by family conflict, divorce, or peer violence and rejection.

Other mental disorders

Incidence of psychotic disorders markedly increases during the post-pubertal years, more evidently in boys than in girls. A possibility that puberty stimulates pathological brain development in individuals with antenatally acquired brain abnormalities underlies neurodevelopmental hypotheses of schizophrenia.[102] The later age of onset for schizophrenia in girls might arise from the different effect of male and female gonadal hormones on brain development.[103] Consistent with this hypothesis is the observation that early menarche predicts later onset of schizophrenic symptoms in females.[104]

Eating disorders are rarely seen before puberty and are marked by differences between the sexes in prevalence from early adolescence. Anorexia nervosa is uncommon in childhood but rises steeply in early adolescence in girls with a peak age of onset around 14 years. Pubertal stage seems to be more important than age as a predictor of subclinical bulimia nervosa, disordered eating, and abnormal eating attitudes.[105-107] For this reason, early developing girls are more likely to have symptoms of eating disorders than are late developers. Speculation has centred on the pubertal increase in body fat contributing to body dissatisfaction and use of dieting, a major risk factor for eating disorders in post-menarcheal girls.[108,109] No association has been reported between anorexia nervosa and menarche or other indices of pubertal stage, but the power of available studies to find such an association has been limited.[110]

Disorders of gender identity typically emerge around age 3–4 years, but undergo dramatic shifts across puberty. The majority of prepubertal gender identity cases do not persist into adolescence. Once past puberty, the likelihood of gender dysphoria persisting is high, although some further shifts may occur through to late adolescence.[111] Although the cause of gender identity disorder remains unclear, it has been suggested that gonadal hormone changes at puberty bring completion of a process of CNS reorganisation that began in prenatal life.[112] However, current understanding of the role of puberty in the development of gender identity and its disorders are limited.

Epilepsy

Frequency of seizures in women with intractable epilepsy changes across the menstrual cycle in response to changing concentrations of oestrogen, which lowers seizure thresholds, and progesterone, which has the reverse effect.[113] These effects prompted investigation of changes in epilepsy around the time of menarche. Retrospective studies of patients with ongoing epilepsy suggest that seizures commonly worsened at around menarche in girls.[114] Some retrospective studies have also shown that rates of seizure onset are higher within 2 years of menarche[114,115] but this has not been so in all series.[116] To date, no prospective study has been done of either the course of childhood onset epilepsy or incident seizures across pubertal stage.

Musculoskeletal disorders, pain and somatic symptoms

The pubertal growth spurt, which is unique to *H sapiens*, might contribute to musculoskeletal morbidities in adolescence. Bone mineral accretion accelerates during puberty under the influence of gonadal steroids, with peak bone mass achieved by the early 20s.[117] Delayed puberty and low weight during puberty can impair bone mineral accretion, leading to osteoporosis and increased fracture risk. So-called growing pains are common in younger adolescents.[118] Major musculoskeletal problems such as adolescent idiopathic scoliosis and slipped capital femoral epiphysis are linked to peak growth velocity during puberty.[119,120] Other poorly studied conditions seem to have a peak onset around puberty, including Scheuermann's disease, Osgood-Schlatter's disease, and osteochondritis dissecans, which can increase risk of chronic musculoskeletal pain in adult life.[121]

Several common pain syndromes begin or worsen in early adolescence. Migraine and tension headaches are commoner in women than men during the reproductive years, a pattern that emerges from around age 11 years and is linked to puberty.[122-124] The early adolescent increase in back, facial, and stomach pains is associated with pubertal status in both sexes.[125-127] It therefore appears that pain, pain perception, or both, are affected by puberty. Possible mechanisms include physical stresses associated with the pubertal growth spurt, a heightened attentiveness to somatic symptoms as a consequence of rapid physical growth, and heightened post-pubertal negative affect in girls leading to a greater awareness of somatic symptoms.[125,128] Gonadal hormones may be directly involved in altering pain thresholds, consistent with the observation of fluctuations in pain perception throughout the menstrual cycle in adult women.[129]

Obesity, polycystic ovarian syndrome, and cardiovascular risk

Childhood body fat affects the timing of puberty in a sexually dimorphic pattern, with an association between higher body-mass index (BMI) and earlier onset of menses in girls.[130] A suggestion that rising childhood obesity has driven a reduction in the age of puberty in the USA[131] seems unlikely, since increasing childhood obesity has not brought change in the timing of puberty elsewhere.[132,133] Whereas boys with higher BMI are more likely to have pubertal delay,[134] in girls obesity is associated with earlier adrenarche and puberty, and with early development of polycystic ovarian changes.[135] The features of polycystic ovarian syndrome commonly emerge around menarche and include hyperandrogenism, menstrual irregularities, an elevated ratio of luteinising hormone to follicle-stimulating hormone, and polycystic ovaries on sonography. This syndrome is the commonest cause of female infertility and is strongly linked with the metabolic syndrome and with premature and excessive mortality in the long term.[136] The emergence of polycystic ovarian syndrome during pubertal transition is thought to be related to maturation in the pattern of luteinising hormone secretion, and the typical pubertal increase in insulin resistance.[11]

Pubertal timing seems to affect cardiovascular risk separately from BMI. Women who report early menarche have an increased BMI in adolescence and adulthood independent of childhood BMI.[137] Some evidence exists of a similar association in men.[138] Blood pressure and lipid profiles seem to be more strongly associated with pubertal stage than with age and body size during adolescence, so that in boys early puberty leads to an earlier transition to male lipid patterns.[139] Intriguingly, individuals with advanced puberty at age 15 years in the 1946 British birth cohort study[140] had a mean adult blood pressure 6·4 mm Hg higher than that of individuals with minimal or no signs of puberty at that age. It is unclear whether this association reflects different pre-existing biological risks or differences in health-risk behaviour in those with early puberty.

Cancer

Early puberty has been linked to cancer in later life through several mechanisms. Longer duration of exposure to gonadal steroids might increase the risk of steroid-dependent cancers such as breast[341] and ovarian cancer[342] in women, and possibly prostate cancer in men.[343] Increased rates of obesity in early developers might heighten oxidative stresses (hyperglycaemia, hyperleptinaemia, increased lipid concentrations in tissue, inadequate antioxidant defenses, increased rates of free radical formation, enzymatic sources within the endothelium, and chronic inflammation) that raise risks for a range of cancers.[344] Hyperinsulinaemia might also promote cell growth to increase risks for colon cancer.[345] There is also a possibility that behaviours associated with cancer, including smoking and poor diet, might differ in those with early puberty, thus affecting future risks of the disease.

Conclusions and implications

Human puberty probably evolved its unique qualities to ensure that an individual possessed the necessary physical, emotional, and social qualities to ensure successful mating and parenting in primitive social groups. Those characteristics included rapid physical development and a readiness to develop attachments outside the immediate family group. The social context of modern industrialised society differs greatly from what prevailed during human evolutionary history. A delay in social role transitions into marriage and parenthood has occurred at a time when a more dominant youth culture, likened to a "super-peer," has had a profound influence on the lifestyles of youth.[146] To the extent that industries from entertainment and fashion to food market through youth culture, so too they will have a major influence on youth lifestyles that in turn will affect health in later life.

Despite this growing recognition that puberty is a phase of high risk for many health problems, preventive work has often had a narrow focus around themes such as the initiation of substance use or risky sexual behaviours. Yet the potential of such work seems much greater, particularly around promotion of mental health. Puberty occurs at a time of neural plasticity, where the effects of earlier adversity may be ameliorated and where experience may shape brain development and later emotional functioning. Major gaps remain in our knowledge of important areas such as the relationship between puberty and CNS development. Pubertal hormones have a demonstrable effect on neuronal function, but whether puberty and cortical maturation merely co-occur temporally or are causally related remains unclear. This question might be relevant for the prevention of mental disorders in adolescence and clinical intervention for childhood emotional and behavioural problems that may or may not persist into adolescence.

The modern mismatch between biological and social maturity is of great significance for health and reproductive success. A prolonged adolescence, shaped by powerful socioeconomic forces, has seen new health problems emerge.[26] For young people without strong family and educational connections, puberty is a high risk period which can mark the beginning of a fast-track to adulthood with early transitions into sexual activity and school leaving as well as the development of psychiatric and substance use disorders. The health consequences for groups such as young offenders may be devastating.[147] Maintaining strong links to family and school will remain a cornerstone of promoting adolescent health social development. Yet success in promoting adolescent health might ultimately rely on the extent to which we can integrate the gains of the 20th century for young people, in terms of education and economic prosperity, with opportunities to assume adult roles closer to the age at which they are biologically equipped to do so.

Conflict of interest statement
We declare that we have no conflict of interest.

Acknowledgments
George Patton receives salary support from the Victorian Health Promotion Foundation.

References
1 Spear LP. Adolescent brain development and animal models. *Ann N Y Acad Sci* 2004; **1021**: 23–26.
2 Delemarre-van de Waal HA. Regulation of puberty. *Best Pract Res Clin Obstet Gynaecol* 2002; **16**: 1–12.
3 Arlt W, Martens JW, Song M, Wang JT, Auchus RJ, Miller WL. Molecular evolution of adrenarche: structural and functional analysis of p450c17 from four primate species. *Endocrinology* 2002; **143**: 4665–72.
4 Goodyer IM, Herbert J, Tamplin A, Altham PME. First episode major depression in adolescents: affective, cognitive and endocrine characteristics of risk status and predictors of onset. *Br J Psychiatry* 2000; **176**: 142–49.
5 Dahl RE. Adolescent brain development: A period of vulnerabilities and opportunities. *Ann N Y Acad Scis* 2004; **1021**: 1–21.
6 Marshall WA, Tanner JM. Variations in the pattern of pubertal changes in boys. *Arch Dis Child* 1970; **45**: 13–23.
7 Marshall WA, Tanner JM. Variations in pattern of pubertal changes in girls. *Arch Dis Child* 1969; **44**: 291–303.
8 Parent AS, Teilmann G, Juul A, Skakkebaek NE, Toppari J, Bouguignon JP. The timing of normal puberty and the age limits of sexual precocity: variations around the world, secular trends, and changes after migration. *Endocr Rev* 2003; **24**: 668–93.
9 van den Berg SM, Setiawan A, Bartels M, Polderman TJ, van der Vaart AW, Boomsma DI. Individual differences in puberty onset in girls: bayesian estimation of heritabilities and genetic correlations. *Behav Genet* 2006; **36**: 1–10.
10 Gluckman PD, Hanson MA. Evolution, development and timing of puberty. *Trends Endocrinol Metab* 2006; **17**: 7–12.
11 Stafford DEJ, Gordon CM. Adolescent androgen abnormalities. *Curr Opin Obstet Gynecol* 2002; **14**: 445–51.
12 Juul A, Teilmann G, Scheike T, et al. Pubertal development in Danish children: comparison of recent European and US data. *Int J Androl* 2006; **29**: 247–55.
13 Herman-Giddens ME, Slora EJ, Wasserman RC, et al. Secondary sexual characteristics and menses in young girls seen in office practice: a study from the Pediatric Research in Office Settings network. *Pediatrics* 1997; **99**: 505–12.
14 Herman-Giddens ME, Wang L, Koch G. Secondary sexual characteristics in boys: estimates from the national health and nutrition examination survey III, 1988–1994. *Arch Pediatr Adolesc Med* 2001; **155**: 1022–28.
15 Viner RM. Splitting hairs: is puberty getting earlier in girls? *Arch Dis Child* 2002; **86**: 8–10.
16 Kaplowitz P. Pubertal development in girls: secular trends. *Curr Opin Obstet Gynecol* 2006; **18**: 487–91.
17 Mul D, Fredriks AM, van Buuren S, Oostdijk W, Verloove-Vanhorick SP, Wit JM. Pubertal development in The Netherlands 1965–1997. *Pediatr Res* 2001; **50**: 479–86.

18 Hall GS. Adolescence: Its psychology and its relations to physiology, anthropology, sociology, sex, crime, religion and education. London: Sidney Appleton; 1905.

19 Freud A. Adolescence as a developmental disturbance. In: Caplan G, Lebovici S, eds. Adolescence. New York: Basic Books; 1969.

20 Kestenberg J. Phases of adolescence with suggestions for a correlation of psychic and hormonal organization. Antecedents of adolescent organization in childhood. *J Am Acad Child Adolesc Psychiatry* 1967; 6: 426–63.

21 Gottlieb G. The roles of experience in the development of behavior and the nervous system. In: Gottlieb G, ed. Neural and behavioral specificity: studies on the development of behavior and the nervous system. New York: Academic Press, 1976.

22 Lerner RM. Concepts and theories of human development. 2nd edn. New York: Random House, 1986.

23 Brooks-Gunn J, Warren MP. Biological and social contributions to negative affect in young adolescent girls. *Child Dev* 1989; 60: 40–55.

24 Schlegel A, Barry H. Adolescence: an anthropological enquiry. New York: Free Press, 1991.

25 Furlong A, Cartmel F. Young people and social change: invidualisation and risk in late modernity. Maidenhead: Open University Press, 1997.

26 Graham P. The end of adolescence. Oxford: Oxford University Press, 2004.

27 Rutter M, Graham P, Chadwick OFD, Yule W. Adolescent turmoil: fact or fiction. *J Child Psychol Psychiat* 1976; 17: 35–56.

28 Jones MC. Psychological correlates of somatic development. *Child Dev* 1965; 36: 899–911.

29 Jones MC, Bayley N. Physical maturing among boys as related to behaviour. *J Educ Psychol* 1950; 41: 129–48.

30 Schofield M. The sexual behaviour of young people. London: Longmans, 1965.

31 Stattin H, Magnusson D. Pubertal maturation in female development. Hillsdale: Erlbaum, 2003.

32 Primus RJ, Kellogg CK. Pubertal-related changes influence the development of environment-related social interaction in the male rat. *Devel Psychobiol* 1989; 22: 633–43.

33 Adriani W, Chiarotti F, Laviola G. Elevated novelty seeking and peculiar d-amphetamine sensitization in periadolescent mice compared with adult mice. *Behav Neurosci* 1998; 112: 1152–66.

34 Insel TR. A neurobiological basis of social attachment. *Am J Psychiatry* 1997; 154: 726–35.

35 Rosenblum LA. A comparative perspective on adolescence. In: Bancroft J, Reinisch JM, eds. Adolescence and puberty. New York: Oxford University Press, 1990: 63–69.

36 Moore J. Dispersal, nepotism, and primate social behaviour. *Int J Primatology* 1992; 13: 361–78.

37 McEwen BS, Alves SE. Estrogen actions in the central nervous system. *Endocrine Rev* 2003; 20: 279–307.

38 Giedd JN, Blumenthal J, Jeffries NO, et al. Brain development during childhood and adolescence: a longitudinal MRI study. *Nature Neurosci* 1999; 2: 861–63.

39 Cameron JL. Interrelationships between hormones, behavior, and affect during adolescence. *Ann N Y Acad Sci* 2004; 1021: 110–23.

40 Young EA, Alemus M. Puberty, ovarian steroids, and stress. *Ann N Y Acad Sci* 2004; 1021: 124–33.

41 Stroud LR, Salovey P, Epel ES. Sex differences in stress responses: social rejection versus achievement stress. *Biol Psychiatry* 2002; 52: 318–27.

42 Francis DD, Diorio J, Plotsky PM, Meaney MJ. Environmental enrichment reverses the effects of maternal separation on stress reactivity. *J Neurosci* 2002; 22: 7840–43.

43 Giedd JN. Structural magnetic resonance imaging of the adolescent brain. *Ann N Y Acad Sci* 2004; 1021: 77–85.

44 Mussen PH, Jones MC. The behavior inferred motivations of late and early maturing boys. *Child Dev* 1958; 29: 61–67.

45 Alsaker FD. The impact of puberty. *J Child Psychol Psychiat* 1996; 37: 249–58.

46 Sowell ER, Thompson PM, Holmes CJ, Jernigan TL, Toga AW. In vivo evidence for post-adolescent brain maturation in frontal and striatal regions. *Nature Neurosci* 1999; 2: 859–61.

47 Thompson PM, Giedd JN, Woods RP, MacDonald D, Evans AC, Toga AW. Growth patterns in the developing brain detected by using continuum mechanical tensor maps. *Nature* 2000; 404: 190–93.

48 Lewis DA. Development of the prefrontal cortex during adolescence: Insights into vulnerable neural circuits in schizophrenia. *Neuropsychopharmacology* 1997; 16: 385–98.

49 Patton GC, Hemphill S, Beyers JM, et al. Pubertal stage and deliberate self-harm in adolescents. *J Am Acad Child Adolesc Psychiatry* (in press).

50 Guerra S, Wright AL, Morgan WJ, Sherrill DL, Holberg CJ, Martinez FD. Persistence of asthma symptoms during adolescence: role of obesity and age at the onset of puberty. *Am J Respir Crit Care Med* 2004; 170: 78–85.

51 Ernst P, Ghezzo H, Becklake MR. Risk factors for bronchial hyperresponsiveness in late childhood and early adolescence. *Eur Respir J* 2002; 20: 635–39.

52 Nicolai T, Illi S, Tenborg J, Kiess W, Mutius E. Puberty and prognosis of asthma and bronchial hyper-reactivity. *Pediatr Allergy Immunol* 2001; 12: 142–48.

53 van Ginkel R, Reitsma JB, Buller HA, van Wijk MR, Taminau JA, Benninga MA. Childhood constipation: longitudinal follow-up study beyond puberty. *Gastroenterology* 2003; 125: 357–63.

54 Watson AR, Taylor CM, McGraw M. Disorders of the urinary system. In: McIntosh N, Helms PJ, Smyth RL, eds. Forfar and Arneil's textbook of pediatrics. 6th edn. Edinburgh: Churchill Livingstone, 2003; 599–650.

55 Varraso R, Siroux V, Maccario J, Pin I, Kauffmann F. Asthma severity is associated with body mass index and early menarche in women. *Am J Respir Crit Care Med* 2005; 171: 334–39.

56 Teilmann G, Juul A, Skakkebaek NE, Toppari J. Putative effects of endocrine disrupters on pubertal development in the human. *Best Pract Res Clin Endocrinol Metab* 2002; 16: 105–21.

57 Pundziute-Lycka A, Dahlquist G, Nystrom L, et al. The incidence of type I diabetes has not increased but shifted to a younger age at diagnosis in the 0–34 years group in Sweden 1983–1998. *Diabetologia* 2002; 45: 783–91.

58 Beeson PB. Age and sex associations of 40 autoimmune diseases. *Am J Med* 1994; 96: 457–62.

59 Gillespie KM, Nolsoe R, Betin VM, et al. Is puberty an accelerator of type I diabetes in IL6-174CC females? *Diabetes* 2005; 54: 1245–48.

60 Verthelyi D. Sex hormones as immunomodulators in health and disease. *Int Immunopharmacol* 2001; 1: 983–93.

61 Lamason R, Zhao P, Rawat R, et al. Sexual dimorphism in immune response genes as a function of puberty. *BMC Immunol* 2006; 7: 2.

62 Brown RT, Borden KA. Hyperactivity at adolescence: Some misconceptions and new directions. *J Clin Child Psychol* 1986; 15: 194–209.

63 Clampit MK, Pickle JB. Stimulant medication and the hyperactive adolescent: myths and facts. *Adolescence* 1983; 18: 811–21.

64 Thorley G. Review of follow-up and follow-back studies of childhood hyperactivity. *Psychol Bull* 1984; 96: 116–32.

65 Willoughby MT. Developmental course of ADHD symptomatology during the transition from childhood to adolescence: a review with recommendations. *J Child Psychol Psychiat* 2003; 44: 88–106.

66 Duke-Duncan P, Ritter PL, Dornbusch SM, Gross RT, Carlsmith JM. The effect of pubertal timing on body image, school behavior, and deviance. *J Youth Adolesc* 1985; 14: 227–35.

67 Flannery DJ, Rowe DC, Gulley BL. Impact of pubertal status, timing and age on adolescent sexual experience and delinquency. *J Adolesc Res* 1993; 8: 21–40.

68 Felson RB, Haynie DL. Pubertal development, social factors and deliquency among adolescent boys. *Criminology* 2002; 40: 967–88.

69 Martin CA, Kelly TH, Raynens MK, et al. Sensation seeking, puberty, and nicotine, alcohol, and marijuana use in adolescence. *J Am Acad Child Adolesc Psychiatry* 2002; 41: 1495–502.

70 Dick DM, Rose RJ, Viken RJ, Kaprio J. Pubertal timing and substance use: associations between and within families across late adolescence. *Dev Psychol* 2000; 36: 180–89.

71 Wichstrom L. The impact of pubertal timing on adolescents: alcohol use. *J Res Adolesc* 2001; 11: 131–50.

72 Anthony JC, Petronis KR. Early-onset drug use and the risk of later drug problems. *Drug Alcohol Depend* 1995; 40: 9–15.

73 Lanza ST, Collins LM. Pubertal timing and the onset of substance use in females during early adolescence. *Prevention Sci* 2002; 3: 69–82.

74 Aro H, Taipale V. The impact of timing of puberty on psychosomatic symptoms among fourteen to sixteen-year-old Finnish girls. *Child Dev* 1987; 58: 261–68.

75 Stattin H, Magnusson D. Pubertal maturation in female development: paths through life. Hillsdale: Erlbaum, 1990.

76 Patton GC, Hemphill S, Toumbourou J, McMorris BJ, Catalano RF. Pubertal stage and the onset of substance abuse. *Pediatrics* 2004; 114: 300–06.

77 Martin CA, Kelly TH, Rayens MK, et al. Sensation seeking, puberty, and nicotine, alcohol, and marijuana use in adolescence. *J Am Acad Child Adolesc Psychiatry* 2002; 41: 1495–502.

78 Shugrue PJ, Merchenthaler I. Estrogen is more than just a "sex hormone": novel sites for estrogen action in the hippocampus. *Front Neuroendocrinol* 2000; 21: 95–101.

79 Book A, Stazyk K, Quinsey V. The relationship between testosterone and aggression: a meta-analysis. *Aggression Violent Behav* 2001; 6: 579–99.

80 Spear LP, Brake SC. Periadolescence: age-dependent behavior and psychopharmacologicla responsitivity in rates. *Devel Psychobiol* 1983; 16: 83–109.

81 Viner RM, Cole TJ, Taylor B. What are the implications of early pubertal development? Findings in adulthood from a national birth cohort. *Arch Dis Child* 2006; 91 (suppl 1): A86.

82 Hayward C, Sanborn K. Puberty and the emergence of gender differences in psychopathology. *J Adolesc Health* 2002; 30 (suppl 4): 49–58.

83 Kessler RC. Epidemiology of women and depression. *J Affect Dis* 2003; 74: 5–13.

84 Rutter M, Smith D. Psychosocial disorders in young people: time trends and their causes. Chichester: Wiley and Sons; 1995.

85 Wade TJ, Cairney J, Pevalin DJ. Emergence of gender differences in depression during adolescence: national panel results from three countries. *J Am Acad Child Adoles Psychiatry* 2002; 41: 190–98.

86 Garrison CZ, Waller JL, Cuffe SP, McKeown RE, Addy CL, Jackson KL. Incidence of major depressive disorder and dysthymia in young adolescents. *J Am Acad Child Adolesc Psychiatry* 1997; 36: 458–65.

87 Hayward C, Killen JD, Hammer LD, et al. Pubertal stage and panic attack history in sixth- and seventh-grade girls. *Am J Psychiatry* 1992; 149: 1239–43.

88 Wichstrom L. The emergence of gender difference in depressed mood during adolescence. *Dev Psychol* 1999; 35: 232–45.

89 Nolen-Hoeksema S, Girgus JS. The emergence of gender differences in depression during adolescence. *Psychol Bull* 1994; 115: 424–43.

90 Petersen AC, Sarigiani PA, Kennedy RE. Adolescent depression: why more girls? *J Youth Adolesc* 1991; 20: 247–71.

91 Simmons RG, Blyth DA, VanCleave EF, Bush DM. Entry into early adolescence: the impact of school structure, puberty and early dating on self-esteem. *Am Sociol Rev* 1979; 44: 948–67.

92 Piccinelli M, Wilkinson G. Gender differences in depression: critical review. *Br J Psychiatry* 2000; 177: 486–92.

93 Resnick MD, Bearman PS, Blum RW, et al. Protecting adolescents from harm: findings from the National Longitudinal Study on Adolescent Health. *JAMA* 1997; 278: 823–32.

94 Bond L, Carlin J, Thomas L, Patton GC. Does bullying cause emotional problems? A longitudinal study of young secondary school students. *BMJ* 2001; 323: 480–84.

95 Paikoff RL, Brooks-Gunn J, Warren MP. Predictive effects of hormonal change on affective expression in adolescent females over the course of one year. *J Youth Adolesc* 1991; 20: 191–214.

96 Patton GC, Hibbert ME, Carlin J, et al. Menarche and the onset of depression and anxiety in Victoria, Australia. *J Epidemiol Community Health* 1996; 50: 661–66.

97 Angold A, Costello EJ, Erkanli A, Worthman CM. Pubertal changes in hormone levels and depression in girls. *Psychol Med* 1999; 29: 1043–53.

98 Angold A, Costello EJ, Worthman CM. Puberty and depression: the roles of age, pubertal status, and pubertal timing. *Psychol Med* 1998; 28: 51–61.

99 Hayward C, Gotlib IH, Schraedley PK, Litt IF. Ethnic differences in the association between pubertal status and symptoms of depression in adolescent girls. *J Adol Health* 1999; 25: 143–49.

100 Goodyer IM, Herbert J, Tamplin A, Altham PM. Recent life events, cortisol, dehydroepiandrosterone and the onset of major depression in high-risk adolescents. *Br J Psychiatry* 2000; 177: 499–504.

101 Cyranowski JM, Frank E, Young E, Shear MK. Adolescent onset of the gender difference in lifetime rates of major depression. *Arch Gen Psychiatry* 2000; 57: 21–27.

102 Weinberger DR. Implication of normal brain development for the pathogenesis of schizophrenia. *Arch Gen Psychiatry* 1987; 44: 660–69.

103 Haefner H, Maurer K, Loeffler W, Riecher-Roessler A. The influence of age and sex on the onset and early course of schizophrenia. *Br J Psychiatry* 1993; 162: 80–86.

104 Cohen RZ, Seeman MV, Gotowiec A, Kopala L. Earlier puberty as a predictor of later onset of schizophrenia in women. *Am J Psychiatry* 1999; 156: 1059–64.

105 Killen JD, Hayward C, Litt IF, et al. Is puberty a risk factor for eating disorders? *Am J Dis Childhood* 1992; 146: 323–25.

106 Cauffman E, Steinberg L. Interactive effects of menarcheal status and dating on dieting and disordered eating among adolescent girls. *Dev Psychol* 1996; 32: 279–87.

107 Swarr A, Richards M. Longitudinal effects of adolescent girls' pubertal development, perceptions of pubertal timing and parental relationships on eating problems. *Dev Psychol* 1996; 32: 636–42.

108 Abraham S, O'Dea JA. Body mass index, menarche, and perception of dieting among peripubertal adolescent females. *Int J Eat Disord* 2001; 29: 23–28.

109 O'Dea JA, Abraham S. Onset of disordered eating attitudes and behaviors in early adolescence: interplay of pubertal status, gender, weight and age. *Adolescence* 1999; 34: 671–79.

110 Stice E, Presnell K, Bearman SK. Relation of early menarche to depression, eating disorders, substance abuse, and comorbid psychopathology among adolescent girls. *Dev Psychol* 2001; 37: 608–19.

111 Bradley SJ, Zucker KJ. Gender identity disorder: a review of the past 10 years. *J Am Acad Child Adolesc Psychiatry* 1997; 36: 872–80.

112 Rahman Q. The neurodevelopment of human sexual orientation. *Neurosci Biobehav Rev* 2005; 29: 1057–66.

113 Herzog AG, Klein P, Ransil BJ. Three patterns of catamenial epilepsy. *Epilepsia* 1993; 38: 1082–88.

114 Klein P, van Passel-Clark L, Pezzullo JC. Onset of epilepsy at the time of menarche. *Neurology* 2003; 60: 495–97.

115 Svalheim S, Tauboll E, Bjornenak T, et al. Onset of epilepsy and menarche—is there any relationship? *Seizure* 2006; 15: 571–75.

116 Hauser WA, Annegers JF, Kurland LT. Incidence of epilepsy and unprovoked seizures in Rochester, Minnesota: 1935–1984. *Epilepsia* 1993; 34: 453–68.

117 Loud KJ, Gordon CM. Adolescent bone health. *Arch Pediatr Adolesc Med* 2006; 160: 1026–32.

118 Friedland O, Hashkes PJ, Jaber L, et al. Decreased bone speed of sound in children with growing pains measured by quantitative ultrasound. *J Rheumatol* 2005; 32: 1354–57.

119 Burwell RG. Aetiology of idiopathic scoliosis: current concepts. *Pediatr Rehabil* 2003; 6: 137–70.

120 Puylaert D, Dimeglio A, Bentahar T. Staging puberty in slipped capital femoral epiphysis: importance of the triradiate cartilage. *J Pediatr Orthop* 2004; 24: 144–47.

121 Harreby MS, Neergaard K, Hesselsoe G, Kjer J. Are low back pain and radiological changes during puberty risk factors for low back pain in adult age? A 25-year prospective cohort study of 640 school children. *Ugeskr Laeger* 1997; 159: 171–74.

122 Bille B. Migraine in school children. *Acta Paediatrica* 1962; 51 (suppl 136): 16–18.

123 Facchinetti F, Sgarbi G, Piccinini F. Hypothalamic resetting at puberty and the sexual dimorphism of migraine. *Funct Neurol* 2000; 15: 137–42.

124 Laurell K, Larsson B, Eeg-Olofsson O. Prevalence of headache in Swedish schoolchildren, with a focus on tension-type headache. *Cephalalgia* 2004; 24: 380–88.

125 Wedderkopp N, Andersen LB, Froberg K, Leboeuf-Yde C. Back pain reporting in young girls appears to be puberty-related. *BMC Musculoskelet Disord* 2005; 6: 52.

126 LeResche L, Mancl LA, Drangsholt MT, Saunders K, Korff MV. Relationship of pain and symptoms to pubertal development in adolescents. *Pain* 2005; 118: 201–09.

127 Rhee H. Relationships between physical symptoms and pubertal development. *J Pediatr Health Care* 2005; **19**: 95–103.

128 Mechanic D. Adolescent health and illness behavior: review of literature and a new hypothesis for the study of stress. *J Hum Stress* 1983; **9**: 4–13.

129 Riley JL, III, Robinson ME, Wise EA, Price DD. A meta-analytic review of pain perception across the menstrual cycle. *Pain* 1999; **81**: 225–35.

130 Biro FM, Khoury P, Morrison JA. Influence of obesity on timing of puberty. *Int J Androl* 2006; **29**: 272–77.

131 Kaplowitz PB, Slora EJ, Wasserman RC, Pedlow SE, Herman-Giddens ME. Earlier onset of puberty in girls: relation to increased body mass index and race. *Pediatrics* 2001; **108**: 347–53.

132 Mul D, Fredriks AM, van Buuren S, Oostdijk W, Verloove-Vanhorick SP, Wit JM. Pubertal development in The Netherlands 1965–1997. *Pediatr Res* 2001; **50**: 479–86.

133 Juul A, Teilmann G, Scheike T, et al. Pubertal development in Danish children: comparison of recent European and US data. *Int J Androl* 2006; **29**: 247–55.

134 Wang Y. Is obesity associated with early sexual maturation? A comparison of the association in American boys versus girls. *Pediatrics* 2002; **110**: 903–10.

135 Dunger DB, Ahmed ML, Ong KK. Effects of obesity on growth and puberty. *Best Pract Res Clin Endocrinol Metab* 2005; **19**: 375–90.

136 Gleicher N, Barad D. An evolutionary concept of polycystic ovarian disease: does evolution favour reproductive success over survival? *Reprod Biomed Online* 2006; **12**: 587–89.

137 Laitinen J, Power C, Jarvelin MR. Family social class, maternal body mass index, childhood body mass index, and age at menarche as predictors of adult obesity. *Am J Clin Nutr* 2001; **74**: 287–94.

138 Sandhu J, Ben Shlomo Y, Cole TJ, Holly J, Davey SG. The impact of childhood body mass index on timing of puberty, adult stature and obesity: a follow-up study based on adolescent anthropometry recorded at Christ's Hospital (1936–1964). *Int J Obes (Lond)* 2006; **30**: 14–22.

139 Shankar RR, Eckert GJ, Saha C, Tu W, Pratt JH. The change in blood pressure during pubertal growth. *J Clin Endocrinol Metab* 2005; **90**: 163–67.

140 Hardy R, Kuh D, Whincup PH, Wadsworth ME. Age at puberty and adult blood pressure and body size in a British birth cohort study. *J Hypertens* 2006; **24**: 59–66.

141 Ahlgren M, Melbye M, Wohlfahrt J, Sorensen TI. Growth patterns and the risk of breast cancer in women. *N Engl J Med* 2004; **351**: 1619–26.

142 Jordan SJ, Webb PM, Green AC. Height, age at menarche, and risk of epithelial ovarian cancer. *Cancer Epidemiol Biomarkers Prev* 2005; **14**: 2045–48.

143 Giles GG, Severi G, English DR, et al. Early growth, adult body size and prostate cancer risk. *Int J Cancer* 2003; **103**: 241–45.

144 Vincent HK, Taylor AG. Biomarkers and potential mechanisms of obesity-induced oxidant stress in humans. *Int J Obes (Lond)* 2006; **30**: 400–18.

145 Frezza EE, Wachtel MS, Chiriva-Internati M. Influence of obesity on the risk of developing colon cancer. *Gut* 2006; **55**: 285–91.

146 Brown JD, Halpern CT, L'Engle KL. Mass media as a sexual super peer for early maturing girls. *J Adolesc Health* 2006; **36**: 420–27.

147 Coffey C, Veit F, Wolfe R, Cini E, Patton GC. Mortality in young offenders: retrospective cohort study. *BMJ* 2003; **326**: 1064–66.

Life Course

[4]

The Life Course as Developmental Theory

Glen H. Elder, Jr.

The pioneering longitudinal studies of child development (all launched in the 1920s and 1930s) were extended well beyond childhood. Indeed, they eventually followed their young study members up to the middle years and later life. In doing so, they generated issues that could not be addressed satisfactorily by available theories. These include the recognition that individual lives are influenced by their ever-changing historical context, that the study of human lives calls for new ways of thinking about their pattern and dynamic, and that concepts of human development should apply to processes across the life span. Life course theory has evolved since the 1960s through programmatic efforts to address such issues.

INTRODUCTION

A central premise ties together the studies presented in this article: *the notion that changing lives alter developmental trajectories.* I address the developmental relevance of these social pathways in the life course, beginning with findings based on *Children of the Great Depression* (Elder, 1974) and their theoretical meaning for life course study and developmentalists in general. Next I turn to the challenges we have pursued over recent decades and the responses that have fostered advances in life course theory. I conclude with some developmental implications of successive life transitions, from the early years to later life.

Empirical Origins

During the late 1920s and early 1930s, three pioneering longitudinal studies of children were launched at the University of California, Berkeley: the Oakland Growth Study (birth years 1920–1921), under the direction of the late Harold and Mary Jones; the Berkeley Guidance Study (birth years 1928–1929), directed by the late Jean Macfarlane; and the Berkeley Growth Study (also 1928–1929), managed by the late Nancy Bayley. No one could have imagined at the time what this collective effort would mean for an emerging field of child development. From their Berkeley Institute of Child Welfare (now called Human Development), the investigators saw few other projects engaged in studying children over time. The modest beginning established by these studies represents a key event in the remarkable growth of longitudinal research, centered on human development across the life course.[1]

1. An account of the three longitudinal studies at the Institute of Human Development can be found in volumes edited by Eichorn, Clausen, Haan, Honzik, and Mussen (1981) and by

I first encountered these studies in the early 1960s after arriving at the institute (now called Human Development) to work with John Clausen on a study of careers using data from the Oakland Growth Study. The archival records from year to year broadened my vision of lives and revealed the dramatic instability of families under changing economic conditions, the Great Depression. A good many study members could say that they were once "well off" and then "quite poor." Life histories noted frequent changes of residence and jobs, such as they were. A child in an economically deprived family who seemed "old beyond his time" recovered his youthful spirit when family income improved. Overall, the Depression children who did well in their adult years left many puzzles behind.

Such events focused my attention on ways of thinking about social change, life pathways, and individual development as modes of behavioral continuity and change. These pathways represent the most distinctive area for exploration. In my view, they refer to the social trajectories of education, work, and family that are followed by individuals and groups through society. Life transitions (e.g., entry into first grade, birth of a child) are always part of social trajectories that give them distinctive meaning and form

Jones, Bayley, Macfarlane, and Honzik (1971). One of the most important studies based on the Oakland Growth and Guidance samples following participants into adulthood was produced by Jack Block (with the assistance of Norma Haan), entitled *Lives through Time* (1971). Other major studies include Clausen's *American Lives* (1993) and Elder's *Children of the Great Depression* (1974). The growth of longitudinal studies has been documented in a number of volumes, including Cairns, Elder, and Costello (1996), Elder (1985), Magnusson and Bergman (1990), Nesselroade and Baltes (1979), and Rutter (1988).

2   Child Development

(Elder, 1998). The multiple trajectories of individuals and their developmental implications are basic elements of the "life course," as conceptualized in research and theory.

Historical forces shape the social trajectories of family, education, and work, and they in turn influence behavior and particular lines of development. Some individuals are able to select the paths they follow, a phenomenon known as human agency, but these choices are not made in a social vacuum. All life choices are contingent on the opportunities and constraints of social structure and culture. These conditions clearly differed for children who grew up during the Great Depression and World War II. Such thinking prompted the way I studied children of the Great Depression, based on the Berkeley Institute studies. It also influenced how I proceeded to carry out a series of investigations of human life and development in different times and places—World War II and the Korean War, the Chinese Cultural Revolution, rural disadvantage in contemporary America, and inner-city poverty.

The Oakland and Berkeley cohorts were subject to the influence of other historical times, including World War II and the Korean conflict. The Oakland males were old enough to serve in World War II, whereas the younger Berkeley males typically experienced this war in terms of mobilized life on the homefront. They served mainly in the Korean War. Later in this article I draw upon accounts of such experiences, as reported in a series of papers (Elder, 1986, 1987; with Clipp [Elder & Clipp, 1988, 1989; see also Clipp & Elder, 1996]). The talented men and women in Lewis Terman's sample (born between 1903 and the 1920s) also encountered the Great Depression and World War II, but later in life (Holahan & Sears, 1995). Our studies show that this later timetable made a lasting imprint on their lives (Elder, Pavalko, & Hastings, 1991), a point well documented by the impact of World War II.

Another effort to examine the role of the state in social mobilization took us to Shanghai and a life history study of the Cultural Revolution in the lives of men and women just prior to the crisis of Tianamen Square (Elder, Wu, & Yuan, 1993). In collaboration with the Institute of Sociology (Shanghai University) and the Carolina Population Center, we used retrospective life history methods in a survey of 1,300 adults in Shanghai during the winter and spring of 1987–1988. Especially among urban young people who were sent to peasant communities and mines, the disruptive forces and sanctions of the Cultural Revolution led to the postponement of family formation and to the loss of education and conventional career prospects. Because prospective longitudinal studies are not available on the near or distant past in developing societies, this study proved unusually valuable in showing us the effectiveness of retrospective life history techniques for recovering knowledge about the enduring effects of past events.

In the 1980s, hard times returned to rural America with a collapse of land values reminiscent of the Great Depression's jolt. This event led to collaboration with Rand Conger and colleagues at Iowa State University on a panel study of economic stress in family relationships and children's life experiences (Conger & Elder, 1994; Elder, 1992). A third of the families in this north central region of Iowa were engaged in farming, and a fifth had no exposure to agriculture, either in childhood or in their adult years. Launched in 1989, this study of 451 families drew upon analytic models in studies of "children of the Great Depression" and also extended them in fruitful ways through better documentation of the "linking" or intervening experiences and processes.

As in the Depression research, we viewed the family and its adaptations as a central link between a generalized economic decline and the well-being of children. Indebtedness, income loss, and unstable work increased the felt economic pressure of families. The stronger this reported pressure, the greater the risk of depressed feelings and marital negativity among parents. These processes tended to undermine nurturant parenting and increased the likelihood of emotional distress, academic trouble, and problem behavior among boys and girls. Countering such cumulative adversities are resourceful paths to adulthood, most commonly associated with families that have ties to the land (Elder & Conger, in press). The Iowa Youth and Families Project is currently following these children into their adult years of advanced education, family formation, and work.

At the same time, inner-city poverty became an important issue, as the rate of poverty climbed steadily higher in the neighborhoods of our large northern cities (Jargowsky, 1997; Wilson, 1987). To understand the implications of this change for minority children in particular, I joined a research team that was beginning to focus on families and young adolescents in the central city of Philadelphia. In neighborhoods that range from a poverty rate of 10% to 40%, we investigated pathways of success and trouble among African American and European American youth ($N = 487$, ages 11–14 in 1991—Elder, Eccles, Ardelt, & Lord, 1995; Furstenberg, Cook, Eccles, Elder, & Sameroff, in press). As in the Iowa study, we identified a similar process by which economic hardship adversely influenced Black and White children.

Glen H. Elder, Jr. 3

Family resources and strategies proved to be more potent in fostering successful outcomes in youth (in academic achievement, social involvement, emotional health, avoidance of problem behavior) than neighborhood influences. There were greater differences within particular neighborhoods, among families and children, than between them. In high-risk neighborhoods, we asked how parents sought to minimize children's exposure to dangers (e.g., keeping children in the house) and maximize opportunities beyond the household (e.g., involving children in recreational and education programs in the area). This project is part of a research program sponsored by the MacArthur Foundation Research Network on Successful Adolescent Development among Youth in High-Risk Settings.

Children of the Great Depression: Some
Theoretical Implications

Longitudinal data at the University of California's Institute of Human Development at Berkeley contributed to these research themes and approaches by encouraging me to think holistically about lives and development over time and across changing contexts. I had to move beyond the early longitudinal projects that were known for child-based studies in single domains, such as problem behavior in the work of Jean Macfarlane (Macfarlane, Allen, & Honzik, 1954) on the Berkeley Guidance sample.

This also applied to the Oakland Growth Study (1930–1931) established by Harold Jones and Herbert Stolz. They were interested in normal growth and development, including physical maturation. Neither developmental nor health effects of the encompassing Depression crisis were on their agenda. Over 30 years later, I was privileged to use the data archive they had constructed and saw the possibility of bringing these larger contextual forces to an understanding of the lives of the Oakland men and women, then in their forties. I asked how the economic depression of the 1930s affected them as children with a background in middle- and working-class families before the economic collapse.

Members of the Oakland Study were born at the beginning of the 1920s, entered childhood during this prosperous decade, and then encountered the economic collapse as adolescents through the hardship experience of parents and relatives. Their historical location placed them at risk of this deprivational event. Some were exposed to severe hardships through the family, whereas others managed to avoid them altogether. These contrasting situations, deprived and nondeprived, established an "experi-

ment in nature" with empirical findings that affirm the principle of (1) *historical time and place:* that *the life course of individuals is embedded in and shaped by the historical times and places they experience over their lifetime.*

The full significance of this principle is clarified by comparing the adolescent experience of the Oakland cohort with that of youth who were born a decade earlier and later. For example, a large number of men and women in Lewis Terman's sample (Holahan & Sears, 1995) of highly able youth were born around 1908–1910. They entered grade school during the First World War, and most experienced the relative prosperity of middle-class life during the 1920s. The Oakland children encountered Depression hardships after a relatively secure phase of early development in the 1920s, and they left home after the worst years of the 1930s for education, work, and family.

This life pattern differed strikingly for children who were born at the end of the 1920s or during the Great Depression. A comparative group, the younger Berkeley Guidance children (born 1928–1929), experienced the vulnerable years of childhood during the worst years of the Great Depression, a period of extraordinary stress and instability (see Figure 1—Elder, 1979, 1981; Elder, Caspi, & Downey, 1986; Elder, Liker, & Cross, 1984). Their adolescence coincided with the "empty households of World War II," when parents worked from sunup to sundown in essential industry. We found that the Berkeley children were more adversely influenced by the economic collapse than were the Oakland adolescents, especially the boys.

Even within their respective cohorts, the Oakland and Berkeley study members experienced differences in the temporal order of life events. Some entered marriage before their twentieth birthday, while others were still unmarried 8 years later. Early marriage tended to produce a cumulation of life disadvantages, from socioeconomic hardship to the loss of education. Early childbearing had similar consequences. Later on in life, children of the study members left home at different times in their parents' lives. Whether relatively early or late, the timing of life transitions has long-term consequences through effects on subsequent transitions. The principle of (2) *timing in lives* states that: *the developmental impact of a succession of life transitions or events is contingent on when they occur in a person's life.*

Historical events and individual experience are connected through the family and the "linked" fates of its members. The misfortune of one member is shared through relationships. For example, Depression hardship tended to increase the explosiveness of

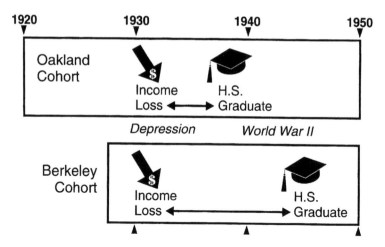

Figure 1   The different historical times of the Oakland and Berkeley cohorts

fathers who were inclined toward irritability. And the more explosive they became under economic stress, the more adversely it affected the quality of marriage and parenting. In these ways, our observations support another principle, that of (3) *linked lives: lives are lived interdependently, and social and historical influences are expressed through this network of shared relationships.*

The Great Depression brings to mind "a world out of control," and yet families often worked out successful adaptations in these circumstances. Parents and children made choices and some engaged in effective adaptations within available options and constraints. I have called this human agency. Under the mounting economic pressures of their households, mothers sought and found jobs amidst scarce options, while their children assumed responsibilities in the home and community. When hard-pressed parents moved their residence to cheaper quarters and sought alternative forms of income, they were involved in the process of "building a new life course." As expressed in this manner, the principle of (4) *human agency* states that *individuals construct their own life course through the choices and actions they take within the opportunities and constraints of history and social circumstances.*

In terms of contemporary knowledge, these early empirical observations already illustrate core principles of life course theory. I use the term "theory" to refer to a framework and orientation (Merton, 1968). Life course theory defines a common field of inquiry by providing a framework that guides research on

matters of problem identification and conceptual development. The key principles are *historical time and place, the timing of lives, linked or interdependent lives,* and *human agency.* Considerations of historical context and social timing enabled us to see how members of the Oakland and Berkeley cohorts were influenced differentially by their life experiences. Moreover, these influences could only be understood through the hardship adaptations of people who were important in their lives—through the agency and dynamic of linked lives.

As one might expect, the principle of historical time is most fully expressed today in the work of historians within the new social history who have played an important role in the development of life course studies. Especially prominent in this group is Tamara Hareven (1978, 1982, 1996), who has pioneered in the historical study of families and lives. In collaboration with her study of Manchester, NH, men, we show that both historical time *and* place (i.e., region) make a difference in life opportunities and adult careers (Elder & Hareven, 1993). Another important contribution is Modell's (1989) study of the emergence of the social institutions of adolescence (such as dating, courtship) across twentieth-century America. A productive collaboration between historians and developmentalists is reported in *Children in Time and Place* (Elder, Modell, & Parke, 1993), and includes an insightful account of ways of studying children in history (see Cahan, Mechling, Sutton-Smith, & White, 1993).

The principle of timing has been associated with

the work of Bernice Neugarten on adult development since the 1950s (see Neugarten, 1968; Neugarten & Datan, 1973; and Hagestad & Neugarten, 1985). In the 1960s, sociological studies of age greatly expanded our understanding of the social and individual implications of the temporal pattern of events (see Riley, Johnson, & Foner, 1972). Planned alterations in the timing of life events is one expression of the principle of human agency. People's choices on timing construct their life course (Clausen, 1993). The primacy of human agency in life course thinking has been strengthened by a number of developments, including Bandura's pioneering research on self-efficacy (Bandura, 1997) and greater knowledge of genetic influences on the selection of environments (Dunn & Plomin, 1990; Scarr & McCartney, 1983). But the chance to make certain choices depends on the opportunities and constraints of history.

The principle of linked lives is a key premise of the earliest social account of *pattern* in human lives (see Thomas & Znaniecki, 1918–1920), and it remains a cornerstone of contemporary life course theory, with its notions of role sequence and synchronization. Today the idea of linked lives is central to the ecology of human development (Bronfenbrenner, 1979) and is expressed in models of personal networks (Granovetter, 1973) and in their convoys of friends and family over time (Kahn & Antonucci, 1980). Synchronization in life planning and action refers to the coordination of lives, usually on matters of timing (Hareven, 1991). The concept of family management (Furstenberg, 1993; Sampson, 1992) generally concerns the effectiveness of life synchronization among members, along with other adaptations. A full account of these applications in life course theory and its contribution to an understanding of child development is available in Volume 1 of the new *Handbook of Child Psychology* (Elder, 1998; see also 1995, 1996).

When work began on *Children of the Great Depression* in the mid-1960s, a field of life course studies or relevant theories did not exist. The concept of life course was rarely discussed in the scholarly literature or in graduate seminars. In putting together a study of children in the Great Depression, I drew upon the ideas and research of many people in the social and behavioral sciences who were beginning to work on relevant problems, such as aging (see Elder, 1998). Though neglected at the time, these contexts of developmental relevance are now gaining appropriate visibility through multilevel studies of neighborhood and community effects in children's lives (Furstenberg et al., in press; Sampson, 1997). With advances in statistical models, we are now able to investigate

the interplay of changing behavior and personality with changing social pathways. However, it is still the case that longitudinal studies *seldom* examine the stability and nature of children's social environments over time (Sameroff, 1993, p. 8). As a result, sources of behavioral continuity and change remain poorly understood.

The work ahead is daunting, to be sure, but life course ideas on time, process, and context have continued to spread throughout the social and behavioral sciences. We find examples in both ecological and life-span developmental psychology, in the new social and cultural history of family and children, and in cultural models from anthropology and the sociology of age (see Elder, 1996, 1998; Featherman, 1983). I think of this diffusion in terms of research issues that were once posed many years ago by the Berkeley longitudinal studies.

Challenges to Life Course Theory

The Berkeley studies were originally designed for assessments of child development. There was no plan to follow the participants into their twenties and thirties. As they continued into adulthood and even the later years, they acquired greater theoretical significance. I see this significance in the fresh momentum they gave to the study of adult development and its implications for children's lives, along with more awareness of the correlated limitations of child-based models of growth and development.

When the study members reached adulthood, investigators had two ways of thinking about social pathways, and neither placed individuals in history. One involved the notion of careers, usually over a person's worklife. The second is known as the "life cycle"—a sequence of social roles that bear upon stages of parenthood, from the birth of children to their departure from the household and their eventual transition to the role of parent, setting in motion another life cycle.

Neither approach proved satisfactory. The career model dealt with single careers, mainly a person's work life, and thus oversimplified the lives of people who were coping with multiple roles at the same time. The large-scale entry of mothers into the labor force produced circumstances that favored a new concept of multiple, interlocking trajectories that varied in synchronization. Career perspectives also failed to incorporate notions of age-graded expectations in a systematic way and did not orient analyses to the historical context of lives across the generations.

Life cycle theory helped to contextualize people's

lives by emphasizing the social dynamic of "linked lives." These connections extend across the generations and serve to integrate young and old. Social ties to significant others become forms of social control and constraint in channeling individual decisions and actions. Socialization occurs through such networks of social relationships. Though notable, these contributions of life cycle theory did not locate people according to their life stage or historical context.

To address these limitations, studies began to draw upon the insights of a deeper knowledge of age in people's lives. The cultural content of child socialization has much to do with the learning of behaviors that are prescribed and proscribed by age. They constitute "age expectations." These cultural expectations include notions about the timing and order of transitions, such as entry into first grade, and about whether the events are early, on time, or late (Hagestad & Neugarten, 1985). Some events are "out of order" according to conventional expectations, such as births before marriage. Ill-timed or off-timed events (too late or too early) can have adverse effects. In addition, birth year orients analysis to people in specific historical locations, and thus according to particular changes. Consider Americans who were born in the late 1930s. They avoided the generalized pressures of family stress and deprivation, but faced another risk—that of the absence and loss of father during the Second World War.

Children of the Great Depression (Elder, 1974) brought the *life cycle model* together with an *age-based concept of timing* in a framework on the life course. Neither perspective was adequate by itself. In the life cycle approach, the notion of "linked lives" enabled us to understand how Depression hardship influenced children through the family. And it proved helpful in thinking about socialization and the role sequences of adult life. But age distinctions were needed to locate families in history and to mark the transitions of adult life. The meanings of age brought a perspective on "timing" to the study.

A more recent study also shows the insights of a life course model that incorporates ideas of career, life cycle, and age, as expressed in the core principles of timing and linked lives. Among African American families in Los Angeles, Burton (1985; see also Burton & Bengtson, 1985) found that the timing of a young daughter's birth had repercussions well into the grandparent generation. A birth in early adolescence multiplied strains and deprivations, reflecting the violation of deep-seated expectations about "how life should be lived." The young mothers expected their own mothers to help care for their child, but this expectation seldom materialized because they felt

"too young" for the grandmother role. As a mother put it, "I can't be a young momma and a grandmomma at the same time."

In this study, the birth of a child defines a life transition, but transitions are frequently a succession of choice points (see Figure 2). In fact, the transition to motherhood in adolescence can be thought of as a *multiphasic process* in which each phase is linked to a choice point. Young girls may choose to engage in premarital sex or not, or to use contraception or not, to seek an abortion or not, and to marry the father or not. Only a handful of options lead to a birth out of wedlock. Not too long ago, unwed motherhood was viewed simply as *one* transition, a concept that obscured appropriate points of preventive intervention along the life course.

What are the consequences of a childbirth that occurs much too early according to expectations? One life course interpretation stresses the *cumulation of disadvantages*—a concatenation of negative events and influences. Birth of a child to an early adolescent may result in the early termination of schooling, with its negative implications for employment. Whether disadvantages cumulate or not depends on the new mother's response to her circumstance. In a Baltimore longitudinal study of African American generations (Furstenberg, Brooks-Gunn, & Morgan, 1987), young mothers who could stay in school through the childcare provided by their mother or who married the father were able to minimize the long-term disadvantage of an ill-timed birth.

As life course theory advanced, it provided a framework for studies that relate social pathways to history and developmental trajectories. In any longitudinal study, the mere step of locating parents in history through their birth year can generate historical insights that would not be achieved otherwise. Consider what we have learned about Lewis Terman's sample of gifted Californians who were born between 1900 and the 1920s (Holahan & Sears, 1995). Selected as the upper 1% of age peers at 19, these "best and brightest" seemed to be invulnerable to the misfortunes of history. However, the twentieth century proved to be no respecter of their high ability (Shanahan, Elder, & Miech, 1997). Men born before 1911 ended up with college degrees and no place to go in the stagnant economy of the 1930s. Their alternative in many cases was to stay in school, piling up degrees. Indeed, they ended up better educated than the younger men, but aspirations had little to do with their achievement.

Life course theory provides a way to study the myriad changes that bear upon children in today's world (see Hernandez, 1993). These include (1) the

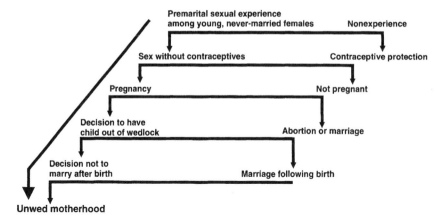

Figure 2 The life course of unwed motherhood

restructuring of the economy through downsizing and other strategies, as expressed through community and family disruption and hardship; (2) the family consequences of expanding levels of economic inequality; (3) the implications of change in the welfare system for children and young families; (4) the concentration of poverty and crime in the inner city; and (5) the redesign of schools and learning through information-age technology. All epochs of social change call for approaches to child development that view children in their changing ecologies. The motivating question focuses on the process by which a particular change is expressed in the way children think, feel, and behave.

More concepts of development are at work today in studies across the life course, and projects are assessing the developmental impact of changing pathways in changing times.[2] The challenge involves the

2. These challenges to life course theory and analysis—thinking about lives, human development, and their relation to changing times—are a large part of the story, but they should be combined with the task of establishing concepts of development that apply across the life course, a major item on the agenda of developmental life-span psychology (Baltes, Lindenberger, & Staudinger, 1998). In "The Life Course and Human Development" (Elder, 1998), I discuss the convergence of these strands in contemporary life course theory. Paul Baltes has been most involved over the years in the development of life-span concepts. In his writings, selection, optimization, and compensation mechanisms aim to minimize the impact of organismic losses and maximize gains. Thus, children may select activities in which they are successful, whether sports or music, and optimize benefits through an investment of time, energy, and relationships. In old age, the musician might restrict the number of pieces and practice more often to compensate for declining physical skill.

analysis of "interlocking trajectories" that connect changing environments with behavioral changes. Consider the following: Using growth curve models, a longitudinal study found that increasing negative life events contributed significantly to the widely documented rise in depressed feelings among girls during early adolescence, especially in the absence of parental warmth (Ge, Lorenz, Conger, Elder, & Simons, 1994). No such effect was observed among boys. In another research example that parallels *Children of the Great Depression* (1974), a nationwide longitudinal study found that mounting economic hardship in families significantly increased the antisocial tendencies and depressed feelings of boys and girls (McLeod & Shanahan, 1996). This type of work provides merely a sampling of the new life course studies.

Transition experiences represent a strategic approach to the possibilities of studying *lives in motion*. Transitions make up life trajectories, and they provide clues to developmental change. The process by which this occurs is captured by the lasting effect of early transitions, my concluding topic.

Transition Experiences in Changing Lives

Early transitions can have enduring consequences by affecting subsequent transitions, even after many years and decades have passed. They do so, in part, through behavioral consequences that set in motion "cumulating advantages and disadvantages." Individual differences are minimized in life transitions when the new circumstances resemble a "total institution" that presses from all angles toward a particular behavior (Caspi & Moffitt, 1993, pp. 265–266). One transition with such impact is military service, a common event for young men in the Oakland and Berkeley studies.

Nine out of 10 males from the Oakland Growth Study served in the military, as did over 70% of the Berkeley Guidance males, most of whom came from economically deprived households in the 1930s (Elder, 1986, 1987). Veterans who entered the service immediately after high school fared better in psychological health and life achievement than nonveterans, regardless of preservice background. This "early entry" occurred before adult careers and thus became a formative influence. In large part, military service accounts for why many "children of the Great Depression" did well in their lives. Three functions of the service offer essential details of this developmental process.

First, military mobilization tends to pull young people from their past, however privileged or deprived, and in doing so creates new beginnings that favor developmental change. This transition, as a Berkeley veteran noted, provided a "passage into manliness."

Second, military service establishes a clear-cut break from the age-graded career, a time-out in which to sort matters and make a new beginning. For another Berkeley veteran, the army "was a place to be for a while, a place for sorting out self."

Third, military service offers a wide range of new experiences for personal growth from group processes, training, and travel. Almost overnight, young men were placed in demanding leadership roles. The G.I. Bill for advanced education was also part of this developmental regime.

Experiences of this kind do not exhaust all features of military service, but they collectively shaped a "developmental turning point" for youth from disadvantaged circumstances. One pathway involved situational changes that made early entrants more ambitious, assertive, and self-directed by mid-life (Elder, 1986). Another pathway led to extensive use of the educational and housing benefits of the G.I. Bill. These trajectories literally changed the kind of parents, husbands, and workers the men became. In this manner, the life change of veterans has special relevance to their children's well-being, a problem explored by Lois Stolz (1954) in the aftermath of World War II.

This research posed important questions regarding the nature of change and continuity in life-span development. Some Guidance Study men experienced dramatic change in their life course, what I describe as a "turning point." The military placed them in a total institution, and the resulting change established a trajectory of greater competence (Clausen, 1995; Rutter, 1996). In other cases, stress symptoms persisted, especially from war combat (Elder & Clipp, 1989). They may have done so through interactions with others that recreated the "trauma" situation or from the progressive cumulation of behavioral consequences (see Caspi, Bem, & Elder, 1989). Explosiveness born of a war experience may elicit responses that legitimize and reinforce such "disruptive" dispositions.

A more complete account of the change mechanisms is presented by a panel study of approximately 1,000 boys from low-income areas of Boston who grew up in the 1920s and 1930s (Sampson & Laub, 1996; see also 1993). More than 70% served in the military. The matched control design of delinquents and controls was originally used for a longitudinal study of delinquency by Sheldon and Eleanor Glueck (Glueck & Glueck, 1968), pioneers in research on juvenile delinquency. Men in both samples generally entered World War II at the age of 18 or 19. Most served at least 2 years and overseas.

As expected, the delinquents were more involved in dishonorable discharges and other forms of official misconduct, but they were also more likely to benefit from the service over their life course, when compared to the controls. And this was especially true for men who entered the service early. These men were young enough to take advantage of such experience through in-service schooling, overseas duty, and the G.I. Bill. In particular, benefits of the G.I. Bill were notably greater for veterans with a delinquent past when they entered the service at a young age. All of these experiences enhanced occupational status, job stability, and economic well-being up to the middle years, independent of childhood differences and socioeconomic origins.

As a whole, these findings provide consistent support for an "early timing hypothesis" on the life course advantages of military service. When military service begins shortly after high school, its training, developmental, and resource advantages are most likely to enhance educational opportunities (e.g., the G.I. Bill) and occupational advancement (e.g., officer training). Later entry, by contrast, is more likely to pull men and women out of adult roles, disrupting their life course. Persistent disadvantages appear among veterans who entered the Second World War at a very late age—in their thirties.

Effects of this kind were observed among California men in Lewis Terman's study of highly able children (Elder, Shanahan, & Clipp, 1994). The older cohort of men hit both the Depression and war years at "an untimely point" in their lives. They tended to follow a path of life-long disadvantage into the later years, when compared to the younger men (Elder & Chan, in press). They suffered more work instability, earned less income over time, experienced a higher rate of divorce, and were at greater risk of an accelerated decline in physical health by their fifties.

"Timeliness," then, represents an important determinant of enduring military influences from the 1940s and its expression in veterans' lives. The service was indeed a bridge to greater opportunity for many, given appropriate timing.

Reflections

In thinking back to the early 1960s at the Berkeley Institute of Human Development, it would be difficult for any of us to appreciate the research challenge of the longitudinal studies. The institute psychologists were students of child development at a time when the study members were entering their middle years. Child-based models of development had little to offer research accounts of the adult years, their pathways, and turning points.

These were the kinds of issues that I recall in exchanges over case histories at the time. The childhood poverty of some adults in the Oakland Growth Study did not square with their high achievements and good health at mid-life. Jean Macfarlane (1963), director of the Berkeley Guidance Study, also noted in the early 1960s that a number of boys in the Guidance Study turned out to be more stable and productive adults than the staff had expected.

Members of the Oakland Growth and Berkeley Guidance studies are "children of the Great Depression," but the central theme of their lives is not the harsh legacy of a deprived family through enduring limitations. It is not the long arm of a Depression childhood. Rather, it is the story of how so many women and men successfully overcame disadvantage in their lives. Some rose above the limitations of their childhood through military service, others through education and a good job, and still others through the nurturing world of family.

These accomplishments amidst adversity were not gained without personal costs, a point that John Clausen (1993) has made so eloquently in *American Lives*. War stresses continue to reverberate through the lives of some combat veterans, though a good many have "learned to manage" (Elder & Clipp, 1988; Hendin & Haas, 1984). Women on the homefront kept families together while working long hours. Other women survived family abuse and have

coped effectively with the stresses of life. Life success can be assessed partly in these terms. Jean Macfarlane (1963, 1971) may have had this in mind some years ago when she spoke about the maturing experience of working through the pain and confusion of life.

But not even great talent and industry can ensure life success over adversity without opportunities. Talented Black youth in our blighted inner cities face this reality every day. Generations of young Chinese also learned this during the Cultural Revolution when important life decisions were made by the work unit, and many thousands were sent down from the city to the rural countryside and mines. Members of this "sent-down generation" were disadvantaged in education, work careers, mate selection, and family formation (Elder, Wu, & Yuan, 1993). Talented women in the Lewis Terman study discovered this lesson when they were barred from career advancement in their chosen fields (Holahan & Sears, 1995, chap. 5). Even some Terman men found their lives going nowhere as they left college for hard times in the Great Depression and later were mobilized into World War II. The constraining realities of social systems are very real.

Life course theory and research alert us to this real world, a world in which lives are lived and where people work out paths of development as best they can. It tells us how lives are socially organized in biological and historical time, and how the resulting social pattern affects the way we think, feel, and act. All of this has something important to say about our field of inquiry. Human development is embedded in the life course and historical time. Consequently, its proper study challenges us to take all life stages into account through the generations, from infancy to the grandparents of old age.

ACKNOWLEDGMENTS

This paper was presented in abbreviated form as a presidential address at the biennial meeting of the Society for Research in Child Development, Washington, DC, April 5, 1997. I wish to express a deep sense of gratitude to many colleagues and students who have been so important in the evolution of my perspective. I am especially pleased that I could share my ideas for the essay with John Clausen before he passed away in February 1996. John brought me to the Institute of Human Development and did much to enhance my accomplishments through this research organization, as did Brewster Smith and Paul Mussen, Jean Macfarlane and Marjorie Honzik, Mary Jones and Dorothy Eichorn, Jeanne and Jack Block, among others. All of us have intellectual homes, and the institute represents one of mine across the years. My professional journey has been blessed by Urie Bronfenbrenner's mentorship. It was he who insisted that I bring my work more fully into the field of developmental science. Lastly, I am indebted to the interdisciplinary vitality of the Carolina Consortium on Human Development (Cairns, Elder, & Costello, 1996). In preparing this essay, I had the benefit of ongoing conversations with Urie Bronfenbrenner. Thanks also to many colleagues and coauthors who have read and commented on drafts of this manuscript. I gratefully acknowledge support by the National Institute of Mental Health (MH 51361, MH 43270, MH 41327, and MH 00567), a contract with the U.S. Army Research Institute, and research support from the MacArthur Foundation Research Network on Successful Adolescent Development Among Youth in High-Risk Settings.

ADDRESS AND AFFILIATION

Corresponding author: Glen H. Elder, Jr., Carolina Population Center, University of North Carolina at Chapel Hill, University Square CB# 8120, 123 West Franklin Street, Chapel Hill, NC 27516-3997; e-mail: glen_elder@unc.edu.

REFERENCES

Baltes, P. M., Lindenberger, U., & Staudinger, U. M. (1998). Life-span theory in developmental psychology. In R. M. Lerner (Ed.), W. Damon (General Ed.), *Handbook of child psychology: Vol. 1. Theoretical models of human development* (5th ed., pp. 1029–1043). New York: Wiley.

Bandura, A. (1997). *Self-efficacy: The exercise of control.* New York: W. H. Freeman.

Block, J., in collaboration with Haan, N. (1971). *Lives through time.* Berkeley, CA: Bancroft.

Bronfenbrenner, U. (1979). *The ecology of human development.* Cambridge, MA: Harvard University Press.

Burton, L. M. (1985). *Early and on-time grandmotherhood in multigenerational black families.* Unpublished doctoral dissertation, University of Southern California.

Burton, L. M., & Bengtson, V. L. (1985). Black grandmothers: Issues of timing and continuity of roles. In V. L. Bengtson & J. F. Robertson (Eds.), *Grandparenthood* (pp. 61–77). Beverly Hills, CA: Sage.

Cahan, E., Mechling, J., Sutton-Smith, B., & White, S. H. (1993). The elusive historical child: Ways of knowing the child of history and psychology. In G. H. Elder, Jr., J. Modell, & R. D. Parke (Eds.), *Children in time and place* (pp. 192–223). New York: Cambridge University Press.

Cairns, R. B., Elder, G. H., Jr., & Costello, E. J. (Eds.). (1996). *Developmental science.* New York: Cambridge University Press.

Caspi, A., Bem, D. J., & Elder, G. H., Jr. (1989). Continuities and consequences of interactional styles across the life course. *Journal of Personality, 57,* 375–406.

Caspi, A., & Moffitt, T. E. (1993). When do individual differences matter? A paradoxical theory of personality coherence. *Psychological Inquiry, 4,* 247–271.

Clausen, J. A. (1993). *American lives: Looking back at the children of the Great Depression.* New York: Free Press.

Clausen, J. A. (1995). Gender, contexts, and turning points in adults' lives. In P. Moen, G. H. Elder, Jr., & K. Lüscher (Eds.), *Examining lives in context: Perspectives on the ecology of human development* (pp. 365–389). Washington, DC: APA Press.

Clipp, E. C., & Elder, G. H., Jr. (1996). The aging veteran of World War II: Psychiatric and life course insights. In P. E. Ruskin & J. A. Talbott (Eds.), *Aging and posttraumatic stress disorder* (pp. 19–51). Washington, DC: American Psychiatric Press, Inc.

Conger, R. D., & Elder, G. H., Jr. (1994). *Families in troubled times: Adapting to change in rural America.* Hawthorne, NY: Aldine DeGruyter.

Dunn, J., & Plomin, R. (1990). *Separate lives: Why siblings are so different.* New York: Basic.

Eichorn, D. H., Clausen, J. A., Haan, N., Honzik, M., & Mussen, P. H. (Eds.). (1981). *Present and past in middle life.* New York: Academic Press.

Elder, G. H., Jr. (1974). *Children of the Great Depression: Social change in life experience.* Chicago: University of Chicago Press.

Elder, G. H., Jr. (1979). Historical change in life patterns and personality. In P. B. Baltes & O. G. Brim, Jr. (Eds.), *Life-span development and behavior* (Vol. 2, pp. 117–159). New York: Academic Press.

Elder, G. H., Jr. (1981). Social history and life experience. In D. H. Eichorn, J. A. Clausen, J. Haan, M. P. Honzik, & P. H. Mussen (Eds.), *Present and past in middle life* (pp. 3–31). New York: Academic Press.

Elder, G. H., Jr. (Ed.). (1985). *Life course dynamics: Trajectories and transitions, 1968–1980.* Ithaca, NY: Cornell University Press.

Elder, G. H., Jr. (1986). Military times and turning points in men's lives. *Developmental Psychology, 22,* 233–245.

Elder, G. H., Jr. (1987). War mobilization and the life course: A cohort of World War II veterans. *Sociological Forum, 2,* 449–472.

Elder, G. H., Jr. (1992, March). *Children of the farm crisis.* Paper presented at the meeting of the Society for Research on Adolescence, Washington, DC.

Elder, G. H., Jr. (1995). The life course paradigm: Social change and individual development. In P. Moen, G. H. Elder, Jr., & K. Lüscher (Eds.), *Examining lives in context: Perspectives on the ecology of human development* (pp. 101–139). Washington, DC: APA Press.

Elder, G. H., Jr. (1996). Human lives in changing societies: Life course and developmental insights. In R. B. Cairns, G. H. Elder, Jr., & E. J. Costello (Eds.), *Developmental science* (pp. 31–62). New York: Cambridge University Press.

Elder, G. H., Jr. (1998). The life course and human development. In R. M. Lerner (Ed.), W. Damon (General Ed.), *Handbook of child psychology: Vol. 1. Theoretical models of human development* (5th ed., pp. 939–991). New York: Wiley.

Elder, G. H., Jr., Caspi, A., & Downey, G. (1986). Problem behavior and family relationships: Life course and inter-generational themes. In A. B. Sørensen, F. E. Weinert, & L. R. Sherrod (Eds.), *Human development and the life course: Multidisciplinary perspectives* (pp. 293–340). Hillsdale, NJ: Erlbaum.

Elder, G. H., Jr., & Chan, C. (in press). War's legacy in men's lives. In P. Moen & D. Dempster-McClain (Eds.), *A nation divided: Diversity, inequality and community in American society.* Ithaca, NY: Cornell University Press.

Elder, G. H., Jr., & Clipp, E. C. (1988). Wartime losses and social bonding: Influences across 40 years in men's lives. *Psychiatry, 51,* 177–198.

Elder, G. H., Jr., & Clipp, E. C. (1989). Combat experience and emotional health: Impairment and resilience in later life. *Journal of Personality, 57,* 311–341.

Elder, G. H., Jr., & Conger, R. D. (in press). *Leaving the land: Rural youth at century's end.* Chicago: University of Chicago Press.

Elder, G. H., Jr., Eccles, J. S., Ardelt, M., & Lord, S. (1995). Inner-city parents under economic pressure: Perspectives on the strategies of parenting. *Journal of Marriage and the Family, 57,* 771–784.

Elder, G. H., Jr., & Hareven, T. K. (1993). Rising above life's disadvantages: From the Great Depression to war. In G. H. Elder, Jr., J. Modell, & R. D. Parke (Eds.), *Children in time and place: Developmental and historical insights* (pp. 47–72). New York: Cambridge University Press.

Elder, G. H., Jr., Liker, J. K., & Cross, C. E. (1984). Parent-child behavior in the Great Depression: Life course and intergenerational influences. In P. B. Baltes & O. G. Brim, Jr. (Eds.), *Life-span development and behavior* (Vol. 6, pp. 109–158). New York: Academic Press.

Elder, G. H., Jr., Modell, J., & Parke, R. D. (Eds.). (1993). *Children in time and place: Developmental and historical insights.* New York: Cambridge University Press.

Elder, Glen H., Jr., Pavalko, E. K., & Hastings, T. J. (1991). Talent, history, and the fulfillment of promise. *Psychiatry, 54,* 215–231.

Elder, G. H., Jr., Shanahan, M. J., & Clipp, E. C. (1994). When war comes to men's lives: Life course patterns in family, work, and health [Special issue]. *Psychology and Aging, 9,* 5–16.

Elder, G. H., Jr., Wu, W., & Yuan, J. (1993). *State-initiated change and the life course in Shanghai, China.* Unpublished project report.

Featherman, D. L. (1983). The life-span perspective in social science research. In P. B. Baltes & O. G. Brim, Jr. (Eds.), *Life-span development and behavior* (Vol. 5, pp. 1–57). New York: Academic.

Furstenberg, F. F., Jr. (1993). How families manage risk and opportunity in dangerous neighborhoods. In W. J. Wilson (Ed.), *Sociology and the public agenda* (pp. 231–258). Newbury Park, CA: Sage.

Furstenberg, F. F., Jr., Brooks-Gunn, J., & Morgan, S. P. (1987). *Adolescent mothers in later life.* New York: Cambridge University Press.

Furstenberg, F. F., Jr., Cook, T., Eccles, J., Elder, G. H., Jr., &

Sameroff, A. (Eds.). (in press). *Managing to make it: Urban families in high-risk neighborhoods.* Chicago: University of Chicago Press.

Ge, X., Lorenz, F. O., Conger, R. D., Elder, G. H., Jr., & Simons, R. L. (1994). Trajectories of stressful life events and depressive symptoms during adolescence. *Developmental Psychology, 30,* 467–483.

Glueck, S., & Glueck, E. (1968). *Delinquents and nondelinquents in perspective.* Cambridge, MA: Harvard University Press.

Granovetter, M. S. (1973). Strength of weak ties. *American Journal of Sociology, 78,* 1360–1380.

Hagestad, G. O., & Neugarten, B. L. (1985). Age and the life course. In R. H. Binstock & E. Shanas (Eds.), *Handbook of aging and the social sciences* (2d ed., pp. 46–61). New York: Van Nostrand Reinhold.

Hareven, T. K. (1978). *Transitions: The family and the life course in historical perspective.* New York: Academic Press.

Hareven, T. K. (1982). *Family time and industrial time.* New York: Cambridge University Press.

Hareven, T. K. (1991). Synchronizing individual time, family time, and historical time. In J. Bender & D. E. Wellbery (Eds.), *Chronotypes: The construction of time* (pp. 167–182). Stanford, CA: Stanford University Press.

Hareven, T. K. (1996). What difference does it make? *Social Science History, 20,* 317–344.

Hendin, H., & Hass, A. P. (1984). *Wounds of war: The psychological aftermath of combat in Vietnam.* New York: Basic.

Hernandez, D. J. (1993). *America's children: Resources from family, government, and the economy.* New York: Russell Sage.

Holahan, C. K., & Sears, R. R. (1995). *The gifted group in later maturity.* Stanford, CA: Stanford University Press.

Jargowsky, P. A. (1997). *Poverty and place: Ghettos, barrios, and the American city.* New York: Russell Sage.

Jones, M. C., Bayley, N., Macfarlane, J. W., & Honzik, M. H. (Eds.). (1971). *The course of human development: Selected papers from the longitudinal studies, Institute of Human Development, the University of California, Berkeley.* Waltham, MA: Xerox College Publishing.

Kahn, R. L., & Antonucci, T. C. (1980). Convoys over the life course: Attachment, roles, and social support. In P. B. Baltes & O. G. Brim, Jr. (Eds.), *Life-span development and behavior* (Vol. 3, pp. 253–286). New York: Academic Press.

Macfarlane, J. W. (1963). From infancy to adulthood. *Childhood Education, 39,* 336–342.

Macfarlane, J. W. (1971). Perspectives on personality consistency and change from the Guidance Study. In M. C. Jones, N. Bayley, J. W. Macfarlane, & M. P. Honzik (Eds.), *The course of human development: Selected papers from the longitudinal studies, Institute of Human Development, the University of California, Berkeley* (pp. 410–415). Waltham, MA: Xerox College Publishing.

Macfarlane, J. W., Allen, L., & Honzik, M. P. (1954). *A developmental study of the behavior problems of normal children between twenty-one months and fourteen years.* Berkeley: University of California Press.

Magnusson, D., & Bergman, L. R. (Eds.). (1990). *Data quality in longitudinal research.* New York: Cambridge University Press.

McLeod, J. D., & Shanahan, M. J. (1996). Trajectories of poverty and children's mental health. *Journal of Health and Social Behavior, 37,* 207–220.

Merton, R. K. (1968). *Social theory and social structure.* New York: Free Press.

Modell, J. (1989). *Into one's own: From youth to adulthood in the United States 1920–1975.* Berkeley: University of California Press.

Nesselroade, J. R., & Baltes, P. B. (Eds.). (1979). *Longitudinal research in the study of behavior and development.* New York: Academic Press.

Neugarten, B. L. (1968). *Middle age and aging: A reader in social psychology.* Chicago: University of Chicago Press.

Neugarten, B. L., & Datan, N. (1973). Sociological perspectives on the life cycle. In P. B. Baltes & K. W. Schaie (Eds.), *Life-span developmental psychology: Personality and socialization* (pp. 53–69). New York: Academic Press.

Riley, M. W., Johnson, M. E., & Foner, A. (Eds.). (1972). *Aging and society: A sociology of age stratification.* New York: Russell Sage.

Rutter, M. (Ed.). (1988). *Studies of psychosocial risk: The power of longitudinal data.* New York: Cambridge University Press.

Rutter, M. (1996). Transitions and turning points in developmental psychopathology: As applied to the age span between childhood and mid-adulthood. *International Journal of Behavioral Development, 19,* 603–626.

Sameroff, A. J. (1993). Models of development and developmental risk. In C. H. Zeanah, Jr. (Ed.), *Handbook of infant mental health* (pp. 3–13). New York: Guilford.

Sampson, R. J. (1992). Family management and child development: Insights from social disorganization theory. In J. McCord (Ed.), *Advances in criminological theory: Vol. 3. Facts, frameworks, and forecasts* (pp. 63–93). New Brunswick, NJ: Transaction Books.

Sampson, R. J. (1997, April). *Child and adolescent development in community context: New findings from a multilevel study of 80 Chicago neighborhoods.* Paper presented at the biennial meeting of the Society for Research in Child Development, Washington, DC.

Sampson, R. J., & Laub, J. H. (1993). *Crime in the making: Pathways and turning points through life.* Cambridge, MA: Harvard University Press.

Sampson, R. J., & Laub, J. H. (1996). Socioeconomic achievement in the life course of disadvantaged men: Military service as a turning point, circa 1940–1965. *American Sociological Review, 61,* 347–367.

Scarr, S., & McCartney, K. (1983). How people make their own environments: A theory of genotype → environment effects. *Child Development, 54,* 424–435.

Shanahan, M. J., Elder, G. H., Jr., & Miech, R. A. (1997). History and agency in men's lives: Pathways to achievement in cohort perspective. *Sociology of Education, 70,* 54–67.

Stolz, L. M. (1954). *Father relations of war-born children.* Stanford, CA: Stanford University Press.

Thomas, W. I., & Znaniecki, F. (1918–1920). *The Polish peasant in Europe and America* (Vols. 1–2). Urbana: University of Illinois Press.

Wilson, W. J. (1987). *The truly disadvantaged: The inner city, the underclass, and public policy.* Chicago: University of Chicago Press.

Resilience

[5]

Implications of Resilience Concepts for Scientific Understanding

MICHAEL RUTTER

Developmental Psychopathology, SGDP Centre, Institute of Psychiatry, De Crespigny Park, Denmark Hill, London, United Kingdom

ABSTRACT: Resilience is an interactive concept that refers to a relative resistance to environmental risk experiences, or the overcoming of stress or adversity. As such, it differs from both social competence positive mental health. Resilience differs from traditional concepts of risk and protection in its focus on individual variations in response to comparable experiences. Accordingly, the research focus needs to be on those individual differences and the causal processes that they reflect, rather than on resilience as a general quality. Because resilience in relation to childhood adversities may stem from positive adult experiences, a life-span trajectory approach is needed. Also, because of the crucial importance of gene–environment interactions in relation to resilience, a wide range of research strategies spanning psychosocial and biological methods is needed. Five main implications stem from the research to date: (1) resistance to hazards may derive from controlled exposure to risk (rather than its avoidance); (2) resistance may derive from traits or circumstances that are without major effects in the absence of the relevant environmental hazards; (3) resistance may derive from physiological or psychological coping processes rather than external risk or protective factors; (4) delayed recovery may derive from "turning point" experiences in adult life; and (5) resilience may be constrained by biological programming or damaging effects of stress/adversity on neural structures.

KEYWORDS: gene–environment interactions; individual differences; stress/adversity; coping processes; turning point experiences; biological effects

INTRODUCTION

The term *resilience* is used to refer to the finding that some individuals have a relatively good psychological outcome despite suffering risk experiences that would be expected to bring about serious sequelae.[1] In other words, it implies

Address for correspondence: Prof. Michael Rutter, Developmental Psychopathology, PO 80, MRC SGDP Centre, Institute of Psychiatry, De Crespigny Park, Denmark Hill, London SE 5 8AF, UK. Voice: 020-7848-0882; fax: 020-7848-0866.
e-mail: j.wickham@iop.kcl.ac.uk

relative resistance to environmental risk experiences, or the overcoming of stress or adversity.[2–4] It is not, however, just social competence[5] or positive mental health.[6] Both of them are important concepts but they refer to something different from resilience. Essentially, resilience is an interactive concept that is concerned with the combination of serious risk experiences and a relatively positive psychological outcome despite those experiences.

There are two sets of research findings that provide a background to the resilience notion. First, there is the universal finding of huge individual differences in people's responses to all kinds of environmental hazard.[1] Before inferring resilience from these individual differences in response there are two major methodological artifactual possibilities that have to be considered. To begin with, apparent resilience might be simply a function of variations in risk exposure. This possibility means that resilience can only be studied effectively when there is both evidence of environmentally mediated risk and a quantitative measure of the degree of such risk. The other possible artifact is that the apparent resilience might be a consequence of measuring too narrow a range of outcomes. The implication is that the outcome measures must cover a wide range of possibly adverse sequelae. The details of the research strategies that need to be employed for these purposes are considered in Rutter[1] and Rutter.[7]

Second, there is the evidence that, in some circumstances, the experience of stress or adversity sometimes *strengthens* resistance to later stress[8]—a so-called "steeling" effect. Although the research literature is much more sparse than that on individual differences in response to environmental hazards, there are some empirically based examples of stress experiences increasing resistance to later stress.[9] For example, it has been shown that experimental stress in rodents leads to structural and functional effects on the neuroendocrine system that are associated with greater resistance to later stress.[9] Similarly, repeated parachute jumping by humans leads to physiological adaptation associated with both a change in the timing and nature of the anticipatory physiological response and also the reduced subjective feeling of stress.[8] It is well known, of course, that exposure to infections (either by natural exposure or through vaccination or immunization) leads to relative immunity to later exposure to the same infectious agents. The experience of happy separations in early childhood may also possibly lead to a better adaptation to hospital admission.[10] Older children's experience of coping successfully with family poverty seemed, in the Californian studies of the Great Depression, to lead to greater psychological strengths later.[11] It is important to question what are the circumstances that lead stress/adversity to result in steeling effects rather than sensitization. There is a paucity of good research data on this matter but it seems that probably the key element is some form of successful coping with the challenge or stress or hazard. This is likely to involve physiological adaptation, psychological habituation, a sense of self-efficacy, the acquisition of effective coping strategies, and/or a cognitive redefinition of the experience.

DOES RESILIENCE ADD TO RISK AND PROTECTION CONCEPTS?

Whenever a new term becomes fashionable, it is always necessary to consider whether it is simply a new way of repackaging old material or whether it introduces some new perspective. In other words, is resilience just a fancy way of reinventing concepts of risk and protection? It is not, because risk and protection both start with a focus on variables, and then move to outcomes, with an implicit assumption that the impact of risk and protective factors will be broadly similar in everyone, and that outcomes will depend on the mix and balance between risk and protective influences. By contrast, resilience starts with a recognition of the huge individual variation in people's responses to the same experiences, and considers outcomes with the assumption that an understanding of the mechanisms underlying that variation will cast light on the causal processes and, by so doing, will have implications for intervention strategies with respect to both prevention and treatment.

Does that mean that resilience concepts reject the traditional study of risk and protective factors? Certainly not, because there is an abundance of evidence that much of the variation in psychopathological outcomes can be accounted for by the summative effects of risk and protective factors. Also, and more importantly, resilience is an interactive concept that can only be studied if there is a thorough measurement of risk and protective factors. In short, resilience requires the prior study of risk and protection but adds a different, new dimension.

A second possibility that has to be considered is that because resilience is an inference based on evidence of an interaction, this means that it can be adequately assessed through finding a statistically significant multiplicative interaction. At first sight, it sounds obvious that that must be the case, but in fact it is wrong. That is because a statistical interaction requires variation in both variables and not just one and because synergistic interactions may involve either an additive or a multiplicative interaction.[12,13] The point about statistical interaction requiring variation in both variables is that there are quite common circumstances in which there clearly is an interaction in a biological sense, but yet this is not reflected in the statistical interaction term. For example, there are major individual differences in people's responses to malaria, and something is known about the genes that moderate this. This will not result in a statistical interaction in areas where malaria is endemic because everyone will have been exposed to more or less the same degree of risk of infection. Similarly, there are big individual differences, again genetically influenced, in atopy. Thus, some people respond to the spring pollens by the development of hay fever, whereas others do not show this response. But, in ordinary circumstances everyone living in the same area is exposed to much the same level of pollens. Accordingly, there will be no statistical interaction, despite the obvious evidence of a biological interaction.

A further possibility that has to be considered is the assumption that it should be possible to measure resilience directly as an observed trait, rather than having to rely on an inference based on some kind of interaction, however, assessed. Numerous researchers and clinicians are searching for such questionnaire or interview measures of this postulated trait. It is a fallacious approach, however, because resilience is not a single quality. People may be resilient in relation to some sort of environmental hazards but not others. Equally they may be resilient in relation to some kinds of outcomes but not others. In addition, because context may be crucial, people may be resilient at one time period in their life but not at others.

GENE–ENVIRONMENT INTERACTION (G × E)

Some of these issues are well illustrated by considering findings on gene–environment interactions (G × E) in relation to some environmental risk influence, as investigated with respect to some psychopathological outcome. For a long time, behavioral geneticists tended to argue that such interactions were sufficiently rare and so minor in their effects that they could be ignored in most genetic analyses. It is clear that this was a mistaken assumption.[14,15] G × E relies on studying an environmental risk factor for which there is good evidence of substantial risk, and of environmental mediation of that risk, as well as heterogeneity in outcome. In other words, despite conventional wisdom suggesting the opposite, the implication is that, in the present state of knowledge, the starting point has to be the study of environmental risk, and not identification of genetic risk.[15–17]

Three key findings from the Dunedin study well illustrate the phenomenon. FIGURES 1, 2, and 3 show the pattern. FIGURE 1 deals with variations in response to childhood maltreatment in terms of the outcome of antisocial behavior, according to moderation by the allelic variation in the gene that regulates MAOA activity. Considered in quantitative terms there was no main effect of genes, there was a small, significant effect of childhood maltreatment, but the big effect came from the interaction. Childhood maltreatment had a rather small effect on the individuals with high MAOA activity but it had a very big effect in relation to those with low MAOA activity. FIGURE 2 shows a comparable pattern with respect to the serotonin transporter gene again with maltreatment as the risk variable, but this time with depression as the outcome. FIGURE 3 shows the findings in relation to the valine variant of the COMT gene in relation to the effects of early heavy use of cannabis, schizophrenia being the outcome variable. In both these latter examples, there was the same overall pattern of no genetic main effect, a significant environmental effect, but with the biggest effect coming from the interaction between the identified gene and the measured risk environment. Each of these findings has now been replicated in one way or another and the serotonin transporter gene finding also has a much broader

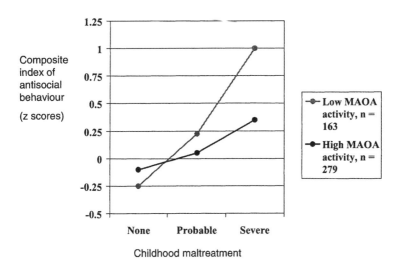

FIGURE 1. Antisocial behavior as a function of MAOA activity and a childhood history of maltreatment.[28]

body of biological research using a range of research strategies including imaging studies of response to stress, rearing studies in rhesus monkeys, and animal models of other kinds.[15] There are a series of quite important methodological checks that need to be undertaken before inferring a G × E but such steps were undertaken in a thorough and resolute fashion by the Dunedin study team and the results are compelling in showing that the interaction is valid, and not artefactual.

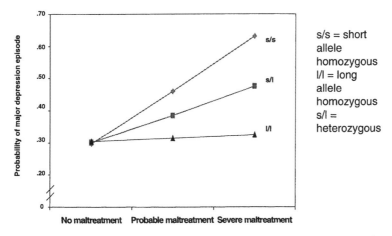

FIGURE 2. Effect of maltreatment in childhood on liability to depression moderated by 5-HTT gene.[29]

Child Development

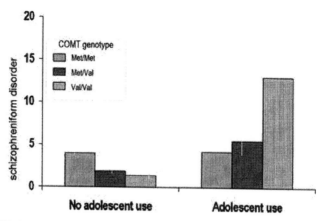

FIGURE 3. Schizophrenia spectrum disorder: cannabis use interacts with genotype.[30]

There are four main lessons from the body of research on G × E. First, as in the three Dunedin study examples, the influence of the genes was only shown through demonstration of the interaction with the environmental hazard. Second, in each case, the G × E was specific to a particular psychopathological outcome. The finding underlines the fact that there is not, and cannot be, a single universally applicable resilience trait. Third, the implication of the G × E is that both the G and the E share the same causal pathophysiological pathway. Of course, that suggestion needs to be tested. Nevertheless, the point is that the resilience finding has causal process implications for both genes and environment. Fourth, the genetic variant is neither a risk nor a protective factor in itself. That is, there is little or no effect on psychopathology in the absence of the environmental risk factor. There could scarcely be any better example of the value of a resilience concept in studying causal processes because it identified a significant and important genetic effect that would not have been detected in the absence of studying the interaction.

OTHER LESSONS FROM RESILIENCE FINDINGS

Obviously, resilience is not just a feature of G × E. There are numerous other circumstances in which resilience is evident. The findings from such studies bring out four more important lessons for scientific understanding. First, resistance to environmental hazards may come from *exposure* to risk in controlled circumstances, rather than *avoidance* of risk. This is best demonstrated, of course, in the natural immunity to infections and that brought about by immunization and vaccination. It is also evident in the rodent studies of stress to which reference has already been made. The Californian studies of the great economic depression[11] provide an interesting example of the benefits of adolescents coping successfully, the contrast being with the findings of adverse effects in younger children who were not able to cope in the same way. Treatment studies of fears and phobias have also shown that exposure is an important (although not necessarily essential) element in their successful treatment.[18,19] Avoidance of the feared object is the action most likely to lead to persistence of the fear. It has to be said that there is a paucity of good evidence on the protective effect of controlled exposure to stress/adversity in relation to psychopathological outcomes, and clearly there is a need to consider both physiological mediation and cognitive/affective mediation. Nevertheless, the parallels with internal medicine are sufficiently compelling to indicate that it is quite likely that there are psychological parallels to the immunity example.

Second, protection may derive from circumstances that are either neutral or risky in the absence of the key environmental hazard. For example, it is apparent in the protection against malaria provided by heterozygote sickle-cell status.[20] Being a carrier of the sickle-cell is not in itself a good thing but it happens to be protective against malaria. It has no particular benefits for people living in a malaria-free area but it has important benefits for those in areas where malaria is endemic. Adoption may well constitute a psychological example. Adoption is an experience that probably carries some risks (albeit small ones) that stem from it being atypical in all societies. If children who are adopted come from a low-risk background, there are no particular advantages to being adopted. By sharp contrast, however, for children who have been exposed in early life to parental abuse or neglect, adoption can be highly advantageous.[21]

FIGURE 4 illustrates the point in a somewhat different way by its indication that actions that are protective in depriving circumstances may be of no particular benefit in advantageous conditions. Quinton and Rutter[22] showed that the

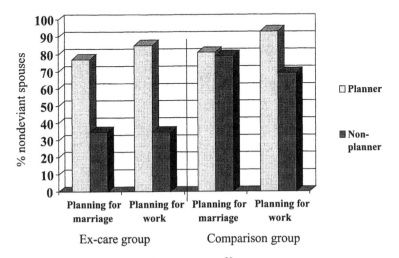

FIGURE 4. Planning and nondeviant spouses.[22]

phenomenon of planning (meaning no more than taking considered decisions rather than acting impulsively) made it much more likely that young people who had been reared in institutions would marry a nondeviant spouse. Moreover, this effect was evident, not just with respect to planning for marriage, but also planning as evident in the work context. By contrast, the planning tendency made no significant difference in a comparison population sample. The point is that the peer group for the children who had been raised in residential group homes was largely a deviant one and when they left the institutions and returned to discordant families there was considerable pressure to marry to get out of the arena of conflict. This did not apply in the comparison group who, if they married entirely by random selection, were most likely to land up with a nondeviant spouse and their circumstances provided no particular pressure to marry in haste.

The third message, therefore, is that protection may derive from what people do to deal with stress or adversity. That is, the notion of resilience focuses attention on coping mechanisms, mental sets, and the operation of personal agency. In other words, it requires a move from a focus on external risks to a focus on *how* these external risks are dealt with by the individual. More generally, this means that resilience, unlike risk and protective factor approaches, forces attention on dynamic *processes*, rather than static factors that act in summative fashion. Such processes may involve neurotransmitters as in the G × E example, neuroendocrine effects as seen in stress adaptation, or cognitive/emotional mechanisms. It should be noted that the study of cognitive/emotional mechanisms may require qualitative methods to generate hypotheses (although quantitative measures will still be required to test the hypothesis so generated). Thus, Hauser et al.,[23] in their study of resilience in young people who had had a prolonged psychiatric hospitalization, found that three features were strongly characteristic of resilience (as compared with average outcomes). These were: personal agency and a concern to overcome adversity; a self-reflective style; and a commitment to relationships.

Fourth, protection may derive from circumstances that come about long after the risk experience. In other words, resilience may sometimes reflect later recovery, rather than an initial failure to succumb. Thus, Laub and Sampson,[24] in their follow-up of the Gluecks' institutionalized sample, showed that a beneficial turning point effect was seen with a supportive marriage. It might have been supposed that the beneficial effect derived solely from a secure attachment relationship, but their findings indicated that the benefits also stemmed from the new extended kin network and friendship group that marriage brought, providing hitherto lacking positive role models. Also, the spouses frequently exerted informal controls as well as support, marital obligations often cut off the antisocial individual from the delinquent peer group, and marriage brought expectations of providing financial support (so that regular employment also provided social controls). Much the same complex mix of influences was seen with the parallel finding of the turning point effect of armed services for young people from a severely disadvantaged background.[25] It was not that serving in the armed services was of itself beneficial but, rather, it provided opportunities for continuing education in a more adult environment. It brought a widening of the peer group and it often delayed marriage until careers were more effectively managed.

IS RESILIENCE UNLIMITED?

Resilience notions have generally been interpreted as conveying great optimism regarding the possibility of surviving adversity. Such optimism is well justified but it is necessary to ask whether resilience is limited. Findings indicate that it is. Thus, our follow-up study of children from profoundly depriving residential institutions in Romania, who were adopted into well-functioning UK families, showed remarkable persistence of adverse sequelae even after more than 7.5 years in the adoptive home.[26,27] As FIGURE 5 indicates, there were no persisting sequelae that could be detected when the children had left the institutions before the age of 6 months but there was then a marked increase in multiple impairments that occurred even within the group of children spending just 6 to 12 months in depriving institutions. Curiously, there was no further increase in risk with persistence of the depriving circumstances beyond the 6-month period (at least up to the age of 42 months). The implication seems to be that the pervasively depriving circumstances took some months to have an effect but when they lasted beyond the age of 6 months, they tended to have effects that endured many years. The inference is that there may have been some form of intraorganismic change—either neural damage or biological programming of some kind.

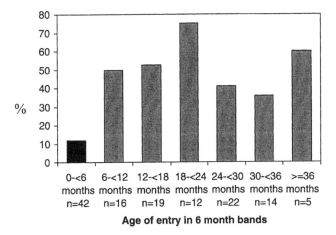

FIGURE 5. Rates of children with 2+ impairments by age of entry pooled in 6-month bands (institution-reared Romanian adoptees) (from Kreppner *et al.*, submitted).

Child Development

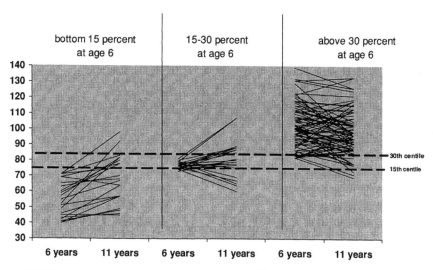

FIGURE 6. Change in IQ between ages 6 and 11.[26]

On the other hand, although the effects were remarkably persistent, there was change between 6 and 11 years as illustrated in FIGURE 6 showing a line scattergram for cognitive change between 6 and 11 years. It is notable that the changes, however, were largely confined to the group that was most impaired at 6 years. Also, it is striking that there was huge heterogeneity in outcome with some children showing superior cognitive functioning despite the prolonged institutional deprivation. Factors promoting resilience in the face of this extraordinarily pervasive and profound deprivation remain unclear.

CONCLUSIONS

There are three broad research implications that derive from resilience findings. Because resilience is not a general quality that represents a trait of the individual, research needs to focus on the processes underlying individual differences in response to environmental hazards, rather than resilience as an abstract entity. Second, because resilience in relation to adverse childhood experiences may stem from positive adult experiences, it is necessary to adopt a life-span trajectory approach that can investigate later turning point effects. Third, because of the importance of G × E, it will be necessary to combine psychosocial and biological research approaches and to use a diverse range of research strategies. These should include functional imaging of cognitive processing, neuroendocrine studies, investigation of mental sets and models, and the use of animal studies of various kinds.

Resilience findings also provide five key implications for scientific understanding of substantive effects. First, resistance to hazards may derive from controlled exposure to risk (rather than its avoidance). Second, resistance may derive from traits or circumstances that are either risky or neutral in the absence of the relevant environmental hazard. Third, resistance may derive from physiological or psychological coping processes, rather than external risk or protective factors. Fourth, delayed recovery may derive from "turning point" effects in adult life. Fifth, resilience may be constrained by biological programming or by the damaging effects of stress/adversity on neural structures.

REFERENCES

1. RUTTER, M. 2006. The promotion of resilience in the face of adversity. *In* Families Count: Effects on Child and Adolescent Development. A. Clarke-Stewart & J. Dunn, Eds.: 26–52. Cambridge University Press. New York & Cambridge. In press.
2. CICCHETTI, D., F.A. ROGOSCH, M. LYNCH & K.D. HOLT. 1993. Resilience in maltreated children: processes leading to adaptive outcome. Dev. Psychopathol. **5:** 629–648.
3. LUTHAR, S. 2003. Resilience and Vulnerability: Adaptation in the Context of Childhood Adversities. Cambridge University Press. New York.
4. MASTEN, A.S. 2001. Ordinary magic: resilience processes in development. Am. Psychol. **56:** 227–238.
5. MASTEN, A.S. 2006. Competence and psychopathology in development. *In* Developmental Psychopathology. Vol. 3: Risk, disorder and psychopathology, 2nd ed. D. Cicchietti & D. Cohen, Eds.: 696–738. J. Wiley & Sons. New York.
6. LAYARD, R. 2005. Happiness: Lessons from a New Science. Allen Lane. London.
7. RUTTER, M. Proceeding from correlation to causal inference: the use of natural experiments. Submitted.
8. RUTTER, M. 1981. Stress, coping and development: some issues and some questions. J. Child Psychol. Psychiatry **22:** 323–356.
9. HENNESSEY, J.W. & S. LEVINE. 1979. Stress, arousal, and the pituitary-adrenal system: a psychoendocrine hypothesis. *In* Progress in Psychobiology and Physiological Psychology. J.M. Sprague & A.N. Epstein, Eds.: 133–178. Academic Press, New York.
10. STACEY, M., R. DEARDEN, R. PILL & D. ROBINSON. 1970. Hospitals, children and their families: the report of a pilot study. Routledge & Kegan Paul. London.
11. ELDER, G.H. 1974. Children of the Great Depression. University of Chicago Press. Chicago.
12. RUTTER, M. 1983. Statistical and personal interactions: facets and perspectives. *In* Human Development: An Interactional Perspective. D. Magnusson & V. Allen, Eds.: 295–319. Academic Press. New York.
13. RUTTER, M. 2006. Genes and Behavior: Nature-Nurture Interplay Explained. Blackwell Publishing. Oxford.
14. RUTTER, M. & J. SILBERG. 2002. Gene-environment interplay in relation to emotional and behavioral disturbance. Annu. Rev. Psychol. **53:** 463–490.
15. RUTTER, M., T.E. MOFFITT & A. CASPI. 2006. Gene-environment interplay and psychopathology: multiple varieties but real effects. J. Child Psychol. Psychiatry **47:** 226–261.

16. MOFFITT, T.E., A. CASPI & M. RUTTER. 2005. Strategy for investigating interactions between measured genes and measured environments. Arch. Gen. Psychiatry **62:** 473–481.

17. MOFFITT, T.E., A. CASPI & M. RUTTER. 2006. Measured gene-environment interactions in psychopathology: concepts, research strategies, and implications for research, intervention, and public understanding of genetics. Perspectives on Psychological Science: **1:** 5–27.

18. MARKS, I.M. 1987. Fears, Phobias, and Rituals: Panic, Anxiety and Their Disorders. Oxford University Press. Oxford.

19. RACHMAN, S.J. 1990. Fear and Courage. W.H. Freeman, New York.

20. ROTTER, J.I. & J.M. DIAMOND. 1987. What maintains the frequencies of human genetic diseases? Nature **329:** 289–290.

21. DUYME, M., A-C. DUMARET & S. TOMKIEWICZ. 1999. How can we boost IQs of "dull children"?: A late adoption study. Proc. Natl. Acad. Sci. USA **96:** 8790–8794.

22. QUINTON, D. & M. RUTTER. 1988. Parenting breakdown: The making and breaking of inter-generational links. Avebury. Aldershot.

23. HAUSER, S., J. ALLEN, E. GOLDEN. 2006. Out of the Woods: Tales of Resilient Teens. Harvard University Press. Cambridge, MA.

24. LAUB, J. & R. SAMPSON. 2003. Shared Beginnings, Divergent Lives: Delinquent Boys to Age 70. Harvard University Press. Cambridge, MA.

25. ELDER, G.H. JR. 1986. Military times and turning points in men's lives. Dev. Psychol. **22:** 233–245.

26. BECKETT, C., B. MAUGHAN, M. RUTTER, *et al.* 2006. Do the effects of early severe deprivation on cognition persist into early adolescence? Findings from the English and Romanian Adoptees Study. Child Dev. **77:** 696–711.

27. KREPPNER, J.M., M. RUTTER, C. BECKETT, *et al.* (submitted). Normality and impairment following profound early institutional deprivation. A longitudinal follow-up into early adolescence.

28. CASPI, A., J. MCCLAY, T.E. MOFFITT, *et al.* 2002. Role of genotype in the cycle of violence in maltreated children. Science **297:** 851–854.

29. CASPI, A., K. SUGDEN, T.E. MOFFITT, *et al.* 2003. Influence of life stress on depression: Moderation by a polymorphism in the 5-HTT gene. Science **301:** 386–389.

30. CASPI, A., T.E. MOFFITT, M. CANNON, *et al.* 2005. Moderation of the effect of adolescent-onset cannabis use on adult psychosis by a functional polymorphism in the COMT gene: Longitudinal evidence of a gene-environment interaction. Biol. Psychiatry **57:** 1117–1127.

Part II
Influences on Development

[6]

Gene–environment interdependence

Michael Rutter

Social, Genetic and Developmental Psychiatry Centre, Institute of Psychiatry, London, UK

Abstract

Behavioural genetics was initially concerned with partitioning population variance into that due to genetics and that due to environmental influences. The implication was that the two were separate and it was assumed that gene–environment interactions were usually of so little importance that they could safely be ignored. Theoretical considerations suggested that that was unlikely to be true and empirical findings are now accumulating on the demonstrated and replicated biological interactions between identified common single genetic variants and the operation of environmentally mediated risks. The paper outlines the evidence and considers why it is changing concepts in ways that matter.

Background to concepts of gene–environment interdependence

The evidence showing the interdependence of genetic (G) and environmental (E) influences as they affect behaviour and psychopathology has changed the ways in which nature and nurture have to be viewed with respect to their operation over the course of the life span (Kendler & Prescott, 2006; Rutter, 2006a). For years, quantitative behavioural genetics had been preoccupied with partitioning population variance into the separable and independent genetic and environmental contributions to individual differences in the liability to a broad range of traits and disorders. The findings were hugely important in making it clear that the dismissal of genetic factors by many behavioural scientists was misguided; indeed, it was wrong. The best research indicated that the heritability findings were generally valid and that genetic influences were operative with respect to almost all behaviours and mental disorders (Rutter, 2006a). Nevertheless, quantification of heritability, on its own, was singularly unhelpful in the elucidation of causal processes and mechanisms; in most cases the heritability accounted for only about half the population variance, and there was increasing evidence of gene–environment correlations and interactions, raising questions about the supposed separateness of G and E.

There was also a growing body of evidence of environmentally mediated risk and protective effects on most mental disorders (Rutter, Pickles, Murray & Eaves, 2001; Rutter, 2005). It was, however, apparent in all research that there was huge individual variation in response to all manner of environmental hazards – both physical and psychosocial (Rutter, 1972, 2006b). This evidence raised the query as to whether genetic factors played a role in this marked heterogeneity in response (Rutter, 2003).

The arrival of molecular genetics transformed the scene in ways that were both helpful and unhelpful. The helpful step was taking genetics out of the 'black box' of 'something genetic' of an unspecified nature into the translucency provided by a knowledge of the actual effects of specific individual identified susceptibility genes. The most convincing example of this kind was provided by the discovery of the risk effects for Alzheimer's disease (AD) of the APO-E4 allelic variation (Strittmatter, Saunders, Schmechel, Pericak-Vance, Enghild, Salvesen & Roses, 1993). The finding has been replicated many times (Saunders, 2000), and clearly it is robust and of sufficient strength to be meaningful. Nevertheless, it remains unclear exactly what the APO-E4 actually does; the genetic risk seems to involve non-specific adverse responses to brain injury (and also cognitive decline in ageing) and not just a specific disease. Also, the strength of effect appears to vary by ethnicity.

It is against that background that genetic–environmental interdependence needs to be considered. Four main varieties of gene–environment interplay occur: epigenetic effects of environments on genes; variations in heritability according to environmental circumstances; gene–environment correlations; and gene–environment interactions (see Rutter, 2006a; Rutter, Moffitt & Caspi, 2006). But before discussing these in turn, it is necessary to note what genes 'do'.

Address for correspondence: Michael Rutter, PO 80, SGDP Centre, Institute of Psychiatry, Denmark Hill, London SE5 8AF, UK; e-mail: j.wickham @iop.kcl.ac.uk

What genes do

The history of genetics goes back to the mid-nineteenth century, when Mendel concluded, on the basis of his study of pea plants, that genes were particulate factors that were passed on from generation to generation, each gene existing in alternate forms (now termed alleles – see Lewin, 2004). In the mid-twentieth century it was shown that deoxyribonucleic acid (DNA) constituted the relevant genetic material. Moreover, it became evident that genes brought about their effects through their influence ('coding' for) on some protein product. It all sounds very straightforward and deterministic, but it proved not to be the case. To begin with, DNA as such has no effect on proteins. Rather, through a process called transcription, it specified the synthesis of messenger RNA which, in turn, undergoes 'translation' through which it specified the synthesis of polypeptides, which ultimately go on to form proteins. The complexities do not end there. The DNA content of all cells is much the same, but the *actions* of DNA are crucially dependent on their functional activation (termed 'expression') in particular cells at particular phases of development. This involves the processes of transcription and translation plus epigenetic mechanisms involving methylation and acetylation (two linked chemical processes). Further down the causal chain, it is these proteins that bring about the relevant effects on phenotypes (meaning the behavioural manifestations in the case of mental traits and disorders).

The key feature of the multi-step causal chain is that it involves not just the effect of a single gene that codes for some protein product, but rather the effect of multiple inherited DNA elements that influence transcription and translation, plus environmental influences (including hormones, diet, chemical substance and rearing experiences). The net effect is that the effects of genes are most appropriately viewed as involving a dynamic process in which the effects of a single gene are influenced by multiple inherited DNA elements *and* by the actions of environments and of random stochastic variation. What seemed to be a quite simple deterministic inheritance of particulate genes has proved to be a much more multifaceted indirect causal chain that brings together the co-action of both genes and environment (through effects on gene expression).

Effects of environments on genes

Traditionally, it has always been assumed that, although environmental circumstances may influence psychological development and functioning (both normal and abnormal), they cannot alter genes. In one sense, that has to be true.

The specific effects of DNA depend on the DNA sequence – meaning the order of base pairs (made up of four chemicals) – that specifies what is inherited. That cannot be altered by the environment. On the other hand, the functional effects of that DNA sequence are entirely dependent on gene expression (as noted above) and that can be influenced (sometimes in a major way) by environmental features. In that sense, environments can and do have effects on genes through a process termed epigenesis (Jaenisch & Bird, 2003).

There are several very striking examples of such epigenetic effects (see Rutter, 2006a) but, in relation to developmental science, the pioneering studies of Michael Meaney and his colleagues, using rats to investigate the effects of early nurturant experiences, provide the best example (Cameron, Parent, Champagne, Fish, Ozaki-Kuroda & Meaney, 2005; Champagne, Chretien, Stevenson, Zhang, Gratton & Meaney, 2004; Meaney & Szyf, 2005; Weaver, Cervoni, Champagne, D'Alessio, Charma, Seckl, Dymov, Szyf & Meaney, 2004). The starting point for their work was the observation that lactating mother rats varied markedly in the extent to which they licked and groomed their neonatal offspring, showing arched back nursing, and that the variation in maternal behaviour was associated with individual differences in the offspring's behaviour and response to stress. The first research question was whether this intergenerational influence was genetically or environmentally mediated. A cross-fostering design clearly showed that the effects were a function of the rearing and not the biological parentage. The next question was, by what mechanism did this come about? It was found that the consequences were mediated by DNA methylation effects on a specific glucocorticoid receptor gene promoter in the hippocampus. In other words, it involved an epigenetic effect on a type of steroid that is concerned with cortisol-related functions (these being implicated in stress responses). The next question was whether this maternally mediated epigenetic marking was irreversible (as implied by the consequences that endured into adult life) or whether there were ways in which it could be altered in later life. If methylation effects were truly responsible, chemical reversal might be possible and, if successful, the key query was whether this would be associated with changes in the endocrine response to stress. Risk reversal always provides a powerful test of causal inferences. It was found that a drug called trichostatin-A did go some way to reversing the methylation effect and that this did indeed change the endocrine response to stress.

The findings are compelling, and are supported by other research, and the question is, how far can the findings be generalized to humans? The field of gene expression is much too new, and the findings so far too limited,

14   Michael Rutter

for any firm conclusions on the range of environmental effects that involve changes in gene expression. The area to which extrapolation seems most likely to apply is the process of so-called developmental programming (Rutter, 2006b). In that connection, it is noteworthy that the known environmental effects apply to normal variations, and not just extremes, and that the consequences tend to have an adaptive function and not a generally good or bad effect in absolute terms. Also, it is quite likely that epigenetic effects will prove to be implicated in a variety of lasting prenatal effects (Coe & Lubach, 2005).

Some commentators have been tempted to assume that the archback nursing influences must have some human equivalents and that these will be mediated by epigenetic effects. In that connection, it is necessary to note that the effects in the rat applied only in the first week of life, and not later. Also, they did not reflect the overall amount of mother–offspring contact. It is unwarranted to conclude that epigenetics is involved in all rearing influences in early childhood. Also, though doubtless there are neural concomitants, it may well be that epigenetics plays little role in environmental effects that derive from how people think about their experiences, or in effects that are essentially interpersonal in operation. These, and other, possibilities have still to be put under the research microscope. In the meanwhile, the main research message is that part of the pattern of nature–nurture interplay involves the environmentally induced chemical changes responsible for methylation and acetylation influences on gene expression.

Variations in heritability according to environmental circumstances

Over the last decade or so, there have been repeated attempts by behavioural geneticists to use observed variation in heritability according to environmental circumstances as a means of elucidating key mediating mechanisms in nature–nurture interplay (see Rutter *et al.*, 2006). In seeking to understand and interpret the research evidence, it is crucial to appreciate that there are at least four competing models for what such variations in heritability might mean (Shanahan & Hofer, 2005). First, it could reflect nothing more than *relative variation*. That is, because heritability is a context-specific, population-specific measure quantifying the relative effect of G and E, heritability will go *down* when there is a massive environmentally mediated risk effect. Conversely, it will go *up* in the context of a major genetic risk. Second, it could reflect a *stress-diathesis* model reflecting gene–environment interaction (G × E). Because heritability estimates include G × E in the G term, this means that they will

go *up* in the context of environmental risk, if genes are influencing individual susceptibility to environmental stressors. Third, there is a *bio-ecological model* that proposes that advantageous proximal environments actualized genetic influences. Fourth, there is an *environmental constraints/opportunities model* in which the proposition is that genetically influenced individual differences will increase heritability if good environmental opportunities mean that they have a greater chance to make a difference, and that heritability will be lower if there are environmental constraints that impede the possibility of genetically influenced individual initiatives making much difference.

It is obvious from this brief summary of models that they have the huge potential advantage of giving rise to different predictions. In principle, therefore, it should be possible to use the empirical findings to identify mediating mechanisms. Unfortunately, the findings (and the inferences to which they give rise) are rather contradictory and therefore inconclusive (see Rutter *et al.*, 2006). That is because, in most cases, key features have had to be inferred rather than measured (this applies, for example, to environmental opportunities and constraints), and because it has been unclear how far the effects of variations in environmental circumstances are environmentally, rather than genetically, mediated. Accordingly, although large variations in heritability over time and place are well demonstrated, and although they clearly must reflect some form of nature–nurture interplay, the mediating mechanisms remain frustratingly unclear.

Gene–environment correlations (rGE)

Gene–environment correlations (rGE) concern genetic influences on individual variations in people's *exposure* to particular sorts of environments. This comes about as a result of 'passive', 'active' and 'evocative' rGE (Plomin, DeFries & Loehlin, 1977). 'Passive' refers to the effects of *parental* genes on parental behaviours that help shape the rearing environments that they provide for their children. The rGE comes about when there is a positive correlation between passing on 'risky' genes and providing a 'risky' rearing environment. 'Active' and 'evocative' are similar in that they refer to the effects of the *child's* genes on those child behaviours that help the child's selection of environments ('active' rGE) or that serve to influence interpersonal interactions and, hence, influence other people's reactions to the child ('evocative' rGE).

The first basic finding is that twin studies have shown that genes are implicated in individual differences in exposure to a wide range of environments having important associations with psychopathology (Rutter *et al.*, 2006). 'Passive' effects need to be assessed through twin studies of parents (Neiderhiser, Reiss, Pedersen, Lichtenstein, Spotts, Hansson, Cederblad & Ellhammer, 2004) and 'active' or 'evocative' effects through either adoptee studies (e.g. Ge, Conger, Cadoret, Neiderhiser, Yates, Troughton & Stewart, 1996; O'Connor, Deater-Deckard, Fulker, Rutter & Plomin, 1998) or children of twins designs (D'Onofrio, Turkheimer, Eaves, Corey, Berg, Solaas & Emery, 2003; Silberg & Eaves, 2004). The evidence indicates that 'passive', 'active' and 'evocative' rGE are all operative, although their relative importance in particular circumstances is less clear. The findings have also begun to indicate the parent and child behaviours that have environmental effects – personality variables in the case of parents and disruptive behaviour in the case of children, but evidence is rather sparse so far. It is important to note that the O'Connor *et al.* (1998) adoptee study showed that the evocative effect on the adoptive parents of the children's disruptive behaviour applied nearly as strongly to those not at genetic risk (at least insofar as that could be indexed by the qualities of the biological mother) as those at genetic risk. The Jaffee *et al.* (Jaffee, Caspi, Moffitt, Polo-Thomas, Price & Taylor, 2004) study, using a twin design, also showed that different aspects of rearing varied in their susceptibility to 'evocative' effects – corporal punishment being quite strongly influenced and overt physical abuse very little influenced.

Three main conclusions on rGE are possible. First, part of the genetic influences on mental disorder derive from the effects of rGE in influencing individual differences in people's exposure to risky or protective environments. Second, part of the risk associated with adverse environments is mediated genetically rather than environmentally (see Plomin & Bergeman, 1991). Third, the priority now is research into the effects of parental and child behaviours in shaping and selecting environments, rather than further quantification of rGE. The key need concerns the identification of the specific behaviours that serve to influence environments in particular ways. The search for genes that provide susceptibility to those behaviours is also important, but it can take place only after the behavioural processes have been identified and understood. To search for genes that code for specific environments would be a misguided enterprise.

Gene–environment interactions (G × E)

The fourth area of nature–nurture interplay concerns gene–environment interactions (G × E). During the 1980s and early 1990s, the generally accepted view in behavioural genetics was that G × E was rare and of such limited importance that it could be ignored in most circumstances. This dismissal of G × E arose partly in a carry-forward of the 'direct' effects implied by Mendelian models and partly because genetic 'black box' analyses of anonymous (i.e. unmeasured) G and anonymous E had failed to find any omnibus interaction between the two. Biological considerations indicated that genetically influenced sensitivities were unlikely to take this general form (Rutter & Pickles, 1991; Rutter & Silberg, 2002). Moreover, there were four key reasons for expecting G × E to be influential (Rutter, 2006a; Rutter *et al.*, 2006). First, evolutionary considerations argue that genetic variation in response to the environment provides the raw material for natural selection (Ridley, 2003).

Second, developmental considerations indicate that biological development at the individual level involves adaptations to the environmental conditions that prevail during the formative period of development; it is implausible that genetic factors do not play a role in moderating that process (Bateson, Barker, Clutton-Brock, Deb, D'Udine, Foley, Gluckman, Godfrey, Kirkwood, Lahr, McNamara, Metcalfe, Monaghan, Spencer & Sultan, 2004).

Third, environmental evidence indicates that, in both humans and other animals, there is great variability in responses to environmental hazards. To argue that response heterogeneity is not influenced by genes would require the assumption that responsiveness to the environment is uniquely outside the sphere of genetic influence (Moffitt, Caspi & Rutter, 2006).

Fourth, there is the biological evidence showing numerous examples of G × E in biology, and increasingly in medicine (Moffitt *et al.*, 2006; Rutter, 2006a). It is clear that the traditional notion that strictly additive, non-interactive, effects for genetic and environmental influences constitute the norm must be rejected. Of course there are some main effects of both G and E that involve no synergism between the two, but G × E is likely often to play some role in multifactorial traits and disorders. Twin and adoptee studies have shown the likely occurrence of G × E with respect to anxiety/depressive disorders, antisocial behaviour/substance abuse disorders, and schizophrenia (Rutter *et al.*, 2006). Nevertheless, although quantitative genetic studies provide a reasonable basis for anticipating G × E, only molecular genetic findings provide direct pointers to interactions between identified susceptibility genes and specific measured environmental circumstances.

Against that background, the evidence from three papers reporting findings from the Dunedin Longitudinal Study may be considered. In brief, on a sample of about 1000 individuals followed from age 3 to 26 years, DNA findings were related to multi-measure, multi-informant measures of psychopathology, as moderated by systematic measures of environmental features for which other research had shown environmentally mediated risk effects. The first

16 Michael Rutter

paper showed a significant main effect of childhood maltreatment on antisocial behaviour, no significant main effect of a gene influencing MAOA activity, and a strong G × E effect (Caspi, McClay, Moffitt, Mill, Martin, Craig, Taylor & Poulton, 2002). The second paper showed an effect of both child maltreatment and life stresses on depression moderated by a 5HTT gene allelic variation (Caspi, Sugden, Moffitt, Taylor, Craig, Harrington, McClay, Mill, Martin, Braithwaite & Poulton, 2003) – again with no significant main effect of the gene in the absence of the environmental hazards. The third paper (Caspi, Moffitt, Cannon, McClay, Murray, Harrington, Taylor, Arseneault, Williams, Braithwaite, Poulton & Craig, 2005) showed that heavy early use of cannabis predisposed to schizophrenia spectrum disorders only in the presence of the val/val allelic variation of the COMT genotype.

Statistical interaction effects are notoriously subject to artefactual influences and, therefore, it was crucial to undertake rigorous methodological checks to ensure that the findings were not in reality due to G × G, rather than G × E, interactions, and were not a result of some scaling artefact. The G × E findings survived all these tests. Moreover, other researchers have shown similar G × E, with the several positive replications outnumbering the few negative findings. Nevertheless, because the interest has to be in the *biology* of G × E, and not just in finding a statistical interaction, the real test lies in the use of other research strategies in humans and other animals to investigate biological processes. It is the fact that these similarly indicate G × E with the same genes and comparable environmental variations that most effectively validates the reality of the G × E.

Thus, the Suomi research group, working with rhesus monkeys, showed that the same short allele of the 5HTT transporter gene was associated with serotonin metabolites in the cerebrospinal fluid (Bennett, Lesch, Heils, Long, Lorenz, Shoaf, Champoux, Suomi, Linnoila & Higley, 2002), with visual orientation to stimuli (Champoux, Bennett, Shannon, Higley, Lesch & Suomi, 2002), and with increased ACTH levels (Barr, Newman, Shannon, Parker, Dvoskin, Becker, Schwandt, Champoux, Lesch, Goldman, Suomi & Higley, 2004).

Human imaging studies (using normal volunteers) have shown greater amygdala neural activity in response to fearful visual stimuli for participants with the short allele (Hariri, Mattay, Tessitore, Koachana, Fera & Goldman, 2002; Hariri, Drabant, Munoz, Kolachana, Venkata, Egan & Weinberger, 2005; Heinz, Braus, Smolka, Wrase, Puls, Hermann, Klein, Grüsser, Flor, Schumann, Mann & Bücher, 2005); greater functional connectivity between the subgenual cingulate and amygdala in response to negative facial expressions in participants with the short allele (Pezawas, Meyer-Lindenberg, Drabant, Verchinski,

Munoz, Kolachana, Egan, Mattay, Hariri & Weinberger, 2005); and variations in anterior cingulate activation according to the MAOA genotype during a response inhibition task (Meyer-Lindenberg, Buckholtz, Kolachana, Hariri, Pezawas, Blasi, Wabnitz, Honea, Verchinski, Callicott, Egan, Mattay & Weinberger, 2006).

The key implication of these G × E findings is that there is a plausible biological mechanism and that it is likely that the gene and the measured environment operate on the *same* causal pathway. The experimental imaging studies also suggest that risk effects are dimensional and operate in the normal population and not just on individuals with identified mental disorders.

Conclusions

The era of simply measuring heritability is over (although quantitative genetics still has an important broader role) and now there is the opportunity to study causal processes. Such study, however, must move beyond the search for susceptibility genes 'for' specific mental disorders, must include a study of environmental risk factors, and must involve the study of the various forms of gene–environment interplay. Particularly as exemplified by epigenetic environmental effects on gene expression, and by G × E, it is not putting it too strongly to refer to the interplay as often (but certainly not always) involving gene–environment interdependence. This type of research is still in its infancy and it remains to be seen just which effects will prove to be important. However, the evidence available to date indicates that there are real effects and that these will necessarily change the way we think about both G and E as they operate over the course of normal and abnormal development.

References

Barr, C.S., Newman, T.K., Shannon, C., Parker, C., Dvoskin, R.L., Becker, M.L., Schwandt, M., Champoux, M., Lesch, K.P., Goldman, D., Suomi, S.J., & Higley, J.D. (2004). Rearing condition and 5-HTTLPR interact to influence limbic-hypothalamic-pituitary-adrenal axis response to stress in infant macaques. *Biological Psychiatry*, **55**, 733–738.

Bateson, P., Barker, D., Clutton-Brock, T., Deb, D., D'Udine, B., Foley, R.A., Gluckman, P., Godfrey, K., Kirkwood, T., Lahr, M.M., McNamara, J., Metcalfe, N.B., Monaghan, P., Spencer, H.G., & Sultan, S.E. (2004). Developmental plasticity and human health. *Nature*, **430**, 419–421.

Bennett, A.J., Lesch, K.P., Heils, A., Long, J.D., Lorenz, J.G., Shoaf, S.E., Champoux, M., Suomi, S.J., Linnoila, M.V., & Higley, J.D. (2002). Early experience and serotonin transporter gene variation interact to influence primate CNS function. *Molecular Psychiatry*, **7**, 118–122.

Cameron, N.M., Parent, C., Champagne, F.A., Fish, E.W., Ozaki-Kuroda, K., & Meaney, M.J. (2005). The programming of individual differences in defensive responses and reproductive strategies in the rat through variations in maternal care. *Neuroscience and Biobehavioral Reviews*, 29, 843–865.

Caspi, A., McClay, J., Moffitt, T.E., Mill, J., Martin, J., Craig, I.W., Taylor, A., & Poulton, R. (2002). Role of genotype in the cycle of violence in maltreated children. *Science*, 297, 851–854.

Caspi, A., Moffitt, T.E., Cannon, M., McClay, J., Murray, R., Harrington, H., Taylor, A., Arseneault, L., Williams, B., Braithwaite, A., Poulton, R., & Craig, I.W. (2005). Moderation of the effect of adolescent-onset cannabis use on adult psychosis by a functional polymorphism in the COMT gene: longitudinal evidence of a gene × environment interaction. *Biological Psychiatry*, 57, 1117–1127.

Caspi, A., Sugden, K., Moffitt, T.E., Taylor, A., Craig, I.W., Harrington, H., McClay, J., Mill, J., Martin, J., Braithwaite, A., & Poulton, R. (2003). Influence of life stress on depression: moderation by a polymorphism in the 5-HTT gene. *Science*, 301, 386–389.

Champagne, F., Chretien, P., Stevenson, C.W., Zhang, T.Y., Gratton, A., & Meaney, M.J. (2004). Variations in nucleus accumbens dopamine associated with individual differences in maternal behavior in the rat. *Journal of Neuroscience*, 24, 4113–4123.

Champoux, M., Bennett, A., Shannon, C., Higley, J.D., Lesch, K.P., & Suomi, S.J. (2002). Serotonin transporter gene polymorphism, differential early rearing, and behavior in rhesus monkey neonates. *Molecular Psychiatry*, 7, 1058–1063.

Coe, C.L., & Lubach, G.R. (2005). Developmental consequences of antenatal dexamethasone treatment in nonhuman primates. *Neuroscience Biobehavioral Review*, 29, 227–235.

D'Onofrio, B., Turkheimer, E., Eaves, L., Corey, L.A., Berg, K., Solaas, M.H., & Emery, R.E. (2003). The role of the children of twins design in elucidating causal relations between parent characteristics and child outcomes. *Journal of Child Psychology and Psychiatry*, 44, 1130–1144.

Ge, X., Conger, R.D., Cadoret, R.J., Neiderhiser, J.M., Yates, W., Troughton, E., & Stewart, M.A. (1996). The developmental interface between nature and nurture: a mutual influence model of child antisocial behavior and parent behaviors. *Developmental Psychology*, 32, 574–589.

Hariri, A., Drabant, E., Munoz, K., Kolachana, B., Venkata, S., Egan, M., & Weinberger, D. (2005). A susceptibility gene for affective disorders and the response of the human amygdala. *Archives of General Psychiatry*, 62, 146–152.

Hariri, A., Mattay, V., Tessitore, A., Koachana, B., Fera, F., Goldman, D., Egan, M.F., & Weinberger, D.R. (2002). Serotonin transporter genetic variation and the response of the human amygdala. *Science*, 297, 400–403.

Heinz, A., Braus, D.F., Smolka, M.N., Wrase, J., Puls, I., Hermann, D., Klein, S., Grüsser, S.N., Flor, H., Schumann, G., Mann, K., & Bücher, C. (2005). Amygdala-prefrontal coupling depends on a genetic variation of the serotonin transporter. *Nature Neuroscience*, 8, 20–21.

Jaenisch, R., & Bird, A. (2003). Epigenetic regulation of gene expression: how the genome integrates intrinsic and environmental signals. *Nature Genetics Supplement*, 33, 245–254.

Jaffee, S.R., Caspi, A., Moffitt, T.E., Polo-Thomas, M., Price, T.S., & Taylor, A. (2004). The limits of child effects: evidence for genetically mediated child effects on corporal punishment but not on physical maltreatment. *Developmental Psychology*, 40, 1047–1058.

Kendler, K.S., & Prescott, C.A. (2006). *Genes, environment and psychopathology: Understanding the causes of psychiatric and substance use disorders*. New York: Guilford Press.

Lewin, B. (2004). *Genes VIII*. Upper Saddle River, NJ: Pearson Prentice Hall.

Meaney, M.J., & Szyf, M. (2005). Maternal care as a model for experience-dependent chromatin plasticity? *Trends in Neuroscience*, 28, 456–463.

Meyer-Lindenberg, A., Buckholtz, J.W., Kolachana, B., Hariri, A.R., Pezawas, L., Blasi, G., Wabnitz, A., Honea, R., Verchinski, B.A., Callicott, J., Egan, M.F., Mattay, V.S., & Weinberger, D.R. (2006). Neural mechanisms of genetic risk for impulsivity and violence in humans. *Proceedings of the National Academy of Sciences of the USA*, 103, 6269–6274.

Moffitt, T.E., Caspi, A., & Rutter, M. (2006). Measured gene-environment interactions in psychopathology: concepts, research strategies, and implications for research, intervention, and public understanding of genetics. *Perspectives on Psychological Science*, 1, 5–27.

Neiderhiser, J.M., Reiss, D., Pedersen, N.L., Lichtenstein, P., Spotts, E.L., Hansson, K., Cederblad, M., & Ellhammer, O. (2004). Genetic and environmental influences on mothering of adolescents: a comparison of two samples. *Developmental Psychology*, 40, 335–351.

O'Connor, T.G., Deater-Deckard, K., Fulker, D., Rutter, M., & Plomin, R. (1998). Genotype–environment correlations in late childhood and early adolescence: antisocial behavioral problems and coercive parenting. *Developmental Psychology*, 34, 970–981.

Pezawas, L., Meyer-Lindenberg, A., Drabant, E.M., Verchinski, B.A., Munoz, K., Kolachana, B., Egan, M.F., Mattay, V.S., Hariri, A.R., & Weinberger, D.R. (2005). 5-HTTLPR polymorphism impacts human cingulate-amygdala interactions: a genetic susceptibility mechanism for depression. *Nature Neuroscience*, 8, 828–834.

Plomin, R., & Bergeman, C.S. (1991). The nature of nurture: genetic influence on 'environmental' measures. *Behavioral and Brain Sciences*, 14, 373–427.

Plomin, R., DeFries, J.C., & Loehlin, J.C. (1977). Genotype-environment interaction and correlation in the analysis of human behavior. *Psychological Bulletin*, 84, 309–322.

Ridley, M. (2003). *Nature via nurture: Genes, experience and what makes us human*. London: Fourth Estate.

Rutter, M. (1972). *Maternal deprivation reassessed*. Harmondsworth, Middlesex: Penguin.

Rutter, M. (2003). Genetic influences on risk and protection: implications for understanding resilience. In S. Luthar (Ed.), *Resilience and vulnerability: Adaptation in the context of childhood adversities* (pp. 489–509). New York: Cambridge University Press.

Rutter, M. (2005). Environmentally mediated risks for psychopathology: research strategies and findings. *Journal of the*

18   Michael Rutter

American Academy of Child and Adolescent Psychiatry, **44**, 3–18.

Rutter, M. (2006a). *Genes and behavior: Nature–nurture interplay explained*. Oxford: Blackwell.

Rutter, M. (2006b). The promotion of resilience in the face of adversity. In A. Clarke-Stewart & J. Dunn (Eds.), *Families count: Effects on child and adolescent development* (pp. 26–52). New York and Cambridge: Cambridge University Press.

Rutter, M., Moffitt, T.E., & Caspi, A. (2006). Gene–environment interplay and psychopathology: multiple varieties but real effects. *Journal of Child Psychology and Psychiatry*, **47**, 226–261.

Rutter, M., & Pickles, A. (1991). Person–environment interactions: concepts, mechanisms, and implications for data analysis. In T.D. Wachs & R. Plomin (Eds.), *Conceptualization and measurement of organism–environment interaction* (pp. 105–141). Washington, DC: American Psychological Association.

Rutter, M., Pickles, A., Murray, R., & Eaves, L. (2001). Testing hypotheses on specific environmental causal effects on behavior. *Psychological Bulletin*, **127**, 291–324.

Rutter, M., & Silberg, J. (2002). Gene–environment interplay in relation to emotional and behavioral disturbance. *Annual Review of Psychology*, **53**, 463–490.

Saunders, A.M. (2000). Apolipoprotein E and Alzheimer disease: an update on genetic and functional analyses. *Journal of Neuropathology and Experimental Neurology*, **59**, 751–758.

Shanahan, M.J., & Hofer, S.M. (2005). Social context in gene–environment interactions: retrospect and prospect. *Journal of Gerontology B Psychological Science and Social Science*, **60**, 65–76.

Silberg, J.L., & Eaves, L.J. (2004). Analysing the contributions of genes and parent–child interaction to childhood behavioural and emotional problems: a model for the children of twins. *Psychological Medicine*, **34**, 347–356.

Strittmatter, W.J., Saunders, A.M., Schmechel, D., Pericak-Vance, M., Enghild, J., Salvesen, G.S., & Roses, A.D. (1993). Apolipoprotein E: high-avidity binding to beta-amyloid and increased frequency of type 4 allele in late-onset familial Alzheimer disease. *Proceedings of the National Academy of Sciences of the USA*, **90**, 1977–1981.

Weaver, I.C.G., Cervoni, N., Champagne, F.A., D'Alessio, A.C., Charma, S., Seckl, J., Dymov, S., Szyf, M., & Meaney, M.J. (2004). Epigenetic programming by maternal behavior. *Nature Neuroscience*, **7**, 847–854.

[7]

How People Make Their Own Environments: A Theory of Genotype → Environment Effects

Sandra Scarr and Kathleen McCartney

Yale University

SCARR, SANDRA, and MCCARTNEY, KATHLEEN. *How People Make Their Own Environments: A Theory of Genotype → Environment Effects.* CHILD DEVELOPMENT, 1983, **54**, 424–435. We propose a theory of development in which experience is directed by genotypes. Genotypic differences are proposed to affect phenotypic differences, both directly and through experience, via 3 kinds of genotype → environment effects: a passive kind, through environments provided by biologically related parents; an evocative kind, through responses elicited by individuals from others; and an active kind, through the selection of different environments by different people. The theory adapts the 3 kinds of genotype-environment correlations proposed by Plomin, DeFries, and Loehlin in a developmental model that is used to explain results from studies of deprivation, intervention, twins, and families.

Introduction

Theories of behavioral development have ranged from genetic determinism to naive environmentalism. Neither of these radical views nor interactionism has adequately explained the process of development or the role of experience in development. In this paper we propose a theory of environmental effects on human development that emphasizes the role of the genotype in determining not only which environments are experienced by individuals but also which environments individuals seek for themselves. To show how this theory addresses the process of development, the theory is used to account for seemingly anomalous findings for deprivation, adoption, twin, and intervention studies.

For the species, we claim that human experience and its effects on development depend primarily on the evolved nature of the human genome. In evolutionary theory the two essential concepts are selection and variation. Through selection the human genome has evolved to program human development. Phenotypic variation is the raw material on which selection works. Genetic variation must be associated with phenotypic variation, or there could be no evolution. It follows from

evolutionary theory that individual differences depend in part on genotypic differences. We argue that genetic differences prompt differences in which environments are experienced and what effects they may have. In this view, the genotype, in both its species specificity and its individual variability, largely determines environmental effects on development, because the genotype determines the organism's responsiveness to environmental opportunities.

A theory of behavioral development must explain the origin of new psychological structures. Because there is no evidence that new adaptations can arise out of the environment without maturational changes in the organism, genotypes must be the source of new structures.

Maturational sequence is controlled primarily by the genetic program for development. As Gottlieb (1976) said, there is evidence for a role of environment in (1) maintaining existing structures and in (2) elaborating existing structures; however, there is no evidence that the environment has a role in (3) inducing new structures. In development, new adaptations or structures cannot arise out of experience per se.

We thank Emily Cahan, Jerome Kagan, Katherine Nelson, Robert Plomin, and Theodore D. Wachs for their critical and helpful comments on several drafts of this paper. Their disagreements with us were stimulating and always constructive. Much of the family research reviewed here was done in collaboration with Richard A. Weinberg and supported by the W. T. Grant Foundation and the National Institute of Mental Health. The day-care studies have the collaboration of J. Conrad Schwarz, Susan Grajek, and Deborah Phillips and were supported by the W. T. Grant Foundation and the Bermuda Government. Requests for reprints should be sent to Sandra Scarr, Department of Psychology, Yale University, Box 11-A Yale Station, New Haven, Connecticut 06520.

The most widely accepted theories of development are vague about how new structures arise; for example, Piaget (1980) fails to make the connection between organism and environment clear in his references to interaction. Nor is development well described by maturation alone (see Connolly & Prechtl, 1981). Neither Gesell and Ilg (1943) nor contemporary nativists (e.g., Chomsky, 1980) appreciate the inextricable links of nature and nurture in a hierachically organized system of development.

We suggest that the problem of new structures in development has been extraordinarily difficult because of a false parallel between genotype and environment, which, we argue, are not constructs at the same level of analysis. The dichotomy of nature and nurture has always been a bad one, not only for the oft-cited reasons that both are required for development, but because a false parallel arises between the two. We propose that development is indeed the result of nature *and* nurture but that genes drive experience. Genes are components in a system that organizes the organism to experience its world. The organism's abilities to experience the world change with development and are individually variable. A good theory of the environment can only be one in which experience is guided by genotypes that both push and restrain experiences.

Behavioral development depends on both a genetic program and a suitable environment for the expression of the human, species-typical program for development. Differences among people can arise from both genetic and environmental differences, but the process by which differences arise is better described as genotype → environment effects. Like Chomsky and Fodor (1980), we propose that the genotype is the driving force behind development, because, we argue, it is the discriminator of what environments are actually experienced. The genotype determines the *responsiveness* of the person to those environmental opportunities. Unlike Chomsky and Fodor, we do not think that development is precoded in the genes and merely emerges with maturation. Rather, we stress the role of the genotype in determining which environments are actually experienced and what effects they have on the developing person.

We distinguish here between environments to which a person is exposed and environments that are actively experienced or "grasped" by the person. As we all know, the relevance of environments changes with development. The toddler who has "caught on" to the idea that things have names and who demands the names for everything is experiencing a fundamentally different verbal environment from what she experienced before, even though her parents talked to her extensively in infancy. The young adolescent who played baseball with the boy next door and now finds herself hopelessly in love with him is experiencing her friend's companionship in a new way.

A model of genotypes and environments. —Figure 1 presents our model of behavioral development. In this model, the child's phenotype (P_c), or observable characteristics, is a function of both the child's genotype (G_c) and her rearing environment (E_c). There will be little disagreement on this. The parents' genotypes (G_p) determine the child's genotype, which in turn influences the child's phenotype. Again, there should be little controversy over this point. As in most developmental theories, transactions occur between the organism and the environment; here they are described by the correlation between phenotype and rearing environment. In most models, however, the source of this correlation is ambiguous. In this model, both child's phenotype and rearing environment are influenced by the child's genotype. Because the child's genotype influences both the phenotype and the rearing environment, their correlation is a function of the genotype. The genotype is *conceptually prior* to both the phenotype and the rearing environment.

It is an unconventional shorthand to suggest that the child's genotype can directly affect the rearing environment. What we want

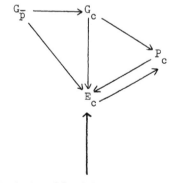

Fig. 1.—A model of behavioral development

426 Child Development

to represent is developmental changes in the genetic program that prompt new experiences, before the full phenotype is developed. An example could be found in the development of productive speech; the child becomes attentive to the language environment receptively months before real words are produced. Our argument is that changes in what is "turned on" in the genotype affect an emerging phenotype both directly through maturation (G_c to P_c) and through prompting new experiences.

The model could just as well specify intermediate phenotypes, such as receptive language in the example of productive speech, but the *idea* that genetic differences (both developmental changes for an individual over time and differences among individuals) affect experiential differences could be lost in a web of path diagrams. The model is designed to present our ideas, not for analysis of variance.

Also clouded by an endless regress of intermediate phenotypes would be the idea that the correlation or transaction between phenotype and environment is determined by developmental changes in the genotype. We recognize that this is not a popular position, but we propose it to account for data to be discussed in the final sections of the paper.

Thus, we intend the path from G_c to E_c to represent the idea that developmental changes in phenotypes are prompted both by changes in the effective genotype and by changes in the salience of environments, which are then correlated.

The path from the G_c to P_c represents maturation, which is controlled primarily by the genetic program. New structures arise out of maturation, from genotype to phenotype. Behavioral development is elaborated and maintained, in Gottlieb's sense, by the transactions of phenotype and environment, but it cannot arise de novo from this interaction. Thus, in this model, the course of development is a function of genetically controlled maturational sequences, although the rate of maturation can be affected by some environmental circumstances, such as the effects of nutrition on physical growth (Watson & Lowrey, 1967). Behavioral examples include cultural differences in rates of development through the sequence of cognitive stages described by Piaget and other theoretical sequences (see Nerlove & Snipper, 1981).

Separation of genetic and environmental effects on development.—The major problem

with attempts to separate environmental from genetic effects and their combinations is that people evoke and select their own environments to a great extent. There may appear to be arbitrary events of fate, such as being hit by a truck (did you look carefully in both directions?), falling ill (genetic differences in susceptibility, or a life-style that lowers resistance to disease?), but even these may not be entirely divorced from personal characteristics that have some genetic variability. Please understand that we do not mean that one's environmental fate is *entirely* determined by one's genotype—only that some genotypes are more likely to receive and select certain environments than others. A theory that stresses either genetic or environmental differences per se cannot account for the processes by which people come to be the way they are. At any one point in time, behavioral differences may be analyzed into variances that can be attributed more or less to genetic and environmental sources (see Plomin, DeFries, & Loehlin, 1977; Scarr & Kidd, in press). A quantitative genetic approach to estimating variances, however, does not attempt to specify the processes by which individuals developed their phenotypes.

Genotype-environment correlations.—Plomin et al. (1977) have described a model of phenotype variation that estimates the amount of variance that arises from genetic and environmental differences. Genotype-environment correlation is a nonlinear component in the additive variance model, included to account for situations in which "genotypes are selectively exposed to different environments." They did not intend to describe developmental processes, as we are doing here. Rather, Plomin and his colleagues were responding to the question, How much of the variation in a phenotype is due to differences among genotypes, differences among environments, dominance effects, genotype-environment interactions, and genotype-environment correlations? Their model addresses sources of individual differences in a population of phenotypes at one point in time. By contrast, our use of the term, genotype → environment effects, is to describe developmental *processes* over time, not to estimate sources of variance in phenotypes. We seek to answer the questions, How do genotypes and environments *combine* to produce human development? and How do genetic and environmental differences *combine* to produce variation in development?

An Evolving Theory of Behavioral Development

Plomin et al. (1977) described three kinds of genotype-environment correlations that we believe form the basis for a developmental theory. The theory of genotype → environment effects we propose has three propositions:

1. The process by which children develop is best described by three kinds of genotype → environment effects: a *passive* kind, whereby the genetically related parents provide a rearing environment that is correlated with the genotype of the child (sometimes positively and sometimes negatively); an *evocative* kind, whereby the child receives responses from others that are influenced by his genotype; and an *active* kind that represents the child's selective attention to and learning from aspects of his environment that are influenced by his genotype and indirectly correlated with those of his biological relatives.

2. The relative importance of the three kinds of genotype → environment effects changes with development. The influence of the passive kind declines from infancy to adolescence, and the importance of the active kind increases over the same period.

3. The degree to which experience is influenced by individual genotypes increases with development and with the shift from passive to active genotype → environment effects, as individuals select their own experiences.

The first, *passive* genotype → environment effects arise in biologically related families and render all of the research literature on parent-child socialization uninterpretable. Because parents provide both genes and environments for their biological offspring, the child's environment is necessarily correlated with her genes, because her genes are correlated with her parents' genes, and the parents' genes are correlated with the rearing environment they provide. It is impossible to know what about the parents' rearing environment for the child determines what about the child's behavior, because of the confounding effect of genetic transmission of the same characteristics from parent to child. Not only can we not interpret the direction of effects in parent-child interaction, as Bell (1968) argued, we also cannot interpret the *cause* of those effects in biologically related families.

An example of a positive kind of passive genotype-environment correlation can be found

in reading; parents who read well and enjoy reading are likely to provide their children with books; thus, the children are more likely to be skilled readers who enjoy reading, both for genetic and environmental reasons. The children's rearing environment is positively correlated with the parents' genotypes and therefore with the children's genotypes as well.

An example of a negative passive genotype-environment correlation can also be found in reading. Parents who are skilled readers, faced with a child who is not learning to read well, may provide a more enriched reading environment for that child than for another who acquires reading skills quickly. The more enriched environment for the less able child represents a negative genotype → environment effect (see also Plomin et al., 1977). There is, thus, an unreliable, but not random, connection between genotypes and environments when parents provide the opportunities for experience.

The second kind of genotype → environment effect is called evocative because it represents the different responses that different genotypes evoke from the social and physical environments. Responses to the person further shape development in ways that correlate with the genotype. Examples of such evocative effects can be found in the research of Lytton (1980), the theory of Escalona (1968), and the review of Maccoby (1980). It is quite likely that smiley, active babies receive more social stimulation than sober, passive infants. In the intellectual area, cooperative, attentive preschoolers receive more pleasant and instructional interactions from the adults around them than uncooperative, distractible children. Individual differences in responses evoked can also be found in the physical world; for example, people who are skillful at electronics receive feedback of a sort very different from those who fail consistently at such tasks.

The third kind of genotype → environment effect is the active, niche-picking or niche-building sort. People seek out environments they find compatible and stimulating. We all select from the surrounding environment some aspects to which to respond, learn about, or ignore. Our selections are correlated with motivational, personality, and intellectual aspects of our genotypes. The active genotype → environment effect, we argue, is the most powerful connection between people and their environments and the most direct expression of the genotype in experience.

428 Child Development

Examples of active genotype → environment effects can be found in the selective efforts of individuals in sports, scholarship, relationships—in life. Once experiences occur, they naturally lead to further experiences. We agree that phenotypes are elaborated and maintained by environments, but the impetus for the experience comes, we argue, from the genotype.

Developmental changes in genotype → environment effects.—The second proposition is that the relative importance of the three kinds of genotype → environment effects changes over development from infancy to adolescence. In infancy much of the environment that reaches the child is provided by adults. When those adults are genetically related to the child, the environment they provide in general is positively related to their own characteristics and their own genotypes. Although infants are active in structuring their experiences by selectively attending to what is offered, they cannot do as much seeking out and niche-building as older children; thus, passive genotype → environment effects are more important for infants and young children than they are for older children, who can extend their experiences beyond the family's influences and create their own environments to a much greater extent. Thus, the effects of passive genotype → environment effects wane when the child has many extrafamilial opportunities.

In addition, parents can provide environments that are negatively related to the child's genotype, as illustrated earlier in teaching reading. Although parents' genotypes usually affect the environment they provide for their biological offspring, it is sometimes positive and sometimes negative and therefore not as direct a product of the young child's genotype as later environments will be. Thus, as stated in proposition 3, genotype → environment effects increase with development, as active replace passive forms. Genotype → environment effects of the evocative sort persist throughout life, as we elicit responses from others based on many personal, genotype-related characteristics from appearance to personality and intellect. Those responses from others reinforce and extend the directions our development has taken. High intelligence and adaptive skills in children from very disadvantaged backgrounds, for example, evoke approval and support from school personnel who might otherwise despair of the child's chances in life (Garmezy, Note 1). In adulthood, personality and intellectual differences evoke different responses in others. Sim-

ilarities in personal characteristics evoke similar responses from others, as shown in the case of identical twins reared apart (Bouchard, Note 2). These findings are also consistent with the third proposition.

A probabilistic model.—The concept of genotype → environment effects is emphasized in this emerging theory for three major reasons: the model results in a testable set of hypotheses for which disconfirmation would come from random association between genotypes and environments, it describes a developmental process, and it implies a *probabilistic* connection between a person and the environment. It is more likely that people with certain genotypes will receive certain kinds of parenting, evoke certain responses from others, and select certain aspects from the available environments; but nothing is rigidly determined. The idea of genetic differences, on the other hand, has seemed to imply to many that the person's developmental fate was preordained without regard to experience. This is absurd. By invoking the idea of genotype → environment effects, we hope to emphasize a probabilistic connection between genotypes and their environments. Although mismatches between the behaviors of parents and children certainly exist (see Nelson, 1973), we argue that on the average there are correlations of parents' characteristics and the rearing environment they provide.

Waddington (1962) postulated a probable but not determinant connection between genotypes and phenotypes through an epigenetic space, in which environmental events deflect the course of the developing phenotype. Figure 2 illustrates Waddington's theory of the probable relationship between genotypic and phenotypic differences. Note that a correlation remains between genotype and phenotype, even though one cannot specify in advance what environmental events will affect phenotypic development. To this conception, we add that genotypes shape many of their own experiences through evocative and active genotype → environment correlations.

The Role of the Environment Revisited

If genotypes are the driving force behind development and the determinants of what environments are experienced, does this mean that environments themselves have no effects? Clearly, environments are necessary for development and have effects on the average levels of development, but they may or may not cause variations among individuals (McCall, 1981). We argue like McCall that nature has not left essential human development at the mercy of experiences that may or may not be encountered; rather, the only necessary experiences are ones that are generally available to the species. Differences in experience per se, therefore, cannot be the major cause of variation among individuals. The major features of human development are programmed genetically and require experiences that are encountered by the vast majority of humankind in the course of living. Phenotypic variation among individuals relies on experiential differences that are determined by genetic differences rather than on differences among environmental effects that occur randomly.

Imposed environments.—In developmental studies, we usually think of environments provided for a child, such as parental interaction, school curricula, and various experimental manipulations. In some cases there are passive and evocative genotype-environment correlations that go unrecognized, as in parent-child interaction and the selection of children into school curricula. In a few cases there may be no correlation of the child's genotype with the treatment afforded an experimental group of which she is a member. On the other hand, it is impossible to ignore the attention and learning characteristics the child brings to the situation, so that the effects of environmental manipulations are never entirely free of individual differences in genotypes. Development is not necessarily constrained by genotype-environment correlations, although most often genotypes and environments are correlated in the real world, so that in fact, if not in principle, there are such constraints.

Sometimes, the influence of genotypes on environments is diminished through unusual positive or negative interventions, so that the environments experienced are less

driven by genotypes and may even be negatively related to genotypes, as in the passive, familial situation. Examples of this effect can be found in studies of deprivation, adoption, and day care. Studies of children reared in isolation (Clarke & Clarke, 1976) and children reared in unstimulating institutions (Dennis & Najarian, 1951; Hunt, 1961, 1980) have demonstrated the adverse effects of deprived environments on many aspects of development. Such studies usually address average responses to these poor environments. In any case, studies of environments that are so extreme as to be outside of the normal range of rearing environments for the species have few implications for environmental variation that the vast majority of human children experience.

In contrast to the extremely poor environments in the deprivation literature, the adoption studies include only rearing environments in the range of adequate to very good. The evidence from studies of biologically related and adoptive families that vary in socioeconomic status from working to upper middle class is that most people experience what Scarr and Weinberg (1978) have called "functionally-equivalent" environments. That is, the large array of individual differences among children and late adolescents adopted in infancy were not related to differences among their family environments—the same array of environmental differences that were and usually are associated with behavioral differences among children born to such families (Scarr, 1981; Scarr & Kidd, in press; Scarr & Weinberg, 1976, 1977, 1978). On the average, however, adopted children profit from their enriched environments, and they score above average on IQ and school achievement tests and on measures of personal adjustment.

Negative genotype-environment correlations.—Environments provided to children that are negatively related to their genotypes can

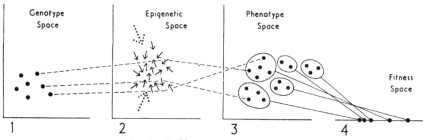

FIG. 2.—Waddington's epigenetic space

430   Child Development

have dramatic effects on average levels of development. Extrafamilial interventions that provide unusual enrichments or deprivations can alter the developmental levels of children from those that would be predicted by their family backgrounds and estimated genotypes. Intervention theories predict these main effects (Caldwell & Richmond, 1968; Hunt, 1980).

Enriched day-care environments have been shown to enhance intellectual development of children from disadvantaged backgrounds (Ramey & Haskins, 1981; McCartney, Note 3). Similarly, less stimulating day-care environments can hamper children's intellectual and social development, even if they come from more advantaged families (McCartney, Scarr, Phillips, Grajek, & Schwarz, 1981; McCartney, Note 3).

These are, however, rather rare opportunities, or lack of same, providing negatively correlated experiences for genotypes. In the usual course of development beyond early childhood, individuals select and evoke experiences that are directly influenced by their genotypes and therefore positively correlated with their own phenotypic characteristics.

Environmental effects on averages versus individuals.—One must distinguish environmental events that on the average enhance or delay development for all children from those that account for *variation* among children. There can be "main effects" that account for variation among groups that are naturally or experimentally treated in different ways. Within the groups of children there still remain enormous individual differences, some of which arise in response to the treatment. It is rare that the variation *between* groups approaches the magnitude of differences *within* groups, as represented in the pervasive overlapping distributions of scores. In developmental psychology, we have usually been satisfied if the treatment observed or implemented produced a statistically reliable difference between groups, but we have rarely examined the sources of differential responsiveness within the groups.

Most often, the same treatments that alter the average performance of a group seem to have similar effects on most members of the group. Otherwise, we would find a great deal of variance in genotype-environment interactions; that is, what's sauce for the goose would be poison for the gander. For the kinds of deprivation or interventions studied most often in developmental psychol-

ogy, the main effects seem not to change the rank orders of children affected. The main effects are real, but they are also small by comparison to the range of individual variation within groups so treated or not. Some children may be more responsive than others to the treatment, but we doubt that there are many situations in which disordinal interactions are the rule. Very few children lose developmental points by participating in Headstart or gain by being severely neglected in infancy. The search for aptitude-treatment interactions (Cronbach & Snow, 1977) and genotype-environment interactions (Erlenmeyer-Kimling, 1972) have not produced dramatic or reliable results.

In studies of adoptive and biologically related families, the correlation of children's IQ scores with the educational level of biological parents is about .35, whether or not the parents rear their children (Scarr & Weinberg, in this issue). Adopted children on the average have higher IQ scores than their biological parents as a result of the influence of their above-average adoptive parents. Taken together, these findings support the claim that treatments can have main effects without overcoming genetic differences in children's responsiveness to those environments. Adopted children have IQ scores above those of their biological parents, yet the *correlations* of adopted children are higher with their biological than their adoptive parents (Scarr & Weinberg, 1977, 1978, in this issue). The average effects of treatments, such as adoption, seem to increase the mean IQ scores, but they do not seem to affect the rank order of the children's scores with respect to their biological parents, and it is on rank orders, not means, that correlations depend. These results imply that the effect of adoptive families is to increase the scores of adopted children above those which would be predicted by their biological parents, but not to alter radically the rank order of individual differences among children they rear. And so it is, we think, with most treatments.

Answering Questions from Previous Research on Twins and Families

Neither extreme genetic determinism nor naive environmentalism can account for seemingly anomalous findings from research on twins and families. Three puzzling questions remain, the first of which concerns the *process* by which monozygotic (MZ) twins come to be more similar than dizygotic (DZ) twins, and biological siblings more similar than adopted siblings on all measurable characteristics, at least by the end of adolescence (Scarr & Weinberg, 1978). The second question concerns the declining similarities between DZ twins and adopted siblings from infancy to adolescence. The third question arises from the unexpected similarities between identical twins reared in different homes.

A theory of genotype-environment correlation can account for these findings by pointing to the degree of genetic resemblance and the degree of similarity in the environments that would be experienced by the co-twins and sibs.

Genetic resemblance determines environmental similarity.—The expected degree of environmental similarity for a pair of relatives can be thought of as the product of a person's own genotype → environment path and the genetic correlation of the pair. Figure 3 presents a model of the relationship between genotypes and environments for pairs of relatives who vary in genetic relatedness. G_1 and G_2 symbolize the two genotypes, E_1 and E_2 their respective environments. The similarity in the two environments (path a) is the product of the coefficient of each genotype with its own environment (path x) and the genetic correlation of the pair (path b). On the assumption that individuals' environments are equally influenced by their own genotypes, the similarity in the environments of two individuals becomes a function of their genetic correlation.

This model can be used to answer question 1 concerning the process by which MZ twins come to be more similar than DZ twins and biological siblings more similar than adopted siblings. For identical twins, for whom $b = 1.00$, the relationship of one twin's environment with the other's genotype is the same as the correlation of the twin's environment with her own genotype. Thus, one would certainly predict what is often observed: that the hobbies, food preferences, choices of friends, academic achievements, and so forth of the MZ twins are very similar (Scarr & Carter-Saltzman, 1980). Kamin (1974) proposed that all of this environmental similarity is imposed on MZ co-twins because they look so much alike. Theories of genetic resemblance do not speak to how close resemblances arise. We propose that the home environments provided by the parents, the responses that the co-twins evoke from others, and the active choices they make in their environments lead to striking similarities through genotypically determined correlations in their learning histories.

The same explanation applies, of course, to the greater resemblance of biological than adopted siblings. The environment of one biological sib is correlated to the genotype of the other as one-half the coefficient of the sibling's environment to her own genotype, because $b = 0.50$, as described in Figure 3. The same is true for DZ twins. There is a very small genetic correlation for intelligence between adopted siblings in most studies that arises from selective placement of the offspring of similar mothers in the same adoptive home. More important for this theory, however, is the selective placement of adopted children to match the intellectual characteristics of the adoptive parents. This practice allows adoptive parents to create a positive, passive genotype-environment correlation for their adopted children in early childhood, when the theory asserts that this kind of correlation is most important. In fact, the selective placement estimates from studies by Scarr and Weinberg (1977) can account for most of the resemblance between adoptive parents and their children. In addition, adoptive parents, like their biological counterparts, can provide negative genotype-environment correlations that assure that their several children will not differ too much on important skills, such as reading.

Changing similarities among siblings.—The second question left unanswered by previous research concerned the declining similarities of dizygotic twins and adopted siblings from infancy to adolescence. It is clear from Matheny, Wilson, Dolan, and Krantz's (1981) longitudinal study of MZ and DZ twins that the DZ correlations for intelligence of .60–.75 are higher than genetic theory would predict in infancy and early childhood. For school age and older twins, DZ correlations were the usual .55. Similarly, the intelligence correlations of a sample of

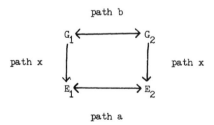

FIG. 3.—A model of environmental similarity based on genetic resemblance.

432 Child Development

late adolescent adopted siblings were zero, compared to the .25–.39 correlations of the samples of adopted children in early to middle childhood (Scarr & Weinberg, 1978).

Neither environmental nor genetic theories can effectively address these data. How can it be that the longer you live with someone, the less like them you become? One could evoke some ad hoc environmental theory about sibling relationships becoming more competitive, or "deidentified," but that would not account for the continued, moderate intellectual resemblance of biological siblings. Genetic theory has, of course, nothing to say about decreasing twin resemblance or any resemblance among young adoptees.

The theory put forward here predicts that the relative importance of passive versus active genotype-environment correlations changes with age. Recall that passive genotype-environment correlations are created by parents who provide children with both genes and environments, which are then correlated. Certainly in the case of DZ twins, whose prenatal environment was shared and whose earliest years are spent being treated in most of the same ways at the same time by the same parents, the passive genotype → environment effect is greater than that for ordinary sibs. Biological and adopted siblings do not, of course, share the same developmental environments at the same time because they differ in age. The passive genotype-environment correlation still operates for siblings, because they have the same parents, but to a lesser extent than for twins. (See Table 1.)

Monozygotic twin correlations for intellectual competence do not decline when active genotype-environment correlations outweigh the importance of the passive ones, because MZ co-twins typically select highly correlated environments anyway. Dizygotic pairs, on the other hand, are no more genetically related than sibs, so that as the intense similarity of their early home environments

gives way to their own choices, they select environments that are less similar than their previous environments and about as similar as those of ordinary sibs.

Adopted sibs, on the other hand, move from an early environment, in which mother may have produced similarity, to environments of their own choosing. Because their genotypes are hardly correlated at all, neither are their chosen environmental niches. Thus, by late adolescence, adopted siblings do not resemble each other in intelligence, personality, interests, or other phenotypic characteristics (Grotevant, Scarr, & Weinberg, 1977; Scarr, Webber, Weinberg, & Wittig, 1981; Scarr & Weinberg, 1978).

Biological siblings' early environments, like those of adopted children, lead to trait similarity as a result of passive genotype → environmental effects. As biological siblings move into the larger world and begin to make active choices, their niches remain moderately correlated because their genotypes remain moderately correlated. There is no marked shift in intellectual resemblance of biological sibs as the process of active genotype → environment influence replaces the passive one.

Identical twins reared apart.—The third question concerned the unexpected degree of resemblance between identical twins reared mostly apart. With the theory of genotype→ environment effects, their resemblance is not surprising. Given opportunities to attend selectively to and choose from varied opportunities, identical genotypes are expected to make similar choices. They are also expected to evoke similar responses from others and from their physical environments. The fact that they were reared in different homes and different communities is not important; differences in their development could arise only if the experiential opportunities of one or both were very restricted, so that similar choices could not have been made. According to previous

TABLE 1

THE SIMILARITY OF CO-TWIN'S AND SIBLING'S GENOTYPES AND ENVIRONMENTS DUE TO:

	GENETIC CORRELATION	CORRELATIONS IN THE ENVIRONMENTS OF RELATED PAIRS	
		Passive Genotype → Environment Effects in Early Development	Active Genotype → Environment Effects in Early Development
MZ twins............	1.00	High	High
DZ twins.............	.52	High	Moderate
Biological siblings......	.52	Moderate	Moderate
Adopted siblings.......	.01	Moderate	Low

studies (Juel-Nielsen, 1980; Newman, Freeman, & Holzinger, 1937; Shields, 1962) and the recent research of Bouchard and colleagues at the University of Minnesota (Bouchard, Note 2), the most dissimilar pairs of MZs reared apart are those in which one was severely restricted in environmental opportunity. Extreme deprivation or unusual enrichment can diminish the influence of genotype and environment and therefore lessen the resemblance of identical twins reared apart.

Research Strategies

The theory we propose can be tested in several ways and prove unable to account for results. First, studies of parental treatment of more than one child would be informative about passive genotype → environment effects. In general, we expect the rearing environment provided for the children in a family to differ in ways that are related to each child's characteristics. Do parents treat all of their children alike, as so many studies of one child per family seem to imply? Can parents be authoritative with one child and permissive with another? Our theory predicts that parents will respond to individual differences in their children, in keeping with Lytton's (1980) research on families with twins. If parent treatment of their children is not related to children's talents, interests, and personalities, the theory is wrong.

Second, studies of responses that individuals evoke from others would test our ideas about evocative genotype → environment effects. The social psychology literature on attractiveness (Bersheid & Walster, 1974; Mursteid, 1972), for example, would seem to support our view that some personal characteristics evoke differential responses from others. Similarly, teachers' responses to children with high versus low intelligence, hyperactivity versus acceptable levels of energy, and so forth provide some evidence for our theory. If others do not respond differentially to individual characteristics for which there is genetic variability, then the theory is wrong.

Third, active niche-building is being studied by the Laboratory of Comparative Human Cognition in their naturalistic observations of children's adaptations to problem-solving situations (Cole & The Laboratory of Comparative Human Cognition, Note 4). Our theory predicts that children select and build niches that are correlated with their talents, interests, and personality characteristics. If not, the theory is wrong.

Fourth, longitudinal studies of adopted children, such as the ongoing work of Plomin and colleagues, can provide valuable evidence of the changing influences of family environments on children. The theory predicts that children's characteristics will be more related to characteristics of the adoptive parents and other adopted siblings in earlier than later development. If adopted children are as similar to their adoptive parents and each other in late adolescence as they were in early childhood, that aspect of the theory is wrong.

Fifth, studies of older adolescents and adults who were adopted in infancy and others who were born into their families can provide evidence on the long-term effects of passive genotype → environment effects within families. Both evocative and active kinds of genotype → environmental effects can be traced through the similarities and dissimilarities of the two kinds of siblings.

In these ways, and others, the theory can be tested. It can fail to account for results obtained, or it can account for the diverse results more adequately than other theories. Given the various results of family studies presented in this paper, we believe that its predictions will be fulfilled. At least, we hope it will encourage more developmentalists to study more than one child per family, genetically unrelated families, and individual differences in experience.

Summary

In summary, the theory of genotype → environment correlations proposed here describes the usual course of human development in terms of three kinds of genotype-environment correlations that posit cooperative efforts of the nature-nurture team, directed by the genetic quarterback. Both genes and environments are constituents in the developmental system, but they have different roles. Genes direct the course of human experience, but experiential opportunities are also necessary for development to occur. Individual differences can arise from restrictions in environmental opportunities to experience what the genotype would find compatible. With a rich array of opportunities, however, most differences among people arise from genetically determined differences in the experiences to which they are attracted and which they evoke from their environments.

The theory also accounts for individual differences in responsiveness to environments —differences that are not primarily interac-

434   Child Development

tions of genotypes and environments but roughly linear combinations that are better described as genotype-environment correlations. In addition, the theory accounts for seemingly anomalous results from previous research on twins and families.

Most important, the theory addresses the issue of process. Rather than presenting a static view of individual differences through variance allocation, this theory hypothesizes processes by which genotypes and environments combine across development to make us both human and unique.

Reference Notes

1. Garmezy, N. *The case for the single case in experimental-developmental psychology.* Paper presented at the annual meeting of the American Psychological Association, Los Angeles, August 1981.
2. Bouchard, T. *The Minnesota study of twins reared apart: Description and preliminary findings.* Paper presented at the annual meeting of the American Psychological Association, August 1981.
3. McCartney, K. *The effect of quality of day care environment upon children's language development.* Unpublished doctoral dissertation, Yale University, 1982.
4. Cole, M., & The Laboratory of Comparative Human Cognition. *Niche-picking.* Unpublished manuscript, University of California, San Diego, 1980.

References

Bell, R. Q. A reinterpretation of the direction of effects in studies of socialization. *Psychological Review,* 1968, **75,** 81–95.

Bersheid, E., & Walster, E. Physical attractiveness. In L. Berkowitz (Ed.), *Advances in experimental social ysychology.* New York: Academic Press, 1974.

Caldwell, B. M., & Richmond, I. The Children's Center in Syracuse. In L. Dittman (Ed.), *Early child: The new perspectives.* New York: Atherton, 1968.

Chomsky, N. On cognitive structures and their development: A reply to Piaget. In M. Piattelli-Palmarini (Ed.), *Language and learning: The debate between Jean Piaget and Noam Chomsky.* Cambridge, Mass.: Harvard University Press, 1980.

Chomsky, N., & Fodor, J. Statement of the paradox. In M. Piattelli-Palmarini (Ed.), *Language and learning: The debate between Jean Piaget and Noam Chomsky.* Cambridge, Mass.: Harvard University Press, 1980.

Clarke, A. M., & Clarke, A. D. B. *Early experience: Myth and evidence.* New York: Free Press, 1976.

Connolly, K. J., & Prechtl, H. F. R. (Eds.), *Maturation and development: Biological and psychological perspectives.* Philadelphia: Lippincott, 1981.

Cronbach, L. J., & Snow, R. E. *Attitudes and instructional methods.* New York: Irvington, 1977.

Dennis, W., & Najarian, P. Infant development under environmental handicap. *Psychological Monographs,* 1951, **71**(7, Whole No. 436).

Erlenmeyer-Kimling, L. Gene-environment interactions and the variability of behavior. In L. Ehrman, G. Omenn, & E. Caspair (Eds.), *Genetics, environment and behavior.* New York: Academic Press, 1972.

Escalona, S. C. *The roots of individuality.* Chicago: Aldine, 1968.

Gesell, A., & Ilg, F. L. *Infant and child in the culture of today.* New York: Harper & Bros., 1943.

Gottlieb, G. The role of experience in the development of behavior in the nervous system. In G. Gottlieb (Ed.), *Studies in the development of behavior and the nervous system.* Vol. **3.** *Development and neural and behavioral specificity.* New York: Academic Press, 1976.

Grotevant, H. D., Scarr, S., & Weinberg, R. A. Patterns of interest similarity in adoptive and biological families. *Journal of Personality and Social Psychology,* 1977, **35,** 667–676.

Hunt, J. McV. *Intelligence and experience.* New York: Ronald, 1961.

Hunt, J. McV. *Early psychological development and experience.* Worcester, Mass.: Clark University Press, 1980.

Juel-Nielsen, N. *Individual and environment: Monozygotic twins reared apart.* New York: International Universities Press, 1980.

Kamin, L. J. *The science and politics of IQ.* Potomac, Md.: Erlbaum, 1974.

Lytton, H. *Parent-child interaction: The socialization process observed in twin and single families.* New York: Plenum, 1980.

McCall, R. B. Nature-nurture and the two realms of development: A proposed integration with respect to mental development. *Child Development,* 1981, **52,** 1–12.

McCartney, K., Scarr, S., Phillips, D., Grajek, S., & Schwarz, J. C. Environmental differences among day care centers and their effects on children's development. In E. F. Zigler & E. W. Gordon (Eds.), *Day care: Scientific and social policy issues.* Boston: Auburn House, 1981.

Maccoby, E. E. *Social development.* New York: Harcourt, Brace, Jovanovich, 1980.

Matheny, A. P., Jr., Wilson, R. S., Dolan, A. B., & Krantz, J. Z. Behavioral contrasts in twinships: Stability and patterns of differences in childhood. *Child Development,* 1981, **52,** 579–598.

Murstein, B. I. Physical attractiveness and marital choice. *Journal of Personality and Social Psychology,* 1972, **22,** 8–12.

Nelson, K. Structure and strategy in learning to talk. *Monographs of the Society for Research in Child Development,* 1973, **38**(1–2, Serial No. 149).

Nerlove, S. B., & Snipper, A. S. Cognitive consequences of cultural opportunity. In R. H. Munroe, R. L. Munroe, & B. B. Whiting (Eds.), *Handbook of cross-cultural human development.* New York: Garland, 1981.

Newman, H. G., Freeman, F. N., & Holzinger, K. J. *Twins: A study of heredity and environment.* Chicago: University of Chicago Press, 1937.

Piaget, J. The psychogenesis of knowledge and its epistemological significance. In M. Piattelli-Palmarini (Ed.), *Language and learning: The debate between Jean Piaget and Noam Chomsky.* Cambridge, Mass.: Harvard University Press, 1980.

Plomin, R., DeFries, J. C., & Loehlin, J. C. Genotype-environment interaction and correlation in the analysis of human behavior. *Psychological Bulletin,* 1977, **84,** 309–322.

Ramey, C. T., & Haskins, R. The modification of intelligence through early experience. *Intelligence,* 1981, **5,** 5–19.

Scarr, S. *IQ: Race, social class and individual differences, new studies of old problems.* Hillsdale, N.J.: Erlbaum, 1981.

Scarr, S., & Carter-Saltzman, L. Twin method: Defense of a critical assumption. *Behavior Genetics,* 1980, **9,** 527–542.

Scarr, S., & Kidd, K. K. Behavior genetics. In M. Haith & J. Campos (Eds.), *Manual of child psychology: Infancy and the biology of development.* (Vol. 2). New York: Wiley, in press.

Scarr, S., Webber, P. L., Weinberg, R. A., & Wittig, M. A. Personality resemblance among adolescents and their parents in biologically-related and adoptive families. *Journal of Personality and Social Psychology,* 1981, **40,** 885–898.

Scarr, S., & Weinberg, R. A. IQ test performance of black children adopted by white families. *American Psychologist,* 1976, **31,** 726–739.

Scarr, S., & Weinberg, R. A. Intellectual similarities within families of both adopted and biological children. *Intelligence,* 1977, **1**(2), 170–191.

Scarr, S., & Weinberg, R. A. The influence of "family background" on intellectual attainment. *American Sociological Review,* 1978, **43,** 674–692.

Scarr, S., & Weinberg, R. A. The Minnesota adoption studies: Genetic differences and malleability. *Child Development,* in this issue.

Scarr-Salapatek, S. An evolutionary perspective on infant intelligence. In M. Lewis (Ed.), *Origins of intelligence: Infancy and early childhood.* N.Y.: Plenum, 1976.

Shields, J. *Monozygotic twins brought up apart and brought up together.* London: Oxford University Press, 1962.

Waddington, C. H. *New patterns in genetics and development.* New York: Columbia University Press, 1962.

Watson, E. H., & Lowrey, G. H. *Growth and development of children.* Chicago: Year Book Medical Publishers, 1967.

[8]

Genetic influences on measures of the environment: a systematic review

KENNETH S. KENDLER[1,2*] AND JESSICA H. BAKER[1,3]

[1] Virginia Institute for Psychiatric and Behavioral Genetics, Department of Psychiatry, Medical College of Virginia of Virginia Commonwealth University, Richmond, VA, USA; [2] Department of Human Genetics, Virginia Commonwealth University, Richmond, VA, USA; [3] Department of Psychology, Virginia Commonwealth University, Richmond, VA, USA

ABSTRACT

Background. Traditional models of psychiatric epidemiology often assume that the relationship between individuals and their environment is unidirectional, from environment to person. Accumulating evidence from developmental and genetic studies has made this perspective increasingly untenable.

Method. Literature search using Medline, PsycINFO, article references and contact with experts to identify all papers examining the heritability of measures of environments of relevance to psychiatry/psychology.

Results. We identified 55 independent studies organized into seven categories: general and specific stressful life events (SLEs), parenting as reported by child, parenting reported by parent, family environment, social support, peer interactions, and marital quality. Thirty-five environmental measures in these categories were examined by at least two studies and produced weighted heritability estimates ranging from 7% to 39%, with most falling between 15% and 35%. The weighted heritability for all environmental measures in all studies was 27%. The weighted heritability for environmental measures by rating method was: self-report 29%, informant report 26%, and direct rater or videotape observation (typically examining 10 min of behavior) 14%.

Conclusion. Genetic influences on measures of the environment are pervasive in extent and modest to moderate in impact. These findings largely reflect 'actual behavior' rather than 'only perceptions'. Etiologic models for psychiatric illness need to account for the non-trivial influences of genetic factors on environmental experiences.

INTRODUCTION

In traditional psychiatric epidemiological models of disease etiology, the causal relationship is conceptualized as moving from the environment to the organism. However, the unidirectionality of this association has been increasingly questioned. In the developmental literature, it is now

* Address for correspondence: Kenneth Kendler, M.D., Virginia Commonwealth University, Virginia Institute for Psychiatric and Behavioral Genetics, Box 980126, Richmond, VA 23298-0126, USA.
(Email: Kendler@vcu.edu)

widely accepted that organisms both impact on and are impacted by their environment (Bell, 1968; Wachs & Plomin, 1991).

Genetic approaches can provide valuable information about the nature of the relationship between individuals and their environment. Many important aspects of human behavior are significantly influenced by genetic factors (Plomin et al. 2003; Kendler & Eaves, 2005; Kendler & Prescott, 2006). If the association between individuals and their environment solely takes the form of environment→person, then genes ought to have no influence on environmental exposures and the heritability of environment experiences should be zero. However, if an individual's own behavior impacts on the environmental exposures and if the relevant aspect of behavior is itself subject to genetic influences, then these environmental measures ought to be heritable.

The concept that individuals play an active role in selecting, modifying and constructing their environment is widely accepted in evolutionary biology (Dawkins, 1982; Odling-Smee *et al.* 2003). In his book *The Extended Phenotype*, Dawkins (1982) provides many examples of genes that 'extend' their phenotype outside the skin of the organism that possesses them. In what has been termed 'niche construction', animals such as beavers, weaver birds and termites modify their physical environment through building dams or constructing nursery environments for their offspring (Odling-Smee *et al.* 2003). In addition to effects on the physical environment, in social animals, genes can impact on key aspects of the social environment such as parent–offspring, mate and adult–peer relationships. In the evolutionary genetics literature, this is called 'indirect genetic effects' (Agrawal *et al.* 2001). Studies in model organisms have found significant genetic effects on a wide range of behaviors influencing the physical and social environment, including nest construction, selection of micro-environments, maternal and affiliative behaviors, infant behaviors that communicate distress to the mother and intra-species aggression (Kendler & Greenspan, 2006). Plomin *et al.* (1977) distinguished between passive, reactive and active forms of genetic influence on environmental measures, or as they termed it: 'genotype–environment correlation'.

In this paper, we review systematically, for the first time to our knowledge, research that uses human genetically informative samples to examine the heritability of measures of the environment, focusing on those environmental constructs of etiological importance for psychiatric and drug use disorders. (Heritability is defined as the proportion of individual differences for a trait in a particular population that results from inter-individual genetic differences.) Examining the heritability of the environmental exposure, which has been variously called

gene–environment covariance, gene–environment correlation or genetic control of exposure to the environment (Kendler & Eaves, 1986), is of interest to the field of mental health because it provides insight into the nature of the causal relationship between humans and their social and physical surroundings.

METHOD

We began with literature searches conducted in Medline and PsycINFO. Search terms included 'twin' or 'genetic' along with: 'stressful life events', 'social support', 'friendship', 'marriage', 'trauma/traumatic', 'parenting', 'peer deviance', 'peer relationship', 'negative life event' and 'parent child relationship'. A blanket search was also conducted with only the terms 'stressful life event' and 'social support' in an effort to ensure that no relevant studies were missed. Next, an extensive review of the references of relevant articles was carried out. Finally, a preliminary list of references was emailed to prominent researchers in their field for review.

Articles were included in this review if they included a methodological design that estimated the genetic influences on an environmental variable. We identified studies using twin, adoption and step-family designs. We only included published articles where the primary language was English and the environment under investigation had been related to risk for psychiatric disorders and/or psychological health. We found at least two studies that examined five broad categories of the environment: social support, parenting behavior, family environment, peer interactions, and stressful life events (SLEs). In general, for a specific variable to be included in this review, we had to identify two articles that examined its heritability. However, exceptions to this rule were made if the article was of particular interest or there were a limited number of studies available in a specific category. To implement this rule it was necessary to make judgments as to whether variables from separate studies were measuring comparable constructs. For example, within the category of SLEs, we concluded that controllable and dependent events (where dependent is defined as probably resulting from the respondent's own behavior), uncontrollable and independent events (where dependent is defined as probably unrelated to the respondent's own behavior), negative and undesirable events and positive and desirable events were sufficiently similar to be combined together. For parenting behavior, warmth, positivity and acceptance, authoritarianism and control, and anger and negativity were treated as equivalent. Finally, within peer interactions, general peer delinquency and peer substance use were sufficiently similar to be examined together. We use the term 'general' SLEs to refer to those events that were typically assessed in a general life event inventory while 'specific' SLEs (such as divorce or combat exposure) were assessed in studies focusing on that single variable.

Although it would have been ideal to conduct formal meta-analyses of this literature, this was not feasible. Very few primary reports provided confidence intervals (or standard errors) of the estimates or primary data (i.e. contingency tables or correlations).

When multiple reports were found from the same data set, we used the one judged most relevant. The exception to this general rule comes within the category of social support, where three different studies from the Virginia Twin Registry (VTR) are reported. Each of these three studies uses a different interview wave for analyses but on overlapping twin subjects. Because of this, a summary statistic was calculated for the overlapping variables between these three VTR studies. Once all relevant articles were obtained, a weighted mean heritability, with the weights based on the sample size, was calculated for those variables that were assessed in at least two studies and the results are summarized in Table 1. We also prepared for this review nine Appendix tables, termed A1 to A9, that provide a study by study summary. These tables are available in the online version of this paper and from our website (www.vipbg.vcu. edu/~jbaker).

RESULTS

General SLEs

Ten twin studies were identified that examined the heritability of general SLEs (Wierzbicki, 1989; Plomin *et al.* 1990; Kendler *et al.* 1993, 1999; Billig *et al.* 1996; Foley *et al.* 1996; Thapar & McGuffin, 1996; Saudino *et al.* 1997;

Bolinskey *et al.* 2004; Wang *et al.* 2005). Six of these studies reported on the heritability of total SLEs (Wierzbicki, 1989; Plomin *et al.* 1990; Kendler *et al.* 1993; Thapar & McGuffin, 1996, Bolinskey *et al.* 2004; Wang *et al.* 2005). In five of these studies (Wierzbicki, 1989; Plomin *et al.* 1990; Kendler *et al.* 1993; Bolinskey *et al.* 2004; Wang *et al.* 2005), the heritabilities ranged from 24 % to 47 %. The weighted mean across all six studies was 28 % (Table 1).

We identified four studies that reported heritabilities of negative and positive SLEs, with the latter being slightly more heritable (Wierzbicki, 1989; Plomin *et al.* 1990; Thapar & McGuffin, 1996; Saudino *et al.* 1997). Seven and five studies respectively examined independent (Plomin *et al.* 1990; Billig *et al.* 1996; Foley *et al.* 1996; Thapar & McGuffin, 1996; Saudino *et al.* 1997; Kendler *et al.* 1999; Bolinskey *et al.* 2004) and dependent SLEs (Plomin *et al.* 1990; Billig *et al.* 1996; Foley *et al.* 1996; Kendler *et al.* 1999; Bolinskey *et al.* 2004). Weighted mean heritabilities were substantially lower for the independent (17 %) than for the dependent stressful events (31 %).

Specific life events

We identified six studies, reviewed in Table A2, that examined the heritability of specific life events (McGue & Lykken, 1992; Lyons *et al.* 1993; Jang *et al.* 2001; Stein *et al.* 2002; Johnson *et al.* 2004; Middeldorp *et al.* 2005). Four of these studies examined the propensity of individuals to select themselves into traumatic situations: three in civilian life (Jang *et al.* 2001; Stein *et al.* 2002; Middeldorp *et al.* 2005) and one in the Vietnam War (Lyons *et al.* 1993). Reported heritabilities ranged from 20 % to 63 %, with a weighted mean of 36 %. Two studies examined the heritability of divorce, reporting heritabilities of 29 % (Middeldorp *et al.* 2005) and 53 % (McGue & Lykken, 1992) with a weighted mean of 35 %. Two studies reported heritabilities of various non-assaultive traumas (Jang *et al.* 2001; Stein *et al.* 2002) that were low, estimated at 7 %.

Parenting behavior

We located a total of 19 individual studies that examined the heritability of various aspects of the parent–child relationship (Rowe, 1981, 1983; Rende *et al.* 1992; Perusse *et al.* 1994;

Table 1. *The weighted mean heritability across studies of various aspects of the environment*

Constructs	No. studies	Studies included	Total N	Weighted mean
Stressful life events				
Total life events	6	Wierzbicki, 1989; Plomin et al. 1990; Kendler et al. 1993; Thapar & McGuffin, 1996; Bolinskey et al. 2004; Wang et al. 2005	6197	0·28
Negative life events	3	Plomin et al. 1990; Wierzbicki, 1989; Thapar & McGuffin, 1996	731	0·39
Positive life events	3	Plomin et al. 1990; Wierzbicki, 1989; Thapar & McGuffin, 1996	731	0·34
Independent life events	6	Plomin et al. 1990; Billig et al. 1996; Thapar & McGuffin, 1996; Foley et al. 1996; Kendler et al. 1999; Bolinskey et al. 2004	5056	0·17
Dependent life events	5	Plomin et al. 1990; Billig et al. 1996; Foley et al. 1996; Kendler et al. 1999; Bolinskey et al. 2004	4459	0·31
Selection into trauma	4	Lyons et al. 1993; Jang et al. 2001; Stein et al. 2002; Middeldorp et al. 2005	6558	0·36
Selection into non-assaultive trauma	2	Jang et al. 2001; Stein et al. 2002	569	0·07
Divorce	2	McGue & Lykken, 1992; Middeldorp et al. 2005	5692	0·35
Child-based reports of parenting behavior				
Maternal warmth	7	Rowe, 1981; Rende et al. 1992; Plomin et al. 1994; O'Connor et al. 1995; Kendler, 1996; Lichtenstein et al. 2003; Neiderhiser et al. 2004	3446	0·37
Paternal warmth	5	Rowe, 1981; Plomin et al. 1994; O'Connor et al. 1995; Kendler, 1996; Lichtenstein et al. 2003	2664	0·34
Maternal control	5	Rende et al. 1992; O'Connor et al. 1995; Kendler, 1996; Lichtenstein et al. 2003; Neiderhiser et al. 2004	2330	0·15
Paternal control	3	O'Connor et al. 1995; Kendler, 1996; Lichtenstein et al. 2003	1448	0·17
Paternal negativity	2	Plomin et al. 1994; O'Connor et al. 1995	377	0·12
Paternal protectiveness	2	Kendler, 1996; Lichtenstein et al. 2003	2198	0·20
Maternal protectiveness	2	Kendler, 1996; Lichtenstein et al. 2003	2198	0·26
Parent-based reports of parenting behavior				
Parental warmth	4	Perusse et al. 1994; Kendler, 1996; Deater-Deckard et al. 1999; Deater-Deckard, 2000	1690	0·35
Parental control	3	Kendler, 1996; Losoya et al. 1997; Spinath & O'Connor, 2003	433	0·20
Parental protectiveness	3	Perusse et al. 1994; Kendler, 1996; Spinath & O'Connor, 2003	1477	0·23
Parental negativity	7	O'Connor et al. 1995; Losoya et al. 1997; Deater-Deckard et al. 1999, 2001; Deater-Deckard, 2000; Neiderhiser et al. 2004; Boivin et al. 2005	4766	0·19
Family environment				
Cohesion/connectedness	4	Plomin et al. 1988, 1989; Jacobson & Rowe, 1999; Jang et al. 2001	1911	0·24
Conflict	3	Plomin et al. 1988, 1989; Jacobson & Rowe, 1999	1428	0·30
Organization	3	Plomin et al. 1988, 1989; Jacobson & Rowe, 1999	1428	0·25
Expressiveness	3	Plomin et al. 1988, 1989; Jacobson & Rowe, 1999	1428	0·24
Active	3	Plomin et al. 1988, 1989; Jacobson & Rowe, 1999	1428	0·26
Control	3	Plomin et al. 1988, 1989; Jacobson & Rowe, 1999	1428	0·18
Social support				
Friend problem	2	Kendler et al. 1997; Agrawal et al. 2002	2860	0·23
Relative problem	2	Kendler et al. 1997; Agrawal et al. 2002	2860	0·38
Friend support	3	Kessler et al. 1992; Kendler et al. 1997; Agrawal et al. 2002	4502	0·17
Relative support	3	Kessler et al. 1992; Kendler et al. 1997; Agrawal et al. 2002	4502	0·31
Confidants	3	Kessler et al. 1992; Kendler et al. 1997; Agrawal et al. 2002	4502	0·31
Social integration	2	Kendler et al. 1997; Agrawal et al. 2002	2860	0·31

Peer interactions				
Peer deviance	4	Iervolino et al. 2002; Rose, 2002; White et al. 2003; Walden et al. 2004	3012	0·21
Marital quality				
Marital satisfaction	2	Spotts et al. 2004b, 2005	752	0·28
Marital conflict	2	Spotts et al. 2005; Spotts, unpublished data	1659	0·13
Marital warmth	3	Spotts et al. 2004b, 2005; Spotts, unpublished data	1985	0·17
Observer/informant reports				
Maternal control	3	Rende et al. 1992; O'Connor et al. 1995; Neiderhiser et al. 2004	639	0·12
Maternal affection	4	Rende et al. 1992; O'Connor et al. 1995; Kendler, 1996; Deater-Deckard, 2000; Neiderhiser et al. 2004	1695	0·14
Maternal negativity	3	O'Connor et al. 1995; Deater-Deckard, 2000; Neiderhiser et al. 2004	635	0·06
Heritability of self-report measures	197 constructs	All studies that gave sample size information	124464	0·29
Heritability of observer-report measures	42 constructs	All studies that gave sample size information	9032	0·14
Heritability of informant-report measures	18 constructs	All studies that gave sample size information	8856	0·26
Heritability of all non-self-report measures	60 constructs	All studies that gave sample size information	16210	0·21
Heritability of all environmental measures	265 constructs	All studies that gave sample size information	141460	0·27

Plomin et al. 1994; O'Connor et al. 1995; Kendler, 1996; Elkins et al. 1997; Losoya et al. 1997; Deater-Deckard et al. 1999, 2001; Deater-Deckard, 2000; Wade & Kendler, 2000; Lichtenstein et al. 2003; Spinath & O'Connor, 2003; Neiderhiser et al. 2004; Walden et al. 2004; Boivin et al. 2005; Herndon et al. 2005). We divided them into studies that examined this relationship from the perspective of the child *versus* from the perspective of the parent. While child-based designs assess the role of genetic factors in the *elicitation* of parental behavior, parent-based designs evaluate how genes impact on the *provision* of parental care. The results are shown in Tables A3–A5.

Child-based designs

As outlined in Tables A3 and A4, we identified 12 studies examining the heritability of parental behavior through child reports. Two or more studies were found that reported on maternal warmth (Rowe, 1981; Rende et al. 1992; Plomin et al. 1994; O'Connor et al. 1995; Kendler, 1996; Lichtenstein et al. 2003; Neiderhiser et al. 2004), paternal warmth (Rowe, 1981; Plomin et al. 1994; O'Connor et al. 1995; Kendler, 1996; Lichtenstein et al. 2003), maternal control (Rende et al. 1992; Kendler, 1996; O'Connor et al. 1998; Lichtenstein et al. 2003; Neiderhiser et al. 2004), paternal control (O'Connor et al. 1995; Kendler, 1996; Lichtenstein et al. 2003), paternal negativity (Plomin et al. 1994; O'Connor et al. 1995), and paternal and maternal protectiveness (Kendler, 1996; Lichtenstein et al. 2003). The weighted heritabilities were highest for measures of parental warmth (34–37%), intermediate for measures of protectiveness (20–26%) and lowest for measures of control and negativity (12–17%).

Parent-based designs

As outlined in Table A4, 10 studies were identified that examined the heritability of parental behavior from parent reports (Perusse et al. 1994; Plomin et al. 1994; Kendler, 1996; Losoya et al. 1997; Deater-Deckard et al. 1999, 2001; Deater-Deckard, 2000; Spinath & O'Connor, 2003; Neiderhiser et al. 2004; Boivin et al. 2005). Two or more studies were found that reported on parental warmth (Perusse et al. 1994; Kendler, 1996; Deater-Deckard et al. 1999,

2001), control (Kendler, 1996; Losoya *et al.* 1997; Spinath & O'Connor, 2003), protectiveness (Perusse *et al.* 1994; Kendler, 1996; Spinath & O'Connor, 2003) and negativity (O'Connor *et al.* 1995; Losoya *et al.* 1997; Deater-Deckard *et al.* 1999, 2001; Deater-Deckard, 2000; Neiderhiser *et al.* 2004; Boivin *et al.* 2005). As shown in Table 1, heritability was substantially higher for the dimension of parental warmth (35%) than for the remaining dimensions of parental behavior (19–23%).

Family environment

We located seven studies that examined various aspects of the environment either in the family of origin or in the current family (Plomin *et al.* 1988, 1989; Hur & Bouchard, 1995; Deater-Deckard *et al.* 1999; Jacobson & Rowe, 1999; Jang *et al.* 2001; Herndon *et al.* 2005) (Table A6). From these reports, we were able to extract weighted estimates for the heritability of six dimensions of family functioning: cohesion (Plomin *et al.* 1988, 1989; Jacobson & Rowe, 1999; Jang *et al.* 2001), conflict (Plomin *et al.* 1988, 1989; Jang *et al.* 2001), organization (Plomin *et al.* 1988, 1989; Jang *et al.* 2001), expressiveness (Plomin *et al.* 1988, 1989; Jang *et al.* 2001), activity (Plomin *et al.* 1988, 1989; Jang *et al.* 2001) and control (Plomin *et al.* 1988, 1989; Jang *et al.* 2001). These estimates were relatively similar across these constructs, varying from 18% to 30%.

Social support

We identified five studies that examined genetic influences on social support (Table A7) (Bergeman *et al.* 1990; Kessler *et al.* 1992; Kendler *et al.* 1997; Agrawal *et al.* 2002; Raynor *et al.* 2002). Three studies come from different interviews with the VTR, from which we could construct six overlapping measures (Kessler *et al.* 1992; Kendler *et al.* 1997; Agrawal *et al.* 2002): friend problems, relative problems, relative support, friend support, confidants, and social integration. Weighted means for these measures ranged from 17% to 38%. Two other studies report heritabilities for constructs closely related to social support that were broadly consistent with those estimated from the VTR samples (Bergeman *et al.* 1990; Raynor *et al.* 2002).

Peer interactions

We found six studies examining the heritability of various aspects of peer relationships (Table A8) (Manke *et al.* 1995; Iervolino *et al.* 2002; Rose, 2002; White *et al.* 2003; Walden *et al.* 2004; Rushton & Bons, 2005). Four studies assessed peer deviancy (Iervolino *et al.* 2002; Rose, 2002; White *et al.* 2003; Walden *et al.* 2004), with a weighted heritability estimate of 21%. Two other studies examined other aspects of friend relationships, suggesting that genetic factors had a significant impact on the chances of having negative interactions with friends (Manke *et al.* 1995) and choosing friends similar to oneself (Rushton & Bons, 2005).

Marital quality

We located four studies that assessed genetic influences on various aspects of marital relationships (Table A9) (Spotts *et al.* 2004 *a*, *b*, 2005; Spotts *et al.* in press). Two or more reports were found that examined three marital dimensions: satisfaction, conflict and warmth. Weighted heritabilities for these constructs ranged from 13% to 28%.

Summary results

The articles we reviewed in Tables A1 to A9 included a total of 265 variables and over 100 000 assessments (although multiple assessments were often performed on the same subject). The total weighted mean heritability for all these environmental measures was 27%.

DISCUSSION

The literature we have reviewed suggests that genetic influences on measures of the environment are pervasive in extent and modest to moderate in impact. Every aspect of the environment that we were able to examine was significantly influenced by genetic factors. However, the role of genetic influences on these behaviors was far from overwhelming. The weighted heritability estimates for the 35 constructs that were assessed in at least two studies ranged from 7% to 39%, with most falling between 15% and 35%. These results are consistent with extensive evidence, from non-genetically informative studies, of 'person–environment covariance' (see, for example, Wachs, 1992, ch. 7).

Three trends in these summary results are noteworthy. First, SLEs that are largely dependent on an individual's own behavior are more heritable than 'fateful' events independent of the individual's actions. Second, whether reported by the parent or the child, parenting behavior reflecting the positive emotional quality of the parent–child relationship is more heritable that parenting behavior related to disciplinary styles (e.g. control or protectiveness). This pattern might arise because positive emotionality in parent–child relationships is strongly impacted by the genetically influenced temperament of both parties. By contrast, disciplinary style may be more like a social attitude – an approach towards parenting learned by the parent during their own life experiences and which they attempt to apply equally to all their children.

Third, consistent with expectation, genes from each party in a relationship appear to contribute to its quality. This can be best seen in the parent–child relationship, where the quality of that relationship appears to be impacted in similar ways by the genotype of the parent and the genotype of the child. These results suggest one obvious reason why the heritabilities of interpersonal environments are modest. That is, the quality of an interpersonal relationship is impacted on by at least two genotypes – that of the informant and that of the other individual. Our assessments only measure the former, while the latter typically comes out in the analyses as 'environment'.

Methodological concerns

These results should be interpreted in the context of four major methodological concerns. First, in nearly all of the studies included in this review, measures of the environment were obtained at a single point in time. If we instead examined the stable aspects of experiences, would the heritability of the environment increase? We know of two studies that address this question. Foley et al. (1996) examined SLEs reported in the previous 12 months at two interviews separated by at least a year. Using a twin 'measurement model', they were able to separate the contribution of random or occasion-specific events on SLEs from those that are stable over time. The model can then partition the influences on the stable liability to

SLEs into its genetic and environmental components. Their best-fitting model indicated that stable individual differences were most important for personal SLEs and only make a small contribution to network events. Of particular interest, they found that about 55% of the variation in personal SLEs results from occasion-specific effects or error. However, the heritability of the stable liability to personal SLEs was 65%. This was approximately twice as high as the standard heritability for SLEs calculated from the same data. That is, correcting for transient environmental and measurement effects, genetic factors were quite important in discriminating those individuals with a stable tendency to have few *versus* large numbers of SLEs.

Using similar methods, Kendler (1997) examined social support assessed twice 5 years apart. Levels of social support were moderately stable over time. The heritability of the temporally stable aspects of social support (which ranged from about 45% to 75%) was more than twice as great as that obtained by measurements on one occasion. These two studies suggest that studies examining one 'snapshot' of the environment might underestimate genetic contributions to environmental experiences. Genetic factors are likely to strongly influence the temporally stable patterns of our environmental interactions.

The second major methodological concern is that a substantial majority of the studies reviewed relied on self-report. Could these studies have examined the heritability of the *perception* of the environment rather than heritability of the actual environmental experiences themselves? We have the ability to address this question because a substantial number of studies that we reviewed assessed the environment by direct observation of behavior (either 'live' or by videotape) or by informant reports, most commonly from relatives. All of these studies are individually summarized in Table 2. As is clear from Table 2, heritability estimates derived from direct behavioral observation are on average substantially lower than those obtained using other assessment methods. By contrast, estimates of heritability obtain from informants appear to be broadly similar in magnitude to that outlined from all sources in Tables 1 and A1–A9.

Table 2.   *Non-self-report measures of the environment*

Study/Construct	Construct assessment	N	h^2
Rende *et al.* (1992)		124	
Maternal control	Observer		0·31
Maternal affection	Observer		0·00
Maternal attention	Observer		0·61
Responsiveness	Observer		0·00
Manke *et al.* (1995)		190	
Delinquency orientation	Maternal report		0·71
Delinquency orientation	Paternal report		0·49
O'Connor *et al.* (1995)			
Adolescent's behavior towards mother		186	
Warmth	Observer		0·25
Assertive	Observer		0·27
Positive mood	Observer		0·11
Control	Observer		0·33
Anger	Observer		0·27
Adolescent's behavior towards father		186	
Warmth	Observer		0·33
Assertive	Observer		0·34
Positive control	Observer		0·35
Control	Observer		0·10
Anger	Observer		0·29
Mother's behavior towards adolescent		186	
Warmth	Observer		0·07
Assertive	Observer		0·00
Positive mood	Observer		0·28
Control	Observer		0·13
Monitoring	Observer		0·08
Anger	Observer		0·00
Father's behavior towards adolescent		186	
Warmth	Observer		0·15
Assertive	Observer		0·00
Positive mood	Observer		0·02
Control	Observer		0·15
Monitoring	Observer		0·18
Anger	Observer		0·00
Kendler (1996)		937	
Paternal warmth	Co-twin report		0·20
Maternal warmth	Co-twin report		0·33
Paternal protectiveness	Co-twin report		0·17
Maternal protectiveness	Co-twin report		0·29
Paternal authoritarianism	Co-twin report		0·46
Maternal authoritarianism	Co-twin report		0·26
Thapar & McGuffin (1996)			
SLE (females)	Parent report	109	0·00
SLE (males)	Parent report	89	0·00
Independent SLE (females)	Parent report	109	0·15
Independent SLE (males)	Parent report	89	0·00
Negative impact events (females)	Parent report	109	0·54
Negative impact events (males)	Parent report	89	0·16
Positive impact events (females)	Parent report	109	0·74
Positive impact events (males)	Parent report	89	0·47
Deater-Deckard (2000)		120	
Maternal negative affect	Observer		0·06
Maternal positive affect	Observer		0·00
Negative control	Observer		0·00
Positive control	Observer		0·00
Responsiveness	Observer		0·49
Child difficult behavior	Observer		0·00
Child conduct problems	Parent report		0·59
Neiderhiser *et al.* (2004)			
Maternal positivity (TM)	Observer	326	0·00
Maternal negativity (TM)	Observer	326	0·09
Maternal control (TM)	Observer	326	0·00

Table 2 (*cont.*)

Study/Construct	Construct assessment	N	h²
Maternal positivity (NEAD)	Observer	138	0·23
Maternal negativity (NEAD)	Observer	138	0·00
Maternal control (NEAD)	Observer	138	0·12
Walden *et al.* (2004)		690	
Peer deviance	Teacher report		0·00
Number of substances used	Maternal report		0·10
Number of substances used	Co-twin report		0·25
Spotts *et al.* (2005)		326	
Wives' marital conflict	Observer		0·02
Wives' marital warmth	Observer		0·21

SLE, Stressful life event; TM, Twin Moms Project; NEAD, Non-shared Environment and Adolescent Development.

To obtain a crude quantitative assessment of the impact of different measurement methods, we calculated a weighted heritability for all of our environmental measures obtained by these three assessment methods: self-report (197 variables) 29%, observer report (42 variables) 14%, and informant report (18 variables) 26%. Only five of the studies we reviewed (Plomin *et al.* 1994; Kendler, 1996; Thapar & McGuffin, 1996; Lichtenstein *et al.* 2003; Neiderhiser *et al.* 2004) included heritability estimates of similar environmental measures by two of these three methods. Similar to what we found when aggregating across a wide variety of environmental measures, in these studies, which permit a more controlled comparison, self-report measures had the highest heritabilities, observer report the least, and informant reports had intermediate results typically only modestly less than those obtained by self-report.

These results provide strong evidence that our estimates of the heritability of the environment are not solely the result of subjective perceptions but reflect 'real' environmental experiences. When the environment of an individual is judged by an external informant, the estimated heritability is only slightly less than when assessed by the individual her/himself. This would suggest that reporting bias contributes only modestly to the estimated heritability of the environment. However, when assessed by direct observation, the heritability of the environment is substantially less than when obtained from self- or informant-report. There are two plausible interpretations of this finding. Self- and informant-reports could share consistent biases that inflate

heritability estimates. Alternatively, the heritabilities obtained from direct observation could be biased downwards because they sample such a small 'slice' of time compared to the two other assessment methods. With the exception of a single report (Rende *et al.* 1992), all the studies reviewed in Table 2 had a duration of observation of only 10 min. Given the two studies outlined above that showed the substantial gain in heritability when correcting for measurement error from self-report measures, it is likely that these very short sampling frames substantially increase the impact of 'error' and other short-term fluctuations. This in turn should result in a downward bias on heritability estimates, which are always limited by unreliability of measurement. We would suggest that the second of these two explanations is the more plausible but this question can only be resolved definitively by further research. We conclude that while reporting bias almost certainly contributes to the evidence for heritability of measures of the environment, most of the findings in the literature probably reflect actual behaviors and not only perceptions.

The third major methodological concern was that we found very few studies that examined the heritability of the environment in a developmental context. One such report, by Elkins *et al.* (1997), shows the possible richness of this approach. In male twins aged 11 and 17, significant genetic influences were found on measures of parent–son conflict, regard, involvement, and overall support. Of particular interest, heritabilities were significantly higher in older twins, demonstrating increased genetic influence with age. These results, consistent with the prior proposal of Scarr and McCartney (1983), suggest that the heritability of the environment might increase during adolescence as individuals become more able to control and influence their environment. In accord with this prediction, we see, in male twins from the VTR, increasing heritability of peer group deviance from childhood through early adulthood (Kendler *et al.* unpublished observations).

The fourth methodological concern is that we relied solely on published reports. If there is a publication bias such that studies reporting higher heritability for environmental measures are more likely to be published than those reporting low or absent heritability, our aggregate heritability estimates will be biased upward.

Possible mediators of the genetic effects on the environment

Clearly, genetic factors do not, in any direct way, 'code' for specific environments. Of the possible mediators between genotype and environmental measures, by far the most studied has been personality, especially neuroticism and extraversion (e.g. Horwood & Fergusson, 1986; Fergusson & Horwood, 1987; Headey & Wearing, 1989; Poulton & Andrews, 1992; Magnus *et al.* 1993; Billig *et al.* 1996; Saudino *et al.* 1997; Krueger *et al.* 2003; Spinath & O'Connor, 2003). Shared genetic influences have been implicated between neuroticism and parenting (Spinath & O'Connor, 2003), while neuroticism scores have also been shown to significantly predict SLEs, the quality of interpersonal relationships (Kendler *et al.* 2003) and to predispose individuals to experiencing more negative life events (Magnus *et al.* 1993). By contrast, extraversion has been shown to significantly predict the occurrence of positive life events (Magnus *et al.* 1993) as well as to share common genetic variance with controllable and desirable life events (Saudino *et al.* 1997).

Implications

The results of this review have three major implications. First, these findings strongly support bidirectional models of person environment inter-relationships (Scarr & McCartney, 1983). Human beings actively create important aspects of their social environment and interpersonal relationships. Second, the results have crucial implications for how we understand gene action in psychiatry. With startling advances in molecular genetics, our field has turned increasingly towards reductionist models of 'inside the skin' gene effects. While such research approaches are likely to be very fruitful, they will not result in a complete understanding of the pathway from genes to disorders. To achieve that goal, it will be necessary to also consider 'outside the skin' pathways, where the impact of genes on disease risk is mediated through self-selection into pathogenic environments (Kendler, 2001). Third, standard heritability estimates cannot discriminate between inside and outside the skin pathways. Our results suggest that a non-trivial proportion of genetic effects assessed by twin and adoption studies for psychiatric and substance use disorders may involve selection into environmental adversity that then feeds back to increase disease risk.

NOTE

Supplementary material accompanies this paper on the Journal's website (http://journals.cambridge.org).

ACKNOWLEDGMENTS

This work was supported in part by NIH grants T32-DA-007027, MH-49492 and DA-11287. Robert Plomin, Nancy Pedersen and Michael Rutter provided helpful comments on earlier versions of this manuscript.

DECLARATION OF INTEREST

None.

REFERENCES

Agrawal, A., Brodie, E. & Wade, M. J. (2001). On indirect genetic effects in structured populations. *American Naturalist* **158**, 308–323.

Agrawal, A., Jacobson, K. C., Prescott, C. A. & Kendler, K. S. (2002). A twin study of sex differences in social support. *Psychological Medicine* **32**, 1155–1164.

Bell, R. Q. (1968). A reinterpretation of the direction of effects in studies of socialization. *Psychology Review* **75**, 81–95.

Bergeman, C. S., Plomin, R., Pedersen, N. L., McClearn, G. E. & Nesselroade, J. R. (1990). Genetic and environmental influences on social support: the Swedish Adoption/Twin Study of Aging. *Journal of Gerontology* **45**, 101–106.

Billig, J. P., Hershberger, S. L., Iacono, W. G. & McGue, M. (1996). Life events and personality in late adolescence: genetic and environmental relations. *Behavior Genetics* **26**, 543–554.

Boivin, M., Perusse, D., Dionne, G., Saysset, V., Zoccolillo, M., Tarabulsy, G. M., Tremblay, N. & Tremblay, R. E. (2005). The genetic–environmental etiology of parents' perceptions and self-assessed behaviours toward their 5-month-old infants in a large twin and singleton sample. *Journal of Child Psychology and Psychiatry* **46**, 612–630.

Bolinskey, P. K., Neale, M. C., Jacobson, K. C., Prescott, C. A. & Kendler, K. S. (2004). Sources of individual differences in stressful life event exposure in male and female twins. *Twin Research* **7**, 33–38.

Dawkins, R. (1982). *The Extended Phenotype: The Gene as the Unit of Selection.* Oxford University Press: Oxford.

Deater-Deckard, K. (2000). Parenting and child behavioral adjustment in early childhood: a quantitative genetic approach to studying family processes. *Child Development* **71**, 468–484.

Deater-Deckard, K., Dunn, J., O'Connor, T. G., Davies, L. & Golding, J. (2001). Using the stepfamily genetic design to examine gene–environment processes in child and family functioning. *Marriage and Family Review* **33**, 131–156.

Deater-Deckard, K., Fulker, D. W. & Plomin, R. (1999). A genetic study of the family environment in the transition to early adolescence. *Journal of Child Psychology and Psychiatry* **40**, 769–775.

Elkins, I. J., McGue, M. & Iacono, W. G. (1997). Genetic and environmental influences on parent–son relationships: evidence for increasing genetic influence during adolescence. *Developmental Psychology* **33**, 351–363.

Fergusson, D. M. & Horwood, L. J. (1987). Vulnerability to life events exposure. *Psychological Medicine* **17**, 739–749.

Foley, D. L., Neale, M. C. & Kendler, K. S. (1996). A longitudinal study of stressful life events assessed at interview with an epidemiological sample of adult twins: the basis of individual variation in event exposure. *Psychological Medicine* **26**, 1239–1252.

Headey, B. & Wearing, A. (1989). Personality, life events, and subjective well-being: toward a dynamic equilibrium model. *Journal of Personality and Social Psychology* **57**, 731–739.

Herndon, R. W., McGue, M., Krueger, R. F. & Iacono, W. G. (2005). Genetic and environmental influences on adolescents' perceptions of current family environment. *Behavior Genetics* **35**, 373–380.

Horwood, L. J. & Fergusson, D. M. (1986). Neuroticism, depression and life events: a structural equation model. *Social Psychiatry* **21**, 63–71.

Hur, Y. M. & Bouchard Jr., T. J. (1995). Genetic influences on perceptions of childhood family environment: a reared apart twin study. *Child Development* **66**, 330–345.

Iervolino, A. C., Pike, A., Manke, B., Reiss, D., Hetherington, E. M. & Plomin, R. (2002). Genetic and environmental influences in adolescent peer socialization: evidence from two genetically sensitive designs. *Child Development* **73**, 162–174.

Jacobson, K. C. & Rowe, D. C. (1999). Genetic and environmental influences on the relationships between family connectedness, school connectedness, and adolescent depressed mood: sex differences. *Developmental Psychology* **35**, 926–939.

Jang, K. L., Vernon, P. A., Livesley, W. J., Stein, M. B. & Wolf, H. (2001). Intra- and extra-familial influences on alcohol and drug misuse: a twin study of gene–environment correlation. *Addiction* **96**, 1307–1318.

Johnson, W., McGue, M., Krueger, R. F. & Bouchard Jr., T. J. (2004). Marriage and personality: a genetic analysis. *Journal of Personality and Social Psychology* **86**, 285–294.

Kendler, K. & Greenspan, R. J. (2006). The nature of genetic influences on behavior: lessons from 'simpler' organisms. *American Journal of Psychiatry* **163**, 1683–1694.

Kendler, K. S. (1996). Parenting: a genetic–epidemiologic perspective. *American Journal of Psychiatry* **153**, 11–20.

Kendler, K. S. (1997). Social support: a genetic–epidemiologic analysis. *American Journal of Psychiatry* **154**, 1398–1404.

Kendler, K. S. (2001). Twin studies of psychiatric illness: an update. *Archives of General Psychiatry* **58**, 1005–1014.

Kendler, K. S. & Eaves, L. J. (1986). Models for the joint effect of genotype and environment on liability to psychiatric illness. *American Journal of Psychiatry* **143**, 279–289.

Kendler, K. S. & Eaves L. J. (2005). *Psychiatric Genetics (Review of Psychiatry).* American Psychiatric Association: Washington, DC.

Kendler, K. S., Gardner, C. O. & Prescott, C. A. (2003). Personality and the experience of environmental adversity. *Psychological Medicine* **33**, 1193–1202.

Kendler, K. S., Karkowski, L. M. & Prescott, C. A. (1999). The assessment of dependence in the study of stressful life events: validation using a twin design. *Psychological Medicine* **29**, 1455–1460.

Kendler, K. S., Neale, M., Kessler, R., Heath, A. & Eaves, L. (1993). A twin study of recent life events and difficulties. *Archives of General Psychiatry* **50**, 789–796.

Kendler, K. S. & Prescott, C. A. (2006). *Genes, Environment, and Psychopathology: Understanding the Causes of Psychiatric and Substance Use Disorders.* Guilford Press: New York.

Kendler, K. S., Sham, P. C. & MacLean, C. J. (1997). The determinants of parenting: an epidemiological, multi-informant, retrospective study. *Psychological Medicine* **27**, 549–563.

Kessler, R. C., Kendler, K. S., Heath, A., Neale, M. C. & Eaves, L. J. (1992). Social support, depressed mood, and adjustment to stress: a genetic epidemiologic investigation. *Journal of Personality and Social Psychology* **62**, 257–272.

Krueger, R. F., Markon, K. E. & Bouchard Jr., T. J. (2003). The extended genotype: the heritability of personality accounts for the heritability of recalled family environments in twins reared apart. *Journal of Personality* **71**, 809–833.

Lichtenstein, P., Ganiban, J., Neiderhiser, J. M., Pedersen, N. L., Hansson, K., Cederblad, M., Elthammar, O. & Reiss, D. (2003). Remembered parental bonding in adult twins: genetic and environmental influences. *Behavior Genetics* **33**, 397–408.

Losoya, S. H., Callor, S., Rowe, D. C. & Goldsmith, H. H. (1997). Origins of familial similarity in parenting: a study of twins and adoptive siblings. *Developmental Psychology* **33**, 1012–1023.

Lyons, M. J., Goldberg, J., Eisen, S. A., True, W., Tsuang, M. T., Meyer, J. M. & Henderson, W. G. (1993). Do genes influence exposure to trauma? A twin study of combat. *American Journal of Medical Genetics* **48**, 22–27.

Magnus, K., Diener, E., Fujita, F. & Pavot, W. (1993). Extraversion and neuroticism as predictors of objective life events: a longitudinal analysis. *Journal of Personality and Social Psychology* **65**, 1046–1053.

Manke, B., McGuire, S., Reiss, D., Hetherington, E. M. & Plomin, R. (1995). Genetic contributions to adolescents extrafamilial social interactions – teachers, best friends, and peers. *Social Development* **4**, 238–256.

McGue, M. & Lykken, D. (1992). Genetic influence on risk of divorce. *Psychological Science* **3**, 368–373.

Middeldorp, C. M., Cath, D. C., Vink, J. M. & Boomsma, D. I. (2005). Twin and genetic effects on life events. *Twin Research and Human Genetics* **8**, 224–231.

Neiderhiser, J. M., Reiss, D., Pedersen, N. L., Lichtenstein, P., Spotts, E. L., Hansson, K., Cederblad, M. & Ellhammer, O. (2004). Genetic and environmental influences on mothering of adolescents: a comparison of two samples. *Developmental Psychology* **40**, 335–351.

O'Connor, T. G., Deater-Deckard, K., Fulker, D., Rutter, M. & Plomin, R. (1998). Genotype–environment correlations in late childhood and early adolescence: antisocial behavioral problems and coercive parenting. *Developmental Psychology* **34**, 970–981.

O'Connor, T. G., Hetherington, E. M., Reiss, D. & Plomin, R. (1995). A twin–sibling study of observed parent–adolescent interactions. *Child Development* **66**, 812–829.

Odling-Smee, F. J., Laland, K. N. & Feldman, M. W. (2003). *Niche Construction: The Neglected Process in Evolution.* Princeton University Press: Princeton.

Perusse, D., Neale, M. C., Heath, A. C. & Eaves, L. J. (1994). Human parental behavior: evidence for genetic influence and potential implication for gene–culture transmission. *Behavior Genetics* **24**, 327–335.

Plomin, R., DeFries, J. C., Craig, I. W. & McGuffin, P. (2003). *Behavioral Genetics in the Postgenomic Era.* American Psychological Association: Washington, DC.

626 *K. S. Kendler and J. H. Baker*

Plomin, R., DeFries, J. C. & Loehlin, J. C. (1977). Genotype–environment interaction and correlation in the analysis of human behavior. *Psychological Bulletin* **84**, 309–322.

Plomin, R., Lichtenstein, P., Pedersen, N. L., McClearn, G. E. & Nesselroade, J. R. (1990). Genetic influence on life events during the last half of the life span. *Psychology of Aging* **5**, 25–30.

Plomin, R., McClearn, G. E., Pedersen, N., Nesselroade, J. R. & Bergeman, C. S. (1988). Genetic influence on childhood family environment perceived retrospectively from the last half of the life span. *Developmental Psychology* **24**, 738–745.

Plomin, R., McClearn, G. E., Pedersen, N., Nesselroade, J. R. & Bergeman, C. S. (1989). Genetic influence on adult's ratings of their current family environment. *Journal of Marriage and the Family* **51**, 791–803.

Plomin, R., Reiss, D., Hetherington, E. M. & Howe, G. (1994). Nature and nurture: genetic contributions to measures of the family environment. *Developmental Psychology* **30**, 32–43.

Poulton, R. G. & Andrews, G. (1992). Personality as a cause of adverse life events. *Acta Psychiatrica Scandinavica* **85**, 35–38.

Raynor, D. A., Pogue-Geile, M. F., Kamarck, T. W., McCaffery, J. M. & Manuck, S. B. (2002). Covariation of psychosocial characteristics associated with cardiovascular disease: genetic and environmental influences. *Psychosomatic Medicine* **64**, 191–203.

Rende, R., Slomkowski, C., Stocker, C., Fulker, D. W. & Plomin, R. (1992). Genetic and environmental influences on maternal and sibling interaction in middle childhood: a sibling adoption study. *Developmental Psychology* **28**, 484–490.

Rose, R. J. (2002). How do adolescents select their friends? A behavior–genetic perspective. In *Paths to Successful Development: Personality in the Life Course* (ed. L. Pulkkinen and C. Avshalom), pp. 106–125. Cambridge University Press: Cambridge, UK.

Rowe, D. C. (1981). Environmental and genetic influences on dimensions of perceived parenting: a twin study. *Developmental Psychology* **17**, 203–208.

Rowe, D. C. (1983). A biometrical analysis of perceptions of family environment: a study of twin and singleton sibling kinships. *Child Development* **54**, 416–423.

Rushton, J. P. & Bons, T. A. (2005). Mate choice and friendship in twins: evidence for genetic similarity. *Psychological Science* **16**, 555–559.

Saudino, K. J., Pedersen, N. L., Lichtenstein, P., McClearn, G. E. & Plomin, R. (1997). Can personality explain genetic influences on life events? *Journal of Personality and Social Psychology* **72**, 196–206.

Scarr, S. & McCartney, K. (1983). How people make their own environments: a theory of genotype greater than environment effects. *Child Development* **54**, 424–435.

Spinath, F. M. & O'Connor, T. G. (2003). A behavioral genetic study of the overlap between personality and parenting. *Journal of Personality* **71**, 785–808.

Spotts, E. L., Prescott, C. P. & Kendler, K. S. (in press). Examining the origins of gender differences in marital quality: a behavioral genetic analysis. *Journal of Family Psychology*.

Spotts, E. L., Lichtenstein, P., Pedersen, N., Neiderhiser, J. M., Hansson, K., Cederblad, M. & Reiss, D. (2005). Personality and marital satisfaction: a behavioural genetic analysis. *European Journal of Personality* **19**, 205–227.

Spotts, E. L., Neiderhiser, J. M., Ganiban, J., Reiss, D., Lichtenstein, P., Hansson, K., Cederblad, M. & Pederson, N. L. (2004*a*). Accounting for depressive symptoms in women: a twin study of associations with interpersonal relationships. *Journal of Affective Disorders* **82**, 101–111.

Spotts, E. L., Neiderhiser, J. M., Towers, H., Hansson, K., Lichtenstein, P., Cederblad, M., Pederson, N. L. & Reiss, D. (2004*b*). Genetic and environmental influences on marital relationships. *Journal of Family Psychology* **18**, 107–119.

Stein, M. B., Jang, K. L., Taylor, S., Vernon, P. A. & Livesley, W. J. (2002). Genetic and environmental influences on trauma exposure and posttraumatic stress disorder symptoms: a twin study. *American Journal of Psychiatry* **159**, 1675–1681.

Thapar, A. & McGuffin, P. (1996). Genetic influences on life events in childhood. *Psychological Medicine* **26**, 813–820.

Wachs, T. D. (1992). *The Nature of Nurture*. Sage Publications, Inc.: Newbury Park, CA.

Wachs, T. D. & Plomin, R. E. (1991). *Conceptualization and Measurement of Organism–Environment Interaction*. American Psychological Association: Washington, DC.

Wade, T. D. & Kendler, K. S. (2000). The genetic epidemiology of parental discipline. *Psychological Medicine* **30**, 1303–1313.

Walden, B., McGue, M., Iacono, W. G., Burt, S. & Elkins, I. (2004). Identifying shared environment contributions to early substance use: the importance of peers versus parents. *Journal of Abnormal Psychology* **113**, 440–450.

Wang, X., Trivedi, R., Treiber, F. & Snieder, H. (2005). Genetic and environmental influences on anger expression, John Henryism, and stressful life events: the Georgia Cardiovascular Twin Study. *Psychosomatic Medicine* **67**, 16–23.

White, V. M., Hopper, J. L., Wearing, A. J. & Hill, D. J. (2003). The role of genes in tobacco smoking during adolescence and young adulthood: a multivariate behaviour genetic investigation. *Addiction* **98**, 1087–1100.

Wierzbicki, M. (1989). Twins' responses to pleasant, unpleasant, and life events. *Journal of Genetic Psychology* **150**, 135–145.

[9]

How social experiences influence the brain
Frances A Champagne and James P Curley

Social experiences throughout life influence gene expression and behavior, however, early in development these influences have a particularly profound effect. In mammals, mother–infant interactions are the primary source of social stimulation and result in long-term changes in offspring phenotype. This has previously been demonstrated in rodents and primates, however, recent studies in rats have advanced our understanding of how these influences are achieved at a mechanistic level, through epigenetic modification, and provide a model for studying the transmission of social behavior across generations. These studies emphasize the importance of a life-history approach to the study of brain development; incorporating information about genetic background, prenatal and postnatal maternal care received, and post-weaning social interactions of an individual, in addition to the social environment experienced by previous generations.

Addresses
Sub-Department of Animal Behaviour, University of Cambridge, High Street Madingley, Cambridge, CB3 8AA, UK

Corresponding author: Champagne, Frances A
(fac25@hermes.cam.ac.uk)

Introduction
Early in development, the parent–offspring relationship is critical for determining survival of offspring, with the quality of this relationship being the primary focus of research examining the impact of social experiences. In mammals, the mother is the principal caregiver, providing both nutritional resources and behavioral stimulation to offspring. Experimental paradigms involving manipulation of the mother–infant relationship have been used extensively to investigate the nature of the developmental impact of these interactions, however, these manipulations are often disruptive to offspring development. In many species, aspects of maternal care show a high degree of stability and these traits can be quantified and associated with more subtle behavioral and neuroendocrine outcomes in offspring [1,2]. Use of these approaches has enabled researchers to address questions about the molecular mechanisms involved in mediating the effects of early rearing experiences and incorporate studies of transgenerational effects in their studies. Thus, when considering the question 'how do social experiences influence the brain?', it is becoming clear that we must take a broad approach; examining studies using multiple paradigms, with inter-species comparisons, and using a life-history approach considering the contribution of genetic background and social experience throughout the lifespan. Here, we discuss current understanding of the role of mother–infant interactions in mediating developmental outcomes, the interaction between social environment and genetic background, and the mechanisms mediating the long-term effects of early social experiences. Recent work illustrating the impact of social experiences beyond the postpartum period and the transmission of social behavior across generations is also explored.

Maternal influence on brain development and behavior
Though considerations of mother–infant interactions are often limited to the postpartum period, in which both behavioral and nutritional aspects of care can be readily observed, events occurring before birth also have a substantial impact on brain development and behavior. Increasing levels of gestational social stress (see glossary) in guinea pigs, experimentally induced by altering the stability of group composition by interchanging females between colonies every few days, alters the behavior and neuroendocrine function of both male and female offspring [3•]. Female offspring are masculinized, displaying male-typical play and courtship behavior, and have higher levels of serum testosterone and increased adrenal tyrosine hydroxylase activity [4]. Androgen receptors (AR) in the medial preoptic area (MPOA) and arcuate nucleus (ARC) of the hypothalamus are upregulated in these females [4]. By contrast, male offspring of these socially stressed mothers are infantilized as adults, resting in body contact with others for longer and integrating courtship behavior into their play behavior [5,6]. Development of the pituitary–adrenocortical system is also delayed in these males and they have decreased adrenal tyrosine hydroxylase activity, and downregulated ARs in the MPOA and ARC [5,6]. Thus, social experiences of the mother can influence offspring development during the prenatal period with consequences for adult reproductive function. These effects are particularly relevant in species such as the guinea pig, which have a prolonged prenatal period and relatively little postpartum mother–infant interaction.

In altricial species, such as rats and mice, which give birth to young that are still dependent on the mother, maternal care is predominantly postnatal. Nevertheless, the prenatal maternal environment plays a crucial role in shaping the adult behavior in these species. For instance, gestational stress (both physical and social) of rat and mouse dams leads to long-term changes in offspring behavior, typically affecting hypothalamic pituitary axis (HPA) activity and cognition in a sex-specific manner [3•,7]. Moreover, it has been recently demonstrated that male mice of the C57BL/6J strain develop anxiety and emotional phenotypes equivalent to those of another inbred strain (Balb/cJ) if they have been both embryo transferred and cross-fostered (see glossary) to Balb/cJ mothers [8]. Embryo transfer (see glossary) alone or cross-fostering alone were insufficient to generate this adult phenotype. Thus, the role of maternal factors in epigenetically shaping brain development and behavior of offspring before birth must be considered, although in most mammals the majority of maternal care and infant development occurs postpartum.

Studies of the neurobiological and behavioral consequences of deprivation of maternal care during infancy in both primates and rodents highlight the role of experiences during this period in the development of stress responsivity and social behavior. In primates, this effect has been best demonstrated in Harlow's artificial rearing paradigm, in which infant rhesus monkeys are reared in complete social isolation for periods of 3–12 months [9,10]. Juveniles reared in this environment display marked deficits in play behavior, learning impairments, heightened fear-related behaviors, and behavioral inhibition. These behavioral effects are associated with a disruption of HPA activity, even among peer-reared infants deprived of maternal stimulation but not completely socially deprived [11]. Similar results are observed in artificially reared rat pups removed from their mother on day 3 postpartum and raised in complete social isolation [12,13•]. As adults, artificially reared pups are more fearful, display cognitive impairments related to attentional-shifting, and are impaired in social recognition compared with the behavior of mother-reared infants. Long periods of daily maternal separation are also associated with increased stress responsivity and cognitive deficits in offspring [14].

However, developmental consequences are not limited to such extreme experiences. Observations of bonnet and pigtail macaques indicate that juvenile offspring of mothers who display high levels of affiliative behavior, such as infant touching and cradling, are more exploratory and engage in more social contact with conspecifics [15]. Natural variations in maternal care can also be characterized in rodents, enabling a more detailed analysis of the mechanisms mediating these changes [1]. In rats, offspring born to mothers who display high levels of licking and grooming (LG) during the first week postpartum are less fearful, have an attenuated corticosterone response to stress, and increased levels of hippocampal glucocorticoid receptor (GR) expression compared with those of offspring of mothers who display low levels of LG [16,17]. Cross-fostering studies indicate that the quality of postpartum maternal care is crucial for the development of these phenotypes [18]. Thus, even variations in social interaction that exist within the normal range of behavior can produce long-term changes in offspring.

Interaction between genes and social environment
Although social experiences early in life play a major role in shaping brain development and adult behavior, individuals vary significantly in the degree to which they are affected by these influences. One explanation for this variability is that the underlying genotype makes individuals more or less susceptible to the effects of early social environments. In rodents, such gene x environment (see glossary) interactions have previously been documented; inbred strains, for instance, vary in the degree to which offspring are affected by maternal separation and neonatal handling [19,20]. Recent molecular genetics work involving the monoamine oxidase A (MAOA) and serotonin transporter genes have highlighted the importance of these interactions in primate and human behavior. In humans, adult males who were maltreated as children and who possess a low-activity form of the MAOA gene (related to the number of variable number tandem repeats in the promoter region), exhibit significantly more violence and conduct disorders than males who either carry the high-activity form and were maltreated, or who carry the low-activity form but were not maltreated [21,22]. Male rhesus monkeys with a similar low activity form of this gene demonstrate increased aggression as infants, but only if they are raised by their mothers; males raised in peer-only groups are not more aggressive [23••]. In both instances, increased aggression is observed in male individuals who have both a copy of the low activity form of the MAOA gene and were exposed to adult aggression during development. Likewise, humans carrying at least one copy of the short form of the serotonin transporter gene (fewer repeats in the promoter region) have an accentuated risk of developing depression if they experienced at least three 'stressful' life events during childhood and adolescence [24]. Rhesus monkeys carrying an

equivalent short form of this gene have higher HPA activity and adrenocorticotropin releasing hormone (ACTH) levels during social separation stress when peer-reared are compared with mother-reared [25–27]. Although these examples of interactions between genotypes and early environment are striking, we are only starting to fully appreciate the complex interplay between genetic backgrounds, social environments and brain development. Indeed, it is likely that such interactions will be found to be common and significant to the development of most behavioral phenotypes.

Mechanisms of social influence on development

Early rearing environments are clearly capable of exerting neurobiological changes that persist into adulthood, but only recently has the molecular mechanism mediating these long-term effects been explored. Expression of glucocorticoid receptors in the hippocampus is thought to mediate the individual differences in stress responsivity observed in offspring born to high and low LG rat dams [16,17,28]. Analysis of the regulatory regions of the glucocorticoid receptor implicates DNA methylation as a possible mechanism for phenotypic differentiation. Attachment of methyl groups to DNA blocks transcriptional factors from gaining access to the gene and, thus, expression of the gene is effectively silenced [29]. This particularly stable epigenetic modification, which is maintained after cell division, is the means by which cellular differentiation occurs during development. Investigation of the methylation status of the exon 1_7 promoter region of the glucocorticoid receptor ($GR1_7$) in hippocampal tissue taken from adult offspring born to low LG mothers indicates elevated levels of DNA methylation compared with that of adult offspring of high LG mothers, which would certainly explain the decreased level of GR expression in low LG offspring [30••]. Analysis of the developmental time course of this methylation pattern in the hippocampus indicates that just before parturition, at embryonic day 20, and immediately after birth, at day 1 postpartum, there are no differences in methylation of the GR 1_7 promoter region. However, group differences in methylation are evident by day 6 postpartum, correlated with a period of differential maternal LG, they persist post-weaning at day 21, and into adulthood at day 90. Hippocampal tissue from offspring born to low LG mothers who are then cross-fostered to high LG mothers indicates a methylation pattern corresponding to the maternal care received during the postnatal period [30••]. These epigenetic changes, thus, provide a stable mechanism whereby the effects of early social experiences can persist throughout the lifespan.

Social influence throughout a lifetime: reversibility

Discussions of the impact of early environment often refer to 'programming', emphasizing the long-term

effects of these experiences, and the association of epigenetic modifications with these effects certainly provides support for this notion of stability. However, plasticity exists whereby social experiences later in life can alter the course of development and, in some cases, compensate for early deprivation. In rats exposed to postnatal maternal separation, enriching the post-weaning social environment through group housing with conspecifics decreases the corticosterone response to stress and reduces behavioral indications of anxiety [31]. Cognitive deficits, as indicated by performance on a Morris water maze, of offspring who receive low levels of LG during the postnatal period can also be reversed using post-weaning social enrichment [32]. These studies also illustrate that the modulation of behavioral phenotype by the post-weaning environment does not involve the same neural mechanisms that mediate the original deficits. Social enrichment did not affect the elevated levels of corticotropin-releasing factor (CRF) in the paraventricular nucleus of the hypothalamus (PVNh) and decreased levels of hippocampal GR mRNA found in maternally separated males. Hippocampal N-methyl-D-aspartate (NMDA) receptor binding in the offspring of low LG mothers was also not altered by these post-weaning manipulations [33]. Thus, social experiences beyond the postnatal period might alter brain development via alternative, yet equally stable mechanisms.

Figure 1

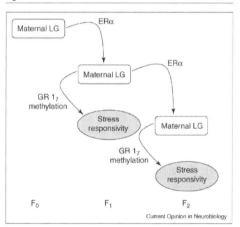

Transmission of maternal care and stress responsivity across generations. Variations in maternal licking and grooming (LG) are transmitted from mother (F0) to female offspring (F1) associated with changes in expression of estrogen receptor α (ERα) in the medial preoptic area. Differential methylation of the GR1$_7$ promoter region of the glucocorticoid receptor (GR) is likewise associated with F0 LG, resulting in individual differences in stress responsivity of offspring. Variation in LG of female offspring (F1) is then transmitted to the F2 generation, as are patterns of GR methylation and stress responsivity.

Transmission of social behavior across generations

Perhaps one of the most interesting advances in our understanding of the impact of social experience on development comes from studies of transgenerational effects. In primates, frequency of contact with infants and abusive behavior are both stable maternal traits that can be transmitted from one generation to the next [2]. In rhesus macaques, primiparous females who engage in high levels of abusive behavior towards infants are also abusive to subsequent offspring [34**,35]. Females born to these mothers display high levels of abuse toward their own infants and this pattern of inheritance is observed in the biological offspring of non-abusive mothers cross-fostered to abusive females. However, females born to abusive mothers who are then cross-fostered to non-abusive mothers are not abusive toward their offspring, indicating an environmentally mediated effect.

Similar work in rats indicates that female offspring reared by mothers who are high in LG behavior are high in LG toward their own offspring, whereas female offspring reared by low LG mothers are themselves low in LG [1,18]. There is some evidence to suggest that estrogen receptor (ER) expression in the MPOA might play a role in regulating this transmission. Levels of ER α in the MPOA are elevated among high LG mothers and their female offspring compared with levels in low LG mothers and their female offspring [36]. In females, the quality of

mother–infant interactions can, thus, affect reproductive behavior and, as a consequence, be passed on to subsequent generations. The implications of this transmission are that the developmental consequences of early rearing experience, such as stress responsivity and epigenetic modification of the glucocorticoid receptor, can be passed from one generation to the next (Figure 1).

Conclusions

Social experiences provide cues to the overall quality of a given environment and the status of an individual within that environment. When there is stability in environmental conditions over time, these experiences enable an individual to predict and possibly be adapted to future conditions, increasing reproductive success and survival [37]. This evolutionary perspective provides an explanation for the developmental impact of social experiences and a framework for understanding what particular aspects of brain and behavior might be the target of regulation by this feature of an individual's environment. The influence of early environment on stress responsivity and social behavior can be interpreted within this context. Disruptions occurring during the prenatal or postnatal period that alter mother–infant interactions might indicate a highly variable environment. Heightened stress responsivity would enable an individual to respond more rapidly to environmental change and increase likelihood of survival. By altering social behavior, these adaptive behavioral responses to stress can then be passed on to subsequent generations.

Figure 2

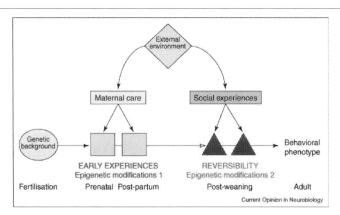

The development of behavioral phenotypes. Adult behavior is a product of the dynamic interplay between genes and social environment. Offspring develop differentially according to both maternal care (including nutritional, hormonal and behavioral cues) during gestation and lactation, and social experiences (predominantly behavioral cues) post-weaning. Recent evidence suggests that these induced changes are associated with epigenetic modifications of the genome. The relative impact of these experiences might be modified by underlying genetic background, with individuals being differentially susceptible to their influence. Finally, social experiences during these periods can have disruptive, neutral or adaptive effects on development. In adaptive terms, the maternal care received during development might be regulated by, and indicative of, the external physical and social environment. Thus, through epigenetic modifications offspring might be better prepared for adult life, whereas in changing external environments, social experience post-weaning offers opportunities to modify and perhaps reverse development via alternative epigenetic mechanisms.

Perhaps a crucial aspect of social experiences that is common to humans, primates and rodents is tactile stimulation. Deprivation of contact or decreased frequency of contact, whether in the form of holding an infant or licking and grooming a pup, directs development along a path involving heightened stress responsivity and decreased social behavior. In artificial rearing paradigms, provision of licking-like tactile stimulation to rat pups reduces behavioral indices of anxiety and improves social learning [12]. Licking and grooming behavior in rats is associated with epigenetic changes that are thought to mediate these behavioral phenotypes; however, we do not yet know whether this mechanism is relevant to other species or whether these mechanisms can be generalized to other forms of social interaction. In humans and primates, social learning is crucial to behavioral development and to the transmission of traits from mother to offspring. Does this transmission involve epigenetic changes? Recent studies of learning and memory would suggest that these processes do involve epigenetic changes, producing long-term effects on hippocampal plasticity [38,39•]. Studies of the role of epigenetic modifications in the context of social behavior would, thus, provide a better understanding of the mechanisms involved in both mediating the effects of early environment and transmitting these effects to future generations.

The interplay between genetic background and environment has clear implications for the developing brain and hence adult behavior (Figure 2). Recent evidence suggests that social experiences in infancy literally build upon this genetic background through epigenetic modification; however, the relevance of this mechanism to social influence at other periods in development is not known. Investigations of the molecular mechanisms mediating the influence of the social environment from the prenatal period through to adulthood are necessary to further our understanding of gene x environment interactions and the role of these experiences in creating stable phenotypes.

Acknowledgements

FA Champagne is funded by a fellowship from the Canadian Institutes of Health Research (CIHR) and JP Curley is supported by the Cambridge-Leverhulme Initiative in Post-Genomics Research. The authors would like to thank W Swaney for providing a critical review of this manuscript.

References and recommended reading

Papers of particular interest, published within the annual period of review, have been highlighted as:

- of special interest
- of outstanding interest

1. Champagne F, Francis D, Mar A, Meaney M: **Variations in maternal care in the rat as a mediating influence for the effects of environment on development.** *Physiol Behav* 2003, 79:359-371.

2. Fairbanks L: **Individual differences in maternal style of old world monkeys.** *Adv Study Behav* 1996, 25:579-611.

3. Kaiser S, Sachser N: **The effects of prenatal social stress on behaviour: mechanisms and function.** *Neurosci Biobehav Rev* 2005, 29:283-294.
This is an excellent review article comprehensively surveying the effects of social stress during pregnancy on offspring development across mammals. The authors describe these behavioural effects, the neuroendocrine pathways mediating them and discuss whether they are pathological or adaptive in nature.

4. Kaiser S, Kruijver FPM, Swaab DF, Sachser N: **Early social stress in female guinea pigs induces a masculinization of adult behavior and corresponding changes in brain and neuroendocrine function.** *Behav Brain Res* 2003, 144:199-210.

5. Kaiser S, Kruijver FPM, Straub RH, Sachser N, Swaab DF: **Early social stress in male guinea-pigs changes social behaviour, and autonomic and neuroendocrine function.** *J Neuroendocrinol* 2003, 15:761-769.

6. Kaiser S, Sachser N: **Social stress during pregnancy and lactation affects the male guinea offsprings' endocrine status and infantilizes their behaviour.** *Psychoneuroendocrinology* 2001, 26:503-519.

7. Welberg LA, Seckl JR: **Prenatal stress, glucocorticoids and the programming of the brain.** *J Neuroendocrinol* 2001, 13:113-128.

8. Francis D, Szegda K, Campbell G, Martin W, Insel T: **Epigenetic sources of behavioral differences in mice.** *Nat Neurosci* 2003, 6:445-446.

9. Harlow H, Dodsworth R, Harlow M: **Total social isolation in monkeys.** *Proc Natl Acad Sci USA* 1965, 54:90-97.

10. Harlow H, Suomi S: **Social recovery by isolation-reared monkeys.** *Proc Natl Acad Sci USA* 1971, 68:1534-1538.

11. Capitanio J, Mendoza S, Mason W, Manninger N: **Rearing environment and hypothalamic-pituitary-adrenal regulation in young rhesus monkeys (Macaca mulatta).** *Dev Psychobiol* 2005, 46:318-330.

12. Gonzalez A, Lovic V, Ward G, Wainwright P, Fleming A: **Intergenerational effects of complete maternal deprivation and replacement stimulation on maternal behavior and emotionality in female rats.** *Dev Psychobiol* 2001, 38:11-32.

13. Lovic V, Fleming A: **Artificially-reared female rats show reduced prepulse inhibition and deficits in the attentional set shifting task - reversal of effects with maternal-like licking stimulation.** *Behav Brain Res* 2004, 148:209-219.
Using an artificial rearing paradigm with rat pups, the authors illustrate the cognitive deficits that occur under conditions of complete maternal deprivation and the role that manual tactile stimulation, using a paintbrush, can have in restoring normal functioning.

14. Lehmann J, Pryce C, Bettschen D, Feldon J: **The maternal separation paradigm and adult emotionality and cognition in male and female Wistar rats.** *Pharmacol Biochem Behav* 1999, 64:705-715.

15. Weaver A, Richardson R, Worlein J, De Waal F, Laudenslager M: **Response to social challenge in young bonnet (Macaca radiata) and pigtail (Macaca nemestrina) macaques is related to early maternal experiences.** *Am J Primatol* 2004, 62:243-259.

16. Caldji C, Tannenbaum B, Sharma S, Francis D, Plotsky P, Meaney M: **Maternal care during infancy regulates the development of neural systems mediating the expression of fearfulness in the rat.** *Proc Natl Acad Sci USA* 1998, 95:5335-5340.

17. Liu D, Dioro J, Tannenbaum B, Caldji C, Francis D, Freedman A, Sharma S, Pearson D, Plotsky P, Meaney M: **Maternal care, hippocampal glucocorticoid receptors, and hypothalamic-pituitary-adrenal responses to stress.** *Science* 1997, 277:1659-1662.

18. Francis D, Dioro J, Liu D, Meaney M: **Nongenomic transmission across generations of maternal behavior and stress responses in the rat.** *Science* 1999, 286:1155-1158.

19. Zaharia MD, Kulczycki J, Shanks N, Meaney MJ, Anisman H: **The effects of early postnatal stimulation on Morris water-maze acquisition in adult mice: genetic and maternal factors.** *Psychopharmacology (Berl)* 1996, 128:227-239.

20. Hennessy MB, Li J, Lowe EL, Levine S: **Maternal behavior, pup vocalizations, and pup temperature changes following handling in mice of 2 inbred strains**. *Dev Psychobiol* 1980, 13:573-584.

21. Caspi A, McClay J, Moffitt TE, Mill J, Martin J, Craig IW, Taylor A, Poulton R: **Role of genotype in the cycle of violence in maltreated children**. *Science* 2002, 297:851-854.

22. Foley DL, Eaves LJ, Wormley B, Silberg JL, Maes HH, Kuhn J, Riley B: **Childhood adversity, monoamine oxidase a genotype, and risk for conduct disorder**. *Arch Gen Psychiatry* 2004, 61:738-744.

23. Newman TK, Syagailo YV, Barr CS, Wendland JR, Champoux M,
•• Graessle M, Suomi SJ, Higley JD, Lesch KP: **Monoamine oxidase A gene promoter variation and rearing experience influences aggressive behavior in rhesus monkeys**. *Biol Psychiatry* 2005, 57:167-172.
Non-human primates provide an excellent model system to study gene x environment interactions, because rearing environments can be easily controlled. This paper, investigating a study group of 45 unrelated adult males, reinforces earlier findings from human studies that the low activity form of the MAOA gene is associated with increased aggression in males but subject to early rearing environment.

24. Caspi A, Sugden K, Moffitt TE, Taylor A, Craig IW, Harrington H, McClay J, Mill J, Martin J, Braithwaite A *et al.*: **Influence of life stress on depression: moderation by a polymorphism in the 5-HTT gene**. *Science* 2003, 301:386-389.

25. Champoux M, Bennett A, Shannon C, Higley JD, Lesch KP, Suomi SJ: **Serotonin transporter gene polymorphism, differential early rearing, and behavior in rhesus monkey neonates**. *Mol Psychiatry* 2002, 7:1058-1063.

26. Barr CS, Newman TK, Shannon C, Parker C, Dvoskin RL, Becker ML, Schwandt M, Champoux M, Lesch KP, Goldman D *et al.*: **Rearing condition and rh5-HTTLPR interact to influence limbic-hypothalamic-pituitary-adrenal axis response to stress in infant macaques**. *Biol Psychiatry* 2004, 55:733-738.

27. Barr CS, Newman TK, Schwandt M, Shannon C, Dvoskin RL, Lindell SG, Taubman J, Thompson B, Champoux M, Lesch KP *et al.*: **Sexual dichotomy of an interaction between early adversity and the serotonin transporter gene promoter variant in rhesus macaques**. *Proc Natl Acad Sci USA* 2004, 101:12358-12363.

28. Liu D, Dioro J, Day J, Francis D, Meaney M: **Maternal care, hippocampal synaptogenesis and cognitive development in rats**. *Nat Neurosci* 2000, 3:799-806.

29. Razin A: **CpG methylation, chromatin structure and gene silencing - a three-way connection**. *EMBO J* 1998, 17:4905-4908.

30. Weaver I, Cervoni N, Champagne F, D'Alessio A, Sharma S,
•• Seckl J, Dymov S, Szyf M, Meaney M: **Epigenetic programming by maternal behavior**. *Nat Neurosci* 2004, 7:847-854.

Exploration of the influence of maternal care on DNA methylation of the GR17 promoter region indicating that low levels of maternal stimulation are associated with hypermethylation of this region preventing binding of the transcription factor NGFI-A. This is an excellent series of studies, and the first paper shows the epigenetic effects of early rearing.

31. Francis D, Dioro J, Plotsky P, Meaney M: **Environmental enrichment reverses the effects of maternal separation on stress reactivity**. *J Neurosci* 2002, 22:7840-7843.

32. Bredy T, Humpartzoomian R, Cain D, Meaney M: **Partial reversal of the effect of maternal care on cognitive function through environmental enrichment**. *Neuroscience* 2003, 118:571-576.

33. Bredy T, Zhang T, Grant R, Dioro J, Meaney M: **Peripubertal environmental enrichment reverses the effects of maternal care on hippocampal development and glutamate receptor subunit expression**. *Eur J Neurosci* 2004, 20:1355-1362.

34. Maestripieri D: **Early experience affects the intergenerational
•• transmission of infant abuse in rhesus monkeys**. *Proc Natl Acad Sci USA* 2005, 102:9276-9279.
The authors combine behavioral characterization under semi-naturalistic conditions and cross-fostering in a longitudinal study of rhesus monkeys to demonstrate the transmission of abusive behavior across generations. This study provides an elegant example of how early rearing environment influences the maternal behavior of female offspring.

35. Maestripieri D, Lindell S, Ayala A, Gold P, Higley JD: **Neurobiological characteristics of rhesus macaque abusive mothers and their relation to social and maternal behavior**. *Neurosci Biobehav Rev* 2005, 29:51-57.

36. Champagne F, Weaver I, Dioro J, Sharma S, Meaney M: **Natural variations in maternal care are associated with estrogen receptor alpha expression and estrogen sensitivity in the medial preoptic area**. *Endocrinology* 2003, 144:4720-4724.

37. Gluckman PD, Hanson MA, Spencer HG, Bateson P: **Environmental influences during development and their later consequences for health and disease: implications for the interpretation of empirical studies**. *Proc Biol Sci* 2005, 272:671-677.

38. Levenson JM, Sweatt JD: **Epigenetic mechanisms in memory formation**. *Nat Rev Neurosci* 2005, 6:108-118.

39. Levenson JM, O'Riordan KJ, Brown KD, Trinh MA, Molfese DL,
• Sweatt JD: **Regulation of histone acetylation during memory formation in the hippocampus**. *J Biol Chem* 2004, 279:40545-40559.
The authors provide evidence that the formation of long-term memory is mediated by epigenetic changes in the hippocampus involving histone acetylation. This work advances our understanding of the molecular basis of learning.

[10]

Cognitive and affective development in adolescence

Laurence Steinberg

Department of Psychology, Temple University, Philadelphia, PA 19122, USA

Questions about the nature of normative and atypical development in adolescence have taken on special significance in the last few years, as scientists have begun to recast old portraits of adolescent behavior in the light of new knowledge about brain development. Adolescence is often a period of especially heightened vulnerability as a consequence of potential disjunctions between developing brain, behavioral and cognitive systems that mature along different timetables and under the control of both common and independent biological processes. Taken together, these developments reinforce the emerging understanding of adolescence as a critical or sensitive period for a reorganization of regulatory systems, a reorganization that is fraught with both risks and opportunities.

Introduction

Adolescence is characterized by an increased need to regulate affect and behavior in accordance with long-term goals and consequences, often at a distance from the adults who provided regulatory structure and guidance during childhood. Because developing brain, behavioral and cognitive systems mature at different rates and under the control of both common and independent biological processes, this period is often one of increased vulnerability and adjustment. Accordingly, normative development in adolescence can profitably be understood with respect to the coordination of emotional, intellectual and behavioral proclivities and capabilities, and psychopathology in adolescence may be reflective of difficulties in this coordination process.

The notion that adolescence is a heightened period of vulnerability specifically because of gaps between emotion, cognition and behavior has important implications for our understanding of many aspects of both normative and atypical development during this period of the life-span. With respect to normative development, for instance, this framework is helpful in understanding age differences in judgment and decision-making, in risk-taking, and in sensation-seeking [1]. With respect to atypical development, the framework helps us to understand why adolescence can be a time of increased risk for the onset of a wide range of emotional and behavioral problems, including depression, violent delinquency and substance abuse [2].

Corresponding author: Steinberg, L. (lds@temple.edu).
Available online 23 December 2004

Questions about the nature of normative and atypical development in adolescence have taken on special significance in the last few years as scientists have begun to recast old portraits of adolescent psychological development in light of new knowledge about adolescent brain development. Recent discoveries in the area of developmental neuroscience have stimulated widespread scientific and popular interest in the study of brain development during adolescence, as well as substantial speculation about the connections between brain maturation and adolescents' behavioral and emotional development. Indeed, the topic has garnered such widespread public interest that it was the subject of a recent cover story in *Time* magazine aimed at parents of teenagers [3], and was raised in arguments submitted in late 2004 to the United States Supreme Court in connection with the Court's consideration of the constitutionality of the juvenile death penalty [4].

Brain development in adolescence

As reviewed in the accompanying article by Paus [5] there is growing evidence that maturational brain processes are continuing well through adolescence. Even relatively simple structural measures, such as the ratio of white-to-gray matter in the brain, demonstrate large-scale changes into the late teen-age years [6–8]. The impact of this continued maturation on emotional, intellectual and behavioral development has yet to be thoroughly studied, but there is considerable evidence that the second decade of life is a period of great activity with respect to changes in brain structure and function, especially in regions and systems associated with response inhibition, the calibration of risk and reward, and emotion regulation. Contrary to earlier beliefs about brain maturation in adolescence, this activity is not limited to the early adolescent period, nor is it invariably linked to processes of pubertal maturation (Figure 1).

Two particular observations about brain development in adolescence are especially pertinent to our understanding of psychological development during this period. First, much brain development during adolescence is in the particular brain regions and systems that are key to the regulation of behavior and emotion and to the perception and evaluation of risk and reward. Second, it appears that changes in arousal and motivation brought on by pubertal maturation precede the development of regulatory competence in a manner that creates a disjunction between the adolescent's affective experience

70   *TRENDS in Cognitive Sciences* Vol.9 No.2 February 2005

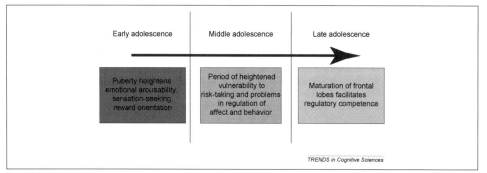

Figure 1. It has been speculated that the impact of puberty on arousal and motivation occurs before the maturation of the frontal lobes is complete. This gap may create a period of heightened vulnerability to problems in the regulation of affect and behavior, which might help to explain the increased potential in adolescence for risk-taking, recklessness, and the onset of emotional and behavioral problems.

and his or her ability to regulate arousal and motivation. To the extent that the changes in arousal and motivation precede the development of regulatory competence – a reasonable speculation, but one that has yet to be confirmed – the developments of early adolescence may well create a situation in which one is starting an engine without yet having a skilled driver behind the wheel [9].

Cognitive development in adolescence

Until recently, much of the work on adolescent cognitive development was devoted to a search for a core mechanism that could account parsimoniously for broad changes in adolescent thinking [10]. After nearly 50 years of searching, what has emerged instead is the necessity of an integrated account. What lies at the core of adolescent cognitive development is the attainment of a more fully conscious, self-directed and self-regulating mind [10]. This is achieved principally through the assembly of an advanced 'executive suite' of capabilities [11], rather than through specific advancement in any one of the constituent elements. This represents a major shift in prevailing views of adolescent cognition, going beyond the search for underlying elements [12] that are formed and operate largely outside awareness.

As Keating [10] has noted, the plausibility of such an integrative account has been substantially enhanced by recent major advances in the neurosciences [6–8,13–18], in comparative neuroanatomy across closely related primate species that illuminate core issues of human cognitive evolution [10,19], and in a deepened understanding of the critical role of culture and context in the shaping of cognitive and brain development [11,20]. Much of the underlying action is focused on specific developments in the prefrontal cortex, but with an equally significant role for rapidly expanding linkages to the whole brain [11,15,21]. This complex process of assembly is supported by increasingly rapid connectivity (through continued myelination of nerve fibers), particularly in communication among different brain regions, and by significant and localized synaptic pruning, especially in frontal areas that are crucial to executive functioning [6–8,18].

Whatever the underlying processes, during early adolescence, individuals show marked improvements in reasoning (especially deductive reasoning), information processing (in both efficiency and capacity), and expertise. These conclusions derive from studies of age differences in logical reasoning on tasks in which participants are asked to solve verbal analogies or analyze logical propositions; basic cognitive processes, such as short- or long-term memory; and in specialized knowledge [10]. There has been broad consensus for more than 25 years that, as a result of these gains, individuals become more capable of abstract, multidimensional, planned and hypothetical thinking as they develop from late childhood into middle adolescence (less is known about cognitive changes during late adolescence). No research in the past several decades has challenge this conclusion.

Implications of new brain maturation research for adolescent cognitive development

After a rather lengthy period during the late 1980s and early 1990s, when the study of adolescent cognitive development was more or less moribund, interest in intellectual development during adolescence has been revitalized in recent years in two ways. First, researchers in the field of developmental neuroscience began to direct attention to the study of structural and functional aspects of brain development during early adolescence [6,8,13,22]. These studies have pointed both to significant growth and significant change in multiple regions of the prefrontal cortex throughout the course of adolescence, especially with respect to processes of myelination and synaptic pruning (both of which increase the efficiency of information processing) [8,17,23]. These changes are believed to undergird improvements in various aspects of executive functioning, including long-term planning, metacognition, self-evaluation, self-regulation and the coordination of affect and cognition [10]. Most research has focused on age differences in skills known to be related to functioning in the dorsolateral region of the prefrontal cortex, such as those involving working memory, spatial working memory and planning [24–26], but two recent studies [27,28] indicate as well that adolescence is a time of improvement

TRENDS in Cognitive Sciences Vol.9 No.2 February 2005 71

in abilities that have been linked to functioning in the ventromedial prefrontal cortex, such as the calibration of risk and reward (Box 1).

In addition, adolescence appears to be a time of improved connectivity between regions of the prefrontal cortex and several areas of the limbic system, a restructuring that further affects the ways in which individuals evaluate and respond to risk and reward [22,29]. Whether and to what extent these changes in brain structure and function are linked to processes of pubertal maturation is not known. Some aspects of brain development are coincident with, and likely linked to, neuroendocrinological changes occurring at the time of puberty, but others appear to take place along a different, and later, timetable. Disentangling the first set from the second is an important challenge for the field [9]. It is also important to note that there are relatively few studies of developmental changes in brain function (as opposed to structure) in adolescence, and that conclusions about the putative links between changes in cognitive performance and changes in brain

structure during adolescence are suggestive, rather than conclusive.

Cognitive development in context

A second relatively new direction in research on adolescent cognitive development has involved the study of cognitive development as it plays out in its social context and, in particular, as it affects the development of judgment, decision-making and risk-taking [30–35]. New perspectives on adolescent cognition-in-context emphasize that adolescent thinking in the real world is a function of social and emotional, as well as cognitive, processes, and that a full account of the ways in which the intellectual changes of adolescence affect social and emotional development must examine the ways in which affect and cognition interact [10]. Studies of adolescents' reasoning or problem-solving using laboratory-based measures of intellectual functioning might provide better understanding of adolescents' potential competence than of their actual performance in everyday settings, where judgment and decision-making are likely affected by emotional states, social influences and expertise [1]. Thus, whereas studies of people's responses to hypothetical dilemmas involving the perception and appraisal of risk show few reliable age differences after middle adolescence, studies of actual risk-taking (e.g. risky driving, unprotected sexual activity, etc.) indicate that adolescents are significantly more likely to make risky decisions than are adults.

One reasonable hypothesis is that adults and adolescents 16 and older share the same logical competencies, but that age differences in social and emotional factors, such as susceptibility to peer influence or impulse control, lead to age differences in actual decision-making [36]. Research that examines developmental changes in cognitive abilities assessed under varying social and emotional conditions (e.g. the same task administered under conditions of high versus low affective arousal, or in the presence versus absence of peers) would be potentially quite informative, as at least one study indicates that adolescents' risk taking is more influenced than that of adults by the presence of peers [37] (Figure 2).

Consistent with findings on the advances in reasoning, characteristic of the transition into adolescence, studies of social cognition demonstrate that the ways in which adolescents think about others becomes more abstract, more differentiated and more multidimensional [38]. More recent studies of changes in social cognition during adolescence have attempted to clarify the conditions under which relatively more advanced displays of social cognition are likely to be seen; to describe gender and cultural differences in certain aspects of social cognition, such as prosocial reasoning [39,40] or impression formation [41]; and to examine the links between social cognition and social behavior. These studies indicate that patterns of social cognitive development in adolescence, like patterns of cognitive development more generally, vary both as a function of the content under consideration and the emotional and social context in which the reasoning occurs [38].

For example, although individuals' thinking about moral dilemmas becomes more principled over the course

---

Box 1. Age differences in ventromedial functioning

The most widely used task in the assessment of ventromedial functioning is the Iowa Gambling Task [56]. Subjects are asked to draw cards from one of four face-down decks; each card provides information on how much has been won and lost on that draw. Cards from two of the decks offer high rewards, but in one deck the rewards are paired either with occasional very high losses, and in the other with frequent modest losses, and continuing to draw from either of these decks results in a net loss over time. By contrast, cards from the other two decks offer low rewards, but these are paired either with frequent small losses, or sporadic, but modest, losses, and these decks lead to net gains over time.

Researchers monitor individuals' pattern of card selection over numerous trials. Healthy adults typically begin by drawing from the decks at random, then gradually increase their pulls from the 'good' decks and decrease their pulls from the 'bad' decks. The notable exceptions to this pattern are patients with lesions to the ventromedial prefrontal cortex, individuals with substance abuse problems, and individuals who report high levels of risk-taking in everyday life, all of whom persist in drawing from the 'bad' decks despite the net losses that result.

Only recently have studies examined age differences on the Iowa Gambling Task. In one study [27] of four age groups – 6–9 year-olds, 10–12 year-olds, 13–15 year-olds and 18–25 year-olds – the youngest subjects drew equally from the good and bad decks. The two middle groups showed modest improvement over time; by the final trial block, they were drawing from the good decks about 55% and 60% of the time, respectively. By the final block, however, the young adults were drawing from the good decks nearly 75% of the time, and they began shifting towards the good decks much earlier than the younger groups.

Another study, of 9- to 17-year-olds, also found significant improvement in performance on this task with age [28]. 14–17 year-olds drew from the good decks more often than 9–10 year-olds (although not more often than 11–13 year olds) and began shifting to the good decks earlier than did either of the younger groups. The researchers also administered two tasks known to activate the dorsolateral prefrontal cortex: a go/no-go task, which assesses response inhibition, and a digit span test, which assesses working memory. As expected, performance on both dorsolateral tasks improved with age. More importantly, however, there were no significant correlations between performance on the ventromedial task and performance on either of the dorsolateral tasks, suggesting that maturation of the ventromedial prefrontal cortex may be a developmentally distinct process from the maturation of other regions of the frontal lobe.

72   *TRENDS in Cognitive Sciences* Vol.9 No.2 February 2005

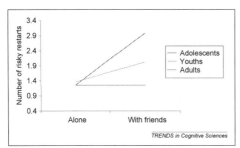

Figure 2. In a study designed to investigate age differences in risk-taking [37], participants were asked to play a computerized game in which they had opportunities to take driving risks, such as continuing to drive after a traffic light had turned yellow in order to drive the car further and earn more points. Individuals were randomly assigned to one of two conditions: playing the game alone, or playing it while two friends were watching and giving advice. The graph shows the number of times individuals risked crashing the car by stopping and then restarting it to try to drive a bit further after the yellow light had appeared. Adolescents (aged 13–16), youths (aged 18–22), and adults (aged 24 and older) demonstrated equivalent degrees of risk-taking when alone, but in the presence of peers, adolescents and youths, but not adults, took more risks.

of adolescence, their reasoning about real-life problems is often not as advanced as their reasoning about hypothetical dilemmas [42]. The correlation between adolescents' moral reasoning and their moral behavior is especially likely to break down when individuals define issues as personal choices rather than ethical dilemmas (for instance, when using drugs is seen as a personal matter rather than a moral issue) [43]. Similarly, when faced with a logical argument, adolescents are more likely to accept faulty reasoning or shaky evidence when they agree with the substance of the argument than when they do not [44,45]. And, although individuals' ability to look at things from another person's perspective increases in adolescence, the extent to which this advanced social perspective taking translates into tolerance for others' viewpoints depends on the particular issue involved [46]. In other words, adolescents' social reasoning, like that of adults, is influenced not only by their basic intellectual abilities, but by their desires, motives and interests.

Affect and cognition

In contrast to most measures of cognitive development in adolescence, which seem to correlate more closely with age and experience rather than the timing of pubertal maturation, there is evidence for a specific link between pubertal maturation and developmental changes in arousal, motivation and emotion. For example, there is evidence that pubertal development directly influences the development of romantic interest and sexual motivation [47,48]. There is also evidence that some changes in emotional intensity and reactivity, such as changes in the frequency and intensity of parent-adolescent conflict, may be more closely linked to pubertal maturation than to age [49]. Some cognitive skills related to human face-processing have also shown intriguing alterations in mid-adolescence – an apparent *decrement* in face processing skills that is associated with sexual maturation (measured by Tanner staging by physical examinations) rather than

with age or grade level [50]. A parallel finding has been reported for voice recognition [51].

There is also evidence that increases in sensation-seeking, risk-taking and reckless behavior in adolescence are influenced by puberty and not chronological age. For example, in a study by Martin *et al.* [29], where sensation-seeking and risk behaviors were examined in a large group of young adolescents aged 11 to 14, there was no significant correlation between age and sensation-seeking, but a significant correlation between sensation-seeking and pubertal stage. There is also evidence in animal and human studies supporting a link between increasing levels of reproductive hormones and sensitivity to social status [52,53], which is consistent with the link between puberty and risk-taking, since several influential theories of adolescent risk-taking [54] suggest that at least some of this behavior is done in the service of enhancing one's standing with peers. Although further research is much needed, it appears that there are important links between pubertal maturation and social information-processing.

In some models of the development of affect regulation there is an explicit emphasis on cognitive systems exerting control over emotions and emotion-related behavior [55]. Many aspects of affect regulation involve the ability to inhibit, delay or modify an emotion or its expression in accordance with some rules, goals or strategies, or to avoid learned negative consequences. However, there is increasing understanding that cognitive-emotional interactions in adolescence also unfold in the other direction in important ways. Thus, just as cognition has an important impact on emotion, emotion has an important impact on basic cognitive processes, including decision-making and behavioral choice.

Decision-making and risk-taking

Behavioral data have often made it appear that adolescents are poor decision-makers (i.e. their high-rates of participation in dangerous activities, automobile accidents, drug use and unprotected sex). This led initially to hypotheses that adolescents had poor cognitive skills relevant to decision-making or that information about consequences of risky behavior may have been unclear to them [56,57]. In contrast to those accounts, however, there is substantial evidence that adolescents engage in dangerous activities *despite* knowing and understanding the risks involved [29,58,59,60–63]. Thus, in real-life situations, adolescents do not simply rationally weigh the relative risks and consequences of their behavior – their actions are largely influenced by feelings and social influences [1].

In contrast to much previous work on adolescent decision-making that emphasized cognitive processes and mainly ignored affective ones, there is now increasing recognition of the importance of emotion in decision-making [64]. The 'decision' to engage in a specific behavior with long-term health consequences – such as smoking a cigarette, drinking alcohol, or engaging in unprotected sex – cannot be completely understood within the framework of 'cold' cognitive processes. ('Cold' cognition refers to thinking processes under conditions of low emotion and/or arousal whereas 'hot' cognition refers to thinking under conditions of strong feelings or high arousal and which

TRENDS in Cognitive Sciences   Vol.9 No.2 February 2005   73

therefore may be much more important to understanding risky choices in real-life situations.) These affective influences are relevant in many day-to-day 'decisions' that are made at the level of 'gut-feelings' regarding what to do in a particular situation (rather than deliberate thoughts about outcome probabilities or risk value). These 'gut feelings' appear to be the products of affective systems in the brain that are performing computations that are largely outside conscious awareness [65,66]. How these feelings develop, become calibrated during maturation, and are influenced by particular types of experiences at particular points in development are only beginning to be studied within the framework of affective neuroscience [29]. It does, however, appear that puberty and sexual maturation have important influences on at least some aspects of affective influences on behavior through new drives, motivations and intensity of feelings, as well as new experiences that evoke strong feelings (such as developing romantic involvement) [67,68].

The development of regulatory competence

During the adolescent transition, regulatory systems are gradually brought under the control of central executive functions, with a special focus on the interface of cognition and emotion. Two important observations are especially important. The first is that the development of an integrated and consciously controlled 'executive suite' of regulatory capacities is a lengthy process. Yet, adolescents confront major, emotionally laden life dilemmas from a relatively early age – an age that has become progressively younger over historic time due to the decline in the age of pubertal onset and in the age at which a wide range of choices are thrust upon young people, as well as a decline in the active monitoring of adolescents by parents as a result of changes in family composition and labor force participation.

The second observation is that the acquisition of a fully coordinated and controlled set of executive functions occurs relatively later in development [10]. As such, it is less likely to be canalized (to the same degree as, say, early language acquisition), leaving greater opportunities for suboptimal trajectories. These suboptimal patterns of development take many different forms, clusters of which are associated with broad categories of psychopathology, such as the excessive down-regulation of mood and motivation that characterizes many internalizing difficulties, or the inadequate control of arousal that is associated with a wide range of risky behaviors typically seen as externalizing problems.

Concluding comments

Like early childhood, adolescence may well be a sensitive or critical developmental period for both normative and maladaptive patterns of development [69–71]. Several aspects of development during this period are especially significant in this regard, among them: the role of puberty in a fundamental restructuring of many body systems and as an influence on social information-processing; the apparent concentration of changes in the adolescent brain in the prefrontal cortex (which serves as a governor of cognition and action) together with the enhanced inter-regional communication between the prefrontal cortex

and other brain regions; and the evidence for substantial synaptic pruning and for non-trivial physiological reversibility of behavioral and neuroendocrine patterns arising from early developmental experiences. Taken together, these developments reinforce the emerging understanding of adolescence as a critical or sensitive period for a reorganization of regulatory systems, a reorganization that is fraught with both risks and opportunities [10]. As we look to the future of research on cognitive and affective development in adolescence, the challenge facing researchers will be integrating research on psychological, neuropsychological and neurobiological development. What we now have are interesting pieces of a complicated puzzle, but the pieces have yet to be fit together in a way that moves the field out of the realm of speculation and towards some measure of certainty.

Acknowledgements

Many of the ideas expressed in this article grew out of the work of the MacArthur Foundation Research Network on Psychopathology and Development. I am especially grateful to Ron Dahl, Dan Keating, David Kupfer, Ann Masten and Danny Pine for their contributions to the enterprise. Thanks also to Marnia Davis for bibliographic assistance.

References

1 Steinberg, L. (2004) Risk-taking in adolescence: What changes, and why? Ann. N. Y. Acad. Sci. 1021, 51–58
2 Steinberg, L. et al. Psychopathology in adolescence: Integrating affective neuroscience with the study of context. In Developmental Psychopathology Vol. 1: Theory and Method (Cicchetti, D. and Cohen, D., eds), Wiley (in press)
3 Wallis, C. (2004) What makes teens tick. Time 10 May, pp. 56–65
4 Wiener, R. and Miller, M. (2004) Determining the death penalty for juveniles. APA Monitor on Psychology 35, 68
5 Paus, T. (2005) Mapping brain maturation and cognitive development during adolescence. Trends Cogn. Sci. 9, 000–000
6 Giedd, J. et al. (1999) Brain development during childhood and adolescence: A longitudinal MRI study. Nat. Neurosci. 2, 861–863
7 Sowell, E.R. et al. (2001) Improved memory functioning and frontal lobe maturation between childhood and adolescence: A structural MRI study. J. Int. Neuropsychol. Soc. 7, 312–322
8 Sowell, E.R. et al. (2002) Development of cortical and subcortical brain structures in childhood and adolescence: A structural MRI study. Dev. Med. Child Neurol. 44, 4–16
9 Dahl, R.E. (2001) Affect regulation, brain development, and behavioral/emotional health in adolescence. CNS Spectr. 6, 1–12
10 Keating, D.P. (2004) Cognitive and brain development. In Handbook of Adolescent Psychology (2nd edn) (Lerner, R.J. and Steinberg, L.D., eds), pp. 45–84, Wiley
11 Donald, M. (2001) A Mind So Rare: The Evolution of Human Consciousness, Norton
12 Dennett, D.C. (1996) Kinds of Minds: Toward an Understanding of Consciousness, Basic Books
13 Casey, B.J. et al. (2000) Structural and functional brain development and its relation to cognitive development. Biol. Psychol. 54, 241–257
14 Johnson, M.H. (2001) Functional brain development in humans. Nat. Rev. Neurosci. 2, 475–483
15 Luna, B. et al. (2001) Maturation of widely distributed brain function subserves cognitive development. Neuroimage 13, 786–793
16 Nelson, C.A. (1999) Neural plasticity and human development. Curr. Dir. Psychol. Sci. 8, 42–45
17 Paus, T. et al. (1999) Structural maturation of neural pathways in children and adolescents: in vivo study. Science 283, 1908–1911
18 Steingard, R.J. et al. (2002) Smaller frontal lobe white matter volumes in depressed adolescents. Biol. Psychiatry 52, 413–417
19 Rilling, J.K. and Insel, T.R. (1999) The primate neocortex in comparative perspective using magnetic resonance imaging. J. Hum. Evol. 37, 191–223

74   *TRENDS in Cognitive Sciences* Vol.9 No.2 February 2005

20 Francis, D.D. *et al.* (2002) Environmental enrichment reverses the effects of maternal separation on stress reactivity. *J. Neurosci.* 22, 7840–7843

21 Newman, J. and Grace, A.A. (1999) Binding across time: The selective gating of frontal and hippocampal systems modulating working memory and attentional states. *Conscious. Cogn.* 8, 196–212

22 Spear, P. (2000) The adolescent brain and age-related behavioral manifestations. *Neurosci. Biobehav. Rev.* 24, 417–463

23 Huttenlocher, P. (1994) Synaptogenesis, synapse elimination, and neural plticity in human cerebral cortex. In *Threats to Optimal Development: Integrating Biological, Psychological, and Social Risk Factors* (Vol. 27) (Nelson, C., ed.), pp. 35–54, Eralbaum

24 Luciana, M. and Nelson, C. (2002) Assessment of neuropsychological function through use of the Cambridge Neuropsychological Testing Automated Battery: Performance in 4- to 12-year-old children. *Dev. Neuropsychol.* 22, 595–624

25 Vuontella, V. *et al.* (2003) Audiospatial and visuospatial working memory in 6-13 year old school children. *Learn. Mem.* 10, 74–84

26 Welsh, M. *et al.* (1991) A normative-developmental study of executive function: A window on prefrontal function in children. *Dev. Neuropsychol.* 7, 131–149

27 Crone, E. and van der Molen, M. (2004) Developmental changes in real-life decision-making: Performance on a gambling task previously shown to depend on the ventromedial prefrontal cortex. *Dev. Neuropsychol.* 25, 251–279

28 Hooper, C. *et al.* (2004) Adolescents' performance on the Iowa Gabling Task: Implications for the development of decision-making and ventromedial prefrontal cortex. *Dev. Psychol.* 40, 1148–1158

29 Martin, C.A. *et al.* (2002) Sensation seeking, puberty and nicotine, alcohol and marijuana use in adolescence. *J. Am. Acad. Child Adolesc. Psychiatry* 41, 1495–1502

30 Cauffman, E. and Steinberg, L. (2000) (Im)maturity of judgment in adolescence: Why adolescents may be less culpable than adults. *Behav. Sci. Law* 18, 1–21

31 Fried, C.S. and Reppucci, N. (2001) Criminal decision-making: The development of adolescent judgment, criminal responsibility, and culpability. *Law Hum. Behav.* 25, 45–61

32 Maggs, J. *et al.* (1995) Risky business: The paradoxical meaning of problem behavior for young adolescents. *J. Early Adolesc.* 15, 344–362

33 Miller, D. and Byrnes, J. (1997) The role of contextual and personal factors in children's risk taking. *Dev. Psychol.* 33, 814–823

34 Scott, E. *et al.* (1995) Evaluating adolescent decision making in legal contexts. *Law Hum. Behav.* 19, 221–244

35 Steinberg, L. and Cauffman, E. (1996) Maturity of judgment in adolescence: Psychosocial factors in adolescent decisionmaking. *Law Hum. Behav.* 20, 249–272

36 Steinberg, L. *Adolescence* (7th edn), McGraw-Hill (in press)

37 Gardner, M. and Steinberg, L. Risk-taking among adolescents, young adults, and adults: The role of peer influence. *Dev. Psychol.* (in press)

38 Eisenberg, N. and Morris, A. (2004) Moral cognitions and prosocial responding in adolescence. In *Handbook of Adolescent Psychology* (Lerner, R. and Steinberg, L., eds), pp. 155–188, Wiley

39 Boehnke, K. *et al.* (1989) Developmental pattern of prosocial motivation: A cross national study. *J. Cross Cult. Psychol.* 20, 219–243

40 Jaffee, S. and Hyde, J.S. (2000) Gender differences in moral orientation: A meta-analysis. *Psychol. Bull.* 126, 703–726

41 Crystal, D. *et al.* (1998) Concepts of human differences: A comparison of American, Japanese, and Chinese children and adolescents. *Dev. Psychol.* 34, 714–722

42 Sobesky, W. (1983) The effects of situational factors on moral judgments. *Child Dev.* 54, 575–584

43 Kuther, T.L. and Higgins-D'Alessandro, A. (2000) Bridging the gap between moral reasoning and adolescent engagement in risky behavior. *J. Adolesc.* 23, 409–422

44 Klaczynski, P.A. (1997) Bias in adolescents' everyday reasoning and its relationships with intellectual ability, personal theories, and self-serving motivation. *Dev. Psychol.* 33, 273–283

45 Klaczynski, P. and Gordon, D. (1996) Everyday statistical reasoning during adolescence and young adulthood: Motivational, general ability, and developmental influences. *Child Dev.* 67, 2873–2891

46 Wainryb, C. *et al.* (2001) Children's, adolescents', and young adults' thinking about different types of disagreements. *Dev. Psychol.* 37, 373–386

47 Neeman, J. *et al.* (1995) The changing importance of romantic relationship involvement to competence from late childhood to late adolescence. *Dev. Psychopathol.* 7, 727–750

48 Udry, J. (1987) Hormonal and social determinants of adolescent sexual initiation. In *Adolescence and Puberty* (Bancroft, J., ed.), pp. 70–87, Oxford University Press

49 Steinberg, L. (1987) The impact of puberty on family relations: Effects of pubertal status and pubertal timing. *Dev. Psychol.* 23, 451–460

50 Diamond, R. *et al.* (1983) Genetic influences on the development of spatial skills during early adolescence. *Cognition* 13, 167–185

51 Mann, V. *et al.* (1979) Development of voice recognition: Parallels with face recognition. *J. Exp. Child Psychol.* 27, 153–165

52 Book, A. *et al.* (2001) The relationship between testosterone and aggression: A meta-analysis. *Aggression & Violent Behavior* 6, 579–599

53 Josephs, R.A. *et al.* (2003) Status, testosterone, and human intellectual performance: Stereotype threat as status concern. *Psychol. Sci.* 14, 158–163

54 Moffitt, T. (1993) Adolescence-limited and life-course-persistent antisocial behavior: A developmental taxonomy. *Psychol. Rev.* 100, 674–701

55 Thompson, R.A. and Fox, N.A. eds (1994) Emotion regulation: A theme in search of definition. Monogr. Soc. Res. Child Dev. 59, No. 240

56 Botvin, G. (1991) Substance abuse prevention: Theory, practice, and effectiveness. In *Crime and Justice* (Tonry, M., ed.), pp. 461–519, University of Chicago Press

57 Tobler, N. (1986) Meta-analysis of 143 adolescent prevention programs: Quantitative outcome results of program participants compared to a control or comparison group. *J. Drug Issues* 16, 537–567

58 Benthin, A. *et al.* (1995) Adolescent health-threatening and health-enhancing behaviors: A study of word association and imagery. *J. Adolesc. Health* 17, 143–152

59 Cauffman, E. and Steinberg, L. (1995) The cognitive and affective influences on adolescent decision-making. *Temple Law Rev.* 68, 1763–1789

60 Slovic, P. (1987) Perception of risk. *Science* 236, 280–285

61 Slovic, P. (1998) Do adolescent smokers know the risks? *Duke Law J.* 47, 1133–1141

62 Slovic, P. (2000) What does it mean to know a cumulative risk? Adolescent's perceptions of short-term and long-term consequences of smoking. *J. Behav. Decis. Making* 13, 259–266

63 Slovic, P. (2000) Rejoinder: The perils of Viscusi's analyses of smoking risk perceptions. *J. Behav. Decis. Making* 13, 273–276

64 Loewenstein, G. and Lerner, J.S. The role of affect in decision-making. In *Handbook of Affective Science* (Goldsmith, H., ed.), Oxford University Press (in press)

65 Bechara, A. *et al.* (2000) Emotion, decision making and the orbitofrontal cortex. *Cereb. Cortex* 10, 295–307

66 Bechara, A. *et al.* (1999) Different contributions of the human amygdala and ventromedial prefrontal cortex to decision-making. *J. Neurosci.* 19, 5473–5481

67 Keating, D.P. and Sasse, D.K. (1996) Cognitive socialization in adolescence: Critical period of a theory of mind. In *Psychosocial Development During Adolescence: Progress in Developmental Contextualism* (Gullota, T.P., ed.), pp. 232–258, Sage

68 Richards, M.H. *et al.* (1998) Developmental patterns and gender differences in the experience of peer companionship during adolescence. *Child Dev.* 69, 154–163

69 Boyce, W.T. and Keating, D.P. Should we intervene to improve childhood circumstances? In *A Life Course Approach to Chronic Disease Epidemiology* (2nd edn) (Kuh, D. and Ben-Shlomo, Y., eds), Oxford University Press (in press)

70 Keating, D.P. and Hertzman, C. (1999) *Developmental health and the wealth of nations: Social, biological, and educational dynamics*, Guilford Press

71 Meaney, M.J. (2001) Maternal care, gene expression, and the transmission of individual differences in stress reactivity across generations. *Annu. Rev. Neurosci.* 24, 1161–1192

[11]

Does Stress Damage the Brain?

J. Douglas Bremner

Studies in animals showed that stress results in damage to the hippocampus, a brain area involved in learning and memory, with associated memory deficits. The mechanism involves glucocorticoids and possibly serotonin acting through excitatory amino acids to mediate hippocampal atrophy. Patients with posttraumatic stress disorder (PTSD) from Vietnam combat and childhood abuse had deficits on neuropsychological measures that have been validated as probes of hippocampal function. In addition, magnetic resonance imaging (MRI) showed reduction in volume of the hippocampus in both combat veterans and victims of childhood abuse. In combat veterans, hippocampal volume reduction was correlated with deficits in verbal memory on neuropsychological testing. These studies introduce the possibility that experiences in the form of traumatic stressors can have long-term effects on the structure and function of the brain. Biol Psychiatry 1999;45:797–805 © 1999 Society of Biological Psychiatry

Key Words: Memory, hippocampus, stress, cortisol, PTSD

Introduction

One hundred years of psychiatry has brought us back to our starting point. At the end of the 19th century, Sigmund Freud made the famous case study of Anna O., who was suffering from hysterical symptoms that appeared to be related to the witnessing of sexual events as a child. Freud originally believed that Anna O. was a victim of exposure to traumatic sexual experiences in childhood. Following this initial observation, he noticed an increasing number of women in his practice who reported exposure to sexual events in childhood. Could it be that Vienna was suffering from an epidemic of childhood sexual abuse? At the time, childhood sexual abuse was considered to be a rare phenomenon. Freud changed his views into the theory that fantasies of childhood sexuality were leading to neurotic behavior in his patients,

rather than the reality of childhood sexual abuse (Nemiah 1998). The rest of the story is the history of American psychiatry for a good part of the 20th century.

American psychiatry was dominated by Freud's theories for the first half of the 20th century. These views held sway until the advance of biologic approaches to psychiatry, which have become increasingly prominent over the past 30 years. Biological psychiatrists aimed to replace Freud's theories of psychopathology (based on ideas of imbalances of psychological forces) with what they felt was a more scientific approach. In their view, psychopathology was secondary to disruptions of physiology that had their foundation in genetic vulnerability. This framework placed greater emphasis on genetic abnormalities leading to physiologic changes, with their phenomenologic expression in psychiatric disorders. In the early phase of biological psychiatry, there was a great emphasis on finding the genetic basis for psychiatric disorders, and little emphasis on the role of environment in the genesis of psychopathology. As is often true in the history of the development of ideas, the biological psychiatrists effectively leaped backward over 50 years of psychoanalysis to psychiatrists such as Kraepelin (1919). He also believed that psychiatric disorders had their basis in constitutional abnormalities that had their expression in the brain, and performed neuroanatomic studies of the brains of schizophrenics in order to find a lesion to explain their illness.

The biological psychiatrists who used this model, however, were really not much different from the psychoanalysts who preceded them. Both groups gave little or no credence to the role that environment could play in the development of psychiatric illness. Biological psychiatry emphasized the deterministic effects of genetics, while psychoanalysts focused on unconscious mechanisms upon which the environment had little impact (e.g., at one time the idea that children should be observed in order to understand their internal psychology was considered radical). Thirty years after the start of the biologic revolution in psychiatry, we still have not found the gene for schizophrenia or mania. It is clear that genetic factors do play an important role in psychiatric disorders. Most likely, a combination of genetic and environmental factors, of nature and nurture, is involved in the development of psychopathology. In terms of possible environmental causes of psychopathology, stress is a good candidate.

One of the most important brain areas that mediates, and in turn is affected by, the stress response is the hippocam-

From the Departments of Diagnostic Radiology and Psychiatry, Yale University School of Medicine, Yale Psychiatric Institute, Yale/VA PET Center, and National Center for PTSD-VA Connecticut Healthcare System, New Haven, CT.

Address reprint requests to J. Douglas Bremner, MD, Yale Psychiatric Institute, POB 208038 Yale Station, New Haven, CT 06520.

Received February 20, 1998; revised October 8, 1998; accepted December 10, 1998.

pus. The hippocampus plays an important role in new learning and memory (Zola-Morgan and Squire 1990). This function is critical to the stress response, for example in assessing potential threat during a life-threatening situation, as occurs with exposure to a predator. Alterations in memory form an important part of the clinical presentation of patients with stress-related psychopathology. PTSD patients demonstrate a variety of memory problems including deficits in declarative memory (remembering facts or lists, as reviewed below), and fragmentation of memories (both autobiographic and trauma-related). PTSD is also associated with alterations in nondeclarative memory (i.e., types of memory that cannot be willfully brought up into the conscious mind, including motor memory such as how to ride a bicycle). These types of nondeclarative memories include conditioned responses and abnormal reliving of traumatic memories following exposure to situationally appropriate cues (Brewin et al 1996).

The important effects of the stress hormones, glucocorticoids, on the hippocampus is consistent with the hypothesis that the hippocampus likely plays a role in stress-related psychiatric disorders. The hippocampus has a rich concentration of receptors for glucocorticoids (McEwen et al 1986). Corticosteroid receptors within the hippocampus include Type I (mineralocorticoid) and Type II (glucocorticoid). Type II receptors have a low affinity for glucocorticoids, but tissues with Type I receptors contain an enzyme which metabolizes cortisol so that the receptor is not exposed to high concentrations of cortisol that is available for binding. This binary system of receptors may allow a more flexible responsiveness of the system, with Type II receptors playing a more important role in modulation of hippocampal function during high release of glucocorticoids as is seen during acute stress (Trapp and Holsboer 1996). The hippocampus also modulates glucocorticoid release through inhibitory effects on the hypothalamic–pituitary–adrenal (HPA) axis. These findings indicate that the hippocampus is an important center piece for integrating cognitive, neurohormonal, and neurochemical responses to stress. We hypothesized that hippocampal dysfunction represents the anatomic basis for alterations in memory, such as fragmented or delayed recall of traumatic memories of childhood abuse (Bremner et al 1996a). The hippocampus may also play a role in other symptoms of PTSD.

Studies in normal human subjects showed that glucocorticoids have direct effects on memory function. Administration of commonly used therapeutic doses of glucocorticoids (Keenan et al 1995), dexamethasone (Wolkowitz et al 1990; Newcomer et al 1994), or cortisol (Kirschbaum et al 1996) resulted in impairments in verbal declarative memory function in healthy human subjects.

Cortisol levels were related to memory function, with evidence of exacerbation of memory deficits with stress-induced cortisol elevations (Kirschbaum et al 1996; Lupien et al 1997) and improvement in memory function with reduction in cortisol levels (Seeman et al 1997; Wolkowitz et al 1997). ACTH (Born et al 1990) and cortisol (Born et al 1987) have effects on a component of the event related potential (ERP) that is a marker for selective attention. Patients with Cushing's Disease, which involves excessive release of cortisol over long periods of time, have deficits in verbal declarative memory that are correlated with hippocampal volume reduction on magnetic resonance imaging (MRI) (Starkman et al 1992). These findings showed that glucocorticoids have direct and reversible effects on memory and cognition that are at least partially mediated through the hippocampus.

Cortisol also represents an important part of the response to stress in human subjects. Healthy human subjects undergoing psychological stressors demonstrate a robust increase in cortisol levels in the periphery (Rose et al 1968; Seeman et al 1995a; Seeman et al 1995b). Soldiers in the Korean War undergoing random artillery bombardment had markedly increased levels of urinary cortisol, with the highest levels in soldiers under the greatest danger, in comparison with their own cortisol levels when away from the battle zone area (Howard et al 1955). These studies showed that extreme stress results in an acute increase in cortisol levels in human subjects.

Work from the laboratories of Robert Sapolsky at Stanford University, Bruce McEwen at Rockefeller University, and others demonstrated in a variety of animal species that high levels of glucocorticoids seen in stress is associated with damage to the hippocampus. When male and female vervet monkeys are caged together, the female monkeys attack the males, leading to extreme stress in the males, which is often fatal. Monkeys who were improperly caged and died spontaneously following exposure to severe stress had multiple gastric ulcers on autopsy, consistent with exposure to chronic stress, and hyperplastic adrenal cortices, consistent with sustained glucocorticoid release. These monkeys also had damage to the CA3 subfield of the hippocampus (Uno et al 1989).

Follow-up studies suggested that hippocampal damage was associated with direct exposure of glucocorticoids to the hippocampus (Sapolsky et al 1990). Studies in a variety of animal species (Sapolsky et al 1988) showed that direct glucocorticoid exposure results in decreased dendritic branching (Wooley et al 1990; Watanabe et al 1992c), alterations in synaptic terminal structure (Magarinos et al 1997), a loss of neurons (Uno et al 1990), and an inhibition of neuronal regeneration (Gould et al 1998) within the CA3 region of the hippocampus. These effects are steroid and tissue specific (Sapolsky et al 1985; Packan and Sapolsky 1990). Prenatal exposure to elevated levels of glucocorticoids also resulted in hippocampal damage (Uno et al 1990), a finding which has implications for the common practice in pediatric medicine of administering dexamethasone to premature infants to prevent intraventricular hemorrhage. Glucocorticoids exert their effect through disruption of cellular metabolism (Lawrence and Sapolsky 1994) and by increasing the vulnerability of hippocampal neurons to a variety of insults, including endogenously released excitatory amino acids (Sapolsky and Pusinelli 1985; Armanini et al 1990; Virgin et al 1991). Glucocorticoids have also been shown to augment extracellular glutamate accumulation (Stein-Behrens et al 1994). Furthermore, reduction of glucocorticoid exposure prevents the hippocampal cell loss associated with chronic stress (Landfield et al 1981; Meaney et al 1988).

Stress also has effects on functions of new learning and memory that are mediated by the hippocampus. Exposure to the stress of an unfamiliar environment resulted in deficits in working memory indicative of hippocampal dysfunction (Diamond et al 1996). High levels of glucocorticoids seen with stress were associated with deficits in new learning, in addition to damage to the hippocampus (Luine et al 1994). Long-term subcutaneous implants of glucocorticoids that mimic the chronic stress situation resulted in deficits in new learning and memory for maze escape behaviors. Moreover, the magnitude of deficits in new learning of maze escape behaviors was correlated with the number of damaged cells in the CA3 region of the hippocampus (Arbel et al 1994). Stress was also shown to affect long-term potentiation (LTP), which is used as a model for the molecular basis of new learning and memory (Diamond et al 1995). These effects may be mediated by glucocorticoids acting through the Type II receptor within the hippocampus (Pavlides et al 1995).

Other neurochemical systems interact with glucocorticoids to mediate the effects of stress on memory and the hippocampus. Stress resulted in a decrease in $5HT_{1A}$ binding within the hippocampus with associated atrophy in the CA3 region of the hippocampus and memory impairment. Tianeptine, which decreases serotonin levels within the hippocampus, blocked the effect of stress on memory and the hippocampus, suggesting that serotonin released during stress may also play a role in the etiology of hippocampal damage (McEwen et al 1997). Brain-derived neurotrophic factor (BDNF) is a recently isolated neuropeptide which has important trophic effects on the hippocampus and other brain regions. Stress resulted in a reduction in brain-derived neurotrophic factor (BDNF) mRNA in the hippocampus, an effect which may be partially related to glucocorticoid release (Smith et al 1995). These effects were blocked by antidepressant drugs and electroconvulsive therapy (Nibuya et al 1995). Stress-induced reductions in BDNF may contribute to hippocampal atrophy associated with stress.

Stress-mediated hippocampal damage may lead to dysregulation of others aspects of the organism's stress response system. The hippocampus has an inhibitory effect on the corticotropin releasing factor (CRF) and the hypothalamic–pituitary–adrenal (HPA) axis (Jacobson and Sapolsky 1991). Intraventricular injection of CRF, which is physiologically released during stress, resulted in a series of physiologic and behavioral responses that are adaptive during stress and are considered to be characteristic of anxiety responses. Stress-induced damage to the hippocampus resulted in increased levels of corticotropin releasing factor (CRF) mRNA in the paraventricular nuclei of the hypothalamus (Herman et al 1989) as well as a decrease in the sensitivity of rats to dexamethasone suppression of HPA function (Feldman and Conforti 1980; Magarinos et al 1988). In human subjects with combat-related PTSD, we found elevated CRF levels in cerebrospinal fluid based on a single lumbar puncture determination (Bremner et al 1997a). CRF is distributed in a number of locations outside of the hypothalamus. The behavioral effects of CRF are not likely to be mediated by hypothalamic CRF, however, and the functional significance of elevations in CRF derived from the hypothalamus for stress-related psychiatric disorders is unclear.

The effects of glucocorticoids on the physiology of the organism exposed to stress are more complex than a simple mediation of hippocampal neuronal cell death. Glucocorticoids have a variety of effects on physiologic systems in addition to effects on the brain, including the modulation of gene expression, immunity, reproduction, and bone formation. These effects may have a protective effect on the organism during certain situations of stress, but in other situations, the effects of glucocorticoids may be damaging (McEwen et al 1992). Stress-induced hippocampal damage may be an example of sacrificing long-term function (i.e., memory function) for the sake of short-term survival. Elevations in glucocorticoids are not invariably associated with hippocampal damage. For instance, the absence of glucocorticoids following adrenalectomy resulted in damage to neurons of the dentate gyrus of the hippocampus (distinct from the CA3 region most commonly affected by stress) (Vaher et al 1994). The authors argued for a more dynamic role of glucocorticoids in sculpting neurons of the hippocampus, with glucocorticoids having the potential to have both protective and damaging effects depending on a variety of factors (McEwen et al 1995).

These studies raised the question, do glucocorticoids result in hippocampal damage and associated memory deficits in humans? With this in mind, we initially used neuropsychological testing to measure declarative memory function in Vietnam combat veterans with PTSD. We selected measures that were validated in studies of patients with epilepsy to be specific probes of hippocampal function. Sass and colleagues in the Yale Neurosurgery Program administered the Wechsler Memory Scale (WMS)-Logical Subscale (paragraph recall) and verbal Selective Reminding Test (vSRT) to patients with epilepsy who subsequently underwent surgical resection of the hippocampus. The investigators found that decreases in percent retention of the WMS paragraph after delayed recall and deficits on the Long Term Retrieval (LTR) subscale of the vSRT were correlated with decreases in neuronal number of the CA3 region of the left hippocampus (Sass et al 1990; Sass et al 1992). The findings were specific to verbal, and not visual, memory. In a study using these measures, we compared Vietnam combat veterans with PTSD ($n = 26$) to control subjects ($n = 16$) matched for gender, age, race, years of alcohol abuse, years of education, handedness, and socioeconomic status. We found deficits in paragraph recall as measured by the WMS-Logical Component, for immediate and delayed recall, as well as percent retention. We also found deficits in short-term verbal memory as measured with the vSRT LTR. There was no difference in IQ between patients and control subjects in this study as measured by the Wechsler Adult Intelligence Sale-Revised (WAIS-R) or visual memory as measured by the WMS-Figural Component (Bremner et al 1993). We followed up studies of memory in male combat veterans with PTSD by examining men and women with PTSD related to severe childhood physical and/or sexual abuse. We studied patients with PTSD related to a history of severe childhood abuse as measured by the Early Trauma Inventory (ETI) ($n = 18$), and compared them to healthy subjects ($n = 17$) matched for age, gender, race, years of education, and years of alcohol abuse. We found deficits in immediate and delayed recall and percent retention on the WMS-Logical Component, as well as the vSRT LTR, in the patients with abuse-related PTSD in comparison to controls. Deficits in short-term memory in the childhood abuse patients were significantly correlated with level of abuse as measured with the composite severity score on the ETI ($r = -.48$; $p < .05$). There was no difference in IQ as measured by the WAIS-R or visual memory as measured by the WMS-Figural Component in early trauma patients in comparison to control subjects (Bremner et al 1995b). Other groups also found deficits in verbal declarative memory in Vietnam combat veterans with PTSD using other measures of verbal declarative memory function (Uddo et al 1993; Yehuda et al 1995) (although see Gurvits et al 1993). Recently, deficits in verbal declarative memory were also reported in Desert Storm veterans with PTSD (Vasterling et al 1997). Future studies are needed to demonstrate that

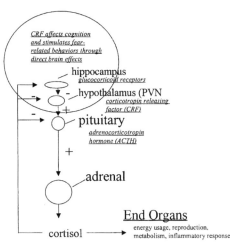

Figure 1. Diagrammatic representation of the relationship between the hippocampus and the hypothalamic–pituitary–adrenal (HPA) axis response to stress in PTSD. Activation of the HPA axis in acute stress results in elevated cortisol in the periphery, which may lead to hippocampal damage. Hippocampal atrophy may cause a release of hypothalamic inhibition, resulting in elevated CRF with associated blunted ACTH response to CRF. Long-term dysregulation in PTSD may lead to decreases in cortisol (the mechanism of which is unclear) or no change.

verbal memory deficits are specifically associated with PTSD, and are not a nonspecific result of exposure to traumatic stress.

In order to test the hypothesis that traumatic stress results in hippocampal damage, we used magnetic resonance imaging (MRI) to quantitate hippocampal volume in living human subjects with a history of traumatic stress and the diagnosis of PTSD. We first looked at hippocampal volume in Vietnam veterans with combat-related PTSD. Healthy control subjects were matched for gender, age, race, years of alcohol abuse, years of education, height, weight, and socioeconomic status. Measurements of the hippocampus were performed using a reliable technique for measurement of hippocampal volume that has been validated by correlating MRI-based volumetrics with hippocampal neuronal number obtained from surgical specimens of the hippocampus in patients with epilepsy. We found an 8% decrease in MRI-based measurement of right hippocampal volume in patients with PTSD ($n = 26$) in comparison to matched control subjects ($n = 22$) [1184 vs 1286 mm^3; 95% confidence interval (CI) 10 to 195 mm^3; $p < .05$]. Decreases in right hippocampal volume in the PTSD patients were associated with deficits in short-term memory as measured by the WMS-Logical, percent retention subcomponent ($r = .64$; $p < .05$). There was no difference in volume of bilateral left temporal lobe (minus hippocampus) or caudate between patients and controls in this study (Bremner et al 1995c). We have subsequently not found a difference in volume of the amygdala between patients with combat-related PTSD and control subjects (Bremner et al 1998). Multiple linear regression including potential confounders not addressed by the matching methodology, years of alcohol abuse, education, and age, did not show a significant relationship between these variables and hippocampal volume (Bremner et al 1996b).

A subsequent study examined hippocampal volume in 17 male and female adults with a history of severe childhood physical and/or sexual abuse and long-term psychiatric consequences in the form of PTSD. They were compared to 17 healthy control subjects matched on a case-by-case basis for age, gender, handedness, race, years of education, and years of alcohol abuse. There was a 12% reduction in left hippocampal volume in the patients with abuse-related PTSD in relation to comparison subjects, which was statistically significant ($p < .05$). A 3.8% reduction in volume of the right hippocampus was not significant. Multivariate analyses utilizing stepwise linear regression continued to show a significant relationship between PTSD and decreased hippocampal volume when the potential confounders of age, education, and alcohol abuse were entered in the model. There were no significant differences between patients and controls for temporal lobe, caudate, or amygdala volumes in this study (Bremner et al 1997b).

Other studies found reductions in hippocampal volume in clinical populations of traumatized subjects. Gurvits and co-workers (1996) compared hippocampal volume in seven patients with Vietnam combat-related PTSD to seven Vietnam combat veterans without PTSD, and eight healthy nonveteran control subjects. The authors found a 26% bilateral decrease in hippocampal volume, which was statistically significant for both left and right hippocampal volume considered separately. Although subjects were not case matched for alcohol abuse, there continued to be a significant difference in hippocampal volume after adjusting for years of alcohol abuse using analysis of covariance. There was no difference in ventricular, amygdala, or whole brain volume between the groups. This study also found a significant correlation between level of combat exposure (measured with the Combat Exposure Scale) and combat exposure, as well as visual delayed recall errors. Stein and colleagues (1997) found a statistically significant 5% reduction in left hippocampal volume in 21 sexually abused women relative to 21 nonabused female control subjects. Hippocampal atrophy in this study was correlated with level of dissociative symptomatology in the abused women. Most (although not all) of the abused women had a current diagnosis of PTSD. In summary, there are several replicated studies in more than one population of traumatized patients showing atrophy of the hippocampus, which appears to be specific to PTSD diagnosis. PTSD patients with early life trauma had a greater reduction in left hippocampal volume, while patients with PTSD from later life (Vietnam combat) had bilateral or right hippocampal atrophy. One possible explanation for this finding is related to the fact that the hippocampus continues to develop after birth. Insults to the hippocampus as different stage of development may have different effects on the hippocampus.

Hippocampal atrophy was also found in patients with major depression. Exposure to stress has been temporally related to the onset of depressive episodes (reviewed in Mazure 1994), and many patients with depression have elevations in plasma cortisol levels. Cognitive deficits consistent with hippocampal dysfunction were also associated with depression. Recently, Sheline and co-workers (1996) found atrophy of the hippocampus in a group of treated patients with major depression compared to control subjects. Our group has also found statistically significant reductions in hippocampal volume after controlling for differences in whole brain volume (Bremner et al, unpublished data, 2/16/98). A previous study, however, did not find evidence for hippocampal atrophy in depression in patients with current depression (Axelson et al 1993). This negative finding may be related in part to limited resolution of early MR imaging techniques and inability to distinguish hippocampus from amygdala. Hippocampal volume reductions in depression could be related to either stress resulting in an increase in cortisol, or to elevated cortisol levels that are associated with depressive episodes in 40% to 50% of patients. More work is needed to comprehensively examine cortisol, memory, and the hippocampus in depressed patients before and after treatment.

The functional implications of hippocampal volume reduction in PTSD are unclear. Volume reductions of 5% to 12% are of a lesser magnitude than in other disorders involving hippocampal pathology such as epilepsy and Alzheimer's dementia. The fact that volume reduction correlated with memory dysfunction in at least two studies indicates that these findings are related to declarative memory dysfunction. The hippocampus may also be involved in fear responding and other behaviors that are relevant to the clinical presentation of PTSD.

There are alternative possible explanations for memory deficits and hippocampal volume reduction in PTSD. Small hippocampal volume and poor memory function that is present from birth could represent a risk factor for the development of PTSD. Consistent with this idea, McNally and Shin (1995) reported that low IQ at the time of entering the service was a risk factor for development of combat-related PTSD. Studies in monozygotic twins (who have identical genetic constitution) are needed in order to assess the relative contribution of genetic and environmental factors to memory deficits and hippocampal volume reduction in PTSD.

The possibility that cortisol may be low in chronic PTSD raises the question of how elevations in cortisol can represent the mechanisms of hippocampal atrophy in PTSD. Several early studies showed decreased cortisol in chronic PTSD (Mason et al 1986; Yehuda et al 1991; reviewed in Yehuda et al 1995b). These findings have not been uniformly replicated, however (Pitman and Orr 1990; Lemieux and Coe 1995), in some cases with larger sample sizes than earlier studies (Mason et al, unpublished data, 9/1/98). We hypothesized that high levels of cortisol at the time of the stressor result in damage to hippocampal neurons, which can persist for many years after the original trauma, leading to reductions in hippocampal volume as measured with MRI (Bremner et al 1995a, 1996; 1998). In this scenario, decreased cortisol characterizes the chronic stages of the disorder due to adaptation and long-term changes in cortisol regulation. The studies reviewed above suggest that acute traumatic stress results in hyperactivity of the CRF/HPA system, while chronic PTSD may lead to long-term dysregulation, which results in a different HPA/cortisol system. It is also possible that sensitivity of hippocampal glucocorticoid receptors to circulating cortisol represents the critical variable in determining vulnerability to stress-induced hippocampal atrophy.

Findings of no increase in cortisol levels in the aftermath of rape in women who subsequently develop PTSD (Resnick et al 1995; Yehuda et al 1998) have also been used to argue against the glucocorticoid hypothesis of stress-induced hippocampal damage. In an initial report, cortisol samples obtained days to weeks after exposure to the trauma of rape found a relationship between low cortisol in the aftermath of rape and prior history of trauma (Resnick et al 1995). In a subsequent analysis of samples obtained 8 to 48 hours after the rape, the authors found a relationship between low cortisol levels in the aftermath of rape and prior history of trauma. However, there was there was no relationship between cortisol and risk for subsequent development of PTSD (Yehuda et al 1998). Given the finding that history of prior trauma increases the risk for PTSD with subsequent victimization, this raises the question of whether these patients had prior PTSD, or were physiologically distinct from the nonstress exposed subjects. The studies also provide no information about cortisol levels at the time of the rape. Studies are needed to examine the relationship between cortisol at the time of the trauma, hippocampal volume, and PTSD.

Findings of memory deficits and hippocampal volume reduction in PTSD have implications for the controversy surrounding delayed recall of childhood abuse (Bremner et al 1996). The hippocampus has been hypothesized to play a role in the binding of individual memory elements at the time of memory retrieval. If the hippocampus is dysfunctional, this may represent the anatomic basis of the fragmentation of memory often seen in patients with PTSD related to childhood abuse. Memory dysfunction in PTSD is also relevant to clinical management. Clinicians should be aware that problems with learning and memory may affect the performance of patients at work or school.

If stress results in hippocampal damage and associated problems with memory, this could have far reaching implications. Our inner cities are plagued by an epidemic of urban violence that affects our nation's children on a daily basis. The hippocampus plays a role in new learning and memory. If stress impairs the ability of children to learn, this could have important public health implications. Consistent with this, one recent study showed that Lebanese teenagers with PTSD related to exposure to bombings and violence in civil war had deficits in academic achievement as measured with the Metropolitan Achievement Test (MAT) in comparison to stressed nonPTSD youths and nonstressed control subjects (Saigh et al 1996).

The question arises, if stress can damage the brain, is there anything that can be done to prevent or reverse this process? The good news is that studies in animals demonstrated several agents with potentially beneficial effects. The group at Rockefeller University found that phenytoin (Dilantin) reverses stress induced hippocampal atrophy, probably through modulation of excitatory amino acid-induced neurotoxicity (Watanabe et al 1992a). Other agents, including tianeptine and dihydroepiandrosterone (DHEA), have similar effects (Watanabe et al 1992b). Serotonin reuptake inhibitor administration was shown to result in an increase in dendritic branching within the hippocampus (Duman et al 1997). We still do not know if hippocampal atrophy is reversible in humans. However, findings that cognitive therapy results in reversal of memory dysfunction in traumatized Lebanese youths with PTSD offers some grounds for hope (Saigh 1988). In addition, studies showing that the hippocampus is unique within the brain in its capacity to regenerate neurons (Gould et al 1998) suggest that reversibility may be possible even in the setting of neuronal death.

This research reviewed in this paper was supported by a NIH-sponsored General Clinical Research Center (GCRC) Clinical Associate Physician (CAP) Award and a VA Research Career Development Award to Dr. Bremner, and the National Center for PTSD Grant.

References

Arbel I, Kadar T, Silberman M, Levy A (1994): The effects of long-term corticosterone administration on hippocampal morphology and cognitive performance of middle-aged rats. *Brain Res* 657:227–235.

Armanini MP, Hutchins C, Stein BA, Sapolsky RM (1990): Glucocorticoid endangerment of hippocampal neurons is NMDA-receptor dependent. *Brain Res* 532:7–1.

Axelson DA, Doraiswamy PM, McDonald WM, et al (1993): Hypercortisolemia and hippocampal damage changes in depression. *Psych Res* 47:163–173.

Born J, Kern W, Fehm-Wolfsdorf G, Fehm HL (1987): Cortisol effects on attentional processes in man as indicated by event-related potentials. *Psychophysiology* 24:286–291.

Born J, Unseld U, Pietrowsky R, Bickel U, Voigt K, Fehm HL (1990): Time course of ACTH 4-10 effects on human attention. *Neuroendocrinology* 52:169–174.

Bremner JD, Innis RB, Charney DS (1996b): Hippocampal volume in posttraumatic stress disorder: Controlling for potential confounders. *Am J Psychiatry* 163:1658–1659.

Bremner JD, Krystal JH, Charney DS, Southwick SM (1996a): Neural mechanisms in dissociative amnesia for childhood abuse: Relevance to the current controversy surrounding the "false memory syndrome." *Am J Psychiatry* 153(7):FS71–82.

Bremner JD, Krystal JH, Southwick SM, Charney DS (1995a): Functional neuroanatomical correlates of the effects of stress on memory. *J Trauma Stress* 8:527–554.

Bremner JD, Licinio J, Darnell A, et al (1997a): Elevated CSF corticotropin-releasing factor concentrations in posttraumatic stress disorder. *Am J Psychiatry* 154:624–629.

Bremner JD, Randall PR, Capelli S, Scott T, McCarthy G, Charney DS (1995b): Deficits in short-term memory in adult survivors of childhood abuse. *Psychiatry Res* 59:97–107.

Bremner JD, Randall PR, Scott TM, et al (1995c): MRI-based measurement of hippocampal volume in posttraumatic stress disorder. *Am J Psychiatry* 152:973–981.

Bremner JD, Randall P, Vermetten E, et al (1997b): MRI-based measurement of hippocampal volume in posttraumatic stress disorder related to childhood physical and sexual abuse: A preliminary report. *Biol Psychiatry* 41:23–32.

Bremner JD, Scott TM, Delaney RC, et al (1993): Deficits in short-term memory in post-traumatic stress disorder. *Am J Psychiatry* 150:1015–1019.

Bremner JD, Vermetten E, Southwick SM, Krystal JH, Charney DS (1998): Trauma, memory, and dissociation: An integrative formulation. In: *Trauma, Memory and Dissociation.* Bremner JD, Marmar C, editors. Washington DC: APA Press, pp 365–402.

Brewin CR, Dalgleish T, Joseph S (1996): A dual representation theory of posttraumatic stress disorder. *Psychol Rev* 103:670–686.

Diamond DM, Branch BJ, Fleshner M, Rose GM (1995): Effects of dehydroepiandrosterone and stress on hippocampal electrophysiological plasticity. *Ann N Y Acad Sci* 774:304–307.

Diamond DM, Fleshner M, Ingersoll N, Rose GM (1996): Psychological stress impairs spatial working memory: Relevance to electrophysiological studies of hippocampal function. *Behav Neurosci* 110:661–672.

Duman RS, Heninger GR, Nestler EJ (1997): A molecular and cellular theory of depression. *Arch Gen Psychiatry* 54:597–606.

Feldman S, Conforti N (1980): Participation of the dorsal hippocampus in the glucocorticoid feedback effect on adrenocortical activity. *Neuroendocrinology* 30:52–55.

Gould E, Tanapat P, McEwen BS, Flugge G, Fuchs E (1998): Proliferation of granule cell precursors in the dentate gyrus of adult monkeys is diminished by stress. *PNAS* 95:3168–3171.

Gurvits TG, Lasko NB, Schacter SC, Kuhne AA, Orr SP, Pitman RK (1993): Neurological status of Vietnam veterans with chronic posttraumatic stress disorder. *J Neuropsychiatry Clin Neurosci* 5:183–188.

Gurvits TG, Shenton MR, Hokama H, et al (1996): Magnetic resonance imaging study of hippocampal volume in chronic combat-related posttraumatic stress disorder. *Biol Psychiatry* 40:192–199.

Herman J, Schafer M, Young E, et al (1989): Evidence for hippocampal regulation of neuroendocrine neurons of hypothalamo-pituitary-adrenocortical axis. *J Neurosci* 9:3072–3082.

Howard JM, Olney JM, Frawley JP, et al (1955): Studies of adrenal function in combat and wounded soldiers. *Annal Surg* 141:314–320.

Jacobson L, Sapolsky R (1991): The role of the hippocampus in feedback regulation of the hypothalamic-pituitary-adrenocortical axis. *Endocr Rev* 12:118–134.

Keenan PA, Jacobson MW, Soleyman RM, Newcomer JW (1995): Commonly used therapeutic doses of glucocorticoids impair explicit memory. *Annal N Y Acad Sci* 761:400–402.

Kirschbaum C, Wolf OT, May M, Wippich W, Hellhammer DH (1996): Stress- and treatment-induced elevations of cortisol levels associated with impaired declarative memory in healthy adults. *Life Sci* 58:1475–1483.

Kraepelin E (1919): *Dementia Praecox and Paraphrenia.* Huntington, NY: Reprinted 1971 by Krieger Publishing Co.

Landfield P, Baskin R, Pitler T (1981): Brain aging correlates: Retardation by hormonal-pharmacological treatments. *Science* 214:581–584.

Lawrence MS, Sapolsky RM (1994): Glucocorticoids accelerate ATP loss following metabolic insults in cultured hippocampal neurons. *Brain Res* 646:303–306.

Lemieux AM, Coe CL (1995): Abuse-related posttraumatic stress disorder: Evidence for chronic neuroendocrine activation in women. *Psychosom Med* 57:105–115.

Luine V, Villages M, Martinex C, McEwen BS (1994): Repeated stress causes reversible impairments of spatial memory performance. *Brain Res* 639:167–170.

Lupien SJ, Gaudreau S, Tchiteya BM, et al (1997): Stress-induced declarative memory impairment in healthy elderly subjects: Relationship to cortisol reactivity. *JCEM* 82:2070–2075.

Magarinos A, Somoza G, DeNicola A (1987): Glucocorticoid negative feedback and glucocorticoid receptors after hippocampectomy in rats. *Horm Metab Res* 19:105–109.

Magarinos AM, Verdugo JM, McEwen BS (1997): Chronic stress alters synaptic terminal structure in hippocampus. *PNAS* 94:14002–14008.

Mason JW, Giller EL, Kosten TR, Ostroff RB, Podd L (1986):

Urinary free cortisol levels in post-traumatic stress disorder patients. *J Nerv Ment Dis* 174:145–149.

Mazure CM, editor (1994): *Stress and Psychiatric Disorders.* Washington, DC: American Psychiatric Press.

McNally RJ, Shin, LM (1995): Association of intelligence with severity of posttraumatic stress disorder symptoms on Vietnam combat veterans. *Am J Psychiatry* 152:936–938.

McEwen BS (1995): Adrenal steroid actions on brain: Dissecting the fine line between protection and damage. In: Friedman MJ, Charney DS, Deutch AY, editors. *Neurobiological and Clinical Consequences of Stress: From Normal Adaptation to PTSD.* New York: Raven Press, pp. 135–151.

McEwen BS, Angulo J, Cameron H, et al (1992): Paradoxical effects of adrenal steroids on the brain: Protection versus degeneration. *Biol Psychiatry* 31:177–199.

McEwen BS, Conrad CD, Kuroda Y, Frankfurt M, Magarinos AM, McKittrick C (1997): Prevention of stress-induced morphological and cognitive consequences. *Eur Neuropsychopharm* 7(3 suppl):S322–S328.

McEwen B, de Kloet E, Rostene W (1986): Adrenal steroid receptors and actions in the nervous system. *Phys Rev* 66:1121–1189.

Meaney M, Aitken D, Bhatnager S, van Berkel C, Sapolsky R (1988): Effect of neonatal handling on age-related impairments associated with the hippocampus. *Science* 239:766–769.

Nemiah J (1998): In: Bremner JD, Marmar C, editors. *Trauma, Memory and Dissociation.* Washington DC: APA Press, pp. 1–18.

Newcomer JW, Craft, S, Hershey, T, Askins, K, & Bardgett, ME (1994). Glucocorticoid-induced impairment in declarative memory performance in adult humans. *Journal of Neuroscience,* 14:2047-2053.

Nibuya M, Morinobu S, Duman RS (1995): Regulation of BDNF and trkB mRNA in rat brain by chronic electroconvulsive seizure and antidepressant drug treatments. *J Neurosci* 15: 7539–7547.

Pavlides C, Watanabe Y, Magarinos AM, McEwen BS (1995): Opposing roles of type I and type II adrenal steroid receptors in hippocampal long-term potentiation. *Neuroscience* 68: 387–394.

Pitman R, Orr S (1990): Twenty-four hour urinary cortisol and catecholamine excretion in combat-related posttraumatic stress disorder. *Biol Psychiatry* 27:245–247.

Resnick HS, Yehuda R, Pitman RK, Foy DW (1995): Effect of previous trauma on acute plasma cortisol level following rape. *Am J Psychiatry* 152:1675–1677.

Rose RM, Poe RO, Mason JW (1968): Psychological state and body size as determinants of 17-OHCS excretion. *Arch Intern Med* 121:406–413.

Saigh PA (1988): Effects of flooding on memories of patients with posttraumatic stress disorder. In: Bremner JD, Marmar C, editors. *Trauma, Memory, and Dissociation.* Washington DC: APA Press, pp. 285–320.

Saigh PA, Mroweh M, Bremner JD (1997): Scholastic impairments among traumatized adolescents. *Behav Res Ther* 35: 429–436.

Sapolsky R, Krey L, McEwen B (1985): Prolonged glucocorticoid exposure reduces hippocampal neuron number: implications for aging. *J Neurosci* 5:1221–1226.

Sapolsky R, Pulsinelli W (1985): Glucocorticoids potentiate ischemic injury to neurons: Therapeutic implications. *Science* 229:1397–1400.

Sapolsky RM (1996): Why stress is bad for your brain. *Science* 273:749–750.

Sapolsky RM, McEwen BS (1988): Why dexamethasone resistance? Two possible neuroendocrine mechanisms. In: Schatzberg AF, Nemeroff CB, editors. *The Hypothalamic-Pituitary-Adrenal Axis: Physiology, Pathophysiology, and Psychiatric Implications.* New York: Raven Press.

Sapolsky RM, Packan DR, Vale WW (1988): Glucocorticoid toxicity in the hippocampus: In vitro demonstration. *Brain Res* 453:367–371.

Sapolsky RM, Uno H, Rebert CS, Finch CE (1990): Hippocampal damage associated with prolonged glucocorticoid exposure in primates. *J Neurosci* 10:2897–2902.

Sass KJ, Sass A, Westerveld M, et al (1992): Specificity in the correlation of verbal memory and hippocampal neuron loss: Dissociation of memory, language, and verbal intellectual ability. *J Clin Exp Neuropsychol* 14:662–672.

Sass KJ, Spencer DD, Kim JH, Westerveld M, Novelly RA, Lencz T (1990): Verbal memory impairment correlates with hippocampal pyramidal cell density. *Neurology* 40:1694–1697.

Seeman TE, Berkman LF, Gulanski BI, Robbins RJ, Greenspan SL, Charpentier P, Rowe JW (1995b): Self esteem and neuroendocrine response to challenge: Macarthur studies of successful aging. *J Psychosom Res* 39:69–84.

Seeman TE, McEwen BS, Singer BH, Albert MS, Rowe JW (1997): Increase in urinary cortisol excretion and memory declines: MacArthur studies of successful aging. *JCEM* 82:2458–2465.

Seeman TE, Singer B, Charpentier P (1995a): Gender differences in patterns of HPA axis response to challenge (1995a): Macarthur studies of successful aging. *Psychoneuroendocrinol* 20:711–725.

Sheline Y, Wang P, Gado M, Csernansky J, Vannier M (1996): Hippocampal atrophy in major depression. *Proc Natl Acad Sci U S A* 93:3908–3913.

Smith MA, Makino S, Kvetnansky R, Post RM (1995): Stress and glucocorticoids affect the expression of brain-derived neurotrophic factor and neurotrophin-3 mRNA in the hippocampus. *J Neurosci* 15:1768–1777.

Starkman MN, Gebarski SS, Berent S, Schteingart DE (1992): Hippocampal formation volume, memory dysfunction, and cortisol levels in patients with Cushing's Syndrome. *Biol Psychiatry* 32:756–765.

Stein MB, Koverola C, Hanna C, Torchia MG, McClarty B (1997): Hippocampal volume in women victimized by childhood sexual abuse. *Psychol Med* 27:951–959.

Stein-Behrens BA, Lin WJ, Sapolsky RM (1994): Physiological elevations of glucocorticoids potentiate glutamate accumulation in the hippocampus. *J Neurochem* 63:596–602.

Trapp T, Holsboer F (1996): Heterodimerization between mineralocorticoid and glucocorticoid receptors increases the functional diversity of corticosteroid action. *TIPS* 17:145–149.

Uddo M, Vasterling JT, Brailey K, Sutker PB (1993): Memory and attention in posttraumatic stress disorder. *J Psychopath Behav Assess* 15:43–52.

Uno H, Lohmiller L, Thieme C, Kemnitz JW, Engle MJ, Roecker EB (1990): Brain damage induced by prenatal exposure to dexamethasone in fetal rhesus monkeys. 1. Hippocampus. *Dev Brain Res* 53:157–167.

Uno H, Tarara R, Else JG, Suleman MA, Sapolsky RM (1989): Hippocampal damage associated with prolonged and fatal stress in primates. *J Neurosci* 9:1705–1711.

Vaher PR, Luine VN, Gould E, McEwen BS (1994): Effects of adrenalectomy on spatial memory performance and dentate gyrus morphology. *Brain Res* 1004;656:71–78.

Vasterling JJ, Brailey K, Constans JI, Sotker PB (1998): Attention and memory dysfunction in posttraumatic stress disorder. *Neuropsychology* 12(1):125-33.

Virgin CE, Taryn PTH, Packan DR, et al (1991): Glucocorticoids inhibit glucose transport and glutamate uptake in hippocampal astrocytes: implications for glucocorticoid neurotoxicity. *J Neurochem* 57:1422–1428.

Watanabe YE, Gould H, Cameron D, Daniels D, McEwen BS (1992a): Phenytoin prevents stress and corticosterone induced atrophy of CA3 pyramidal neurons. *Hippocampus* 2:431–436.

Watanabe YE, Gould H, Daniels D, Cameron D, McEwen BS (1992b): Tianeptine attenuates stress-induced morphological changes in the hippocampus. *Eur J Pharm* 222:157–162.

Watanabe Y, Gould E, McEwen BS (1992c): Stress induces atrophy of apical dendrites of hippocampal CA3 pyramidal neurons. *Brain Res* 588:341–345.

Wolkowitz OM, Reus VI, Roberts E, et al (1997): Dehydroepiandosterone (DHEA) treatment of depression. *Biol Psychiatry* 41:311–318.

Wolkowitz OM, Reus VI, Weingartner H, (1990): Cognitive effects of corticosteroids. *Am J Psychiatry* 147:1297–1303.

Wooley CS, Gould E, McEwen BS (1990): Exposure to excess glucocorticoids alters dendritic morphology of adult hippocampal pyramidal neurons. *Brain Res* 531:225–231.

Yehuda R, Giller EL, Levengood RA, Southwick SM, Siever LJ (1995b): Hypothalamic-pituitary adrenal (HPA) functioning in posttraumatic stress disorder: The concept of the stress response spectrum. In: Friedman MJ, Charney DS, Deutch AY, editors. *Neurobiological and Clinical Consequences of Stress: From Normal Adaptation to PTSD.* New York: Raven Press, pp. 367–380.

Yehuda R, Keefer RSE, Harvey PD, et al (1995a): Learning and memory in combat veterans with posttraumatic stress disorder. *Am J Psychiatry* 152:137–139.

Yehuda R, Resnick HS, Schmeidler J, Yang R-K, Pitman RK (1998): Predictors of cortisol and 3-methoxy-4-hydroxyphenylglycol responses in the acute aftermath of rape. *Biol Psychiatry* 43:855–859.

Yehuda R, Southwick SM, Nussbaum EL, Giller EL, Mason JW (1991): Low urinary cortisol in PTSD. *J Nerv Ment Dis* 178:366–369.

Zola-Morgan SM, Squire LR (1990): The primate hippocampal formation: evidence for a time-limited role in memory storage. *Science* 250:288–290.

[12]

The influence of family, school, and the environment

Barbara Maughan

Introduction

Like adult disorders, most child psychiatric problems are now regarded as multifactorially determined: both genetic and environmental factors play a role in their development. This chapter provides an overview of some of the key environmental elements in that equation. Subsequent chapters discuss risks for specific disorders; the focus here is on the more general issues that arise when considering the effect of environmental influences on the onset or persistence of psychopathology in childhood.

Environments and development

As in all aspects of child psychiatry, a developmental perspective is crucial when considering environmental risks. Some developmental periods may be especially sensitive for neurodevelopment, and show heightened effects of environmental insults. In addition, key sources of environmental influence change with age, and the meaning and impact of events will vary with the child's stage of cognitive, emotional, and social development. The family is the central source of early environmental influences, charged as it is in most societies with prime responsibility for the care, nurture, and socialization of the young. As children develop, so their social worlds expand; childcare and school settings take on increased importance, as do relationships with friends and peers. Throughout, each of these proximal contexts is shaped by influences from the wider culture and society. Any comprehensive assessment of

a child's environment needs to take each of these types and levels of influence into account.

Nature-nurture interplay

At one time, causal associations between adverse experiences and childhood disorder were assumed to run in just one direction. Today, it is clear that the situation is vastly more complex. Children are not simply passive recipients of experience; they influence, as well as being influenced by, those around them, and they play an active role in constructing and interpreting their social worlds.[1] Even very young infants influence the nature of their interactions with caregivers, and children's capacities for shaping and selecting their experiences increase as they mature. The temperamentally difficult child is likely to evoke more negative responses from parents; when parents themselves are under stress, or find it hard to maintain consistency, troublesome child behaviours can play a key role in fuelling harsh or punitive responses. Delinquent adolescents may seek out delinquent peers, who further encourage their antisocial activities. Associations between environmental factors and disorder often involve complex reciprocal patterns of effects.

Some of the evocative effects of children's behaviour will reflect heritable traits.[2] The advent of behaviour–genetic studies in child psychiatry has provided important insights into environmental as well as genetic risks. Genetic analyses have shown, for example, that many ostensibly 'environmental' factors include some element of genetic mediation.[3] Parents provide children not only with their environments but also with their genes, so that in biologically related families, nature and nurture are inevitably interwoven. Musical parents will encourage their children to enjoy music, buy them a violin, and may also pass on musical talents. In a similar way, antisocial parents may rear children in hostile and punitive environments, provide models of antisocial behaviour, and also pass on genes that predispose to disruptive behaviours. In all likelihood, genes and environments will often be *correlated* in this way.

Genetically informative studies have also highlighted other key mechanisms in *gene-environment interplay*.[4] First, environments may *moderate* genetic influences, such that the heritability of some traits may vary systematically with qualities of the environment. Second, genetic factors may contribute to *differential sensitivity to environmental risks*. Research has consistently shown marked individual differences in children's responses to all but the most severe forms of psychosocial adversity. As yet, reasons for these differences are not well understood. They may reflect variations in the severity of exposure; individual differences in resilience or coping strategies, or in environmental sources of protection; or variations in vulnerability. Genetic predispositions clearly constitute one source of such vulnerability, and several examples of gene x environment interactions have now been documented. Finally, pre-clinical studies provide clear evidence that environments can influence *gene expression* through *epigenesis*; as yet, the extent to which processes of this kind apply in humans is unknown.

Risk variables and risk mechanisms

Identifying environmental factors that show links with children's adjustment is only the first step in understanding *how* they function to increase risk for disorder. A variety of different mechanisms has been proposed here. Some may run through the effects of stress on the biological substrate. Exposure to aggression and hostility may influence children's cognitive processing, leading to the development of negative cognitive sets and attributional biases. In a related way, disrupted early attachments are argued to affect the psychological structures needed for later relationship formation. Adverse experiences may lead to direct increases in negative emotionality, disruptive behaviours, and impulsiveness, or to negative interactional styles that impact on social relationships. And finally, stress may affect children's self-concepts, or compromise their coping skills in ways that increase the risks for disorder. Any given environmental risk may be associated with a number of risk mechanisms, and the processes involved in the persistence of disorder may differ from those involved in its onset.

Family influences

Pre- and early post-natal development

Some vulnerability to psychopathology is laid down in foetal development. The potential for adverse effects of maternal substance use on the developing foetus have been known for many years; much recent attention has focussed on associations between prenatal cigarette smoking and risk for externalizing disorders in offspring. In addition, current estimates suggest that as much as 15 per cent of the load of childhood emotional/behavioural problems may be attributable to exposure to maternal anxiety and stress

in pregnancy. Though the mechanisms involved here remain to be elucidated, there is speculation that these effects may reflect foetal programming of stress response systems akin to those posited in studies of early life influences on risk for cardiovascular disease.

Post-natally, as children progress from the complete dependence of infancy to increasing independence, they need stable and secure family relationships to provide emotional warmth, responsiveness, and constructive discipline. The influential work of Bowlby[5] and others has shown that a child's need to be attached to others is a basic part of our biological heritage. Infants become increasingly socially responsive over the first 6 months of life. At 6 to 8 months of age they begin to form selective attachments to particular individuals; they seek proximity to these attachment figures if distressed or frightened, and protest if the person they are attached to leaves. In evolutionary terms, these behaviours function to provide protection for the infant, and to reduce anxiety and distress.

Almost all infants—even those neglected or maltreated by their carers—develop attachment relationships of this kind. Their quality varies, however, depending on characteristics of the parent, the child, and the mesh between the two. Infants who have received sensitive and responsive care tend to show *secure* attachment patterns; *insecure* attachments are more likely to develop when parents themselves are stressed or unsupported, and are unresponsive to their children. Two main types of insecure attachment have been identified: avoidant attachments (associated with rejecting or highly intrusive parental care) and resistant–ambivalent patterns (associated with inconsistent or unresponsive parenting). More recently, a third disorganized category has been described, in which infants show a variety of contradictory behaviours after brief separations, and often appear confused, depressed, or apprehensive. This seems especially associated with parental behaviours that are frightening, unpredictable, or abusive.

Attachment theorists argue that the quality of these early relationships may have long-term implications. Though not entirely resistant to change, infants' attachment patterns do tend to be stable over time. Some of this stability may reflect continuity in the quality of family care. In addition, attachment theory proposes that early attachment experiences are internalized in internal working models of self and others, which function as templates for future relationship formation. Children who have experienced responsive early care come to expect others to be caring and reliable; those who have been ignored or rejected develop less positive expectancies of others, of relationships, and of themselves. Later in development, new relationships may be created in line with these expectancies.

Although many aspects of these models await confirmation, securely attached infants are known to go on to be more sociable and co-operative in their social relationships, and to show more positive affect and self-esteem. Insecurely attached infants show less positive relationships, and are at some increased risk for psychopathology. Taken alone, attachment security in infancy is only a weak predictor of global functioning in early adulthood, suggesting that early attachment experiences work with and through other experiences—including peer relationships, later family experiences, and eventually mature intimate relationships—to contribute to later functioning. In addition, both ICD-10 and DSM-IV recognize two varieties of attachment disorders: non-attachment with emotional withdrawal, typically associated with abuse, and non-attachment with indiscriminate sociability, most usually observed when children have been exposed to repeated changes of caretaker or institutional care. Although as many as 40 per cent of infants receive insecure attachment classifications, these more severe forms of attachment disorder are rare.

Family relationships and parenting

Many other aspects of family life and relationships, and of parenting styles and behaviours, have been examined for their impact on children's development. Research on families emphasizes the complexity of family relationships; each dyadic relationship is influenced by other relationships in the family, and normative transitions in family life—the birth of a sibling, or mother starting work—reverberate to affect all family members.[6] Relationships with parents and siblings change as children develop, and both these, and specific aspects of parenting, may impact on risks for disorder.

The implications of the most severely compromised parenting, involving abuse or neglect, are examined in Chapter 9.3.3, and family-based risks for individual childhood disorders are discussed in detail in the chapters dealing with each specific condition. In general, these reflect four broad themes:

- ◆ discordant, dysfunctional relationships between parents, or in the family system as a whole;
- ◆ hostile or rejecting parent-child relationships, or those markedly lacking in warmth;
- ◆ harsh or inconsistent discipline;
- ◆ ineffective monitoring and supervision.

Within this broad pattern, differential treatment of siblings is known to increase conflict between children, and may have important implications for psychopathology. In addition, outcomes are markedly poorer when children face multiple family-related risks.

Family life can also provide important sources of protective influences for children facing life events and other stressors. Cohesion and warmth within the family, the presence of one good relationship with a parent, close sibling relationships, and the nature of parental monitoring and supervision have all been found to show protective influences of this kind.

Parent and family characteristics

Psychopathology in parents is associated with increased risks of emotional and behavioural problems in children. Recent estimates suggest that as many as 60 per cent of the children of parents with major depression will develop psychiatric problems in childhood or adolescence, and their risks of affective disorder are increased fourfold. Psychosis, alcohol and drug abuse, and personality disorders in parents are also associated with increased risks of disorder in offspring, and parental criminality is a strong risk factor for conduct problems and delinquency.

In most instances, these links will reflect a complex interplay between genetic and environmental effects. Disorder in parents is frequently associated with disturbed marital relationships, and parental psychopathology may also impair parenting capacities. Depressed mothers, for example, are less sensitive and responsive to their infants, and attend less, and respond more negatively, to older children. Alcohol and drug abuse and major mental disorders in parents may impair parenting in more wide-ranging ways. When parents are antisocial, effects may also be mediated through the endorsement of antisocial attitudes and social learning.

Young maternal age is associated with increased risk for child and adolescent conduct problems. In part, these associations are likely to reflect the educational and social disadvantages that predict very early parenthood; in part, the poor social conditions and lack of support faced by many young mothers; and in part, less than optimal parenting styles. Delinquency is also associated with large family size. Once again, the more proximal risks involved are likely to be complex: parental supervision may be less effective in large families, and opportunities to 'learn' from delinquent siblings higher. Beyond this, family size shows few consistent links with childhood disorder. Only children are not at increased psychiatric risk, and they share with other first-borns some small advantages in terms of cognitive development. Birth order also appears to have few implications for behavioural adjustment, although youngest children show some increased rates of school refusal.

Changing family patterns

Recent decades have seen massive changes in the pattern of many children's family lives. The most obvious markers are the dramatic increases in rates of divorce, single parenthood, and step-family formation, along with major increases in maternal employment. In the years immediately after the Second World War, just 6 per cent of British couples divorced within 20 years of marriage. By the mid-1960s that figure had increased four-fold, and divorce rates continued to rise into the 1980s. For most children, parental divorce will be followed by a period in a single-parent household; for a substantial minority, further family transitions will mean that they become part of a step family. In the early years of the 21st century more than 10 per cent of UK families with dependent children were step-families, and approaching a quarter of children lived in single parent households.

Parental divorce

There is now extensive evidence that divorce is associated with negative consequences for children.[7] Psychological and behavioural distress are common, especially in the period immediately following divorce; more severe disturbance is not. Boys in particular are at increased risk for conduct problems. Educational attainments and motivation are often compromised, and subsequent relationships may also be affected. As they approach adulthood, children of divorce move into close relationships earlier than their peers, but also experience higher risks of relationship breakdowns.

Events both before and after the separation seem central in understanding these effects. Longitudinal studies, for example, have shown that children in divorcing families often show disturbed behaviour well before their parents separate. Exposure to the discord and conflict that frequently precede divorce thus seem to be key components of risk. After separation, problematic relationships between parents may continue, and the parents' own distress may compromise their capacity to respond sensitively and consistently to their children's needs. Many families face a sharp decline in economic circumstances after divorce, and for many children their parents' separation may involve house moves, school changes, and other disruptions to their established social networks. Each of this constellation of factors may contribute to subsequent outcomes.

Single parents and step families

Research on the effects of growing up in single-parent and step families illustrates the complexity of family-related influences.[8]

Overall, children in single-parent and step families show higher mean levels of emotional and behavioural problems than those in non-divorced two-parent families; they also have an increased probability of health problems and educational underachievement. But there are also marked differences within each family type and associations between the quality of mother–child relationships and children's adjustment is similar across family settings. In addition, single-parent and reconstituted families often differ from stable two-parent families in a plethora of other ways; in particular, they are much more likely to face economic pressures, poor social support, and higher levels of maternal depression. Once these variations and the degree of negativity in family relationships are taken into account, family type *per se* shows few consistent links with children's adjustment.

Peer influences

Beyond the family, relationships with peers are now recognized to provide a unique and essential contribution to children's social, emotional, and cognitive development.[9] By the end of the pre-school period most children have at least one reciprocated friendship. In childhood and adolescence, peers take on increasing importance; in middle childhood, more than 30 per cent of children's social interactions are with peers, and adolescents are estimated to spend more than twice as much time with peers than they do with parents or other adults. The functions of friendship change with development, expanding to encompass companionship and stimulation, help and sharing, social and emotional support and intimacy.

With friends and peers children acquire skills, attitudes, and experiences that contribute to many aspects of their adaptation. By the same token, children who have poor social skills, or who are rejected or neglected by peers, are at risk of a range of adverse outcomes including poor school performance, school drop-out, and psychiatric disorder. Social rejection may increase children's feelings of loneliness, reduce supports that can buffer against stressors, and also mean that isolated children miss out on important social learning experiences. Since many children with psychiatric disorders also show difficulties in relationships with peers, processes of this kind may well compound their problems. In adolescence, affiliations with behaviourally deviant peers have attracted particular interest as correlates of conduct disorder and delinquency. Here, reciprocal influences have been demonstrated: aggressive disruptive children are more likely to associate with deviant peers, but relationships with peers also show an independent effect on both the onset and persistence of delinquency.

Child care and schooling

By the late 1990s approaching 50 per cent of mothers in the UK returned to full- or part-time work before their infants reached one year of age. This major increase in early maternal employment has prompted extensive research on the impact of alternative childcare on children's development. Recent evidence[10] suggests that multiple features of early care need to be considered in assessing effects. Higher child-care *quality* (as indexed by features such as sensitive and responsive care-giving, and cognitive and language stimulation), is associated with improved performance on tests of cognitive, language, and early academic skills, and with more prosocial skills and fewer behaviour problems, By contrast, higher *quantity*

of child care (as indexed by hours per week in any kind of non-maternal care), is associated with some increased risks of problem behaviours in both the preschool and early school years.

School life then brings its own demands and challenges. Starting and changing schools are significant, sometimes troublesome, events for children; although most young children adapt well, a significant minority show some disturbance when they start school, and both attainment levels and self-perceptions are affected for many young adolescents after the transition from primary to secondary school. Tests and examinations rank high on children's lists of fears, and levels of psychological distress are elevated at times of major examinations. Although fears of this kind are not generally severe, they do show links with clinically significant symptoms. Bullying is a further problem especially associated with the school context. Self-report surveys suggest that over 15 per cent of young children experience some bullying at school, mostly unknown to parents or teachers. Although rates fall with age, up to 5 per cent of adolescents continue to face bullying in secondary school. Persistently victimized children have identifiable characteristics, with histories of anxious insecure behaviours and social isolation often beginning before they started school; bullying then increases their risks of adjustment problems.

Like families, schools differ in their atmosphere and social climate, and these variations show an independent impact on children's academic progress and behaviour. In part, these variations reflect differences in initial pupil intakes. In addition, they show systematic links with organizational characteristics of schools. Schools with more positive outcomes are characterized by purposeful leadership, constructive classroom management techniques, an appropriate academic emphasis, and consistent but not oversevere sanctions. In relation to behavioural outcomes, the composition of pupil groupings may also be influential. Young children are more likely to become aggressive if placed in highly aggressive classes, and risks of delinquency are increased in secondary schools where intakes include large proportions of less able children. For some severely disadvantaged groups, however, schooling may offer an important source of positive experiences. Experimental studies of preschool programmes, for example, have shown important long-term gains in terms of reduced risks of delinquency and unemployment many years after participants left school.

Wider social and environmental influences

Poverty and social disadvantage

Poverty and social disadvantage are most strongly associated with deficits in children's cognitive skills and educational achievements.[11] In the behavioural domain, disruptive behaviours also show links with family poverty. Effects appear to be more marked for boys than for girls, and seem to be stronger in childhood than in adolescence. Intermittent hardship is associated with some increased risk for conduct problems, but the impact is most marked for children in families facing persistent economic stress. Most current evidence suggests that these effects are indirect. Poverty imposes stress on parents, and reduces the supports available to them; these in turn increase the risks of harsh or coercive parenting, and reduce parents' emotional availability to their children's needs. Some studies suggest that relative deprivation—the perception that one is disadvantaged by comparison with others—may be more important than income levels *per se*.

Neighbourhood and community contexts

Rates of childhood disorder vary in different neighbourhoods and communities. Urbanization is frequently associated with increased risks of disorder, and rates may be especially high in chronically disadvantaged inner-city neighbourhoods. In early childhood, many of these effects seem to be indirect; neighbourhood disadvantage increases stress on families, and these in turn largely account for associations with children's difficulties. In severely disadvantaged settings, however, even quite young children may be directly exposed to community violence, and in adolescence, neighbourhood influences may be mediated through associations with delinquent peers.

Multiple stressors

For many children, exposure to these differing types of adversity will covary. Stressed families frequently live in poor neighbourhoods, where schools are under pressure and peer groups deviant. Early epidemiological findings suggested that isolated single risks have relatively little impact on disorder, but that rates rise sharply when risk factors combine. More recently, studies have shown that child, sociocultural, parenting, and peer-related risks each add uniquely to the prediction of behaviour problems. In addition, the total number of risks a child faces explains further variance in outcomes.

Secular trends in disorder and psychosocial risks

Finally, it is important to consider how psychosocial risks may impact on overall levels of disorder. There is now clear evidence that rates of many adolescent disorders—including depression, suicide, alcohol and drug use, and delinquency—have risen since the Second World War.[12] Since it is implausible that changes in the gene pool could occur so rapidly, environmental risk factors must be implicated. Some of these may overlap with risks for individual differences in disorder, but others may be quite distinct. Based on an extensive review of available evidence, Rutter and Smith[12] concluded that a variety of factors are likely to be implicated:

1 increased rates of family breakdown, with their associated effects on the disruption of relationships and exposure to conflict and discord;

2 a change in the meaning of adolescence, with prolonged education and economic dependence on parents occurring alongside increased autonomy in other spheres;

3 a possibly increased disparity between young people's aspirations and the opportunities available to meet them;

4 increased alcohol consumption and illegal drug use;

5 changing social attitudes to acceptable behaviour, possibly enhanced by influences from the mass media.

Other specific factors may affect rates of juvenile crime. In particular, the increasing commercialization of youth culture, providing more goods to steal, may have coincided with diminished surveillance and increased situational opportunities for property crime.

Further information

Clarke-Stewart, A. and Dunn, J. (2006). *Families count: effects on child and adolescent development.* Cambridge University Press, Cambridge.
Rutter M. (2005). Environmentally mediated risks for psychopathology: Research strategies and findings. *Journal of the American Academy of Child and Adolescent Psychiatry,* 44, 3–18.

References

1. Lytton, H. (1990). Child and parent effects in boys' conduct disorder: a reinterpretation, *Developmental Psychology,* 5, 683–97.
2. Scarr, S. and McCartney, K. (1983). How people make their own environments: a theory of genotype–environment effects. *Child Development,* 54, 424–35.
3. Plomin, R. and Bergeman, C.S. (1991). The nature of nurture. Genetic influences on 'environmental' measures. *Behavioural and Brain Sciences,* 14, 373–86.
4. Rutter, M., Moffitt, T., and Caspi, A. (2006). Gene–environment interplay and psychopathology: Multiple varieties but real effects. *Journal of Child Psychology and Psychiatry,* 47, 226–61.
5. Bowlby, J. (1988). *A secure base: clinical applications of attachment theory.* Routledge, London.
6. Dunn, J. (1994). Family influences. In *Development through life: a handbook for clinicians* (eds. M. Rutter and D.F. Hay), pp. 112–31. Blackwell Science, Oxford.
7. Rodgers, B. and Pryor, J. (1998). *Divorce and separation: the outcomes for children.* Joseph Rowntree Foundation, York.
8. Dunn, J., Deater-Deckard, K., Pickering, K., *et al.* (1998). Children's adjustment and prosocial behaviour in step-, single-parent, and non-stepfamily settings: findings from a community study. *Journal of Child Psychology and Psychiatry,* 39, 1083–95.
9. Rubin, K.H., Bukowski, W., and Parker, J.G. (1998). Peer interactions, relationships, and groups. In *Handbook of child psychology,* Vol. 3 *Social, emotional and personality development* (ed. N. Eisenberg), pp. 619–700. Wiley, New York.
10. NICHD Early Child Care Research Network (2006). Child-care effect sizes for the NICHD Study of Early Child Care and Youth Development. *American Psychologist,* 61, 99–116.
11. Duncan, G.J. and Brooks-Gunn, J. (ed.) (1997). *Consequences of growing up poor.* Russell Sage, New York.
12. Rutter, M. and Smith, D.J. (1995). *Psychosocial disorders in young people: times trends and their causes.* Wiley, Chichester.

[13]

How Families Matter in Child Development

Reflections from Research on Risk and Resilience

Ann S. Masten and Anne Shaffer

Throughout the history of child development, the family has played a ubiquitous role in theory, research, practice, and policy aimed at understanding and improving child welfare and development. From grand theories to heated controversies, family processes and roles have been invoked in numerous ways in developmental science over the past century to explain or debate whether and how families matter (Collins, Maccoby, Steinberg, Hetherington et al., 2000; Maccoby, 1992). Psychoanalytic theory (Freud, 1933/1964; Munroe, 1955), attachment theory (e.g., Bowlby, 1969, Carlson & Sroufe, 1995; Sroufe & Waters, 1977), ecological and developmental systems theory (e.g., Bronfenbrenner, 1979, Ford & Lerner, 1992; Sameroff, 2000), family systems theory (Davies & Cicchetti, 2004; Fiese, 2000; Fiese & Spagnola, in press), social learning and social cognitive theory (Bandura, 1977, 2001; Gewirtz, 1969), coercion theory (e.g., Patterson, 1982), parenting styles theory (Baumrind, 1967, 1973), and a variety of other influential frameworks have emphasized the family in diverse ways. Theories about the origins of competence and about the origins of psychopathology also have focused on family roles and processes (Cummings, Davies, & Campbell, 2000; Fiese, Wilder, & Bickham, 2000; Masten & Coatsworth, 1995; Masten, Burt, & Coatsworth, in press). Family-based adversity in many forms, including loss (Bowlby, 1980; Brown & Harris, 1978, Sandler, Wolchik, Davis, Haine et al., 2003), deprivation and institutional rearing (Rutter, Chapter 2 in this book; 1972; Zeanah et al., 2003, Zeanah, Smyke, & Settles, in press), divorce (Amato, Chapter 8 in this book; Hetherington, Chapter 9 in this book; Hetherington, Bridges, & Insabella, 1998; Walper, Chapter 10 in this book), interparental conflict or domestic violence (Cummings & Davies, 2002; Graham-Bermann & Edelson, 2001; Wolfe, Crooks, Lee, McIntyre-Smith et al., 2003), maltreatment (Belsky, 1984; Cicchetti & Carlson, 1989), and poverty (Brooks-Gunn & Duncan, 1997; Luthar, 1999; McLoyd, 1990), has been the focus of extensive study, often with the goal of learning how to prevent or ameliorate the impact of such adversity on children. Not surprisingly, families also have been the target of many kinds of interventions aimed at altering family interaction or parenting behavior in order to change the course of child development (Albee & Gullotta, 1997; Szapocznik & Williams, 2000; Cicchetti & Hinshaw, 2002; Masten et al., in press; Weissberg, Kumpfer, & Seligman, 2003).

As developmental psychopathology emerged over the past four decades, family functioning has played a central role in theory and research on competence, risk, and resilience, reflecting the salience of family-oriented concepts and intervention strategies in the disciplines from which developmental psychopathology evolved: child development, psychiatry, pediatrics, and related social sciences (Cicchetti, 1990; Cummings et al., 2000; Fiese & Spagnola, in press; Luthar, 2003, in press; Masten, 2001; Masten & Coatsworth, 1998; Masten et al., in press; Rutter, 1990; Sameroff & Chandler, 1975; Sroufe, Carlson, Levy, & Egeland, 1999). In developmental psychopathology, the role of family in development has been particularly salient in the study of risk and resilience. For this reason, and because developmental psychopathology is such a broad and integrative approach to understanding and attempting to redirect development, we believe the research focused on risk and resilience in developmental psychopathology can provide a useful lens through which to consider the broader mission of this volume to delineate the case for how "families count" for development in childhood and adolescence. Based on the studies of risk and resilience, we aim in this chapter to frame how one might think about the diverse ways families could matter in human development.

Basic Models of the Ways Families Matter

Perusing the evidence in studies of risk and resilience, it is clear that there are several key ways that families may matter, including the fundamental fact that parents pass their genes on to their biological children (cf. Grant, Compas, Stuhlmacher, Thrum et al., 2003; Luthar, 2003, in press; Masten, 2001; Masten et al., in press; Repetti, Taylor, & Seeman, 2002). In Figure 1.1, we illustrate some of the basic models of family effects on child behavior and development. These are described generally here, with elaboration and examples to follow in this chapter.

Families can function as direct influences on child behavior, in positive or negative ways (Figure 1.1A). When a direct family effect is positive on desired child outcomes, the family effect is described as *promotive* (see discussion by Sameroff, Chapter 3 in this book) or the feature of the family under observation is termed a *resource* or *asset* for children. On the other hand, if a family attribute predicts psychopathology or negative outcomes on a desired child behavior such as academic achievement, it could be described as a *risk factor*. Sometimes positive family effects are viewed as

How Families Matter in Child Development   7

A. Direct family effects

B. Mediated indirect family effects

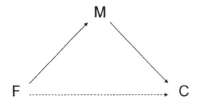

C. Family as mediator

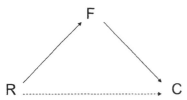

FIGURE 1.1. Basic models of family effects on child behavior [Note. R = Risk Factor; F = Family; C = Child behavior; M = Mediator (M_G = Geneticmediator; M_E = Environmental mediator).]

counterbalancing the effects of independent risk factors (R in Figure 1.1A), such as bad neighborhoods or deviant peer influences; in this case, the positive family effect is sometimes termed a *compensatory factor*. These are all relatively simple, additive models about how families matter, although the processes accounting for these influences could be very complex in nature. More complex variations of this model include more family factors or more additional risk factors. *Cumulative risk models,* for example, often include multiple features of the family or environment that are composited into a global index of overall riskiness for child behavior or development (see Sameroff, Chapter 3 in this book). Scores on composited risk indices of this kind typically indicate that child problems increase as a function of the number of risk factors, forming a *risk gradient*. Nonetheless, even cumulative risk models, which could reflect enormously complex processes, are variations on this basic model of direct influences.

8   *Ann S. Masten and Anne Shaffer*

D. Complex mediated family effects

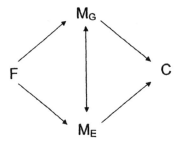

E. Family as moderator

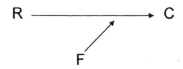

F. Transactional family-child effects

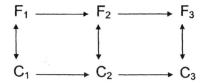

FIGURE 1.1. *continued.* Basic models of family effects on child behavior [Note. R = Risk Factor; F = Family; C = Child behavior; M = Mediator (M_G = Geneticmediator; M_E = Environmental mediator).]

The influences of families on child outcomes can also be indirect. Figure 1.1B illustrates a simple indirect effect of some family feature on a child outcome, where the effects of family on child are entirely mediated by some intervening factor and the processes the factor represents (which are often unknown). The mediator could be a feature of the child, the child's diet, the school, neighborhood, or health care system, or any other system that influences a child's behavior. A parent's income, for example, can influence where the family lives, which determines many features of a child's day-to-day context, including the quality of the school the child attends and how much violence the child observes in the surrounding environs. Families, of course, can influence many aspects of a child's life, at many levels. Thus, the same family could produce all kinds of risks, assets, and opportunities to the same child over the course of development, varying from genes to nice neighbors to actions resulting in tutors or college admission. Model D in Figure 1.1 illustrates a more complex variation on the indirect model, where family effects are mediated by both genes and environment and the interaction of those mediators.

Family can also function as the mediator of more distal conditions on children, as illustrated in Figure 1.1C. In this model, a risk factor alters family functioning (e.g., parenting) in some way, which in turn affects the child. Many models of distal risk factors such as social class or economic hardship are thought to be mediated by their effects on parents.

There are also models of family in a moderating role, where something about the family alters the impact of a risk factor on a child, as shown in Figure 1.1E. In this case of family as *moderator*, family alters the effect of another condition or factor on the child, in either a negative or a positive way. When the effect is positive, the family role is called a *protective factor*. Protective processes can be activated by adverse events, in much the way that an airbag is triggered by the impact of an automobile accident; analogously, parents may be spurred to protective action by perceived threats in the lives of their children. These moderating roles all imply some kind of interaction, where the influence of adversity depends on the family in some way. Families have been implicated in many studies as protective factors when child development is threatened by adversity of some kind (discussed further below and by Rutter, Chapter 2 in this book). Of course, families may also exacerbate negative effects, boosting the negative impact of a risk factor.

There are also models of more dynamic, complex interaction over time. A relatively simple example of a transactional model is illustrated in Figure 1.1F (adapted from the seminal work of Arnold Sameroff). In this model, ongoing interactions of child and family influence the family, the child, and their future interactions. Transactional models are based on systems theory, in which changes in one system (such as the family) can lead to changes in all other systems connected directly and indirectly to a family. There have been many elaborations on how this may work in development among systems theorists (Bronfenbrenner, 1979; Ford & Lerner, 1992; Sameroff, 2000; Thelen & Smith, 1998). All these models posit that many interactions among many systems at multiple levels (e.g., genes, central nervous system, peers, family, school, neighborhood, culture) give rise to child development, with bi-directional influences connecting multiple levels.

Intervention can also be conceptualized and modeled in relation to these basic models of family influence on children. If the family is the target of intervention, then the intervener must have a model of how the intervention will change the family (a theory of intervention) and how that in turn will change the child (a theory of family influence). As described later, a number of preventive interventions are designed to support positive parenting as a mediator in order to protect a child from the potentially deleterious effects of a risk factor such as divorce or poverty. In such cases, the intervention can be viewed as an effort to alter the mediator. Holmbeck (1997) illustrated such a model in his depiction of a moderated mediational model. In a family systems therapy model, in contrast, the intervention could be directed at the child, the parent, or their interaction, because changing any part of the system would theoretically change the other parties of interaction; in this case, the chosen target for change might be based on a theory about where in the family the intervener believes there is the greatest motivation or leverage for change.

In the following sections, we highlight examples of models of how families matter based on findings from the literature on risk and resilience. We focus particularly on models of families as adaptive systems for human development, as mediators and moderators of change, and as targets of intervention.

Families as Major Adaptive Systems for Human Development

In the risk and resilience literature, quality of parenting and the parent-child relationship have been implicated over and over again as correlates of positive development, both in normative situations and under adverse conditions, leading to the observation that families and parenting comprise a complex and fundamental system for human development, biologically and culturally evolved to promote and protect development (Masten, 2001; Fiese & Spagnola, in press). Effective parenting is pervasively associated with positive adjustment, in both normative and high-risk situations (Damon & Eisenberg, 1998; Fiese & Spagnola, in press; Luthar, in press; Maccoby, 1980; 1992; Masten & Coatsworth, 1998). In the resilience literature, relationships with competent and caring adults, who function in parenting or mentoring roles, top the list of the most widely observed correlates of good adaptation among children in risky or hazardous rearing environments or among children enduring or recovering from trauma (Luthar, 2003, in press; Masten & Powell, 2003; Masten & Reed, 2002; Wright & Masten, 2005). Moreover, moving a child from a context with poor caregiving to one with good caregiving, as happened with many Romanian orphans adopted around 1991 following the fall of the Ceausescu regime, has been followed in many cases by dramatic improvements in development (Rutter, Chapter 2; Rutter & the English and Romanian Adoptees (ERA) Study Team, 1998).

Families are charged by most societies with the job of socializing children to live in the society, and hence function as conduits of culture and standards of behavior. Other people, including teachers or mentors, certainly play important roles in a child's life, but parents typically have the primary role in child socialization, particularly early in development when children depend on adults for satisfying many needs and spend most of their time with family or designated surrogate caregivers. Some of the key debates and issues of the past few decades have focused on the importance of how well parents do this job or delegate it to others – whether or not, for example, day care or divorce is detrimental to child development. Parent-child relationships also are viewed as key regulators of child behavior, through such actions as soothing, monitoring, or providing security. Although the general aim of these regulatory functions to help children regulate their emotions and behavior may be similar over time, the actual behavior and function of families in this regard should change with development, as children grow up, because what is appropriate and effective for an infant, toddler, or adolescent may be vastly different and require very different kinds of parental behavior.

Attachment and Family Functions. Attachment relationships are fundamental to the role of the family as an adaptive system and to the development of emotion regulation as outlined earlier. The multiple functions of attachment relationships have been delineated by numerous scholars (Carlson & Sroufe, 1995; Sroufe & Waters, 1977; Cicchetti, 1990; Maccoby, 1980; Waters, Vaughn, Posada, & Kondo-Ikemura, 1995) since John Bowlby (1969) so eloquently described the nature of human attachment in terms of adaptive functions. In attachment theory, as in the empirical work supporting this theory, the special relationship initially formed between a child and primary caregiver can influence learning, reactions to threat, exploration, and many other behaviors associated with competence and maladaptation. Children who form insecure attachments or who do not have the opportunity to form such a relationship in early development because of severe privation or impaired functioning exhibit major developmental problems, and these findings have been replicated in studies of primates as well as humans (Cicchetti & Carlson, 1989; Hinde, 1974; Shonkoff & Phillips, 2000; Suomi, 2000; Zeanah, Smyke, & Settles, in press).

Family as Regulator. The attachment relationship and the larger family context serve regulatory functions of diverse kinds (Fiese & Spagnola, in press; Gunnar, in press; Sroufe, 1996). Arousal regulation is provided by the parent who soothes a fussing baby, comforts a frightened child, or encourages an adolescent to try something new. Under high threat conditions, separation from the attachment figure(s) is associated with high levels of distress in children, as observed long ago by Bowlby (1969), Spitz (1945) and others, and also, more recently, in systematic studies of children following traumatic life events, ranging from war and terrorism to hospitalization and natural disasters (Garmezy & Rutter, 1983; Pine, Costello, &

Masten, in press). Gradually, the parent's role in child regulation becomes less direct, and developmental theories have proposed for nearly a century that there are processes of *internalization* by which what is initially mother-child or family-based regulatory function gradually shifts to self-regulation, through various processes of learning, scaffolding, and assimilation (e.g., Breger, 1974). Recent studies of caregiver-offspring interactions are beginning to examine how such transfer from family to self-regulation occurs. Brain development research suggests that stress regulation provided by mothers (both animal and human) can alter the organization of the brain or gene expression so as to affect future behavior and development (Gunnar & Donzella, 2002; Pine et al., in press). Similarly, it has been argued that risky families may create or exacerbate vulnerabilities in their children, with lasting consequences on the child's regulatory capacity (Boyce, in press; Gunnar, in press; Gunnar & Donzella, 2002; Repetti et al., 2002; Shonkoff & Phillips, 2000). Such phenomena would represent biological embedding of context related to family function. In this new work, for example, stress regulation in parent-offspring interactions alters the stress-emotional response systems in the offspring, sometimes with lasting impact (Gunnar, in press).

Parent as Teacher, Socializer, Protector, and Cultural Conduit. In social development, parents have been accorded many roles as teachers, role modelers, and socializers who demonstrate, reward, punish, and otherwise shape behavior in children; reciprocally, parents are also shaped in turn by the behaviors of their children over the course of many interactions (Belsky, 1984; Bornstein, 1995; Collins, Maccoby, Steinberg, Hetherington et al., 2000; Fiese, 2000; Fiese & Spagnola, in press; Maccoby, 1992; Masten & Gewirtz, in press; Sameroff, Chapter 3 in this book). Parents also teach or expose children to cultural traditions that serve a regulatory function in human adaptation, including religious practices and ethnic traditions. Children may learn to pray or meditate, and to participate in culturally-specific rituals, such as a healing ceremony, to deal with loss or adversity (Crawford, Wright, & Masten, in press). Families also have their own internal culture and rituals that may serve many functions for children, such as imparting family values or life lessons (Fiese & Spagnola, in press). In these ways, parents play a major part in the establishment of children's social and cultural identity, both through direct education and the indirect provision of the child's earliest context for development.

Family as Provider, Broker or Purveyor of Resources and Opportunities. Parents also provide food, shelter, clothing, books, performing art lessons, sports team access, and many other resources and opportunities for children. Additionally, parent education, jobs, and choices often determine the nature of the neighborhood and school in which a child lives and learns; thus family can directly and indirectly influence many aspects of the daily context of a child's life, including the quality of education and the availability of social relationships, and recreational opportunities. (Collins et al., 2000; Sameroff, Chapter 3 in this book). Parents talk and read to children, and the degree to which they do so predicts vocabulary and school success (Hart & Risley, 1995). However, this relation could be confounded to some degree by shared verbal aptitude of parents and children that is, in part, genetically mediated, thus highlighting the complex interactions among family-related factors and their impact on child development.

Family as Source of Risks and Threat

In the risk literature, the family also can be the source of threats to development, in a number of different ways. Some are more *passive* in nature. At the biological level, for example, a parent may pass on the genes that convey risk for a specific disorder, such as schizophrenia (Gottesman & Hanson, 2005), or a biological disposition or temperament that may render the child more vulnerable to risky social environments. Families can also be risky social environments in and of themselves (Repetti et al. 2002). Although such actions may not be deliberate, family members may harm their children through neglect or incompetence. Parents who are impaired themselves, by mental or physical illness or disability, may not be able to provide normative levels of nutrition, security, or teaching for their children, or to see impending danger and take protective action, and thus place their child at risk for many negative outcomes. In fact, it is not surprising to find that a host of variables related to child competence and achievement are related to the socioeconomic status or functional competence of parents (Masten & Coatsworth, 1995; 1998; McLoyd, 1998; Repetti et al., 2002). There are a number of candidate processes that could explain the mechanisms by which parent competence or SES are linked to child outcomes; for example, less competent or less affluent parents may increase the exposure of the children to danger, toxins, deviant peers, or other bad influences in the environment due to their circumstances, choices, or behaviors (Collins et al., 2000; Masten & Gewirtz, in press). Very young children are particularly vulnerable to hazards posed by lack of attention or monitoring for safety (Masten & Gewirtz, in press).

In some cases, parent behavior or family functioning itself is the *active* source of threat. For example, child maltreatment perpetrated by a parent is a direct threat to children, and studies suggest that maltreatment by an attachment figure has greater effects on a child than maltreatment by a stranger (Masten & Wright, 1998). This is consistent with the idea of family as a key adaptive system for human development, such that disturbances to this system have particularly deleterious outcomes. Harsh, inconsistent parenting has also been consistently related to problems in child development (Repetti et al., 2002; Dodge, Malone, Lansford, Miller-Johnson et al., Chapter 5 in this book), most commonly being linked with later externalizing behavior problems. Finally, the relations of family conflict and aggressive behavior to child outcomes are not necessarily limited to those actions directed at the child. Observing domestic violence or interparental conflict may be highly disturbing to children, disrupting their sense of security; even toddlers react to observed conflict between strangers with distress (Cummings & Davies, 2002).

Cumulative Risk. Because of the multiple ways, both direct and indirect, that parents and families may play a role in the lives of children, studies that consider aggregate risk in the lives of children often consider multiple aspects of family attributes and function (see Sameroff, Chapter 3 in this book). These indices often include, for example, risk factors such as low parent education, low family income, parental unemployment, mental illness, incarceration, foster placement, large family size, child abuse, domestic violence, harsh or inconsistent parenting, divorce, and many other events and conditions that implicate family functioning. Cumulative risk indices and risk gradients that reflect the overall level of psychosocial risk in the lives of children often index family functioning in complex and diverse ways (Jessor, 1993; Masten & Gewirtz, in press; Rutter, 1979; 1983; Sameroff, Chapter 3 in this book; Sameroff & Fiese, 2000; Wyman, Sandler, Wolchik, & Nelson, 2000). Numerous studies have shown that the accumulation of risk factors is inversely related to a wide variety of indicators of positive adaptation, yet the processes underlying these effects may be obscured by the complexity of multiple risks when they are considered together. Paradoxically, aggregating risks may be more consistent with the reality of risks that interact and pile up in the lives of families and at the same time are so complex that the processes involved cannot be uncovered. Risk investigators have struggled with this dilemma in family research as well and developed creative strategies for detecting specific ways in which risk and protective factors operate in affecting children's lives or proximal causes that interact to influence developmental pathways.

Family as Proximal Mediator of Distal Events or Conditions

Ecological theory and systems theory have provided a great deal of guidance in the conceptualization of risk and resilience processes. In this view, child development is embedded in the family system, which is in turn embedded in other systems, including the parents' work, the community, and culture. Sometimes the family or particular individuals within the family become the proximal *mediators* of risks or protection arising outside the family system. Thus, for example, a father or mother can experience problems at work that affect his or her parenting and thereby the behavior of the child (see Crouter, Chapter 6 in this book). Economic situations at the national or regional level can also affect family life in many ways that then affect the children within those families. Many studies have examined the indirect effects of parent-related adversity on child adaptation via the deleterious impact on parental functioning (Grant et al., 2003). In a classic study of the Great Depression and development, Elder observed such effects among children and adolescents who were part of ongoing longitudinal studies of child development when this major historical event unfolded (Elder, 1974/1999). In recent years, Conger and colleagues have documented such effects in their important studies of farm families in Iowa, where economic conditions affected the parents and their relationship, which in turn affected the adolescents in the family (Conger, Ge, Elder, Lorenz et al., 1994; Elder & Conger, 2000).

Thus, research has examined how the processes of family adaptation unfold over time (Gest, Neemann, Hubbard, Masten et al., 1993), and analytic strategies that address these longitudinal relations enhance the possibility of empirically describing these theoretical processes of familial adaptation (e.g., Hinshaw, 2002; Kraemer, Stice, Kazdin, Offord et al., 2001). Through such research, it has become increasingly possible to demonstrate empirically the mediating role of parenting in understanding the negative yet indirect impact of many environmental stressors on child functioning, findings which are notably consistent with the theoretical models of family systems approaches.

Intervention strategies with foundations in systems theories have been developed explicitly to capitalize on parents' mediating role in the relations between risk factors and child outcomes. For example, Brody and colleagues have recently reported on a parenting intervention program implemented with African American families that specifically targeted improving regulated and communicative parenting behaviors in order to indirectly support and enhance protective factors for their children (Brody, Murry, Gerrard, Gibbons et al., 2004). This directed effort to "regulate the regulator" or moderate the mediator (as noted earlier) represents an important translation of theory and empirical research findings into applied efforts to intervene with families. Such intervention research has shown, quite promisingly, that the hypothesized mediating role of the parent in children's adaptation to risk and adversity is subject to change.

Parents as Mediators of Genetic Risk or Vulnerability

Parenting has also been shown to mediate the effects of genetic risks to adaptation in adverse circumstances. Specifically, in a recent study of genetic and environmental effects in the development of resilience among children living in poverty, results suggested that maternal warmth was associated with resilience, partly mediated by genetic processes and partly mediated by environmental processes (Kim-Cohen et al., 2004).

Family as Moderator of Risk and as Moderated by Other Influences

In the resilience literature, moderating effects of family on risk or vulnerability of children also have been posited, with growing corroborative evidence (Luthar, in press; Masten & Powell, 2003; Rutter, Chapter 2 in this book). In all the cases where a moderating effect is postulated, some kind of conditional or joint effect is proposed (indicating interactions among predictors). The quality of parenting is more important under certain conditions (presence or absence of a gene; good or poor neighborhood); other factors (such as deviant peers) vary in influence depending on the quality of family functioning; or there is a good versus poor fit of family (e.g., parenting style) with child (e.g., personality). In one kind of interaction, the family functions to buffer a child from the worst exposure to or impact of adversity. A family may provide an island of safety and security in a dangerous neighborhood (e.g., Richters & Martinez, 1993). In other instances, family factors may serve to exacerbate the effects of already negative contexts. For example, poor parenting may be particularly dangerous to children in bad neighborhoods because they are left unprotected or put at increased risk.

The quality of monitoring by parents in risky environments has been strongly implicated as a moderator (Dishion & McMahon, 1998; Fiese & Spagnola, in press; Repetti et al., 2002). Evidence also suggests that the influence of deviant peers depends on parenting (Galambos, Barker, & Almeida, 2003; Pettit, Bates, Dodge, & Meece, 1999). Deviant peers appear to be less influential in the context of positive parenting behavior and relationships. Families are also affected by the quality of neighborhood functioning (Sampson, Morenoff, & Earls, 1999).

Age and individual differences in children can also moderate family effects. In ways too numerous and complex to describe, parents change their perceptions and behavior in relation to developmental changes in their children and also according to how their children respond and how they expect their children to respond. Individual differences in child temperament and personality, for example, have been extensively investigated as moderators of parent behavior, and these ways of relating to the world change over the course of development (Caspi & Shiner, in press; Rothbart & Bates, 1998; Kochanska, 1995).

In all of the ways described that families may function to promote and protect development, child qualities could moderate the effects of the parent or family (see Sameroff, Chapter 3 in this book). Gene-by-family interactions are also possible, as suggested by recent work on the joint effects of genes and context (see Rutter, Chapter 2 in this book). Caspi and colleagues (Caspi, McClay, Moffitt, Mill et al., 2002), for example, observed that variations in the genotype producing high versus low levels of monoamine oxidase A (MAOA) showed an interaction with serious maltreatment in predicting antisocial behavior problems. The combination of low MAOA expression and maltreatment was associated with substantially higher risk for antisocial behavior.

The quality of parenting can also be moderated by the systems that regulate parent behavior, such as the marital relationship, the extended family, and the social systems of work, culture, or community. A supportive spouse or grandparent can serve as a protective factor for the children in a family during times of strain, adversity, or parental impairment, not only by direct actions toward the children, but also by regulating the arousal, affect, and behavior of the parent (Dunn, Fergusson & Maughan Chapter 12 in this book; Hetherington, Chapter 9 in this book; Sameroff, Chapter 3 in this book).

Ever More Complex Models of Family Influence

In addition to the effects described earlier, families vary in the degree to which they are affected by other systems or by negative life experiences, and a number of factors are likely to account for these individual differences in adaptation and functioning. Thus it is possible to imagine ways in which the mediating and moderating processes described might work together. For example, there are individual differences in the degree to which parenting itself is affected by adverse conditions. In some families, parenting is undermined by adversity, while in other families, parents take action to protect their parenting from the effects of adversity, by seeking social support or other kinds of assistance. In other words, there may be parents and families that are more resilient in the face of adversity in terms of how well they function to protect and care for children.

In considering the phenomenon of naturally occurring resilience, a child may appear to be more resilient under adversity, but a closer look reveals that the child's adaptation actually reflects the resilience of the parenting or family system; the child has simply not been exposed to the same level of risk as a child whose parenting has deteriorated in the face of adversity.

Interventions to Protect or Improve Family Functioning

In prevention science over the past two decades, there are many examples of interventions designed to help children through changing family interaction or parenting (Kumpfer & Alvarado, 2003; Luthar, in press; Masten et al., in press; Sameroff, Chapter 3 in this book; Sameroff & Fiese, 2000). Many interventions can be viewed as attempts to create moderating effects akin to the protective effects discussed above, in order to influence the course of development. In van den Boom's (1994, 1995) work with high-risk, irritable babies, mothers in the experimental group were trained to be more sensitive and tuned to their babies, in accordance with attachment theory (using strategies developed by van IJzendoorn, Juffer, & Duyvesteyn [1995]); experimental babies subsequently showed more secure attachment and also better competence. Investigators at the Oregon Social Learning Center have developed effective strategies for changing families (e.g., Forgatch & DeGarmo, 1999; Martinez & Forgatch, 2001). Forgatch and DeGarmo (1999), for example, demonstrated that parenting could be altered for families undergoing divorce, with the consequence of better outcomes for their children. Investigators at Arizona State University, in another experimental clinical trial with divorcing families, demonstrated significant effects on parenting and child outcomes in the experimental as compared with control families, with effects holding up for at least six years (Wolchik, Sandler, Millsap, Plummer et al., 2002). Successful efforts also have been made to improve mother-toddler interaction when mothers are depressed, as a preventive intervention for children (Cicchetti, Toth, & Rogosch, 1999). These interventions, as well as the intervention for African-American parents described earlier (Brody et al., 2004) illustrate successful interventions to alter parenting as a mediator of developmental risk factors such as divorce, maternal psychiatric illness, and poverty.

If one aims to alter family processes such as parenting, then an important step is to identify the influences on the nature and quality of parenting. Belsky (1984), in his article on the determinants of parenting, discussed a number of possible influences, including characteristics of the parent, social context, and child. Parenting itself has a developmental history, as Belsky observed, and thus may have long-term antecedents. At the same time, parenting may also be influenced by a host of more contemporary conditions, such as contextual challenges and supports. Social support in various forms was noted by Belsky and later by numerous others (e.g., Repetti et al., 2002) as a key empirically supported influence on parenting. Belsky also argued persuasively that because of its multiple determinants, the parenting system was buffered to some degree from harmful disruptions.

More complex models also have been used to capture the ongoing dynamics of family systems, both in interaction with other systems (e.g., schools, and peer groups) and in terms of the internal dynamics of interaction among subgroups of the family. Even in studies that focus on a single dyad, such as mother-child, it is not easy to model or study the ongoing complexities of relationships and their bi-directional effects on the people in the relationship (Fiese & Spagnola, in press). The role of transactional processes arising in the family for resilience have been noted (e.g., Egeland, Carlson, & Sroufe, 1993; Gest et al., 1993; Sameroff, Chapter 3 in this book) but rarely demonstrated in longitudinal designs with repeated measures over multiple points in time. As time goes on, there are more data sets with the kind of panel data that make it possible to investigate transactional effects over time involving family members (see Ge, Conger,

Lorenz, Shanahan et al., 1995, for example). Recent advances in growth curve and structural equation modeling provide powerful new tools for examining dynamic models of such bi-directional influences, and no doubt there will be more examples testing transactional models involving the family.

The Jacobs Conference

The 2003 Jacobs Conference brought together an exciting group of scholars to discuss the issues and evidence about how families matter. In the chapters that follow, these scholars highlight much of the best evidence for and against many of the processes delineated here, as well as the conceptual and methodological gaps and issues that will motivate future research. As often observed in the history of science, ideas and theories about important, complex topics tend to get ahead of the execution of the empirical research with the design and power to test the ideas. Numerous gaps remain in the database on how families matter for development. Nonetheless, promising signs abound in the pages of this volume that suggest we are on the horizon of a new era, in which dynamic, multilevel models about family processes in development, spanning genes to culture, will be put to the test in elegant, longitudinal studies.

References

Albee, G. W., & Gullotta, T. P. (1997). Primary prevention works. *Issues in children's and families' lives, Vol. 6* (pp. 3–22). Thousand Oaks, CA: Sage Publications.

Bandura, A. (1977). *Social learning theory.* New York: General Learning Press.

Bandura, A. (2001). Social cognitive theory: An agentive perspective. *Annual Review of Psychology, 52,* 1–26.

Baumrind, D. (1967). Child care practices anteceding three patterns of preschool behavior. *Genetic Psychology Monographs, 75,* 43–88.

Baumrind, D. (1973). The development of instrumental competence through socialization. In A. D. Pick (Ed.), *Minnesota Symposium on Child Psychology: Vol. 7* (pp. 3–46). Minneapolis: University of Minnesota Press.

Belsky, J. (1984). The determinants of parenting: A process model. *Child Development, 55,* 83–96.

Bornstein, M. H. (Ed.) (1995). *Handbook of parenting.* Mahwah, NJ: Erlbaum.

Bowlby, J. (1969). *Attachment and loss.* New York: Basic Books.

Bowlby, J. (1980). *Attachment and loss: Vol. 3 Loss: Sadness & depression.* New York: Basic Books.

Boyce, W. T. (in press). The biology of misfortune: Stress reactivity, social context, and the ontogeny of psychopathology in early life. In A. S. Masten (Ed.), *Developmental psychopathology: Integrating multiple levels of analysis. 33rd Minnesota Symposium on Child Psychology.* Minneapolis: University of Minnesota Press.

Breger, L. (1974). *From instinct to identity.* Englewood Cliffs, NJ: Prentice-Hall.

Brody, G. H., Murry, V. M., Gerrard, M., Gibbons, F. X., Molgaard, V., McNair, L. et al. (2004). The Strong African American Families Program: Translating research into prevention programming. *Child Development, 75,* 900–917.

Bronfenbrenner, U. (1979). *The ecology of human development: Experiments by nature and design.* Cambridge, MA: Harvard University Press.

Brooks-Gunn, J., & Duncan, J. (1997, Summer/Fall). The effects of poverty on children. *The future of children, 7,* 55–71.

Brown, G. W., & Harris, T. (1978). *Social origins of depression.* London: Tavistock.

Carlson, E. A., & Sroufe, L. A. (1995). Contributions of attachment theory to developmental psychopathology. In D. Cicchetti & D. Cohen (Eds.), *Developmental Psychopathology: Vol. 1. Theory and methods* (pp. 581–617). New York: Wiley.

Caspi, A., McClay, J., Moffitt, T. E., Mill, J., Martin, J., Craig, J. W., Taylor, A., & Poulton, R. (2002). Role of genotype in the cycle of violence in maltreated children. *Science, 297,* 851–854.

Caspi, A., & Shiner, R. L. (in press). Personality development. In W. Damon & R. Lerner (Series Eds.) & N. Eisenberg (Vol. Ed.), *Handbook of child psychology: Vol. 3. Social, emotional, and personality development* (6th ed.). New York: Wiley.

Cicchetti, D. (1990). An historical perspective on the discipline of developmental psychopathology. In J. Rolf, A. S. Masten, D. Cicchetti, K. H. Nuechterlein, & S. Weintraub (Eds.), *Risk and protective factors in the development of psychopathology* (pp. 2–28). New York: Cambridge University Press.

Cicchetti, D., & Carlson, V. (1989). *Child maltreatment.* New York: Cambridge University Press.

Cicchetti, D., & Hinshaw, S. P. (2002). Editorial: Prevention and intervention science: Contributions to developmental theory. *Development and Psychopathology, 14,* 667–671.

Cicchetti, D., Toth, S. L., & Rogosch, F. A. (1999). The efficacy of toddler-parent psychotherapy to increase attachment security in offspring of depressed mothers. *Attachment and Human Development, 1,* 34–66.

Collins, W. A., Maccoby, E. E., Steinberg, L., Hetherington, E. M., & Bornstein, M. (2000). Contemporary research on parenting: The case for nature and nurture. *American Psychologist, 55,* 218–232.

Conger, R. D., Ge, X., Elder, G. H., Lorenz, F. O., & Simons, R. L. (1994). Economic stress, coercive family process, and developmental problems of adolescents. *Child Development, 65,* 541–561.

Crawford, E., Wright, M. O'D., Masten, A. S. (in press). Resilience and spirituality in youth. In P. L. Benson, E. C. Roehlkepartain, P. E. King, & L. Wagener (Eds.), *The handbook of spiritual development in childhood and adolescence.* Newbury Park, CA: Sage Publications.

Cummings, E. M., & Davies, P. T. (2002). Effects of marital conflict on children: Recent advances and emerging themes in process-oriented research. *Journal of Child Psychology and Psychiatry, 43,* 31–63.

Cummings, E. M., Davies, P. T., & Campbell, S. B. (2000). *Developmental psychopathology and family process.* New York: Guilford.

Damon, W. (Editor-in-Chief), & Eisenberg, N. (Vol. Ed.) (1998). *Handbook of child psychology: Vol. 3. Social, emotional, and personality development* (5th ed.). New York: Wiley.

Davies, P. T., & Cicchetti, D. (Eds.) (2004). Family systems and developmental psychopathology [Special issue], *Development and Psychopathology, 16,* 477–81.

Dishion, T. J., & McMahon, R. J. (1998). Parental monitoring and the prevention of child and adolescent problem behavior: A conceptual and empirical foundation. *Clinical Child and Family Psychology Review, 1*, 61–75.

Egeland, B., Carlson, E. A., & Sroufe, L. A. (1993). Resilience as process. *Development and Psychopathology, 5*, 517–528.

Elder, G. H. (1974/1999). *Children of the Great Depression*. Chicago: University of Chicago Press.

Elder, G. H., & Conger, R. D. (2000). *Children of the land: Adversity and success in rural America*. Chicago: University of Chicago Press.

Fiese, B. H. (2000). Family matters: A systems view of family effects on children's cognitive health. In R. J. Sternberg & E. L. Grigorenko (Eds.), *Environmental effects on cognitive abilities* (pp. 39–57). Mahwah, NJ: Erlbaum.

Fiese, B. H., & Spagnola, M. (in press). The interior life of the family: Looking from the inside out and outside in. In A. S. Masten, L. A. Sroufe, & B. Egeland (Eds.), *Developmental psychopathology: Integrating multiple levels of analysis. 33rd Minnesota Symposium on Child Psychology*. Minneapolis: University of Minnesota Press.

Fiese, B., Wilder, J., & Bickham, N. (2000). Family context in developmental psychopathology. In A. Sameroff, M. Lewis & S. Miller (Eds.), *Handbook of Developmental Psychopathology* (2nd ed., pp. 115–134). New York: Kluwer Academic / Plenum Publishers.

Ford, D. H., & Lerner, R. M. (1992). *Developmental systems theory: An integrative approach*. Newbury Park, CA: Sage Publications.

Forgatch, M. S., & DeGarmo, D. S. (1999). Parenting through change: An effective prevention program for single mothers. *Journal of Consulting and Clinical Psychology, 67*, 711–724.

Freud, S. (1933/1964). *New introductory lectures on psychoanalysis*. New York: W. W. Norton.

Galambos, N. L., Barker, E. T., & Almeida, D. M. (2003). Parents do matter: Trajectories of change in externalizing and internalizing problems in early adolescence. *Child Development, 74*, 578–594.

Garmezy, N., & Rutter, M. (1983). *Stress, coping, and development in children*. New York: McGraw-Hill.

Ge, X., Conger, R. D., Lorenz, F. O., Shanahan, M., & Elder, G. H. (1995). Mutual influences in parent and adolescent psychological distress. *Developmental Psychology, 31*, 406–419.

Gest, S. D., Neemann, J., Hubbard, J. J., Masten, A. S., & Tellegen, A. (1993). Parenting quality, adversity, and conduct problems in adolescence: Testing process-oriented models of resilience. *Development and Psychopathology, 5*, 663–682.

Gewirtz, J. R. (1969). Mechanisms of social learning: Some roles of stimulation and behavior in early human development. In D. A. Goslin (Ed.), *Handbook of socialization theory and research* (pp. 57–212). Chicago: Rand McNally.

Gottesman, I. I., & Hanson, D. R. (2005). Human development: Biological and genetic processes. *Annual Review of Psychology, 56*, 263–286.

Graham-Bermann, S. A., & Edelson, J. L. (2001). *Domestic violence in the lives of children: The future of research, intervention and social policy*. Washington, DC: American Psychological Association.

Grant, K. E., Compas, B. E., Stuhlmacher, A. F., Thrum, A. E., McMahon, S. D., & Halpert, J. A. (2003). Stressors and child and adolescent psychopathology: Moving from markers to mechanisms of risk. *Psychological Bulletin, 129*, 447–466.

Gunnar, M. R. (in press). Social regulation of stress in early child development. In K. McCartney & D. A. Phillips (Eds.), *Handbook of early child development*. New York: Blackwell.

Gunnar, M. R., & Donzella, B. (2002). Social regulation of the L-HPA axis in early human development. *Psychoneuroendocrinology, 27*, 199–220.

Hart, B., & Risley, T. R. (1995). *Meaningful differences in the everyday experiences of young American children*. Baltimore: Paul H. Brooks.

Hetherington, E. M., Bridges, M., & Insabella, G. M. (1998). What matters and what does not? Five perspectives on the association between marital transitions and children's adjustment. *American Psychologist, 53*, 167–184.

Hinde, R. A. (1974). *Biological bases of human social behaviour*. New York: McGraw-Hill Book Co.

Hinshaw, S. P. (2002). Process, mechanism, and explanation related to externalizing behavior in developmental psychopathology. *Journal of Abnormal Child Psychology, 30*, 431–446.

Jessor, R. (1993). Successful adolescent development among youth in high-risk settings. *American Psychologist, 48*, 117–126.

Kim-Cohen, J., Moffitt, T. E., Caspi, A., & Taylor, A. (2004). Genetic and environmental processes in young children's resilience and vulnerability to socioeconomic deprivation. *Child Development, 75*, 651–668.

Kochanska, G. (1995). Children's temperament, mothers' discipline, and security of attachment: Multiple pathways to emerging internalization. *Child Development, 66*, 597–615.

Kraemer, H. C., Stice, E., Kazdin, A., Offord, D., & Kupfer, D. (2001). How do risk factors work together? Mediators, moderators, and independent, overlapping, and proxy risk factors. *American Journal of Psychiatry, 158*, 848–856.

Kumpfer, K. L., & Alvarado, R. (2003). Family-strengthening approaches for the prevention of youth problem behaviors. *American Psychologist, 58*, 457–465.

Luthar, S. S. (1999). *Poverty and children's adjustment*. Newbury Park, CA: Sage Publications.

Luthar, S. S., Ed. (2003). *Resilience and vulnerability: Adaptation in the context of childhood adversities*. New York: Cambridge University Press.

Luthar, S. S. (in press). Resilience in development: A synthesis of research across five decades. In D. Cicchetti & D. J. Cohen (Eds.), *Developmental psychopathology: Risk disorder, and adaptation* (2nd ed.). New York: Wiley.

Maccoby, E. E. (1980). *Social development: Psychological growth and the parent-child relationship*. San Diego, CA: Harcourt Brace Jovanovich.

Maccoby, E. E. (1992). The role of parents in the socialization of children: An historical overview. *Developmental Psychology, 28*, 1006–1017.

Martinez, C. R., & Forgatch, M. S. (2001). Preventing problems with boys' noncompliance: Effects of a parent training intervention for divorcing mothers. *Journal of Consulting and Clinical Psychology, 69*, 416–428.

Masten, A. S. (2001). Ordinary magic: Resilience processes in development. *American Psychologist, 56*, 227–238.

Masten, A. S., Burt, K., & Coatsworth, J. D. (in press). Competence and psychopathology in development. In D. Cicchetti & D. Cohen (Eds.), *Handbook of developmental psychopathology* (2nd ed.) New York: Wiley.

Masten, A. S., & Coatsworth, J. D. (1995). Competence, resilience, and psychopathology. In D. Cicchetti & D. Cohen (Eds.), *Developmental psychopathology: Vol. 2. Risk, disorder, and adaptation* (pp. 715–752) New York: Wiley.

Masten, A. S., & Coatsworth, J. D. (1998). The development of competence in favorable and unfavorable environments: Lessons from research on successful children. *American Psychologist, 53,* 205–220.

Masten, A. S., & Gewirtz, A. H. (in press). Vulnerability and resilience in early childhood development. In K. McCartney & D. A. Phillips (Eds.), *Handbook of early childhood development.* New York: Blackwell.

Masten, A. S., & Powell, J. L. (2003). A resilience framework for research, policy, and practice. In S. S. Luthar (Ed.), *Resilience and vulnerability: Adaptation in the context of childhood adversities* (pp. 1–25). New York: Cambridge University Press.

Masten, A. S., & Reed, M-G J. (2002). Resilience in development. In C. R. Snyder & S. J. Lopez (Eds.), *Handbook of positive psychology* (pp. 74–88). London: Oxford University Press.

Masten, A. S., & Wright, M. O. (1998). Cumulative risk and protection models of child maltreatment. *Journal of Aggression, Maltreatment and Trauma, 2,* 7–30. Also published as a monograph, in B. B. R. Rossman & M. S. Rosenberg (Eds.), *Multiple victimization of children: Conceptual, developmental, research and treatment issues* (pp. 7–30). Binghamton, NY: Haworth.

McLoyd, V. C. (1990). The impact of economic hardship on black families and children: Psychological distress, parenting, and socioemotional development. *Child Development, 61,* 311–346.

McLoyd, V. C. (1998). Socioeconomic disadvantage and child development. *American Psychologist, 53,* 185–204.

Munroe, R. L. (1955). *Schools of analytic thought: An exposition, critique, and attempt at integration.* New York: Holt, Rinehart, & Winston.

Patterson, G. R. (1982). *Coercive family processes.* Eugene, OR: Castalia Press.

Pettit, G. S., Bates, J. E., Dodge, K. A., & Meece, D. W. (1999). The impact of after-school peer contact on early adolescent externalizing problems is moderated by parental monitoring, perceived neighborhood safety, and prior adjustment. *Child Development, 70,* 768–778.

Pine, D. S., Costello, J., & Masten, A. S. (in press). Trauma, proximity, and developmental psychopathology: The effects of war and terrorism on children. *Neuropsychopharmacology.*

Repetti, R. L., Taylor, S. E., & Seeman, T. E. (2002). Risky families: Family social environments and the mental and physical health of offspring. *Psychological Bulletin, 128,* 330–366.

Richters, J. E., & Martinez, P. (1993). The NIMH community violence project: I. Children as victims of and witnesses to violence. *Psychiatry, 56,* 7–21.

Rothbart, M. K., & Bates, J. E. (1998). Temperament. In N. Eisenberg (Ed.), *Handbook of child psychology: Vol. 4. Social, emotional, and personality development* (pp. 105–76). New York: Wiley.

Rutter, M. (1972). *Maternal Deprivation Reassessed.* Harmondsworth: Penguin.

Rutter, M. (1979). Protective factors in children's responses to stress and disadvantage. *Annals of the Academy of Medicine, Singapore, 8,* 324–338.

Rutter, M. (1983). Stress, coping, and development: Some issues and some questions. In N. Garmezy & M. Rutter (Eds.), *Stress, coping, and development in children* (pp. 1–42). New York: McGraw-Hill.

Rutter, M. (1990). Psychosocial resilience and protective mechanisms. In J. Rolf, A. S. Masten, D. Cicchetti, K. H. Nuechterlein, & S. Weintraub (Eds.), *Risk and protective factors in the development of psychopathology* (pp. 181–214). New York: Cambridge University Press.

Rutter, M., & the English and Romanian Adoptees (ERA) Study Team (1998). Developmental catch-up and deficit following adoption after severe global early privation. *Journal of Child Psychology and Psychiatry, 39,* 465–476.

Sameroff, A. J. (2000). Developmental systems and psychopathology. *Development and Psychopathology, 12,* 297–312.

Sameroff, A. J., & Chander, M. J. (1975). Reproductive risk and the continuum of caretaking casualty. *Review of Child Development Research, 4,* 187–244.

Sameroff, A. J., & Fiese, B. H. (2000). Transactional regulation: The developmental ecology of early intervention. In J. P. Shonkoff & S. J. Meisels (Eds.), *Handbook of early childhood intervention* (pp. 135–159). New York: Cambridge University Press.

Sampson, R. J., Morenoff, J., & Earls, F. (1999). Beyond social capital: Spatial dynamics of collective efficacy for children. *American Sociological Review, 64,* 633–660.

Sandler, I., Wolchik, S., Davis, C., Haine, R., & Ayers, T. (2003). Correlational and experimental study of resilience in children of divorce and parentally bereaved children. In S. Luthar (Ed.), *Resilience and vulnerability: Adaptation in the context of childhood adversities* (pp. 213–242). Cambridge: Cambridge University Press.

Shonkoff, J., & Phillips, D. A. (2000). Nurturing relationships. In *Neurons to neighborhoods: The science of early childhood development* (pp. 225–266). Washington, DC: National Academies Press.

Spitz, R. A. (1945). Hospitalism: An inquiry into the genesis of psychiatric conditions in early childhood. *Psychoanalytic Study of the Child, 1,* 53–74.

Sroufe, L. A. (1996). *Emotional development: The organization of the emotional life in the early years.* New York: Cambridge University Press.

Sroufe, L. A., Carlson, E. A., Levy, A. K., & Egeland, B. (1999). Implications of attachment theory for developmental psychopathology. *Development and Psychopathology, 11,* 1–13.

Sroufe, L. A., & Waters, E. (1977). Attachment as an organizational construct. *Child Development, 48,* 1184–1199.

Suomi, S. J. (2000). A biobehavioral perspective on developmental psychopathology: Excessive aggression and serotonergic dysfunction in monkeys. In A. Sameroff, M. Lewis, & S. M. Miller (Eds.), *Handbook of developmental psychopathology* (pp. 237–256). New York: Kluwer Academic Publishers.

Szapocznik, J., & Williams, R. A. (2000). Brief Strategic Family Therapy: Twenty-five years of interplay among theory, research and practice in adolescent behavior problems and drug abuse. *Clinical Child and Family Psychology Review, 3,* 117–134.

Thelen, E., & Smith, L. (1998). Dynamic systems theories. In R. M. Lerner (Ed.), *Handbook of Child Psychology: Vol. 1. Theoretical models of human development* (pp. 563–634). New York: Wiley.

van den Boom, D. C. (1994). The influence of temperament and mothering on attachment and exploration: An experimental manipulation of sensitive responsiveness among lower-class mothers with irritable infants. *Child Development, 65,* 1457–1477.

van den Boom, D. C. (1995). Do first-year intervention effects endure? Follow-up during toddlerhood of a sample of Dutch irritable infants. *Child Development, 66,* 1798–1816.

van IJzendoorn, M. H., Juffer, F., & Duyvesteyn, M. G. C. (1995). Breaking the intergenerational cycle of insecure attachment: A review of the effects of attachment-based interventions on maternal sensitivity and infant security. *Journal of Child Psychology & Psychiatry & Allied Disciplines, 36,* 225–248.

Waters, E., Vaughn, B. E., Posada, G., & Kondo-Ikemura, K. (1995). Caregiving, cultural, and cognitive perspectives on secure-base behavior and working models. *Monographs of the Society for Research in Child Development: Vol. 60.* Chicago: University of Chicago Press.

Weissberg, R. P., Kumpfer, K. L., & Seligman, M. E. P. (2003). Prevention that works for children and youth. *American Psychologist, 58,* 425–432.

Wolchik, S. A., Sandler, I. N., Millsap, R. E., Plummer, B. A., Greene, S. M., Anderson, E. R., et al. (2002). Six-year follow-up of preventive interventions for children of divorce. A randomized controlled trial. *JAMA: Journal of the American Medical Association, 288,* 1874–1881.

Wolfe, D. A., Crooks, C. V., Lee, V., McIntyre-Smith, A., & Jaffe, P. G. (2003). The effects of children's exposure to domestic violence: A meta-analysis and critique. *Clinical Child and Family Psychology Review, 6,* 171–187.

Wright, M. O'D., & Masten, A. S. (2005). Resilience processes in development: Fostering positive adaptation in the context of adversity. In S. Goldstein & R. Brooks (Eds.), *Handbook of resilience in children.* New York: Kluwer Academic/Plenum.

Wyman, P. A., Sandler, I., Wolchik, S., & Nelson, K. (2000). Resilience as cumulative competence promotion and stress protection: Theory and intervention. In D. Cicchetti, J. Rappaport, I. Sandler, & R. P. Weissberg (Eds.), *The promotion of wellness in children and adolescents* (pp. 133–184). Thousand Oaks, CA: Sage Publications.

Zeanah, C. H., Nelson, C. A., Fox, N. A., Smyke, A. T., Marshall, P., Parker, S. W., & Koga, S. (2003). Designing research to study the effects of institutionalization on brain and behavioral development: The Bucharest Early Intervention Project. *Development and Psychopathology, 15,* 885–907.

Zeanah, C. H., Smyke, A. T., & Settles, L. D. (in press). Orphanages as a developmental context for early childhood. In K. McCartney & D. A. Phillips (Eds.), *Handbook of early childhood development.* New York: Blackwell.

[14]

SOCIOECONOMIC STATUS AND CHILD DEVELOPMENT

Robert H. Bradley and Robert F. Corwyn

Center for Applied Studies in Education, University of Arkansas at Little Rock, 2801 S. University Ave., Little Rock, Arkansas 72204; e-mail: rhbradley@ualr.edu

Key Words   socioeconomic status, poverty, achievement, adjustment, child well-being

■ **Abstract**   Socioeconomic status (SES) is one of the most widely studied constructs in the social sciences. Several ways of measuring SES have been proposed, but most include some quantification of family income, parental education, and occupational status. Research shows that SES is associated with a wide array of health, cognitive, and socioemotional outcomes in children, with effects beginning prior to birth and continuing into adulthood. A variety of mechanisms linking SES to child well-being have been proposed, with most involving differences in access to material and social resources or reactions to stress-inducing conditions by both the children themselves and their parents. For children, SES impacts well-being at multiple levels, including both family and neighborhood. Its effects are moderated by children's own characteristics, family characteristics, and external support systems.

CONTENTS

INTRODUCTION 372
HISTORY AND DEFINITION 372
SES & WELL-BEING 373
   Health 373
   Cognitive and Academic Attainment 375
   Socioemotional Development 377
   Models of Mediating Processes 378
   Resources 379
   Stress Reactions 383
   Health-Relevant Behaviors/Lifestyle 385
   Models of Moderation 387
COLLECTIVE SES 388
FUTURE DIRECTIONS 391

INTRODUCTION

Socioeconomic status (SES) remains a topic of great interest to those who study children's development. This interest derives from a belief that high SES families afford their children an array of services, goods, parental actions, and social connections that potentially redound to the benefit of children and a concern that many low SES children lack access to those same resources and experiences, thus putting them at risk for developmental problems (Brooks-Gunn & Duncan 1997). The interest in SES as a global construct persists despite evidence that there is wide variability in what children experience within every SES level, despite evidence that the link between SES and child well-being varies as a function of geography, culture, and recency of immigration, and despite evidence that the relation between SES and child well-being can be disrupted by catastrophes and internal strife (Bradley & Corwyn 1999, Wachs 2000).

In this chapter we review the history of SES and provide an overview of the association between SES and children's well-being for three major domains of development (cognitive, socioemotional, health). Attention is given to models that attempt to explicate the connection between SES and these aspects of development. Finally, we offer a rationale for expanding attention to collective SES as a way of more fully instantiating the concepts of developmental systems theory into research on SES.

HISTORY AND DEFINITION

Social scientists have shown continued interest in SES even though there has never been complete consensus on precisely what it represents (Liberatos et al. 1988, McLoyd 1997). There has been something of a tug-of-war between proponents of SES as representing class (or economic position) and proponents of SES as representing social status (or prestige). The idea of capital (Coleman 1988) perhaps best embodies the current meaning psychologists hold of SES (Entwistle & Astone 1994, Guo & Harris 2000). Capital (resources, assets) has become a favored way of thinking about SES because access to financial capital (material resources), human capital (nonmaterial resources such as education), and social capital (resources achieved through social connections) are readily connectible to processes that directly affect well-being. Capital is linked to historic ideas about SES, such as social and material "deprivation," and it brings into focus the important dimension of social relationships (Krieger et al. 1997).

Most widely used measures of SES only partially map onto the concepts of capital described by Coleman. Financial capital is reasonably well assessed by household income, but is more often indexed by occupational status. However, neither fully captures the notion of wealth as described by economists (Smith 1999); wealth may be a better measure of the financial resources available in that it is often a more accurate barometer of access to opportunities (Oliver & Shapiro 1995, Ostrove et al. 1999, Williams & Collins 1995). Income is considered a rather volatile indicator of financial capital (Hauser 1994), and the best way of ordering occupations in terms of their actual contributions to financial well-being has been hotly debated for decades (Davies 1952, Entwisle & Astone 1994, Miller 1991, Grusky & Van Rompaey 1992, Nam & Powers 1983). Most social scientists agree that a combination of income and occupational status provides a better approximation to financial capital than either alone. To more fully capture financial capital, Entwisle & Astone (1994) recommend gathering data on what the family pays for rent or housing. Ostrove and his coworkers (1999) simply asked respondents to estimate the total value of their assets.

Entwisle & Astone (1994) also recommend expanding data collections pertaining to social capital (e.g., number of parents in the home, presence of a grandparent in the home), a suggestion that may garner increasing support given that many children live in households with only one parent. Research showing that occupation often partially determines one's social network suggests that occupational status may also provide some indication of social capital. Likewise, research showing a link between the type of employment parents engage in and parenting practices suggests that occupational status may also capture some of human capital (Kohn & Schooler 1982, Parcel & Menaghan 1990, Rodrigo et al. 2001).

Although there is general consensus that income, education, and occupation together represent SES better than any of these alone (White 1982), there is no consensus on (*a*) how best to composite the set of indicators; (*b*) whether it works best to examine relations between SES and child outcomes using a composite, a statistical procedure that includes each indicator, or each indicator singly; or (*c*) how best to measure each component (Krieger et al. 1997). The predictive value of specific composites have been compared with inconsistent results (Gottfried 1985, Liberatos et al. 1988, White 1982). At times the different indicators seem to be tapping into the same underlying phenomenon, as indicated by their intercorrelations and their similar correlations with outcome measures. At other times, they appear to be tapping into different underlying phenomena and seem to be connected to different paths of influence, as indicated by only modest correlations even among different SES composites and links with different mediating variables (Ostrove et al. 1999). Relatedly, there remains some uncertainty as to whether SES has the same underlying meaning in all ethnic and cultural groups (Williams & Collins 1995).

In overview, the choice of how to measure SES remains open. Part will be determined by the question being examined, part by practical considerations concerning the acquisition of data, and part by the population from whom the data are collected. Regarding this last issue, both theory and empirical findings indicate that SES indicators are likely to perform differently across cultural groups (Bradley 1994, Bronfenbrenner 1995).

SES & WELL-BEING

Health

For years, studies of adults have documented a relation between SES and health (Adler et al. 1994). The data on children is somewhat less complete and less consistent, but evidence points to a substantial relation that begins before birth (US Dep. Health & Human Services 2000b). Children from low-SES families are more likely to experience growth retardation and inadequate neurobehavioral development in utero (DiPietro et al. 1999, Kramer 1987). They are more likely to be born prematurely, at low birth weight, or with asphyxia, a birth defect, a disability, fetal alcohol syndrome, or AIDS (Crooks 1995, Hawley & Disney 1992, US Dep. Health & Human Services 2000b, Cassady et al. 1997, Vrijheid et al. 2000, Wasserman et al. 1998). Early health problems often emanate from poor prenatal care, maternal substance abuse, poor nutrition during pregnancy, maternal lifestyles that increase the likelihood of infections (smoking, drug use), and living in a neighborhood that contains hazards affecting fetal development (toxic waste dumps) (US Dep. Health & Human Services 2000a).

After birth, low-SES infants are more likely to suffer injuries and to die (Overpeck et al. 1998, Scholer et al. 1999). During childhood, SES is implicated in many diseases, including respiratory illnesses (Cohen 1999, Haan et al. 1989, Johnston-Brooks et al. 1998, Klerman 1991, Rosenbaum 1992). Low SES is associated with an increased likelihood of dental caries (US Dep. Health & Human Services 2000b), higher blood lead levels (Brody et al. 1994a, Starfield 1982, Tesman & Hills 1994), iron deficiency (US Dep. Health & Human Services 2000b, Starfield 1989), stunting (Brooks-Gunn & Duncan 1997, Korenman & Miller 1997, Kotch & Shackelford 1989), and sensory impairment (US Dep. Health & Human Services 2000b, Starfield 1989, Wilson 1993). These outcomes likely reflect an array of conditions associated with low SES, including inadequate nutrition, exposure to tobacco smoke, failure to get recommended immunizations, and inadequate access to health care (US Dep. Health & Human Services 2000a,b; Pollitt et al. 1996; Raisler et al. 1999; Sandel & Schrfstein 1999).

On the other hand, SES is not implicated in all illnesses, and the SES/health gradient appears less steep in more egalitarian nations (Adler et al. 1999). Moreover, the relations between particular SES indicators and health factors may be quite complex. For example, the impact of low income appears to depend on how long poverty lasts and the child's age when the family is poor (Bradley & Whiteside-Mansell 1997, Duncan & Brooks-Gunn 1997, Miller & Korenman 1994).

When low-SES children experience health problems, the consequences are often more severe. Low-SES children born preterm are far more likely to suffer health and developmental consequences than their more affluent counterparts (Parker et al. 1988). Children from low-income families are two to three times as likely to suffer complications from appendicitis and bacterial meningitis and to die from injuries and infections at every age (US Dep. Health & Human Services 2000b). The average length of stay for poor children in acute care hospitals is longer than the average for nonpoor children (Bradley & Kelleher 1992). Equally important are findings that early insults to health may have long-term consequences (McLoyd 1998, Bradley et al. 1994). For example, premature children who lived in poverty for the first 3 years of life manifested more problems in growth, health status, intelligence, and behavior (Bradley et al. 1994); children with high lead levels are at increased risk of long-term neurological problems (Needleman et al. 1990);

and low-birthweight children who also had perinatal illnesses experienced more school failure (McGauhey et al. 1991).

Among adolescents, SES is related to health status, but relations are less consistent than for adults (Macintyre & West 1991). Goodman (1999) found that SES was related to depression, obesity, and self-rated overall health (US Dep. Health & Human Services 2000a,b; Call & Nonnemaker 1999). Data from NHANES II indicate that poor teens are more likely to show stunting (Brooks-Gunn & Duncan 1997). However, SES was not associated with asthma and was inconsistently related to suicide attempts and STDs (Goodman 1999).

Biologic impacts during childhood create vulnerabilities that result in adverse health outcomes in adulthood. Power (1991) found that SES measured in middle childhood and adolescence was related to health status at age 23, even controlling for SES at age 23. Hertzman (1999) refers to this as the "biological embedding" of early experience and notes that there is evidence for "latent" effects of early biologic damage (e.g., a higher propensity for adult cardiovascular disease for low-birthweight children). Specifically, he offers the hypothesis that "systemic differences in the quality of early environments, in terms of stimulation and emotional and physical support, will affect the sculpting and neurochemistry of the central nervous system in ways that will adversely affect cognitive, social, and behavioral development" (p. 89). Little research has been completed on this hypothesis, but research shows that anthropometric indicators of undernutrition during infancy predict cognitive performace in middle childhood and adolescence (Pollitt et al. 1996). Also, Treiber and his coworkers (1999) found evidence that low SES was associated with increased systolic blood pressure and increased left ventricular mass among adolescents.

Cognitive and Academic Attainment

For over 70 years findings on the relationship between SES and intellectual/academic competence has accumulated. McCall (1981) presented evidence that the association between SES and cognitive performance begins in infancy. Numerous studies have documented that poverty and low parental education are associated with lower levels of school achievement and IQ later in childhood (Alexander et al. 1993, Bloom 1964, Duncan et al. 1994, Escalona 1982, Hess et al. 1982, Pianta et al. 1990, Walberg & Marjoribanks 1976, Zill et al. 1995). Kennedy and colleagues (1963) reported results from a random sample of first- through sixth-grade African American children selected to represent African Americans living in the southeastern United States. The mean IQ of the highest SES group was 25 points higher than the mean of the lowest SES group.

There has been some debate regarding which aspects of SES most strongly connect to cognitive development. Mercy & Steelman (1982) found that each SES measure used in the Health Examination Survey (family income, maternal education, paternal education) predicted intellectual attainment, with education being the best predictor. Maternal education was a stronger predictor than paternal education. Scarr & Weinberg (1978) found maternal and paternal education to

376   BRADLEY ▪ CORWYN

be equally good predictors. This discrepancy may reflect differences in the ages of the children assessed. Mercy & Steelman studied 6- to 11-year-olds, whereas Scarr & Weinberg (1978) studied 15-year-olds. In his meta-analysis White (1982) found that SES accounted for about 5% of the variance in academic achievement. Among the traditional measures of SES, family income accounted for the greatest amount of variance, but SES measures that combined two or more indicators accounted for more variance than single indicators. In a recent study DeGarmo and colleagues (1999) found that each SES indicator (income, education, occupation) was associated with better parenting, which in turn affected school achievement via skill-building activities and school behavior.

Few researchers have concentrated on the relation between parental occupation and cognitive development. However, Parcel & Menaghan (1990) found that mothers who worked in occupations with a variety of tasks and problem solving opportunities provided more warmth and support and a greater number of stimulating materials. Their children manifested more advanced verbal competence. Such findings are consistent with the classic argument of Kohn & Schooler (1982): what parents experience at work, they incorporate into their style of parenting.

There is evidence that the connection between SES and cognitive performance applies to many societies. Mpofu & Van de Vijver (2000) found that among Zimbabwean children social class predicted the frequency with which children used taxonomic rather than functional classification strategies. In their cross-cultural review Bradley and colleagues (1996) found that SES indicators were strongly related to cognitive development from infancy through middle childhood. Evidence suggests a particularly strong relation between SES and verbal skills (Mercy & Steelman 1982). Hart & Risley (1995) found major differences in the language proficiency of children from high-SES and low-SES families. Hoff-Ginsberg (1991) also found substantial SES differences in language performance for children, beginning early in life.

In his meta-analysis White (1982) found some evidence that the relation between SES and intellectual/academic attainment diminishes with age. However, Smith and colleagues (1997) found that the effects of family income on achievement among 7-year-olds were similar to the effects on intelligence for 3-year-olds. Likewise, Walberg & Marjoribanks (1976) suggested that adolescents may benefit as much as younger children from a stimulating family environment. "Uncorrected regression can underestimate environmental effects when there are substantial errors in measuring the environment" (p. 546). Their results suggest that for intellectual and academic attainment there may be a kind of accumulated value to family environment and SES, but thus far there is little evidence to substantiate this.

The relation between SES and cognitive attainment may be quite complex, with different components of SES contributing to the development of particular cognitive skills in different ways and with some components of SES serving to moderate the effects of other components. DeGarmo and colleagues (1999) examined the paths between maternal education, occupation, and income and found evidence of both similarities and differences in their connections to school achievement among 6- to 9-year-olds. Several analyses have indicated that the relations for family income and parental education depend on the number of siblings present in the household (Anastasi 1956, Mercy & Steelman 1982, Walberg & Marjoribanks 1976). Others have discussed the importance of unpacking the effects of socio-economic status owing to the high level of confounding between socioeconomic and family demographic indicators, but few studies have done so (Brooks-Gunn & Duncan 1997, McLoyd 1998).

SES also appears to affect school attendance and number of years of schooling completed (Haverman & Wolf 1995, Brooks-Gunn & Duncan 1997). The impact on years completed appears to be less than the impact on school achievement. Even so, SES remains one of the most consistent predictors of early high school drop-out, with evidence suggesting that it is connected both to low parental expectations and to early initiation of sexual activity (Battin-Pearson et al. 2000).

Socioemotional Development

Although the link between SES and children's social and emotional well-being is not as consistent as the link with cognitive attainment, there is substantial evidence that low-SES children more often manifest symptoms of psychiatric disturbance and maladaptive social functioning than children from more affluent circumstances (Bolger et al. 1995, Brooks-Gunn & Duncan 1997, Lahey et al. 1995, McCoy et al. 1999, McLeod & Shanahan 1993, Moore et al. 1994, Patterson et al. 1989, Sameroff et al. 1987, Starfield 1989, Takeuchi et al. 1991). It is not easy to state the precise relation between SES and socioemotional problems in children. It is often difficult to identify mental illness in young children, owing to the various standards and methods used to assess mental illness. For very young children, there is little evidence of a relation between SES and socioemotional well-being (Earls 1980, Richman et al. 1975). However, the relation emerges in early childhood and becomes reasonably consistent (especially for externalizing problems) in middle childhood (Achenbach et al. 1990, Duncan et al. 1994, McLeod & Shanahan 1993). Among adolescents, low SES is often associated with poor adaptive functioning, an increased likelihood of depression, and delinquent behavior (McLoyd 1997). Conger and colleagues (1997), however, did not find a relation between poverty and adolescent problems. Part of the difference in findings may pertain to who reports on social and emotional well-being. Most often parents and teachers are the reporters, but in the Conger et al. study adolescents reported on their own behavior.

The strength of the relationship between SES and mental disorders varies by type of disorder and race (McLoyd 1997). The relationship is most consistent with schizophrenia and personality disorders, reasonably consistent with mild depression, and inconsistent with neuroses and affective disorders (Ortega & Corzine 1990). Among children 6–17 years old referred to a psychiatric clinic, SES was associated with parent and teacher reports of aggressiveness and delinquency (McCoy et al. 1999).

Higher rates of substance abuse have been reported for low-SES teens, but findings are inconsistent (Wills et al. 1995). The relation is often mediated through

378   BRADLEY ▪ CORWYN

friends' use of substances, academic competence, and parental supportiveness. It is also connected with the experience of negative life events (Wills et al. 1992).

Ortega & Corzine (1990) identified a number of factors that complicate our ability to understand relations between SES and socioemotional adjustment. The two leading theories (social causation and social selection/drift) imply opposite causation. The social causation explanation holds that mental disorder results from poverty and its cofactors; the social selection explanation holds that those with mental disorders gradually drift into lower SES strata. For children, there has been little study of the drift hypothesis because it was generated to explain the gradual decline in status for seriously mentally ill adults. A second complication in interpreting research on SES and mental illness derives from the fact that the poor are more likely to be defined as mentally ill even when they manifest the same level of symptomatology as do more affluent individuals.

In overview, there is substantial evidence linking low SES to less optimal outcomes in nearly every area of functioning. Unfortunately, most studies examined only a single outcome and, even when they examined more than one outcome, little attention was given to whether individual children experienced multiple bad outcomes. According to developmental systems theory, it is very difficult to predict developmental pathways with precision in highly complex, self-constructing organisms like humans (Ford & Lerner 1992, Wachs 2000). The same set of circumstances may potentiate any of a number of outcomes (the principle of equipotentiality) depending on individual strengths and vulnerabilities and other conditions present both concurrent and subsequent to the experience of those circumstances.

For low-SES children, it is quite difficult to predict whether a particular health, cognitive, or emotional problem may eventually emerge. However, it is somewhat easier to predict that low-SES children are likely to experience more developmental problems than affluent children. Results from the Infant Health and Development Program showed that 40% of children born prematurely and who lived in chronic poverty had deficiencies in at least two areas of functioning at age three (Bradley et al. 1994). Likewise, Bradley and his colleagues (2000) found that the quality of the home environment was correlated about 0.40 with the number of developmental problems manifested by adolescents from five different sociocultural groups. Correlations with specific problems varied across groups, but the correlation with the number of problems was virtually identical.

Models of Mediating Processes

The SES literature offers a variety of proposed mechanisms linking SES and child well-being. The MacArthur Network on SES and health placed linking mechanisms in two broad categories: environmental resources/constraints and psychological influences (Adler & Ostrove 1999). Most hypothesized mechanisms have not been adequately explored, especially in terms of applicability to different cultural groups; in effect, most have verisimilitude, not established credibility. Many proposed intervening processes are themselves disconnected from broader developmental systems models that not only stipulate moderating and mediating processes but mediated moderating and moderated mediating processes as well (Baron & Kenny 1986). In sum, the literature mostly provides bits and pieces of the larger person-process-context-time tableaux described by Bronfenbrenner (1995).

It is not easy to determine with precision the processes through which SES influences child well-being, partly because low SES frequently co-occurs with other conditions that purportedly affect children (e.g., minority and immigrant status, single parenthood, a family member with a disability or serious mental illness, exposure to teratogens and other potentially hazardous environmental conditions)— the classic "third variable" problem. It is difficult to disentangle SES from such cofactors when there is evidence that they may exacerbate the effects of SES (i.e., they function as moderators). Direct biological damage may also contribute to SES differences. To be more specific, brain disorders, such as those connected with mental illness, can also result from trauma or exposure to pathogens, both of which are more common among individuals who are low SES. Low-SES children are more often the victims of child abuse, peer aggression, and community violence (Garbarino 1999).

In overview, for a given child from a low-SES family, the mechanism leading to a poorer developmental outcome could be one connected to family SES, a particular SES cofactor (such as single parenthood or minority status), a combination of the two, or even a third variable connected to both (e.g., family conflict). During the course of childhood, the meaning and significance of particular cofactors can change (Moen et al. 1995). For preschool children, living in a deteriorated neighborhood may mean less access to stimulating resources and recreational facilities. For an adolescent, the same neighborhood may mean increased likelihood of affiliation with deviant peers.

Resources

NUTRITION   Among the most oft-cited linkages between SES and well-being is access to resources (Klerman 1991). Klerman's model includes seven paths linking low income to health, inability to purchase goods and services essential for health and inability to secure appropriate health services. Mortorell (1980) identified inadequate dietary intake as a key pathway to poor health. According to his model, inadequate dietary intake results in defective nutrient absorption, defective nutrient utilization, and poor defenses against infection. Poor nutritional status, in turn, contributes to an array of morbidities and mortality. Pollitt and colleagues (1996) offer a similar formulation. In addition, they present evidence that poor nutritional status affects brain growth both pre- and postnatally.

Overall evidence supporting the "nutrition pathway" is incomplete, but research showing nutritionally mediated SES impacts on (*a*) growth (Adler et al. 1999, Brooks-Gunn & Duncan 1997, Miller & Korenman 1994), (*b*) the increased likelihood of neural tube defects owing to inadequate intake of folic acid during pregnancy (Wasserman et al. 1998), (*c*) the prevalence of iron deficiency owing to

380   BRADLEY ■ CORWYN

inadequate intake of meats and vegetables rich in iron (US Dep. Health & Human Services 2000a, Oski 1993, Starfield 1989), and (*d*) poor long-term memory following lengthy episodes of poor nutrition (Korenman & Miller 1997) offer support for such a path. Valenzuela (1997) offers evidence that chronic undernutrition can deplete the energy resources of both parent and child, making the child more lethargic and less able to elicit attention from the parent and the parent less sensitive and supportive of the child. The result is not only compromised growth but increased likelihood of insecure attachment, negative affect, and limited mastery motivation.

ACCESS TO HEALTH CARE   It is difficult to determine how much poor nutrition contributes to developmental problems because children who lack access to adequate nutrition also tend to lack access to other resources, such as adequate medical care. It is not easy to determine if a condition connected to poor nutrition actually results from poor nutrition or whether it reflects inadequate prenatal care (Blendon et al. 1989; US Dep. Health & Human Services 2000a,b), inadequate preventive care for the child (e.g., failure to obtain all recommended immunizations) (US Dep. Health & Human Services 2000a, Raisler et al. 1999, Sandel & Schrfstein 1999), failure to obtain necessary medical treatment for acute or chronic medical conditions (US Dep. Health & Human Services 2000b), or increased exposure to infection owing to poor personal hygiene (Rushing & Ortega 1979). For example, prematurity and low birthweight are also associated with delayed or absent prenatal care (Crooks 1995, Frank et al. 1992).

Many poor families cannot purchase needed health care services. Poor children often have no medical insurance and, thus, are more likely to use emergency rooms for medical care and may be in more advanced stages of illness before being treated. The generally inadequate educational backgrounds of many poor adults (and the greater prevalence of ethnic minorities and recent immigrants among the poor) may also reduce the likelihood of their seeking help for symptoms of illness because of beliefs about the causes and cures for symptoms that do not square with modern medical practice. In effect, there may be both a lack of money to purchase service and a lack of fit between the care that is available and the care that is wanted (Bradley & Kelleher 1992).

Research does not make clear how significant a role inadequate medical care plays in the health and developmental problems of low-SES children. Social status differences remain even when there is universal health coverage (Baum et al. 1999). In industrialized countries relative material deprivation, rather than absolute material deprivation, may account for much of the SES differential in well-being. Low social status may limit one's social ties (capital) and lead to feelings of helplessness and lack of control, the first reducing one's protection from potential threats to well-being, the second limiting one's own efforts to deal effectively with those threats (Marmot 1999).

HOUSING   Dilapidated, crowded housing has long been cited as one of the factors responsible for the SES gradient in child health (Marmot 1999). Poor children often live in homes that have cracks in the floor, inadequate heat, pests, open heating appliances, unprotected stairwells, lead paint, and leaky ceilings, and are crowded (Bradley et al. 2001a, Guo & Harris 2000, Mayer 1997). These conditions lead to increased illnesses and injuries (US Dep. Health & Human Services 2000b). Brooks-Gunn and coworkers (1995), Guo & Harris (2000), and Bradley & Caldwell (1980) have also linked the physical quality of the home environment to children's intellectual and social well-being. Evans and colleagues (1999) have, likewise, linked household crowding to cognitive and emotional functioning.

COGNITIVELY STIMULATING MATERIALS AND EXPERIENCES   For over 50 years researchers have argued that low-SES children lack access to cognitively stimulating materials and experiences, which not only limits their cognitive growth but reduces their chances of benefiting from school (Bloom 1964, Hunt 1961). Data from the National Longitudinal Survey of Youth and the National Household Education Survey (Bradley et al. 2001a, Corwyn & Bradley 2000) indicate that children from poor families have less access to a wide variety of different recreational and learning materials from infancy through adolescence. They are less likely to go on trips, visit a library or museum, attend a theatrical performance, or be given lessons directed at enhancing their skills. Access to such material and cultural resources mediates the relation between SES (or family income) and children's intellectual and academic achievement from infancy through adolescence (Bradley 1994, Bradley & Corwyn 2001, Brooks-Gunn et al. 1995, Entwisle et al. 1994, Guo & Harris 2000). The impact becomes greater as the number of negative life events (e.g., family dissolution, loss of employment) and risk conditions (e.g., household crowding, presence of a mentally ill parent) increases (Brooks-Gunn et al. 1995, Sameroff et al. 1993).

Bradley & Corwyn (2001) also found that access to stimulating materials and experiences mediated the relation between SES and children's behavior problems. The connection between SES, stimulating experiences, and children's cognitive functioning is well established (Bradley & Corwyn 1999, Brooks-Gunn & Duncan 1997, McLoyd 1998). Such experiences provide both direct and indirect (i.e., mediated through more capable peers and adults) learning opportunities for children as well as serving as a motivational base for continued learning (Saegert & Winkel 1990). However, the connection between SES, access to stimulating experiences, and behavior problems has been less intensively investigated. Part of the connection would appear to be direct. Human beings are self-constructing organisms that thrive on a diversity of experiences; potentially enriching materials and experiences engage cognitive arousal mechanisms (Ford & Lerner 1992). Learning materials and experiences also afford opportunities for social exchanges and, thereby, engage social arousal mechanisms in a generally productive way. Absent such opportunities, children may become bored and frustrated, leading them to engage in behavior that arouses negative responses from parents and peers. These behaviors may contribute to the kind of coercive styles of parenting that have been hypothesized to

382 BRADLEY ■ CORWYN

increase later behavioral maladjustment (Conger et al. 1997, Dodge et al. 1994, McLoyd 1998).

PARENT EXPECTATIONS AND STYLES   Part of the observed connection between SES, cognitively stimulating experiences, and child well-being probably reflects parental attitudes, expectations, and styles of interacting with children. Adams (1998) identified eight major differences in patterns of socialization for children from different social classes: among them, the emphasis given to verbal skills, independence, achievement, and creativity. High-SES parents engage children in more conversations, read to them more, and provide more teaching experiences (Shonkoff & Phillips 2000). Their conversations are richer, contain more contingent responsiveness, and include more efforts to elicit child speech (Hoff-Ginsberg & Tardif 1995, Hart & Risley 1995). Their teaching style includes more scaffolding and complex verbal strategies (Borduin & Henggeler 1981). Bradley & Corwyn (1999), in their review of research on the home observation for measurement of the environment (HOME) inventory, found that these effects applied to children from infancy through adolescence and generally hold for children from diverse ethnic backgrounds. Such differences in parenting practice are strongly implicated in the relation between SES and children's intellectual and academic performance (Hoff-Ginsberg & Tardif 1995, Walberg & Marjoribanks 1976). Even so, the relation between SES and child cognitive and language competence via the stimulation found in the home appears to be a complex one that is associated with both the degree of crowding in the residence and the number of siblings present (Bradley et al. 1994, Evans et al. 1999, Mercy & Steelman 1982, Walberg & Marjoribanks 1976). The distresses and distractions connected with crowding result in fewer and less-rich exchanges between parent and child. Having more siblings results in less allocation of time and attention to each child.

Low-SES parents are less likely to purchase reading and learning materials for their children, less likely to take their children to educational and cultural events, and less likely to regulate the amount of TV their children watch (Bradley et al. 2001a, Hess et al. 1982). As a result, low-SES children more frequently experience school failure (even in the early grades), which moves them on a trajectory of either conduct problems or withdrawal behaviors (Battin-Pearson et al. 2000).

TEACHER ATTITUDES AND EXPECTATIONS   Teacher attitudes and expectations may also be part of a complex set of mediators linking low SES to school failure and behavior problems via learning materials and experiences. McLoyd (1998) has argued that teachers tend to perceive low-SES pupils less positively (both in terms of their academic and self-regulatory skills). Teachers provide poor children with less positive attention and less reinforcement for good performance. If children, both prior to school entry and during their school years, have less experience with cognitively stimulating materials and experiences at home, they are more likely to fulfill teachers' negative stereotypes. This increases the likelihood of negative interactions with teachers, a problem that may be exacerbated for minority children or recently immigrated children without good skills in English. Over time, the frustrations connected with school failure and negative exchanges with teachers are likely to increase acting out behaviors (or depression for some children). It also increases the likelihood that children will affiliate with deviant peers.

Stress Reactions

Researchers have consistently argued that stress accounts for much of the difference in outcomes between low-SES and high-SES children (Adler et al. 1999, Bradley & Whiteside-Mansell 1997, McLoyd 1998, Shonkoff & Phillips 2000). Low-SES families experience more threatening and uncontrollable life events, are disproportionately exposed to environmental hazards and violence, and are at increased risk of experiencing destabilizing events such as family dissolution and household moves (Bradley & Whiteside-Mansell 1997, Gad & Johnson 1980). The chronic strain associated with unstable employment and persistent economic hardship can lead to diminished self-esteem, a diminished sense of control over one's life, anger, and depression (Amato & Zuo 1992, Dohrenwend 1990, Pearlin et al. 1981). It also increases the likelihood of partner and child abuse (Garbarino 1992). Coping with these strains also reduces the likelihood that one can engage in health-promoting activities (National Center for Children in Poverty 1990).

ALLOSTATIC LOAD   There are immediate (and more long-term) physiologic responses to stresses associated with low SES and its cofactors (e.g., crowded housing, household and neighborhood violence). Health scientists have proposed the concepts of allostatis and allostatic load to help explain the impact of stress on adaptive functioning (Johnston-Brooks et al. 1998, McEwen & Seeman 1999). Allostatis refers to the body's capacity to adapt and adjust to the demands imposed by environmental stressors via physiological changes. The constant turning on and turning off of stress-related physiologic responses creates allostatic load, including more long-term changes (e.g., persistent elevation in blood pressure). Research done mostly with primates and human adults indicates that allostatic load is connected to a wide array of both biologic and behavioral differences, including growth, the timing of pubertal changes, cognitive functioning, metabolism, and susceptibility to illness.

There has been limited research specifically targeted to children, so the impact of stress mediators during childhood is less clear. There is some evidence for disregulated hypothalamic-pituitary-adrenal axis activity (leading to increased activity level), disregulated serotonergic function (which may lead to increased hostility and suicide), and impaired immune system functioning (which leads to increased illness via changes in cardiovascular activity) (Johnston-Brooks et al. 1998, McEwen & Seeman 1999). What seems clearer is that allostatic load (with its myriad mediating processes) can have numerous lifelong negative consequences, some of which are seriously damaging; however, much remains to be determined

384   BRADLEY ■ CORWYN

about the precise pathways for particular outcomes during each stage of the life course (Francis et al. 1999).

PARENTING   Allostatic load appears to affect parenting (Francis et al. 1999, McEwen & Seeman 1999). The stresses, uncertainties, and low social standing connected to low SES bring about a sense of powerlessness, low self-esteem, learned helplessness, and reduced orientation toward mastery and efficacy (Baum et al. 1999, McLoyd 1998). Longitudinal research on health indicates that living in a low-SES environment over a prolonged period of time tends to deplete energy reserve capacity and leads to negative emotional states such as anxiety, depression, and hostility, which in turn, lead to poorer relationships with family members and friends (Gallo & Matthews 1999, Wilkinson 1999). The MacArthur SES and Health Psychosocial Working Group have termed this set of behaviors "reactive responding" (Taylor & Seeman 1999). Reactive responding includes chronic vigilance, acting on the basis of environmental demands rather than self-generated goals, having simple, short-term goals, developing a narrow range of skills, maintaining a present orientation, reacting emotionally, and using few options to deal with environmental demands.

McLoyd (1990) found that the distress among poor parents can lead to the over use of negative control strategies, low warmth and responsiveness, and failure to adequately monitor children. Animal studies suggest that early caregiving responses help determine the infant's stress reactivity, which then affects risk for disease and, in the longer term, interest in providing care for one's own offspring (Francis et al. 1999). For older children, such parenting behaviors can result in low self-esteem and poor adaptive functioning. McLoyd has also argued that if a parent reacts by becoming too restrictive, it can lead to bonding with peers rather than parents (see also Elder et al. 1985).

Longitudinal studies provide substantial empirical support for the path linking low SES to lower competence and maladaptive behavior via harsh or neglectful parenting and compromised parent-child relationships (Bradley & Corwyn 2001; Conger et al. 1992, 1997; Elder et al. 1985; Felner et al. 1995; Luster et al. 1995; Lempers et al. 1989; McCoy et al. 1999; McLoyd et al. 1994; Morrison & Eccles 1995). Research shows that it is the absence of positive parenting, not just the presence of negative parenting, that links low SES to child well-being (Bolger et al. 1995, Brody et al. 1999, McCoy et al. 1999). For example, Bolger and colleagues (1995) found that maternal involvement mediated 34% of the variance for externalizing behavior problems, 31% of the variance for self-esteem, and 14% of the variance for popularity. Brody and colleagues (1999) reported that economic hardship reduced the likelihood that mothers would set high developmental goals for their children and engage in competency promoting activities. This resulted in poorer self-regulation and less academic and psychosocial competence on the part of African American children ages 6–9. In an earlier study Brody and colleagues (1994b) found that if parents remained optimistic, despite being poor, it served as a protective factor against negative parenting.

Despite general support for the "stress reactions" path, there have been some exceptions (Felner et al. 1995, McLeod & Shanahan 1993), and there is some evidence that age and ethnicity moderate the relation (Bradley & Corwyn 2001). There has also been less support for the hypothesis that parent's emotional responsiveness mediates the relation between low SES and child well-being (McLeod & Shanahan 1993).

Health-Relevant Behaviors/Lifestyle

A third class of processes often mentioned as mediators between SES and child well-being is health-relevant (or lifestyle) behaviors (Adler & Ostrove 1999, Klerman 1991, Williams & Collins 1995). Members of the lower social classes use tobacco and alcohol more but tend to diet and exercise less (Baum et al. 1999, Dohrenwend 1990, Harrell et al. 1998). To some extent these behavioral differences are derivative of the attitudes that distinguish higher and lower social classes (Rank 2000), but they may also reflect stress reactions and social affiliations (Paltiel 1988). These factors are associated with poorer physical and mental health, which may make it harder for low SES parents to provide warm, responsive, stimulating care or to monitor their children (Garbarino 1992, Natl. Res. Counc. 1993). Such parents also provide a less desirable role model for children, albeit the role-modeling hypothesis has not received strong scientific support for all areas of child functioning (McLoyd 1998).

There has been relatively little study of most lifestyle behaviors as mediators of the SES/child well-being relation, although there is evidence of the intergenerational transmission of substance abuse. Wills and coworkers (1995) found that low parental education increased the likelihood of smoking, which was related to adolescent academic and behavioral competence. This, in turn, increased the likelihood that the adolescent would use drugs and would affiliate with friends who also used drugs.

As children move toward adolescence, their own health-relevant behaviors become conduits for adaptive functioning (Harrell et al. 1998, Natl. Res. Counc. 1993). Sedentary lifestyles, poor eating habits, and early engagement in risky behaviors (smoking, substance use, sexual behavior, criminal activities) frequently lead to more serious health and adjustment difficulties. Although the health-relevant behavior path is appealing as a link between SES and child well-being, research findings are inconsistent. These lifestyle behaviors do not appear to account for most of the SES/well-being gradient (Adler et al. 1999, Harrell et al. 1998, O'Malley & Johnston 1999, Wohlfarth & Van den Brink 1998).

In overview, families with more money, higher levels of education, and higher occupational status are likely to purchase an array of goods and services that directly benefit their children. High-SES families may also use their wealth to live in good houses in safe neighborhoods, thereby affording their children protection from harm. The goods and services also become part of more elaborate paths involving chains of mediators (wherein particular goods and services may more

386   BRADLEY ■ CORWYN

indirectly affect child outcomes) (Brody et al. 1999, Conger et al. 1997, Guo & Harris 2000). However, few such models have been tested on multiple populations and few have been tested on children of different ages.

Perhaps most importantly, many of the proposed models reflect developmentally restricted conceptualizations of life-span processes. Some attention has been given to the timing and duration of poverty in its effects on child well-being, with ample evidence to support the hypothesis that persistent poverty has long-term negative consequences (Bradley & Whiteside-Mansell 1997, Duncan & Brooks-Gunn 1997, McEwen & Seeman 1999). There is less evidence for timing effects. Nonetheless, studies on both animals and humans provide some support for the hypothesis that early deprivation has long-term negative consequences (Duncan & Brooks-Gunn 1997, McEwen & Seeman 1999). There is even some tantalizing evidence that changes in family income, somewhat independent of parental education, have consequences for child development (Garrett et al. 1994).

The principles of parallel, convergent, and reciprocal causation are very important to bear in mind when interpreting results of completed studies or when planning future studies on mediation (Anderson 1999). The principle of parallel causation stipulates that several different processes or factors may be sufficient, but not necessary, to produce a particular developmental outcome. The principle of convergent causation stipulates that a particular process may be necessary but not sufficient to produce a particular outcome; its effect depends on the presence of a second factor. The principle of reciprocal causation stipulates that bidirectional influences among several processes and factors interacting across time are required to produce a particular developmental outcome. Bradley et al. (2001b) examined the relation between three aspects of children's home environments (learning stimulation, maternal responsiveness, and spanking) from infancy through adolescence using hierarchical linear modeling. They found that each contributed, independent of the other, to reading achievement and that learning stimulation and spanking contributed to behavior problems, independent of the others.

One of the main limitations of research on SES is the failure to simultaneously consider correlated mediating processes or factors when studying how one particular process operates to influence a specific developmental outcome. Consider again, for example, the nutrition pathway. The same children who experience inadequate nutrition are also more likely to be exposed to environmental hazards pre- and postnatally and to receive inadequate parenting (Pollitt et al. 1996). Low-SES children are more likely to be exposed to drugs (including alcohol and tobacco) prenatally. These exposures are connected to prematurity, low birthweight, interuterine growth retardation, and perinatal complications, not to mention longer-term health, growth, and cognitive difficulties (Hawley & Disney 1992, Korenman & Miller 1997, McLoyd 1998). If one is interested in a possible link between SES and cognitive functioning via poor nutrition, it may be critical to include a consideration of one or more of these other processes. Otherwise, one may attribute cognitive problems to poor nutrition when they actually result from poor parenting or a combination of poor nutrition and prenatal exposure to drugs. The practice of nutrition researchers in controlling for cognitively stimulating materials and experiences when studying the impact of inadequate nutrition on cognitive development is a step in the right direction (Pollitt et al. 1996). A few researchers have used techniques such as structural equation modeling to examine the joint function of multiple mediation processes connecting SES to child functioning (Brody et al. 1999, Dodge et al. 1994). However, model misspecification remains a major impediment to understanding the precise mechanisms that link SES and most child outcomes.

Models of Moderation

Although most research on SES and child outcomes has focused on mediating processes, it is generally acknowledged that these processes are not the same for all children (McLoyd 1998, Wills et al. 1995). For any given mediator model, certain characteristics of children and certain environmental conditions serve as moderators (Wachs 2000). Whereas mediator models are concerned with a process through which SES operates to influence children's development, moderator models are concerned with the conditions in which the process operates. The two models complement one another, with each adding insights into the nature of relations between SES and child outcomes (Baron & Kenny 1986). If researchers obtain weak or inconsistent results when investigating a particular association, it often implicates a moderator effect.

The discovery of a moderator often provides clues regarding a mediating process that underlies the relation between a predictor and outcome variable (Rutter 1990). The connection between mediators and moderators is often tighter (i.e., more fundamental) than may be initially apparent. Although Baron & Kenny (1986) went to great lengths to point out the distinctions between mediators and moderators, they also discussed how each often implicates the other.

The potential value of searching for moderators in regard to SES and child well-being would seem particularly great in light of the two principle classes of mechanisms thought to connect them: access to resources and stress reactions. Taylor & Seeman (1999) compiled a list of possible moderators of the relation between physical and/or psychological health. Belief in personal control, dispositional optimism, social support, self-esteem, coping strategies, and reactive responding were frequently (although not inevitably) observed to be moderators of the SES and health relationship, with social support exhibiting a particularly strong relation to psychological health. Their review emphasized the fact that these same variables may also partially mediate the relation between SES and health. In each case, the characteristic of the individual either increased or decreased resources or increased or decreased harmful stressors. The frequent finding that SES/child development relations differ by race offers another example of a moderator that likely implicates either access to resources or stress exposure as connecting paths. The discrimination and oppression often faced by members of minority groups both reduces the likelihood of accessing resources and increases the likelihood of experiencing stress (Garcia Coll et al. 1996, McLoyd 1990).

388   BRADLEY ■ CORWYN

Resiliency researchers have identified several factors that may serve as moderators of the relation between SES and child well-being, with emphasis on those that help children cope with the kinds of adversity connected with low SES (Garmezy 1993, Masten & Coatsworth 1998, Rutter 1990). Garmezy (1993) recognizes three broad categories that may function as moderators: (*a*) personality/dispositional features such as self-esteem, locus of control, self-efficacy, optimism, stress reactivity, humor, active coping strategies, communication skills, cognitive competence, affective responses to others, and predictability; (*b*) family characteristics, such as cohesion, shared values, patience, conflict, consistency of rules, orderliness, and the presence of supportive adults; and (*c*) availability of external support systems. Each of these either changes the likelihood of accessing needed goods and services, changes the likelihood of encountering stress, or changes one's reactions to stress-inducing events and conditions. An example from the attachment literature is the finding that infants with difficult temperaments who are in low-resource environments tend to form insecure attachments (Vaughn & Bost 1999). Compas and colleagues (2001) call for research that investigates how social context (e.g., SES) may moderate the relation between individual differences (e.g., temperament) and coping responses to stress.

In contrast to the paucity of research on moderators of the SES child outcome relation, SES is frequently conceptualized as a moderator of relationships effecting children. Examples include the relation between maternal depression and parenting practices (Lovejoy et al. 2000) and the relation between risk factors and adolescent substance abuse (Wills et al. 1995).

COLLECTIVE SES

It is generally acknowledged that SES operates at multiple levels to affect well-being (Adler et al. 1999, Krieger et al. 1997, Leventhal & Brooks-Gunn 2000). Community-level SES measurement can provide information about exposures to violence and hazards as well as access to recreational and institutional resources. For children, it is important to consider community-level SES because there is evidence that neighborhood of residence is associated with health, achievement, and behavioral outcomes even when individual-level income and education are controlled (Baum et al. 1999, Leventhal & Brooks-Gunn 2000, Wasserman et al. 1998). The effects appear to begin prior to birth, with research indicating that living in a lower SES neighborhood increases the likelihood of neural tube defects (Vrijheid et al. 2000, Wasserman et al. 1998). Neighborhood effects on health appear to continue through childhood. Sargent and coworkers (1995) found that living in a densely populated, high poverty community was associated with a ninefold increase in lead burden. Also, adolescent females with a family history of cardiovascular disease showed higher levels of blood pressure and left ventricular mass if they lived in low-SES neighborhoods (Treiber et al. 1999).

Research relating neighborhood SES to health is quite limited and not fully consistent. According to Leventhal & Brooks-Gunn (2000), the most consistent finding is that living in a high-SES neighborhood has positive benefits for school readiness and school achievement, perhaps more so for European Americans than members of minority groups. There is also evidence that living in a low-SES neighborhood may contribute to development of behavior problems and increase the likelihood of nonmarital childbearing (Crane 1991, Loeber & Wikstrom 1993). Osofsky (1999) argued that children growing up in poor urban environments are frequently exposed to guns, knives, drugs, and acts of random violence. As a result, many children manifest posttraumatic stress disorder symptoms. Exposure to such violence also interrupts a child's ability to think clearly and solve problems (Garbarino 1999).

According to the general ecological hypothesis, as the number of stresses in a neigborhood increases and as the number of supports decreases, distress among those living in the neighborhood rises (Zuvarin 1989). Social disorganization theory posits that neighborhoods characterized by a high percentage of low-SES residents, and cofactors of low SES such as single parenthood and ethnic heterogeneity, decrease the likelihood of social order (Sampson 1992). Wilson (1991) stated that neighborhoods with high rates of joblessness and single-parent families tend to produce a feeling of "social isolation" for adults caring for children. This, over time, undermines family management and results in socialization practices and family lifestyles that are not conducive to adaptive functioning (e.g., active problem solving, household organization, warm and stimulating parenting, a focus on schooling, adequate monitoring). It also results in a loss of self- and group identification that sustains customary behavior and prevents deviant behavior (Harrell & Peterson 1992).

Jencks & Mayer (1990) identified four kinds of theories relating neighborhood poverty to maladaptive social behavior: (*a*) contagion theories—the idea that peers influence the spread of problem behaviors; (*b*) collective socialization theories—the idea that role models and monitoring are critical to healthy and adaptive functioning; (*c*) competition theories—the concept that people compete for scarce resources; and (*d*) relative deprivation theories—the theory that individuals evaluate their standing relative to the standing of their neighbors. Duncan & Brooks-Gunn (1997) examined aspects of these theories with both very young children and adolescents. The presence of affluent neighbors had a positive effect on IQ, teenage births, and school dropout, suggesting the influence of adult role models and monitoring as mediating variables. Evidence in favor of the "contagion" effect occurred only for adolescents.

Leventhal & Brooks-Gunn (2000) used a somewhat more concise approach in their review of potential mechanisms linking neighborhood poverty to child well-being. They recognized three classes of mediators: (*a*) institutional resources (e.g., schools, child care facilities, medical facilities, employment opportunities), (*b*) relationships (the characteristics of parents and support networks available to assist parents), and (*c*) norms/collective efficacy. Social and health scientists contend that social capital in the form of social affiliation and social cohesion within neighborhoods and communities may help reduce the risk of morbidity and maladaptive functioning (Kawachi 1999). They argue that informal social control, maintenance of healthy norms, and access to various forms of social support can

390   BRADLEY ■ CORWYN

contribute to both healthier lifestyles and positive well-being. Collective efficacy involves the extent to which there are social connections in the neighborhood and to which residents monitor and supervise the behavior of others in accordance with social standards (Sampson et al. 1997). There is also some support for the collective efficacy hypothesis in the form of the social control of children and affiliation with deviant peers functioning to mediate the relation between neighborhood SES and adolescent behavior, mental health, and achievement (Darling & Steinberg 1997, Elliott et al. 1996, Sampson et al. 1997).

Support for institutional resources as mediators of relations between neighborhood SES and child well-being is quite limited. Few studies have examined the mediating role played by the child care options available, medical resources found in the community, or recreational facilities present. Ennett and coworkers (1997) found that characteristics of schools partially mediated the relation between neighborhood characteristics and rates of cigarette and alcohol use. Entwisle and colleagues (1994) found that mathematics reasoning skills of school-age boys were related to the type of neighborhood the boys lived in. They speculated that this difference may derive from differential opportunities to participate in complex rule-based games with peers.

A companion set of hypotheses relates to how the physical and social quality of neighborhoods affects parenting, Leventhal & Brooks-Gunn's (2000) third class of potential mediators. Parental decisions regarding how far children are allowed to travel from home without supervision depends on the parent's appraisal of potential harm present in the neighborhood (Jacobs & Bennet 1993). Earls and coworkers (1994) reported that parents who live in dangerous neighborhoods admit using more harsh control and verbal aggression with their children. Young & Gately (1988) found that the rates of maltreatment by females was lower when substantial numbers of women with access to material resources were available for support. Garbarino (1999) also demonstrated a relationship between social cohesion and abuse rates. However, few studies have examined the extent to which differences in parenting practices actually mediate the relation between neighborhood SES and child well-being. Klebanov and colleagues (1998) found that the quality of learning experiences in the home mediated the relation between neighborhood and IQ for 3-year-olds. Greenberg and colleagues (1999) also found that the home environment mediated the relation between neighborhood risk and teacher-reported social competence and achievement. Even so, research suggests that most of the variance in parenting is not accounted for by neighborhood of residence (Caspi et al. 2000, Furstenberg et al. 1999).

It is methodologically difficult to establish causal relationships between complex social settings such as neighborhoods and individual behavioral outcomes because results are often consistent with more than one explanation (Duncan & Raudenbush 1999, Natl. Res. Counc. 1993). There are a number of potentially confounding factors that make interpretations about neighborhood effects difficult. Most notably, any differences observed in the incidence of negative behaviors or outcome may be due to the characteristics of those people who selected to live there (a "selection effect" or "omitted variables bias"). Also, major social stressors may have a direct effect on a large proportion of neighborhood residents (an "aggregation effect"). Even so, for certain classes of child outcomes (e.g., congenital anomalies), living in particular low-SES neighborhoods (i.e., near a toxic waste dump) carries a significantly elevated risk of poor development (Vrijheid et al. 2000).

FUTURE DIRECTIONS

The literature reviewed above presents a complex portrait of the relation between SES and child development. Rearchers have specified, and at least partially examined, numerous mechanisms linking SES and child well-being. Not yet fully known is how the various components of SES interact synergistically with each other or with other aspects of family, neighborhood, peer, and institutional contexts to affect the course of development (McLoyd 1998). It is also difficult to attribute causality to SES because children's environments interact with their genetic makeup to impact well-being in many different ways (Huston et al. 1997, Wachs 2000). Children with different genetic attributes will respond differentially to the same environmental circumstances. In the diathesis-stress model of psychopathology, individuals who are genetically predisposed to a particular stress-related problem will be more sensitive to stress-inducing experiences (Paris 1999). On the other side of the equation, environments help determine how genes express themselves (Plomin & Crabbe 2000). Genes could have greater or lesser effects depending on environment. Research in the next decade should help explicate how SES operates through multiple mechanisms simultaneously to affect developmental course, how those paths vary across ethnic and cultural groups, and how different components of SES function conjointly to effect different developmental systems.

Visit the Annual Reviews home page at www.AnnualReviews.org

LITERATURE CITED

Achenbach T, Bird H, Canino G, Phares V, Gould M, Rubio-Stipec M. 1990. Epidemiological comparisons of Puerto Rican and U.S. mainland children: parent, teacher and self reports. *J. Am. Acad. Child Adolesc. Psychiatry* 29:84–93

Adams BN. 1998. *The Family: a Sociological Interpretation.* New York: Harcourt Brace

Adler NE, Boyce T, Chesney MA, Cohen S, Folkman S, et al. 1994. Socioeconomic status and health: the challenge of the gradient. *Am. Psychol.* 49:15–24

Adler NE, Marmot M, McEwen BS, Stewart J, eds. 1999. *Socioeconomic Status and Health in Industrialized Nations.* New York: NY Acad. Sci.

Adler NE, Ostrove JM. 1999. Socioeconomic status and health: what we know and what we don't. See Adler et al. 1999, pp. 3–15

Alexander KL, Entwisle DR, Dauber SL. 1993. First-grade behavior: its short- and long-term consequences for school performance. *Child Dev.* 64:801–14

Amato PR, Zuo J. 1992. Rural poverty, urban

392   BRADLEY ■ CORWYN

poverty, and psychological well-being. *Sociol. Q.* 33:229–40

Anastasi A. 1956. Intelligence and family size. *Psychol. Bull.* 53:187–209

Anderson NB. 1999. Solving the puzzle of socioeconomic status and health: the need for integrated, multilevel, interdisciplinary research. See Adler et al. 1999, pp. 302–3

Baron R, Kenny D. 1986. The moderator-mediator variable distinction in social psychological research. *J. Pers. Soc. Psychol.* 11: 1173–82

Battin-Pearson S, Newcomb MD, Abbott RD, Hill KG, Catalano RF, Hawkins JD. 2000. Predictors of early high school drop-out: a test of five theories. *J. Educ. Psychol.* 92: 568–82

Baum A, Garofalo JP, Yali AM. 1999. SES and chronic stress: does stress account for SES effects on health? See Adler et al. 1999, pp. 131–44

Blendon R, Aiken L, Freeman H, Corey C. 1989. Access to medical care for black and white Americans. *JAMA* 261:278–81

Bloom B. 1964. *Stability and Change in Human Characteristics*. New York: Wiley

Bolger KE, Patterson CJ, Thompson WW, Kupersmidt JB. 1995. Psychosocial adjustment among children experiencing persistent and intermittent family economic hardship. *Child Dev.* 66:1107–29

Borduin CM, Henggeler N. 1981. Social class, experimental setting and task characteristics as determinants of mother-child interactions. *Dev. Psychol.* 17:209–14

Bradley RH. 1994. The HOME Inventory: review and reflections. In *Advances in Child Development and Behavior*, ed. H Reese, pp. 241–88. San Diego, CA: Academic

Bradley RH, Caldwell BM. 1980. The relation of the home environment, cognitive competence, and IQ among males and females. *Child Dev.* 51:1140–48

Bradley RH, Corwyn RF. 1999. Parenting. In *Child Psychology: A Handbook of Contemporary Issues*, ed. C Tamis-LeMonda, L Balter, pp. 339–62. New York: Psychology Press

Bradley RH, Corwyn RF. 2001. *Age and ethnic variations in family process mediators of SES*. Presented at Conf. Socioeconomic Status, Parenting, Child Dev., Minneapolis, MN

Bradley RH, Corwyn RF, Burchinal M, McAdoo HP, Garcia Coll C. 2001a. The home environments of children in the United States. Part 2: relations with behavioral development through age 13. *Child Dev.* In press

Bradley RH, Corwyn RF, Caldwell BM, Whiteside-Mansell L, Wasserman GA, et al. 2000. Measuring the home environments of children in early adolescence. *J. Res. Adolesc.* 10:247–89

Bradley RH, Corwyn RF, McAdoo HP, Garcia Coll C. 2001b. The home environments of children in the United States. Part 1: variations by age, ethnicity, and poverty status. *Child Dev.* In press

Bradley RH, Corwyn RF, Whiteside-Mansell L. 1996. Life at home: same time, different places. *Early Dev. Parent.* 5:251–69

Bradley RH, Kelleher KJ. 1992. *Childhood morbidity and mortality: the growing impact of social factors*. Presented at Conf. Social Sci. Health Policy: Building Bridges Between Research and Action, Washington, DC

Bradley RH, Whiteside-Mansell L. 1997. Children in poverty. In *Handbook of Prevention and Treatment With Children and Adolescents*, ed. RT Ammerman, M Hersen, pp. 13–58. New York: Wiley

Bradley RH, Whiteside-Mansell L, Mundfrom DJ, Casey PH, Kelleher KJ, Pope SK. 1994. Early indications of resilience and their relation to experiences in the home environments of low birthweight, premature children living in poverty. *Child Dev.* 65:346–60

Brody DJ, Pirkle JL, Kramer RA, Flegal KM, Matte TD, et al. 1994a. Blood lead levels in the U.S. population. *JAMA* 272:277–81

Brody GH, Flor DL, Gibson NM. 1999. Linking maternal efficacy beliefs, developmental goals, parenting practices, and child competence in rural single-parent African American families. *Child Dev.* 70:1197–208

Brody GH, Stoneman Z, Flor D, McCrary C,

Hastings L, Conyers O. 1994b. Financial resources, parent psychological functioning, parent co-caregiving, and early adolescent competence in rural two-parent African-American families. *Child Dev.* 65:590–605

Bronfenbrenner U. 1995. Developmental ecology through space and time: a future perspective. See Moen et al. 1995, pp. 619–48

Brooks-Gunn J, Duncan GJ. 1997. The effects of poverty on children. *Future Child.* 7(2):55–71

Brooks-Gunn J, Klebanov PK, Liaw F. 1995. The learning, physical, and emotional environment of the home in the context of poverty: The Infant Health and Development Program. *Child. Youth Serv. Rev.* 17:251–76

Call KT, Nonnemaker J. 1999. Socioeconomic disparities in adolescent health: contributing factors. See Adler et al. 1999, pp. 352–55

Caspi A, Taylor A, Moffitt TE, Plomin R. 2000. Neighborhood deprivation affects children's mental health: environmental risks, identified in genetic design. *Psychol. Sci.* 11:338–42

Cassady C, Farel A, Guild P, Kennelly J, People-Sheps M, et al. 1997. *Maternal and Child Health Model Indicators.* Washington, DC: Maternal Child Health Bur., US Dep. Health Human Serv.

Cohen S. 1999. Social status and susceptibility to respiratory infections. See Adler et al. 1999, pp. 246–53

Coleman JS. 1988. Social capital in the creation of human capital. *Am. J. Sociol.* 94 (Suppl.):S95–120

Compas BE, Connor-Smith JK, Saltzman H, Thomsen AH, Wadsworth ME. 2001. Coping with stress during childhood and adolescence: problems, progress, and potential in theory and research. *Psychol. Bull.* 127:87–127

Conger RD, Conger KJ, Elder GH. 1997. Family economic hardship and adolescent adjustment: mediating and moderating processes. See Duncan & Brooks-Gunn 1997, pp. 288–310

Conger RD, Conger KJ, Elder GH, Lorenz F,

Simons R, Whitbeck L. 1992. A family process model of economic hardship and adjustment in early adolescent boys. *Child Dev.* 63:526–41

Corwyn RF, Bradley RH. 2000. *Developmental accomplishments and family-child activities of preschoolers in the United States: comparisons across three major ethnic groups and poverty status.* Presented at Meet. Southwest. Soc. Res. Hum. Dev., Eureka Springs, AR, April 13–15

Crane J. 1991. The epidemic theory of ghettos and neighborhood effects on dropping out and teenage childbearing. *Am. J. Sociol.* 96:1126–59

Crooks D. 1995. American children at risk: poverty and its consequences for children's health, growth, and school achievement. *Yearb. Phys. Anthropol.* 38:57–86

Darling N, Steinberg L. 1997. Assessing neighborhood effects using individual-level data. In *Neighborhood Poverty: Policy Implications in Studying Neighborhoods*, ed. J Brooks-Gunn, GJ Duncan, JL Aber, 2:120–31. New York: Russell Sage Found.

Davies AF. 1952. Prestige of occupations. *Br. J. Sociol.* 3:134–47

DeGarmo DS, Forgatch MS, Martinez CR. 1999. Parenting of divorced mothers as a link between social status and boys' academic outcomes: unpacking the effects of socioeconomic status. *Child Dev.* 70:1231–45

DiPietro JA, Costigan KA, Hilton SC, Pressman EK. 1999. Effects of socioeconomic status and psychosocial stress on the development of the fetus. See Adler et al. 1999, pp. 356–58

Dodge KA, Petit FS, Bates JE. 1994. Socialization mediators of the relation between socioeconomic status and child conduct problems. *Child Dev.* 65:649–65

Dohrenwend B. 1990. Socioeconomic status (SES) and psychiatric disorders. *Soc. Psychiatry Psychiatr. Epidemiol.* 25:41–47

Duncan GJ, Brooks-Gunn J. 1997. *Consequences of Growing Up Poor.* New York: Russell Sage Found.

Duncan GJ, Brooks-Gunn J, Klebanov P. 1994.

394   BRADLEY ■ CORWYN

Economic deprivation and early childhood development. *Child Dev.* 65:296–318

Duncan GJ, Raudenbush SW. 1999. Assessing the effects of context in studies of children and youth development. *Educ. Psychol.* 34:29–41

Earls F. 1980. Prevalence of behavior problems in 3-year-old children: a cross-national replication. *Arch. Gen. Psychiatry* 37:1153–57

Earls F, McGuire J, Shay S. 1994. Evaluating a community intervention to reduce the risk of child abuse: methodological strategies in conducting neighborhood surveys. *Child Abuse Negl.* 18:473–85

Elder G, Caspi A, Van Nguyen T. 1985. Resourceful and vulnerable children: family influences in hard times. In *Development as Action in Context*, ed. R Silbereisen, H Eyferth, pp. 167–86. Berlin: Springer-Verlag

Elliott D, Wilson WJ, Huizinga D, Sampson R, Elliott A, Rankin B. 1996. The effects of neighborhood disadvantage on adolescent development. *J. Res. Crime Delinq.* 33:389–426

Ennett ST, Flewelling RL, Lindrooth RC, Norton EC. 1997. School and neighborhood characteristics associated with school rates of alcohol, cigarette, and marijuana use. *J. Health Soc. Behav.* 38:55–71

Entwisle DR, Alexander KL, Olson LS. 1994. The gender gap in math: its possible origins in neighborhood effects. *Am. Sociol. Rev.* 59:822–38

Entwisle DR, Astone NM. 1994. Some practical guidelines for measuring youth's race/ethnicity and socioeconomic status. *Child Dev.* 65:1521–40

Escalona S. 1982. Babies at double hazard: early development of infants at biologic and social risk. *Pediatrics* 70:670–75

Evans GW, Maxwell LE, Hart B. 1999. Parental language and verbal responsiveness to children in crowded homes. *Dev. Psychol.* 35:1020–23

Felner RD, Brand S, DuBois DL, Adan AM, Mulhall PF, Evans EG. 1995. Socioeconomic disadvantage, proximal environmental experiences, and socioemotional and academic adjustment in early adolescence: investigation of a mediated effects model. *Child Dev.* 65:296–318

Ford DH, Lerner RM. 1992. *Developmental Systems Theory: An Integrated Approach.* Newbury Park, CA: Sage

Francis D, Champagne FA, Liu D, Meaney MJ. 1999. Maternal care, gene expression, and the development of individual differences in stress reactivity. See Adler et al. 1999, pp. 66–84

Frank R, Strobino D, Salkever D, Jackson C. 1992. Updated estimates of the impact of prenatal care on birthweight outcomes by race. *J. Hum. Resourc.* 27:629–42

Furstenberg FF, Cook TE, Eccles J, Elder G, Sameroff A. 1999. *Managing To Make It: Urban Families and Adolescent Success.* Chicago: Univ. Chicago Press

Gad M, Johnson J. 1980. Correlates of adolescent life stresses related to race, SES, and levels of perceived support. *J. Clin. Child. Psychol.* 9:13–16

Gallo LC, Matthews KA. 1999. Do negative emotions mediate the association between socioeconomic status and health? See Adler et al. 1999, pp. 226–45

Garbarino J. 1992. The meaning of poverty in the world of children. *Am. Behav. Sci.* 35:220–37

Garbarino J. 1999. The effects of community violence on children. In *Child Psychology, A Handbook of Contemporary Issues*, ed. L Balter, C Tamis–LaMonda, pp. 412–25. New York: Psychology Press

Garcia Coll C, Lamberty G, Jenkins R, McAdoo HP, Crnic K, et al. 1996. An integrative model for the study of developmental competencies in minority children. *Child Dev.* 67:1891–914

Garmezy N. 1993. Children in poverty: resilience despite risk. *Psychiatry* 56:127–36

Garrett P, Ng'andu N, Ferron J. 1994. Poverty experiences of young children and the quality of their home environments. *Child Dev.* 65:331–45

Goodman E. 1999. The role of socioeconomic status gradients in explaining differences in

US adolescents' health. *Am. J. Public Health* 89:1522 28

Gottfried AW. 1985. Measures of socioeconomic status in child development research: data and recommendations. *Merrill-Palmer Q.* 31:85–92

Greenberg MT, Lengua LJ, Coie JD, Pinderhughes EE. 1999. Predicting developmental outcomes at school entry using a multiple-risk model: four American communities. *Dev. Psychol.* 35:403–17

Grusky DB, Van Rompaey SE. 1992. The vertical scaling of occupations: some cautionary comments and reflections. *Am. J. Sociol.* 97:1712–28

Guo G, Harris KM. 2000. The mechanisms mediating the effects of poverty on children's intellectual development. *Demography* 37:431–47

Haan MN, Kaplan GA, Syme SL. 1989. Socioeconomic status and health: old observations and new thoughts. In *Pathways to Health: The Role of Social Factors*, ed. JP Bunker, DS Gomby, BH Kehrer, pp. 176–233. Palo Alto, CA: Henry J. Kaiser Found.

Harrell AV, Peterson GE. 1992. *Drugs, Crime, and Social Isolation: Barriers to Urban Opportunities*. Washington, DC: Urban Inst. Press

Harrell JS, Bangdiwala SI, Deng S, Webb JP, Bradley C. 1998. Smoking initiation in youth: the roles of gender, race, socioeconomics, and developmental status. *J. Adolesc. Health* 23:271–79

Hart B, Risley TR. 1995. *Meaningful Differences in the Everyday Experience of Young American Children*. Baltimore, MD: Brookes

Hauser RM. 1994. Measuring socioeconomic status in studies of child development. *Child Dev.* 65:1541–45

Haverman R, Wolfe R. 1995. The determinants of children's attainments: a review of methods and findings. *J. Econ. Lit.* 33:1829–78

Hawley T, Disney E. 1992. Crack's children: the consequences of maternal cocaine abuse. *Soc. Policy Rep. Soc. Res. Child Dev.* 6(4):1–22

Hertzman C. 1999. The biological embedding of early experience and its effects on health in adulthood. See Adler et al. 1999, pp. 85–95

Hess RD, Holloway S, Price G, Dickson WP. 1982. Family environments and the acquisition of reading skills. In *Families As Learning Environments of Children*, ed. LM Laosa, IE Sigel, pp. 87–113. New York: Plenum

Hoff-Ginsberg E. 1991. Mother-child conversation in different social classes and communicative settings. *Child Dev.* 62:782–96

Hoff-Ginsberg E, Tardif T. 1995. Socioeconomic status and parenting. In *Handbook of Parenting*, ed. MH Bornstein, 4:161–87. Mahweh, NJ: Erlbaum

Hunt JM. 1961. *Intelligence and Experience*. New York: Ronald

Huston AC, McLoyd VC, Garcia Coll C. 1997. Poverty and behavior: the case for multiple methods and levels of analysis. *Dev. Rev.* 17:376–93

Jacobs J, Bennett M. 1993. Decision-making in one parent and two parent families: influence and information selection. *J. Early Adolesc.* 13:245–66

Jencks C, Mayer S. 1990. The social consequences of growing up in a poor neighborhood. In *Inner City Poverty in the United States*, ed. L Lynn, M McGeary, pp. 111–86. Washington, DC: Natl. Acad. Press

Johnston-Brooks CH, Lewis MA, Evans GW, Whalen CK. 1998. Chronic stress and illness in children: the role of allostatic load. *Psychosom. Med.* 60:597–603

Kawachi I. 1999. Social capital and community effects on population and individual health. See Adler et al. 1999, pp. 120–30

Kennedy W, Van de Riet V, White JA. 1963. A normative sample of intelligence and achievement of Negro elementary school children in southeastern United States. *Monogr. Soc. Res. Child Dev.* 28(6) whole issue

Klebanov PK, Brooks-Gunn J, McCarton CM, Mccormick MC. 1998. The contribution of neighborhood and family income upon developmental test scores over the first three years of life. *Child Dev.* 69:1420–36

396 BRADLEY ▪ CORWYN

Klerman LV. 1991. *Alive and Well?* New York: Natl. Cent. Children Poverty, Columbia Univ.

Kohn ML, Schooler C. 1982. Job conditions and personality: a longitudinal assessment of their reciprocal effects. *Am. J. Soc.* 87:1257–83

Korenman S, Miller JE. 1997. Effects of long-term poverty on the physical health of children in the National Longitudinal Survey of Youth. See Duncan & Brooks-Gunn 1997, pp. 70–99

Kotch J, Shackelford J. 1989. *The nutritional status of low-income preschool children in the United States: a review of the literature.* ERIC Doc. ED 308 965 PS 018 152

Kramer MS. 1987. Determinants of low birthweight: methodological assessment and meta-analysis. *Bull. WHO* 65:663–737

Krieger N, Williams DR, Moss HW. 1997. Measuring social class in US public health research: concepts, methodologies, and guidelines. *Annu. Rev. Public Health* 18:341–78

Lahey BB, Loeber R, Hart EL, Frick PJ, Applegate B, et al. 1995. Four-year longitudinal study of conduct disorders in boys: patterns and predictors of persistence. *J. Abnorm. Psychol.* 104:83–93

Lempers JD, Clark-Lempers D, Simons RL. 1989. Economic hardship, parenting, and distress in adolescence. *Child Dev.* 60:25–39

Leventhal T, Brooks-Gunn J. 2000. The neighborhoods they live in: the effect of neighborhood residence on child and adolescent outcomes. *Psychol. Bull.* 126:309–37

Liberatos P, Link BG, Kelsey JL. 1988. The measurement of social class in epidemiology. *Epidemiol. Rev.* 10:87–121

Loeber R, Wikstrom PH. 1993. Individual pathways to crime in different types of neighborhoods. In *Integrating Individual and Ecological Aspects of Crime*, ed. DP Farrington, RJ Sampson, P Wikstrom, pp. 169–204. Stockholm: Natl. Counc. Crime Prev.

Lovejoy MC, Graczyk PA, O'Hare E, Neuman G. 2000. Maternal depression and parenting behavior: a meta-analytic review. *Clin. Psychol. Rev.* 20:561–92

Luster T, Reischl T, Gassaway J, Gomaa H. 1995. *Factors related to early school success among African-American children from low income families.* Presented at Bienn. Meet. Soc. Res. Child Dev, Indianapolis, IN

Macintyre S, West P. 1991. Lack of class variation in health in adolescence: an artifact of an occupational measure of class. *Soc. Sci. Med.* 30:665–73

Marmot M. 1999. Epidemiology of socioeconomic status and health: Are determinants within countries the same as between countries? See Adler et al. 1999, pp. 16–19

Masten AS, Coatsworth JD. 1998. The development of competence in favorable and unfavorable environments. *Am. Psychol.* 53:205–20

Mayer S. 1997. *What Money Can't Buy.* Cambridge, MA: Harvard Univ. Press

McCall RB. 1981. Nature-nurture and the two realms of development: a proposed integration with respect to mental development. *Child Dev.* 52:1–12

McCoy MB, Firck PJ, Loney BR, Ellis ML. 1999. The potential mediating role of parenting practices in the development of conduct problems in a clinic-referred sample. *J. Child. Fam. Stud.* 8:477–94

McEwen BS, Seeman T. 1999. Protective and damaging effects of mediators of stress. See Adler et al. 1999, pp. 30–47

McGauhey P, Starfield B, Alexander C, Ensminger M. 1991. Social environment and vulnerability of low birth weight children: a social-epidemiological perspective. *Pediatrics* 88:943–53

McLeod J, Shanahan M. 1993. Poverty, parenting, and children's mental health. *Am. Sociol. Rev.* 58:351–66

McLoyd VC. 1997. The impact of poverty and low socioeconomic status on the socioemotional functioning of African-American children and adolescents: mediating effects. In *Social and Emotional Adjustment and Family Relations in Ethnic Minority Families*, ed. RD Taylor, M Wang, pp. 7–34. Mahwah, NJ: Erlbaum. 239 pp.

McLoyd VC. 1998. Socioeconomic disadvantage and child development *Am. Psychol.* 53:185–204

McLoyd VC. 1990. The impact of economic hardship on black families and children: psychological distress, parenting, and socioemotional development. *Child Dev.* 61:311–46

McLoyd VC, Jayaratne TE, Ceballo R, Borquez J. 1994. Unemployment and work interruption among African American single mothers: effects on parenting and adolescent socioemotional functioning. *Child Dev.* 65:562–89

Mercy JA, Steelman LC. 1982. Familial influence on the intellectual attainment of children. *Am. Sociol. Rev.* 47:532–42

Miller DC. 1991. *Handbook of Research Design and Social Measurement.* Newbury Park, CA: Sage. 5th ed.

Miller JE, Korenman S. 1994. Poverty and children's nutritional status in the United States. *Am. J. Epidemiol.* 140:233–42

Moen P, Elder GH, Luscher K, eds. 1995. *Examining Lives in Context.* Washington, DC: Am. Psychol. Assoc.

Moore KA, Morrison DR, Zaslow M, Glei DA. 1994. *Ebbing and flowing, learning and growing: family economic resources and children's development.* Presented at Res. Brief., Board Child. Fam. Washington, DC: Child Trends, Inc.

Morrison LA, Eccles J. 1995. *Poverty, parenting, and adolescents' achievement.* Presented at Bienn. Meet. Soc. Res. Child Dev. Indianapolis, IN

Mortorell R. 1980. Interrelationships between diet, infectious disease, and nutritional status. In *Social and Biological Predictors of Nutritional Status, Physical Growth and Neurological Development,* ed. HS Greene, FE Johnson, pp. 188–213. New York: Academic

Mpofu E, Van de Vijver FJR. 2000. Taxonomic structure in early to middle childhood: a longitudinal study of Simbabwean schoolchildren. *Int. J. Behav. Dev.* 24:204–312

Nam CB, Powers MG. 1983. *The Socioeconomic Approach to Status Measurement.* Houston, TX: Cap & Gown

Natl. Cent. Child. Poverty. 1990. *Five Million Children: A Statistical Profile of Our Poorest Young Children.* New York: Columbia Univ. Sch. Public Health

Natl. Res. Counc. 1993. *Losing Generations.* Washington, DC: Natl. Acad. Press

Needleman HL, Schell A, Bellinger D, Leviton A, Allred E. 1990. The long-term effects of low doses of lead in childhood: an 11-year follow-up report. *N. Engl. J. Med.* 322:83–88

Oliver ML, Shapiro TM. 1995. *Black Wealth, White Wealth.* New York: Routledge

O'Malley PM, Johnston LD. 1999. Drinking and driving among US high school seniors, 1984–1997. *Am. J. Public Health* 89:678–84

Ortega ST, Corzine J. 1990. Socioeconomic status and mental disorders. *Res. Commun. Ment. Health* 6:149–82

Oski F. 1993. Iron deficiency in infancy and childhood. *N. Engl. J. Med.* 329(3):190–93

Osofsky JD. 1999. The impact of violence on children. *Future Child.* 9(3):33–49

Ostrove JM, Feldman P, Adler NE. 1999. Relations among socioeconomic indicators and health for African-Americans and whites. *J. Health Psychol.* 4:451–63

Overpeck MD, Brenner RA, Trumble AC, Trifiletti LB, Berendes HW. 1998. Risk factors for infant homicide in the United States. *N. Engl. J. Med.* 339:1211–16

Paltiel FL. 1988. Is being poor a mental health hazard? *Women's Health* 12:189–211

Parcel TL, Menaghan EG. 1990. Maternal working conditions and children's verbal facility: studying the intergenerational transmission of inequality from mothers to young children. *Soc. Psychol. Q.* 53:132–47

Paris J. 1999. *Genetics and Psychopathology: Predisposition-Stress Interactions.* Washington, DC: Am. Psychiatr. Press

Parker S, Greer S, Zuckerman B. 1988. Double jeopardy: the impact of poverty on early child development. *Pediatr. Clin. N. Am.* 35:1127–241

Patterson G, DeBarsyshe B, Ramsey E. 1989.

398   BRADLEY ■ CORWYN

A developmental perspective on antisocial behavior. *Am. Psychol.* 44:329–35

Pearlin Ll, Menaghan EG, Lieberman MA, Mullan JT. 1981. The stress process. *J. Health Soc. Behav.* 22:337–56

Pianta RC, Egeland B, Sroufe LA. 1990. Maternal stress and children's development: prediction of school outcomes and identification of protective factors. See Rolf et al. 1990, pp. 215–35

Plomin R, Crabbe J. 2000. DNA. *Psychol Bull.* 126:806–28

Pollitt E, Golub M, Gorman K, Grantham-McGregor S, Levitsky D, et al. 1996. A reconceptualization of the effects of undernutrition on children's biological, psychosocial, and behavioral development. *Soc. Policy Rep. Soc. Res. Child Dev.* 10(5):1–24

Power C. 1991. Social and economic background and class inequalities in health among young adults. *Soc. Sci. Med.* 32:411–17

Raisler J, Alexander C, O'Campo P. 1999. Breast-feeding and infant illness: a dose response relationship? *Am. J. Public Health* 89:25–30

Rank MR. 2000. Socialization of socioeconomic status. In *Handbook of Family Development and Intervention*, ed. WC Nichols, pp. 129–42. New York: Wiley

Richman N, Stevenson J, Graham P. 1975. Prevalence of behavior problems in three-year-old children: an epidemiological study in a London borough. *J. Child Psychol. Psychiatry* 16:277–87

Rodrigo MJ, Janssens JM, Ceballos E. 2001. Reasoning and action complexity: sources and consequences on maternal child-rearing behavior. *Int. J. Behav. Dev.* 25:50–59

Rolf J, Masten A, Cicchetti D, Nuechterlein K, Weintraub S, eds. 1990. *Risk and Protective Factors in Development of Psychopathology.* New York: Cambridge Univ. Press

Rosenbaum S. 1992. Child health and poor children. *Am. Behav. Sci.* 35:275–89

Rushing WA, Ortega ST. 1979. Socioeconomic status and mental disorder: new evidence and a sociomedical formulation. *Am. J. Sociol.* 84:1175–200

Rutter M. 1990. Psychosocial resilience and protective mechanisms. See Rolf et al. 1990, pp. 181–214

Saegert S, Winkel GH. 1990. Environmental psychology. *Annu. Rev. Psychol.* 41:441–77

Sameroff AJ, Seifer R, Baldwin A, Baldwin C. 1993. Stability of intelligence from preschool to adolescence: the influence of social and family risk factors. *Child Dev.* 64:80–97

Sameroff AJ, Seifer R, Zax M, Barocas R. 1987. Early indicators of developmental risk: the Rochester longitudinal study. *Schizophr. Bull.* 13:383–94

Sampson RJ. 1992. Family management and child development: insights from social disorganization theory. In *Advances in Criminological Theory*, ed. J McCord, 3:63–93. New Brunswick, NJ: Transaction Books

Sampson RJ, Raudenbush SW, Earls F. 1997. Neighborhoods and violent crime: a multilevel study of collective efficacy. *Science* 277:918–24

Sandel M, Schrfstein J. 1999. *Not Safe at Home: How America's Housing Crisis Threatens the Health of Its Children.* Boston: Boston Med. Cent. Children's Hosp., The Doc4Kids Project

Sargent JD, Brown MJ, Freeman A, Bailey D, Goodman D, Freeman DH. 1995. Childhood lead poisoning in Massachusetts's communities: its association with sociodemographic and housing characteristics. *Am. J. Public Health* 85:528–34

Scarr S, Weinberg RA. 1978. The influence of "family background" on intellectual attainment. *Am. Sociol. Rev.* 43:674–92

Scholer SJ, Hickson GB, Ray WA. 1999. Sociodemographic factors identify US infants at high risk for injury mortality. *Pediatrics* 103:1183–88

Shonkoff JP, Phillips DA, eds. 2000. *From Neurons to Neighborhoods: The Science of Early Childhood Development.* Washington, DC: Natl. Acad. Press

Smith JP. 1999. Healthy bodies and thick wallets: the dual relation between health and economic status. *J. Econ. Perspect.* 13:145–66

Smith JR, Brooks-Gunn J, Klebanov P. 1997.

The consequences of living in poverty for young children's cognitive and verbal ability and early school achievement. See Duncan & Brooks-Gunn 1997, pp. 132–89

Starfield B. 1982. Family income, ill health and medical care of U.S. children. *J. Public Healthy Policy* 3:244–59

Starfield B. 1989. Child health care and social factors: poverty, class, race. *Bull. NY Acad. Med.* 65:299–306

Takeuchi DT, Williams DR, Adair RK. 1991. Economic stress in the family and children's emotional and behavioral problems. *J. Marriage Fam.* 53:1031–41

Taylor SE, Seeman TE. 1999. Psychosocial resources and the SES-health relationship. See Adler et al. 1999, pp. 210–25

Tesman JR, Hills A. 1994. Developmental effects of lead exposure in children. *Soc. Policy Rep. Soc. Res. Child Dev.* 8(3):1–16

Treiber R, Harshfield G, Davis H, Kapuku G, Moore D. 1999. Stress responsivity and body fatness: links between socioeconomic status and cardiovascular risk factors in youth. See Adler et al. 1999, pp. 435–38

US Dep. Health Hum. Serv. 2000a. *Child Health USA 2000.* Washington, DC: US GPO

US Dep. Health Hum. Serv. 2000b. *Healthy People 2010.* Washington, DC: US GPO

Valenzuela M. 1997. Maternal sensitivity in a developing society: the context of urban poverty and infant chronic undernutrition. *Dev. Psychol.* 33:845–55

Vaughn BE, Bost KK. 1999. Attachment and temperament: redundant, independent, or interacting influences on interpersonal adaptation and personality development? In *Handbook of Attachment: Theory, Research, and Clinical Applications,* ed. J Cassidy, PR Shaver, pp. 198–225. New York: Guilford

Vrijheid M, Dolk H, Stone D, Alberman E, Scott JES. 2000. Socioeconomic inequalities in risk of congenital anomaly. *Arch. Dis. Child.* 82:349–52

Wachs TD. 2000. *Necessary but Not Sufficient.* Washington, DC: Am. Psychol. Assoc.

Walberg HJ, Marjoribanks K. 1976. Family environment and cognitive development:

twelve analytic models. *Rev. Educ. Res.* 46: 527–51

Wasserman CR, Shaw GM, Selvin S, Gould JB, Syme SL. 1998. Socioeconomic status, neighborhood social conditions, and neural tube defects. *Am. J. Public Health* 88:1674–80

White KR. 1982. The relation between socioeconomic status and academic achievement. *Psychol. Bull.* 91:461–81

Wilkinson RG. 1999. Health, hierarchy, and social anxiety. See Adler et al. 1999, pp. 48–63

Williams DR, Collins C. 1995. U. S. socioeconomic and racial differentials in health: patterns and explanations. *Annu. Rev. Sociol.* 21:349–86

Wills TA, McNamara G, Vaccaro D. 1995. Parental education related to adolescent stress-coping and substance use: development of a mediational model. *Health Psychol.* 14:464–78

Wills TA, Vaccaro D, McNamara G. 1992. Live events, family support, and competence in adolescent substance use. *Am. J. Commun. Psychol.* 20:349–74

Wilson AL. 1993. Poverty and children's health. *Child Youth Fam. Serv. Q.* 16:14–16

Wilson WJ. 1991. Studying inner-city social dislocation: the challenge of public agenda research. *Am. Sociol. Rev.* 56:1–14

Wohlfarth T, Van den Brink W. 1998. Social class and substance use disorders: the value of social class as distinct from socioeconomic status. *Soc. Sci. Med.* 47:51–68

Young G, Gately T. 1988. Neighborhood impoverishment and child maltreatment. *J. Fam. Issues* 9:240–54

Zill N, Moore K, Smith E, Stief T, Coiro M. 1995. The life circumstances and development of children in welfare families: a profile based on national survey data. In *Escape From Poverty: What Makes a Difference For Children?* ed. PL Chase-Lansdale, J Brooks-Gunn, pp. 38–59. New York: Cambridge Univ. Press

Zuvarin SJ. 1989. The ecology of child abuse and neglect: review of the literature and presentation of data. *Violence Vict.* 4:101–20

[15]

Lasting Consequences
of the Summer Learning Gap

Karl L. Alexander
Johns Hopkins University

Doris R. Entwisle
Johns Hopkins University

Linda Steffel Olson
Johns Hopkins University

Prior research has demonstrated that summer learning rooted in family and community influences widens the achievement gap across social lines, while schooling offsets those family and community influences. In this article, we examine the long-term educational consequences of summer learning differences by family socioeconomic level. Using data from the Baltimore Beginning School Study youth panel, we decompose achievement scores at the start of high school into their developmental precursors, back to the time of school entry in 1st grade. We find that cumulative achievement gains over the first nine years of children's schooling mainly reflect school-year learning, whereas the high SES–low SES achievement gap at 9th grade mainly traces to differential summer learning over the elementary years. These early out-of-school summer learning differences, in turn, substantially account for achievement-related differences by family SES in high school track placements (college preparatory or not), high school noncompletion, and four-year college attendance. We discuss implications for understanding the bases of educational stratification, as well as educational policy and practice.

Comparisons of school-year and summer learning inform fundamental questions of educational stratification and help parse school, family, and community influences on children's academic development. With children "in" their homes, schools, and communities during the school year, but just "in" their homes and communities over the summer months, the academic calendar approximates a natural experiment that affords leverage for isolating the distinctive role of schooling in children's cognitive development. This was the great insight exploited by Barbara Heyns in her 1978 book *Summer Learning*, which established that achievement

gaps by family SES (socioeconomic status) and race/ethnicity widen more during the summer months than during the school year.

Although the detailed results of subsequent research on the seasonality of learning do not line up perfectly (see Cooper and colleagues' [1996] meta-analysis for an overview), the patterns documented by Heyns in the 1970s for middle school children in public schools in Atlanta, Georgia appear to have considerable generality. This is especially the case for her conclusions regarding family socioeconomic background, which have been replicated in our Baltimore research on the early elementary years with data from the 1980s (e.g., Entwisle, Alexander, and Olson 1997), in studies conducted in other localities (Murnane 1975; O'Brien 1998), and in national data from earlier (Heyns 1987; Karweit, Ricciuti, and Thompson 1994; Phillips 2000) and more recent periods (Burkam et al. 2004; Downey, von Hippel, and Broh 2004; Reardon 2003).

Direct correspondence to Karl Alexander, Department of Sociology, Johns Hopkins University, 3400 N. Charles Street, Baltimore, MD 21218. This analysis was supported by the Spencer Foundation (Grant 20030057) and the W. T. Grant Foundation (Grants No. 9819298 and 95164195).

Using the national Early Child Longitudinal Study data (ECLS) over kindergarten and 1st grade, these recent analyses address a potentially critical source of bias in that they adjust seasonal comparisons for school year beginning and ending dates in relation to when students were actually tested. Other studies of seasonal learning patterns define in-school and summer learning around fall and spring testing dates—for example, the September through June "school year" becomes October through May, if that is the testing schedule. Consequently, the school year is typically understated and summer is overstated, such that an indeterminate portion of school-year learning is allocated to the summer months. While this imprecision probably moderates seasonal differences, ECLS analyses still find that "children from higher-SES families learn more over the summer than do their less-advantaged counterparts" (Burkham et al. 2004:18).

Findings from this literature support two conclusions: 1) prior to high school, the achievement gap by family SES traces substantially to unequal learning opportunities in children's home and community environments; and 2) with learning gains across social lines more nearly equal during the school year, the experience of schooling tends to offset the unequalizing press of children's out-of-school learning environments. Schooling thus appears to play a compensatory role, although we caution that this conclusion holds only for the experience of schooling writ large. It does not imply parity, or even near equivalence, in access to particular school resources or opportunities to learn, which often are quite unequally distributed (e.g., Dougherty 1996).

These insights inform our understanding of the roles played by families, neighborhoods, and schools in cognitive development over the short-term, but do they have consequences for later patterns of educational stratification? It seems reasonable that they would, yet research on the seasonality of learning has yet to inform the question. Rather, studies have been narrowly focused on establishing the seasonal pattern, and to a lesser extent on trying to account for it (e.g., investigating differences in the summer experiences of low-income and upper-income youth). Still, two bodies of evidence suggest there *ought* to be lasting consequences of summer learning differences over the elementary grades—consequences that are likely substantial.

First, achievement scores at any level of schooling predict success at the next level. This holds for high school completion, college attendance, college completion (see Entwisle et al. 1997, table 7.2), and later successes in the labor market (e.g., Kerckhoff, Raudenbush, and Glennie 2001). Second, cognitive achievement scores at the individual level are moderately to highly correlated across time. Most immediately relevant is the patterning of scores from the early elementary grades into middle school and high school. In national data, test scores measured in kindergarten and 1st grade correlate .5 and above with scores at 5th and 10th grade (e.g., Pope, Lehrer, and Stevens 1980; Weller, Schnittjer, and Tuten 1992), while in the present project fall and spring subtests from 1st grade on the California Achievement Test battery on average correlate .54 with their counterpart measures nine years later.

Here, then, is the argument in propositional form: (1) if the achievement gap by family SES during the elementary school years traces substantially to summer learning differences, and (2) if achievement scores are highly correlated across stages of young people's schooling, and (3) if academic placements and attainments at the upper grades are selected on the basis of achievement scores, then (4) summer learning differences during the foundational early grades help explain achievement-dependent outcome differences across social lines in the upper grades, including the transition out of high school and, for some, into college.

Though the argument seems plausible enough, it has yet to be put to the test. Using data from the Baltimore-based Beginning School Study (BSS) youth panel, our analysis examines consequences of seasonal learning differences during the elementary school years for children's later schooling.

SAMPLE AND METHODS

The BSS panel consists of a representative random sample of Baltimore school children whose educational progress has been monitored from 1st grade through age 22. The project began in the fall of 1982, when the study participants (N = 790), randomly selected from 20 public elementary schools within strata defined by school racial composition and socioeconomic level, were starting 1st grade. We use testing data from Baltimore City Public School System (BCPSS) records to track learning patterns, school records and student reports to identify students' high school curriculum placement (college preparatory versus others), and student interview data from an age 22/23 Young Adult Survey (YAS) to determine high school completion and college attendance. Questionnaire data from parents are combined with school record data about parents to rank children's family socioeconomic standing in elementary school. (For more detail on the BSS sampling and research design, see Entwisle and colleagues [1997]; see Table A1 in the Appendix for variable descriptions.)

We analyze scores on the Reading Comprehension subtest of the California Achievement Test (CAT-R) battery from school records over BSS years 1 through 5 (California Achievement Test 1979), fall and spring separately, and from a BSS administration of this same subtest in year 9 (analyses using the Math Concepts subtest yield quite similar results). The twice annual testing schedule for the early years allows separate calculation of school-year (fall to spring) and summer (spring to fall) learning gains over the entire elementary school period for children promoted regularly (repeaters are covered through the highest grade attained over these five years). The BCPSS discontinued fall achievement testing in BSS year 7 (the 1988 to 1989 school year), and after year 8 they discontinued use of the CAT battery altogether, but in spring 1991 (the end of 9th grade for children promoted regularly) the BSS did its own administration of the Reading Comprehension and Math Concepts subtests, achieving 75 percent coverage of the original panel.[1] The interval between the end of BSS year 5 and spring of year 9 spans the middle school years and the first year of high school. With no fall scores for those years, gains cannot be calculated separately by season, so overall gains are reported.

We use 11 testing points in the analysis (fall and spring for each of the first five years plus

spring of year 9). This is an uncommonly rich set of testing data, but owing to absences, transfers outside the city school system, and other complications, not all children were tested on every occasion. Case coverage when screened on complete testing data is 326 (from 790 originally). Additionally, some positive selection is evident—while fall of 1st grade scores are close (281.7 for the listwise sample and 280.6 for the full sample), by year 9 the listwise group's spring average is .18 SD above the full sample average. However, the 464 excluded cases include many with nearly complete testing records, and some useful testing data are available for just about everyone. For example, 81 percent of cases have observed data for at least 6 of the 11 testing occasions, and 92 percent have data for at least four test scores.[2] To take advantage of this circumstance, we generated an imputed version of the raw data (based on 10 imputations) using multiple imputation methods (e.g., Allison 2002). These methods predict missing scores from the available data (including spring scores over years 6 through 8, which are not used in the substantive analyses), plus race, sex, and family SES background (the continuous version), which are known for all but three cases, and high school track placement. We used STATA software to carry out the imputation procedure.[3] The final imputed data set of test scores and seasonal components includes 787 cases (three cases that lacked data on family SES were dropped). Data were not imputed for high school track and the age 22 educational outcome variables used as dependent variables in the regression models.

The imputed achievement data were derived as the average of the 10 versions generated by the imputation process. We then used these scores (fall and spring over the elementary years and spring of year 9) to calculate the four achievement components used in the analyses: fall of 1st grade score, cumulative school-year gain over the elementary grades, cumulative summer gain over the elementary grades, and total gain over years 6 through 9. Because this

---

[1] Testing continued for roughly 18 months. Using exact testing dates, a linear interpolation referenced scores back to the spring of year 9.

[2] Missing data range from 6 percent to 31 percent across the 11 tests, averaging 22 percent.

[3] See Royston (2004, 2005) for documentation of the user-written programs Ice and Micombine, which implement multiple implementation in STATA.

is a somewhat unusual application of the multiple imputation methodology, we have carefully checked the robustness of the results it yields. The patterns of interest in analyses based on the pooled imputed data (including patterns of statistical significance) are evident also in each of the 10 replicate data sets separately, as well as the N = 326 full information subsample, which though small and probably somewhat atypical, nevertheless has strong internal validity. Accordingly, we report the results based on the pooled imputed data matrix, with supplementary points of interest from the checks mentioned as results are presented.

DISAGGREGATING YEAR 9 ACHIEVEMENT SCORES

The spring year 9 achievement average for the imputed analytic sample is 547.6 scale score points, with a standard deviation of 80.4 (see Table 1). The developmental foundation for this level of assessed performance early in high school (or, for repeaters, just before) is as follows: 1) a baseline average of 279.8 points from the fall of 1st grade; 2) an average *cumulative school-year gain* of 195.0 points fall to spring during elementary school; 3) an average *cumulative summer gain* of 11.1 points spring to fall over summers during the elementary years; and 4) an average cumulative school-year plus summer gain of 61.7 points over school years 6 though 9 (years for which we are unable to distinguish school-year from summer gains).

These achievement scores are vertically calibrated across years so as to approximate a continuous metric, but the distribution lacks a meaningful zero point (the fall of 1st grade *floor,* or lowest possible score, is 133). However, winter gains over the elementary school years account for 195.0 points of the 267.7 point increment from the baseline over this nine-year period, by far the largest of the three components in Table 1.

Important curricular placement decisions are made at the beginning of high school, and Table 1 shows that achievement assessed at that point mainly reflects skill differentials already in place when children enter 1st grade, as well as skills built up in elementary school. Summer learning in this instance is a small part of the overall picture. But what of *differences across social lines* in year 9 achievement levels? Does the breakdown look the same? The right-most column of Table 1 addresses this question, comparing the learning patterns of children classified as "low" and "high" SES in terms of family background (see Table A1 in the Appendix for measurement detail).

We focus here on comparisons across the SES extremes, but we keep in mind that the BCPSS enrollment is largely low income (half the BSS sample is classified low SES) and that few wealthy families send their children to public schools in low-income, high-poverty school systems. "Extreme," then, is relative to the local context. Still, within the BSS, low SES parents are mainly high school dropouts and high SES parents on average have attained some college, so this is a meaningful contrast, even if truncated relative to family differences nationally. In year 9, the high SES achievement average is 73.2 points above the low SES average (.88 SD, referenced to the standard deviation for high and

Table 1. Reading Comprehension Test Score Decomposition over the First Nine Years of School by Family SES

Reading Comprehension CAT Score Gains, Years 1–9	Total	Family SES			Gap High-Low
		Low SES	Mid SES	High SES	
Initial Test Score, Fall 1st Grade	279.81	271.99	277.89	298.47	26.48*
Winter Gain (5 winters)	194.97	191.30	210.19	186.11	−5.19
Summer Gain (4 summers)	11.12	−1.90	4.12	46.58	48.48*
Gain Over Years 6–9	61.69	60.95	60.73	64.34	3.39
Test Score, End Year 9	547.55	522.33	552.94	595.49	73.16*
(N)	(787)	(397)	(204)	(186)	

Note: Significant t-tests for mean differences between Low SES and High SES groups are shown in Gap column.
* $p \le .05$ (two-tailed tests).

low SES youth combined). About a third of that SES difference, 26.5 points, traces to disparities in place when these children started 1st grade, implicating experiences and family resources that predate school entry.[4] The remainder of the difference is built up over the school years, and Table 1 shows that the largest component, 48.5 points, or about two-thirds of the total, traces to summer learning differences over the elementary years. The low SES group actually gains a bit more during the corresponding school years than does the high group (5.2 points, not a significant difference), but this favorable showing while in school is more than offset by their summer shortfall.

Importantly, and so far as we can tell, this pattern is not an artifact of ceiling limits on high SES children's school-year gains. This was checked on the full information, nonimputed cases, 64 of whom scored at the ceiling on one or more of the spring assessments (28 high SES youth, 15 mid SES, and 21 low SES). Excluding these 64 cases reduces the high SES–low SES gap as would be expected, but the summer differential remains the largest component and winter gains still favor the low SES group by a small, nonsignificant margin. Additionally, as shown elsewhere (Alexander, Entwisle, and Olson 2001), SES differences in summer learning are robust in HLM (hierarchical linear models) within-person growth models over the five school years for which we can distinguish summer learning from school year, with the summer learning difference significant each summer.

The early years of schooling are foundational in that the skills acquired then support all later learning. Our analytic comparisons support this point, insomuch as achievement levels at the start of high school substantially trace back to

those early years. Moreover, most of that learning happens when children are in school, so schooling indeed makes a difference for low SES youth and high SES youth alike (for more on this point, see Downey et al. 2004). But with respect specifically to the year 9 achievement gap by SES background, experiences outside school apparently make an even bigger difference, as that gap substantially originates over the years before 1st grade and summer periods during the elementary school years.

SUMMER LEARNING DIFFERENCES AND SCHOOLING OUTCOMES

Do these large cognitive differences that trace back to the period before high school matter in practical terms? The top panel of Table 2 shows attainment outcomes in high school and at selected later benchmarks for the imputed sample, again comparing children classified by family SES. Sixty-two percent of high SES children were enrolled in a college preparatory program in high school versus just 13 percent of the low SES group. There are large differences in high school noncompletion and college attendance as well. Based on information covering the four years after the panel's on-time high school graduation in spring 1994,[5] over a third of the low SES group and just 3 percent of the high group are "permanent dropouts," meaning high school dropouts who at approximately age 22 still lack high school certification of any type. Whereas almost 60 percent of the high SES group attended a four-year college by age 22, just 7 percent of low SES youth did so.

To illustrate how summer learning differences *might be* implicated in the socioeconomic patterning of educational accomplishment in high school and after, the bottom two panels of Table 2 repeat the decomposition exercise from Table 1 across the socioeconomic extremes, but for subsets of youth whose social backgrounds and later experiences align: first, low SES youth in the non-college track and high SES youth in the college track; second, low SES permanent dropouts and high SES youth who attended four-year colleges.

---

[4] With kindergarten now nearly universal and preschool education common, it cannot be said that 1st grade represents children's first encounter with formal schooling. However, many children still attend half-day kindergartens (45 percent in the late 1990s [West, Denton, and Reaney 2001]), and many kindergartens stress social skills over academic learning. That said, children's achievement levels do improve over the kindergarten year, but at a slower rate than they do in 1st grade (Downey et al. 2004). In the early 1980s, when the BSS began, kindergarten was not yet mandatory in Baltimore.

---

[5] Owing to grade retention, dropouts, and other circumstances, fewer than half (45 percent) actually finished high school at that time.

Table 2.   Reading Comprehension Test Score Decomposition Over the First Nine Years of School by Family SES, High School Track Placement, and Educational Attainment at Age 22

	Family SES			
	Low SES	Mid SES	High SES	Gap
Proportion College-Prep High School Track	.13	.30	.62	.49*
(N)	(320)	(176)	(160)	
Educational Attainment, Age 22				
Proportion Permanent Dropout	.36	.13	.03	−.33*
Proportion High School Graduate/GED	.35	.35	.11	−.24*
Proportion Trade School/Two-Year College	.21	.34	.27	−.06
Proportion Four-Year College	.07	.18	.59	.52*
(N)	(313)	(158)	(159)	

Reading Comprehension CAT Score Gains, Years 1–9	Low SES Non-College Track	High SES College Prep Track	Gap
Initial Test Score, Fall 1st Grade	269.88	310.30	40.42*
Winter Gain (5 winters)	188.20	180.58	−7.62
Summer Gain (4 summers)	−1.85	74.63	76.48*
Gain Over Years 6–9	60.44	67.21	6.77
Test Score, End Year 9	516.67	632.72	116.05*
(N)	(278)	(99)	

Reading Comprehension CAT Score Gains, Years 1–9	Low SES Permanent Dropouts	High SES 4-Year College	Gap
Initial Test Score, Fall 1st Grade	268.06	311.04	42.98*
Winter Gain (5 winters)	183.32	180.19	−3.13
Summer Gain (4 summers)	−11.04	75.53	86.57*
Gain Over Years 6–9	62.93	69.54	6.61
Test Score, End Year 9	503.26	636.30	133.04*
(N)	(114)	(94)	

Note: Significant t-tests for mean differences between Low SES and High SES groups are shown in Gap column.
* $p \leq .05$ (two-tailed tests).

Consider first the college track/high SES–non-college track/low SES comparison. There is a 116.1 point (1.3 SD) difference between the two groups' year 9 achievement averages, more than half of which (76.5 points) traces to summer learning differences carried forward from elementary school. The second largest component is the 40.4 point fall of 1st grade disparity.

The situation is much the same when comparing low SES permanent dropouts against high SES youth who attended four-year colleges, for whom the year 9 achievement difference is 133.0 points (1.4 SD). This huge disparity again traces substantially to the groups' unequal experience of summer learning over the early formative years, which accounts for 86.6 scale points, or 65 percent of the total. The next largest component, at 43.0 points, again is the fall of 1st grade difference.

The groups involved in these comparisons certainly are not distinguished solely by their achievement scores early in high school. For this reason, the comparisons in Table 2 cannot be said to isolate causality. In strictly empirical terms, out-of-school experiences account for the majority of the achievement differences registered in 9th grade, and these achievement differences, in turn, anticipate vastly different high school placements, modes of high school exit, and patterns of postsecondary attendance. More to the point, though, it seems certain that achievement levels at the start of high school *play some role* in the schooling outcomes in Table 2—for example, achievement scores and the competencies they signal are used in making curricular placement decisions; they inform parents', teachers', and counselors' thinking about students' academic prospects; and they are used in a self-referential way to inform a student's own sense of self in the student role.

It is a familiar pattern of educational stratification that disadvantaged social origins anticipate disadvantaged social destinations. Academic skill development, we know, plays a role in cementing that link. Low achievement scores at the start of high school do not auger well for later success, and it is low SES students and those who are socially disadvantaged in other ways who tend to fall toward the low end of the achievement distribution. But comparisons made only in the upper grades obscure the developmental history upon which students' high school records are built. Our results show how out-of-school learning during the elementary grades is linked to the year 9 achievement gap by family SES: a gap that, in turn, separates college track youth from non-college track youth, and that distinguishes those who fall off the path to high school completion from those who attend four year colleges.

REGRESSION ADJUSTED COMPARISONS

It may be the case that the comparisons in Table 2 exaggerate the role of summer differences by focusing on extreme cases. No doubt there is some truth to that. To gauge more formally the

descriptive differences just reviewed, Table 3 presents high SES–low SES comparisons adjusted for background attributes. The entries, derived from group-specific logistic regression equations, are predicted probabilities of being in a college preparatory program in high school (estimated for the high SES and the low SES subsamples), of being a permanent dropout (versus any other educational status, estimated for the low SES sample only), and of attending a four-year college (versus any other educational status, estimated for the high SES subsample only). The equations adjust for differences associated with race (a dummy variable distinguishing blacks from whites), sex (females versus males), family SES (the full metric version to control for SES differences within the nominal "low" and "high" classifications), and four variables that make up the components of year 9 achievement: a baseline score from the fall of 1st grade; a measure of cumulative school-year gains over years 1 through 5; a measure of cumulative summer gains over summers 1 through 4; and a measure of total gains, summer and school-year, over years 6 through 9. The estimates in this way disaggregate effects of year 9 achievement scores, with some statistical controls to isolate group differences.

Table 3. Predicted Probabilities of Educational Outcomes from Logistic Regression Models

	Predicted Probability from Logistic Model[a]	Predicted Probability Substituting CAT Means for Opposite SES Group	Predicted Probability Substituting Only Summer CAT Gain for Opposite SES Group
Probability of College-Prep Curriculum for Low SES Sample	.07	.29	.16
Probability of College-Prep Curriculum for High SES Sample	.71	.32	.40
Probability of Permanent Dropout for Low SES Sample	.35	.23	.26
Probability of Attendance at Four-Year College for High SES Sample	.67	.24	.34

[a] Predicted probabilities come from logistic models predicting three different outcomes: permanent dropout, attendance at a four-year college, and enrollment in a college-prep high school curriculum. Each regression controls on demographic factors (gender, race, and a continuous composite measure of family SES). The regressions are estimated separately for low and high SES groups. Predicted probabilities are calculated for a sample member who scores at the mean on each predictor.

As one would expect, year 9 achievement effects themselves are predictive of all three outcomes. To establish the point, using the unimputed data we substituted year 9 achievement scores for the four components in Table 3. For analyses screened on just year 9 scores (N's 514–576), the analytic sample with complete testing data (N = 326), and the smaller high SES–low SES comparison subsamples, with race, sex, and family SES (metric version) controlled, effects of achievement in year 9 are statistically significant and substantively large throughout. Table 3 shows, in summary fashion, the extent to which mean differences across SES levels in the developmental components of year 9 achievement contribute to high SES–low SES differences in college track enrollment at the secondary level, high school noncompletion through age 22, and attendance at a four-year college.

Three predicted probabilities are reported for each outcome. The first is derived by evaluating the logistic equation for the focal group at that group's mean regressor values—high SES youth in the case of college track placement and four-year college enrollment; low SES youth in the case of college track placement and permanent dropout. This simply uses the group's own properties and regression results to generate an expected probability for the event at issue. The second and third estimates are a form of statistical experimentation, in the nature of regression decomposition as applied to least squares regression analyses (e.g., Althauser and Wigler 1972; Iams and Thornton 1975; Jones and Kelley 1984). In these instances, we apply the *other group's* mean achievement values (but not the three background measures) to the focal group's logistic coefficients—for example, applying the low SES group's achievement means to the high SES group's coefficients when predicting the high SES probability of college track enrollment. The first estimate substitutes all four achievement means; the second substitutes just the summer gain component (retaining the focal group's means for the other three components).

This exercise explores a "what if" counterfactual: What if everything else about the group at issue remains the same, but instead of having the achievement averages observed for them, they have the other group's averages? How would that affect, for example, their expected

probability of college-prep enrollment? This is clearly an artificial exercise—it's hard to imagine changes in achievement averages of this magnitude with nothing else changing. Still, the calculations usefully highlight interesting properties of the data and allow us to go beyond simple descriptions to controlled comparisons (i.e., outcome differences adjusted for race, sex, and family socioeconomic background in metric form).

With college track enrollment the criterion, there are enough low SES and high SES youths to perform the experiment for both groups (this holds for both the imputed data and the original listwise sample). Based on their respective logistic results and own regressor averages, the estimated probability of enrolling in a college-preparatory high school program is .71 among high SES youth and .07 among low SES youth. Substituting the low SES achievement means into the high SES equation reduces the former group's predicted probability of college track enrollment to .32, or by more than half, as a function of the two groups' very different achievement averages. At the other extreme, substituting the high SES averages in the low SES equation increases college track enrollment prospects four-fold, from .07 to .29.[6]

When we instead substitute *just* the low SES youth's lower average summer gain for the high SES youth's higher average summer gain (and vice versa) in the third column, the estimates are midrange, with the predicted probability for the high SES group increasing to .40 (but still well short of their own estimate of .71) and the low SES group decreasing to .16 (but still double their own estimate of .07). The former reduces the initial .64 point difference in the probability of college track enrollment by roughly 48 percent—$(.71 - .07) - (.40 - .07)/(71 - .07)$; the latter yields a 14 percent reduction.

There are hardly any unimputed high SES permanent dropouts or low SES youth who attended four-year colleges, so the other two sets of calculations in Table 3 are done for one group only. For high SES youth, the *estimated* probability of enrolling in a four-year college is .67. This drops to .24 (a .43 point reduction) when

---

[6] The logistic model is nonlinear and nothing in the logic or mechanics of this technique obliges symmetric results.

the calculations are based on low SES youth's achievement averages throughout and to .34 (a .33 point reduction) when just the mean value for the summer component is substituted. Both changes are large, and again the summer component alone produces most of the reduction in the predicted probability.[7]

The calculations predicting permanent high school dropout status indicate a smaller role for achievement differences altogether, but a consequential one nonetheless. The predicted probability of permanent dropout status for low SES youth is .35. This improves to .23 when all four high SES achievement means are substituted and to .26 when just the summer mean is used.

DISCUSSION

Our analysis adds an important practical dimension to research on the seasonality of learning, with implications for how the out-of-school institutional contexts of family and community that frame young children's academic development contribute to patterns of educational stratification. Stability in cognitive achievement over the course of young people's schooling is the bridge between summer learning shortfall over the elementary school years and later schooling outcomes. *Since it is low SES youth specifically whose out-of-school learning lags behind, this summer shortfall relative to better-off children contributes to the perpetuation of family advantage and disadvantage across generations.*

Low SES youth, we find, are less likely to find their way to a college-preparatory high school program, partly because their test scores are low at the very time these placements are made. And because their scores are low, they also are more prone to leave school without degrees and less likely to attend a four-year college. In light of these, and no doubt other, serious consequences, the question of why achievement levels at the start of high school are so disparate takes on great importance.

It is well established that there are vast differences across social lines in preschool children's out-of-school learning environments (e.g., Hart and Risley 1995). This helps explain not just why disadvantaged youth start school already far behind in kindergarten or 1st grade (Lee and Burkam 2002), but also why they continue to lag behind later (Farkas and Beron 2004; Phillips, Crouse, and Ralph 1998). Now we see that summer learning differences after children start school follow a like pattern, but what might not have been expected is the extent to which the *continuing press* of school-age children's family and neighborhood environments contributes to the year 9 achievement differential between high and low SES youth: summer shortfall over the five years of elementary school accounts for more than half the difference, a larger component than that built up over the preschool years.[8] And too, these learning differences from the early years that present themselves in 9th grade reverberate to constrain later high school curriculum placements, high school dropout, and college attendance. This lasting legacy of early experience typically is hidden from view.

The BSS is a local study and the analytic sample before imputation is small, just over 300. This is obviously limiting. Yet, the local context is urban and high poverty and thus policy relevant. Though the analytic sample may not be, strictly speaking, representative, these nevertheless are typical urban youth. But more to the point, to our knowledge there is no better data source, *anywhere,* for informing the issues addressed in this article. The national ECLS data, for example, include fall tests in kindergarten and 1st grade only, and so cover just the summer between kindergarten and 1st grade. Other samples used to study learning patterns by season also typically include data for just one summer, and none offer the long-term perspective of the BSS. Our results are best considered suggestive, and certainly the detailed percentages and probabilities reported should not be generalized. That said, BSS findings

---

[7] Using the imputed data, we get a .03 probability of four-year college attendance for low SES youth. This increases to .13 when calculated using high SES youth's four CAT-R means and to .07 when just the summer mean is substituted.

[8] For perspective on the time line of the black–white achievement gap, see Phillips and colleagues (1998). They estimate that half or more of the gap measured in 12th grade reflects continuity of differences evident at the start of 1st grade.

align well with a now sizeable literature on summer learning differentials, and the links seen in this analysis to later outcomes certainly have surface plausibility. With these caveats understood, we now discuss several implications of the findings presented here.

Surely the point made by David Berliner (2006) in his Invited Presidential Speech at the 2005 American Educational Research Association (AERA) annual meeting is correct: to moderate the achievement gap, the most compelling need is to reduce family and youth poverty. However, there also is a critical role for school reform. Achievement differentials by race/ethnicity and along lines of family advantage/disadvantage over the last 50 years have exhibited more volatility than many seem to realize (e.g., Krueger 1998; Lee 2002). Using National Assessment of Educational Progress (NAEP) testing data, for example, Hauser (1995) estimates that the I.Q. gap separating white and black youths declined by almost a third between 1970 and 1990, while Grissmer and colleagues (1994) conclude that progress during this period was too great to be accounted for by improvements in family life alone. They, and the others mentioned, direct attention to the likely role played by school improvements, including increased funding and class size reduction.

It is unlikely school resources can compensate *wholly* for the limited learning opportunities outside school that hold back many minority and low SES youth. Nevertheless, seasonal comparisons of learning make a compelling case that schooling indeed "makes a difference" in these children's lives, echoing the "differential sensitivity" hypothesis originally advanced in the Equality of Educational Opportunity report (Coleman et al. 1966). But how and when can interventions be most effectively targeted? What is the role of schools in educational stratification? And how should schools be held accountable when achievement scores persist in falling short of expectations? These are large issues, and the realization that much of the problem traces to out-of-school time during the early elementary years has implications for them all.

First, attempting to close the gap after it has opened wide is a rear guard action. Most of the gap increase happens early in elementary school, which is where corrective interventions would be most effective—or even before. To catch up,

youth who have fallen behind academically need to make larger than average gains. That is expecting a great deal, perhaps too much, of struggling students. Early interventions to keep the achievement gap from opening wide in the first place should be a high priority, and the earlier the better, with the kinds of preschool compensatory education initiatives that have proven effective (e.g., Ramey, Campbell, and Blair 1998; Schweinhart and Weikart 1998; Reynolds and Temple 1998).

Second, once in school, disadvantaged children need year-round, supplemental programming to counter the continuing press of family and community conditions that hold them back. The school curriculum in the elementary years often is self-consciously pursued at home, as when, for example, parents work with their children on letter and number skills or reading. Parents of means generally did well in school themselves. They understand the skills and behaviors valued there and exemplify them in family life. For their part, poor parents often themselves struggled at school and have low literacy levels, and thus they undoubtedly have difficulties cultivating valued educational skills in their children. While low income, low SES parents generally want the same kinds of enriching experiences for their children as do well-off parents, they often lack the means to provide them (e.g., Chin and Phillips 2004).

Seasonal studies of learning suggest that schooling compensates, to some degree, for a lack of educationally enriching experiences in disadvantaged children's family life—these youth come closer to keeping up with better-off students during the school year than they do during the summer months. But if some school helps, does that mean more school is necessarily better? Summer and after-school programs are the most obvious approaches,[9] but what counts is how that extra learning time is used. Summer schools that incorporate so-called best practice principles have proven effective (Borman and Dowling 2006; Cooper et al. 2000), but to address the achievement gap specifically, programs will need to target dis-

---

[9] Some have also called for more far-reaching reform of the traditional school-year calendar to eliminate the long summer break (e.g., Cooper 2004; Gandara and Fish 1994; McCabe 2004).

advantaged students specifically. All children can benefit from high quality "universal" programs—preschools for all; summer schools for all—but they will not benefit in equal measure. Families of privilege will tend to find their way to higher quality programs, and their children will be positioned to profit more from programs of like quality (e.g., Cooper et al. 2000). As a result, rather than moderate the achievement gap, across-the-board programming for academic remediation and/or enrichment would likely exacerbate it, making the problem worse rather than better (Ceci and Papierno 2005). This poses a challenge to policy: what to do when two educational goals, each commendable, are in conflict?

Third, the school-year pattern of achievement gain parity (or near parity) across social lines flies in the face of widely held (if often only whispered) assumptions about the learning abilities of poor and minority youth. It also flies in the face of widely held assumptions about the failures of the public schools and school systems burdened by high poverty enrollments. Perhaps these schools and school systems are doing a better job than is generally recognized (e.g., Alexander 1997; Berliner and Biddle 1995; Krueger 1998), with family disadvantages mistaken for school failings (e.g., Rothstein 2002) and the occasional but very real horror story (e.g., Kozol 1991) overgeneralized.

Finally, a seasonal perspective on learning also has implications for school accountability. The No Child Left Behind (NCLB) standard of "adequate yearly progress" is intended to monitor school effectiveness based on annual achievement testing in grades 3 through 8. Schools that fail to meet local NCLB standards in math and reading for two consecutive years are designated "in need of improvement," with increasingly severe correctives required the longer they remain so designated. Certainly schools that chronically fall short need help; however, the punitive cast of NCLB may be misplaced. Indeed, annual assessments confound school-year and summer learning in

unknown proportions, and schools that enroll mainly disadvantaged students will be held accountable not just for what happens to their pupils during the school year, but also for their students' summer learning, over which they have no control. If the BSS pattern is at all typical, this will show many schools in a poor light even when their students move ahead during the school year at a rate comparable to that of students in schools deemed to be performing adequately. An accountability system that monitors progress fall to spring, perhaps relative to an expected summer gain baseline (Downey, von Hippel, and Hughes 2005), would be more appropriate for gauging a school's effectiveness. The current arrangement is useful for identifying need, but little more, and certainly not for apportioning blame.

Karl L. Alexander *is John Dewey Professor of Sociology at the Johns Hopkins University. His interests center on problems of educational stratification that can be addressed via organizational, social psychological, and life course perspectives. With Doris Entwisle and Susan Dauber, he recently published a revised updated version of their 1994 evaluation of grade retention,* On the Success of Failure. *He is also working on several projects that examine the early adult transition through the lens of the* Beginning School Study.

Doris R. Entwisle *is Research Professor of Sociology at the Johns Hopkins University. Her main area of interest is the sociology of human development over the life course, with an emphasis on issues of inequality. Her current research concerns the ways in which members of the Beginning School Study panel make the transition to adulthood and how social and financial disadvantage early in life alters the life situations of adults in their early 20s. Her most recent book (with Karl L. Alexander and Linda S. Olson),* Children, Schools, and Inequality, *explores the ways in which social structure shapes the paths that children take through elementary school.*

Linda Steffel Olson *is an associate research scientist in the Department of Sociology at the Johns Hopkins University. She has been associated with the Beginning School Study for the past 19 years. Her interests center on the effects of social structure on schooling outcomes.*

Table A1. Definitions, Means, and Standard Deviations of Variables in Seasonal Gain Analysis

Variable	Mean	(SD)	N	Description
Background Characteristics				
Student Gender	.51	(.50)	787	1 = Female; 0 = Male
Student Race	.55	(.50)	787	1 = Black; 0 = White
Family Socioeconomic Status Composite	−.04	(.80)	787	Average of both parents' educational level, a ranking of mother's and father's occupational status (TSEI2, see Featherman and Stevens 1982), and participation in federal meal subsidy program (all measures converted to z-scores).
Mother's Years of Education	11.7	(2.6)	750	
Father's Years of Education	12.2	(2.7)	529	
Mother's TSEI2 Job Status	31.9	(15.8)	610	
Father's TSEI2 Job Status	33.3	(18.1)	518	
Proportion Meal Subsidy	.66	(.47)	754	
Family SES Composite Trichotomized				Composite variable trichotomized: Low SES = 0, Mid SES = 1, and High SES = 2. The family SES composite was trichotomized into low (50 percent of sample), medium (26 percent), and high (24 percent) SES categories in such a way that the mean educational level for parents was around 10 years for the low group, 12 years for the medium group, and around 15 years for the high SES group. The skew in the data toward the low SES group reflects the socioeconomic makeup of the Baltimore City student population.
Student Achievement, Years 1–9 (Imputed data)				
CAT Reading Score, Fall 1st Grade	279.8	(40.7)	787	California Achievement Test (CAT), Form C, Reading Comprehension, scale scores. BCPS tested students in the fall and spring of each year through year 6, and in spring only in years 7 and 8. In the spring of year 9, the BSS administered the CAT to students (testing continued over an 18 month period), then using exact testing dates, interpolated scores back to the spring of year 9. See Entwisle and colleagues (1997, Appendix), for data on psychometric properties of CAT. Seasonal components of reading achievement, years 1 to 5, were computed by subtracting fall from spring scores (winter gains) and spring from the following fall scores (summer gains). Yearly seasonal gains were then summed for a total Summer Gain and Winter Gain. Years 6 to 9 Gain was calculated by subtracting the spring year 5 score from the spring of year 9 score.
CAT Reading Score, Spring Year 9	547.6	(80.4)	787	
High School and Postsecondary Attainment				
Proportion College-Prep High School Curriculum	.30	(.46)	656	Data on high school curriculum come from BCPS school records. Students attending one of the magnet high schools with strong college-prep tracks were designated as "College Prep." Data on students from non-BCPC schools came from student responses to questions on the high school program.
Educational Attainment Age 22				
Proportion Permanent Dropout	.22	(.42)	630	Data from Young Adult Survey at age 22. Highest level of education completed or enrolled in by age 22. For postsecondary schooling, highest level attended whether or not completed the program.
Proportion Terminal High School	.29	(.45)	630	
Proportion Trade School/Two-Year College	.26	(.44)	630	
Proportion Four-Year College	.23	(.42)	630	

REFERENCES

Alexander, Karl L. 1997. "Public Schools and the Public Good." *Social Forces* 76:1–30.

Alexander, Karl L., Doris R. Entwisle, and Linda S. Olson. 2001. "Schools, Achievement and Inequality: A Seasonal Perspective." *Educational Evaluation and Policy Analysis* 23:171–91.

Allison, Paul D. 2002. *Missing Data.* Thousand Oaks, CA: Sage Publications.

Althauser, Robert P. and Michael Wigler. 1972. "Standardization and Component Analysis." *Sociological Methods and Research* 1:97–135.

Berliner, David. 2006. "Our Impoverished View of Educational Reform." *Teachers College Record* 108:949–95.

Berliner, David C. and Bruce J. Biddle. 1995. *The Manufactured Crisis: Myths, Fraud and the Attack on America's Public Schools.* Reading, MA: Addison-Wesley.

Borman, Geoffrey D. and N. M. Dowling. 2006. "The Longitudinal Achievement Effects of Multi-Year Summer School: Evidence from the Teach Baltimore Randomized Field Trial." *Educational Evaluation and Policy Analysis* 28:25–48.

Burkam, David T., Douglas D. Ready, Valerie E. Lee, and Laura F. LoGerfo. 2004. "Social-Class Differences in Summer Learning Between Kindergarten and First Grade: Model Specification and Estimation." *Sociology of Education* 77:1–31.

California Achievement Test. 1979. *Technical Bulletin 1, Forms C and D, Levels 10–19.* Monterey, CA: McGraw-Hill.

Ceci, Stephen J. and Paul B. Papierno. 2005. "The Rhetoric and Reality of Gap Closing: When the 'Have-Nots' Gain but the 'Haves' Gain Even More." *American Psychologist* 60:149–60.

Chin, Tiffani and Meredith Phillips. 2004. "Social Reproduction and Child-Rearing Practices: Social Class, Children's Agency, and the Summer Activity Gap." *Sociology of Education* 77:185–210.

Coleman, James S., Ernest Q. Campbell, Charles J. Hobson, James McPartland, Alexander Mood, Frederic D. Weinfeld, and Robert L. York. 1966. *Equality of Educational Opportunity.* Washington, DC: U.S. Government Printing Office.

Cooper, Harris. 2004. "Is the School Calendar Dated? Education, Economics, and the Politics of Time." Pp. 3–23 in *Summer Learning, Research, Policies, and Programs,* edited by G. D. Borman and M. Boulay. Mahweh, NJ: Lawrence Erlbaum Associates.

Cooper, Harris, Kelly Charlton, Jeff C. Valentine, and Laura Muhlenbruck. 2000. *Making the Most of Summer School: A Meta-Analytic and Narrative Review.* Monograph Series for the Society for Research in Child Development, vol. 65, no. 1, Serial No. 260. Ann Arbor, MI: Society for Research in Child Development.

Cooper, Harris, Barbara Nye, Kelly Charlton, James Lindsay, and Scott Greathouse. 1996. "The Effects of Summer Vacation on Achievement Test Scores: A Narrative and Meta Analytic Review." *Review of Educational Research* 66:227–68.

Dougherty, Kevin J. 1996. "Opportunity-to-Learn Standards: A Sociological Critique." *Sociology of Education* Extra issue:40–66.

Downey, Douglas B., Paul T. von Hippel, and Beckett Broh. 2004. "Are Schools the Great Equalizer? Cognitive Inequality During the Summer Months and the School Year." *American Sociological Review* 69:613–35.

Downey, Douglas B., Paul T. von Hippel, and Melanie Hughes. 2005. "Are 'Failing' Schools Really Failing? Using Seasonal Comparisons to Evaluate School Effectiveness." Presented at the American Sociological Association, Education Section, August, Montreal, Canada.

Entwisle, Doris R., Karl L. Alexander, and Linda S. Olson. 1997. *Children, Schools and Inequality.* Boulder, CO: Westview Press.

Farkas, George and Kurt Beron. 2004. "The Detailed Age Trajectory of Oral Vocabulary Knowledge: Differences by Class and Race." *Social Science Research* 33:464–97.

Featherman, David L. and Gillian Stevens. 1982. "A Revised Socioeconomic Index of Occupational Status: Application in Analysis of Sex Differences in Attainment." Pp. 141–82 in *Social Structure and Behavior: Essays in Honor of William Hamilton Sewell,* edited by R. M. Hauser, D. Mechanic, A. O. Haller, and T. Hauser. New York: Academic Press.

Gandara, P. C. and Judy Fish. 1994. "Year-Round Schooling as an Avenue to Major Structural Reform." *Educational Evaluation and Policy Analysis* 16:67–85.

Grissmer, David W., Shelia Nataraj Kirby, Mark Berends, and Stephanie Williamson. 1994. *Student Achievement and the Changing American Family.* Santa Monica, CA: The Rand Corporation.

Hart, Betty and Todd R. Risley. 1995. *Meaningful Differences in the Everyday Experience of Young American Children.* Baltimore, MD: Paul H. Brookes Publishing Co.

Hauser, Robert M. 1995. "The Bell Curve." *Contemporary Sociology* 24:149–53.

Heyns, Barbara. 1978. *Summer Learning and the Effects of Schooling.* New York: Academic.

———. 1987. "Schooling and Cognitive Development: Is There a Season for Learning?" *Child Development* 58:1151–60.

Iams, Howard M. and Arland Thornton. 1975. "Decomposition of Differences: A Cautionary Note." *Sociological Methods and Research* 3:341–51.

Jones, F. L. and Jonathan Kelley. 1984. "Decomposing Differences Between Groups: A

Cautionary Note on Measuring Discrimination." *Sociological Methods and Research* 12:323–43.

Karweit, Nancy, Anne Ricciuti, and Bill Thompson. 1994. "Summer Learning Revisited: Achievement Profiles of Prospects' First Grade Cohort." Abt Associates, Washington, DC. Unpublished manuscript.

Kerckhoff, Alan C., Stephen W. Raudenbush, and Elizabeth Glennie. 2001. "Education, Cognitive Skill, and Labor Force Outcomes." *Sociology of Education* 74:1–24.

Kozol, Jonathan. 1991. *Savage Inequalities: Children in America's Schools.* New York: Crown Publishing.

Krueger, Alan B. 1998. "Reassessing the View that American Schools are Broken." *FRBNY Economic Policy Review* March:29–43.

Lee, Jaekyung. 2002. "Racial and Ethnic Achievement Gap Trends: Revising the Progress Toward Equity." *Educational Researcher* 31:3–12.

Lee, Valerie E. and David T. Burkam. 2002. *Inequality at the Starting Gate.* Washington, DC: Economic Policy Institute.

McCabe, Melissa. 2004. "Year-Round Schooling." *Education Week on the Web,* January 27. Education issues A–Z. Retrieved November 20, 2006 (http://www.edweek.org).

Murnane, Richard J. 1975. *The Impact of School Resources on the Learning of Inner City Children.* Cambridge, MA: Ballinger.

O'Brien, Daniel M. 1998. "Family and School Effects on the Cognitive Growth of Minority and Disadvantaged Elementary Students." Presented at the Association for Public Policy Analysis and Management, October 29–31, New York.

Phillips, Meredith. 2000. "Understanding Ethnic Differences in Academic Achievement: Empirical Lessons from National Data." Pp. 103–32 in *Analytic Issues in the Assessment of Student Achievement,* edited by U. S. Department of Education. Washington, DC: U. S. Department of Education, National Center for Education Statistics.

Phillips, Meredith, James Crouse, and John Ralph. 1998. "Does the Black-White Test Score Gap Widen After Children Enter School?" Pp. 229–72

in *The Black-White Test Score Gap,* edited by C. Jencks and M. Phillips. Washington, DC: Brookings.

Pope, Jean, Barry Lehrer, and James Stevens. 1980. "A Multiphasic Reading Screening Procedure." *Journal of Learning Disabilities* 13:98–102.

Ramey, Craig T., Frances A. Campbell, and Clancy Blair. 1998. "Enhancing the Life Course for High-Risk Children: Results from the Abecedarian Project." Pp. 163–83 in *Social Programs That Work,* edited by J. Crane. New York: Russell Sage Foundation.

Reardon, Sean F. 2003. *Sources of Inequality: The Growth of Racial/Ethnic and Socioeconomic Test Score Gaps in Kindergarten and First Grade.* Working Paper No. 03005, Population Research Institute, University Park, PA, Pennsylvania State University.

Reynolds, Arthur J. and Judy A. Temple. 1998. "Extended Early Childhood Intervention and School Achievement: Age Thirteen Findings from the Chicago Longitudinal Study." *Child Development* 69:231–46.

Rothstein, Richard. 2002. *Classes and Schools: Using Social, Economic, and Educational Reform to Close the Black-White Achievement Gap.* Washington, DC: Economic Policy Institute.

Royston, Patrick. 2004. "Multiple Imputation of Missing Values." *Stata Journal* 4:227–41.

———. 2005. "Multiple Imputation of Missing Values: Update." *Stata Journal* 5:88–102.

Schweinhart, Lawrence J. and David P. Weikart. 1998. "High/Scope Perry Preschool Program Effects at Age Twenty-Seven." Pp. 148–83 in *Social Programs That Work,* edited by J. Crane. New York: Russell Sage.

Weller, L. David, Carl J. Schnittjer, and Bertha A. Tuten. 1992. "Predicting Achievement in Grades Three Through Ten Using the Metropolitan Readiness Test." *Journal of Research in Childhood Education* 6:121–29.

West, Jerry, Kristin Denton, and Lizabeth M. Reaney. 2001. *The Kindergarten Year: Findings from the Early Childhood Longitudinal Study.* Technical Report No. NCES 2001-023. Washington, DC: National Center for Educational Statistics.

[16]

Personality differences in childhood and adolescence: measurement, development, and consequences

Rebecca Shiner[1] and Avshalom Caspi[2]

[1]Colgate University, USA; [2]Institute of Psychiatry, King's College London, UK &
University of Wisconsin-Madison, USA

Child psychologists and psychiatrists are interested in assessing children's personalities. This interest is fueled by the practical desire to identify differences between children that have predictive utility, and by recognition that future advances in developmental theory, especially in relation to gene-environment interplay, can only be as good as the measures on which they rely. The aim of this article is to facilitate these practical and theoretical advances. First, we delineate a taxonomy of measurable individual differences in temperament and personality in childhood, and point the reader to proven and/or promising measuring instruments. Second, we describe the processes through which early temperament differences may become elaborated into adult personality structure and lifelong adaptation, and identify gaps in the empirical research that need to be filled. Third, we explore the various connections between temperament/ personality traits and psychopathology, and direct attention to promising questions and strategies.

It is not necessary to conduct research to appreciate that children and adolescents differ in their personalities. Parents, teachers, child psychologists and psychiatrists, and other close observers of human nature can plainly see these differences. Some children are exuberant whereas others are reserved; some are irritable, others are even-tempered; some are aggressive, others gentle. However, research is needed to answer more nuanced questions about the measurement and consequences of such individual differences: What taxonomy best captures the variation in children's behavioral tendencies? How do children's earliest temperamental traits develop into later personality? Does childhood personality shape important life outcomes? How might childhood personality influence the emergence of psychopathology? Answers to these questions are crucial for those who wish to describe, explain, and predict the nature of individual lives across time. Research on personality development has been especially productive over the past 15 years, paralleling a similarly active period of research on personality psychology in general (Funder, 2001; Lubinski, 2000). In this article, we examine findings emerging from this research on personality development across childhood into adulthood. First, we delineate a taxonomy of measurable individual differences in temperament and personality in childhood. Second, we address the processes through which early individual differences shape adult personality and life adaptation. Third, we explore the mechanisms by which childhood personality may be linked with the emergence of psychiatric disorders. In short, we hope to (a) demonstrate that the existing data point to the reality and consequential nature of personality differences among children and adolescents, (b) orient the reader to proven and/or promising measuring

instruments and assessment tools, and (c) identify existing gaps in the empirical research that need to be filled.

What individual differences exist among children and adolescents, and how can these be measured?

Individual differences in childhood and adolescence are variously described as *temperament* traits or as *personality* traits. Most developmental models of temperament have emphasized behavioral consistencies that appear early in life, that are frequently but not exclusively emotional in nature, and that have a presumed biological basis (Cohen, 1999; Kagan, 1998; Rothbart & Bates, 1998; Shiner, 1998). Whereas temperament traits are typically considered the whole of personality in infancy, they form but a subset of personality differences in later childhood and adulthood. Personality refers more inclusively to people's tendencies to behave, think, and feel in certain consistent ways. Although temperament and personality have been demarcated as theoretically discrete domains, there is reason to believe that the two domains may be less distinct than often assumed (McCrae et al., 2000). Like temperament traits, nearly all personality traits – whether measured by self-reports or observer-reports – show moderate genetic influence (Bouchard & Loehlin, 2001), and individual differences in 'personality traits' have been identified in non-human animals as well (Gosling, 2001). Like personality traits, temperament traits are not immune from experience. Behavioral genetic studies have established that individual differences in temperament, measured even during the first few years of life, are only partially heritable and are influenced significantly by unique environmental events (Emde & Hewitt, 2001), including both pre- and postnatal experiences. Moreover, not all temperament traits can be measured in infancy, because some aspects of temperament come on-line later in development (e.g., some emotions, motor skills, arousal and attentional systems) (Rothbart, Ahadi, & Evans, 2000a, p. 124). Although most researchers and clinicians are reluctant to characterize infants and young children as having 'personalities,' the distinction between temperament and personality becomes increasingly unclear as children move out of infancy. Consequently, we discuss temperament and personality systems together throughout this review.

In thinking about how to measure and study individual differences in personality, it is important to acknowledge the galvanizing role of Thomas and Chess who, four decades ago, focused research and clinical attention on temperament differences between children. They conceptualized temperament 'as the stylistic component of behavior – that is, the *how* of behavior as differentiated from motivation, the *why* of behavior, and abilities, the *what* of behavior' (Goldsmith et al., 1987, p. 508). On the basis of this conceptualization, in 1956 they initiated a study of 141 infants and their parents (Thomas, Chess, Birch, Hertzig, & Korn, 1963; Thomas, Chess, & Birch, 1968). They submitted the first 22 parent interviews to an inductive content analysis to determine which categories of behavior appeared in all children and seemed to have potential significance for psychological development; they identified nine categories of behavior as important. Thomas and Chess's model of temperament continues to be highly influential, and their ideas about temperament are ubiquitous in popular guides to parenting.

Recent work on the measurement of temperament has revealed some limitations of Thomas and Chess's original temperament model. First, it has become increasingly clear that it is difficult to distinguish between the stylistic components of behavior and the motivation and content of behavior. For example, a particular child may be described as showing a positive approach tendency toward new situations; but this 'approach' trait contains both a motivational component (the child may be motivated to explore in novel situations) and specific content (the child expresses high levels of positive emotions). Second, factor analyses of parent and teacher questionnaires tapping the nine temperament traits have revealed that fewer than nine traits are captured in these measures (Martin, Wisenbaker, & Huttunen, 1994; Presley & Martin, 1994). Across studies, the most consistent evidence is found for the traits of irritable distress, social inhibition, activity level, and attention – four traits that are described more fully later in this review. Third, in the original model, mood was conceptualized as a continuum ranging from positive to negative mood. More recent

studies have demonstrated that children's tendencies toward positive and negative moods are independent and represent two different temperament traits (Rothbart, 1981; Goldsmith, 1996); the same is true for adults (Watson, Wiese, Vaidya, & Tellegen, 1999). By combining positive and negative emotions into opposite poles of a single dimension, the original Thomas and Chess model may have underestimated the developmental significance of children's temperamental tendencies toward positive emotions. Although some of the specifics of the Thomas–Chess taxonomy have not withstood the test of time, their keen clinical insights continue to provide the impetus for developing classification systems that can be used to describe individual differences between children.

Who needs a personality taxonomy?

One of the most daunting tasks in the study of individual differences in children (and adults) has been to develop a taxonomy of traits: How can we measure the traits that are the most robust and important, in the most parsimonious way? What are the most reliable patterns of covariation of traits across individuals? Students of personality development have used a bewildering array of measures and scales to describe individual differences between children, with the unfortunate consequence that results can be difficult to compare from one study to the next. Moreover, measures with the same name sometimes measure concepts that are not the same, and measures with different names sometimes measure constructs that overlap considerably in their content (Block, 1996). As long as 'each assessor has his own pet units and uses a pet battery of diagnostic devices' (Allport, 1958, p. 258), it will continue to be challenging to integrate the isolated empirical findings on children's individual differences.

Fortunately, there is increasing recognition that existing models of temperament and personality share many traits in common (Caspi, 1998; Church, 1994; Rothbart & Bates, 1998; Shiner, 1998; Watson, Clark, & Harkness, 1994). Progress in synthesizing disparate models of temperament and personality has been facilitated, in part, by the recognition that personality is organized hierarchically (Eysenck, 1947; Hampson, John, & Goldberg, 1986; Kohnstamm, Halverson, Mervielde, & Havill, 1998). At the highest level are those broad traits (e.g., extraversion) representing the most general dimensions of individual differences in personality. At successively lower levels are more specific traits (e.g., sociability, dominance) that are, in turn, composed of more specific responses (e.g., talkative, enthusiastic, good at leading others). In this hierarchical scheme, higher-order constructs can be shown to account for the observed covariation among lower-order constructs (Digman, 1990). By using a hierarchically organized structure like this, it is possible for developmental researchers to relate lower order traits to each other in a coherent taxonomic framework. To date, much of the developmental research on individual differences has focused on single lower-order traits (e.g., activity level, social inhibition, impulsivity, aggression) without examining those traits in relation to children's other traits. As a result, research on personality development is filled with many studies of convergent validity and relatively fewer studies of discriminant validity for individual traits (Revelle, 1993). The use of a personality taxonomy in developmental research could serve as a powerful antidote to this undesirable situation.

A personality taxonomy has three useful functions (Briggs, 1989). First, it can improve communication among researchers who are using different variables to study closely related phenomena; connecting multiple and different measures of personality to an established and validated personality structure helps to organize and integrate diffuse research findings. Second, it can provide researchers with a structure to use when they develop new measures of personality; locating new measures in relation to what is already known eliminates redundancy and elucidates psychological constructs. Third, it can enable researchers to connect personality measures to more elaborate nomological networks and thereby to interpret research and generate new hypotheses about the origins of individual differences in personality.

Linking personality structure in childhood and adulthood

In the last decade, adult personality researchers have moved toward increasing consensus about the higher-order structure of adult personality. These structural models of personality emphasize the importance of a smaller number of higher-order factors rather than a large number of more specific traits. Among the best established models is the five-factor model (or 'the Big Five'; Digman, 1990; John & Srivastava, 1999; McCrae & Costa, 1999), which emphasizes five broad dimensions that encompass numerous more specific dispositions. Several three-factor models have also received support (e.g., Eysenck's (1991) three-factor system; Tellegen's (1985) model of personality structure; Cloninger's model of temperament (Cloninger, Svrakic, & Przybeck, 1993)). For example, biologically oriented theorists have often pointed toward three higher-order domains that correspond with postulated neural structures underlying personality: an approach domain manifested in positive emotions; an avoidance domain manifested in negative emotions; and a constraint domain, manifested as tendencies to inhibit or express emotion and impulse. Although there are important differences among these various models, they overlap to a considerable degree. *Extraversion or*

Positive Emotionality is common to all systems; it describes the extent to which the person actively engages the world or avoids intense social experiences. *Neuroticism or Negative Emotionality* is also common to all systems; it describes the extent to which the person experiences the world as distressing or threatening. *Conscientiousness or Constraint* describes the extent and strength of impulse control: whether the person is able to delay gratification in the service of more distant goals or is unable to modulate impulsive expression. To these three dimensions, the five-factor model adds two more: Agreeableness and Openness to Experience. *Agreeableness* describes a person's interpersonal nature on a continuum from warmth and compassion to antagonism. Agreeable persons are empathic, altruistic, helpful, and trusting, whereas antagonistic persons are abrasive, ruthless, manipulative, and cynical. *Openness to Experience* describes the depth, complexity, and quality of a person's mental and experiential life.

Consensus about the structure of adult personality traits has important implications for developmental research: We now have greater clarity about the adult personality traits that developmental studies should be trying to predict over time. Developmental researchers have explored the possibility that childhood personality structure may share important similarities with adult personality structure, and there is now some evidence that such is the case, at least from preschool-age through adolescence (Halverson, Kohnstamm, & Martin, 1994; Kohnstamm et al., 1998). In a number of studies, four of the Big Five traits – Extraversion, Neuroticism, Conscientiousness, and Agreeableness – consistently have been obtained in factor analyses of parent and teacher ratings of adjective lists, questionnaires, and the California Child Q-Set (summarized in Shiner, 1998; also De Fruyt, Mervielde, Hoekstra, & Rolland, 2000; Goldberg, 2001; Halverson, Havill, & Deal, in press; McCrae et al., 2000; Mervielde & De Fruyt, 1999, 2002; Resing, Bleichrodt, & Dekker, 1999). The trait of Openness to Experience has been obtained in some studies of elementary-school age children and adolescents and includes potentially important characteristics such as curiosity, creativity, imagination, and intellect (Mervielde, De Fruyt, & Jarmuz, 1998); however, findings for this trait are less consistent than those obtained for the other four. An international study of parents' descriptions of their children's personalities has documented that the vast majority of these descriptors can be rationally classified as part of one of the Big Five traits (Kohnstamm et al., 1998); thus, the Big Five traits include domains seen as important to parents in describing their children.

Using a different model of childhood temperament, Rothbart and colleagues have examined parent ratings on the Children's Behavior Questionnaire (CBQ) in several studies of children ages 3 to 8 (Ahadi, Rothbart, & Ye, 1993; Rothbart et al., 2000a;

Rothbart, Ahadi, Hershey, & Fisher, 2001). These researchers discovered evidence for three higher-order factors similar to the adult traits of Extraversion/Surgency, Neuroticism/Negative Emotionality, and Conscientiousness/Constraint. Table 1 presents sample items measuring the four higher-order traits consistently obtained in the childhood Big Five studies and the three comparable higher-order traits obtained in the CBQ.

A proposed taxonomy of personality traits in children and adolescents

On the basis of research conducted with children and adolescents, we propose a preliminary taxonomy of individual differences in personality traits that can be measured in children from approximately preschool-age up (Shiner, 1998). For each higher-order trait, we describe the lower-order traits that are likely to be subsumed within it (Table 2). We assign the lower-order traits to the superfactors on the basis of current research relating lower- and higher-order traits in children and adults and on the basis of conceptually coherent links between the two. Our conceptualization of the higher-order traits largely draws on questionnaire studies in children, but our formulation of lower-order traits draws also on observational and lab-based research.

Extraversion/Positive Emotionality. Children vary in their tendencies to be vigorously, actively, and surgently involved with the world around them. In Big Five studies, children who are high on Extraversion are described as outgoing, expressive, energetic, and dominant with peers and adults. In contrast, those who are low on this superfactor are described as more quiet, inhibited, lethargic, and content to follow other children's lead. Rothbart and colleagues (2001) found evidence for a similar superfactor termed Surgency, which taps children's pleasure in high intensity situations, quick responsiveness, high activity level, and lack of distress in novel social situations. In adults, the trait of Extraversion is linked with the frequent experience of positive moods (Watson & Clark, 1997). Infants likewise exhibit individual differences in the expression of positive emotions (Goldsmith, 1996; Lemery, Goldsmith, Klinnert, & Mrazek, 1999), a temperament trait that predicts extraversion and approach later in childhood (Fox, Henderson, Rubin, Calkins, & Schmidt, 2001). Several researchers have argued that traits encompassed by Extraversion or Positive Emotionality may represent a biological system promoting active approach and exploration of the environment, including the social environment (Depue & Collins, 1999, Panksepp, 1998; Rothbart & Bates, 1998). Research with adults suggests that individuals high on these traits are particularly sensitive to potential rewards (Lucas, Diener, Grob, Suh, & Shao, 2000).

Extraversion/Positive Emotionality encompasses several lower-order traits: social inhibition, sociability, dominance, and activity level. *Social inhibition* reflects reluctance to act and feelings of discomfort in encounters with strangers or possibly other groups of people (Buss & Plomin, 1984). Clear evidence documents individual differences in 'social inhibition with strangers,' from early childhood through middle childhood and into adulthood (Kagan, 1998). Children who are high on this trait are withdrawn, fearful, and hesitant to interact when encountering new people. Over time, inhibition with strangers appears to become differentiated from 'shyness with known others.' Shyness with known others is sometimes linked with being rebuffed by other children, whereas stranger wariness shows no such detrimental outcomes (Asendorpf, 1990). Although social inhibition with strangers has been studied more frequently in children, shyness with known others may well prove to have greater significance for children's functioning by middle childhood.

Shyness is distinguishable from *sociability*, the preference to be with others rather than alone (Asendorpf & Meier, 1993). This distinction is especially apparent by middle childhood (Harrist, Zaia, Bates, Dodge, & Pettit, 1997; Mathiesen & Tambe, 1999), when children have increasing control over how they spend their time and whether they spend it alone or with others; at this point in development, individual differences in sociability and shyness may increasingly represent two different behavioral systems. Sociability may primarily tap elements of approach and positive emotionality, as it does in adults (Church, 1994; Tellegen & Waller, 1992). In contrast, shyness is more likely to be a multidimensional trait combining elements of low approach, high negative emotionality, and high behavioral avoidance (Eisenberg, Fabes, & Murphy, 1995; Nigg, 2000; Rothbart & Bates, 1998). The causes of shyness may, in fact, be quite heterogeneous; low levels of approach or high levels of fear-behavioral inhibition may each predominate in different individuals.

Dominance represents the extent to which a child exerts influence on others' (particularly other children's) behavior, in part through organizing their behavior. This dimension also encompasses a child's ability to act cooperatively and competitively to procure desirable resources (Charlesworth & Dzur, 1987; Hawley, 1999; Hawley & Little, 1999). In adults, this aspect of extraversion includes an individual's tendency to capture others' attention in social situations and to enjoy such attention (Tellegen, 1985; Watson & Clark, 1997). Not surprisingly, children who are dominant over their peers tend to excel in organizing activities and games (Sherif, Harvey, White, Hood, & Sherif, 1961); interestingly, such children also appear to be skilled in deceiving others through careful control of their nonverbal behavior (Keating & Heltman, 1994). Children's dominance may be important for understanding

6   Rebecca Shiner and Avshalom Caspi

Table 1 Examples of trait adjectives, California Child Q-sort items, and Child Behavior Questionnaire items defining four higher-order personality traits in children

Higher-Order Personality Trait	Trait descriptors[a]	Sample items	
		Child Q-sort items[b]	Child Behavior Questionnaire items[c]
Extraversion/ Positive Emotionality	Gregarious Energetic Directive Withdrawn (rev.)	Emotionally expressive A talkative child Fast-paced; moves and reacts to things quickly Inhibited or constricted (rev.)	Seems always in a hurry to get from one place to another Takes a lot of time in approaching new situations (rev.) Seems to be at ease with almost any person Likes rough and rowdy games
Neuroticism/ Negative Emotionality	Tense Concerned about acceptance Touchy Adaptable (rev.)	Fearful and anxious Tends to go to pieces under stress; becomes rattled and disorganized Self-reliant, confident (rev.) Appears to feel unworthy; thinks of self as 'bad'	Gets quite frustrated when prevented from doing something s/he wants to do Is very difficult to soothe when s/he has become upset Tends to become sad if the family's plans don't work out Is quite upset by a little cut or bruise
Conscientiousness/ Constraint	Persevering Planful Careful of personal belongings Diligent	Persistent in activities, does not give up easily Attentive and able to concentrate Planful; thinks ahead Reflective; thinks and deliberates before speaking or acting	When drawing or coloring in a book, shows strong concentration Is good at following instructions Prepares for trips and outings by planning things s/he will need Approaches places s/he has been told are dangerous slowly and cautiously
Agreeableness	Considerate Spiteful (rev.) Rude (rev.) Self-centered (rev.)	Warm and kind toward others Helpful and cooperative Teases other children (rev.) Tends to give, lend, and share	Not applicable

Note: Rev. = Item is scored in the reversed direction.

[a]Trait descriptors defining the higher-order factor in one of two studies. The first study included 2,572 Hawaiian elementary-school children whose teachers ranked the children in each class from highest to lowest on each descriptor (presented in 'Analyses of Digman's child-personality data: Derivation of Big-Five factor scores from each of six samples,' by L.R. Goldberg, 2001, *Journal of Personality*, 69, Appendix Table 1, pp. 732–737. Copyright 2001 by Blackwell Publishers. Adapted by permission.). The second study included 480 Russian children aged 8–10 whose teachers rated them on each descriptor (The structure of temperament and personality in Russian children' by J.M. Digman & A.G. Shmelyov, 1996, *Journal of Personality and Social Psychology, 71,* Table 4, p. 345. Copyright 1996 by the American Psychological Association. Adapted with permission).

[b]Abbreviated California Child Q-sort items defining the factor in two independent studies: (a) a study of 720 Dutch boys and girls who were Q-sorted by parents and teachers (van Lieshout & Haselager, 1993, 1994), and (b) a study of 350 African American and Caucasian boys aged 12–13 enrolled in the Pittsburgh Youth Study who were Q-sorted by their mothers (John, Caspi, Robins, Moffitt, & Stouthamer-Loeber, 1994). Items are from the *California Child Q-Set* by J.H. Block & J. Block, 1980, distributed by Mind Garden, www.mindgarden.com. Copyright 1980 by Consulting Psychologists Press. All rights reserved. Reprinted with permission.

[c]Children's Behavior Questionnaire items defining the factor in several studies of children aged 3–7 (Rothbart et al., 2001). Items are from the *Children's Behavior Questionnaire* by M.K. Rothbart, 1996, unpublished manuscript, University of Oregon. Copyright 1996 by the author. Reprinted with permission.

Table 2 A proposed taxonomy of higher-order and lower-order personality traits in childhood and adolescence

Higher-order traits	Extraversion/ Positive Emotionality	Neuroticism/ Negative Emotionality	Conscientiousness/ Constraint	Agreeableness
Lower-order traits	Social Inhibition/ Shyness Sociability Dominance Energy/ Activity Level	Anxious Distress Irritable Distress	Attention Inhibitory Control Achievement Motivation	Antagonism Prosocial tendencies

their emerging capacities for leadership; given the potential significance of this trait, it deserves more research attention than it has received in recent years.

In some studies, *energy/activity level* emerges as another component of extraversion or surgency (Goldberg, 2001; Rothbart et al., 2001). Children vary in their motor activity from infancy through at least early adolescence. Because children are much more motorically active than adults, activity level may be more salient in children and therefore may be more easily distinguished from related personality dimensions such as sociability (John, Caspi, Robins, Moffitt, & Stouthamer-Loeber, 1994). Eaton (1994) has argued persuasively that over time the high energy and motor activity of some children may become transformed into the greater talkativeness associated with extraversion in adults.

Neuroticism/Negative Emotionality. Just as children vary in their predisposition toward positive emotions, they vary in their susceptibility to negative emotions, including sadness, anxiety, anger, frustration, insecurity, and fear. Clinicians and researchers have been particularly interested in these traits, because they have rightly believed that children high in negative emotionality are at risk for psychiatric problems. Consequently, dimensions tapping negative emotionality emerge in all temperament and personality models. In Big Five studies, children who are high on Neuroticism are described as easily frightened, high-strung, 'falling apart' under stress, prone to feel guilty, low in self-esteem, angry, and insecure about relationships with others. Fewer descriptors define the lower end of this dimension; these include traits such as adaptability in novel situations, self-reliance, and self-confidence. In Rothbart and colleagues' work (2001), a Negative Affectivity superfactor encompasses children's tendencies toward fear, anger/frustration, sadness, and discomfort in the face of irritating or painful sensory stimuli. Children high on this trait also have difficulty settling and soothing themselves when aroused. In adults, a similar Negative Emotionality trait is defined by the tendency to experience a wide variety of negative emotions, to have negatively charged relationships, and to be vulnerable to the adverse effects of stress (Tellegen, 1985; Watson & Clark, 1984). Thus, research on personality superfactors suggests that children and adults who are prone to experience one type of negative emotion are also prone to experience other types of negative emotions as well.

A number of researchers have suggested that Negative Emotionality encompasses two related but distinct lower-order traits, one tapping fear and anxiety and the other tapping anger and irritability. Rothbart and Bates (1998) provide compelling evidence for two traits they label 'fearful distress' and 'irritable distress' in both infancy and early childhood. In older children, the former trait may be more appropriately labeled *anxious distress* because anxiety connotes a broader range of negative emotions, including fear. Anxious distress appears to tap inner-focused distress, including a child's tendency to withdraw fearfully from new situations; Big Five studies of children suggest that fearfulness is also linked with tendencies toward anxiety, insecurity, and guilt. This tendency to experience inner-directed negative emotions has been identified as both a vulnerability factor for and a core feature of many types of adult psychopathology, particularly the anxiety and depressive disorders (Mineka, Watson, & Clark, 1998; Watson et al., 1994). A more detailed understanding of the development of this trait could be extremely helpful in elucidating the pathways that lead to a variety of adult disorders.

In contrast, *irritable distress* taps distress directed outward, including children's tendencies toward irritability, anger, and frustration; these hostile emotions are often evoked by external limitations placed on children by adults (John et al., 1994; Rothbart & Bates, 1998). It is possible that this tendency toward irritability is more easily observed in children and adolescents than in adults, because individuals typically become more adroit at controlling the expression of negative emotions with age (Saarni, 1999). With age, irritable distress may be as strongly related to Agreeableness as it is to Negative Emotionality. Because irritable distress and anxious distress are likely to follow different developmental paths and predict different outcomes, these two lower-order traits should be investigated separately in many instances.

Conscientiousness/Constraint. Children vary widely in their capacities for cognitive, behavioral, and emotional control (Strayhorn, 2002). As Block

(1996) noted, 'with different terminology and with different orientation and intentions, there long has been recognition in developmental psychology and in personality psychology of the crucial importance of behavior monitoring and behavior modulation' (p. 28). An overarching Conscientiousness/Constraint higher-order dimension taps children's individual differences in control. In Big Five studies of children and adolescents, the Conscientiousness superfactor encompasses descriptors such as responsible, attentive, persistent, orderly and neat, planful, and thinks before acting; the low end of the dimension includes traits such as irresponsible, unreliable, careless, quits easily, and distractible. Rothbart and colleagues (2001) have identified a similar superfactor termed Effortful Control, which includes children's capacities to plan behavior, inhibit inappropriate responses, focus and shift attention, take pleasure in low intensity situations, and perceive subtle external stimuli. Posner and Rothbart (2000) have argued that children's individual differences in control and constraint may be related to biological differences in executive attentional systems that develop across early childhood and the early school years. In fact, evidence suggests that the ability to focus attention in infancy predicts Effortful Control later in childhood (Kochanska, Murray, & Harlan, 2000).

The traits of Conscientiousness and Constraint are typically seen as involving voluntary control of behavior, as implied by the labels 'Effortful Control' (Rothbart et al., 2001) and 'Will' (Digman & Inouye, 1986). It is important to distinguish this type of executive control from other types of relatively more involuntary tendencies toward inhibited behavior (Eisenberg, Fabes, Guthrie, & Reiser, 2000; Nigg, 2000). Children's behavior may be inhibited because of low approach tendencies (i.e., low levels of extraversion/positive emotionality) or because of high levels of fear or other negative emotions (i.e., high levels of neuroticism/negative emotionality). These distinctions among different sources of inhibited behavior are crucial for resolving the thorny issue of whether high levels of behavioral constraint ought to be seen as positive or negative. Block and Block (1980) have argued that it is possible to manifest too much constraint, because individuals whose behavior is too inhibited may not have their needs met in the environment. Although inhibition due to low approach or high fear may be problematic or adaptive, depending on the context, high *voluntary* control is likely to be an asset in most life circumstances. In fact, active, effortful control in early childhood predicts better self-regulation of anger and joy later in childhood (Kochanska et al., 2000). Children's emerging capacities for executive control may serve, in part, to regulate the approach and negative emotional systems.

Conscientiousness/Constraint includes at least three lower-order traits: attention, inhibitory control,

and achievement motivation. *Attention* taps children's capacity to regulate attention by shifting mental sets, focus attention, and persist at tasks in the face of distractions. Individual differences in this trait are measured by many neuropsychological tests requiring a high level of focus (e.g., White et al., 1994). Because deficits in attention have implications for children's academic achievement and conduct, a great deal of research has focused on the negative end of this personality dimension, particularly as the trait is expressed in Attention Deficit/Hyperactivity Disorder (ADHD). A second lower-order dimension of Constraint encompasses *inhibitory control* vs. behavioral impulsivity, a dimension that ranges from the tendency to be planful, cautious, and controlling of one's behavior to the tendency to be incautious, careless, and undercontrolled (Kochanska et al., 2000).

A third component appears to be *achievement motivation* (Halverson et al., in press; Mervielde & De Fruyt, 1999, 2002); children who are high on this trait strive for high standards, work hard, and are persistent in completing activities. This trait is similar to *mastery motivation*, a trait frequently studied in children (Gottfried, 1990; Harter, 1981; Eccles, Wigfield, & Schiefele, 1998). Children high on mastery motivation are motivated by curiosity or interest, take great pleasure in mastering their environments, and prefer challenging tasks to easy ones (Shiner, 2000). Achievement motivation emphasizes the role of self-control, whereas mastery motivation emphasizes the role of positive emotions and pleasure in striving. It is possible that both types of striving are important for children's development and that individuals who are high on both types of motivation are particularly effective in school and work environments.

Other lower-order components of Conscientiousness/Constraint may certainly exist, such as orderliness (Mervielde & De Fruyt, 1999, 2002), but have not been investigated as separable dimensions. Further work is needed to untangle the primary traits underlying cognitive, behavioral, and emotional control in children, as these components are not well differentiated in most personality measures.

Agreeableness. Agreeableness has been an important trait in research on both children and adults (Graziano & Eisenberg, 1997). In the Big Five model, the high end of this trait includes children's tendencies toward prosocial behavior; for example, descriptors such as cooperative, considerate, empathic, close to others, generous, polite, kind, and gets along well with others. At the low end, this trait includes antagonistic and disagreeable trait descriptors such as selfish, aggressive, rude, spiteful, teases others, stubborn, and manipulative. In some studies (e.g., Halverson et al., in press; Mervielde & De Fruyt, 1999, 2002), some items measure how manageable the child is for parents and teachers, a developmental distinction from the adult Agreeableness trait. The low end of the Agreeableness dimension is linked to the aforementioned trait of irritable distress; both traits involve the expression of anger and irritability. However, disagreeableness can still be seen as distinct from irritable distress because it is possible for children to experience frequent feelings of anger, irritability, and frustration without directing those feelings toward others and behaving in a hostile manner. Aggressive and disagreeable children may be those whose strong feelings of anger and frustration are not tempered by good self-control. Overall, children who are high on the overarching Agreeableness dimension tend to exhibit traits that foster congenial relationships with peers and adults; these same children tend *not* to exhibit traits that engender hostility.

It is interesting that, although Agreeableness has emerged consistently in questionnaire studies that tap a wide range of child behavior, the traits encompassed by this superfactor are not included in most temperament questionnaires. Perhaps these traits have been seen as less 'basic' than other temperamental traits; in other words, temperament researchers may have considered prosocial and hostile tendencies as the developmental products of more basic, early-emerging temperament traits. There is some evidence supporting this assumption. For example, parent-reported aggression at age 7 is predicted moderately to strongly by infant laboratory measures of frustration and activity level (Rothbart, Derryberry, & Hershey, 2000b). Thus, infants who exhibit strong approach tendencies and high levels of irritable distress may be at risk for developing into more aggressive children. Although Agreeableness may be a complex product of earlier traits and environmental influences, it is still an individual difference dimension that is worthy of study in childhood, and it is unfortunate that this cluster of traits has been left out of most temperament models for older children (Laursen, Pulkkinen, & Adams, 2002).

The two poles of Agreeableness – *antagonism* and *prosocial tendencies* – have been studied separately as distinct traits (Bohart & Stipek, 2001). Quite understandably, developmental researchers have been very interested in the processes that support the development of prosocial traits and the inhibition of antisocial traits. There is abundant evidence that children differ significantly in their levels of physical aggression (Tremblay, 2000) and relational aggression, which includes gossiping and social exclusion (Crick et al., 2001). Children also differ markedly in their levels of empathy and prosocial behavior (Eisenberg, 2000). It will be important for developmental researchers to continue to study these two lower-order straits separately from one another. Graziano and Eisenberg (1997) have suggested that antisocial and prosocial tendencies may eventually prove not to be opposite ends of a single dimension, although they tend to covary negatively. Support for this view comes from research pointing to etiological distinctions between antisocial and prosocial behavior (Krueger, Hicks, & McGue, 2001): Antisocial tendencies are most clearly linked to high Negative Emotionality and low Constraint whereas prosocial tendencies are more clearly linked to low Negative Emotionality and high Positive Emotionality. Also, whereas genetic influences account for a majority of the variance in antisocial tendencies, shared, family-wide environmental experiences account for a significant amount of the variance in prosocial tendencies. Apparently, antisocial and prosocial tendencies can exist in the same person because they spring from different developmental influences.

Maintaining a developmental perspective on childhood personality

Five caveats must be noted, in closing this review of a personality taxonomy for childhood and adolescence. First, a personality taxonomy is an *evolving* classification system whose purpose is to integrate and guide research. This also means that any such system must be open to empirical refutation and requisite modification. There are historical parallels between the use of structural models in personality psychology and the use of a standardized model for describing and diagnosing mental illness in psychiatry. Prior to the advent of the American Psychiatric Association's *Diagnostic and Statistical Manual of Mental Disorders III* (DSM-III), clinicians and researchers did not have available explicit criteria to define the boundaries of diagnostic categories. Clinical diagnoses were difficult to compare and cross-sample replications were hard to conduct. The development of DSM-III was a big improvement because it provided a common language with which clinicians and researchers could communicate about the disorders they were treating or investigating. DSM-III had its share of problems, and subsequent modifications (DSM-III-R, DSM-IV) testify to the need for a flexible and evolving system that can accommodate new empirical information, as do recommended modifications in anticipation of DSM-V (Widiger & Clark, 2000). We can similarly hope that the use of a generally accepted trait taxonomy will help to impose structure on unintegrated research findings, reduce the likelihood that old traits will be reinvented under new labels, and advance the study of personality development across the life span.

Second, although we have described a hierarchical system for organizing personality information, we do not mean to advocate studying personality variation only at the highest level of abstraction; that is, in terms of higher-order, general superfactors. These superfactors are too broad to capture all the interesting variation in children's personality, and distinctions at the level of more specific, lower-order traits are necessary (McAdams, 1992). Such is the case, for example, if using structural models of personality traits to distinguish between different personality disorders (Lynam & Widiger, 2001; Widiger, Trull, Clarkin, Sanderson, & Costa, 2002); recent work suggests that categorical personality disorders are distinguished by particular patterns of dimensional lower-order personality traits. The advantage of broad, higher-order superfactors is their substantial bandwidth; the disadvantage of broad superfactors is their low fidelity (Robins, John, & Caspi, 1994). There is much to learn from studying variation at different levels of the personality trait hierarchy, but this does not obviate the need to understand how different levels are related hierarchically to each other.

Third, more research is needed about the cross-cultural generalizability of the taxonomic system reviewed here. The evidence for it comes almost exclusively from studies of children in Western Europe and North America (albeit with some ethnic heterogeneity). Cross-cultural studies of adult personality structure have been pursued vigorously over the past decade (Church, 2001), but children have been left out of these studies. In pursuing cross-cultural comparisons, it is worth bearing in mind that such comparisons can address at least three different questions (McCrae, 2001): *Transcultural* studies seek to identify human universals in trait structure and developmental processes; *intracultural* studies seek to examine the unique expressions that personality traits may have in specific cultures; *intercultural* studies seek to understand different cultures in terms of their differences in mean levels of personality traits.

Fourth, children should be viewed holistically (Bergman & Cairns, 2000). Children's behavioral tendencies are likely to be inter-related and to influence each other over time. For example, a boy who frequently experiences a high level of negative emotions may have a more difficult time mastering self-control, because he has to contend with stronger surges of anger and sadness. This points to a possible limitation of existing structural models of personality which represent a *dimensional*, or variable-centered, approach to classification concerned with systematizing the enormous differences *between* individuals. In contrast, a *typological*, or person-centered approach, aims to develop a taxonomy not of personality variables but of personality types, and is concerned with the overall structure of personality dimensions *within* individuals. Efforts to classify people rather than variables are still in their early stages of development. Moreover, the descriptive and predictive efficiency and utility of dimensional versus typological approaches await more explicit evaluation (Asendorpf, Caspi, & Hostee, 2002).

Fifth, children's maturation permits the development and expression of new behaviors, which may result in a different personality structure over development (Shiner, Tellegen, & Masten, 2001). The

development of motor skills, language, cognition, self-awareness, self-concept, and empathy all influence the personality characteristics that children can have or display. Although it is tempting to make conceptual links between early temperament dimensions and later personality, empirical work is needed to test the reality of those links and to elucidate the processes by which early temperamental differences between children become elaborated into full-fledged personality differences in later life. We now turn to this topic.

Personality across the life course

From temperament to personality: The process of elaboration

If temperament is the core around which subsequent personality dimensions develop, it is important to understand how phenotypes emerge out of person–environment transactions. The process of developmental elaboration refers to the mechanisms by which those temperament attributes that are part of each individual's genetic heritage accumulate response strength through their repeated reinforcement and become elaborated into cognitive and affective representations that are quickly and frequently activated. This elaboration may involve at least six processes (Table 3), which we now describe in the order of their hypothesized developmental emergence. For example, 'learning processes' and 'environmental elicitation' are hypothesized to influence the course of subsequent personality development already in the first few months of life; 'environmental construal' and 'social comparison processes' can influence personality development only following the emergence of necessary cognitive functions in early and middle childhood; and environmental 'selection' and 'manipulation' require the emergence of self-regulatory functions in later childhood and adolescence.

Learning processes. Temperament differences may influence several learning mechanisms that are involved in the elaboration process, including discrimination learning, extinction, reinforcement, and punishment. For example, Eysenck (1977), in his autonomic conditioning theory of adult antisocial personality disorder, hypothesized that stimulus generalization should be enhanced through parents' verbal labeling of misbehaviors as 'naughty,' 'bad,' or 'wicked.' But children with verbal-skill deficits might not profit from the labeling of a class of behaviors as punishment-attracting; they may have to learn by trial and error. Verbally impaired children thus experience more frequent punishment events than verbally adept children, but with proportionately less result in curbing their problem behaviors. More generally, different parenting socialization practices interact with childhood temperament in

Table 3 Processes through which early temperament/personality may shape the development of later personality, adaptation, and psychopathology

Process	Definition	Example
Learning processes	Temperament shapes the child's experience of classical and operant conditioning.	Children low on Anxious Distress may have difficulty learning through punishment.
Environmental elicitation	Temperament shapes the response of adults and peers to the child.	Children high on Positive Emotionality may attract peers to play with them.
Environmental construal	Temperament shapes the ways that children interpret the environment and their experiences.	Children high on Antagonism may interpret requests from adults as hostile impositions on their freedom.
Social and temporal comparisons	Temperament shapes the ways children evaluate themselves relative to others and to themselves across time.	Children high on Anxious Distress may wrongly view themselves as inadequate relative to their peers.
Environmental selection	Temperament shapes children's choices about their day-to-day environments.	Children high on Achievement Motivation may pursue challenging activities.
Environmental manipulation	Temperament shapes the ways that children alter, modify, and manipulate their environments.	Children high on Dominance may actively persuade other children to choose them as leaders of school groups.

the development of personality (Kochanska, 1991, 1997). For example, fearful children show more positive conscience development when mothers use subtle, gentle, psychological discipline than when mothers use strongly power-assertive discipline. In contrast, parental discipline is less predictive of conscience development for fearless children; rather, these children tend to develop stronger internalization when they are securely attached to their mothers and when their mothers are more responsive to them.

Environmental elicitation. Temperament differences also elicit different reactions from the environment and influence how other people react to children, beginning already in the first few months of life (Bell & Chapman, 1986). Research about this process is especially well developed in relation to 'difficult' temperament and related behavior problems; much less is known about other temperament differences. However, research has shown that individual differences in temperament and personality traits are reliably expressed in unique verbal and nonverbal behaviors, and that other persons in the immediate environment react to these behaviors and use this information to make inferences and attributions (Borkenau & Liebler, 1995; Gifford, 1994).

Perhaps most striking is evidence linking individual differences in adolescent personality and psychopathology to facial expressions of discrete emotions. For example, Extraversion predicts facial expressions of social approach; Agreeableness is negatively correlated with facial expressions of anger; and Conscientiousness is associated with reduced facial expressions of negative emotion and with embarrassment (Eisenberg, Fabes, Miller, Fultz, Shell, et al., 1989; Keltner, 1998; Keltner, Moffitt, & Stouthamer-Loeber, 1995). Facial expressions convey information to other people about the individual's personality. It is possible that these observable 'markers' of personality lead primary caretakers and other adults to attribute psychological

qualities to children, which are subsequently internalized as part of children's emerging self concept.

Research on developmental changes in children's understanding of personality – and the relation of this changing understanding to internalization – suggests that children may be especially sensitive to feedback from adults and peers starting in middle childhood (Sameroff & Haith, 1996). Adults' and peers' verbal messages (reinforcements, attributions) to children about their personal characteristics and behavior may especially influence children's personality development around middle childhood for several reasons. During this period children increasingly develop an understanding of personality consistency (see Eisenberg et al., 1987; Grusec & Redler, 1980). Children also increasingly can describe themselves using trait labels and can see themselves in more complex ways, such as possessing simultaneously attributes that are opposite in valence (e.g., smart and dumb) (Harter, 1998). Thus, because children can hold more complex self-views during middle childhood, children may respond more strongly to feedback about their dispositions during this period.

It should be noted that temperament characteristics may elicit not only behaviors on the part of others, but also *expectations*. Adults have implicit theories about developmental trajectories that they associate with particular temperament attributes. As such, children's temperament-based behaviors elicit expectancy-based reactions from adult caregivers (Graziano, Jensen-Campbell, & Sullivan-Logan, 1998).

Environmental construal. With the emergence of belief systems and expectations, temperament differences may also begin to influence how environmental experiences are construed, thus shaping each person's 'effective experience' of the environment (Hartup & van Lieshout, 1995). For example, temperament differences in impulse control may influence children's reaction to demands for effortful attention and concentration in educational settings (e.g., Mischel, Shoda, & Peake, 1988), turning school into a frustrating experience for some and an engaging experience for others. Research about the construal process stems from the cognitive tradition in personality psychology that emphasizes each person's subjective experience and unique perception of the world. This research focuses on what people 'do' mentally (Cantor, 1990), demonstrating that social information processing – including attention, encoding, retrieval, and interpretation – is a selective process shaped by individual differences in temperament and personality (Fiske & Taylor, 1991).

The role of cognitive factors in personality and psychopathology has been detailed by Crick and Dodge (1994), whose social information-processing model of children's social adjustment includes five steps: (1) to encode information about the event; (2) to interpret the cues and arrive at some decision about their meaning and significance; (3) to search for possible responses to the situation; (4) to consider the consequences of each potential response and to select a response from the generated alternatives; and (5) to carry out the selected response. Research has identified individual differences in processing social information at all of these steps (e.g., Quiggle, Garber, Panak, & Dodge, 1992). Individual differences in social information-processing may play a more important role in automatic rather than in controlled processing of social information (e.g., Rabiner, Lenhart, & Lochman, 1990) and may be especially influential in cognitive processing of emotional information (Rusting, 1998). For example, functional imaging reveals that extraversion is correlated with brain reactivity to positive stimuli in localized brain regions whereas neuroticism is correlated with brain reactivity to negative stimuli in localized brain regions (Canli et al., 2001). Although research on temperament and information processing is well developed in regard to introversion-extraversion and neuroticism in adults, much less is known about other individual differences (Derryberry & Reed, 1994a).

Social and temporal comparisons. With increased cognitive sophistication (e.g., role-taking skills), two social-psychological processes are hypothesized to influence self-evaluations: Children learn about themselves by comparing and contrasting themselves to others (social comparisons) as well as to themselves over time (temporal comparisons). The salience and relative importance of social and temporal comparisons may change across the life course (Suls & Mullen, 1982). Age-related changes in social cognition, as well as changing social roles, suggest that social comparisons may be especially influential from childhood to adolescence and into adulthood, and that temporal comparisons may become increasingly more important during the adult years. The maturational changes that transpire beginning

in middle childhood are accompanied by environmental changes that increasingly facilitate social comparisons. Once in school, children spend significantly more time with peers, participate in more structured activities, and are evaluated with more stringent standards by a greater variety of adults (Harter, 1998). The period of adolescence and young adulthood is devoted to identity construction in new social roles and with new social contacts (Arnett, 2000), thus continuing to favor social comparisons. However, later periods of life may favor temporal comparisons, in part because social contacts tend to be with others with whom people already have shared histories (Carstensen, 1995).

Most of the research on comparison processes has focused on achievement-related behaviors with non-family members; less is known about how these processes are related to the course of personality development. This area of research is potentially fertile. Social comparisons in sibling relationships represent a potent source of environmental influence on personality development in childhood (Dunn, 1996), but there is surprisingly little research on how within-family comparisons shape personality traits and self-evaluations (Tesser, 1980). In adulthood, co-construction of the past is an important part of adults' social relationships, and temporal comparisons may have important implications for adult development (Pasupathi, 2001). However, little is known about which personality traits are most influenced by comparison processes, and how individual differences in temperament and personality influence such comparisons (Derryberry & Reed, 1994b). It is possible that attentional biases shape the type of comparison information to which different persons attend. Temperament and personality differences may also influence responsivity to different types of comparison information and thereby influence emotional reactions (e.g., fear, sadness, or shame) to both social and temporal comparisons.

Environmental selection. As self-regulatory competencies increase with age, individuals begin to make choices and display preferences that may reinforce and sustain their characteristics. Processes of environmental selection are likely to become increasingly important across the years from childhood to adulthood (Scarr & McCartney, 1983). As children move into middle childhood, they are given greater freedom to choose the environments in which they spend their time (Cole & Cole, 1996). In adulthood, individuals make choices regarding education, occupation, and intimate relationships which shape their day-to-day environments. Indeed, by adulthood the most striking personality differences between individuals are to be found not by studying their responses to the same situation but by studying how they choose and construct new situations (Wachtel, 1973). Although the mechanisms that produce such person–situation correlations are not entirely understood, it is apparent that different personalities, by virtue of their behaviors and characteristics, construct social contexts and generate life situations that are congruent with their personalities (Ickes, Snyder, & Garcia, 1997). A person's selection and creation of environments is thus one of the most individualizing and pervasive expressions of his or her personality, and research has shown that individuals' dispositions can lead them to select situations that, in turn, reinforce and sustain those same dispositions (e.g., Magnus et al., 1993).

Environmental manipulation. Once the self-concept is firmly established, and with the development of more sophisticated self-regulatory capacities, individuals also begin to alter, modify, and manipulate the environments in which they find themselves (Buss, 1987). These processes may become particularly important as children become more skilled in regulating their own behavior and more insightful about the causes of others' behaviors. Observational studies point to individual differences in the strategies children use to influence and change the behavior of others (Raush, 1965). Experimental studies with adults likewise show that people alter social situations so that they receive feedback from their environment that confirms their personality characteristics. They do this by adopting behavioral strategies that confirm their self-conceptions and by resisting feedback that clashes with their self-conceptions (Swann, 1996). Environmental manipulation need not be confined to behavioral acts; especially in later periods of life, it may also involve reconstructing the personal past in ways that are consistent with current self-conceptions (McAdams, 1996).

We have described six processes through which endogenous-biological and experiential-learning sources of influence may serve to elaborate an initial disposition over time so that it increasingly organizes emotion, thought, and action. Research is now needed about each of these processes in relation to different temperament and personality traits. The emergence of a consensual, taxonomic system for describing individual differences in temperament and personality may facilitate such a research program and enable students of personality development to shift their concern from studies of structure (e.g., describing the structure of individual differences) to studies of developmental processes (e.g., the elaboration of a temperament trait over time).

Stability of personality traits across the life span

Personality traits are thought, by definition, to reflect stable individual differences. But what does the longitudinal evidence actually show? Stability is most often indexed by the correlation between personality scores across two points in time (i.e., test-retest correlations). These differential, or rank-order,

correlations reflect the degree to which the relative ordering of individuals on a given trait is maintained over time. Rank-order stability is influenced by maturational or experiential factors that differentially affect people, as well as by measurement error.

Two contradictory predictions have been proposed about the rank-order stability of personality traits. The *classical trait perspective* argues that personality traits in adulthood are biologically based 'temperaments' that are not susceptible to the influence of the environment and thus do not change over time (McCrae et al., 2000). From this 'essentialist' perspective, we would expect the test-retest correlations to be high, even in childhood and adolescence. In contrast, the *contextual perspective* emphasizes the importance of life changes and role transitions in personality development and suggests that personality should be fluid, prone to change, and yield low test-retest correlation coefficients, particularly earlier in life (Lewis, 2001).

Existing longitudinal studies do not support either of these extreme positions. A recent meta-analysis of the rank-order stability of personality led to four major conclusions (Roberts & DelVecchio, 2000): Correlations over time (a) are moderate in magnitude, even from childhood to early adulthood, (b) increase as the age of the subjects increases, (c) decrease as the time interval between observations increases, and (d) do not vary markedly from trait to trait.

Two deductions can be drawn from this meta-analysis. First, personality continuity in childhood and adolescence is much higher than originally expected (cf. Lewis, 2001), especially after age three. Although character is by no means fate in childhood, there are striking continuities from childhood through adulthood that point to the importance of childhood temperament and the effects of cumulative continuity from childhood through adolescence (Caspi, 2000). Second, personality continuity in adulthood peaks later than expected. According to one prominent perspective, personality traits are essentially fixed and unchanging after age 30 (Costa & McCrae, 1994). However, the meta-analytic findings show that rank-order stability peaks some time after age 50, but at a level well below unity; test-retest correlations (unadjusted for measurement error) increased from .41 in childhood to .55 at age 30, and then reached a plateau around .70 between ages 50 and 70. Thus, individual differences in personality traits continue to change throughout adulthood, but only modestly after age 50.

Childhood personality and life outcomes

Early individual differences have the potential to shape how children experience, interpret, and respond to the world around them (Caspi, 1998). Childhood personality plays an important role in children's relative success or failure at the future developmental tasks they face; for example, in the cultivation of social relationships, the mastery of educational and work tasks, and the promotion and maintenance of health. Likewise, children's personalities leave them vulnerable to or protect them from maladaptation and psychopathology (Ingram & Price, 2001; Zuckerman, 1999).

Before turning to ask whether (and if so, which) personality traits in childhood and adolescence influence which particular life outcomes, it is important to comment about the ontological status of personality traits. There is much waffling about whether traits are descriptive summaries of observable consistencies in a person's behavior or explanatory concepts. The former view has contributed to the caricature of traits as static, nondevelopmental conceptions of personality, whereas the latter view sees personality traits as organizational constructs that influence how individuals meet environmental demands and new developmental challenges. We take sides with Allport (1937, p. 48; see also, Funder, 1991) who argued for a realist conception of traits as explanatory concepts: 'Personality is and does something ... It is what lies behind specific acts and within the individual.' However, traits are hypothetical constructs rather than observable entities, and their usefulness needs to be demonstrated through a process of construct validation (Tellegen, 1991; Zuroff, 1986). Traits are not an end, but 'placeholders' in an evolving search for social, psychological, and biological processes that provide fuller explanations of behavior (Fletcher, 1993). Structural models of personality will be most useful when traits are linked to these processes that shape characteristic adaptations across the life course (McCrae & Costa, 1999).

To examine how personality shapes the course of life, one must also have a way of thinking about the life course itself. Three conceptual approaches can be identified. An *organizational-adaptational perspective* focuses on tasks and milestones that are encountered during the course of development and on how these are met by different personalities (Masten & Coatsworth, 1995; Sroufe, Carlson, & Shulman, 1993; van Lieshout, 2000). According to this perspective, personality traits influence problem-solving modalities that individuals use when meeting new developmental challenges at different points in the life course (e.g., developing competent peer relationships in childhood, establishing appropriate cross-sex relationships in adolescence, learning to parent in early adulthood, providing for dependent parents in middle age). Especially beyond childhood, as the individual increasingly negotiates social roles defined by the culture, a purely psychological approach to the study of personality coherence may be insufficient. Some researchers have thus found it useful to also adopt a *sociocultural perspective* and to conceive of the life course as a sequence of culturally defined, age-graded roles that

the individual enacts over time (Caspi, 1987). In this fashion, personality coherence can be explored by investigating consistencies in the ways different persons select and perform different social-cultural roles (e.g., Helson, Mitchell, & Moane, 1984; Gest, 1997). Finally, evolutionary psychologists note that a purely sociocultural perspective is inadequate for understanding how personality differences shape the life course, and suggest that it is critical to explore how personality differences are related to those adaptively important problems with which human beings have had to repeatedly contend (Bouchard, 1995). An *evolutionary-psychology perspective* thus focuses attention on the coherence of behavioral strategies that people use in, for example, mate selection, mate retention, reproduction, parental care, kin investment, status attainment, and coalition building (Buss, 1999). These three approaches, or 'road maps for studying personality across the life course,' share an important assumption: Continuities of personality across the life course are expressed not merely through the constancy of behavior across time and in diverse circumstances, but also through the consistency over time in the ways that persons characteristically modify their changing contexts as a function of their behavior. Below, we provide three illustrations of how early personality differences shape different developmental domains.

Cultivating relationships: Friendships, intimate relationships, and parenting. One of the most important tasks faced by children and adolescents is the establishment of friendships and acceptance among peers (Hartup & Stevens, 1999; Masten & Coatsworth, 1998). Among children, all of the higher-order personality traits described previously are important predictors of social competence. Perhaps so many aspects of personality predict social competence because social functioning requires a wide array of skills, including emotional expression, emotional understanding, and emotional and behavioral regulation (Denham, 1998; Rubin et al., 1998). More Agreeable and Extraverted children show better social competence concurrently and across time (Gest, 1997; Jensen-Campbell & Graziano, 2001; Shiner, 2000). Children high on Negative Emotionality or low on Constraint have a variety of social difficulties concurrently and across time (Eisenberg et al., 1997); the interaction of these traits may be especially problematic for social functioning (Eisenberg et al., 2000).

Personality continues to be an important predictor of relationships in adulthood. Attaining a satisfying intimate relationship is the most important goal in many people's lives (Roberts & Robins, 2000). Negative Emotionality is the strongest and most consistent personality predictor of negative relationship outcomes – including relationship dissatisfaction, conflict, abuse, and, ultimately, dissolution (Karney

& Bradbury, 1995). These effects have been uncovered in long-term studies following samples of
children into adulthood, as well as in shorter-term
longitudinal studies of adults. The potential contribution of stable personality differences to shaping
abusive relationships has been further underscored
by several longitudinal studies that found associations between early developing aggressive behavior
patterns in childhood and subsequent abusive behavior in adult romantic relationships (Moffitt &
Caspi, 1998). One study that followed a large sample
of adolescents across their multiple relationships in
early adulthood discovered that the influence of
Negative Emotionality on relationship quality
showed cross-relationship generalization; that is, it
predicted the same relationship experiences across
relationships with different partners (Robins, Caspi,
& Moffitt, in press).

There are three transactional processes by which
personality traits may affect relationship outcomes,
partly by altering micro-interactional processes in
the course of the relationship. Consider the case of
Negative Emotionality – why might individuals high
in Negative Emotionality grow up to have unhappy
relationships? First, they may *select* partners who
are similar to themselves. Assortative mating – the
tendency for people to form unions with similar
others – has known genetic and social consequences,
and it may also have implications for the course of
personality development because similarities between couple members create interpersonal experiences that reinforce initial tendencies (Caspi &
Herbener, 1990). Second, people high in Negative
Emotionality may *react* to and interpret the behaviors of their partners in trait-correlated ways. For
example, high Negative Emotionality individuals are
more likely to be physiologically reactive and to es-
calate negative affect during conflict (e.g., Gottman,
Coan, Carrere, & Swanson, 1998). Cognitive processes also come on line in creating trait-correlated
experiences. For example, high Negative Emotionality individuals may overreact to minor criticism from
their partner, believe they are no longer loved when
their partner does not call, or assume infidelity on
the basis of mere flirtation. Trait-correlated anticipatory attitudes lead individuals to project particular
interpretations onto new social relationships, and
individuals also transfer trait-correlated affective
responses developed in the context of previous relationships to new relationships (e.g., Andersen &
Baum, 1994). People bring histories to relationships,
and these histories are captured in part by stable
personality traits (Epstein, 1991). Third, people high
in Negative Emotionality may *evoke* behaviors from
their partner that contribute to the demise of their
relationships. For example, high Negative Emotionality individuals are prone to express four behaviors
identified as detrimental to relationships: criticism,
contempt, defensiveness, and stonewalling (Gottman, 1994). In short, individuals create trait-cor-

related micro-interactional processes that affect the
course and quality of intimate relationships; these
processes do not occur in a vacuum or arise *de novo*.

Whereas a great deal of research has investigated
the influence of personality on friendships and intimate relationships, fewer studies have considered
the possibility that parents' personalities may shape
their parenting styles and relationships with their
children (Belsky & Barends, 2002). This is a curious
omission because parental personality forms a critical part of children's developmental context (Goldsmith et al., 1994). Moreover, behavioral genetic
studies show that many parenting behaviors are
highly heritable (Plomin, 1994). This does not, of
course, mean that there is a gene for parenting
styles. What it does suggest is that individual differences in parenting behaviors are related to certain
psychological characteristics that are strongly influenced by genetic factors. The handful of studies
that have examined personality → parenting associations – using self-reports as well observations of
parenting – suggest that parental Positive Emotionality and Agreeableness are related to sensitive and
responsive parenting, whereas aspects of parental
Negative Emotionality, such as anxiety and irritability, are related to less competent parenting (e.g.,
Belsky, Crnic, & Woodsworth, 1995; Clark, Kochanska, & Ready, 2000; Kochanska, Clark, &
Goldman, 1997; Losoya, Callor, Rowe, & Goldsmith,
1997; Mangelsdorf et al., 1990). Much more work
needs to be done. First, most of the research to date
has focused on parents of very young children to the
virtual exclusion of adolescents. Second, most of the
research has not tested mediators (e.g., parental attributions) of observed personality → parenting
associations. Third, most of the research has focused on the main effects of personality and has not
yet addressed the conditions under which particular
personality attributes are more or less important in
explaining parenting behavior (e.g., are personality
main effects moderated by the marital relationship
or by the child's temperament?) (Belsky & Barends,
2002). An especially powerful strategy for studying
personality → parenting associations, and for addressing these empirical gaps, is to study the
influence of personality on parenting behavior in
relation to multiple children in the same family.

Striving and achieving. Across the life course, individuals assume multiple performance tasks (e.g.,
pursuing an education, assuming a job, managing
and allocating resources). Personality traits from the
domain of Conscientiousness/Constraint are widely
considered the most important non-cognitive predictors of educational achievement, occupational
attainment, and subsequent job performance
(Judge, Higgins, Thoreson, & Barrick, 1999). Conscientiousness encompasses many traits that are
necessary for completing work effectively: the capacities to sustain attention, to strive toward high

standards, and to inhibit impulsive behavior. In fact, childhood conscientiousness predicts improvements in academic achievement across time into early adulthood (Shiner, 2000). Additional evidence suggests that childhood Positive Emotionality and Agreeableness predict adolescent academic performance (Shiner, 2000); aspects of these same higher-order traits also predict adult job performance in a more limited set of occupational groups (Mount, Barrick, & Stewart, 1998). Predictive associations between temperament and personality traits and achievement are apparent already early in life, at the time that children first enroll in school (Miech, Essex, & Goldsmith, 2001). The finding that temperament affects school performance early in life is important, because school adjustment and academic performance have cumulative effects over time (Entwisle & Alexander, 1993).

Research with children, adolescents, and adults demonstrates that the links between temperament/personality traits and various indices of achievement obtain after controlling for individual differences in ability. These associations beg the question, How? The personality processes involved may vary across different stages of development. In childhood, the association may be accounted for, in part, by the influence that children's personalities have on their emerging relationships with their teachers (Birch & Ladd, 1998). Later in adolescence, and throughout adulthood, there are at least three candidate processes (Schneider, Smith, Taylor, & Fleenor, 1998). First, it is possible that the personality → achievement associations reflect 'attraction' effects, or 'active niche-picking' (Scarr & McCartney, 1983), whereby people actively choose educational and work experiences whose qualities are concordant with their own personalities. Second, it is possible that the personality → achievement associations reflect 'recruitment' effects, whereby people are selectively recruited into jobs on the basis of their personality characteristics (e.g., employers preferentially give opportunities to nice and assertive applicants; those high in Positive Emotionality). Third, it is possible that personality → achievement associations emerge as consequences of 'attrition' or 'deselection pressures,' whereby people leave educational settings or jobs that do not fit with their personality or are released from jobs because of their personality. For example, there is evidence that young children who exhibit a combination of high Negative Emotionality and low Constraint are at heightened risk of unemployment (Caspi, Wright, Moffitt, & Silva, 1998).

Health promotion and maintenance. The lifelong interplay between psyche and soma are nowhere more apparent than in research documenting that personality traits contribute to the maintenance of physical integrity and health. Especially impressive are life-span studies that document links between personality traits of Positive Emotionality and Conscientiousness/Constraint with longevity (Danner, Snowdon, & Friesen, 2001; Friedman et al., 1993). Individuals high in traits related to Disagreeableness (e.g., anger and hostility) appear to be at greatest risk of disease (e.g., cardiovascular illness) (Miller, Smith, Turner, Guijarro, & Hallet, 1996). The evidence for the involvement of Negative Emotionality/Neuroticism in ill health is mixed (Watson & Pennebaker, 1989).

The study of health also serves to illustrate the utility of hierarchical structural models of personality in integrating and interpreting research findings. For example, some of the inconsistency that has been observed in studies of hostility and cardiovascular disease may be due to the fact that hostility is a facet or component of both Neuroticism and Agreeableness (vs. Antagonism) (Smith & Williams, 1992). Measures of hostility that reflect overt interpersonal expressions of anger are facets of Agreeableness that may be the lethal personality risk factor for coronary heart disease, whereas measures of hostility that tap irritation and self-focused negativity are facets of Neuroticism and may be better predictors of health complaints rather than actual health outcomes. A taxonomic model of personality can help researchers to make conceptual and measurement refinements in testing psychosomatic hypotheses.

Personality–health associations may reflect at least three distinct processes (Contrada, Cather, & O'Leary, 1999; Rozanski, Blumenthal, & Kaplan, 1999). First, personality differences may be related to pathogenesis, mechanisms that promote disease. This has been evaluated most directly in studies relating various facets of Disagreeableness/Negative Affectivity to, for example, stress-induced cardiovascular reactivity (Gallo & Mathews, 1999). Second, personality differences may be related to physical-health outcomes because they are associated with health-promoting or health-damaging behaviors. For example, individuals high in Conscientiousness appear to lead well-structured lives that are conducive to health, and Positive Emotionality may foster social relationships, social support, and social integration which are positively associated with health outcomes (Berkman et al., 2000). In contrast, individual differences among adolescents in traits related to low Agreeableness and low Conscientiousness are related to health-risk behaviors such as smoking, unprotected sexual intercourse, and dangerous driving habits (Caspi et al., 1997; Wills et al., 2000). Future research on this 'risky' personality profile could be usefully integrated with developmental research from a decision-theory perspective to better understand how decision-making processes may mediate the links between personality dispositions and later health-risk. Such research also has the potential to contribute to a psychology of public health. Third, personality differences may be related to reactions to illness. This includes a wide class of behaviors, including the possibility that personality differences affect the selection and execution of coping behaviors, modulate distress reduction, and shape treatment adherence. The three aforementioned processes are not mutually exclusive. Moreover, different personality traits may affect health via different processes at different life stages. For example, facets of Disagreeableness may be most directly linked to disease pathogenesis, facets of low Conscientiousness may be more clearly implicated in health-damaging behaviors, and facets of Neuroticism may contribute to ill-health by shaping reactions to illness.

Predicting all of behavior all of the time?

Although personality traits have been shown to shape developmental outcomes in multiple domains and in different age groups, a common refrain is that these predictive associations only account for a fraction of the variance in outcomes of interest. This observation must be balanced by four considerations. First, it seems necessary to periodically re-issue the reminder that even small effect sizes are of theoretical and practical significance (McCartney & Rosenthal, 2000). By way of comparison, epidemiological and clinical studies repeatedly uncover associations whose effect sizes range between .1 and .3 (e.g., the association between decreased bone mineral density and risk of hip fracture; between nicotine patch and smoking abstinence), leading a recent expert panel to recommend rethinking conventional interpretations of psychological research; given adequate attention to sampling considerations, researchers should be 'pleased' with associations around .2 to .3 (Meyer et al., 2001). Second, debates about the size of personality effects are based on the implicit assumption that every behavior is the product of a single trait. This is implausible, because each individual is characterized by a personal pattern of multiple traits working additively and interactively to influence behavior. This multiple-trait perspective has important implications for effect-size estimates; simulation studies demonstrate that it is unreasonable and statistically inconceivable in multiply-determined systems for any single trait to explain much more than 10% of the variance (Ahadi & Diener, 1989). Third, social behavior is a product of multiple personality traits acting in concert and influencing one another (Asendorpf, 2002). Consider the case of relationship outcomes. If personality effects are additive across partners, the 'true' impact of a personality trait on a relationship should be regarded as the summed effect of two personalities, not a single individual's trait (Moffitt, Robins, & Caspi, 2001). Fourth, because the effects of personality differences accumulate over a lifetime, a focus on a single outcome variable measured at a single point in time may underestimate the contribution of personality to the course of developmental trajectories. Abelson (1985) makes this point in noting that differences between baseball players are trivial if considered on the basis of a single at-bat but become meaningful over the course of a game, a season, and a career.

Early temperament/personality and the emergence of psychopathology

Just as individual differences in personality shape individuals' adaptation over time, childhood personality plays an important role in the development of psychopathology. Much of the current research on personality and psychopathology simply documents correlations between temperament or personality traits and aspects of psychopathology, without articulating how the two domains may be connected (Hoyle, 2000; Rothbart & Bates, 1998). We present a conceptual model of possible associations between temperament/personality and psychopathology in childhood and adolescence. In laying out this conceptual model, we draw on models elaborated by Clark, Watson, and Mineka (1994) and Widiger, Verheul, and van den Brink (1999). As much as possible, we borrow their terminology to describe the possible associations, in order to avoid unnecessarily introducing new labels. First, psychopathology may represent the extreme end of a continuously-distributed personality trait or cluster of traits (*spectrum association*). Second, personality may set in motion processes that cause the development of psychopathology (*vulnerability association*). Third, personality may protect against the development of psychopathology in the face of stress and adversity (*resilience association*). Fourth, personality may influence the form and prognosis of a disorder, even if the personality trait is not a component or a cause of the disorder (*pathoplastic association*). Fifth, psychopathology may influence the course of personality development itself (*scarring association*). Below, we elaborate on these possible associations from a developmental perspective.

Spectrum association: Psychopathology may be an extreme manifestation of personality

Although psychiatric disorders are typically measured categorically, it is possible that some disorders are not discrete conditions, but rather represent extreme ends of continuously-distributed personality dimensions or clusters of dimensions (Sonuga-Barke, 1998; Widiger & Clark, 2000). For example, some researchers have argued that ADHD may be an extreme variant of an underlying temperament or personality trait, rather than a discrete condition that is clearly separable from normal functioning (Jensen et al., 1997). Children with ADHD may have a basic deficit in inhibiting a prepotent response when faced with potential reinforcement for that response; i.e., ADHD may represent the extreme low ends of the traits of attention and inhibitory control (Barkley, 1997), aspects of the Conscientiousness/Constraint superfactor (see Table 2).

An understudied area where spectrum relationships are likely is childhood and adolescent personality disorders. Extensive work has been done attempting to link dimensional personality traits with categorical personality disorders in adults, and some researchers have argued that adult personality disorders should be conceptualized as complex combinations of adaptive and maladaptive personality traits rather than as categorically distinct conditions (Costa & Widiger, 2002; Widiger et al., 1999). Little is known, however, about how child and adolescent personality is related both to concurrent personality disorders and to later-appearing personality disorders in adulthood, although some recent theoretical work has elaborated on potential links (Geiger & Crick, 2001; Kernberg, Weiner, & Bardenstein, 2000). Children's early personalities are likely to be important predictors of the processes through which personality functioning goes away and becomes set into maladaptive, rigid patterns.

Several research strategies have been and can be harnessed to study spectrum relationships. First, taxometric methods can be used to distinguish whether differences between groups of individuals (e.g., depressed vs. not depressed persons) represent quantitative differences of degree or qualitative differences in kind (Meehl, 1992). The increasing availability of these methods for addressing the continuum-category debate, and their application to a wide range of psychological phenomena (e.g., Ruscio & Ruscio, 2000), is valuable because the resulting answers can be used to inform different etiological hypotheses and recommend different treatment approaches.

Second, psychopharmacological studies can also be used to generate evidence about whether personality traits and psychiatric disorders exist on a continuum (e.g., Ekselius & von Knorring, 1999). For example, the anti-depressant paroxetine has been shown to reduce negative affect levels in persons without a history of mental disorder in themselves and their first-degree relatives (Knutson et al., 1998). That is, some treatments thought to be targeted at specific syndrome disorders may, in fact, exert their influence via broader personality variables.

Third, methods in behavioral genetics research (such as DF extreme analysis; see Plomin, DeFries, McClearn, & McGuffin, 2001) can be used to address the question of whether the heritability of a disorder (e.g., ADHD) is the same or different from that of individual differences in a trait (e.g., continuously-distributed symptoms of hyperactivity and inattention). For example, with regard to ADHD, genetic analyses suggest that DSM-III-R ADHD may be best viewed as an extreme end of a dimension which varies genetically in the population (Levy, Hay, McStephan, Wood, & Waldman, 1997).

Fourth, multivariate quantitative genetic methods can be used to determine the extent to which the etiologies of normal and abnormal variation overlap. For example, one study showed that most of the observed correlation between the personality trait of Neuroticism and the liability to a diagnosis of major depression was attributable to genetic factors involved in both Neuroticism and major depression (Kendler, Neale, Kessler, Heath, & Eaves, 1993). Another study showed that that correlation between the personality trait of behavioral undercontrol and alcohol dependence was attributable, in part, to genetic factors involved in both (Slutske et al., 2002). It is possible that molecular genetic analyses will increasingly prove useful in studying spectrum relationships by testing the hypothesis that quantitative trait loci (QTLs) associated with personality traits are also associated with psychiatric disorders.

More generally, it is interesting to note that the revival of interest in personality psychology has been spurred by advances in molecular genetics (Benjamin, Ebstein, & Belmaker, 2002). Psychiatric geneticists have turned to personality psychology and its dimensional models for both statistical and conceptual reasons. Unlike classical single-gene disorders in which a single gene is necessary and sufficient to produce the disorder, there is little evidence for such major effects of genes in psychiatry. Rather, genetic influence is more likely to involve multiple genes of variable but small effect size, greatly increasing difficulty in detecting them. Statistically, the use of quantitative personality traits (rather than categorical psychiatric diagnoses) facilitates the detection of such genes. Conceptually, personality traits are of interest to psychiatrists because they may represent endophenotypes for psychiatric disorders; that is, traits that are intermediate on a causal chain from genes to disorder.

Vulnerability association: Personality may put children at risk for the development of psychopathology

Although researchers have examined many models linking personality and psychopathology, the one that has garnered the most interest is that of personality as a causal risk factor for the development of psychopathology. Numerous studies have examined associations between temperament and psychopathology, both concurrently and longitudinally. Longitudinal studies in which temperament is measured prior to the emergence of psychopathology provide the most compelling evidence of a possible causal association. Rothbart and Bates (1998) summarized this literature and reported the following predictive associations between early temperament and later psychopathology: High social inhibition predicts later internalizing symptoms; high unmanageability predicts later externalizing symptoms; low self-control (poor persistence and low predictability) predicts later externalizing symptoms; and high negative emotionality predicts both internalizing and externalizing symptoms. In general, these links are modest in magnitude, which is to be expected to the extent that the development of psychopathology is multifactorial. Although the findings are promising, limitations continue to compromise both the external and internal validity of many studies: Most samples are small or unrepresentative, and reports of temperament and psychopathology are often obtained from the same source. Further, measures of temperament and symptoms often overlap in content, a problem which can be rectified effectively by eliminating overlapping items from both kinds of measures (Lengua, West, & Sandler, 1998).

Fewer studies have tackled the processes through which early temperament might put children at risk for psychiatric disorders. Previously we outlined six processes through which early temperament differences become elaborated into more broad personality dispositions. These same six processes are likely to be the ones through which childhood individual differences put children at risk for psychopathology as well. Research on the development of conduct disorder serves to demonstrate how these six processes may operate. Longitudinal research shows that conduct disorder and severe antisocial behavior are predicted by an early history of high negative emotionality, poor self-control, and high unmanageability (Sanson & Prior, 1999). How might early temperament contribute to the development of severe antisocial behavior over time? Answers to this question are likely to emerge not necessarily from longitudinal studies, but from experimental and observational studies that train their lenses on specific social, cognitive, and behavioral processes at different points in development. First, children with conduct disorder are especially sensitive to signals of reward (O'Brien & Frick, 1996) but are relatively insensitive to punishing stimuli (Lytton, 1990). *Learning processes* may be at work here; these children may have temperament traits that lead to difficulty learning to inhibit behavior when faced with potential rewards. Second, observational studies show that adopted children who are at genetic risk for antisocial behavior receive more negative control and coercive parenting from their adoptive parents than do adopted children not at genetic risk (O'Connor, Deater-Deckard, Fulker, Rutter, & Plomin, 1998). These findings point to *environmental elicitation* in which children's genetically influenced temperaments evoke coercive parenting behaviors. *Environmental construal* may be seen in the way that aggressive children misinterpret the intentions of others. For example, such children seek less information about social situations and are more likely to assume hostile intent on the part of other persons (Coie & Dodge, 1998). Related to the process of en-

vironmental construal are *social comparison processes,* in which temperament shapes the way that individuals evaluate themselves in relation to others. In some studies, externalizing children overestimate their social competence relative to others (Hughes, Cavell, & Grossman, 1997; Patterson, Kupersmidt, & Griesler, 1990); it is possible that such overestimation is related to temperament and may precede the emergence of psychopathology. *Environmental selection* may be seen in the ways by which some children 'select' situations that can then reinforce particular behaviors. For example, children with poor self-control are more likely to form ties to delinquent peers who, in turn, promote their antisocial behavior (Wright, Moffitt, Caspi, & Silva, 2001). Finally, through *environmental manipulation* an individual's personality alters and shapes the environment. For example, disagreeable youth not only perceive more interpersonal conflict in their environment, but also attempt to resolve conflict with destructive tactics (Jensen-Campbell & Graziano, 2001).

It is essential to emphasize that the environment plays a role in all of these processes, either by introducing some input to which the child must respond, or by being an output that the child shapes in some way. Moreover, in some cases, the environment may exert such a strong influence that the child's personality is relatively less important in determining the child's outcome. For example, boys low in self-control are likely to become involved in antisocial behavior if they are reared in poor, criminogenic neighborhoods. However, this personality disposition does not confer risk for antisocial behavior if they are reared in better neighborhoods (Lynam et al., 2000). In other cases, the child's temperament may be so extreme that the environment has less influence on the child's development. For example, parenting quality appears to have little impact on children who are highly callous and unemotional (Wootton, Frick, Shelton, & Silverthorn, 1997); such children have been described as 'fledgling psychopaths' (Lynam, 1996).

Just as QTLs can be used to advance research about spectrum associations, they can also – and may increasingly – be used to study vulnerability associations (Rutter & Silberg, 2002). Specifically, the identification of QTLs in personality research may revolutionize research on personality and psychopathology by providing measured genotypes for investigating two types of gene–environment interplay (Plomin & Caspi, 1999). *Gene–environment correlations* refer to genetic differences in exposure to environments; literally, a correlation between genes and environments. Gene–environment correlations subsume processes such as environmental elicitation, environmental construal, and environmental selection. Although we know of no molecular genetic findings on such gene–environment correlations, the basic strategy seems a sensible one. For example, consider the possible association between the serotonin transporter gene polymorphism (5HTT), neuroticism, and depression (Lesch et al., 1996). If this association proves robust, it will be important to understand the mechanism by which gene–behavior associations develop. For example, this association may be mediated by environmental experience in the sense that children with a short variant of 5HTT are more likely to encounter stressful life events than children with the long variant, either because they generate more stress (environmental selection) or are prone to perceive the same situations as more stressful (environmental construal). *Gene–environment interactions* refer to genetic differences in sensitivity to environments; literally, an interaction between genes and environments. Using 5HTT as an example, children who have a short variant may be at greater risk of developing depression if they are exposed to stressful life events. We predict that tracing the developmental pathways between specific genes and psychopathology through environmental mechanisms is likely to be one of the most important advances that emerges from applications of specific genes associated with temperament and personality traits (Caspi et al., 2002).

Resilience association: Personality may avert the development of psychopathology in the face of stress

Although some personality traits may put children at risk of psychopathology in adverse environments, other traits may promote resilience in the face of adversity; that is, some personality traits may be protective factors in conditions that, on average, put children at risk for psychopathological outcomes (Luthar, Cicchetti, & Becker, 2000; Masten, 2001; Masten & Coatsworth, 1998). In high-risk samples, it is possible to study side-by-side the role of personality in shaping both negative and positive outcomes. For example, Werner and Smith (1992) studied a group of high-risk children who were exposed to perinatal stress, poverty, and multiple family problems. Children who showed positive, resilient adult outcomes were described in infancy as very active; males were also described as easygoing, and females were also described as affectionate.

It seems obvious that attention must be given to the possibility that some personality factors protect against a psychopathological outcome whereas others predispose to it. However, to the extent that protective and risk factors operate dimensionally – at opposite ends of a continuum – there is little to be gained, either in terms of theory or in terms of practice, from focusing on the beneficial effects of, for example, low Negative Emotionality than on the harmful effects of high Negative Emotionality. But there is a great deal of value in testing two hypotheses: (a) That some personality factors provide protection in the presence of risk, even though they

have no effect in the absence of such risk (Rutter, in press) and (b) that higher levels of a trait are necessary for protection under adverse conditions than are necessary for competent functioning in low-risk conditions. Such may be the case in relation to Positive Emotionality, which is associated with creative problem solving (Fredrickson, 1998). Theoretically, the processes through which individual differences in children's temperament and personality promote resilience should be the same as those six processes described in reference to personality as a risk factor.

Although research has been conducted on the protective role of individual differences in IQ (White et al., 1989), much remains to be learned about the potential protective role of individual differences in children's personality. Resilience researchers have called for increasing focus on the processes underlying resilience (Luthar et al., 2000; Masten, 1999), and personality research should be an important part of future work in this area. It is curious, also, that genetic studies, which are so integral to research on vulnerability associations, have played such a minor role in research on resilience. From an evolutionary perspective genes are equally likely to protect against environmental insult as they are to create vulnerability to disease (Hill, 1999).

Pathoplastic association: Personality may affect the presentation and course of psychopathology

Temperament and personality traits may influence the manifestation and course of a disorder, even if such traits are distinct from the disorder itself (i.e., if they are not etiologically related to the disorder). For example, research on tobacco dependence shows that persons with high Negative Emotionality are more likely to relapse following participation in smoking cessation treatments (Kenford et al., 2002), and some personality traits may increase the risk of recurrence of psychiatric conditions (Teasdale & Barnard, 1993). Although these types of pathoplastic relationships have been studied in adults (Widiger et al., 1999), they have received very little attention in research with children, despite their potential developmental significance. However, research on psychiatric comorbidity, which shows that a comorbid disorder may influence the presentation and course of another disorder, underscores the importance of examining pathoplastic relationships between personality traits and psychiatric disorders. For example, children with conduct disorder who have a co-morbid anxiety disorder are less aggressive (Walker et al., 1991) and show less persistence of antisocial behavior over time (Pine, Cohen, Cohen, & Brook, 2000). Similar findings have been obtained for children with co-morbid ADHD and an anxiety disorder: Such children are less impulsive (Newcorn et al., 2001) and show more positive responsiveness to behavioral treatment (Jensen et al., 2001). Taken together, these findings suggest that co-morbid anxiety disorders exert a generally positive influence on the manifestation and course of externalizing disorders. The exploration of pathoplastic relationships may help to uncover sub-types of childhood disorders characterized by distinctive personality profiles and may also help clinicians in their treatment planning (Harkness & Lilienfeld, 1997).

Scarring association: Psychopathology may alter personality functioning

The experience of significant psychopathology has the potential to alter children's personalities in lasting ways. Such a relationship is often referred to as a 'scarring' effect of psychopathology on personality (e.g., Rohde, Lewinsohn, & Seeley, 1990). Personality changes that are secondary to physical disorders are well documented, but, at least in adulthood, there is little solid evidence of lasting changes to personality secondary to psychopathology (Shea et al., 1996). The situation may be very different earlier in life. Because identity and a sense of self are under construction throughout childhood and adolescence (Harter, 1998), children may be particularly vulnerable to the negative effects of psychopathology that emerges early in the life course. This hypothesis has received practically no research attention. However, at least one longitudinal study has shown that children who were involved in antisocial behavior at age 10 showed increases in Negative Emotionality from age 10 to age 20 years; that is, they became increasingly more high strung, alienated, and hostile (Shiner, Masten, & Tellegen, 2002).

Conclusion

The goal of this article was to review recent advances in research on individual differences in personality that may be especially relevant to child psychologists and psychiatrists. First, we have highlighted some breakthroughs toward a working taxonomy of personality differences. Because progress in understanding personality development depends on sound measurement, the Appendix following this review provides a staring point – listing some considerations and some instruments – for researchers who may wish to incorporate personality measurement into their research. Second, although many longitudinal studies have tracked their samples over time in order to document cross-time consistencies of individual differences in personality, longitudinal research is not always developmental research. In fact, little is known about how early-emerging individual differences become elaborated into the consistent ways of behaving, thinking and feeling that we call personality. We have therefore listed some ideas and working hypotheses that we hope will stimulate further research about this topic. Finally, we noted

that the historically unproductive bifurcation of personality and clinical psychology is drawing to an end, aided in part by psychiatrists' renewed interest in the dimensional constructs of personality. We reviewed several ways in which personality differences may be related to psychopathology. Research on childhood and adolescent personality has the potential to yield insights into the processes leading to psychopathology, not just in childhood but across the entire life span.

Author notes

Preparation of this article was supported by grants from the Colgate Research Council, the National Institute of Mental Health (MH-49414, MH-45070), the Medical Research Council, and the William T. Grant Foundation.

Correspondence to

Rebecca Shiner, Colgate University, Department of Psychology, 13 Oak Drive, Hamilton, NY 13346, USA; Email: rshiner@mail.colgate.edu

References

Abelson, R. (1985). A variance explanation paradox: When a little is a lot. *Psychological Bulletin, 97,* 129–133.

Ablow, J.C., Measelle, J.R., Kraemer, H.C., Harrington, R., Luby, J., Smider, N., Dierker, L., Clark, V., Dubicka, B., Heffelfinger, A., Essex, M.J., & Kupfer, D.J. (1999). The MacArthur Three-City Outcome Study: Evaluating multi-informant measures of young children's symptomatology. *Journal of the American Academy of Child and Adolescent Psychiatry, 38,* 1580–1590.

Ahadi, S., & Diener, E. (1989). Multiple determinants and effects sizes. *Journal of Personality and Social Psychology, 56,* 398–406.

Ahadi, S.A., Rothbart, M.K., & Ye, R.M. (1993). Children's temperament in the US and China: Similarities and differences. *European Journal of Personality, 7,* 359–377.

Allport, G.W. (1937). *Personality: A psychological interpretation.* New York: Holt.

Allport, G.W. (1958). What units shall we employ? In G. Lindzey (Ed.), *Assessment of human motives* (pp. 238–260). New York: Rinehart.

Andersen, S.M., & Baum, A. (1994). Transference in interpersonal relations: Inferences and affect based on significant-other representations. *Journal of Personality, 62,* 459–497.

Arnett, J.J. (2000). Emerging adulthood: A theory of development from the late teens through the twenties. *American Psychologist, 55,* 469–480.

Asendorpf, J.B. (1990). Development of inhibition during childhood: Evidence for situational specificity and a two-factor model. *Developmental Psychology, 26,* 721–730.

Asendorpf, J.B. (2002). Personality effects on personal relationships over the life span. In A.L. Vangelisti, H.T. Reis & M.A. Fitzpatrick (Eds.), *Stability and change in relationships* (pp. 35–56). Cambridge University Press.

Asendorpf, J.B., Caspi, A., & Hofstee, W. (Eds.). (2002). Special issue: Personality types. *European Journal of Personality, 16*.

Asendorpf, J.B., & Meier, G.H. (1993). Personality effects on children's speech in everyday life: Sociability-mediated exposure and shyness-mediated reactivity to social situations. *Journal of Personality and Social Psychology, 64*, 1072–1083.

Barkley, R.A. (1997). *ADHD and the nature of self-control*. New York: Guilford.

Bell, R.Q., & Chapman, M. (1986). Child effects in studies using experimental or brief longitudinal approaches to socialization. *Developmental Psychology, 22*, 595–603.

Belsky, J., & Barends, N. (2002). Personality and parenting. In M. Bornstein (Ed.), *Handbook of parenting* (2nd edn, pp. 415–438). Mahwah, NJ: Erlbaum.

Belsky, J., Crnic, K., & Woodworth, S. (1995). Personality and parenting: Exploring the mediating role of transient mood and daily hassles. *Journal of Personality, 63*, 905–929.

Benjamin, J., Ebstein, R.P., & Belmaker, R.H. (Eds.). (2002). *Molecular genetics and the human personality*. Washington, DC: American Psychiatric Publishing.

Bergman, L.R., & Cairns, R.B. (Eds.). (2000). *Developmental science and the holistic approach*. Mahwah, NJ: Erlbaum.

Berkman, L.F., Glass, T., Brissette, I., & Seeman, T.E. (2000). From social integration to health. *Social Science and Medicine, 51*, 843–857.

Birch, S.H., & Ladd, G.W. (1998). Children's interpersonal behaviors and the teacher–child relationship. *Developmental Psychology, 34*, 934–946.

Block, J. (1996). Some jangly remarks on Baumeister & Heatherton. *Psychological Inquiry, 7*, 28–32.

Block, J. (1961/1978). *The Q-sort in personality assessment and psychiatric research*. Palo Alto, CA: Consulting Psychologists Press.

Block J., & Block, J.H. (1969/1980). *The California Child Q-set*. Palo Alto, CA: Consulting Psychologists Press.

Block, J.H., & Block, J. (1980). The role of ego-control and ego-resiliency in the organization of behavior. In W.A. Collins (Ed.), *The Minnesota symposium on child psychology* (vol. 13, pp. 39–101). Hillsdale, NJ: Erlbaum.

Bohart, A.C., & Stipek, D.J. (2001). *Constructive and destructive behavior*. Washington DC: American Psychological Association.

Borkenau, P., & Liebler, A. (1995). Observable attributes as manifestations and cues of personality and intelligence. *Journal of Personality, 63*, 1–25.

Bouchard, T.J., Jr. (1995). Longitudinal studies of personality and intelligence: A behavior genetic and evolutionary psychology perspective. In D. Saklofske & M. Zeidner (Ed.), *International handbook of personality and intelligence* (pp. 81–106). New York: Plenum.

Bouchard, T.J., Jr., & Loehlin, J.C. (2001). Genes, evolution, and personality. *Behavior Genetics, 31*, 243–274.

Briggs, S.R. (1989). The optimal level of measurement for personality constructs. In D.M. Buss & N. Canto (Eds.), *Personality psychology: Recent trends and emerging directions* (pp. 246–260). New York: Spring-Verlag.

Buss, A.H., & Plomin, R. (1984). *Temperament: Early developing personality traits*. Hillsdale, NJ: Erlbaum.

Buss, D.M. (1987). Selection, evocation, and manipulation. *Journal of Personality and Social Psychology, 53*, 1214–1221.

Buss, D.M. (1999). *Evolutionary psychology: The new science of the mind*. Boston: Allyn & Bacon.

Canli, T., Zhao, Z., Desmond, J.E., Kang, E., Gross, J., & Gabrieli, J.D.E. (2001). An fMRI study of personality influences on brain reactivity to emotional stimuli. *Behavioral Neuroscience, 115*, 33–42.

Cantor, N. (1990). From thought to behavior: 'Having' and 'doing' in the study of personality and cognition. *American Psychologist, 45*, 735–750.

Carstensen, L.L. (1995). Evidence for a life-span theory of socioemotional selectivity. *Current Directions in Psychological Science, 4*, 151–156.

Caspi, A. (1987). Personality in the life course. *Journal of Personality and Social Psychology, 53*, 1203–1213.

Caspi, A. (1998). Personality development across the life course. In W. Damon (Series Ed.) & N. Eisenberg (Vol. Ed.), *Handbook of child psychology: Vol. 3. Social, emotional, and personality development* (5th edn, pp. 311–388). New York: Wiley.

Caspi, A. (2000). The child is the father of the man: Personality continuities from childhood to adulthood. *Journal of Personality and Social Psychology, 78*, 158–172.

Caspi, A., Begg, D., Dickson, N., Harrington, H., Langley, J., Moffitt, T.E., & Silva, P.A. (1997). Personality differences predict health-risk behaviors in young adulthood: Evidence from a longitudinal study. *Journal of Personality and Social Psychology, 73*, 1052–1063.

Caspi, A., Block, J., Block, J.H., Klopp, B., Lynam, D., Moffitt, T.E., & Stouthamer-Loeber, M. (1992). A 'common-language' version of the California Child Q-set for personality assessment. *Psychological Assessment, 4*, 512–523.

Caspi, A., & Herbener, E.S. (1990). Continuity and change: Assortative marriage and the consistency of personality in adulthood. *Journal of Personality and Social Psychology, 58*, 250–258.

Caspi, A., McClay, J., Moffitt, T.E., Mill, J., Martin, J., Craig, I.W., Taylor, A., & Poulton, R. (2002). Role of genotype in the cycle of violence in maltreated children. *Science, 297*, 851–854.

Caspi, A., Wright, B., Moffitt, T.E., & Silva, P.A. (1998). Early failure in the labor market: Childhood and adolescent predictors of unemployment in the transition to adulthood. *American Sociological Review, 63*, 424–451.

Charlesworth, W.R., & Dzur, C. (1987). Gender comparisons of preschoolers' behavior and resource utilization in group problem solving. *Child Development, 58*, 191–200.

Church, T.A. (1994). Relating the Tellegen and Five Factor models of personality structure. *Journal of Personality and Social Psychology, 67*, 898–909.

Church, T.A. (Ed.). (2001). Culture and personality. _Journal of Personality, 69._

Clark, L.A., Kochanska, G., & Ready, R. (2000). Mothers' personality and its interaction with child temperament as predictors of parenting behavior. _Journal of Personality and Social Psychology, 79,_ 274–285.

Clark, L.A., Watson, D., & Mineka, S. (1994). Temperament, personality, and the mood and anxiety disorders. _Journal of Abnormal Psychology, 103,_ 103–116.

Cloninger, C.R., Svrakic, D.M., & Przybeck, T.R. (1993). A psychobiological model of temperament and character. _Archives of General Psychiatry, 39,_ 1242–1247.

Cohen, P. (1999). Personality development in childhood: Old and new findings. In C.R. Cloninger (Ed.), _Personality and psychopathology_ (pp. 101–127). Washington DC: American Psychiatric Press.

Coie, J.D., & Dodge, K.A. (1998). Aggression and antisocial behavior. In W. Damon (Series Ed.) & N. Eisenberg (Vol. Ed.), _Handbook of child psychology: Vol. 3. Social, emotional, and personality development_ (5th edn, pp. 779–862). New York, Wiley.

Cole, M., & Cole, S.R. (1996). _The development of children_ (3rd edn). New York: W.H. Freeman.

Contrada, R.J., Cather, C., & O'Leary, A. (1999). Personality and health: Dispositions and processes in disease susceptibility and adaptation to illness. In L.A. Pervin & O.P. John (Eds.), _Handbook of personality: Theory and research_ (2nd edn, pp. 576–604). New York: Guilford.

Costa, P.T., Jr., & McCrae, R.R. (1994). Set like plaster: Evidence for the stability of adult personality. In T.F. Heatherton & J.L. Weinberger (Eds.), _Can personality change?_ (pp. 21–40). Washington, DC: American Psychological Association.

Costa, P.T., & Widiger, T.A. (Eds.). (2002). _Personality disorders and the five-factor model of personality_ (2nd edn). Washington, DC: American Psychological Association.

Crick, N.R., & Dodge, K.A. (1994). A review and reformulation of social information processing mechanisms in children's social adjustment. _Psychological Bulletin, 115,_ 74–101.

Crick, N.R., Nelson, D.A., Morales, J.R., Cullerton-Sen, C., Casas, J.F., & Hickman, S. (2001). Relational victimization in childhood and adolescence: I hurt you through the grapevine. In J. Juvonen & S. Graham (Eds.), _Peer harassment in school: The plight of the vulnerable and victimized_ (pp. 196–214). New York: Guilford.

Danner, D.D., Snowdon, D.A., & Friesen, W.V. (2001). Positive emotions in early life and longevity: Findings from the nun study. _Journal of Personality and Social Psychology, 80,_ 804–813.

De Fruyt, F., Mervielde, I., Hoekstra, H.A., & Rolland, J. (2000). Assessing adolescents' personality with the NEO PI-R. _Assessment, 7,_ 329–345.

Denham, S.A. (1998). _Emotional development in young children._ New York: Guilford.

Depue, R.A., & Collins, P.F. (1999). Neurobiology of the structure of personality: Dopamine, facilitation of incentive motivation, and extraversion. _Behavioral and Brain Sciences, 22,_ 491–569.

Derryberry, D., & Reed, M.A. (1994a). Temperament and attention: Orienting toward and away from positive and negative signals. _Journal of Personality and Social Psychology, 66,_ 1128–1139.

Derryberry, D., & Reed, M.A. (1994b). Temperament and the self-organization of personality. _Development and Psychopathology, 6,_ 653–676.

Digman, J.M. (1990). Personality structure: Emergence of the Five-Factor Model. _Annual Review of Psychology, 41,_ 417–440.

Digman, J.M., & Inouye, J. (1986). Further specification of the five robust factors of personality. _Journal of Personality and Social Psychology, 50,_ 116–123.

Digman, J.M., & Shmelyov, A.G. (1996). The structure of temperament and personality in Russian children. _Journal of Personality and Social Psychology, 71,_ 341–351.

Dunn, J. (1996). Children's relationships: Bridging the divide between cognitive and social development. _Journal of Child Psychology and Psychiatry, 37,_ 507–518.

Eaton, W.O. (1994). Temperament, development, and the Five-Factor Model: Lessons from activity level. In C.F. Halverson, G.A. Kohnstamm, & R.P. Martin (Eds.), _The developing structure of temperament and personality from infancy to adulthood_ (pp. 173–187). Hillsdale, NJ: Erlbaum.

Eccles, J.S., Wigfield, A., & Schiefele, U. (1998). Motivation to succeed. In W. Damon (Series Ed.) & N. Eisenberg (Vol. Ed.), _Handbook of child psychology: Vol. 3. Social, emotional, and personality development_ (5th edn, pp. 1017–1095). New York: Wiley.

Eder, R. (1990). Uncovering young children's psychological selves: Individual and developmental differences. _Child Development, 61,_ 849–863.

Eisenberg, N. (2000). Emotion, regulation, and moral development. _Annual Review of Psychology, 51,_ 665–697.

Eisenberg, N., & Fabes, R.A. (1998). Prosocial development. In W. Damon (Series Ed.) & N. Eisenberg (Vol. Ed.), _Handbook of child psychology: Vol. 3. Social, emotional, and personality development_ (5th edn, pp. 701–778). New York: Wiley.

Eisenberg, N., Fabes, R.A., Guthrie, I.K., & Reiser, M. (2000). Dispositional emotionality and regulation: Their role in predicting quality of social functioning. _Journal of Personality and Social Psychology, 78,_ 136–157.

Eisenberg, N., Fabes, R.A., Miller, P.A., Fultz, J., Shell, R., Mathy, R.M., & Reno, R.R. (1989). Relation of sympathy and personal distress to prosocial behavior: A multimethod study. _Journal of Personality and Social Psychology, 57,_ 55–66.

Eisenberg, N., Fabes, R.A., & Murphy, B.C. (1995). Relations of shyness and low sociability to regulation and emotionality. _Journal of Personality and Social Psychology, 68,_ 505–517.

Eisenberg, N., Fabes, R.A., Shepard, S.A., Murphy, B.C., Guthrie, I.K., Jones, S., Friedman, J., Poulin, R., & Maszk, P. (1997). Contemporaneous and longitudinal prediction of children's social functioning from regulation and emotionality. _Child Development, 68,_ 642–664.

Eisenberg, N., Shell, R., Pasternack, J., Lennon, R., Beller, R., & Mathy, R.M. (1987). Prosocial development during middle childhood: A longitudinal study. _Developmental Psychology, 23,_ 712–718.

Emde, R.N., & Hewitt, J.K. (Eds.). (2001). *Infancy to early childhood: Genetic and environmental influences on developmental change*. New York: Oxford University Press.

Ekselius, L., & Von Knorring, L. (1999). Changes in personality traits during treatment with sertraline or citalopram. *British Journal of Psychiatry, 174*, 444–448.

Entwisle, D.R., & Alexander, K.L. (1993). Entry into school. *Annual Review of Sociology, 19*, 401–423.

Epstein, S. (1991). Cognitive-experiential self-theory: Implications for developmental psychology. In M. Gunnar & L.A. Sroufe (Eds.), *Minnesota symposia on child psychology* (vol. 23, pp. 79–123). Hillsdale, NJ: Erlbaum.

Eysenck, H.J. (1947). *Dimensions of personality*. London: Routledge & Kegan Paul.

Eysenck, H.J. (1977). *Crime and personality*. London: Routledge & Kegan Paul.

Eysenck, H.J. (1991). Dimensions of personality: 16, 5 or 3? Criteria for a taxonomic paradigm. *Personality and Individual Differences, 12*, 773–790.

Fiske, S.T., & Taylor, S. (1991). *Social cognition*. New York: McGraw-Hill.

Fletcher, G.J.O. (1993). The scientific credibility of commonsense psychology. In K.H. Craik, R. Hogan, & R.N. Wolfe (Eds.), *Fifty years of personality psychology* (pp. 251–268). New York: Plenum.

Fredrickson, B.L. (1998). What good are positive emotions? *Review of General Psychology, 2*, 300–319.

Friedman, H.S., Tucker, J.S., Tomlinson-Keasey, C., Schwartz, J.E., Wingard, D.L., & Criqui, M.H. (1993). Does childhood personality predict longevity? *Journal of Personality and Social Psychology, 65*, 176–185.

Funder, D.C. (1991). Global traits: A neo-Allportian approach to personality. *Psychological Science, 2*, 31–39.

Funder, D.C. (2001). Personality. *Annual Review of Psychology, 52*, 197–221.

Fox, N.A., Henderson, H.A., Rubin, K.H., Calkins, S.D., & Schmidt, L.A. (2001). Continuity and discontinuity of behavioral inhibition and exuberance: Psychophysiological and behavioral influences across the first four years of life. *Child Development, 72*, 1–21.

Gallo, L.C., & Mathews, K.A. (1999). Do negative emotions mediate the association between socioeconomic status and health? *Annals of the New York Academy of Sciences, 896*, 226–300.

Geiger, T.C., & Crick, N.R. (2001). A developmental psychopathology perspective on vulnerability to personality disorders. In R.E. Ingram & J.M. Price (Eds.), *Vulnerability to psychopathology* (pp. 57–102). New York: Guilford.

Gest, S.D. (1997). Behavioral inhibition: Stability and associations with adaptation from childhood to early adulthood. *Journal of Personality and Social Psychology, 72*, 467–475.

Gifford, R. (1994). A lens-mapping framework for understanding the encoding and decoding of interpersonal dispositions in nonverbal behavior. *Journal of Personality and Social Psychology, 66*, 398–412.

Goldberg, L.R. (1992). The development of markers for the Big-Five factor structure. *Psychological Assessment, 4*, 26–42.

Goldberg, L.R. (2001). Analyses of Digman's child-personality data: Derivation of Big Five Factor Scores from each of six samples. *Journal of Personality, 69*, 709–743.

Goldsmith, H.H. (1996). Studying temperament via construction of the Toddler Temperament Behavior Assessment Questionnaire. *Child Development, 67*, 218–235.

Goldsmith, H.H., Buss, A., Plomin, R., Rothbart, M.K., Thomas, A., Chess, S., Hinde, R.A., & McCall, R.B. (1987). Roundtable: What is temperament? *Child Development, 58*, 505–529.

Goldsmith, H.H., Losoya, S.H., Bradshaw, D.L., & Campos, J.J. (1994). Genetics of personality: A twin study of the five-factor model and parent–offspring analyses. In C.F. Halverson, Jr., G.A. Kohnstamm, & R.P. Martin (Eds.), *The developing structure of temperament and personality from infancy to adulthood* (pp. 241–265). Hillsdale, NJ: Erlbaum.

Goldsmith, H.H., & Rieser-Danner, L. (1990). Assessing early temperament. In C.R. Reynolds & R. Kamphaus (Eds.), *Handbook of psychological and educational assessment of children. (Vol. 2) Personality, behavior, and context* (pp. 345–378). New York: Guilford Press.

Gosling, S.D. (2001). From mice to men: What can we learn about personality from animal research? *Psychological Bulletin, 127*, 45–86.

Gottfried, A.E. (1990). Academic intrinsic motivation in young elementary school children. *Journal of Educational Psychology, 82*, 525–538.

Gottman, J.M. (1994). *What predicts divorce? The relationship between marital processes and marital outcomes*. Hillsdale, NJ: Erlbaum.

Gottman, J.M., Coan, J., Carrere, S., & Swanson, C. (1998). Predicting marital happiness and stability from newlywed interactions. *Journal of Marriage and the Family, 60*, 5–22.

Graziano, W.G., & Eisenberg, N. (1997). Agreeableness: A dimension of personality. In R. Hogan, J. Johnson, & S. Briggs (Eds.), *Handbook of personality psychology* (pp. 795–824). San Diego, CA: Academic Press.

Graziano, W.G., Jensen-Campbell, L.A., & Finch, J.F. (1997). The self as a mediator between personality and adjustment. *Journal of Personality and Social Psychology, 73*, 392–404.

Graziano, W.G., Jensen-Campbell, L.A., Steele, R.G., & Hair, E.C. (1998). Unknown words in self-reported personality: Lethargic and provincial in Texas. *Personality and Social Psychology Bulletin, 24*, 893–905.

Graziano, W.G., Jensen-Campbell, L.A., & Sullivan-Logan, G. (1998). Temperament, activity, and expectations for later personality development. *Journal of Personality and Social Psychology, 74*, 1266–1277.

Grusec, J.E., & Redler, E. (1980). Attribution, reinforcement, and altruism: A developmental analysis. *Developmental Psychology, 16*, 525–534.

Halverson, C.F., Havill, V.L., & Deal, J. (in press). Personality structure as derived from parental ratings of free descriptions of children: The Inventory of Child Individual Differences. *Journal of Personality*.

Halverson, C.F., Kohnstamm, G.A., & Martin, R.P. (Eds.). (1994). *The developing structure of temperament and personality from infancy to adulthood*. Hillsdale, NJ: Erlbaum.

Hampson, S.E., John, O.P., & Goldberg, L.R. (1986). Category breadth and hierarchical structure in personality: Studies of asymmetries in judgments of trait implications. *Journal of Personality and Social Psychology, 51,* 37–54.

Harkness, A.R., & Lilienfeld, S.O. (1997). Individual differences science for treatment planning: Personality traits. *Psychological Assessment, 9,* 349–360.

Harrist, A.W., Zaia, A.F., Bates, J.E., Dodge, K.A., & Pettit, G.S. (1997). Subtypes of social withdrawal in early childhood: Sociometric status and social-cognitive differences across four years. *Child Development, 68,* 278–294.

Harter, S. (1981). A new self-report scale of intrinsic versus extrinsic orientation in the classroom: Motivational and information components. *Developmental Psychology, 17,* 300–312.

Harter, S. (1998). The development of self-representations. In W. Damon (Series Ed.) & N. Eisenberg (Vol. Ed.), *Handbook of child psychology: Vol. 3. Social, emotional, and personality development* (5th edn, pp. 553–617). New York: Wiley.

Hartup, W.W., & Stevens, N. (1999). Friendships and adaptation across the life span. *Current Directions in Psychological Science, 8,* 76–79.

Hartup, W.W., & van Lieshout, C.F.M. (1995). Personality development in social context. *Annual Review of Psychology, 46,* 655–687.

Hawley, P.H. (1999). The ontogenesis of social dominance: A strategy-based evolutionary perspective. *Developmental Review, 19,* 97–132.

Hawley, P.H., & Little, T.D. (1999). On winning some and losing some: A social relations approach to social dominance in toddlers. *Merrill Palmer Quarterly, 45,* 185–214.

Helson, R., Mitchell, V., & Moane, G. (1984). Personality and patterns of adherence and nonadherence to the social clock. *Journal of Personality and Social Psychology, 46,* 1079–1096.

Hill, A.V.S. (1999). Genetics and genomics of infectious disease susceptibility. *British Medical Bulletin, 55,* 401–413.

Hoyle, R.H. (2000). Personality processes and problem behaviors. *Journal of Personality, 68,* 953–966.

Hughes, J., Cavell, T., & Grossman, P. (1997). A positive view of self – risk or protection for aggressive children? *Development and Psychopathology, 9,* 75–94.

Ingram, R.E., & Price, J.M. (Eds.). (2001). *Vulnerability to psychopathology.* New York: Guilford.

Ickes, W., Snyder, M., & Garcia, S. (1997). Personality influences on the choice of situations. In R. Hogan, J. Johnson, & S. Briggs (Eds.), *Handbook of personality psychology* (pp. 166–198). San Diego: Academic Press.

Jensen, P.S., Hinshaw, S.P., Kraemer, H.C., Lenora, N., Newcorn, J.H., Abikoff, H.B., March, J.S., Arnold, L.E., Cantwell, D.P., Conners, C.K., Elliott, G.R., Greenhill, L.L., Hechtman, L., Hoza, T., Pelham, W.E., Severe, J.B., Swanson, J.M., Wells, K.C., Wigal, T., & Vitiello, B. (2001). ADHD comorbidity findings from the MTA Study: Comparing comorbid subgroups. *Journal of the American Academy of Child and Adolescent Psychiatry, 40,* 146–158.

Jensen, P.S., Mrazek, D., Knapp, P.K., Steinberg, L., Pfeffer, C., Schowalter, J., & Shapiro, T. (1997).

Evolution and revolution in child psychiatry: ADHD as a disorder of adaptation. *Journal of the American Academy of Child and Adolescent Psychiatry, 36,* 1672–1679.

Jensen-Campbell, L.A., & Graziano, W.G. (2001). Agreeableness as a moderator of interpersonal conflict. *Journal of Personality, 69,* 323–362.

John, O.P., Caspi, A., Robins, R.W., Moffitt, T.E., & Stouthamer-Loeber, M. (1994). The 'Little Five': Exploring the five-factor model of personality in adolescent boys. *Child Development, 65,* 160–178.

John, O.P., & Srivastava, S. (1999). The Big Five trait taxonomy: History, measurement, and theoretical perspectives. In L.A. Pervin & O.P. John (Eds.), *Handbook of personality: Theory and research* (2nd edn, pp. 102–138). New York: Guilford.

Judge, T.A., Higgins, C.A., Thoreson, C.J., & Barrick, M.R. (1999). The Big Five personality traits, general mental ability, and career success across the life span. *Personnel Psychology, 52,* 621–652.

Kagan, J. (1998). Biology and the child. In W. Damon (Series Ed.) & N. Eisenberg (Vol. Ed.), *Handbook of child psychology: Vol. 3. Social, emotional, and personality development* (5th edn, pp. 177–235). New York: Wiley.

Kagan, J., Reznick, J.S., Clarke, C., Snidman, N., & Garcia-Coll, C. (1984). Behavioral inhibition to the unfamiliar. *Child Development, 55,* 2212–2225.

Kagan, J., Reznick, J.S., & Snidman, N. (1987). The physiology and psychology of behavioral inhibition in children. *Child Development, 58,* 1459–1473.

Karney, B., & Bradbury, T.N. (1995). The longitudinal course of marital quality and stability: A review of theory, methods, and research. *Psychological Bulletin, 118,* 3–34.

Keating, C.F., & Heltman, K.R. (1994). Dominance and deception in children and adults: Are leaders the best misleaders? *Personality and Social Psychology Bulletin, 20,* 312–321.

Keltner, D. (1998). Facial expressions of emotion and personality. In C. Malatesta-Magai & S.H. McFadden (Eds.), *Handbook of emotion, aging, and the lifecourse.* New York: Academic Press.

Keltner, D., Moffitt, T.E., & Stouthamer-Loeber, M. (1995). Facial expressions of emotion and psychopathology in adolescent males. *Journal of Abnormal Psychology, 104,* 644–652.

Kendler, K.S., Health, M.C., Kessler, R.C., Heath, A.C., & Eaves, L.J. (1993). A longitudinal twin study of personality and major depression in women. *Archives of General Psychiatry, 50,* 853–862.

Kenford, K.L., Smith, S.S., Wetter, D.W., Journey, D.E., Fiore, M.C., & Baker, T.B. (2002). Predicting relapse back to smoking: Contrasting affective and physical models of dependence. *Journal of Consulting and Clinical Psychology, 70,* 216–227.

Kernberg, P.F., Weiner, A.S., & Bardenstein, K.K. (2000). *Personality disorders in children and adolescents.* New York: Basic Books.

Kochanska, G. (1991). Socialization and temperament in the development of guilt and conscience. *Child Development, 62,* 1379–1392.

Kochanska, G. (1997). Multiple pathways to conscience for children with different temperaments: From toddler hood to age 5. *Developmental Psychology, 33,* 228–240.

Kochanska, G., Clark, L., & Goldman, M. (1997). Implications of mothers' personality for parenting and their young children's developmental outcomes. *Journal of Personality, 65*, 389–420.

Kochanska, G., Murray, K.T., & Harlan, E.T. (2000). Effortful control in early childhood: Continuity and change, antecedents, and implications for social development. *Developmental Psychology, 36*, 220–232.

Kochanska, G., Murray, K.T., Jacques, T.Y., Koenig, A.L., & Vantages, K. (1996). Inhibitory control in young children and its role in emerging internalization. *Child Development, 67*, 490–507.

Kohnstamm, G.A., Halverson, C.F., Mervielde, I., & Avilla, V. (1998). *Parental descriptions of child personality: Developmental antecedents of the Big Five?* Mahwah, NJ: Erlbaum.

Knutson, B., Walkouts, O.M., Cole, S.W., Chan, T., More, E.A., Johnson, R.C., Torstar, J., Turner, R.A., & Rues, V. (1998). Selective alteration of personality and social behavior by serotonergic intervention. *American Journal of Psychiatry, 155*, 373–379.

Krueger, R.F., Hicks, B.M., & McGue, M. (2001). Altruism and antisocial behavior: Independent tendencies, unique personality correlates, distinct etiologies. *Psychological Science, 12*, 397–402.

Laursen, B., Pulkkinen, L., & Adams, R. (2002). The antecedents and correlates of Agreeableness in adulthood. *Developmental Psychology, 38*, 591–603.

Lemery, K.S., Goldsmith, H.H., Klinnert, M.D., & Mrazek, D.A. (1999). Developmental models of infant and childhood temperament. *Developmental Psychology, 35*, 189–204.

Lengua, L.J., West, S.G., & Sandler, I.N. (1998). Temperament as a predictor of symptomatology in children: Addressing contamination of measures. *Child Development, 69*, 164–181.

Lesch, K.P., Bengel, D., Heils, A., et al. (1996). Association of anxiety-related traits with a polymorphism in the serotonin transporter gene regulatory region. *Science, 274*, 1527–1531.

Levy, F., Hay, D.A., McStephen, M., Wood, C., & Waldman, I. (1997). Attention-deficit hyperactivity disorder: A category or a continuum? Genetic analysis of a large-scale twin study. *Journal of the American Academy of Child and Adolescent Psychiatry, 36*, 737–744.

Lewis, M. (2001). Issues in the study of personality development. *Psychological Inquiry, 12*, 67–83.

Losoya, S., Callor, S., Rowe, D.C., & Goldsmith, H.H. (1997). Origins of familial similarity in parenting. *Developmental Psychology, 33*, 1012–1023.

Lubinski, D. (2000). Scientific and social significance of assessing individual differences: 'Sinking shafts at a few critical points'. *Annual Review of Psychology, 51*, 405–444.

Lucas, R.E., Diener, E., Grob, A., Suh, E.M., & Shao, L. (2000). Cross-cultural evidence for the fundamental features of extraversion. *Journal of Personality and Social Psychology, 79*, 452–468.

Luthar, S.S., Cicchetti, D., & Becker, B. (2000). The construct of resilience: A critical evaluation and guidelines for future work. *Child Development, 71*, 543–562.

Lynam, D.R. (1996). Early identification of chronic offenders: Who is the fledgling psychopath? *Psychological Bulletin, 120*, 209–234.

Lynam, D.R., Caspi, A., Moffitt, T.E., Wikstrom, P.H., & Loeber, R. (2000). The effects of impulsivity on delinquency are stronger in poor neighborhoods. *Journal of Abnormal Psychology, 109*, 563–574.

Lynam, D.R., & Widiger, T.A. (2001). Using the five-factor model to represent the DSM-IV personality disorders: An expert consensus approach. *Journal of Abnormal Psychology, 110*, 401–412.

Lytton, H. (1990). Child and parent effects in boys' conduct disorder: A reinterpretation. *Developmental Psychology, 26*, 683–697.

Magnus, K., Diener, E., Fujita, F., & Payot, W. (1993). Extraversion and neuroticism as predictors of objective life events: A longitudinal analysis. *Journal of Personality and Social Psychology, 65*, 1046–1053.

Mangesldorf, S.C., Gunnar, M., Kestenbaum, R., Lang, S., & Andreas, D. (1990). Infant proneness-to-distress temperament, maternal personality, and mother–infant attachment. *Developmental Psychology, 61*, 820–831.

Mangelsdorf, S.C., Schoppe, S.J., & Buur, H. (2000). The meaning of parental reports: A contextual approach to the study of temperament and behavior problems in childhood. In V.J. Molfese & D.L. Molfese (Eds.), *Temperament and personality development across the life span* (pp. 121–140). Mahwah, NJ: Erlbaum.

Martin, R.P., Wisenbaker, J., & Huttunen, M. (1994). Review of factor analytic studies of temperament measures based on the Thomas–Chess structural model: Implications for the Big Five. In C.F. Halverson, G.A. Kohnstamm, & R.P. Martin (Eds.), *The developing structure of temperament and personality from infancy to adulthood* (pp. 157–172). Hillsdale, NJ: Erlbaum.

Masten, A.S. (1999). Resilience comes of age: Reflections on the past and outlook for the next generation of research. In M.D. Glantz & J.L. Johnson (Eds.), *Resilience and development: Positive life outcomes* (pp. 281–296). New York: Kluwer.

Masten, A.S. (2001). Ordinary magic: Resilience processes in development. *American Psychologist, 56*, 227–238.

Masten, A.S., & Coatsworth, J.D. (1995). Competence, resilience, & psychopathology. In D. Cicchetti & D. Cohen (Eds.), *Developmental psychopathology: Vol. 2. Risk, disorder, and adaptation* (pp. 715–752). New York: Wiley.

Masten, A.S., & Coatsworth, J.D. (1998). The development of competence in favorable and unfavorable environments: Lessons from research on successful children. *American Psychologist, 53*, 205–220.

Masten, A.S., Morison, P., & Pellegrini, D.S. (1985). A revised class method of peer assessment. *Developmental Psychology, 21*, 523–533.

Mathiesen, K.S., & Tambe, K. (1999). The EAS Temperament Questionnaire – Factor structure, age trends, reliability, and stability in a Norwegian sample. *Journal of Child Psychology and Psychiatry, 40*, 431–439.

McAdams, D.P. (1992). The five-factor model in personality: A critical appraisal. *Journal of Personality, 60*, 329–361.

McAdams, D.P. (1996). Personality, modernity, and the storied self: A contemporary framework for studying persons. *Psychological Inquiry, 7*, 295–321.

McCartney, K., & Rosenthal, R. (2000). Effect size, practical importance, and social policy for children. *Child Development, 71*, 173–180.

McCrae, R.R. (2001). Trait psychology and culture: Exploring intercultural comparisons. *Journal of Personality, 69*, 819–846.

McCrae, R.R., & Costa, P.T., Jr. (1999). A five-factor theory of personality. In L.A. Pervin & O.P. John (Eds.), *Handbook of personality theory and research* (pp. 139–153). New York: Guilford.

McCrae, R.R., Costa, P.T., Ostendorf, F., Angleitner, A., Hrebickova, M., Avia, M.D., Sanz, J., & Sanchez-Bernardos, M.L. (2000). Nature over nurture: Temperament, personality, and life span development. *Journal of Personality and Social Psychology, 78*, 173–186.

Measelle, J.R., Ablow, J.C., Cowan, P.A., & Cowan, C.P. (1998). Assessing young children's views of their academic, social, and emotional lives: An evaluation of the Self-Perception Scales of the Berkeley Puppet Interview. *Child Development, 69*, 1556–1576.

Meehl, P.E. (1992). Factors and taxa, traits and types, differences of degree and differences in kind. *Journal of Personality, 60*, 117–172.

Mervielde, I., & De Fruyt, F. (1999). Construction of the Hierarchical Personality Inventory for Children (Hi-PIC). In I. Mervielde, I. Deary, F. De Fruyt, & F. Ostendorf (Eds.). *Personality psychology in Europe: Proceedings of the Eighth European Conference on Personality* (pp. 107–127). Tilburg University Press.

Mervielde, I., & De Fruyt, F. (2000). The Big Five personality factors as a model for the structure of children's peer nominations. *European Journal of Personality, 14*, 91–106.

Mervielde, I., & De Fruyt, F. (2002). Assessing children's traits with the Hierarchical Personality Inventory for Children. In B. De Raad & M. Perugini (Eds.), *Big Five assessment* (pp. 129–142). Ashland, OH: Hogrefe & Huber.

Mervielde, I., De Fruyt, F., & Jarmuz, S. (1998). Linking openness and intellect in childhood and adulthood. In G.A. Kohnstamm, C.F. Halverson, I. Mervielde, & V.L. Havill (Eds.), *Parental descriptions of child personality: Developmental antecedents of the Big Five?* (pp. 105–126). Mahway, NJ: Erlbaum.

Meyer, G.J., Finn, S.E., Eyde, L.D., Kay, G.G., Moreland, K.L., Dies, R.R., Eisman, E.J., Kubiszyn, T.W., & Reed, G.M. (2001). Psychological testing and psychological assessment: A review of evidence and issues. *American Psychologist, 56*, 128–165.

Miech, R., Essex, M.J., & Goldsmith, H.H. (2001). Self-regulation as a mediator of the status-attainment process: Evidence from early childhood. *Sociology of Education, 74*, 102–120.

Miller, T.Q., Smith, T.W., Turner, C.W., Guijarro, M.L., & Hallet, A.J. (1996). A meta-analytic review of research on hostility and physical health. *Psychological Bulletin, 119*, 322–348.

Mineka, S., Watson, D.B., & Clark, L.A. (1998). Psychopathology: Comorbidity of anxiety and unipolar mood disorders. *Annual Review of Psychology, 49*, 377–412.

Mischel, W., Shoda, Y., & Peake, P.K. (1988). The nature of adolescent competencies predicted by preschool delay of gratification. *Journal of Personality and Social Psychology, 54*, 687–696.

Moffitt, T.E., & Caspi, A. (1998). Implications of violence between intimate partners for child psychologists and psychiatrists. *Journal of Child Psychology and Psychiatry, 39*, 137–144.

Moffitt, T.E., Robins, R.W., & Caspi, A. (2001). A couples analysis of partner abuse with implications for abuse prevention. *Criminology and Public Policy, 1*, 5–36.

Mount, M., Barrick, M.R., & Stewart, G.L. (1998). Five-factor model of personality and performance in jobs involving interpersonal interactions. *Human Performance, 11*, 145–165.

Newcorn, J.H., Halperin, J.M., Jensen, P.S., Abikoff, H.B., Arnld, L.E., Cantwell, D.P., Conners, C.K., Elliott, G.R., Epstein, J.N., Greenhill, L.L., Hechtman, L., Hinshaw, S.P., Hoza, B., Kraemer, H.C., Pelham, W.E., Severe, J.B., Swanson, J.M., Wells, K.C., Wigal, T., & Vitiello, B. (2001). Symptom profiles in children with ADHD: Effects of comorbidity and gender. *Journal of the American Academy of Child and Adolescent Psychiatry, 40*, 137–146.

Nigg, J.T. (2000). On inhibition/disinhibition in developmental psychopathology: Views from cognitive and personality psychology and a working inhibition taxonomy. *Psychological Bulletin, 126*, 220–246.

O'Brien, B.S., & Frick, P.J. (1996). Reward dominance: Associations with anxiety, conduct problems, and psychopathy in children. *Journal of Abnormal Child Psychology, 24*, 223–240.

O'Connor, T.G., Deater-Deckard, K., Fulker, D., Rutter, M., & Plomin, R. (1998). Genotype–environment correlations in late childhood and early adolescence: Antisocial behavioral problems and coercive parenting. *Developmental Psychology, 34*, 970–981.

Ozer, D. (1993). The Q-sort method. In D.C. Funder, C. Tomlinson-Keasy, R.D. Parke, & Widaman, K. (Eds.), *Studying lives through time: Approaches to personality and development* (pp. 343–376). Washington, DC: American Psychological Association.

Panksepp, J. (1998). *Affective neuroscience: The foundations of human and animal emotions.* New York: Oxford University Press.

Pasupathi, M. (2001). The social construction of the personal past and its implications for adult development. *Psychological Bulletin, 127*, 651–672.

Patterson, C., Kupersmidt, J., & Griesler, P. (1990). Children's perceptions of self and of relationships with others as a function of sociometric status. *Child Development, 61*, 1335–1349.

Pine, D.S., Cohen, E., Cohen, P., & Brook, J.S. (2000). Social phobia and the persistence of conduct problems. *Journal of Child Psychology and Psychiatry, 41*, 657–665.

Pfeifer, M., Goldsmith, H.H., Davidson, R.J., & Rickman, M. (in press). Continuity and change in inhibited and uninhibited children. *Child Development.*

Plomin, R. (1994). *Genetics and experience: The interplay between nature and nurture.* Thousand Oaks, CA: Sage.

Plomin, R., & Caspi, A. (1999). Behavioral genetics and personality. In L.A. Pervin & O.P. John (Eds.), *Handbook of personality: Theory and research* (2nd edn, pp. 251–276). New York: Guilford.

Plomin, R., DeFries, J.C., McClearn, J., & McGuffin, P. (2001). *Behavior genetics* (3rd edn). New York: Freeman.

Posner, M.I., & Rothbart, M.K. (2000). Developing mechanisms of self-regulation. *Development and Psychopathology, 12,* 427–441.

Presley, R., & Martin, R.P. (1994). Toward a structure of preschool temperament: Factor structure of the Temperament Assessment Battery for Children. *Journal of Personality, 62,* 415–448.

Quiggle, N.L., Garber, J., Panak, W.F., & Dodge, K.A. (1992). Social information processing in aggressive and depressed children. *Child Development, 63,* 1305–1320.

Rabiner, D.L, Lenhart, L., & Lochman, J.E. (1990). Automatic versus reflective social problem solving in relation to children's sociometric status. *Developmental Psychology, 26,* 1010–1016.

Raush, H.L. (1965). Interaction sequences. *Journal of Personality and Social Psychology, 2,* 487–499.

Resing, W.C.M., Bleichrodt, N., & Dekker, P.H. (1999). Measuring personality traits in the classroom. *European Journal of Personality, 13,* 493–509.

Revelle, W. (1993). Individual differences in personality and motivation: 'Non-cognitive' determinants of cognitive performance. In A. Baddeley & L. Weiskrantz (Eds.), *Attention: Selection, awareness, and control* (pp. 346–373). Oxford: Oxford University Press.

Rohde, P., Lewinsohn, P.M., & Seeley, J.R. (1990). Are people changed by the experience of having an episode of depression? A further test of the scar hypothesis. *Journal of Abnormal Psychology, 99,* 264–271.

Roberts, B.W., & DelVecchio, W.F. (2000). The rank-order consistency of personality traits from childhood to old age: A quantitative review of longitudinal studies. *Psychological Bulletin, 126,* 30–25.

Roberts, B.W., & Robins, R.W. (2000). Broad dispositions, broad aspirations: The intersection of personality and major life goals. *Personality and Social Psychology Bulletin, 26,* 1284–1296.

Robins, R.W., Caspi, A., & Moffitt, T.E. (in press). It's not just who you're with, it's who you are: Personality and relationship experiences across multiple relationships. *Journal of Personality.*

Robins, R.W., John, O.P., & Caspi, A. (1994). Major dimensions of personality in early adolescence: The Big Five and beyond. In C.F. Halverson, G.A. Kohnstamm, & R.P. Martin (Eds.), *The developing structure of temperament and personality from infancy to adulthood* (pp. 267–291). Hillsdale, NJ: Erlbaum.

Rothbart, M.K. (1981). Measurement of temperament in infancy. *Child Development, 52,* 569–578.

Rothbart, M.K., Ahadi, S.A., & Evans, D.E. (2000a). Temperament and personality: Origins and outcomes. *Journal of Personality and Social Psychology, 78,* 122–135.

Rothbart, M.K., Ahadi, S.A., Hershey, K.L., & Fisher, P. (2001). Investigations of temperament at three to seven years: The Children's Behavior Questionnaire. *Child Development, 72,* 1394–1408.

Rothbart, M.K., & Bates, J.E. (1998). Temperament. In W. Damon (Series Ed.) & N. Eisenberg (Vol. Ed.), *Handbook of child psychology: Vol. 3. Social, emotional, and personality development* (5th edn, pp. 105–176). New York: Wiley.

Rothbart, M.K., Derryberry, D., & Hershey, K. (2000b). Stability of temperament in childhood: Laboratory infant assessment to parent report at seven years. In

V.J. Molfese & D.L. Molfese (Eds.), *Temperament and personality development across the life span* (pp. 85–119). Mahwah, NJ: Erlbaum.

Rozanski, A., Blumenthal, J.A., & Kaplan, J. (1999). Impact of psychological factors on the pathogenesis of cardiovascular disease and implications for therapy. *Circulation, 99,* 2192–2217.

Rubin, K.H., Bukowski, W., & Parker, J.G. (1998). Peer interactions, relationships, and groups. In W. Damon (Series Ed.) & N. Eisenberg (Vol. Ed.), *Handbook of child psychology: Vol. 3. Social, emotional, and personality development* (5th edn, pp. 619–700). New York, Wiley.

Ruscio, J., & Ruscio, A.M. (2000). Informing the continuity controversy: A taxometric analysis of depression. *Journal of Abnormal Psychology, 109,* 473–487.

Rusting, C.L. (1998). Personality, mood, and cognitive processing of emotional information: Three conceptual frameworks. *Psychological Bulletin, 124,* 165–196.

Rutter, M. (in press). Crucial paths from risk factors to risk mechanisms. In B. Lahey, T.E. Moffitt & A. Caspi (Eds.), *The causes of conduct disorder and serious juvenile delinquency.* New York: Guilford.

Rutter, M., & Silberg, J. (2002). Gene-environment interplay in relation to emotional and behavioral disturbance. *Annual Review of Psychology, 53,* 463–490.

Saarni, C. (1999). *The development of emotional competence.* New York: Guilford.

Sameroff, A.J., & Haith, M.M. (1996). *The five to seven year shift.* Chicago: University of Chicago Press.

Sanson, A., & Prior, M. (1999). Temperament and behavioral precursors to oppositional defiant disorder and conduct disorder. In H.C. Quay & A.E. Hogan (Eds.), *Handbook of disruptive behavior disorders* (pp. 397–417). New York: Kluwer Academic/Plenum.

Scarr, S., & McCartney, K. (1983). How people make their own environments: A theory of genotype to environment effects. *Child Development, 54,* 424–435.

Scholte, R.H.J., van Aken, M.A.G., & van Lieshout, C.F.M. (1997). Adolescent personality factors in self-ratings and peer nominations and their prediction of peer acceptance and peer rejection. *Journal of Personality Assessment, 69,* 534–554.

Schneider, B., Smith, D.B., Taylor, S., & Fleenor, J. (1998). Personality and organizations: A test of the homogeneity of personality hypothesis. *Journal of Applied Psychology, 83,* 4.

Shea, M.T., Leon, A.C., Mueller, T.I., Solomon, D.A., Warshw, M.G., & Keller, M.B. (1996). Does major depression result in lasting personality change? *American Journal of Psychiatry, 153,* 1404–1410.

Sherif, M., Harvey, O., White, B.J., Hood, W.R., & Sherif, C. (1961). *Intergroup conflict and cooperation: The robbers' cave experiment.* Norman, OK: University of Oklahoma Press.

Shiner, R.L. (1998). How shall we speak of children's personalities in middle childhood?: A preliminary taxonomy. *Psychological Bulletin, 124,* 308–332.

Shiner, R.L. (2000). Linking childhood personality with adaptation: Evidence for continuity and change across time into late adolescence. *Journal of Personality and Social Psychology, 78,* 310–325.

Shiner, R.L., Masten, A.S., & Tellegen, A. (2002). A developmental perspective on personality in emerging adulthood: Childhood antecedents and concurrent adaptation. *Journal of Personality and Social Psychology, 83,* 1165–1177.

Shiner, R.L., Tellegen, A., & Masten, A.S. (2001). Exploring personality across childhood into adulthood: Can one describe and predict a moving target? *Psychological Inquiry, 12,* 96–100.

Slutske, W., Heath, A.C., Madden, P.A.F., Bucholz, K.K., Statham, D.J., & Martin, N.G. (2002). Personality and the genetic risk for alcohol dependence. *Journal of Abnormal Psychology, 111,* 124–133.

Sonuga-Barke, E.J.S. (1998). Categorical models of childhood disorder: A conceptual and empirical analysis. *Journal of Child Psychology and Psychiatry, 39,* 115–133.

Smith, T.W., & Williams, P.G. (1992). Personality and health: Advantages and limitations of the five-factor model. *Journal of Personality, 60,* 395–423.

Sroufe, L.A., Carlson, E., & Shulman, S. (1993). Individuals in relationships: Development from infancy through adolescence. In D.C. Funder, R.D. Parke, C. Tomlinson-Keasey, & K. Widaman (Eds.), *Studying lives through time* (pp. 315–342). Washington, DC: American Psychological Association.

Strayhorn, J.M. (2002). Self-control: Theory and research. *Journal of the American Academy of Child and Adolescent Psychiatry, 41,* 7–16.

Suls, J., & Mullen, B. (1982). From the cradle to the grave: Comparison and self-evaluation across the life-span. In J. Suls (Ed.), *Psychological perspectives on the self* (vol. 1, pp. 97–125). Hillsdale, NJ: Erlbaum.

Swann, W.B., Jr. (1996). *Self traps: The elusive quest for higher self esteem.* New York: Freeman.

Teasdale, J.D., & Barnard, P.J. (1993). *Affect, cognition, and change: Remodeling depressive thought.* Hove, England: Erlbaum.

Tellegen, A. (1985). Structure of mood and personality and their relevance to assessing anxiety, with an emphasis on self-report. In A.H. Tuma & J.D. Maser (Eds.), *Anxiety and the anxiety disorders* (pp. 681–706). Hillsdale, NJ: Erlbaum.

Tellegen, A. (1991). Personality traits: Issues of definition, evidence, and assessment. In W.M. Grove & D. Cicchetti (Eds.). *Thinking clearly about psychology: Vol. 2. Personality and psychopathology* (pp. 10–35). Minneapolis, MN: University of Minnesota.

Tellegen, A., & Waller, N.G. (1992). Exploring personality through test construction: Development of the Multi-dimensional Personality Questionnaire (MPQ). Minneapolis: Unpublished manuscript, University of Minnesota.

Tesser, A. (1980). Self-esteem maintenance in family dynamics. *Journal of Personality and Social Psychology, 39,* 77–91.

Thomas, A., Chess, S., & Birch, H. (1968). *Temperament and behavior disorders in children.* New York: New York University Press.

Thomas, A., Chess, S., Birch, H., Hertzig, M., & Korn, S. (1963). *Behavioral individuality in early childhood.* New York: New York University Press.

Tremblay, R.E. (2000). The development of aggressive behavior during childhood: What have we learned in the past century. *International Journal of Behavioral Development, 24,* 129–141.

Vance, H.B., & Pumariega, A.J. (2001) (Eds). *Clinical assessment of child and adolescent behavior.* New York: Wiley.

van Lieshout, C.F.M. (2000). Lifespan personality development: Self-organizing goal-oriented agents and developmental outcome. *International Journal of Behavioral Development, 24,* 276–288.

van Lieshout, C.F.M., & Haselager, G.J.T. (1993). *The Big Five personality factors in the Nijmegen California Child Q-set (NCCQ).* Nijmegen, The Netherlands: University of Nijmegen.

van Lieshout, C.F.M., & Haselager, G.J.T. (1994). The Big Five personality factors in Q-sort descriptions of children and adolescents. In C.F. Halverson, Jr., G.A. Kohnstamm & R.P. Martin (Eds.). *The developing structure of temperament and personality from infancy to adulthood* (pp. 293–318). Hillsdale NJ: Erlbaum.

Wachtel, P.L. (1973). Psychodynamics, behavior therapy, and the implacable experimenter: An inquiry into the consistency of personality. *Journal of Abnormal Psychology, 82,* 324–334.

Walker, J.L., Lahey, B.B., Russo, M.F., Frick, P.J., Christ, M.A.G., McBurnett, K., Loeber, R., Stouthamer-Loeber, M., & Green, S.M. (1991). Anxiety, inhibition, and conduct disorder in children: I. Relation to social impairment. *Journal of the American Academy of Child and Adolescent Psychiatry, 30,* 187–191.

Watson, D., & Clark, L.A. (1984). Negative affectivity: The disposition to experience aversive emotional states. *Psychological Bulletin, 96,* 465–490.

Watson, D., & Clark, L.A. (1997). Extraversion and its positive emotional core. In R. Hogan, J. Johnson, & S. Briggs (Eds.), *Handbook of Personality Psychology* (pp. 767–793). San Diego, CA: Academic Press.

Watson, D., Clark, L.A., & Harkness, A.R. (1994). Structures of personality and their relevance to psychopathology. *Journal of Abnormal Psychology, 103,* 18–31.

Watson, D., & Pennebaker, J.W. (1989). Health complaints, stress, and distress: Exploring the central role of negative affectivity. *Psychological Review, 96,* 234–254.

Watson, D., Wiese, D., Vaidya, J., & Tellegen, A. (1999). The two general activation systems of affect: Structural findings, evolutionary considerations, and psychobiological evidence. *Journal of Personality and Social Psychology, 76,* 820–838.

Werner, E.E., & Smith, R.S. (1992). *Overcoming the odds: High risk children from birth to adulthood.* Ithaca, NY: Cornell University Press.

White, J.L., Moffitt, T.E., Caspi, A., Bartusch, D.J., Needles, D.J., & Stouthamer-Loeber (1994). Measuring impulsivity and examining its relationship to delinquency. *Journal of Abnormal Psychology, 103,* 192–205.

White, J., Moffitt, T.E., & Silva, P.A. (1989). A prospective replication of the protective effects of IQ in subjects at high risk for juvenile delinquency. *Journal of Clinical and Consulting Psychology, 57,* 719–724.

Widiger, T.A., & Clark, L.A. (2000). Toward DSM-V and the classification of psychopathology. *Psychological Bulletin, 126,* 946–963.

Widiger, T.A., Trull, T.J., Clarkin, J.F., Sanderson, C., & Costa, P.T. (2002). A description of the DSM-IV personality disorders with the five-factor model of personality. In P.T. Costa & T.A. Widiger (Eds.), *Personality disorders and the five-factor model of personality* (2nd edn, pp. 89–99). Washington, DC: American Psychological Association.

Widiger, T.A., Verheul, R., & van den Brink, W. (1999). Personality and psychopathology. In L.A. Pervin & O.P. John (Eds.), *Handbook of personality: Theory and research* (2nd edn, pp. 347–366). New York: Guilford.

Wills, T.A., Sandy, J.M., & Yaeger, A. (2000). Temperament and adolescent substance use: An epigenetic approach to risk and protection. *Journal of Personality, 68*, 1127–1152.

Wootton, J.M., Frick, P.J., Shelton, K.K., & Silverthorn, P. (1997). Ineffective parenting and childhood conduct problems: The moderating role of callous-unemotional traits. *Journal of Consulting and Clinical Psychology, 65*, 292–300.

Wright, B.R.E., Caspi, A., Moffitt, T.E., & Silva, P.A. (2001). The effects of social ties on crime vary by criminal propensity: A life-course model of interdependence. *Criminology, 39*, 321–351.

Zuckerman, M. (1999). *Vulnerability to psychopathology: A biosocial model.* Washington, D.C: American Psychological Association.

Zuroff, D.C. (1986). Was Gordon Allport a trait theorist? *Journal of Personality and Social Psychology, 51*, 993–1000.

Manuscript accepted 5 July 2002

Appendix: Measures of child and adolescent temperament and personality

Temperament and personality in children can be measured using a variety of methods, including questionnaires (parent, teacher, peer, and self-report), peer nominations, Q-sorts, naturalistic observations, and lab assessments. Few measures assess the full range of individual differences described in this article, and fewer still provide information about both higher- and lower-order traits; the development of reliable, valid, and comprehensive measures of child and adolescent personality remains an important task. Researchers have debated the validity of the different methods. Parent questionnaires, which are the most popular measures of temperament, have particularly come under fire because of the potential biases shown by parents (Kagan, 1998). However, the empirical evidence shows that each measurement method possesses strengths and weaknesses, and none of the methods should be categorically dismissed as invalid (Rothbart & Bates, 1998).

Researchers need to consider several issues when selecting methods and instruments for measuring temperament or personality. First, ideally more than one method should be used to provide a more valid assessment of a particular trait; data from different sources capture information on children's behavior in different contexts. Second, more than one trait should be measured, even in studies focused primarily on a single trait. Developmental researchers have often focused on single traits in isolation. By using a comprehensive measurement battery that assesses multiple traits, researchers can obtain critical information about the etiological specificity and the discriminant validity of the target trait. Third, researchers need to consider carefully whether a measure truly taps the trait of interest; labels for measures (e.g., scale names on questionnaires) are often misleading. Fourth, it is important to consider not just what is included in a particular instrument, but also what is left out. For example, many temperament questionnaires do not tap the full range of individual differences observable in children. To obtain information about a wider range of behaviors, supplemental measures may be necessary.

Below we present information about available measures of childhood and adolescent temperament and personality. The accompanying table lists the various methods for measuring individual differences from preschool age through adolescence. We have included sample measures for each method of assessment. Our list of sample measures is by no means comprehensive; the list is intended simply to give some suggestions for potential measures. For a more comprehensive list of temperament measures in infancy and childhood, we refer readers to Goldsmith and Rieser-Danner (1990).

Questionnaires, Q-sorts, and a puppet interview: Parent, teacher, peer, and self-report

Questionnaires are the most popular method for measuring childhood temperament and personality. Parent questionnaires are used most often, but teacher- and self-report questionnaires are used as well. All questionnaires share several strengths: They aggregate information about children's behavior across a number of situations and over a period of time; they are inexpensive to use; and they are efficient ways of gathering a lot of information. Questionnaires also allow researchers to solicit information about relatively rare but potentially significant behaviors, such as intense expressions of negative emotions. Although critics of questionnaires have argued that these measures are plagued by reporter bias, research suggests that 'parent-report measures are more than just perceptions' (Mangelsdorf, Schoppe, & Buur, 2000, p. 134). Further, other methods of assessment may contain some bias as well. Researchers may choose to obtain questionnaire reports and aggregate reports from more than one informant (e.g., mother and father, parent and teacher) in order to address the issue of bias; presumably different reporters will not share identical biases.

Although it may be useful to aggregate reports from different informants, it is important to recognize that reports from different informants possess different characteristics. *Parents* typically see a wide range of their children's behavior, including behavior that may be inhibited outside the home (e.g., tantrums in older children). Parents may know relatively less about their children's behavior with peers. Some parents may not have observed the behavior of a variety of children; these parents therefore may have difficulty comparing their children to the 'average' child. In contrast, *teachers* have seen a range of children and can make experience-based comparisons among them, and teachers presumably can report effectively on children's behavior with peers.

In several studies, *peers* have provided reports about other children's personalities. Two types of peer measurement are possible: Peers can nominate other students who are 'best' or 'least well' described by a particular item (similar to the peer-reputation measures frequently used in developmental research), or peers can fill out a questionnaire describing another student. Peer-nomination ratings from two studies of adolescents produced fewer factors than are sometimes found in reports provided by adults (Mervielde & De Fruyt, 2000; Scholte, van Aken, & van Lieshout, 1997); it is possible that peers provide less differentiated views of their fellow students. It is not clear at what age peers can provide valid reports on other children's personalities. To date, personality-nomination studies have included adolescents only, but measures of peer reputation outside the personality literature (e.g., measures of aggression or likeability) are frequently administered to preschool and school-age children (Masten, Morison, & Pellegrini, 1985; Rubin, Bukowski, & Parker, 1998).

Self-report measures can also be obtained. As with peer report measures, it is not clear at what age self-report questionnaires demonstrate validity. Although it is common to use self-report inventories to assess aspects of psychopathology in school-age children (Vance & Pumariega, 2001), self-report measures of personality typically are used only with adolescents. There is interesting recent evidence, however, that children as young as age 4 years may be able to provide reliable self-reports for certain aspects of their behavior and emotions. The Berkeley Puppet Interview is a modified version of a puppet interview method originally developed by Eder (1990) to measure symptomatology and school adjustment among 4- to 8-year-old children, an age group once thought to be incapable of providing reliable self-reports (Ablow et al., 1999; Measelle, Ablow, Cowan, & Cowan, 1998). Several of the scales (e.g., achievement motivation, social competence, depression-anxiety, and aggression-hostility) measure central aspects of individual differences in person-

ality. Children's self-perceptions on these scales showed modest to moderate convergence with mother and teacher ratings.

A method similar to the questionnaire is the Q-sort (Block, 1961/1978; Caspi et al., 1992; Ozer, 1993), in which an informant sorts a set of cards (with an item on each) into a forced, quasi-normal distribution based on how well each item describes the child. Q-sorts can be completed by parents, teachers, trained observers, or clinicians. The Q-sort method shares the strengths and weaknesses of questionnaires, with two exceptions. First, the Q-sort method requires the informant to make a large number of decisions about the relative descriptiveness of different items, which makes the procedure longer but which may also enhance the thoughtfulness of the informant's eventual ratings. Second, the Q-sort method offers multiple scoring and analytic possibilities for researchers and clinicians, thereby enhancing the ultimate yield from the collected data.

Naturalistic observations and laboratory assessments

As an alternative to questionnaires, researchers have used naturalistic observations and laboratory tasks to assess individual differences in children. Although there are relatively comprehensive home observation measures available for infants, we are not aware of any comprehensive observation systems for normal-range temperament or personality traits in children. Developmental researchers have developed coding procedures for observing a variety of specific behavioral tendencies, such as social withdrawal, aggression, and dominance (Rubin et al., 1998), prosocial behaviors (Eisenberg & Fabes, 1998), and activity level (Eaton, 1994). Researchers have also used laboratory tasks to measure a variety of individual differences in children, including reactivity and inhibition (Kagan, Reznick, Clarke, Snidman, & Garcia-Coll, 1984; Kagan, Reznick, & Snidman, 1987), effortful control (Kochanska, Murray, Jacques, Koenig, & Vandegeest, 1996), and attention/persistence (White et al., 1994). A more comprehensive battery of laboratory tasks assessing temperament in preschool and childhood has been developed by Goldsmith and colleagues (e.g., Pfeifer, Goldsmith, Davidson, & Rickman, in press). Strengths of laboratory tasks include the controlled nature of the observations, the opportunity for fine-grained analysis of specific behaviors, and the potential for making on-line links to brain functioning. Both naturalistic observations and laboratory assessments share some weaknesses: Both methods are time and labor intensive, may be vulnerable to strong situational effects on children's behavior, and may not allow for observation of low frequency behaviors.

32 Rebecca Shiner and Avshalom Caspi

Appendix table Sample measures of temperament and personality in children and adolescents

Type of measure	Age range or grades[a]	Scales
Questionnaire		
Big Five questionnaires		
Inventory of Child Individual Differences (ICID, Halverson et al., in press)	Ages 3–12	Big Five and 15 lower-order scales
Hierarchical Personality Inventory for Children		Big Five and 18 lower-order facet scales
HiPIC (Mervielde & De Fruyt, 1999, 2002)	Ages 6–12 (parent)	
HiPIC (De Fruyt et al., 2000)	Ages 12–17 (self-report)	Big Five and 18 lower-order facet scales
Big Five adjective checklists		
Goldberg (2001)	Grades 1–6	Big Five
Goldberg (1992) used with youth (e.g., Graziano, Jensen-Campbell, & Finch, 1997; Graziano, Jensen-Campbell, Steele, & Hair, 1998; Jensen-Campbell & Graziano, 2001)	Grades 6 through adolescence	Big Five
Child Behavior Questionnaire (Rothbart et al., 2001)	Ages 3–7	Extraversion/Surgency, Negative Affectivity, Effortful Control, and 15 lower-order scales
Q-sort		
California Child Q-Set (Block & Block, 1969/1980; Common-Language Version of the California Child Q-set, Caspi et al., 1992)	Ages 3 through adolescence	Big Five; Ego-resiliency and Ego-control
Peer nominations		
Bipolar nomination scales (Mervielde & De Fruyt, 2000)	Ages 9–12	Agreeableness, Extraversion-Emotional Instability, Intellect-Conscientiousness
Revised Class Play (Masten, Morison, & Pellegrini, 1985)	Grades 3–6	Sociable-Leader, Aggressive-Disruptive, Sensitive-Isolated
Puppet Interview		
Berkeley Puppet Interview (Measelle et al., 1998)	Ages 4–7	Academic competence, Achievement motivation, Social competence, Peer acceptance, Depression-anxiety, Aggression-hostility

[a]The age ranges and grades listed in the table are those for which the measures have been tested. In some cases, it is possible that the measures could be used with children younger or older than those listed.

Part III
Impairment and Disorder

[17]

10-Year Research Update Review: The Epidemiology of Child and Adolescent Psychiatric Disorders: I. Methods and Public Health Burden

E. JANE COSTELLO, PH.D., HELEN EGGER, M.D., AND ADRIAN ANGOLD, M.R.C.PSYCH.

ABSTRACT

Objective: To review recent progress in child and adolescent psychiatric epidemiology in the area of prevalence and burden. **Method:** The literature published in the past decade was reviewed under two headings: methods and findings. **Results:** Methods for assessing the prevalence and community burden of child and adolescent psychiatric disorders have improved dramatically in the past decade. There are now available a broad range of interviews that generate *DSM* and *ICD* diagnoses with good reliability and validity. Clinicians and researchers can choose among interview styles (respondent based, interviewer based, best estimate) and methods of data collection (paper and pencil, computer assisted, interviewer or self-completion) that best meet their needs. Work is also in progress to develop brief screens to identify children in need of more detailed assessment, for use by teachers, pediatricians, and other professionals. The median prevalence estimate of functionally impairing child and adolescent psychiatric disorders is 12%, although the range of estimates is wide. Disorders that often appear first in childhood or adolescence are among those ranked highest in the World Health Organization's estimates of the global burden of disease. **Conclusions:** There is mounting evidence that many, if not most, lifetime psychiatric disorders will first appear in childhood or adolescence. Methods are now available to monitor youths and to make early intervention feasible. *J. Am. Acad. Child Adolesc. Psychiatry,* 2005;44(10):972–986. **Key Words:** epidemiology, services, methods.

The focus of these two 10-year reviews is, unlike most in this series, not on a disorder or treatment but on an approach to thinking about disease. Many years ago, Tony Earls (1979) defined epidemiology as "an exact and basic science of social medicine and public health." Epidemiology provides the scientific underpinnings for the prevention and control of disease across the spectrum of medicine, from infectious diseases like acquired immunodeficiency syndrome to chronic conditions like diabetes. Here we discuss how epidemiology in the past decade has increased our understanding of psychiatric disorders of childhood and adolescence.

Child and adolescent psychiatry came late to epidemiological research, and in one respect this is fortunate because a tremendous amount of empirical, theoretical, and statistical work has been done in other branches of medicine and psychology, from which we have been able to benefit. In the past 30 years, and outstandingly in the past decade, research in our area has caught up, and even, as in the innovative use of longitudinal epidemiological samples to study gene–environment interactions (Caspi et al., 2002, 2003; Foley et al., 2004), moved to the forefront of epidemiological research.

First, we explain what an epidemiological approach to child and adolescent psychiatry can offer, making clear Earls's distinction between "public health epidemiology," whose task is to monitor and reduce the burden of disease on the community, and "scientific epidemiology," which uses epidemiological methods to

Accepted April 25, 2005.

All of the authors are with the Center for Developmental Epidemiology, Duke University Medical School, Durham, NC.

Work on this paper was supported in part by grants 06937, 01002, and 01167 from the National Institute of Mental Health, grants 011301 and 016977 from the National Institute on Drug Abuse, and a Pfizer Faculty Scholar Award in Clinical Epidemiology to Dr. Egger.

Correspondence to Dr. E. Jane Costello, Box 3454, Duke University Health Systems, Durham NC 27710; e-mail: elizabeth.costello@duke.edu.

0890-8567/05/4410–0972©2005 by the American Academy of Child and Adolescent Psychiatry.

DOI: 10.1097/01.chi.0000172552.41596.6f

understand the causes of mental illness (Earls, 1979). Then, we review how far epidemiology has progressed in its "public health" task of monitoring the burden of child and adolescent psychiatric disorder in the past decade. In Part II, we focus on epidemiology's other task: to build a body of scientific information about what causes psychiatric disorders to occur when and where they do. We describe a major paradigm shift that has occurred in recent years: like child and adolescent psychiatry in general, epidemiology is beginning to incorporate developmental psychopathology into a new approach with a new name: developmental epidemiology.

WHAT IS EPIDEMIOLOGY?

Epidemiology is the study of patterns of disease in human populations (Kleinbaum et al., 1982). Patterns are nonrandom distributions, and patterns of disease distribution occur in both time and space. Whenever we observe a nonrandom distribution, we have the opportunity to identify causal factors that influence who gets a disease and who does not. For example, we observe that depression rises rapidly after puberty in girls, but not to the same extent in boys (Angold and Worthman, 1993). This nonrandom distribution in time suggests that there may be something about puberty in girls that is causally related to depression (Angold et al., 1998a). An example of disease distribution in space can be seen in the Methods for the Epidemiology of Child and Adolescent Mental Disorders (MECA) study of five sites in the United States and Puerto Rico (Shaffer et al., 1996). Although the prevalence of psychiatric disorders was fairly similar across sites, the likelihood that a psychiatric diagnosis was accompanied by significant functional impairment was much higher in children at the mainland sites than in Puerto Rico. This offers the opportunity to study between-site differences that may result in differences in the level of impairment caused by psychiatric disorders. The task of epidemiology is to understand these observed patterns in time and space and to use this understanding as a basis for the prevention and control of disease.

Epidemiology has similarities to and differences from clinical medicine. Like clinical medicine, epidemiology is an action-oriented discipline whose goal is interventions to prevent and control disease. Scientific knowledge about the cause and course of disease is another common goal. Epidemiology also reflects clinical medicine

in using two methods of attack on disease: tactical methods, concerned with the practical and administrative problems of disease control at the day-to-day level, and strategic methods, concerned with finding out what causes disease so that new weapons of prevention and control can be engineered (Earls, 1980; Susser, 1973). Thus, for example, in their tactical or public health role, epidemiologists can be found reporting on the prevalence of adolescent drug abuse and advising on how to control its spread, whereas others working at the strategic level may be exploring the science underlying environmental constraints on gene expression.

Epidemiology diverges from clinical medicine to the extent that it concentrates on understanding and controlling disease processes in the context of the population at risk, whereas the primary focus of clinical medicine is the individual patient. This does not mean that epidemiology is not concerned with the individual; on the contrary, it is very much concerned with understanding the individual s illness and the causes of that illness. The difference lies in the frame of reference. Put crudely, clinical medicine asks, "What is wrong with this person and how should I treat him or her?" Epidemiology asks, "What is wrong with this person and what is it about him or her that has resulted in this illness?" Why is this child depressed, but not her brother? If her mother is also depressed, then is the child's depression a cause, a consequence, or an unrelated, chance co-occurrence? Such questions immediately set the individual child within a frame of reference of other children, or other family members, or other people of the same sex or race or social class.

As the study of patterns of disease distribution in time and space, epidemiology encompasses a great deal more than simply counting noses. "Epidemiology counts" (Freedman, 1984), but it does far more than that. This review of the past decade shows just how much more epidemiology has begun to do in one of its final frontiers: child and adolescent psychiatric disorder.

EPIDEMIOLOGICAL METHODS: ASSESSING CHILD AND ADOLESCENT PSYCHIATRIC DISORDERS IN NONCLINICAL SAMPLES

Counting cases is an important first step toward measuring the social burden caused by a disease and the effectiveness of prevention. For most diseases, simply counting the number of individuals presenting for treatment will produce estimates that are seriously biased by referral practices, ability to pay, and other factors; a particular

COSTELLO ET AL.

problem in child psychiatry because parents, teachers, and pediatricians all serve as "gatekeepers" to treatment (Horwitz et al., 1998). Community surveys are needed to measure the extent of need and unmet need for prevention or treatment.

A major task facing child and adolescent psychiatric epidemiologists is to develop assessment measures that accurately identify "true" cases. In recent decades, this task has been understood as one of translating the disease taxonomies in current use (in practice, the *ICD* [World Health Organization, 1978, 1987] and the *DSM* [American Psychiatric Association, 1980, 1987, 1994]) into questionnaires, interviews, and other means for collecting the relevant information from individuals and coding it into diagnostic categories. A decade ago, child and adolescent psychiatric epidemiology was still struggling with the task of developing measures that accurately performed this task for nonclinical samples, preferably for reasons of cost, measures that could be administered without long-term clinical training. The process was made more challenging by the rapid revisions of the taxonomies, which kept moving the target, and by a lack of clarity in many areas of the symptom criteria. Several kinds of measures were needed, ranging in detail from those that mirrored best-practice clinical diagnosis as closely as possible to shorter screening questionnaires for use in the many settings in which full diagnostic assessments were not feasible.

Diagnostic Interviews

The decade since *DSM-IV* appeared has been marked by what could be seen either as surrender in the face of an insoluble problem or as a more mature approach to assessment. It became clear that (1) there is a limit to the degree of test-retest reliability achievable in psychiatric interviews, caused to a considerable extent by problems at the level of the taxonomy (what does "often loses temper" really mean?); (2) diagnostic instruments now available, whether for parents, adolescents, or children older than 8 years, match the test-retest reliability of comparable instruments for adults (Angold and Fisher, 1999; Shaffer et al., 1999); (3) different informants will disagree not because the measuring instrument is faulty but because they really do see different aspects of a child (Kraemer et al., 2003); (4) there is no single best way to identify psychiatric disorders using face-to-face psychiatric interviews. All of the various types of diagnostic interview (e.g., respondent-based interviews, interviewer-based interviews, best-estimate diagnostic interviews) have shown similar levels of test-retest reliability and validity (Angold and Fisher, 1999). Statistical methods are being developed for optimally combining data from multiple informants (Kraemer et al., 2003) and across studies (Festa et al., 2000).

A result of these developments is that the National Institute of Mental Health (NIMH) has ended its period of special support for the development of a single psychiatric interview (the Diagnostic Interview Schedule for Children (DISC; Shaffer et al., 2000). Researchers should decide which diagnostic interview to use based on the core questions that they want to answer in their study and the resources available; for example, will the interviewers come from a survey research company or will they be trained and supervised by the research team?

The former tend to be good at conducting respondent-based interviews such as the DISC, in which each question is fixed. When more intensive training and supervision of interviewers are possible, it has been shown that lay interviewers using a structured interview such as the Child and Adolescent Psychiatric Assessment (CAPA; Angold and Costello, 2000) are capable of making what would once have been called "clinical judgments" about the presence and severity of symptoms and are less likely to overidentify rare symptoms, such as those of psychosis (Breslau, 1987).

Are clinically qualified "best estimators" available to make a final judgment if the fixed questions leave the interviewer unsure of how to code a symptom? If so, then it is feasible to use an interview such as the Development and Well-Being Assessment (DAWBA; Goodman et al., 2000), which combines highly structured questions with additional material, if necessary.

Do the Study Questions Require Categorical Diagnoses or Symptom Scales or Both? All of the interviews described here generate diagnoses. Most also produce symptom scales created by adding the number of positive symptoms. These can be useful provided that the focus is on the symptoms that go into a formal diagnosis and not on any other related symptoms, or on the frequency, duration, or intensity of symptoms. If this kind of information is needed, however, the choice is between instruments such as the CAPA, which incorporate these features, and interviews designed for clinicians, such as the Schedule for Affective Disorders and Schizophrenia for School-Age Children (Ambrosini, 2000; Shanee et al., 1997).

Extensions of Psychiatric Interviews

A great deal of progress has been made in expanding the range of instruments and modalities available for making formal psychiatric diagnoses. Here, we describe some of these developments.

Assessing Psychiatric Disorders in Preschool Children. Just as the in the 1980s, child and adolescent psychiatrists discovered that it was possible to generate reliable diagnostic information from structured interviews with school-age children, so in the past decade, they have discovered that structured interviews with parents of children 2 to 5 years old yield reliable responses that map onto *DSM-IV* diagnostic categories.

Major efforts have been made to create a clear taxonomy of early childhood disorders (Angold and Egger, 2004; Boris et al., 2004; Luby et al., 2003; Scheeringa et al., 2003; Stafford et al., 2003). Several new instruments have been developed for this age group (Carter et al., 2004; Egger and Angold, 2004; Wakschlag et al., 2002). A young child version of the DISC is under development (see http://www.c-disc.com). Work is also going on at several sites to integrate these parent measures with reliable assessments of affect and behavior that can be used directly with young children, such as the MacArthur Story-Stem Battery (Emde et al., 2003) and the Berkeley Puppet Interview (Ablow and Measelle, 1993; Measelle et al., 1998).

Assessing Psychiatric Disorders in Young Adults. When participants in a longitudinal study are interviewed with a measure designed for children one year and one designed for adults the next, year-to-year differences may reflect changes in method as much as developmental changes. Two diagnostic interviews for children and adolescents have developed instruments relevant to adolescents moving out of the home and into independent lives. The DISC has a young adult version in preparation (see http://www.c-disc.com) and the CAPA has a version available for adolescents living away from home and for young adults (the Young Adult Psychiatric Assessment [Angold et al., 1999]). Both are designed to be used with the participant alone, without supporting information from a parent, as is customary with younger individuals.

Alternative Methods of Data Collection. The standard method of data collection until recently has been, as in the clinical field, the face-to-face interview with the child and/or parent. The interviewer usually asked questions from a printed schedule and recorded responses the same way; the latter were then entered into computer files and coded using specially written algorithms that followed the logic of the diagnostic taxonomy (*DSM* or *ICD*). Many alternatives are being developed and tested. First, most interviews have or are developing computerized versions of the standard interview. These may simply transfer the paper-and-pencil interview to a laptop computer, so that the interviewer reads the same questions from the screen as he or she would from the paper schedule and keys in the responses. The advantage here is that the data are entered directly into a database, cutting out an expensive and error-prone phase in data collection. These programs may also prevent the interviewer from entering out-of-range information and guide him or her through sets of branching questions. Examples of computerized interviews are the DISC, a version of the Diagnostic Interview for Children and Adolescents (Reich, 2000), and the Preschool Age Psychiatric Assessment (Egger and Angold, 2004).

A second development has been to provide the child or parent with direct access to the computerized interview, cutting out the interviewer. The respondent may read the questions on the screen or listen to them through earphones, or both. Examples of this approach are the "voice DISC" (see http://www.c-disc.com), and the audio-CASI (computer-assisted self-completed interviewing) sections of the CAPA (see http://devepi.mc.duke.edu). There is evidence that respondents will report more information, particularly about sensitive topics such as abuse and drug use, than they will face to face with an interviewer (Des Jarles et al., 1999; Metzger et al., 2000; Taylor et al., 1999).

Third, investigators have been working on adding visual cues to the verbal forms of questioning in the hope that this will improve the validity of psychiatric interviewing with younger children or those with lower levels of cognitive development. Picture interviews based on earlier versions of the DISC have been developed by a group in Quebec (Valla et al., 1994, 1997, 2000). There are various versions, using both African American and white boys and girls in the pictures. Reliability appears to be comparable to that of the verbal version.

Other Languages. Most of the major assessment instruments have now been translated into Spanish. The DAWBA, which was used for the recent national survey of British children, has online versions in English, Norwegian, Portuguese, and Spanish (http://www.dawba.com/b0.html), and the DISC is available in at least 10 languages (Web site under construction), whereas the CAPA and Preschool Age Psychiatric Assessment also exist in several languages, including Spanish and French. International comparisons are becoming a real possibility.

Screening for Psychiatric Disorder

Brief lists of questions or questionnaires completed by the child, teacher, parent, and/or clinician are widely used to assess psychopathology, much more so than are full psychiatric interviews. Screening instruments are often used in schools, primary care pediatric offices, and with high-risk groups such as children in juvenile justice settings, as well as in national surveys. Thus, it is important to review progress in this field.

Screens have two main types of use: to estimate prevalence rates of a given problem at the level of the population and to identify individual children as being at high risk of a disorder so that they can be selected for further evaluation, clinical services, or preventive interventions. Evidence from the past decade has shown that there are important differences in the utility of brief screens, depending on the purpose for which they are used.

Screens as Epidemiological Tools. Brief screening measures are widely used as components of nationally representative "surveillance

studies," discussed later in this section. They may be completed by parent, teacher, or child or some combination of these. When children themselves have completed such questionnaires in school settings, these have tended to be anonymous surveys (e.g., Alcohol and Drug Defense Program, 1991; Johnston et al., 1996; Stevens et al., 1995; Swanson et al., 1992).

Screening or "indicator" measures may be used in several ways in studies of representative population samples. They may be used as a substitute for, or approximation of, psychiatric interviews, in studies short on time or trained staff. If the sensitivity (proportion of true cases identified) and specificity (proportion of true noncases identified) of the screen in relationship to an accepted criterion, such as a psychiatric interview, are acceptable, then it can be used to estimate population prevalence rates. Screens are used in this way, for example, in the National Longitudinal Survey of Children and Youth (Bennett and Offord, 2001) and the Dutch national survey (Verhulst et al., 1997). Work to develop a screen for use in conjunction with the National Health Interview Survey in the United States is in progress (Bourdon et al., 2005). They may be used as the first stage in a multistage protocol designed to increase the number of likely "cases" for more detailed assessment at a later stage, e.g., Isle of Wight study (Rutter et al., 1970), the Great Smoky Mountains Study (Costello et al., 1996b), Caring for Children in the Community (Angold et al., 2002), the Pittsburgh Youth Study (Loeber et al., 2001). They may be used for follow-up of subjects in longitudinal protocols where frequent contact is required (Farmer et al., 1999) and where change in symptom levels may be more important than change in diagnostic status.

Screening instruments make two sorts of errors: they identify children as cases when they are not (false positives) and they miss true cases (false negatives). Nevertheless, when a screening instrument has good test-retest reliability and validity relative to the criterion measure, it can do three useful things:

1. It can provide a useful approximation of population prevalence, even when it makes errors, provided that the false-positive and false-negative errors are reasonably balanced.
2. Screens tend to be inexpensive and intensive interviews expensive. It is sometimes possible to screen a large sample and randomly select a certain proportion with different screen scores for detailed assessment. With the right sampling design, this can help to reduce sample size (and cost) without too great an increase in variance; indeed, if correctly used it can reduce variance and increase power (Erkanli et al., 1997, 1998, 1999).
3. A screening questionnaire can reduce subject burden, which is particularly important in nonclinical and longitudinal studies.

In short, screens can be useful epidemiological tools, if carefully used.

Screens as Tools for Identifying High-Risk Children. Physicians, social workers, teachers, and other professionals working with a broad range of children are anxious for epidemiologists to use their expertise in instrument development to produce "indicators" for service use (Kohler and Rigby, 2003). The idea is that primary care professionals and others can use a brief measure to identify children who should be offered treatment or referred for specialist evaluation. Screens are often used by nonpsychiatric professionals who have a responsibility, whether legal (mandatory) or professional (ethical), to identify children who they believe could be helped by psychiatric or social work treatment. Front-line professionals are uniquely well placed to serve as gatekeepers to specialty care (Gardner et al., 2004; Sayal and Taylor, 2004). They deserve all of the help that

COSTELLO ET AL.

we can give them. Surprisingly little work has been done recently to examine the validity of the measures that they most often use to identify high-risk children or the decisions that they may base on them (Armbruster and Kazdin, 1994; Cassidy and Jellinek, 1998; Farrington et al., 1996; Horwitz et al., 1998; Stancin and Palermo, 1997) or to develop new, more sensitive instruments for them.

Different traditions of screening have grown up in school and primary care clinics. Screens in schools tend to use a teacher as informant (e.g., Teacher's Report Form [Achenbach, 1991], Rutter B Scale [McGee et al., 1985], Conners Teacher Rating Scale [Conners et al., 1998], or to use child self-report, as for example in screening for suicidality [Shaffer et al., 2004]). On the whole, teachers have done better at identifying children with behavioral problems than children with emotional problems (Kolko and Kazdin, 1993; Verhulst et al., 1994). The evidence that suicide screens are adequate for case identification is not encouraging (Patton et al., 1997; Pfeffer et al., 2000; Shaffer et al., 2004). For example, using the Columbia Suicide Screen, of 100 youths identified as high risk on this screen, only 7 met the DISC criterion of suicidal ideation or attempt, plus depression or dysthymia or substance abuse/dependence (Shaffer et al., 2004).

Primary care research, in contrast, has tended to employ parents as informants (Campo et al., 1999; Horwitz et al., 1992; Jellinek et al., 1999; Lavigne et al., 1993; Merritt et al., 1995; Riekert et al., 1999; Simonian et al., 1991). Some pediatricians are beginning to experiment with adolescent screens for drug or alcohol abuse, and, less frequently, depression (Ellen et al., 1998; Middleman et al., 1995; Schwartz and Wirtz, 1990).

The usefulness of available brief questionnaires as "indicators" of service need is under review in an NIMH-funded study (A. Erkanli, personal communication). An NIH work group is exploring the feasibility of using analyses of existing data sets to develop a brief set of "indicators" of need for mental health referral, for use by parents, teachers, or primary care providers (Jensen, personal communication).

The demands on screening measures used to identify individuals are much higher than the demands on those used for prevalence studies. They must accurately indicate that this particular child is at high risk. False positives and false negatives do not cancel out in this case but do compound the inaccuracy of the screen.

Evidence about the value of available screens for identifying high-risk individuals is depressing. As would be expected when the task is to identify uncommon disorders in the general population, most measures show good ability to select out noncases (i.e., good predictive value negative), but they identify far too many children as potential cases who do not meet full diagnostic criteria at interview (poor predictive value positive). They also miss a substantial proportion of those with the disorder (poor sensitivity), even when they are good at identifying those who do not have the disorder (good specificity). However, even good specificity can be dangerous if it is not good enough. If a disorder is rare, then most of the cases identified by even a pretty good screen will be false positives. There are financial, emotional, ethical, and possibly legal costs to both false positives and false negatives.

An example of the pitfalls of screens as indicators at the individual level is presented by Patton et al. (1999), who screened adolescents for depression using modules of a self-completion computerized version of the Clinical Interview Schedule, a structured psychiatric interview (Monck et al., 1994). The criterion measure was the widely used Composite International Diagnostic Interview (Wittchen et al., 1991). Even using a highly detailed screen, only 49% of those identified were true cases, whereas the screen missed 82% of the adolescents with diagnosed with depression by the Composite International Diagnostic Interview. This level of accuracy throws serious doubts on our ability at present to use brief screens to identify individual children at risk, however useful they may be at the level of population estimates. This is a critical area of work for epidemiology in the next decade.

SURVEILLANCE FOR CHILD AND ADOLESCENT PSYCHIATRIC DISORDERS: ESTIMATING THE BURDEN OF DISEASE

In the past decade, progress has been made not only in epidemiological methods but also in using them to assess the prevalence of child psychiatric disorder. In a world of scarce healthcare resources, it is important to understand the size of the burden to the community caused by these disorders. Burden, in terms of numbers affected, have an impact on the individual, and cost to the community is a crucial factor in the battle for resources for treatment and prevention. One of the most important developments in epidemiology in the past decade is not specific to child and adolescent psychiatry but extends to the way the burden of illness in general is perceived and measured. In 1996, the World Health Organization (WHO), together with the World Bank and the Harvard School of Public Health, published the first volume of *The Global Burden of Disease* (Murray and Lopez, 1996), whose subtitle is *A Comprehensive Assessment of Mortality and Disability From Diseases, Injuries, and Risk Factors in 1990 and Projected to 2020.* Until this publication, diseases tended to be ranked in public health importance in terms of their impact on mortality rates. The WHO project has undertaken the task of weighing the impact of diseases in terms of nonfatal as well as fatal health outcomes. The unit of measurement adopted is disability-adjusted life-years (DALYs), which measure the number of expectable years of life lost (to death) or lived with disability.

Using this unit of measurement has revealed a drastically different picture of the global burden of disease from that seen when only mortality is counted. Above all, it has demonstrated the public health burden of psychiatric disorders. For example, Table 1 shows the 10 leading causes of DALYs in developed regions of the world, for the age range 15–44 (data for children older than age 4 years are not available separately). Unipolar major depression has the highest number of DALYs associated with it, and all but one (osteoarthritis) of the 10 leading causes of DALYs is either a psychiatric disorder (schizophrenia, bipolar disorder, obsessive-compulsive disorders) or strongly associated with psychiatric disorder

TABLE 1

Ten Leading Causes of DALYs at 15–44 Years Old, Developed Regions, 1990

	Both Sexes			Males			Females		
Rank	Disease or Injury	DALYs (thousands)	Cumulative %	Disease or Injury	DALYs (thousands)	Cumulative %	Disease or Injury	DALYs (thousands)	Cumulative %
	All causes	61,707		All causes	36,943		All causes	24,764	
1	Unipolar major depression	7,574	12.3	Alcohol use	4,677	12.7	Unipolar major depression	4,910	19.8
2	Alcohol use	5,477	21.2	Road traffic accidents	4,167	23.9	Schizophrenia	1,450	25.7
3	Road traffic accidents	5,304	29.7	Unipolar major depression	2,664	31.1	Road traffic accidents	1,137	30.3
4	Schizophrenia	3,028	34.7	Self-inflicted injuries	2,072	36.8	Bipolar disorder	1,106	34.7
5	Self-inflicted injuries	2,641	38.9	Schizophrenia	1,578	41.0	OCDs	933	38.5
6	Bipolar disorder	2,241	42.6	Drug use	1,404	44.8	Alcohol use	801	41.7
7	Drug use	1,829	45.5	Violence	1,196	48.1	Osteoarthritis	783	44.9
8	OCDs	1,652	48.2	Ischemia heart disease	1,160	51.2	Chlamydia	599	47.3
9	Osteoarthritis	1,634	50.9	Bipolar disorder	1,135	54.3	Self-inflicted injuries	569	49.6
10	Violence	1,507	53.3	HIV	911	56.7	Rheumatoid arthritis	549	51.8

in the epidemiological literature (alcohol use, road traffic accidents, self-inflicted injuries, drug use, violence). Together the nine psychiatry-related conditions cause more than 50% of all DALYs. Thus, policymakers are being forced to pay serious attention to psychiatric disorders as leading causes of suffering, lost opportunity, and economic cost to their communities.

As we discuss in Part II, there is ever-increasing evidence that many psychiatric disorders are already present, or nascent, in childhood and adolescence. Attempts to reduce the burden of mental illness must out of necessity pay attention to the early years. It is also clear from the population-based studies reviewed later in this article that a large number of children and adolescents suffer from psychiatrically induced disability. This has become a focus of much research in the past decade (Canino et al., 1999; Costello et al., 1996a; Ezpeleta et al., 2000; Foley et al., 2003; Giaconia et al., 2001; Hodges and Gust, 1995; Pickles et al., 2001), especially since WHO published the *International Classification of Functioning* (World Health Organization, 2001), a radical revision of its 1980 *International Classification of Impairments, Disabilities, and Handicaps* (World Health Organization, 1980). Work is progressing on a screening questionnaire for children and adolescents to accompany WHO's brief Disability Assessment Schedule for adults (Janca et al., 1996).

Public Health Surveillance of Child and Adolescent Psychiatric Disorder

For most medical conditions, it is the public health agencies, chiefly the Centers for Disease Control and Prevention (CDC), who keep tabs on the impact of diseases on the public health. CDC is the surveillance arm of medicine, producing regular reports on morbidity, mortality, and, in some cases, risk factors. In the past 10 years, and especially after the publication of the *Global Burden of Disease*, the CDC has paid a great deal more attention to child and adolescent mental disorder. Since 1991, the CDC's Youth Risk Behavior Surveillance System has surveyed suicidality, drug use, and risk-taking behaviors, using anonymous questionnaires administered in schools. The data are useful for tracking rises and falls of these problems, at least as reported by youths attending school. On the whole, rates have been fairly steady since 1991 (see http://www.cdc.gov/HealthyYouth/yrbs/factsheets.htm). For example, rates of physical violence have decreased somewhat, and 12-month rates of attempted suicide have remained constant at around 8%, whereas rates of contemplating or planning suicide have fallen. Reported cigarette use has fallen steadily, use of marijuana rose through 1997 and has since fallen, whereas use of cocaine doubled through 1999 and has since held steady. This kind of tracking is important for deciding whether a problem is becoming more or less of a public health burden and can also be used on occasion to check the effects of a preventive intervention. Other sources of information for tracking risk behaviors are CDC's National Health Interview Survey and the National Health and Nutrition Examination Survey, both of which are seeking ways to incorporate more information about psychiatric disorders into their surveillance of the national burden of disease. The National Health Interview Survey is using a psychiatric screening questionnaire for children 4–17 years old in its national household surveys of health and service use. The Strengths and Difficulties Questionnaire (Goodman, 1999) is widely used in the United Kingdom and many other countries. The full Strengths and Difficulties Questionnaire was used in the National Health Interview Survey in 2001, 2003, and 2004, and CDC developed a brief (six-item) version for use in 2002 and in future years (Bourdon et al., 2005). Preliminary results extrapolated from interviews of 9,878 families in 2002 show that 5.5% of U.S. children 4–17 years old were reported by a parent to have definite or severe difficulties with emotions, concentration, behavior, or being able to get along with other people. Twice as many boys as girls (7.5% versus 3.5%) were reported to have "mental health problems." The percentage of children with mental health problems was higher in families with incomes below the federal poverty level (11%).

These estimates are much lower than those from detailed psychiatric interview studies and need to be validated against full psychiatric assessments. Data should be available soon from studies around the world using both the Strengths and Difficulties Questionnaire and detailed psychiatric interviews, including the latest round of the National Comorbidity Study in the United States, which includes a sample of some 3,000 adolescents (Ron Kessler, personal communication), a study of 300 preschool children (Egger and Angold, 2004), and a sample of 1500 9–17 year olds recruited from a primary care pediatric setting (A. Erkanli, personal communication).

Other Surveys of Prevalence and Burden

There has never been a nationally representative survey of the prevalence and burden of child and adolescent psychiatric disorder in the United States. The United Kingdom has recently carried out a national prevalence

study (Ford et al., 2003; Meltzer et al., 2003b), and it deserves attention as a first for child and adolescent psychiatry.

The British survey was conducted by the Office for National Statistics, with funding from the Department of Education and other agencies. The primary purpose was to produce prevalence estimates of conduct, emotional, and hyperkinetic disorders as well as pervasive developmental disorders, eating disorders, and tic disorders, using both *ICD-10* and *DSM-IV* criteria. The second aim was "to determine the *impact* or *burden* of children's mental health. *Impact* covers the consequences for the child; *burden* reflects the consequences for others" (Meltzer et al., 1999). Third, the study measured service use. A stratified random sampling plan for England, Scotland, and Wales produced a sample of 10,438 children ages 5–15 years. Parent and child were interviewed using the DAWBA (Goodman et al., 2000), a computer-assisted lay interview that uses a "best-estimate" approach to diagnosis. The first interview wave, conducted in 1999, was followed by a mailed questionnaire 18 months later and a second interview 3 years after the first.

Nationally representative data on older adolescents can also be extrapolated from the 479 15- to 17-year-olds included in the first U.S. National Comorbidity Survey (NCS; Kessler, 1994). Although publications from the NCS have not focused much on the adolescents (Kessler and Walters, 1998; Miller et al., 2000), the data set is publicly available for analysis of this subgroup, and the NCS replication study in progress will oversample adolescents ages 13 and older. Other studies have carried out similar single-wave surveys of child and adolescent psychiatric disorders based on smaller geographic areas, and some updates from longitudinal epidemiological studies have also been published in the past decade (reviewed in Costello et al., 2004). Figure 1 presents a summary of data from these studies.

A few general conclusions can be drawn from the data. First, between 3% and 18% of children have a psychiatric disorder causing significant functional impairment (the federal definition of serious emotional disturbance [Federal Register, 1993]). The median estimate of serious emotional disturbance is 12%, more than twice that generated from the National Health Interview Survey screen. The implication for clinicians and policymakers is that at any time one child in eight has an impairing psychiatric disorder.

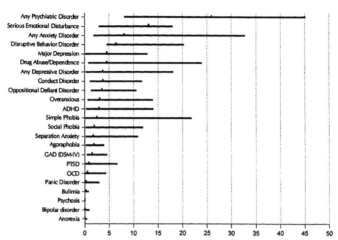

Fig. 1 Summary of results of prevalence studies since 1993: highest, lowest, and median estimates for ages 5–17.

Research in the past decade has made it clear that prevalence rates are highly dependent on the extent to which the algorithms used to make the diagnosis include or ignore functional impairment. The *DSM-IV* itself is somewhat inconsistent on this topic: Some symptoms and diagnoses require impaired functioning to be present, and others do not. It is clear from two papers that present prevalence estimates with and without impairment (Canino et al., 2004; Shaffer et al., 1996) that rates can be dramatically affected by this; for example, in the Methods for the Epidemiology of Child and Adolescent Mental Disorders study, the prevalence of *DSM-III-R* simple phobias varied 30-fold, from 0.7% to 21.6%, depending on how impairment criteria were applied.

Use of Mental Health Services

Serious emotional disturbance is the federal criterion for who should receive services, including income support and mental health care. Another job of public health epidemiology is to monitor the extent to which those who need care are receiving it and to help with the complex task of measuring the effectiveness of treatment and prevention programs in the "real world" outside the research laboratory.

Since the first studies of mental health service use in the 1980s, it has been clear that most children who need care are not getting it (Costello et al., 1988; Dulcan et al., 1990; Leaf et al., 1990; Horwitz et al., 1992).

Additional studies in the past decade have only served to confirm this (Briggs-Gowan et al., 2000; Burns et al., 1995; Horwitz et al., 1998; Leaf et al., 1996; Sawyer et al., 2001; Wu et al., 1999). They have, however, added depth to our understanding of who receives services and why.

Evidence has accumulated for child mental health care disparities associated with age (Olfson et al., 1998), income (Witt et al., 2003), insurance status (Briggs-Gowan et al., 2000), geographical location (Sturm et al., 2003), and family characteristics (Angold et al., 1998b). The NCS and the Ontario Health Survey both showed that the likelihood of receiving treatment during the year of onset of a depressive disorder was 14 to 15 times higher for adults 30–54 years old than it was for children 0–12 years old (Olfson et al., 1998). A similar, though somewhat smaller, disparity in likelihood of prompt treatment was seen for many other disorders. Family income has a confused relationship with access to care. The National Health Interview Survey Disability Supplements showed family financial burden as a barrier to care (Witt et al., 2003), but the survey study of Horwitz et al. of public assistance in Connecticut showed no association with use of mental health care for children (Briggs-Gowan et al., 2000). Whereas health insurance would be expected to mediate access to care, there is growing evidence that children with private insurance are at a disadvantage as compared with publicly insured children in obtaining access to needed care (Burns et al., 1997; Weller et al., 2003; Witt et al., 2003). The gap between need and use is seen not only in the United States but also in countries with more comprehensive healthcare systems (John et al., 1995; Meltzer et al., 2003a; Sawyer et al., 2001; Waddell et al., 2002). Within the United States, geographical disparities in access to services have also been documented (Sturm et al., 2003), often outweighing the effects of race/ethnicity or income. Thomas and Holzer (1999) have pointed out that in the United States, the distribution of child and adolescent psychiatrists is inversely proportional to that of children living in poverty.

An important consideration in children's access to mental health care is their dependence on others, primarily parents, to negotiate the system, make appointments, physically transport them, and pay for treatment. Characteristics of the family such as the perceived burden of the child's problems (Angold et al., 1998b; Teagle, 2002) and family history of mental illness (Johnson et al., 2001) have been shown to have a major impact on a child's chance of receiving needed care in the specialty mental health system. Only when school-based services are available are children sometimes able to seek help for themselves (Farmer et al., 1999, 2003).

A worrisome finding from epidemiological studies of mental health service use is the race/ethnic disparities in access to needed care. A review of the literature (Elster et al., 2003) found that in six of nine studies, African American adolescents received fewer mental health services than did white youths, whereas the other three showed no differences. In three of six studies, Hispanic youths received fewer mental health services, whereas the other three studies showed no differences. Two studies of rural youths in North Carolina found that African American youths were as likely as white youths to receive mental health services through schools, juvenile justice, child welfare, or pediatric primary care providers, but were only half as likely to receive care from psychiatrists or psychologists in specialty mental health settings (Angold et al., 2002). Another study compared white with Native American youths (Costello et al., 1997). There was no overall difference in the likelihood of receiving mental health care, but Native American youths were more than twice as likely as white youths to have used inpatient services at some time.

Another index of access to care is the distribution of spending on mental health treatment across different age groups. We know enough from prevalence studies to be able to say with some confidence that the proportion of children having a psychiatric disorder, with or without impairment, is remarkably similar to that estimated for adults (Costello et al., 1998; Kessler et al., 1994, 1996; U.S. Public Health Service, 1999). A recent study of national spending for mental health and substance abuse (MH/SA) treatment (Harwood et al., 2003) shows the following distribution of expenditures: 11% on those younger than age 18 and 89% on the rest of the population. Another way to look at the picture is to estimate spending on MH/SA treatment as a proportion of all healthcare spending. Harwood and colleagues estimate that 9% of the healthcare spending on children and adolescents went to MH/SA treatment ($9.6 billion), compared with 11% of the healthcare spending on adults ($65.2 billion). It should be noted, however, that these figures do not include counseling and psychological treatment provided through the educational system, which provides mental health care to more children (although not necessarily more treatment sessions) than do medical or specialty mental health services (Burns et al., 1995; Farmer et al., 1999; Wu et al., 1999). The fact remains that one ninth of the money devoted to MH/SA treatment in the United States is being devoted to the youngest one fourth of the population.

There have been major changes during the past decade in the conditions under which mental health services are being provided and the settings in which they are provided. The dramatic move from inpatient to outpatient treatment of young people was already under way in the late 1980s (Kiesler and Simpkins, 1991), whereas a move to managed behavioral health is more recent, and an increase in pharmacologic treatments occurred in the 1990s for two of the most common disorders, attention-deficit/hyperactivity disorder and depression. Probably as a result of this, the extent to which mental health conditions are diagnosed and treated in pediatric primary care settings has risen dramatically: from 1.1 million visits in the mid-1980s to 4.5 million visits in the late 1990s (Glied and Cuellar, 2003).

Effectiveness of Interventions to Prevent and Treat Child Psychiatric Disorder

It may be argued that the reason for the gap between need for and use of mental health services is the lack of effective MH/SA treatments for children and adolescents. The topic of how effective child mental health treatments are, how far they have improved in the past decade, and how the perception that treatment is appropriate and effective influences service use, is too unwieldy for this review (Kazdin, 1996). There is no doubt, as recent surveys have shown (Burns et al., 1999), that treatments that work are available for a wide range of child and adolescent disorders. The question for epidemiology is whether interventions of known effect are really having an impact at the community level.

Since the 1980s, John Weisz's meta-analytic reviews of the effectiveness of psychotherapy have shown that even treatments that worked well in the controlled environment of a research clinic had minimal effects in the real world (Weisz and Jensen, 1999). In the past decade, controlled trials in real-world settings, such as the Fort Bragg experiment (Bickman et al., 1995) have shown disappointing outcomes using traditional data analytic methods (Salzer et al., 1999).

A major methodological problem with observational studies of real-world treatment settings is that children who receive needed care may be different in many ways from those who do not receive treatment. The usual method for dealing with this problem—random allocation to treatment and control status—is often impossible in the real world. Two recent studies have found ways to overcome the problem to some extent. Foster (2003) reanalyzed the Fort Bragg data using propensity score modeling (Rosenbaum and Rubin, 1983), a method that matches cases and controls using a composite score of potential confounders of the treatment-outcome relationship. Foster found a dose-response relationship between number of treatment sessions and children's level of functioning, but no dose-response effect on symptoms (measured using the Child Behavior Checklist). Taking a different approach, Angold et al. (2000a) suggested that treated and untreated children with psychiatric symptoms may differ in the trajectory of their symptoms before entering treatment. They found that treated individuals were more severely disturbed and showed deterioration in their clinical status, even before they received treatment, indicating that comparisons with untreated individuals required controls not only for pretreatment clinical status but also for pretreatment clinical trajectory. A significant dose-response relationship was found between the number of specialty mental health treatment sessions received and improvement in symptomatology at follow-up.

No effect of treatment on secondary psychosocial impairment or parental impact was identified, however.

Psychotropic Medication. Monitoring the use of mental health care also requires monitoring the use of psychotropic medications, and this has been an area of growing concern. A review of two Medicaid databases and a large health maintenance organization, published in 2003 but referring to 1987–1996, found that the 1-year period prevalence of psychotropic medication use grew to 6% of youths younger than 20 years old, a two- to almost a threefold increase over 10 years. Most of the temporal change occurred between 1991 and 1996 (Zito et al., 2003). Medication rates for children are approaching those of adults. For example, the 1996 federal Medical Expenditure Panel Survey showed a 4.1% psychotropic medication rate for 6–17 year olds and a 5.0% rate for 18–44 year olds (Zuvekas and Taliaferro, 2003), and Stein et al. (2001) found that in a population with private insurance in 1998, there was a 4.3% psychotropic medication rate for 1–17 year olds as compared with 4.7% for adults. There is no evidence that the use of psychotropic medications for children and adolescents is falling since these papers were published.

Recent research has begun to document a worrisome aspect of the treatment of psychiatric disorders in children and adolescents—its lack of consistency with treatment guidelines. Olfson (2003) used the Medical Expenditure Panel Survey data to show that whereas many children with depression (especially uninsured and African American youths) did not receive treatment, "antidepressant medications were used far more commonly than would be expected on the basis of published treatment recommendations." In a study of the use of stimulant medication in the general population, Angold et al. (2000b) found that "stimulant treatment was being used in ways substantially inconsistent with current diagnostic guidelines." Whereas three fourths of children with attention-deficit/hyperactivity disorder received stimulants, the majority of children receiving stimulants was never, during a 3-year period, reported by parents to have any impairing attention-deficit/hyperactivity disorder symptoms.

There is no question that many psychiatric disorders impose a huge social burden in terms of disability and public and private expenditures (e.g., Cohen et al., 1994; Glied and Neufeld, 2001; Harwood et al., 1998; Kind and Sorensen, 1993; Scott et al., 2001). There is also evidence that improved treatment and/or case management

COSTELLO ET AL.

can reduce these costs (Dubowitz, 1990; Lave et al., 1998). For example, Foster et al. (2004) used data from two evaluation studies to show that better mental health services reduced the risk of involvement with the juvenile justice system by around 30%. Furthermore, effects were more pronounced for the more serious offenses. One of the tasks of epidemiology in the next decade will be to monitor trends in treatment and prevention and the impact on the prevalence and burden of child and adolescent mental illness.

CONCLUSIONS: WHAT HAVE WE LEARNED IN THE PAST DECADE ABOUT THE BURDEN OF CHILD AND ADOLESCENT PSYCHIATRIC DISORDERS?

From the public health viewpoint, child and adolescent psychiatric epidemiology in the past decade can be said to have come to terms with reality. It has stopped agonizing over how many children have this or that disorder as if there were a "true" answer to the question. It is now clear that measures of psychopathology, whether they take the form of interviews, questionnaires, or so-called objective tests, can be set to generate a wide range of prevalence estimates, depending on the severity of the scoring criteria used. Also, they can only be as good as the taxonomy that they are designed to operationalize. Given the status of our taxonomies (currently *DSM-IV* and *ICD-10*), the highly structured psychiatric interviews developed by epidemiologists are the closest that we are going to get to a gold standard for diagnosis. As was established decades ago for adults, structured interviews are infinitely more reliable than clinical judgment and have high validity vis-à-vis clinicians (Robins et al., 1982). There is little difference in psychometric properties among the various styles of interview, whether they are respondent based, such as the DISC, or interviewer based, such as the CAPA, or use a best-estimate approach, such as the DAWBA. Choice should be dictated by the task at hand. If screening questionnaires are needed, then there is a large range available, most of which work reasonably well at the population level. However, screens cannot be used to replace detailed psychiatric assessments, and even if used to identify high-risk children for more detailed assessment, they will identify large numbers of false positives and false negatives.

Substantively, we can say with certainty that only a small proportion of children with clear evidence of functionally impairing psychiatric disorder receive treatment. Once upon a time, when effective treatments for child and adolescent psychiatric disorders were rare, this was regrettable but not a major public health issue. Now it is. The tragedy is compounded by powerful evidence that most psychiatric disorders have their origins early in life: risk even for adult-onset disorders is often increased by childhood adversities, and disorders manifesting themselves in the early years often recur in adulthood. So the public health directive to intervene early is clear (Insel and Fenton, 2005), but the reality is different. The youngest one fourth of the population receives one ninth of the treatment dollars. A review of NIMH research funding shows that research on children is seriously underfunded. The role of primary and secondary prevention in child and adolescent mental health has never been the focus of serious planning at the federal level. The WHO has made it inescapably clear that psychiatric disorders with their origins in childhood are a major contributor to the "global burden of disease." The task of the next decade is to develop national and international policies to move research, prevention, and treatment resources to where they are most needed. The task of child and adolescent psychiatric epidemiology, in its public health role, is to monitor that process.

Disclosure: Dr. Egger holds a Pfizer Foundation Faculty Scholar Award in Clinical Epidemiology. The other authors have no financial relationships to disclose.

REFERENCES

Ablow JC, Measelle JR (1993), *The Berkeley Puppet Interview (BPI): Interviewing and Coding System Manuals.* Berkeley: University of California at Berkeley

Achenbach TM (1991), *Child Behavior Checklist: Teacher's Report Form.* Burlington: University of Vermont

Alcohol and Drug Defense Program (1991), *Alcohol and Other Drug Use Patterns Among Students in North Carolina Public Schools Grades 7–12: Results of a 1991 Student Survey.* Raleigh: North Carolina Department of Public Instruction

Ambrosini PJ (2000), Historical development and present status of the schedule for affective disorders and schizophrenia for school-age children (K-SADS). *J Am Acad Child Adolesc Psychiatry* 39:49–58

American Psychiatric Association (1980), *Diagnostic and Statistical Manual of Mental Disorders, 3rd edition (DSM-III).* Washington, DC: American Psychiatric Press

American Psychiatric Association (1987), *Diagnostic and Statistical Manual of Mental Disorders, 3rd edition- revised (DSM-III-R).* Washington, DC: American Psychiatric Press

American Psychiatric Association (1994), *Diagnostic and Statistical Manual of Mental Disorders, 4th Edition (DSM-IV).* Washington, DC: American Psychiatric Press

Angold A, Costello EJ (2000), The Child and Adolescent Psychiatric Assessment (CAPA). *J Am Acad Child Adolesc Psychiatry* 39:39–48

Angold A, Costello EJ, Burns BJ, Erkanli A, Farmer EMZ (2000a), The effectiveness of non-residential specialty mental health services for children and adolescents in the "real world". *J Am Acad Child Adolesc Psychiatry* 39:154–160

Angold A, Costello EJ, Worthman CM (1998a), Puberty and depression: the roles of age, pubertal status, and pubertal timing. *Psychol Med* 28:51–61

Angold A, Cox A, Prendergast M et al. (1999), *The Young Adult Psychiatric Assessment (YAPA).* Durham, NC: Duke University Medical Center

Angold A, Egger HL (2004), Psychiatric diagnosis in preschool children. In: *Handbook of Infant, Toddler, and Preschool Mental Health Assessment,* DelCarmen-Wiggins R, Carter A, eds. New York: Oxford University Press, pp 123–139

Angold A, Erkanli A, Egger HL, Costello EJ (2000b), Stimulant treatment for children: a community perspective. *J Am Acad Child Adolesc Psychiatry* 39:975–984

Angold A, Erkanli A, Farmer EMZ et al. (2002), Psychiatric disorder, impairment, and service use in rural African American and white youth. *Arch Gen Psychiatry* 59:893–901

Angold A, Fisher PW (1999), Interviewer-based interviews. In: *Diagnostic Assessment in Child and Adolescent Psychopathology,* Shaffer D, Lucas C, Richters J, eds. New York: Guilford, pp 34–64

Angold A, Messer SC, Stangl D, Farmer EMZ, Costello EJ, Burns BJ (1998b), Perceived parental burden and service use for child and adolescent psychiatric disorders. *Am J Public Health* 88:75–80

Angold A, Worthman CW (1993), Puberty onset of gender differences in rates of depression: a developmental, epidemiologic and neuroendocrine perspective. *J Affect Disord* 29:145–158

Armbruster P, Kazdin AE (1994), Attrition in child psychotherapy. In: *Advances in Clinical Child Psychology, volume 16,* Ollendick TH, Prinz RJ, eds. New York: Plenum, pp 81–108

Bennett KJ, Offord DR (2001), Screening for conduct problems: does the predictive accuracy of conduct disorder symptoms improve with age? *J Am Acad Child Adolesc Psychiatry* 40:1418–1425

Bickman L, Guthrie PR, Foster EM et al. (1995), *Evaluating Managed Mental Health Services: The Fort Bragg Experiment.* New York: Plenum

Boris NW, Hinshaw-Fuselier SS, Smyke AT, Scheeringa MS, Heller S, Zeanah C (2004), Comparing criteria for attachment disorders: establishing reliability and validity in high-risk samples. *J Am Acad Child Adolesc Psychiatry* 43:568–577

Bourdon KH, Goodman R, Rae DS, Simpson MS, Koretz DS (2005), The Strengths and Difficulties Questionnaire: U.S. normative data and psychometric properties. *J Am Acad Child Adolesc Psychiatry* 44:557–564

Breslau N (1987), Inquiring about the bizarre: false positives in Diagnostic Interview Schedule for Children (DISC) ascertainment of obsessions, compulsions, and psychotic symptoms. *J Am Acad Child Adolesc Psychiatry* 26:639–644

Briggs-Gowan MJ, Horwitz SM, Schwab-Stone ME, Leventhal JM, Leaf PJ (2000), Mental health in pediatric settings: distribution of disorders and factors related to service use. *J Am Acad Child Adolesc Psychiatry* 39: 841–849

Burns BJ, Costello EJ, Angold A et al. (1995), Children's mental health service use across service sectors. *Health Aff* 14:147–159

Burns BJ, Costello EJ, Erkanli A, Tweed DL, Farmer EMZ, Angold A (1997), Insurance coverage and mental health service use by adolescents with serious emotional disturbance. *J Child Fam Stud* 6:89–111

Burns BJ, Hoagwood K, Mrazek P (1999), Effective treatment for mental disorders in children and adolescents. *Clin Child Fam Psychol Rev* 2:199–254

Campo JV, Jansen-McWilliams L, Comer DM, Kelleher KJ (1999), Somatization in pediatric primary care: association with psychopathology, functional impairment, and use of services. *J Am Acad Child Adolesc Psychiatry* 38:1093–1108

Canino G, Costello EJ, Angold A (1999), Assessing functional impairment and social adaptation for child mental health services research: a review of measures. *J Ment Health Serv* 1:93–108

Canino G, Shrout P, Rubio-Stipec M et al. (2004), The DSM-IV rates of child and adolescent disorders in Puerto Rico. *Arch Gen Psychiatry* 61:85–93

Carter AS, Briggs-Gowan MJ, Margaret J, Jones SM, Little TD (2003), The Infant-Toddler Social and Emotional Assessment (ITSEA): factor structure, reliability, and validity. *J Abnorm Child Psychol* 31:495–514

Caspi A, McClay J, Moffitt TE et al. (2002), Role of genotype in the cycle of violence in maltreated children. *Science* 297:851–854

Caspi A, Sugden K, Moffitt T et al. (2003), Influence of life stress on depression: moderation by a polymorphism in the 5-HTT gene. *Science* 301:386–389

Cassidy LJ, Jellinek MS (1998), Approaches to recognition and management of childhood psychiatric disorders in pediatric primary care. *Pediatr Clin North Am* 45:1037

Cohen MA, Miller TR, Rossman SB (1994), The cost and consequences of violent behavior in the United States. In: *Understanding and Preventing Violence, Volume III: Social Influences, Volume 4,* Reiss AJ, Roth JA, eds. Washington, DC: National Research Council, National Academy Press, pp 67–166

Conners CK, Sitarenios G, Parker JD, Epstein JN (1998), Revision and re-standardization of the Conners Teacher Rating Scale (CTRS-R): factor, structure, reliability, and criterion validity. *J Abnorm Child Psychiatry* 26:279–291

Costello E, Farmer E, Angold A, Burns B, Erkanli A (1997), Psychiatric disorders among American Indian and White youth in Appalachia: The Great Smoky Mountains Study. *Am J Public Health* 87:827–832

Costello EJ, Angold A, Burns BJ, Erkanli A, Stangl DK, Tweed DL (1996a), The Great Smoky Mountains Study of Youth: functional impairment and severe emotional disturbance. *Arch Gen Psychiatry* 53:1137–1143

Costello EJ, Angold A, Burns BJ et al. (1996b), The Great Smoky Mountains Study of Youth: goals, designs, methods, and the prevalence of DSM-III-R disorders. *Arch Gen Psychiatry* 53:1129–1136

Costello EJ, Burns BJ, Costello AJ, Edelbrock C, Dulcan M, Brent D (1988), Service utilization and psychiatric diagnosis in pediatric primary care: the role of the gatekeeper. *Pediatrics* 82:435–440

Costello EJ, Messer SC, Reinherz HZ, Cohen P, Bird HR (1998), The prevalence of serious emotional disturbance: a re-analysis of community studies. *J Child Fam Stud* 7:411–432

Costello EJ, Mustillo S, Keeler G, Angold A (2004), Prevalence of psychiatric disorders in childhood and adolescence. In: *Mental Health Services: A Public Health Perspective,* Lubotsky Levin B, Petrila J, Hennessy K, eds. New York: Oxford University Press, pp 111–128

Des Jarles D, Paone D, Milliken J et al. (1999), Audio-computer interviewing to measure risk behaviour for HIV among injecting drug users: a quasi-randomised trial. *Lancet* 353:1657–1661

Dubowitz H (1990), Costs and effectiveness of interventions in child maltreatment. *Child Abuse Negl* 14:177–186

Dulcan MK, Costello EJ, Costello AJ, Edelbrock C, Brent D, Janiszewski S (1990), The pediatrician as gatekeeper to mental health care for children: do parents' concerns open the gate? *J Am Acad Child Adolesc Psychiatry* 29:453–458

Earls F (1979), Epidemiology and child psychiatry: historical and conceptual development. *Compr Psychiatry* 20:256–269

Earls F (1980), Prevalence of behavior problems in 3-year-old children: a cross-national replication. *Arch Gen Psychiatry* 37:1153–1157

Egger HL, Angold A (2004), The Preschool Age Psychiatric Assessment (PAPA): a structured parent interview for diagnosing psychiatric disorders in preschool children. In: *Handbook of Infant, Toddler, and Preschool Mental Assessment,* DelCarmen-Wiggins R, Carter A, eds. New York: Oxford University Press, pp 223–243

Ellen JM, Franzgrote M, Irwin CE Jr, Millstein SG (1998), Primary care physicians' screening of adolescent patients: a survey of California physicians. *J Adolesc Health* 22:433–438

Elster A, Jarosik J, VanGeest J, Fleming M (2003), Racial and ethnic disparities in health care for adolescents: a systematic review of the literature. *Arch Pediatr Adolesc Med* 157:867–874

Emde R, Wolfe DP, Oppenheim D (2003), *Revealing the Inner Worlds of Young Children: The MacArthur Story Stem Battery and Parent-Child Narratives.* New York: Oxford University Press

COSTELLO ET AL.

Erkanli A, Soyer R, Angold A (1998), Optimal Bayesian two-phase designs. *J Stat Planning Inference* 66:175–191

Erkanli A, Soyer R, Costello EJ (1999), Bayesian inference for prevalence in longitudinal two-phase studies. *Biometrics* 55:1145–1150

Erkanli A, Soyer R, Stangl D (1997), Bayesian inference in two-phase prevalence studies. *Stat Med* 16:1121–1133

Ezpeleta L, Granero R, de la Osa N, Guillamon N (2000), Predictors of functional impairment in children and adolescents. *J Child Psychol Psychiatry* 41:793–801

Farmer E, Burns B, Phillips S, Angold A, Costello E (2003), Pathways into and through mental health services for children and adolescents. *Psychiatr Serv* 54:60–66

Farmer EMZ, Stangl DK, Burns BJ, Costello EJ, Angold A (1999), Use, persistence, and intensity: patterns of care for children's mental health across one year. *Community Ment Health J* 35:31–46

Farrington DP, Loeber R, Stouthamer-Loeber M, Van Kammen WB, Schmidt L (1996), Self-reported delinquency and a combined delinquency seriousness scale based on boys, mothers, and teachers: concurrent and predictive validity for African-Americans and Caucasians. *Criminology* 34:501–525

Festa A, D'Agostino RB, Howard G, Mykkanen L, Tracy RP, Haffner SM (2000), Chronic subclinical inflammation as part of the insulin resistance syndrome: the insulin resistance atherosclerosis study (IRAS). *Circulation* 102:42–47

58 Fed Reg 29425 (1993)

Foley D, Neale M, Gardner CO, Pickles A, Kendler KS (2003), Major depression and associated impairment: same or different genetic and environmental risk factors? *Am J Psychiatry* 160:2128–2133

Foley DL, Eaves LJ, Wormley B et al. (2004), Childhood adversity, monoamine oxidase A genotype, and risk for conduct disorder. *Arch Gen Psychiatry* 61:738–744

Ford T, Goodman R, Meltzer H (2003), The British Child and Adolescent Mental Health Survey: the prevalence of DSM-IV disorders. *J Am Acad Child Adolesc Psychiatry* 42:1203–1211

Foster EM (2003), Propensity score matching: an illustrative analysis of dose response. *Med Care* 41:1183–1192

Foster EM, Qaseem A, Connor T (2004), Can better mental health services reduce the risk of juvenile justice system involvement? *Am J Public Health* 94:859–865

Freedman DX (1984), Psychiatric epidemiology counts. *Arch Gen Psychiatry* 41:931–933

Gardner W, Kelleher KJ, Pajer KA, Campo JV (2004), Primary care clinicians' use of standardized psychiatric diagnoses. *Child Care Health Dev* 30:401–412

Giaconia RM, Reinherz HZ, Paradis AD, Carmola Hauf AM, Stashwick C (2001), Major depression and drug disorders in adolescence: general and specific impairments in early adulthood. *J Am Acad Child Adolesc Psychiatry* 40:1426–1433

Glied S, Cuellar AE (2003), Trends and issues in child and adolescent mental health. *Health Aff* 22:39–50

Glied S, Neufeld A (2001), Service system finance: implications for children with depression and manic depression. *Biol Psychiatry* 49:1128–1135

Goodman R (1999), The extended version of the strengths and difficulties questionnaire as a guide to child psychiatric caseness and consequent burden. *J Child Psychol Psychiatry* 40:791–799

Goodman R, Ford T, Richards H, Gatward R, Meltzer H (2000), The Development and Well-Being Assessment: description and initial validation of an integrated assessment of child and adolescent psychopathology. *J Child Psychol Psychiatry* 41:645–656

Harwood H, Fountain D, Livermore G (1998), Economic costs of alcohol abuse and alcoholism. *Recent Dev Alcohol* 14:307–330

Harwood HJ, Mark TL, McKusick DR, Coffey RM, King EC, Genuardi JS (2003), National spending on mental health and substance abuse treatment by age of clients, 1997. *J Behav Health Serv Res* 30:433–443

Hodges K, Gust J (1995), Measures of impairment for children and adolescents. *J Ment Health Adm* 22:403–413

Horwitz SM, Leaf PJ, Leventhal JM (1998), Identification of psychosocial problems in pediatric primary care. *Arch Pediatr Adolesc Med* 152:367–371

Horwitz SM, Leaf PJ, Leventhal JM, Forsyth B, Speechley KN (1992), Identification and management of psychosocial and developmental problems in community-based, primary care pediatric practices. *Pediatrics* 89:480–485

Insel TR, Fenton WS (2005), Psychiatric epidemiology: it's just about counting anymore. *Arch Gen Psychiatry* 62.590–592

Janca A, Kastrup M, Katschnig H, Lopez-Ibor J (1996), The World Heath Organization Short Disability Assessment Schedule (WHO DAS-S): a tool for the assessment of difficulties in selected areas of functioning of patients with mental disorders. *Soc Psychiatry Psychiatr Epidemiol* 31:349–354

Jellinek MS, Murphy JM, Little M, Pagano ME, Comer DM, Kelleher KJ (1999), Use of the Pediatric Symptom Checklist to screen for psychosocial problems in pediatric primary care. *Arch Pediatr Adolesc Med* 153:254–260

John LH, Offord DR, Boyle MH, Racine YA (1995), Factors predicting use of mental health and social services by children 6–16 years old: findings from the Ontario Child Health Study. *Am J Orthopsychiatry* 65:76–86

Johnson SD, Stiffman A, Hadley-Ives E, Elze D (2001), An analysis of stressors and co-morbid mental health problems that contribute to youth's paths to substance-specific services. *J Behav Health Serv Res* 28:412–426

Johnston LD, O'Malley PM, Bachman JG (1996), *National Survey Results on Drug Use from the Monitoring the Future Study 1975-1995; Volume 1, Secondary School Students* (NIH Publication No. 96-4139). Rockville, MD: U.S. Department of Health and Human Services, Public Health Service, NIH/NIDA.

Kazdin A (1996), Dropping out of child psychotherapy: issues for research and implications for practice. *Clin Child Psychol Psychiatry* 1:133–156

Kessler RC (1994), The National Comorbidity Survey of the United States. *Int Rev Psychiatry* 6:365–376

Kessler RC, Berglund PA, Leaf PJ et al. (1996), The 12-month prevalence and correlates of serious mental illness (SMI). In: *Mental Health, United States, 1996* (DHHS Pub. No. (SMA)96-3098, Vol. DDHHS Pub. (SMA)96-3098), Manderscheid RW, Sonnenschein MA, eds. Washington, DC: Superintendent of Documents, U.S. Government Printing Office, pp 59–70

Kessler RC, McGonagle KA, Zhao S et al. (1994), Lifetime and 12-month prevalence of DSM-III-R psychiatric disorders in the United States: results from the National Comorbidity Study. *Arch Gen Psychiatry* 51:8–19

Kessler RC, Walters EE (1998), Epidemiology of DSM-III-R major depression and minor depression among adolescents and young adults in the National Comorbidity Survey. *Depress Anxiety* 7:3–14

Kiesler CA, Simpkins C (1991), Changes in psychiatric inpatient treatment of children and youth in general hospitals: 1980–1985. *Hosp Community Psychiatry* 42:601–604

Kind P, Sorensen J (1993), The costs of depression. *Int Clin Psychopharmacol* 7:191–195

Kleinbaum DG, Kupper LL, Morgenstern H (1982), *Epidemiologic Research: Principles and Quantitative Methods*. New York: Van Nostrand Reinhold

Kohler L, Rigby M (2003), Indicators of children's development: considerations when constructing a set of national Child Health Indicators for the European Union. *Child Care Health Dev* 29:551–558

Kolko DJ, Kazdin AE (1993), Emotional/behavioral problems in clinic and nonclinic children: correspondence among child, parent, and teacher reports. *J Child Psychol Psychiatry* 34:991–1006

Kraemer HC, Measelle JR, Ablow JC, Essex MJ, Boyce WT, Kupfer DJ (2003), A new approach to integrating data from multiple informants in psychiatric assessment and research: mixing and matching contexts and perspectives. *Am J Psychiatry* 160:1566–1577

Lave J, Frank R, Schulberg H, Kamlet M (1998), Cost-effectiveness of treatments for major depression in primary care practice. *Arch Gen Psychiatry* 55:645–651

Lavigne JV, Binns HJ, Christoffel KK et al., Pediatric Practice Research Group (1993), Behavioral and emotional problems among preschool children in pediatric primary care: prevalence and pediatricians' recognition. *Pediatrics* 91:649–655

Leaf PJ, Alegria M, Cohen P et al. (1996), Mental health service use in the community and schools: results from the four-community MECA study. *J Am Acad Child Adolesc Psychiatry* 35:889–897

Leaf PJ, Horwitz SM, Leventhal JM et al. (1990), Primary care pediatrics: what is detected, what is done. Presented at the Annual Meeting of the Academy of Child and Adolescent Psychiatry, Chicago, October

Loeber R, Farrington DP, Stouthamer-Loeber M, Moffitt TE, Caspi A, Lynam D (2001), Male mental health problems, psychopathy, and personality traits: key findings from the first 14 years of the Pittsburgh Youth Study. *Clin Child Fam Psychol Rev* 4:273–297

Luby J, Mrakotsky C, Heffelfinger A, Brown K, Hessler M, Spitznagel E (2003), Modification of DSM-IV criteria for depressed preschool children. *Am J Psychiatry* 160:1169–1172

McGee R, Williams S, Bradshaw J, Chapel JL, Robins A, Silva PA (1985), The Rutter Scale for completion by teachers: factor structure and relationships with cognitive abilities and family adversity for a sample of New Zealand children. *J Child Psychol Psychiatry* 26:727–739

Measelle JR, Ablow JC, Cowan PA, Cowan CP (1998), Assessing young children's views of their academic, social, and emotional lives: an evaluation of the self-perception scales of the Berkeley Puppet Interview. *Child Dev* 69:1556–1576

Meltzer H, Gatward R, Corbin T, Goodman R, Ford T (2003a), *Persistence, Onset, Risk Factors and Outcomes of Childhood Mental Disorders*. London: Office for National Statistics

Meltzer H, Gatward R, Goodman R, Ford T (1999), *The Mental Health of Children and Adolescents in Great Britain*. London: Office for National Statistics

Meltzer H, Gatward R, Goodman R, Ford T (2003b), Mental health of children and adolescents in Great Britain. *Int Rev Psychiatry* 15:185–187

Merritt KA, Thompson RJ Jr, Keith BR, Gustafson KE, Murphy LB, Johndrow DA (1995), Screening for child-reported behavioral and emotional problems in primary care pediatrics. *Percept Mot Skills* 80:323–329

Metzger DS, Koblin B, Turner CF et al., HIVNET Vaccine Preparedness Study Protocol Team (2000), Randomized controlled trial of audio computer-assisted self-interviewing: utility and acceptability in longitudinal studies. *Am J Epidemiol* 152:99–106

Middleman AB, Binns HJ, Durant RH (1995), Factors affecting pediatric residents' intentions to screen for high risk behaviors. *J Adolesc Health* 17:106–112

Miller L, Davies M, Greenwald S (2000), Religiosity and substance use and abuse among adolescents in the National Comorbidity Survey. *J Am Acad Child Adolesc Psychiatry* 39:1190–1197

Monck E, Graham P, Richman N, Dobbs R (1994), Adolescent girls I: self-reported mood disturbance in a community population. *Br J Psychiatry* 165:760–769

Murray CJL, Lopez AD (1996), *The Global Burden of Disease, Vol. 1*, Murray CJL, Lopez AD, eds. Geneva, Switzerland: World Health Organization

Olfson M, Gameroff MJ, Marcus SC, Waslick BD (2003), Outpatient treatment of child and adolescent depression in the United States. *Arch Gen Psychiatry* 60:1236–1242

Olfson M, Kessler RC, Berglund PA, Lin E (1998), Psychiatric disorder onset and first treatment contact in the United States and Ontario. *Am J Psychiatry* 155:1415–1422

Patton G, Coffey C, Posterino M, Carlin J, Wolfe R, Bowes G (1999), A computerised screening instrument for adolescent depression: population-based validation and application to a two-phase case-control study. *Soc Psychiatry Psychiatr Epidemiol* 34:166–172

Patton GC, Harris R, Carlin JB et al. (1997), Adolescent suicidal behaviours: a population-based study of risk. *Psychol Med* 27:715–724

Pfeffer CR, Jiang H, Kakuma T (2000), Child-Adolescent Suicidal Potential Index (CASPI): a screen for risk for early onset suicidal behavior. *Psychol Assess* 12:304–318

Pickles A, Rowe R, Simonoff E, Foley D, Rutter M, Silberg J (2001), Child psychiatric symptoms and psychosocial impairment: relationship and prognostic significance. *Br J Psychiatry* 179:230–235

Reich W (2000), Diagnostic interview for children and adolescents (DICA). *J Am Acad Child Adolesc Psychiatry* 39:59–66

Riekert KA, Stancin T, Palermo TM, Drotar D (1999), A psychological behavioral screening service: use, feasibility, and impact in a primary care setting. *J Pediatr Psychol* 24:405–414

Robins LN, Helzer JE, Ratcliff KS, Seyfried W (1982), Validity of the Diagnostic Interview Schedule, Version II: DSM-III diagnoses. *Psychol Med* 12:855–870

Rosenbaum PR, Rubin DB (1983), The central role of the propensity score in observational studies for causal effects. *Biometrika* 70:41–55

Rutter M, Tizard J, Whitmore K (1970), *Education, Health, and Behaviour*. London: Longman

Salzer MS, Bickman L, Lambert EW (1999), Dose-effect relationship in children's psychotherapy services. *J Consult Clin Psychol* 67:228–238

Sawyer M, Arney P, Baghurst J et al. (2001), The mental health of young people in Australia: key findings from the child and adolescent component of the national survey of mental health and well-being. *Aust N Z J Psychiatry* 35:806–814

Sayal K, Taylor E (2004), Detection of child mental health disorders by general practitioners. *Br J Gen Pract* 54:348–352

Scheeringa MS, Zeanah C, Myers L, Putnam F (2003), New findings on alternative criteria for PTSD in preschool children. *J Am Acad Child Adolesc Psychiatry* 42:561–571

Schwartz RH, Wirtz PW (1990), Potential substance abuse: detection among adolescent patients—using the drug and alcohol problem (DAP) quick screen, a 30-item questionnaire. *Clin Pediatr* 29:38–43

Scott S, Knapp M, Henderson J, Maughan B (2001), Financial cost of social exclusion: follow up study of antisocial children into adulthood. *BMJ* 323:191–194

Shaffer D, Fisher P, Lucas CP, Dulcan MK, Schwab-Stone ME (2000), NIMH diagnostic interview schedule for children version IV (NIMH DISC-IV): description, differences from previous versions, and reliability of some common diagnoses. *J Am Acad Child Adolesc Psychiatry* 39:28–38

Shaffer D, Fisher PW, Dulcan M et al. (1996), The NIMH diagnostic interview schedule for children (DISC 2.3): description, acceptability, prevalences, and performance in the MECA study. *J Am Acad Child Adolesc Psychiatry* 35:865–877

Shaffer D, Fisher PW, Lucas CP (1999), Respondent-based interviews. In: *Diagnostic Assessment in Child and Adolescent Psychopathology*, Shaffer D, Lucas CP, Richters JE, eds. New York: Guilford, pp 3–33

Shaffer D, Scott M, Wilcox H et al. (2004), The Columbia Suicide Screen: validity and reliability of a screen for youth suicide and depression. *J Am Acad Child Adolesc Psychiatry* 43:71–79

Shanee N, Apter A, Weizman A (1997), Psychometric properties of the K-SADS-PL in an Israeli adolescent clinical population. *Isr J Psychiatry Relat Sci* 34:179–186

Simonian SJ, Tarnowski KJ, Stancin T, Friman PC, Atkins MS (1991), Disadvantaged children and families in pediatric primary care settings: II. Screening for behavior disturbance. *J Clin Child Psychol* 20:360–371

Stafford B, Zeanah C, Sheeringa M (2003), Exploring psychopathology in early childhood: PTSD and attachment disorders in DC: 0-3 and DSM-IV. *Infant Ment Health J* 24:383–409

Stancin T, Palermo TM (1997), A review of behavioral screening practices in pediatric settings: do they pass the test. *J Dev Behav Pediatr* 18:183–194

Stein BD, Sturm R, Kapur K, J (2001), Datapoints: psychotropic medication costs among youth with private insurance in 1998. *Psychiatr Serv* 52:152

Stevens M, Youells F, Whaley F, Linsey S (1995), Drug use prevalence in a rural school-age population: the New Hampshire survey. *Am J Prev Med* 11:105–113

Sturm R, Ringel JS, Andreyeva T (2003), Geographic disparities in children's mental health care. *Pediatrics* 112:e308–e315

Susser M (1973), *Causal Thinking in the Health Sciences: Concepts and Strategies in Epidemiology*. New York: Oxford University Press

Swanson JW, Linskey AO, Quintero-Salinas R, Pumariega AJ, Holzer CE (1992), A binational school survey of depressive symptoms, drug use, and suicidal ideation. *J Am Acad Child Adolesc Psychiatry* 31:669–678

Taylor A, Goldberg DP, Dempsey K (1999), Audio-computer interviewing to measure HIV-risk behaviour. *Lancet* 354:678–679

Teagle S (2002), Parental problem recognition and child mental health service use. *Ment Health Serv Res* 4:257–266

Thomas CR, Holzer CE (1999), National distribution of child and adolescent psychiatrists. *J Am Acad Child Adolesc Psychiatry* 38:9–15

COSTELLO ET AL.

U.S. Public Health Service (1999), *Mental Health: A Report of the Surgeon General.* Rockville, MD: Department of Health and Human Services

Valla JP, Bergeron L, Bérubé H, Gaudet N, St-Georges M (1994), A structured pictorial questionnaire to assess DSM-III-R based diagnoses in children (6-11 years): development, validity, and reliability. *J Abnorm Child Psychol* 22:403–423

Valla JP, Bergeron L, Bidaut-Russell M, St-Georges M, Gaudet N (1997), Reliability of the Dominic-R: a young child mental health questionnaire combining visual and auditory stimuli. *J Child Psychol Psychiatry* 38: 717–724

Valla J-P, Bergeron L, Smolla N (2000), The Dominic-R: a pictorial interview for 6- to 11-year-old children. *J Am Acad Child Adolesc Psychiatry* 39:85–93

Verhulst FC, Koot HM, Van der Ende J (1994), Differential predictive value of parents and teachers' reports of children's problem behaviors: a longitudinal study. *J Abnorm Child Psychol* 22:531–546

Verhulst FC, van der Ende J, Ferdinand RF, Kasius MC (1997), The prevalence of DSM-III-R diagnoses in a national sample of Dutch adolescents. *Arch Gen Psychiatry* 54:329–336

Waddell C, Offord D, Shepherd C, Hua J, McEwan K (2002), Child psychiatric epidemiology and Canadian public policy-making: the state of the science and the art of the possible. *Can J Psychiatry* 47:825–832

Wakschlag LS, Leventhal BL, Danis B et al. (2002), *Manual for Disruptive Behavior Diagnostic Observational Schedule.* Chicago: University of Chicago

Weisz JR, Jensen PS (1999), Efficacy and effectiveness of child and adolescent psychotherapy and pharmacotherapy. *Ment Health Serv Res* 1: 125–157

Weller WE, Minkovitz CS, Anderson GF (2003), Utilization of medical and health-related services among school-age children and adolescents with special health care needs (1994 National Health Interview Survey on Disability [NHIS-D] Baseline Data). *Pediatrics* 112:593–603

Witt WP, Kasper JD, Riley AW (2003), Mental health services use among school-aged children with disabilities: the role of sociodemographics, functional limitations, family burdens, and care coordination. *Health Serv Res* 38:1441–1466

Wittchen H-U, Robins LN, Cottler LB, Sartorius N, Burke JD, Regier D (1991), Cross-cultural feasibility, reliability, and sources of variance of the Composite International Diagnostic Interview (CIDI). *Br J Psychiatry* 159:645–653

World Health Organization (1978), *Manual of the International Classification of Diseases, Injuries, and Causes of Death, 9th Edition.* Geneva, Switzerland: World Health Organization

World Health Organization (1980), *International Classification of Impairments, Disabilities, and Handicaps: A Manual of Classification Relating to the Consequences of Disease.* Geneva, Switzerland: World Health Organization

World Health Organization (1987), *Tenth Revision of the International Classification of Diseases Chapter V (F): Mental, Behavioural and Developmental Disorders—Clinical Descriptions and Diagnostic Guidelines.* Geneva, Switzerland: World Health Organization

World Health Organization (2001), *ICF: International Classification of Functioning, Disability and Health.* Geneva, Switzerland: World Health Organization

Wu P, Hoven CW, Bird HR et al. (1999), Depressive and disruptive disorders and mental health utilization in children and adolescent. *J Am Acad Child Adolesc Psychiatry* 38:1081–1090

Zito JM, Safer DJ, DosReis S et al. (2003), Psychotropic practice patterns for youth: a 10-year perspective. *Arch Pediatr Adolesc Med* 157: 17–25

Zuvekas SH, Taliaferro GS (2003), Pathways to access: health insurance, the health care delivery system, and racial/ethnic disparities, 1996–1999. *Health Aff* 22:139–153

[18]

10-Year Research Update Review: The Epidemiology of Child and Adolescent Psychiatric Disorders: II. Developmental Epidemiology

E. JANE COSTELLO, Ph.D., DEBRA L. FOLEY, Ph.D., AND ADRIAN ANGOLD, M.R.C.Psych.

ABSTRACT

Objective: To describe the growth of developmental epidemiology in the past decade and to illustrate it with examples of recent studies. **Method:** A review of publications on developmental epidemiology in the past 10 years and a discussion of some key examples. **Results:** The authors describe how the interaction between developmental psychopathology and psychiatric epidemiology has produced developmental epidemiology, the study of patterns of distribution of psychiatric disorders in time as well as in space. They give two examples of the kinds of questions that developmental epidemiology can help to answer: (1) Is the prevalence of autism increasing? Does the use of vaccines explain the increase? (2) Is there an epidemic of child and adolescent depression? Finally, they describe two areas of science that are beginning to inform developmental epidemiology: molecular genetics and the use of biological measures of stress. **Conclusions:** While child and adolescent psychiatric epidemiology continues, as described in the first of these reviews, to address questions of prevalence and burden, it has also expanded into new areas of research in the past decade. In the next decade, longitudinal epidemiological data sets with their rich descriptive data on psychopathology and environmental risk over time and the potential to add biological measures will provide valuable resources for research into gene–environment correlations and interactions. *J. Am. Acad. Child Adolesc. Psychiatry*, 2006;45(1):8–25. **Key Words:** epidemiology, development, review.

As we discussed in the first of these two reviews (see the October 2005 issue of the journal), epidemiology wears two hats: it supports public health by identifying the extent of mental illness and service needs and it aids in the scientific search for causes of mental disorders (Earls, 1979). The first of these reviews discussed the contributions of epidemiology to knowledge about the public health burden of child and adolescent psychiatric disorders. This review deals with epidemiology as a scientific tool for understanding how psychiatric disorders develop.

In this article, we first describe the process by which child psychiatric epidemiology has morphed into developmental epidemiology by incorporating ideas from developmental psychopathology, which in turn used developmental science to change our thinking about psychopathology. Next, we review what has been learned about the development of psychiatric disorders from an epidemiological point of view in the past decade: what we have learned about changes in disease prevalence over recent decades, about age at onset, comorbidity, and the order in which disorders first appear. Third, from the wealth of new knowledge, we highlight two "hot" topics in psychiatric epidemiology: (1) Is autism caused by vaccines? and (2) Is there an epidemic of child or adolescent depression? Finally, we look to the future in two areas that are likely to produce huge dividends in the next decade: the development of biomarkers for stress, and the integration of molecular genetics and environmental risk studies.

Accepted August 5, 2005.

Drs. Costello and Angold are with the Center for Developmental Epidemiology, Duke University Medical School, Durham, NC; and Dr. Foley is with the Virginia Institute for Psychiatric and Behavioral Genetics, Virginia Commonwealth University, Richmond.

Work on this article was supported in part by grants 06937, 01002, and 01167 from the National Institute of Mental Health, and grants 011301 and 016977 from the National Institute on Drug Abuse.

Correspondence to Dr. E. Jane Costello, Box 3454, Duke University Health Systems, Durham NC 27710; e-mail: elizabeth.costello@duke.edu.

0890-8567/05/4501–0008©2005 by the American Academy of Child and Adolescent Psychiatry.

DOI: 10.1097/01.chi.0000184929.41423.c0

FROM DEVELOPMENTAL PSYCHOPATHOLOGY TO DEVELOPMENTAL EPIDEMIOLOGY

To understand how the epidemiological study of child and adolescent psychiatric disorders has changed in the past decade, we need to go back in history to the 1980s and examine the integration of child psychiatric and normative developmental research that created a new discipline: developmental psychopathology.

The relationship between child and adolescent psychiatry and developmental psychology has waxed and waned during the past century. In its earliest decades, child and adolescent psychiatry tended to equate "development" with psychodynamic concepts. In the 1980s, this situation changed radically, with landmark papers by Cicchetti (1984), Garber (1984), Rutter and Garmezy (1983), Sroufe and Rutter (1984) and others, introducing *developmental psychopathology* as an integrative discipline seeking to unify, within a developmental, lifespan framework, contributions from multiple fields of inquiry including biology and developmental science. Sroufe and Rutter (1984) defined developmental psychopathology as "the study of the origins and course of individual patterns of behavioral maladaptation, whatever the age of onset, whatever the causes, whatever the transformations in behavioral manifestation, and however complex the course of the developmental pattern may be." Developmental psychopathology strives to understand psychopathology in relationship to normative adaptation, integrating knowledge across scientific disciplines at multiple levels of analysis and multiple domains, rather than espousing a single theory that would account for all developmental phenomena (Rutter and Sroufe, 2000).

The unifying developmental orientation of the discipline posed new types of questions in new ways. The developmental psychopathologist is concerned not simply with differences in symptom presentation at different developmental periods but rather with the degree of convergence or divergence in the organization of biological, psychological, and social-contextual systems as they relate to symptom manifestation and disorder (Boyce et al., 1998; Cicchetti and Toth, 1998, 1995). This means that rather than being satisfied with a static comparison between children with a given psychiatric disorder and a "control group," for example, a developmental psychopathologist will use a research design that illuminates ways in which the evolution of symptoms over development leads to the creation of a group that could be defined as having a disorder (Cicchetti and Sroufe, 2000).

Developmental Epidemiology

This view of developmental psychopathology has several implications for epidemiological research: (1) it presupposes change and novelty, (2) it underscores the importance of timing in the establishment and organization of behavior, (3) it expects that a causal factor may have many outcomes, whereas several causal factors may have the same outcome (Cicchetti and Cohen, 1995), and (4) therefore leads us not to expect invariant relationships between causes and outcomes across the span of development (Costello and Angold, 1995). These characteristics have been woven into several epidemiological studies in recent years, under the label *developmental epidemiology*.

The term was first coined in the 1970s to describe a longitudinal community study in Woodlawn, IL (Kellam and Werthamer-Larsson, 1986). It has been revived in the past decade to describe an approach to child and adolescent psychiatric epidemiology that incorporates principles of developmental psychopathology into epidemiological research. The task is to understand the mechanisms by which developmental processes affect risk of specific psychiatric disorders and to propose preventive strategies appropriate to the various stages of risk. Such strategies must be appropriate to the developmental stage of both the individual at risk and the development of the disorder. An example of this approach is the work of Tremblay and colleagues in Montreal, showing that physical aggression in the population has a "normal" developmental trajectory; it "increases during the first 3 years after birth and then decreases steadily until adulthood" (Tremblay, 2004). Children who will grow up to be unusually aggressive have their own dysfunctional, developmental trajectory. In one study, for instance, children who were consistently highly aggressive as preschoolers were already significantly more likely to have a difficult temperament by 5 months of age (Tremblay et al., 2004).

A second theme of developmental epidemiology is the need to disentangle how the trajectories of symptoms, environment, and individual development intertwine to produce psychopathology. For example, the "difficult" children of Tremblay et al. (2004) were also

9

COSTELLO ET AL.

more likely to be born into stressed and dysfunctional families.

In another example, Jaffee et al. (2004) sought to clarify whether physical maltreatment leads to the development of antisocial behavior via an environmental causal pathway or via a genetic pathway. Associations between children's physical maltreatment and their antisocial behavior may reflect genetic transmission because parents provide both their child's genotype and their rearing environment. A child's genotype may be correlated with his or her rearing environment (passive genotype-environment correlation). Parental physical maltreatment of a child may also be correlated with other antisocial acts, and adult antisocial behavior is partly heritable. A childhood history of maltreatment may therefore be associated with future antisocial behavior because the genes that parents transmit to their children are the same genes that influence adult antisocial behavior, because childhood maltreatment is causally related to antisocial outcomes, or for both reasons. Developmental, genetically informative epidemiological data are required to tease out these pathways. Parental antisocial behavior may not perfectly capture all genetic risk factors for juvenile antisocial behavior if there are age-specific genetic effects that vary across the life span. Genetically informative designs that control for age-specific effects, such as juvenile twin data in which twins are perfectly correlated for age, permit such effects to be controlled for. Jaffee et al. (2004) used a longitudinal-epidemiological study of twins and their parents to show that physical maltreatment plays a causal role in the development of children's antisocial behavior.

RECENT RESEARCH ON PREVALENCE, ONSET, AND COMORBIDITY

There are two important measures of disorder in the population: prevalence, the proportion of the population with a disorder, and incidence, the rate at which new cases arise. Changes in the prevalence of a disorder over time can provide clues about etiology. We briefly review some recent findings from studies of both children and adults and then discuss two cases in which the possibility of recent increases in prevalence has caused a public furor: autism and early-onset depression. Then we review recent information about the age at incidence of major psychiatric disorders in the population and developmental effects on comorbidity.

Is the Prevalence of Psychiatric Disorders Changing?

Recent national surveys of adults have made it clear that many cases of psychiatric disorder have their origins well before adulthood. For example, Kessler et al. (1993) used data from the first National Comorbidity Survey to demonstrate that in half of the cases of major depression, the first episode had occurred by the mid-20s. The mean age at onset of bipolar disorder was 21 in both sexes (Kessler et al., 1997). In another article, Kessler et al. (1999) found that the reported onset of suicidal ideation, plans, and attempts rose to its highest point in the late teens and early 20s, with the median in the mid-20s. In the case of social phobia and simple phobia, about two thirds of cases had their onset by age 18 (Magee et al., 1996). When respondents had both addictive and other mental disorders in their lifetime, the median age at onset of the mental disorder was 11 years (Kessler et al., 1999) as compared with 21 years for the addictive disorders (Kessler et al., 1996a). Publications from other studies of adults confirmed these findings; for example, in a comparison of seven population samples, Vega et al. (2002) found that hazard rates for first use of alcohol, cannabis, and other drugs peaked in the late teens.

Several researchers have used these and other kinds of prevalence data to argue that there have been secular changes in the proportion of the population of a given age with a lifetime history of a psychiatric disorder; that is, controlling for age, prevalence is higher in more recent cohorts. Here, we discuss three examples in which different methods have been used to test this belief: conduct disorder (CD), depression, and autism.

CD Example. Robins (1999) recently updated the evidence first presented by Rutter et al. in 1984 (see Rutter et al., 1998) that the prevalence of CD has increased in recent decades. Both, however, pointed out the difficulties of drawing conclusions across time, particularly for CD, in which the changes from *DSM-III* to *DSM-III-R*, for example, resulted in a dramatic "masculinization" of the criteria and a shift in the sex ratio (Robins, 1999).

Collishaw and colleagues (2004) recently made ingenious use of three British birth cohort studies to circumvent this problem. Each birth cohort contained subjects 15 to 16 years old, and each measured conduct problems. A calibration study was carried out to ensure that the measures used in the three cohorts were comparable.

(However, they did not map directly on to *DSM-IV* CD.) The authors found a significant increase in mean scores between the cohorts born in 1958 and 1970, and the cohorts born in 1970 and 1983 to 1984. Also, the proportion scoring above a predetermined cut point identifying severe conduct problems rose from 6.8% to 10.4% to 14.9% across the three cohorts, so that by 1999 (when the latest-born cohort was 15 to 16 years old), more than twice as many children fell into the "severe" range as in 1974, when the earliest-born cohort was assessed at the same age. Trends were the same for boys and girls. It really looks as though there has been a significant increase in the proportion of young people with conduct problems and perhaps of CD.

Depression Example. A disturbing conclusion from many adult surveys is the suggestion that recent cohorts of adults (i.e., those born later than the oldest participants in the studies) had higher rates of psychiatric disorders, particularly depression, than did older cohorts when they were the same age (Lewinsohn et al., 1993; Wickramaratne et al., 1989). For example, Kessler et al. (1996b) used the National Comorbidity Survey (NCS) data to argue that depression is a growing public health problem because about 20% of respondents born before 1965 had their onset of pure or primary major depressive disorder by age 18, whereas in the youngest cohort, born between 1965 and 1974, 50% had their first episode by age 18. They make the same case in a recent analysis of the NCS replication study (Kessler et al., 2003).

As several investigative teams have pointed out (Giuffra and Risch, 1994; Patten, 2003; Paykel, 2000; Simon et al., 1995; Wittchen et al., 1994), these studies have a major methodological weakness: they asked adults anywhere up to 54 years old (in the NCS) or even in their 90s (for the Epidemiologic Catchment Area [ECA] and NCS replication) to date the earliest episode of a given psychiatric disorder. Dating of symptoms is unreliable even over short periods of time and varies with the age of the respondent and the time elapsed since the occurrence (Angold et al., 1996; Sanford et al., 1999). Therefore, it is possible that the oldest cohorts have simply forgotten how young they were at their first episode. The result of this would be the appearance that in earlier-born cohorts, fewer children and adolescents had psychiatric disorders than do today's youths (Foley et al., 1998; Pickles et al., 1998).

We recently reviewed this question using a different methodology. Rather than asking adults to recall the onset of their illness, we reviewed the 30 years of studies of children and adolescents (Costello et al., submitted), asking the question: "Do successive birth cohorts of young people report increasing rates of depression?" Data are available for cohorts born in the 1960s to cohorts born in the 1990s. A meta-analysis of 26 studies with close to 60,000 observations showed absolutely no evidence for an "epidemic" of child or adolescent depression, controlling for subjects' age at interview, sex, diagnostic taxonomy, psychiatric interview used, or time frame of the interview (3 months, 6 months, etc.). This was true of major depressive disorder and also of any depressive diagnosis. This sort of study may provide more valid evidence about whether rates of depression are increasing because subjects are being asked about something that occurred or did not occur in the past few months rather than decades ago. Analysis of this type is only possible with cohorts born since the 1960s because before that there were neither epidemiological methods to diagnose depression in children nor studies of representative epidemiological samples. There may have been an increase in the past 30 years compared with earlier decades.

Autism Example. An impassioned argument in recent epidemiological publications concerns the possibility that the prevalence of autism and other pervasive developmental disorders is increasing. Fombonne (2003a) provided a masterly review of the literature up to 2001, which serves as a fine primer on the methodological problems presented by the study of rare disorders in service-poor situations, particularly when our understanding of the clinical phenomenology of those disorders leads to the use of varying diagnostic criteria over time. More recent studies have suggested that autism is far more common than we thought 20 years ago, when a published prevalence rate of about 4 to 6/10,000 was the norm (Lotter, 1980). Summarizing the results from 32 studies published since 1966, Fombonne concluded that at least 10 children per 10,000 suffer from core autism, whereas twice that number have other pervasive developmental disorders (PDDs), including estimates of 2.5 and 0.2/10,000 for Asperger syndrome and childhood disintegrative (Heller) syndrome, respectively. The more recent of the studies reviewed, and others published since 2001 (Fombonne, 2003b; Fombonne et al., 2003; Jick and Kaye, 2003; Yeargin-Allsopp et al., 2003) suggest that the true rates are probably even higher, with a total prevalence of PDD of about

60/10,000, of whom 15/10,000 meet full *DSM-IV* or *ICD-10* criteria for autism. Rett syndrome probably occurs in at least one girl per 10,000, about three fourths of typical cases having a mutation at the MECP2 locus on the X chromosome, which is usually lethal in males (Chakrabarti and Fombonne, 2001; Fombonne et al., 2003; Leonard et al., 1997; Van den Veyver and Zoghbi, 2002), but we can expect this figure to be revised as we learn more about the phenotypes associated with MECP2 dysfunction (Kerr and Ravine, 2003). In this case, unlike the CD example discussed earlier, the most likely explanations for the apparent increase in the prevalence of autism are methodological: (1) changes in the definition of PDDs and (2) increased sophistication of case finding approaches (Fombonne, 2003b; Jick and Kaye, 2003).

These three cases illustrate the pitfalls on the road to the truth about changing rates of child psychiatric disorders. One day we will have regular nationally representative studies that will enable us to monitor the rise and (perhaps) fall in rates of psychiatric disorders in the same way that we now monitor changes in drug use and abuse through regular surveys by the Centers for Disease Control and Prevention.

Age at Onset of Psychiatric Disorders

The first data on age at onset of various psychiatric disorders came from single-wave, cross-sectional studies of adults, who were asked to recall the onset of their first episode. The ECA studies, five community surveys of adults 18 years old and older conducted in the 1980s, first demonstrated that the onset age of several psychiatric disorders was much earlier than had been thought from clinical research (Burke et al., 1990; Christie et al., 1988). In the ECA, close to 80% of respondents with a history of major depressive disorder, an anxiety disorder, or a drug use disorder dated its onset to before age 20 (Christie et al., 1988), and the peak hazard rate for major depression, mania, obsessive-compulsive disorder, phobias, and drug and alcohol disorders was in childhood or adolescence (Burke et al., 1990).

Recent studies, both clinical and epidemiological, show a group of disorders in which the majority of cases begin in childhood (attention-deficit/hyperactivity disorder [ADHD], autism and nonautistic PDD, separation anxiety, specific phobia, oppositional defiant disorder) and a different group that usually begin in adolescence (social phobia, panic disorder, substance abuse, depression, anorexia nervosa, bulimia nervosa). Most of the childhood-onset disorders have more male than female cases, whereas most adolescent disorders have more female than male cases (Rutter et al., 2003). Conduct disorder is a special case; it has been argued (Moffitt, 1993; Moffitt et al., 2002) that, for boys at least, antisocial behavior beginning in childhood has antecedents and a course different from those of adolescent-onset deviance. The seriousness of early-onset deviant behaviors, long emphasized by Moffitt (1993) as a predictor of life-course criminal offending, has been confirmed in several studies (Tolan and Thomas, 1995), although many have also pointed out that environmental characteristics may account for the early onset (Stouthamer-Loeber et al., 1999; Tolan and Thomas, 1995). Studies that report the onset of CD show that in the majority of cases, the onset of the first symptoms is early in life. Lahey et al. (2000), using the Methodology for Epidemiology in Children and Adolescents data on subjects 9 to 17 years old, found that 72% of those meeting criteria for CD by age 17 had their first symptom before age 10. This finding was replicated in the Great Smoky Mountains Study (GSMS), a longitudinal community study beginning at age 9, where unpublished analyses show that of youths who had CD by age 16, 75% had their first symptom before age 10 and 89% before age 13. This would imply that the vast majority of cases of child and adolescent CD are in fact early-onset cases. Future research will need to be careful to specify whether it is concerned with *DSM* CD, which includes a range of symptoms that do not necessarily involve delinquent behavior, or the more extreme forms of behavioral deviance. It makes sense that children who actually break the law at an early age may be different from adolescent law breakers and have different antecedents (Kim-Cohen et al., 2005; National Research Council and Institute of Medicine, 2001; Raine et al., 2005). The *DSM-IV* criteria for CD, which include fighting, lying, bullying, and committing acts of cruelty to animals are less likely to produce markedly different groups as a function of sex or age at onset than are "official" categories resulting from arrest or conviction (National Research Council and Institute of Medicine, 2001).

Data from the past decade of research show that depression is one of the later developing disorders of childhood and adolescence. Lewinsohn et al. (1994), using the Oregon Adolescent Depression Project, found that in cases occurring by age 18, the mean onset age for major depressive disorder was 14.7 years for girls and 15.4 years for boys. Other adolescent-onset disorders are panic disorder (13.9 in GSMS), anorexia nervosa and bulimia nervosa (peak onset ages 16 to17; Lewinsohn et al., 2000), and drug abuse (Costello et al., 1999). It is important to distinguish between age at onset of the full *DSM* disorder and onset of the first symptom in children who will go on to develop the full disorder. The GSMS and Oregon studies found similar age at onset of the full *DSM-IV* diagnosis through age 16, but in GSMS, the mean age at first symptom in those who developed depression by age 16 was 10.7 (SE = 3.9). This was 2 years earlier than the mean onset of the first depressive symptom in those who did not develop the full syndrome (12.4, SE = 3.3).

"Follow-back" analyses that track the onset of psychiatric disorders in adults are just beginning to appear. An important report from the Dunedin study in New Zealand, which has followed a birth cohort since the 1970s, found that of individuals with a psychiatric diagnosis at age 26, three fourths had a diagnosis at age 18, and 50% had one by age 15 (Kim-Cohen et al., 2003). In most cases, a childhood disorder predicted the same diagnosis later on, but there were exceptions. Early CD and/or oppositional disorders predicted a wide range of adult diagnoses, and conversely adult anxiety and schizophreniform disorders were predicted by a wide range of diagnoses. Of course, the prospective studies reviewed here cannot tell us what proportion of all cases have their onset in childhood or adolescence because they do not cover the entire period of risk for most disorders, but they do show that a large proportion of adults with psychiatric disorders had an early onset and that the cumulative prevalence of many disorders is similar in preadult studies to that seen in adult studies. This implies that onset before adulthood may be a characteristic of the majority of adult psychiatric disorders.

Developmental Comorbidity

In the past decade, we have learned a great deal more about comorbidity among child and adolescent psychiatric disorders. A review (Angold et al., 1999) presents data from approximately 20 studies in a form that enables readers to see for themselves the numbers of cases of each disorder and their co-occurrence in each

study. The report also presents, for the first time, a meta-analysis of co-occurring disorders that takes into account other forms of comorbidity; for example, comorbidity between depression and ADHD controlling for comorbidity between ADHD and other disorders. A similar meta-analysis of comorbidity with substance abuse/dependence has also been carried out (Armstrong and Costello, 2002). A summary of the findings of both studies can be seen in Figure 1. The highest levels of comorbidity were between disruptive behavior disorders and ADHD, and anxiety disorders and depression. The lowest were between anxiety and disruptive behavior disorders; however, these were still statistically significant.

In other analyses of comorbidity among anxiety disorders in GSMS (Costello et al., 2004), much of the comorbidity between anxiety disorders and depression was confined to overanxious disorder and generalized anxiety disorders, what have been called the worry disorders as opposed to fear disorders such as separation anxiety and the phobias (Costello et al., 2004), and to panic disorder and posttraumatic stress disorder. Lewinsohn et al. (1997) found significant lifetime comorbidity between depression and all of the anxiety

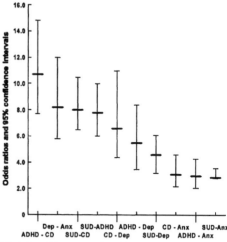

Fig. 1 Comorbidity among psychiatric disorder: the results of meta-analysis. ADHD = attention-deficit/hyperactivity disorder; CD = conduct disorder or oppositional defiant disorder; Dep = depression; Anx = anxiety; SUD = substance use disorder (substance abuse and/or dependence).

COSTELLO ET AL.

disorders except obsessive-compulsive disorder, controlling for comorbidity.

An important caveat in interpreting these data is that many of the studies took a broad view of the time frame for defining comorbidity. Comorbidity refers to co-occurrence in the same time interval, but that interval may be defined narrowly (at the same moment), or more broadly (within the same 6 months or year) or even to refer to the whole lifetime. Further work has been done recently to examine differences between concurrent comorbidity and successive comorbidity (Angold et al., 1999). Using longitudinal data from the GSMS on youths 9 through 16 years old (Costello et al., 2003), although there was a high degree of concurrent comorbidity among almost all of the disorders assessed (25 of 30 tests of association), a different picture appeared when the question asked is which diagnoses predict which over time. Table 1 shows the results of these lagged analyses. In every case, there was significant homotypic continuity, that is, each disorder increased the risk of the same disorder in the future. In contrast, there was relatively little heterotypic continuity, that is, an increased likelihood of a disorder following a different disorder. Heterotypic continuity was significant, controlling for other comorbidities, only for anxiety–depression and depression–anxiety, anxiety–substance abuse/dependence (substance use disorder), and ADHD–oppositional defiant disorder. Furthermore, heterotypic continuity was significantly more likely in girls than in boys.

In our current state of knowledge, comorbidity can be expected in almost every child seen in a mental health setting. An important task for future research is to distinguish between "real" comorbidity and comorbidity caused by a faulty taxonomy or other artifacts of our diagnostic process.

Developmental Ordering of Psychiatric and Substance Abuse Disorders

Related questions for developmental epidemiology deal with the order in which psychiatric disorders appear and the extent to which one disorder increases the risk or accelerates the onset of other disorders.

Lewinsohn et al. (1997) used three waves of data from the Oregon Adolescent Depression Project to examine age at onset of other disorders relative to depressive disorders in adolescents. They found that the mean age at onset of affective disorder in both males and females who developed bipolar disorder during adolescence was 11.75 years, significantly younger than the onset age of youths with major depression but no bipolar disorder (14.95). Simple phobia, separation anxiety, overanxious disorder, and social phobia typically preceded the onset of major depressive disorder, whereas panic disorder and obsessive-compulsive disorder tended to have later onsets. This temporal ordering is consistent with genetic studies (Silberg et al., 2001) suggesting that early symptoms of anxiety influence liability to depressive symptoms expressed in middle to late adolescence.

Both the Oregon Adolescent Depression Project and the GSMS have shown that childhood psychiatric disorders affect both the likelihood and the age at onset of substance use disorders (Costello et al., 1999; Orvaschel et al., 1995; Sung et al., 2004). For example, Sung et al. (Sung et al., 2004) found that CD by age 13 greatly increased the risk of substance use disorder in early adolescence, whereas CD occurring later in adolescence had much less effect as a predictor of substance use

TABLE 1

Homotypic and Heterotypic Continuity, With and Without Controls for Comorbidity

	Past Depression	Past Anxiety	Past Conduct Disorder	Past ODD	Past ADHD	Past Substance Abuse
Predicting for depression	7.0 (3.1, 15.9)***	3.0 (1.7, 5.4)***				
Controlling for comorbidity	4.2 (2.1, 8.3)***	2.7 (1.8, 5.2)**				
Anxiety	5.7 (2.2, 14.5)***	2.4 (1.6, 3.7)***				
Controlling for comorbidity	2.8 (1.2, 6.5)*	2.0 (1.2, 3.4)*				
Conduct disorder			11.2 (5.9, 21.1)***			
Controlling for comorbidity			10.3 (4.3, 24.7)***			
ODD				3.7 (2.2, 6.2)***	2.0 (1.1, 3.8)*	

Note: ODD = oppositional defiant disorder; ADHD = attention-deficit/hyperactivity disorder.
*$p < .05$; **$p < .01$; ***$p < .001$.

14

disorder. This may be because substance use disorder was much less common in younger adolescents, and the cases needed a more toxic risk environment before they developed (see Flavell et al., 2005, for an example with diabetes). Kaplow et al. (2001), using the same data set, found that an apparent lack of association between anxiety disorders and alcohol use was in fact the result of two contradictory processes: children with generalized anxiety disorder were more likely to use alcohol and did so at an earlier age than other children, whereas children with separation anxiety disorder were less likely to use alcohol and began later.

Among the anxiety disorders, there has been a clinical tradition that separation anxiety disorder in childhood is a developmental precursor of panic disorder in adolescence and adulthood (Klein, 1995; Silove et al., 1996). This has been challenged in three epidemiological studies (Hayward et al., 2000; Pine et al., 1998; A. Bittner, unpublished). Using large samples and prospective data, none found any association between separation anxiety disorder and later panic attacks or panic disorder. Future longitudinal studies will, we hope, clarify the developmental course of the anxiety disorders.

New studies are not always needed, however. There is a wealth of information about the developmental organization of psychopathology hiding within existing longitudinal data sets. Recent developments in design and statistics (Cairns et al., 1998; Muthen and Muthen, 2000; Nagin and Tremblay, 2001; Sullivan, 1998) will help with this task. One important conclusion to be drawn from recent studies (Angold et al., 1999; Ford et al., 2003) is that some examples of comorbidity may turn out to be "epiphenomenal" (Angold et al., 1999); for example, what appears in bivariate analyses to be comorbidity between anxiety and CD turns out, when all possible comorbidities are considered in the model, to be the result of comorbidity between (1) anxiety and oppositional defiant disorder, and (2) oppositional defiant disorder and CD.

EARLY RISK FOR PSYCHIATRIC DISORDERS

Developmental science has expanded our understanding of risk and protective factors so dramatically in the past decade that it is beyond the scope of this review to cover the whole area. Instead, we focus on two topics of particular interest for child and adolescent psychiatry: the interrelationship between medical and

psychiatric risk factors and outcomes and the causal role of vaccines in autism and PDD.

Interrelationship Between Medical and Psychiatric Risk Factors and Outcomes

The birth cohort studies of the 1960s and 1970s, which have been so important in demonstrating the early onset and widespread prevalence of psychiatric disorders, are now increasingly being used to illuminate both the psychosocial origins of the "medical" chronic diseases of middle age (Barker, 2003) and the role of early physiological problems in the development of psychiatric disorders (e.g., Brown and Susser, 2002; Opler et al., 2004). Here, we look at one example: effects of low birth weight on later psychopathology. Evidence is emerging linking undernutrition of the fetus, indexed by low birth weight, with depression in adolescence (Saigal et al., 2003), adulthood (Bellingham-Young and Adamson-Macedo, 2003; Gale and Martyn, 2004), and old age (Thompson et al., 2001). Attention deficit problems have long been reported to be more prevalent in children who were preterm or of low birth weight (Breslau et al., 1996; Pharoah et al., 1994; Whitaker et al., 1997), although other studies question the association (Sommerfelt et al., 1996) or suggest that this may have more to do with socioeconomic deprivation or mental retardation than low birth weight itself (Kreppner et al., 2001; Levy et al., 1996). The link between other kinds of conduct problems and low birth weight is unclear (Breslau et al., 1996; Sommerfelt et al., 1993). Few differences have been found in anxiety disorders (Breslau et al., 1996; Saigal et al., 2003), although Whitaker and colleagues noted increased separation anxiety in a subgroup (Whitaker et al., 1997).

There are several mechanisms by which low birth weight may mark permanent changes that increase later vulnerability to depression and other psychiatric disorders. Thompson et al. (2001) suggest three. Programming of the hypothalamus-pituitary-adrenal axis could lead to raised plasma cortisol level, which is a consistently demonstrated biological abnormality in primary depressive disorder (Lopez et al., 1998; Murphy, 1991; Nemeroff et al., 1984). Second, median 24-hour plasma growth hormone concentrations are related to weight at 1 year (Fall et al., 1998), and in depression, the control of growth hormone secretion is known to be disturbed in both children and adults (Birmaher et al., 2000;

COSTELLO ET AL.

Checkley, 1996; Sakkas et al., 1998). Third, reduced plasma thyrotropin levels coupled with impaired response to thyrotropin-releasing hormone are associated with depression (Oomen et al., 1996), and thyroid function may be set during fetal growth and infant feeding (Phillips et al., 1993).

Low birth weight is just one example of a "biological" developmental risk factor that seems to serve as a risk marker for both medical and psychiatric disorders later in life. There is also growing evidence of a common core group of socioeconomic and developmental risk and protective factors that influence the course of both sets of conditions. Poverty, lack of attachment to primary caregivers, poor family relationships, maternal depression, poor school achievement, and disrupted family structure certainly predict child psychiatric disorders, but they also predict chronic medical conditions (Mantymaa et al., 2003; Steptoe et al., 2000; Wright et al., 1998), including cancer (via their link to tobacco use; see Swan et al., 2003).

Vaccines, Autism, and PDD

The suspicion that the true rates of autism and other PDDs are rising has fueled research on what could cause such an increase. The prime suspect has been measles-mumps-rubella (MMR) vaccine (specifically its live, attenuated measles virus component). The putative MMR-autism link story began to attract international attention with case reports of 12 children with PDD presenting with a chronic enterocolitis characterized by nongranulomatous ileocolonic lymphonodular hyperplasia (Wakefield et al., 1998b), although this was not the first clinical suggestion that there may be a link (Gupta, 1996). That initial study gave some prominence to reports of eight of the children's parents or physicians that their first behavioral symptoms had begun shortly (1 to 14 days) after receiving MMR immunizations. This, and a subsequent report on an extended sample of 60 children with histories of normal development followed by developmental regression, was followed by a storm of contentious debate that resulted in a significant fall in the uptake of MMR vaccination (and a subsequent rise in outbreaks of measles) in more than one country (Horton, 2004a,b; Noble and Miyasaka, 2004; Wakefield, 1999; Wakefield et al., 2000). Several years later, 10 of the 13 authors of the 1998 paper (Wakefield et al., 1998b) retracted the interpretation that autism may be causally linked to MMR

(Murch et al., 2004). This confusing story needs to be broken into several components if we are to make sense of it.

PDDs and Gut Disorders. First is the question of whether there is an association between PDDs and a novel (and probably immunopathological) gut disorder distinct from both Crohn's disease and ulcerative colitis. There is clinical evidence in support of this idea, and it certainly deserves further investigation (Ashwood et al., 2003; Furlano et al., 2001; Horvath et al., 1999; Wakefield et al., 2000). The second question concerns whether such a bowel disease may itself be a cause of PDDs, with some cases of the latter constituting what Wakefield et al. (2002) have called enterocolonic encephalopathies. This argument is based on various clinical analogies and is, at present, entirely speculative, but already faces some disconfirmatory epidemiological evidence (Black et al., 2002).

PDDs and Measles. Is bowel disease an aberrant response to exposure to measlesvirus? There is again clinical evidence of the presence of measles antigen in the affected bowel (Kawashima et al., 2000; Martin et al., 2002; Uhlmann et al., 2002; Wakefield et al., 1998a), but similar findings have also been reported in Crohn's disease and ulcerative colitis in the absence of PDD (Hendrickson and Turner, 2002; Wakefield and Montgomery, 2000), so it is unlikely to be related to a specific PDD gut disorder. None of the measles findings in any of these diseases is securely associated with measles antigens rather than cross-reacting host antigens (Ghosh et al., 2001; Hendrickson and Turner, 2002; Iizuka et al., 2000; Morris et al., 2000). We must also bear in mind that the presence of apparent viral antigens could be a result of gut immunological disorder rather than its cause (Hendrickson and Turner, 2002).

PDD and MMR. Is MMR immunization directly (perhaps an aberrant long-term outcome analogous to subacute sclerosing panencephalitis following wild-type measles) or indirectly associated with PDDs? A number of relatively large-scale studies have now reported on this question, using several different strategies. The least satisfactory are demonstrations of a lack of correlation between apparent increases in records of the number of individuals with autism and rates of MMR immunization uptake in the United States and the United Kingdom (Dales et al., 2001; Kaye et al., 2001). More convincing are studies showing that there was no clustering of PDD onsets around the time of immunization, no correlation between the timing of immunization and the timing of onsets of PDDs, and no difference between the age of PDD onset in the unimmunized versus the immunized (DeStefano et al., 2004; Madsen et al., 2002; Taylor et al., 1999). Most convincing of all are studies with a sufficient representation of unimmunized participants to permit a reasonably powered straightforward test of the association between immunization (yes/no) and PDDs (Madsen et al., 2002; Smeeth et al., 2004). Again, the results provided absolutely no support for the existence of an MMR-PDD link. A recent study from Japan showed that the incidence of autism increased in the decade following the withdrawal of MMR (Honda et al., 2005). Although none of these studies was by any means perfect, the concordance of their negative results across several countries and data collection and analysis approaches is impressive. It may be theoretically impossible to prove the null, but it is difficult in the face of all this accumulated evidence to believe that there is a PDD risk from MMR immunization that outweighs the risks of remaining unimmunized.

Thimerosal and PDDs. A second vaccine-autism link concerns vaccines containing thimerosal (sodium ethyl mercury thiosalicylate, 49% mercury by weight, also known as thimerosal in some countries), which has been used to prevent bacterial and fungal contamination since the 1930s (Verstraeten et al., 2003). The situation with respect to thimerosal is conceptually straightforward: Methyl mercury poisoning involves prominent neurological symptoms, characteristically ataxia, dysarthria, constricted visual fields, and peripheral neuropathy, so perhaps autism, despite its different clinical presentation (Nelson and Bauman, 2003), results from thimerosal (although ethyl mercury crosses the blood-brain barrier much less easily than the methylated form). It has also now been found that blood hemoglobin concentrations in infants following vaccination are low and that ethyl mercury is rapidly eliminated via the stool (Pichichero et al., 2002). A recent study found, however, that an autoimmune disease–susceptible strain of mice, but not nonsusceptible mice, showed behavioral and neural morphological and histochemical responses to thimerosal in doses meant to mimic those used in human vaccination schedules (Hornig et al., 2004). This compound is also not a good candidate for explaining any supposed recent increases in autism incidence because it has been absent from vaccines in the

United Kingdom and Denmark during periods in which higher rates of autism and other PDDs have been reported (e.g., Madsen, 2004). Nelson and Bauman (2003) provided a helpful summary of a range of earlier work, but only since then has a small flurry of general population studies of the question appeared. One has reported positive associations (Geier and Geier, 2003)—a study of reports to the Vaccine Adverse Events Reporting System of the U.S. Centers for Disease Control and Prevention related to diphtheria, tetanus, acellular pertussis (DTP) vaccine, which contained thimerosal (administered in years 1992–2000) versus those relating to non-thimerosal-containing DTP (1997–2000). The relative risks for reports of autism and mental retardation were 6, whereas that for speech disorders was 2.2 (with mean postvaccination onset times of 8–22 days). The authors claim that the fact that the thimerosal-containing vaccines were administered over a longer period (1992–2000) would help to preclude the possibility of reporting biases based on popular media publicity. In Denmark, for instance, thimerosal had already been eliminated from vaccines by 1992. Those concerned with this issue could surely have influenced reporting to the Centers for Disease Control and Prevention during this period. It would be helpful to know whether the incidence of adverse reports in those who received thimerosal-containing vaccines increased during the period of the study. Such an increase would not be expected under the hypothesis that thiomersal caused autism and mental retardation but probably would have occurred if reporting bias were responsible for the apparent differences. Nor is it true that biased reporting would have been reflected in an increased incidence rate of acute adverse reaction (Geier and Geier, 2003) because the expectation of activists in this area would relate specifically to neurodevelopmental disorders, not to vasculitis or death.

Much more reliable evidence comes from Hviid and colleagues (2003) and from Madsen et al. (2003), large, representative Danish studies that found no evidence that thimerosal was associated with PDDs, but that rates of official record diagnoses of autism continued to rise after the removal of thimerosal from all vaccines. Similarly negative results have been reported from an HMO database study (Verstraeten et al., 2003), the U.K. General Practice Research Database (Jick and Kaye, 2004), and a United States-Sweden-Denmark comparison of average thimerosal exposures and rates of PDDs

17

COSTELLO ET AL.

(Stehr-Green et al., 2003). In summary, then, there is little evidence that thimerosal has been a substantial cause of autism or other PDDs.

AREAS OF FUTURE GROWTH IN DEVELOPMENTAL EPIDEMIOLOGY

It would be agreeable to think that the tasks involved in monitoring the prevalence and burden of child and adolescent psychiatric disorders—the "public health" duties of epidemiology—would in the next decade be taken over by the agencies tasked to carry out surveillance studies of disease, above all the Centers for Disease Control and Prevention. Then the research funding available from the National Institutes of Health could be used, as intended, for scientific, etiological research rather than for "counting noses." Even if epidemiology has to divide its resources between its two functions, it will nevertheless make progress in two important and interesting areas: genetics and biomarkers.

Genetically Informed Psychiatric Epidemiology

The idea that genes "cause" psychiatric disorders has a long history. What has changed recently is the relationship between genetics and mainstream epidemiology (Rutter et al., 1999a). Both disciplines have altered their attitudes and approach. In 1999, Rutter and colleagues published two comprehensive papers summarizing advances in quantitative and molecular genetics (Rutter et al., 1999b) and reviewing empirical findings related to child and adolescent psychiatric disorders (Rutter et al., 1999a). These remain essential background reading on the genetics of child and adolescent psychiatric disorders. In the past few years there have been several advances that deserve comment here.

First, the behavioral genetic studies of the past decade that focus on children and adolescents have paid much more attention to issues of sampling and generalizability to the population (an obsession of epidemiologists) than used to be the case. Researchers have become much more sensitive to the problems inherent in trying to generalize from adoption or family-based high-risk studies. Twin studies have increasingly used representative sampling frames rather than relying on volunteers or members of twin parents' groups, and sample sizes have also increased. For example, the Virginia Twin Study of Adolescent Behavioral Development (Eaves et al., 1997; Hewitt et al., 1997; Simonoff et al., 1997) used school records to identify all of the twin pairs in Virginia 9 to 17 years old and recruited 1,400 of them, and a nationwide birth registry was used to identify 1,200 infant twin pairs for the Environmental Risk (E-risk) Longitudinal Twin Study currently under way in the United Kingdom (Caspi et al., 1995). Representative sampling, always a major concern to epidemiologists, is particularly important in genetic studies in which there is a possibility that the genes involved in a disorder may vary in different subpopulation groups (Risch et al., 2002).

Second, recognizing the genome as, in a sense, a blueprint for development, recent behavioral genetics studies have moved toward developmentally informative designs. This has yielded important insights. For example, analyses from Virginia Twin Study of Adolescent Behavioral Development (Silberg et al., 2001) suggest that self-reported depression before and after puberty may be etiologically distinct syndromes, with genetic risk for postpubertal depression expressed as overanxious disorder and specific phobias before puberty. In the behavioral problem area, the E-risk study has shown that although genetic factors did not account for significant variation in children's experience of physical maltreatment, maltreatment assessed at age 5 predicted antisocial behavior 2 years later, even after controlling for any genetic transmission of antisocial behavior (Jaffee et al., 2004).

The third and most dramatic development in the genetic epidemiology of child and adolescent psychopathology is the result of recent technological developments in molecular genetics, which have made the collection of biodata for DNA feasible in large field studies using cheek scrapes or small blood samples from finger sticks, and have made testing for candidate genes economically feasible for large samples. In two landmark studies, Caspi et al. (2002, 2003) used data from the Dunedin, New Zealand, longitudinal study to demonstrate that gene–environment interactions predicted psychiatric problems more powerfully than either genes or environmental risk on their own. In the first study (Caspi et al., 2002), the group genotyped the variable number tandem repeat polymorphism at the promoter of the monoamine oxidase A (MAOA) gene, which is known to affect its expression. (Because the MAOA gene is located on the X chromosome, only boys were used in this analysis.) Using data from the early waves of this study, whose participants are now young adults, they created a measure of maltreatment between the ages of 3 and 11.

Maltreatment groups did not differ on MAOA activity, suggesting (as in the E-risk twin study discussed earlier [Jaffee et al., 2004]) that genotype did not influence exposure to maltreatment. Four measures of adolescent and adult antisocial behavior were derived from later waves of the Dunedin data. In each case, the effect of early maltreatment on later antisocial behavior was significant for those with low MAOA activity, but not for those with high MAOA activity.

The interaction of low MAOA activity with early adversity was replicated recently in a study using different measures of both CD and early stressors (Foley et al., 2004). This is important in showing that the gene–environment interaction is robust to measurement methods.

In a second study (Caspi et al., 2003), the group examined the interaction of life stress in young adulthood and human serotonin transporter (5-HTT) genotype on depression at age 26. Both males and females with one or two copies of the short allele of the 5-HTT promoter polymorphism showed more depressive symptoms, diagnosable depression, and suicidality after stressful life events than did participants who were homozygous for the long allele. Three replications of this finding, two positive and one negative, are under review.

These studies are particularly important for child and adolescent psychiatric epidemiology in that they use a regular population sample rather than requiring a special "genetically informative" subgroup of the population such as twins, adoptees, or children of affected parents. This means that existing epidemiological samples, provided that they are large enough and can obtain biodata for DNA extraction, can be used to examine both candidate genes and the role of environmental factors as a function of genetic vulnerabilities.

Another implication of these important studies is that they demonstrate the value of genetic and environmental data collected prospectively from early in life (Foley et al., 2004) as well as accurate assessments of psychopathology over time. Epidemiological studies that meet these criteria (and there are several) have the potential to contribute importantly to developments in psychiatric genetics in the next decade (Jaffee et al., 2004).

Biological Markers of Stress and Psychiatric Disorder

A new and exciting phase in epidemiological research is opening with the development of methods, previously available only in the laboratory, for exploring biological processes that mediate environmental stressors in children's lives. So far, in psychiatric epidemiology as in much clinical work, we have been dependent on verbal descriptions of symptoms and stressors. We have had to assume a causal connection between stressors and symptoms via an unmeasured construct "stress." Now we are beginning to be able to look at possible markers of stressor exposure, such as cortisol reactivity (Granger et al., 1998; Strickland et al., 2002) at baseline or in response to a challenge, using saliva or small amounts of blood collected using the kind of finger-stick technique familiar from diabetes testing.

The use of autonomic tone as a measure of response to stressors has a long history in laboratory studies; for example, Snidman et al. (1995) have demonstrated that shy and inhibited children also show a shift in autonomic balance favoring sympathetic over parasympathetic tone. Portable electrocardiographic monitors now make this kind of research possible in field studies.

A third approach to stress measurement is to use immunocompetence as a marker for response to stressors. Antibodies to resident viruses reflect immunocompetence in keeping the virus in check, which capacity is eroded by stress. On the one hand, in individuals infected with the Epstein-Barr virus, circulating levels of viral antibody have been consistently linked to daily stress levels (Kiecolt-Glaser, 1999; Sarid et al., 2001) and negative affective states (Esterling et al., 1993). On the other hand, social integration and support and stress management interventions are paralleled by lower Epstein-Barr virus antibodies (Esterling et al., 1992; Lutgendorf et al., 1994). The relationship of immunocompetence to stress means that Epstein-Barr virus antibodies represent an ongoing bioassay of chronic stress and immunocompetence: the higher the titer, the greater the level of ongoing stress-related immunocompromise (Glaser et al., 2005). Simply put, more antibody indicates more stress. Preliminary results (McDade, 2002) show promise for this as an ecologically valid measure of medium- to long-term stress.

Fourth, research on adults is beginning to explore the use of C-reactive protein (CRP) and other proteins that mediate inflammatory response as useful biomarkers of risk for leading causes of adult morbidity and mortality, including cardiovascular disease, diabetes, and, most recently, depression. The dominant acute phase protein mediating innate immunity, CRP was the first discovered component of inflammatory response and as such

COSTELLO ET AL.

had long been exclusively related to systemic infection (Du Clos and Mold, 2001; Gabay and Kushner, 1999; Mold et al., 1999). Recently, CRP has been identified as perhaps the most powerful predictor of cardiovascular disease (Danesh et al., 2000; Koenig et al., 1999; Kuller et al., 1996; Ridker et al., 2003). CRP both indexes the degree of systemic wear and tear and plays an atherogenic role in plaque formation from childhood onward (Mold et al., 1999). Mildly and moderately increased levels have been linked to all of the components of the metabolic syndrome (upper body obesity, abnormal glucose, hypertension, low high-density lipoprotein, and elevated triglycerides [Festa et al., 2000; Han et al., 2002; Ridker et al., 2003; Tamakoshi et al., 2003]). Increased CRP has also been associated with reduced activity and physical fitness among children and adolescents (Cook et al., 2000; Isasi et al., 2003). Ongoing psychological distress and disorder may reinforce the systemic burden indexed by CRP (Miller et al., 2001, 2002; Roose et al., 2001). Depression is prospectively linked to coronary artery disease (Glassman and Shapiro, 1998) and has been associated with increased CRP and other inflammatory risk markers (Danner et al., 2003; Dentino et al., 1999; Ford and Erlinger, 2004; Maes, 1999). Similar associations have been found with posttraumatic stress disorder (Miller et al., 2001). So far, this work has been carried out on adult samples, but longitudinal epidemiological studies that collect blood routinely will be able to explore the value of CRP as a marker of the extent to which children experience stressors, such as maltreatment and trauma, as stress, that is, the "allostatic load" (McEwen, 2002) or cost of coping, and the implications for the development of psychiatric disorder.

CONCLUSIONS AND IMPLICATIONS FOR TREATMENT AND PREVENTION

In summary, developmental epidemiology has made considerable progress in the past decade as both a descriptive and an analytic science. Descriptively, it has shown that there are clear timing patterns in the onset of different psychiatric disorders, that the onset of one disorder affects the timing of others, and that individual development intertwines with the development of the disease process. Analytically, it has begun to make use of new techniques to move beyond what epidemiologists Mervin and Ezra Susser (Susser and Susser,

1996) have criticized as "the identification rather than the explanation of causal factors" and begun to search for "mediation and causal chains" (Schwartz, 1998).

In the past decade, developmental epidemiology has come to see itself as part of a more general activity called life course epidemiology (Ben-Shlomo and Kuh, 2002; Elder, 1996, 1998; Singer and Ryff, 1999). A life course approach to epidemiology has been defined as "the study of long-term effects on chronic disease risk of physical and social exposures during gestation, childhood, adolescence, young adulthood and later adult life. It includes studies of the biological, behavioral and psychosocial pathways that operate across an individual's life course, as well as across generations" (Ben-Shlomo and Kuh, 2002). A major reason for the absorption of psychiatric epidemiology into life course epidemiology is the growing tendency to think of psychiatric disorders as chronic diseases, amenable to the same epidemiological research methods as diabetes or cardiovascular disease. A single risk marker, such as low birth weight, can lead to many different outcomes via different pathways.

Role of Developmental Epidemiology in Treatment and Prevention

Treatment interventions attempt to reduce the prevalence of disease in the community by reducing the duration of illness and the likelihood of relapse, whereas preventive interventions try to reduce the incidence of new cases (Rothman and Greenland, 1998). The goal of prevention science is to create an environment in which children (even genetically vulnerable children) are not exposed to risk factors for disease or are protected from their effects. This may be achieved by reducing the spread or strength of risk factors for a disease ("primary" or "universal" prevention) or by breaking the link between risk factors and disease ("secondary" or "targeted" prevention). The main role of epidemiology has been to provide basic information, measurement tools, and research designs for preventive interventions (although clinical epidemiologists play an important role in treatment interventions, too, especially in the conduct of complex, multisite clinical trials).

It follows, then, that developmental epidemiologists will have a strong interest in identifying the risk factors that predict incidence and that are amenable to preventive interventions, and a great deal of work has been done in this area in the past decade. It has often been the older studies, with birth cohorts from the 1960s and 1970s, that have begun to yield the most valuable information about risk. The reason for this is that their participants are now adults, some even middle aged. They have passed through the highest period of risk for the onset of childhood disorders and even, as discussed earlier, for many adult psychiatric disorders. So prevention scientists can look back and identify not only key risk factors but also key critical periods when exposure was most dangerous, and therefore when prevention programs may be most effective. An interesting example discussed earlier is low birth weight, an eminently preventable condition that is only now emerging as a key risk factor for both medical (Barker, 2003) and psychiatric (Gunnell et al., 2003) disorders of adulthood. Here, the critical period of risk lies years, even decades, before the disease outcome. It is also an example of a risk factor probably best attacked through universal prevention programs rather than by targeting small high-risk groups such as pregnant women with a family history of schizophrenia.

The literature on risk for child and adolescent psychiatric disorders was summarized recently in a series of papers from the National Institute of Mental Health. The link between developmental epidemiology and current progress in prevention science is laid out in several recent papers (Anonymous, 2002; Dodge, 2001; Hawkins et al., 2002; Kellam et al., 1999; Spoth et al., 2002) and is too big an issue to be adequately covered here. For the future, developmental epidemiology can contribute to its goal of working even more closely with prevention scientists and clinicians to develop the range of interventions needed to reduce the burden of child and adolescent mental illness.

Disclosure: The authors have no financial relationships to disclose.

REFERENCES

Angold A, Costello EJ, Erkanli A (1999), Comorbidity. *J Child Psychol Psychiatry* 40:57–87

Angold A, Erkanli A, Costello EJ, Rutter M (1996), Precision, reliability and accuracy in the dating of symptom onsets in child and adolescent psychopathology. *J Child Psychol Psychiatry* 37:657–664

Anonymous (2002), The implementation of the Fast Track program: an example of a large-scale prevention science efficacy trial. *J Abnorm Child Psychol* 30:1–17

Armstrong TD, Costello EJ (2002), Community studies on adolescent substance use, abuse, or dependence and psychiatric comorbidity. *J Consult Clin Psychol* 70:1224–1239

Ashwood P, Anthony A, Pellicer AA, Torrente F, Walker-Smith JA, Wakefield AJ (2003), Intestinal lymphocyte populations in children with regressive autism: evidence for extensive mucosal immunopathology. *J Clin Immunol* 23:504–517

Barker D (2003), The developmental origins of adult disease. *Eur J Epidemiol* 18:733–736

Bellingham-Young DA, Adamson-Macedo EN (2003), Foetal origins theory: links with adult depression and general self-efficacy. *Neuroendocrinol Lett* 24:412–416

Ben-Shlomo Y, Kuh D (2002), A life course approach to chronic disease epidemiology: conceptual models, empirical challenges and interdisciplinary perspectives. *Int J Epidemiol* 31:285–293

Birmaher B, Dahl RE, Williamson DE et al. (2000), Growth hormone secretion in children and adolescents at high risk for major depressive disorder. *Arch Gen Psychiatry* 57:867–872

Black C, Kaye JA, Jick H (2002), Relation of childhood gastrointestinal disorders to autism: nested case-control study using data from the UK General Practice Research Database. *BMJ* 325:419–421

Boyce WT, Frank E, Jensen PS, Kessler RC, Nelson CA, Steinberg L; MacArthur Foundation Research Network on Psychopathology and Development (1998), Social context in developmental psychopathology: recommendations for future research from the MacArthur Network on Psychopathology and Development. *Dev Psychopathol* 10:143–164

Breslau N, Chilcoat H, DelDotto J, Andreski P, Brown G (1996), Low birth weight and neurocognitive status at six years of age. *Soc Biol Psychiatry* 40:389–397

Brown AS, Susser ES (2002), In utero infection and adult schizophrenia. *Ment Retard Dev Disabil Res Rev* 8:51–57

Burke KC, Burke JD, Regier DA, Rae DS (1990), Age at onset of selected mental disorders in five community populations. *Arch Gen Psychiatry* 47:511–518

Cairns RB, Cairns BD, Rodkin P, Xie H (1998), New directions in developmental research: models and methods. In: *New Perspectives on Adolescent Risk Behavior*, Jessor R, ed. London: Cambridge University Press, pp 13–40

Caspi A, Henry B, McGee RO, Moffitt TE, Silva PA (1995), Temperamental origins of child and adolescent behavior problems: from age three to fifteen. *Child Dev* 66:55–68

Caspi A, McClay J, Moffitt TE et al. (2002), Role of genotype in the cycle of violence in maltreated children. *Science* 297:851–854

Caspi A, Sugden K, Moffitt T et al. (2003), Influence of life stress on depression: moderation by a polymorphism in the 5-HTT gene. *Science* 301:386–389

Chakrabarti S, Fombonne E (2001), Pervasive developmental disorders in preschool children. *JAMA* 285:3093–3099

Checkley S (1996), The neuroendocrinology of depression and chronic stress. *Br Med Bull* 52:597–617

Christie KA, Burke JD, Regier DA, Rae DS, Boyd JH, Locke BZ (1988), Epidemiologic evidence for early onset of mental disorders and higher risk of drug abuse in young adults. *Am J Psychiatry* 145:971–975

Cicchetti D (1984), The emergence of developmental psychopathology. *Child Dev* 55:1–7

Cicchetti D, Cohen DJ (1995), Perspectives on developmental psychopathology. In: *Developmental Psychopathology, Volume 1: Theory and Methods*, Cicchetti D, Cohen DJ, eds. New York: John Wiley & Sons, pp 3–20

Cicchetti D, Sroufe LA (2000), The past as prologue to the future: the times, they've been a-changin'. *Dev Psychopathol* 12:255–264

Cicchetti D, Toth S (1998), The development of depression in children and adolescents. *Am Psychol* 53:221–241

Cicchetti D, Toth SL (1995), A developmental psychopathology perspective on child abuse and neglect. *J Am Acad Child Adolesc Psychiatry* 34:541–565

Collishaw S, Maughan B, Goodman R, Pickles A (2004), Time trends in adolescent mental health. *J Child Psychol Psychiatry* 45:1350–1362

Cook DG, Mendall MA, Whincup P, Isasi CR (2000), C-reactive protein concentration in children: relationship to adiposity and other cardiovascular risk factors. *Atherosclerosis* 149:139–150

COSTELLO ET AL.

Costello EJ, Angold A (1995), Developmental epidemiology. In: *Developmental Psychopathology, Volume 1*, Cicchetti D, Cohen D, eds. New York: John Wiley & Sons, pp 23–56

Costello EJ, Egger HL, Angold A (2004), The developmental epidemiology of anxiety disorders. In: *Phobic and Anxiety Disorders in Children and Adolescents: A Clinician's Guide to Effective Psychosocial and Pharmacological Interventions*, Ollendick T, March J, eds. New York: Oxford University Press, pp 61–91

Costello EJ, Erkanli A, Federman E, Angold A (1999), Development of psychiatric comorbidity with substance abuse in adolescents: effects of timing and sex. *J Clin Child Psychol* 28:298–311

Costello EJ, Mustillo S, Erkanli A, Keeler G, Angold A (2003), Prevalence and development of psychiatric disorders in childhood and adolescence. *Arch Gen Psychiatry* 60:837–844

Dales L, Hammer S, Smith N (2001), Time trends in autism and in MMR immunization coverage in California. *JAMA* 285:1183–1185

Danesh J, Whincup P, Walker M et al. (2000), Low grade inflammation and coronary heart disease: prospective study and updated meta-analyses. *BMJ* 321:199–204

Danner M, Kasl SV, Abramson JL, Vaccarino V (2003), Association between depression and elevated C-reactive protein. *Psychosom Med* 65:347–356

Dentino AN, Pieper CF, Rao KM et al. (1999), Association of interleukin-6 and other biologic variables with depression in older people living in the community. *J Am Geriatr Soc* 47:6–11

DeStefano F, Bhasin TK, Thompson WW, Yeargin-Allsopp M, Boyle C (2004), Age at first measles-mumps-rubella vaccination in children with autism and school-matched control subjects: a population-based study in metropolitan Atlanta. *Pediatrics* 113:259–266

Dodge K (2001), The science of youth violence prevention: progressing from developmental epidemiology to efficacy to effectiveness to public policy. *Am J Prev Med* 20:63–70

Du Clos TW, Mold C (2001), The role of C-reactive protein in the resolution of bacterial infection. *Curr Opin Infect Dis* 14:289–293

Earls F (1979), Epidemiology and child psychiatry: historical and conceptual development. *Compr Psychiatry* 20:256–269

Eaves LJ, Silberg JL, Maes HH et al. (1997), Genetics and developmental psychopathology: 2. The main effects of genes and environment on behavioral problems in the Virginia Twin Study of adolescent behavior development. *J Child Psychol Psychiatry* 38:965–980

Elder GH (1996), Human lives in changing societies: life course and developmental insights. In: *Developmental Science*, Cairns R, Elder GH Jr, Costello EJ, eds. London: Cambridge University Press, pp 31–62

Elder GH Jr. (1998), The life course as developmental theory. *Child Dev* 69:1–12

Esterling BA, Antoni MH, Kumar M, Schneiderman N (1993), Defensiveness, trait anxiety, and Epstein-Barr viral capsid antibody titers in healthy college students. *Health Psychol* 12:132–139

Esterling BA, Antoni MH, Schneiderman N et al. (1992), Psychosocial modulation of antibody to Epstein-Barr viral capsid antigen and human herpesvirus type-6 in HIV-1-infected and at-risk gay men. *Psychosom Med* 54:354–371

Fall C, Hindmarsh P, Dennison E, Kellingray S, Barker D, Cooper C (1998), Programming of growth hormone secretion and bone mineral density in elderly men: a hypothesis. *J Clin Endocrinol Metab* 83:135–139

Festa A, D'Agostino RB, Howard G, Mykkanen L, Tracy RP, Haffner SM (2000), Chronic subclinical inflammation as part of the insulin resistance syndrome: the insulin resistance atherosclerosis study (IRAS). *Circulation* 102:42–47

Flavell DM, Ireland H, Stephens JW et al. (2005), Peroxisome proliferator-activated receptor alpha gene variation influences age of onset and progression of type 2 diabetes. *Diabetes* 54

Foley DL, Eaves LJ, Wormley B et al. (2004), Childhood adversity, monoamine oxidase A genotype, and risk for conduct disorder. *Arch Gen Psychiatry* 61:738–744

Foley DL, Neale MC, Kendler KS (1998), Reliability of a lifetime history of major depression: implications for heritability and comorbidity. *Psychol Med* 28:857–870

Fombonne E (2003a), Epidemiological surveys of autism and other pervasive developmental disorders: an update. *J Autism Dev Disord* 33:365–382

Fombonne E (2003b), The prevalence of autism. *JAMA* 289:87–89

Fombonne E, Simmons H, Ford T, Meltzer H, Goodman R (2003), Prevalence of pervasive developmental disorders in the British nationwide survey of child mental health. *Int Rev Psychiatry* 15:158–165

Ford DE, Erlinger TP (2004), Depression and C-reactive protein in US adults: data from the Third National Health and Nutrition Examination Survey. *Arch Intern Med* 164:1010–1014

Ford T, Goodman R, Meltzer H (2003), The British child and adolescent mental health survey 1999: The prevalence of DSM-IV disorders. *J Am Acad Child Adolesc Psychiatry* 42:1203–1211

Furlano RI, Anthony A, Day R et al. (2001), Colonic CD8 and gamma delta T-cell infiltration with epithelial damage in children with autism. *J Pediatr* 138:366–372

Gabay C, Kushner I (1999), Mechanisms of disease: acute-phase proteins and other systemic responses to inflammation. *N Engl J Med* 340:448–454

Gale CR, Martyn CN (2004), Birth weight and later risk of depression in a national birth cohort. *Br J Psychiatry* 184:28–33

Garber J (1984), Classification of childhood psychopathology: a developmental perspective. *Child Dev* 55:30–48

Geier MR, Geier DA (2003), Neurodevelopmental disorders after thimerosal-containing vaccines: a brief communication. *Exp Biol Med* 228:660–664

Ghosh S, Armitage E, Wilson D, Minor PD, Afzal MA (2001), Detection of persistent measles virus infection in Crohn's disease: current status of experimental work. *Gut* 48:748–752

Giuffra LA, Risch N (1994), Diminished recall and the cohort effect of major depression: a simulation study. *Psychol Med* 24:375–383

Glaser R, Padgett DA, Litsky ML et al. (2005), Stress-associated changes in the steady-state expression of latent Epstein-Barr virus: implications for chronic fatigue syndrome and cancer. *Brain Behav Immun* 19:91–103

Glassman AH, Shapiro PA (1998), Depression and the course of coronary artery disease. *Am J Psychiatry* 155:4–11

Granger DA, Serbin LA, Schwartzman A, Lehoux P, Cooperman J, Ikeda S (1998), Children's salivary cortisol, internalising behaviour problems, and family environment: results from the Concordia Longitudinal Risk Project. *Int J Behav Dev* 22:707–728

Gunnell D, Rasmussen F, Fouskakis D, Tynelius P, Harrison G (2003), Patterns of fetal and childhood growth and the development of psychosis in young males: a cohort study. *Am J Epidemiol* 158:291–300

Gupta S (1996), Immunology and immunologic treatment of autism. *Proc Natl Autism Assoc* 1996:455–460

Han TS, Sattar N, Williams K, Gonzalez-Villalpando C, Lean ME, Haffner SM (2002), Prospective study of C-reactive protein in relation to the development of diabetes and metabolic syndrome in the Mexico City Diabetes Study. *Diabetes Care* 25:2016–2021

Hawkins JD, Catalano RF, Arthur MW (2002), Promoting science-based prevention in communities. *Addict Behav* 27:951–976

Hayward C, Killen J, Kraemer H, Taylor CB (2000), Predictors of panic attacks in adolescents. *J Am Acad Child Adolesc Psychiatry* 39:207–214

Hendrickson BA, Turner JR (2002), MMR vaccination, ileal lymphoid nodular hyperplasia, and pervasive developmental disorder. *Lancet* 359:2051–2052

Hewitt JK, Silberg JL, Rutter M et al. (1997), Genetics and developmental psychopathology: I. Phenotypic assessment in the Virginia Twin Study of Adolescent Behavioral Development. *J Child Psychol Psychiatry* 38:943–963

Honda H, Shimizu Y, Rutter M (2005), No effect of MMR withdrawal on the incidence of autism: a total population study. *J Child Psychol Psychiatry* 46:572–579

Hornig M, Chian D, Lipkin WL (2004), Neurotoxic effects of postnatal thimerosal are mouse strain dependent. *Mol Psychiatry* 9:833–845

Horton R (2004a), The lessons of MMR. *Lancet* 363:747–749

Horton R (2004b), A statement by the editors of *The Lancet*. *Lancet* 363:820–821

Horvath K, Papadimitriou JC, Rabsztyn A, Drachenberg C, Tildon JT (1999), Gastrointestinal abnormalities in children with autistic disorder. *J Pediatr* 135:559–563

Hviid A, Stellfeld M, Wohlfahrt J, Melbye M (2003), Association between thimerosal-containing vaccine and autism. *JAMA* 290:1763–1766

Iizuka M, Chiba M, Yukawa M et al. (2000), Immunohistochemical analysis of the distribution of measles related antigen in the intestinal mucosa in inflammatory bowel disease. *Gut* 46:163–169

Isasi CR, Deckelbaum RJ, Tracy RP, Starc TJ, Berglund L, Shea S (2003), Physical fitness and C-reactive protein level in children and young adults: The Columbia University Biomarkers Study. *Pediatrics* 111:332–338

Jaffee S, Caspi A, Moffitt T, Taylor A (2004), Physical maltreatment victim to antisocial child: evidence of an environmentally mediated process. *J Abnorm Psychol* 113:44–55

Jick H, Kaye JA (2003), Epidemiology and possible causes of autism. *Pharmacotherapy* 23:1524–1530

Jick H, Kaye JA (2004), Autism and DPT vaccination in the United Kingdom. *N Engl J Med* 350:2722–2723

Kaplow JB, Curran PJ, Angold A, Costello EJ (2001), The prospective relation between dimensions of anxiety and the initiation of adolescent alcohol use. *J Clin Child Psychol* 30:316–326

Kawashima H, Mori T, Kashiwagi Y, Takekuma K, Hoshika A, Wakefield A (2000), Detection and sequencing of measles virus from peripheral mononuclear cells from patients with inflammatory bowel disease and autism. *Dig Dis Sci* 45:723–729

Kaye J, Melero-Montes del Mar M, Hershel J (2001), Mumps, measles, and rubella vaccine and the incidence of autism recorded by general practitioners: a time trend analysis. *BMJ* 322:460–463

Kellam SG, Koretz D, Moscicki E (1999), Core elements of developmental epidemiologically based prevention research. *Am J Community Psychol* 27:463–482

Kellam SG, Werthamer-Larsson L (1986), Developmental epidemiology: a basis for prevention. In: *A Decade of Progress in Primary Prevention*, Kessler M, Goldston SE, eds. Hanover, NH: University Press of New England, pp 154–180

Kerr AM, Ravine D (2003), Review article: breaking new ground with Rett syndrome. *J Intellect Disabil Res* 47:580–587

Kessler RC, Berglund P, Demler O et al. (2003), The epidemiology of major depressive disorder: results from the National Comorbidity Survey Replication (NCS-R). *JAMA* 289:3095–3105

Kessler RC, Borges G, Walters EE (1999), Prevalence of and risk factors for lifetime suicide attempts in the National Comorbidity Survey. *Arch Gen Psychiatry* 56:617–626

Kessler RC, McGonagle KA, Swartz MS, Blazer DG, Nelson CB (1993), Sex and depression in the National Comorbidity Survey: I. Lifetime prevalence, chronicity and recurrence. *J Affect Disord* 29:85–96

Kessler RC, Nelson CB, McGonagle KA, Edlund MJ, Frank RG, Leaf PJ (1996a), The epidemiology of co-occurring addictive and mental disorders: implications for prevention and service utilization. *Am J Orthopsychiatry* 66:17–31

Kessler RC, Nelson CB, McGonagle KA, Liu J, Swartz M, Blazer DG (1996b), Comorbidity of DSM-III-R major depressive disorder in the general population: results from the US National Comorbidity Survey. *Br J Psychiatry* 168:17–30

Kessler RC, Rubinow DR, Holmes C, Abelson JM, Zhao S (1997), The epidemiology of DSM-III-R bipolar I disorder in a general population survey. *Psychol Med* 27:1079–1089

Kiecolt-Glaser JK (1999), Norman Cousins Memorial Lecture 1998. Stress, personal relationships, and immune function: health implications. *Brain Behav Immun* 13:61–72

Kim-Cohen J, Arseneault L, Caspi A, Tomas MP, Taylor A, Moffitt TE (2005), Validity of DSM-IV conduct disorder in 4½–5-year-old children: a longitudinal epidemiological study. *Am J Psychiatry* 162:1108–1117

Kim-Cohen J, Caspi A, Moffitt T, Harrington H, Milne B, Poulton R (2003), Prior juvenile diagnoses in adults with mental disorder: developmental follow-back of a prospective-longitudinal cohort. *Arch Gen Psychiatry* 60:709–717

Klein RG (1995), Is panic disorder associated with childhood separation anxiety disorder? *Clin Neuropharmacol* 18:S7–S14

Koenig W, Sund M, Froelich M et al. (1999), C-reactive protein, a sensitive marker of inflammation, predicts future risk of coronary heart disease in initially healthy middle-aged men: results from the MONICA (monitoring trends and determinants in cardiovascular disease) Augsburg Cohort Study, 1984 to 1992. *Circulation* 99:237–242

Kreppner JM, O'Connor TG, Rutter M, English Romanian Adoptees Study Team (2001), Can inattention/overactivity be an institutional deprivation syndrome? *J Abnorm Child Psychol* 29:513–528

Kuller LH, Tracy RP, Shaten J, Meilahn EN (1996), Relation of C-reactive protein and coronary heart disease in the MRFIT nested case-control study. *Am J Epidemiol* 144:537–547

Lahey B, Miller T, Schwab-Stone M et al. (2000), Age and gender differences in oppositional behavior and conduct problems: a cross-sectional household study of middle childhood and adolescence. *J Abnorm Psychol* 109:488–503

Leonard H, Bower C, English D (1997), The prevalence and incidence of Rett syndrome in Australia. *Eur Child Adolesc Psychiatry* 6(suppl 1): 8–10

Levy F, Hay D, McLaughlin M, Wood C, Waldman I (1996), Twin-sibling differences in parental reports of ADHD, speech, reading and behaviour problems. *J Child Psychol Psychiatry* 37:569–578

Lewinsohn P, Zinbarg J, Lewinsohn M, Sack W (1997), Lifetime comorbidity among anxiety disorders and between anxiety disorders and other mental disorders in adolescents. *J Anxiety Disord* 11:377–394

Lewinsohn PM, Clarke GN, Seeley JR, Rohde P (1994), Major depression in community adolescents: age of onset, episode duration, and time to recurrence. *J Am Acad Child Adolesc Psychiatry* 33:809–818

Lewinsohn PM, Rohde P, Seeley JR, Fischer SA (1993), Age-cohort changes in the lifetime occurrence of depression and other mental disorders. *J Abnorm Psychol* 102:110–120

Lewinsohn PM, Striegel-Moore RH, Seeley JR (2000), Epidemiology and natural course of eating disorders in young women from adolescence to young adulthood. *J Am Acad Child Adolesc Psychiatry* 39:1284–1292

Lopez JF, Chalmers DT, Little KY, Watson SJ, AE Bennett Research Award (1998), Regulation of serotonin1A, glucocorticoid, and mineralocorticoid receptor in rat and human hippocampus: implications for the neurobiology of depression. *Biol Psychiatry* 43:547–573

Lotter V (1980), Methodological problems in cross-cultural epidemiologic research: illustrations from a survey of childhood autism in Africa. In: *Studies of Children*, Earls F, ed. New York: Neale Watson, pp 126–144

Lutgendorf SK, Antoni MH, Kumar M, Schneiderman N (1994), Changes in cognitive coping strategies predict EBV-antibody titre change following a stressor disclosure induction. *J Psychosom Res* 38:63–78

Madsen K, Hviid A, Vestergaard M et al. (2002), A population-based study of measles, mumps and rubella vaccination and autism. *N Engl J Med* 347:1477–1482

Madsen KM (2004), Response. *N Engl J Med* 348:953

Madsen KM, Lauritsen MB, Pedersen CB et al. (2003), Thimerosal and the occurrence of autism: negative ecological evidence from Danish population-based data. *Pediatrics* 112:604–606

Maes M (1999), Major depression and activation of the inflammatory response system. *Adv Exp Med Biol* 461:25–46

Magee W, Eaton W, Wittchen H, McGonagle K, Kessler R (1996), Agoraphobia, simple phobia, and social phobia in the National Comorbidity Survey. *Arch Gen Psychiatry* 53:159–168

Mantymaa M, Puura K, Luoma I et al. (2003), Infant-mother interaction as a predictor of child's chronic health problems. *Child Care Health Dev* 29:181–191

Martin CM, Uhlmann V, Killalea A, Sheils O, O'Leary JJ (2002), Detection of measles virus in children with ileo-colonic lymphoid nodular hyperplasia, enterocolitis and developmental disorder. *Mol Psychiatry* 7:S47–S48

McDade TW (2002), Status incongruity in Samoan youth: a biocultural analysis of culture change, stress, and immune function. *Med Anthropol Q* 16:123–150

McEwen BS (2002), The neurobiology and neuroendocrinology of stress. Implications for post-traumatic stress disorder from a basic science perspective. *Psychiatr Clin North Am* 25:469–494

Miller GE, Stetler CA, Carney RM, Freedland KE, Banks WA (2002), Clinical depression and inflammatory risk markers for coronary heart disease. *Am J Cardiol* 90:1279–1283

Miller RJ, Sutherland AG, Hutchinson JD, Alexander DA (2001), C-reactive protein and interleukin 6 receptor in post-traumatic stress disorder: a pilot study. *Cytokine* 13:253–255

COSTELLO ET AL.

Moffitt TE (1993), Adolescence-limited and life-course-persistent-offending: a complementary pair of developmental theories. In: *Developmental Theories of Crime and Delinquency*, Thornberry TP, ed. New Brunswick, NJ: Transaction, pp 11–55

Moffitt TE, Caspi A, Harrington H, Milne BJ (2002), Males on the life-course persistent and adolescence-limited antisocial pathways: follow-up at age 26. *Dev Psychopathol* 14:179–207

Mold C, Gewurz H, DuClos TW (1999), Regulation of complement activation by C-reactive protein. *Immunopharmacology* 42:23–30

Morris DL, Montgomery SM, Thompson NP, Ebrahim S, Pounder RE, Wakefield AJ (2000), Measles vaccination and inflammatory bowel disease: a national British Cohort Study. *Am J Gastroenterol* 95:3507–3512

Murch SH, Anthony A, Casson DH et al. (2004), Retraction of an interpretation. *Lancet* 363:750

Murphy BE (1991), Steroids and depression. *J Steroid Biochem Mol Biol* 38:537–559

Muthen B, Muthen LK (2000), Integrating person-centered and variable-centered analyses: growth mixture modeling with latent trajectory classes. *Alcohol Clin Exp Res* 24:882–891

Nagin DS, Tremblay RE (2001), Analyzing developmental trajectories of distinct but related behaviors: a group-based method. *Psychol Methods* 6:18–34

National Research Council and Institute of Medicine (2001), Juvenile Crime, Juvenile Justice. Panel on Juvenile Crime: Prevention, Treatment, and Control, McCord J, Widom CS, Crowell NA, eds. Washington, DC: National Academies Press

Nelson KB, Bauman ML (2003), Thimerosal and autism? *Pediatrics* 111:674–679

Nemeroff CB, Widerlov E, Bissette G et al. (1984), Elevated concentrations of CSF corticotropin-releasing factor-like immunoreactivity in depressed patients. *Science* 226:1342–1344

Noble KK, Miyasaka K (2004), Letter to the editor. *N Engl J Med* 348:952–953

Oomen HA, Schipperijn AJ, Drexhage HA (1996), The prevalence of affective disorder and in particular of a rapid cycling of bipolar disorder in patients with abnormal thyroid function tests. *Clin Endocrinol* 45:215–223

Opler MG, Brown AS, Graziano J et al. (2004), Prenatal lead exposure, delta-aminolevulinic acid, and schizophrenia. *Environ Health Perspect* 112:548–552

Orvaschel H, Lewinsohn PM, Seeley JR (1995), Continuity of psychopathology in a community sample of adolescents. *J Am Acad Child Adolesc Psychiatry* 34:1525–1535

Patten SB (2003), Recall bias and major depression lifetime prevalence. *Soc Psychiatry Psychiatr Epidemiol* 38:290–296

Paykel ES (2000), Not an age of depression after all? Incidence rates may be stable over time. *Psychol Med* 30:489–490

Pharoah PD, Stevenson CJ, Cooke RI, Stevenson RC (1994), Prevalence of behaviour disorders in low birthweight infants. *Arch Dis Child* 70:271–274

Phillips DI, Barker DJ, Osmond C (1993), Infant feeding, fetal growth and adult thyroid function. *Acta Endocrinol* 129:134–138

Pichichero ME, Cernichiari E, Lopreiato J, Treanor J (2002), Mercury concentrations and metabolism in infants receiving vaccines containing thiomersal: a descriptive study. *Lancet* 360:1737–1741

Pickles A, Pickering K, Simonoff E, Silberg J, Meyer J, Maes H (1998), Genetic "clocks" and "soft" events: a twin model for pubertal development and other recalled sequences of developmental milestones, transitions, or ages at onset. *Behav Genet* 28:243–253

Pine DS, Cohen P, Gurley D, Brook J, Ma Y (1998), The risk for early-adulthood anxiety and depressive disorders in adolescents with anxiety and depressive disorders. *Arch Gen Psychiatry* 55:56–64

Raine A, Moffitt TE, Caspi A, Loeber R, Stouthamer-Loeber M, Lynam D (2005), Neurocognitive impairments in boys on the life-course persistent antisocial path. *J Abnorm Psychol* 114:38–49

Ridker PM, Buring JE, Cook NR, Rifai N (2003), C-reactive protein, the metabolic syndrome, and risk of incident cardiovascular events: an 8-year follow-up of 14,719 initially healthy American women. *Circulation* 107:391–397

Risch N, Burchand E, Ziv E, Tang H (2002), Categorization of humans in biomedical research: genes, race and disease. *Genome Biol* 3:1–12

Robins L (1999), A 70-year history of conduct disorder: variations in definition, prevalence, and correlates. In: *Historical and Geographical Influences on Psychopathology*, Cohen P, Slomkowski C, Robins L, eds. Mahwah, NJ: Lawrence J. Erlbaum Associates, pp 37–56

Roose SP, Glassman AH, Seidman SN (2001), Relationship between depression and other medical illnesses. *JAMA* 286:1687–1690

Rothman KJ, Greenland S (1998), *Modern Epidemiology*, 2nd ed., Rothman KJ, Greenland S, eds. Philadelphia: Lippincott-Raven

Rutter M, Caspi A, Moffitt T (2003), Using sex differences in psychopathology to study causal mechanisms: unifying issues and research strategies. *J Child Psychol Psychiatry* 44:1092–1115

Rutter M, Garmezy N (1983), Developmental psychopathology. In: *Handbook of Child Psychology, Volume 4*, Mussen P, ed. New York: John Wiley & Sons, pp 775–911

Rutter M, Giller H, Hagell A (1998), *Antisocial Behavior by Young People*. New York: Cambridge University Press

Rutter M, Silberg T, O'Connor T, Simonoff E (1999a), Genetics and child psychiatry: II. Empirical research findings. *J Child Psychol Psychiatry* 40:19–56

Rutter M, Silberg J, O'Connor, Simonoff E (1999b), Genetics and child psychiatry: I. Advances in quantitative and molecular genetics. *J Child Psychol Psychiatry* 40:3–18

Rutter M, Sroufe LA (2000), Developmental psychopathology: concepts and challenges. *Dev Psychopathol* 12:265–296

Saigal S, Pinelli J, Hoult L, Kim MM, Boyle M (2003), Psychopathology and social competencies of adolescents who were extremely low birth weight. *Pediatrics* 111:969–975

Sakkas PN, Soldatos CR, Bergiannaki JD, Paparrigopoulos TJ, Stefanis CN (1998), Growth hormone secretion during sleep in male depressed patients. *Prog Neuropsychopharmacol Biol Psychiatry* 22:467–483

Sanford M, Boyle MH, Szatmari P, Offord DR, Jamieson E, Spinner M (1999), Age-of-onset classification of conduct disorder: reliability and validity in a prospective cohort study. *J Am Acad Child Adolesc Psychiatry* 38:992–999

Sarid O, Anson O, Yaari A, Margalith M (2001), Epstein-Barr virus specific salivary antibodies as related to stress caused by examinations. *J Med Virol* 64:149–156

Schwartz S (1998), The role of values in the nature/nurture debate about psychiatric disorders. *Soc Psychiatry Psychiatr Epidemiol* 33:356–362

Silberg J, Rutter M, Eaves L (2001), Genetic and environmental influences on the temporal association between earlier anxiety and later depression in girls. *Biol Psychiatry* 49:1040–1049

Silove D, Manicavasagar V, Curtis J, Blaszczynski A (1996), Is early separation anxiety a risk factor for adult panic disorder? A critical review. *Compr Psychiatry* 37:167–179

Simon GE, Vonkorff M, Ustun TB, Gater R, Gureje O, Sartorius N (1995), Is the lifetime risk of depression actually increasing? *J Clin Epidemiol* 48:1109–1118

Simonoff E, Pickles A, Meyer JM et al. (1997), The Virginia Twin Study of adolescent behavioral development: influences of age, sex and impairment on rates of disorder. *Arch Gen Psychiatry* 54:801–808

Singer B, Ryff CD (1999), Hierarchies of life histories and associated health risks. *Ann N Y Acad Sci* 896:96–115

Smeeth L, Cook C, Fombonne E et al. (2004), MMR vaccination and pervasive developmental disorders: a case-control study. *Lancet* 364:963–969

Snidman N, Kagan J, Riordan L, Shannon DC (1995), Cardiac function and behavioral reactivity during infancy. *Psychophysiology* 32:199–207

Sommerfelt K, Ellertsen B, Markestad T (1993), Personality and behaviour in eight-year-old, non-handicapped children with birth weight under 1500 g. *Acta Pediatr* 82:723–728

Sommerfelt K, Troland K, Ellertsen B, Markestad T (1996), Behavioral problems in low-birthweight preschoolers. *Dev Med Child Neurol* 38:927–940

Spoth RL, Kavanagh KA, Dishion TJ (2002), Family-centered preventive intervention science: toward benefits to larger populations of children, youth, and families. *Prev Sci* 3:145–152

Sroufe LA, Rutter M (1984), The domain of developmental psychopathology. *Child Dev* 55:17–29

Stehr-Green P, Tull P, Stellfeld M, Mortenson P-B, Simpson D (2003), Autism and thimerosal-containing vaccines: lack of consistent evidence for an association. *Am J Prev Med* 25:101–106

Steptoe A, Lundwall K, Cropley M (2000), Gender, family structure and cardiovascular activity during the working day and evening. *Soc Sci Med* 50:531–539

Stouthamer-Loeber M, Drinkwater M, Loeber R (1999), Family functioning profiles, early onset of offending, and disadvantaged neighborhoods. *Int J Child Fam Welfare* 3:247–256

Strickland PL, Deakin JW, Percival C, Dixon J, Gater RA, Goldberg DP (2002), Bio-social origins of depression in the community: interactions between social adversity, cortisol and serotonin neurotransmission. *Br J Psychiatry* 180:168–173

Sullivan ML (1998), Integrating qualitative and quantitative methods in the study of developmental psychopathology in context. *Dev Psychopathol* 19:377–393

Sung M, Erkanli A, Angold A, Costello E (2004), Effects of age at first substance use and psychiatric comorbidity on the development of substance use disorders. *Drug Alcohol Depend* 75:287–299

Susser M, Susser E (1996), Choosing a future for epidemiology: 2. From black box to chinese boxes and eco-epidemiology. *Am J Public Health* 86:674–677

Swan G, Hudmon K, Jack L et al. (2003), Environmental and genetic determinants of tobacco use: methodology for a multidisciplinary, longitudinal family-based investigation. *Cancer Epidemiol Biomarkers Prev* 12:994–1005

Tamakoshi K, Yatsuya H, Kondo T et al. (2003), The metabolic syndrome is associated with elevated circulating C-reactive protein in healthy reference range, a systemic low-grade inflammatory state. *Int J Obes Relat Metab Disord* 27:443–449

Taylor B, Miller E, Farrington CP et al. (1999), Autism and measles, mumps, and rubella vaccine: no epidemiological evidence for a causal association. *Lancet* 353:2026–2029

Thompson C, Syddall H, Rodin I, Osmond C, Barker DJ (2001), Birth weight and the risk of depressive disorder in late life. *Br J Psychiatry* 179:450–455

Tolan PH, Thomas P (1995), The implications of age of onset for delinquency risk II: longitudinal data. *J Abnorm Child Psychol* 23:1995

Tremblay RE (2004), The development of human physical aggression: how important is early childhood? In: *Social and Moral Development: Emerging Evidence on the Toddler Years*, Leavitt LA, Hall DB, eds. Brunswick, NJ: Johnson & Johnson Pediatric Institute, pp 221–38

Tremblay RE, Nagin DS, Seguin JR et al. (2004), Physical aggression during early childhood: trajectories and predictors. *Pediatrics* 114:e43–e50

Uhlmann V, Martin CM, Sheils O et al. (2002), Potential viral pathogenic mechanism for new variant inflammatory bowel disease. *Mol Pathol* 55:84–90

Van den Veyver IB, Zoghbi HY (2002), Genetic basis of Rett syndrome. *Ment Retard Dev Disabil Res Rev* 8:82–86

Vega W, Aguilar-Gaxiola S, Andrade L et al. (2002), Prevalence and age on onset for drug use in seven international sites: results from the International Consortium of Psychiatric Epidemiology. *Drug Alcohol Depend* 68:285–297

Verstraeten T, Davis RL, DeStefano F et al. Vaccine Safety Datalink Team (2003), Safety of thimerosal-containing vaccines: a two-phased study of-computerized health maintenance organization databases. *Pediatrics* 112:1039–1048

Wakefield A (1999), MMR vaccination and autism. *Lancet* 1999:949–950

Wakefield AJ, Anthony A, Murch SH et al. (2000), Enterocolitis in children with developmental disorders. *Am J Gastroenterol* 95:2285–95

Wakefield AJ, Anthony A, Schepelmann S et al. Royal Free Hospital School of Medicine (1998a), Persistent measles virus (MV) infection and immuno-deficiency in children with autism, ileo-colonic lymphonodular hyperplasia and non-specific colitis. *Gut* 42:A86

Wakefield AJ, Montgomery SM (2000), Measles virus as a risk for inflammatory bowel disease: an unusually tolerant approach. *Am J Gastroenterol* 95:1389–1392

Wakefield AJ, Murch SH, Anthony A et al. (1998b), Ileal-lymphoid-nodular hyperplasia, non-specific colitis, and pervasive developmental disorder in children. *Lancet* 351:637–641

Wakefield AJ, Puleston JM, Montgomery SM, Anthony A, O'Leary JJ, Murch SH (2002), Review article: the concept of entero-colonic encephalopathy, autism and opioid receptor ligands. *Aliment Pharmacol Ther* 16: 663–674

Whitaker AG, Rossem RV, Feldman JF et al. (1997), Psychiatric outcomes in low-birth-weight children at age 6 years: relation to neonatal cranial ultrasound abnormalities. *Arch Gen Psychiatry* 54:847–856

Wickramaratne PJ, Weissman MM, Leaf PJ, Holford TR (1989), Age, period, and cohort effects on the risk of major depression: results from five United States communities. *J Clin Epidemiol* 43:333–344

Wittchen HU, Knauper B, Kessler RC (1994), Lifetime risk of depression. *Br J Psychiatry* 26(suppl):16–22

Wright LB, Treiber F, Davis H, Bunch C, Strong WB (1998), The role of maternal hostility and family environment upon cardiovascular functioning among youth two years later: socioeconomic and ethnic differences. *Ethn Dis* 8:367–376

Yeargin-Allsopp M, Rice C, Karapurkar T, Doernberg N, Boyle C, Murphy C (2003), Prevalence of autism in a US metropolitan area. *JAMA* 289:49–55

[19]

Natural categories or fundamental dimensions: On carving nature at the joints and the rearticulation of psychopathology

ANDREW PICKLES[a] AND ADRIAN ANGOLD[b]
[a]University of Manchester; and [b]Duke University Medical Center

Abstract

The question of whether to view psychopathology as categorical or dimensional continues to provoke debate. We review the many facets of this argument. These include the pragmatics of measurement; the needs of clinical practice; our ability to distinguish categories from dimensions empirically; methods of analysis appropriate to each and how they relate; and the potential theoretical biases associated with each approach. We conclude that much of the debate is misconceived in that we do not observe pathology directly; rather, we observe its properties. The same pathology can have some properties that are most easily understood using a dimensional conceptualization while at the same time having other properties that are best understood categorically. We suggest replacing Meehl's analogy involving qualitatively distinct species with an alternative analogy with the "duality" of light, a phenomenon with both wave- and particle-like properties.

For many years a debate has raged over whether child and adolescent psychopathology should be regarded as consisting of a series of categorical phenomena (with individuals being either cases or noncases of various disorders) or as dimensions with psychopathology being just their negative extremes (Achenbach, 1966, 1985, 1991b; Sonuga–Barke, 1998). At the moment, the official nosologies, *Diagnostic and Statistical Manual of Mental Disorders* (4th ed.; *DSM-IV*; American Psychiatric Association, 1994); and the *International Classification of Diseases* (10th ed.; *ICD-10*); World Health Organization [WHO], 1994) and the research diagnostic interviews that implement them

This work was partially supported by Grants MH45268 and MH48604 to the first author and MH57761–04 and DA11301–05 to the second author from the US NIMH and NIDA.

Address correspondence and reprint requests to: Andrew Pickles, Biostatistics Group, School of Epidemiology and Health Science, University of Manchester, Stopford Building, Oxford Road, Manchester M13 9PT, UK. E-mail: andrew.pickles@man.ac.uk.

(Angold & Fisher, 1999; Shaffer, Fisher, & Lucas, 1999) fall firmly on the side of categorical diagnoses based on increasingly complex algorithms. However, for many purposes, questionnaires based on an explicitly dimensional conception of psychopathology, such as the Child Behavior Checklist (CBCL) and its congeners (e.g., Achenbach, 1991a, 1991c, 1992; Achenbach & Edelbrock, 1991; Achenbach & Rescorla, 2000) continue to be very widely used in both research and clinical practice. In this paper we revisit this debate from both theoretical and empirical perspectives and argue that both sides have been fighting under false colors because the questions at issue have been misframed. The central question is not "Is psychopathology scalar or categorical?" but *"Under what circumstances* does it make sense to regard psychopathology as being scalar and *under what circumstances* does it make sense to regard psychopathology as being categorical?" An essential part of our argument is that it is necessary to shift the debate away from trying to determine whether there are categorical states or dimensional levels of psychopathology toward considering the forms of *relationships with* other processes, either epidemiological or clinical. In both research and clinical practice it is these process-oriented issues that are usually of primary concern; and the form of these relatioships, whether discrete or continuous, does not necessarily correspond to the supposed from of the psychopathology. For instance, even the most hardened categorialist will accept reductions in levels of symptomatology as evidence of treatment efficacy, regardless of whether study participants still meet criteria for suffering from the disorder at the end of the study. On the other side of the coin, it is hard not to imagine someone espousing a basically continuous view of aggressive behavior and refusing to acknowledge that it was important to decide categorically whether some individual was or was not a murderer. We will argue that most forms of psychopathology (indeed, most forms of pathology of any sort) manifest both continuous and discontinuous relationships with other phenomena. In coming to these conclusions, we intend to show that at every level, from the design of measures to the analysis of data, continuous and discontinuous functions are inextricably interwoven. To illustrate these points, we will use examples drawn mainly from two general population studies of children and adolescents: the Great Smoky Mountains Study (Costello et al., 1996) and the Virginia Twin Study of Adolescent Behavioral Development (VTSABD, Eaves et al., 1993).

A Brief Summary of the Debate Over Scales and Categories to Date

In the period following World War II through the 1960s, diagnostic categories for child and adolescent psychiatric disorders were defined only in the crudest terms (e.g., American Psychiatric Association, 1952, 1968) and most general population research was conducted with questionnaire measures of numerous specific behaviors or overall "disturbance" (Cullen & Boundy, 1966; Cummings, 1944; Gould, Wunsch–Hitzig, & Dohrenwend, 1981; Griffiths, 1952; Haggerty, 1925; Lapouse, 1966; Lapouse & Monk, 1958, 1964; Long, 1941; McFie, 1934; Olson, 1930; Srole, Langner,

Mitchell, Opler, & Rennie, 1962; Wickman, 1928; Young–Masten, 1938; Yourman, 1932). Factor analytic studies began to appear in the 1940s. These formed the basis for what later emerged as a fairly consistent set of factors resulting from parent-report questionnaires. (See Achenbach & Edelbrock, 1978, for a scholarly summary of the earlier work.) For most psychopathology research, "diagnosis," insofar as it was considered at all, was defined in terms of scoring above some percentile on the particular scale employed. Wilson (1993) argued that this dimensional view blurred the distinction between normal and abnormal and, being associated with a plethora of unsubstantiated theorizing about psychosocial causes of mental ill-health, contributed to a breakdown of clinical consensus and to the low professional status of psychiatry within US medicine. While this is probably laying too much blame for the ills of psychiatry at the door of dimensional models, these approaches certainly led to wildly varying estimates of the prevalence of psychopatholgy in children (Gould et al., 1981). However, the factor analytic tradition proved capable of generating some highly reliable, replicable, and internationally reproducible dimensions of psychopathology (Achenbach, Conners, Quay, Verhulst, & Howell, 1989; Achenbach & Edelbrock, 1978; Crijnen, Achenbach, & Verhulst, 1997).

By 1980 the basis for the categorical approach had been substantially strengthened. The first major diagnostic general population study of child and adolescent psychiatric disorders was conducted on the Isle of Wight during the 1960s. Similar methods were then used in a second study in an inner city London borough and in a follow-up on the Isle of Wight (Berger, Yule, & Rutter, 1975; Graham & Rutter, 1973; Rutter, 1965, 1976; Rutter, Graham, Chadwick, & Yule, 1976; Rutter, Tizard, & Whitmore, 1970; Rutter, Yule, Morton, & Bagley, 1975; Rutter, Yule, & Berger, 1974; Rutter, Yule, & Quinton, 1974; Yule, Berger, Rutter, & Yule, 1975). Second, Rutter and colleagues developed a multiaxial classification scheme that resulted in the WHO publishing an addendum to the *ICD-9* on the classification of child and adolescent psychiatric disorders (Rutter et al., 1969; Rutter, Shaffer, & Sturge, 1979). These studies and the diagnostic scheme upon which they depended showed that categorical child psychiatric diagnoses were both feasible and capable of yielding results that were scientifically interesting and valuable for planning purposes. They contributed to the neo-Kraepelinian synthesis that was moving to dominate US psychiatry, in which mental illness "consist(s) of a finite number of disease entities, each with a distinct pattern of symptoms and course, and with distinct causes, treatments and neuropathologies" (Kendall, 1991, p. 1). That domination reached fruition, of course, in the third edition of the *DSM* (*DSM-III;* American Psychiatric Association, 1980). However, in order to cover a full range of child symptomatology, the *DSM-III* defined a variety of diagnostic categories for which there was little available validation (Rutter & Shaffer, 1980). Despite its many limitations, and much trenchant criticism of weaknesses in its scientific underpinnings (see, e.g., Blashfield, 1982), the basic approach adopted by the *DSM* has been incorporated into the *ICD-10* (Taylor, 1994; WHO, 1993, 1994), and now provides the leading paradigm for child and adolescent psychiatric research.

Clarifying Some Rhetorical Terminology

What is "empirical?"

In discussions of the relative merits of *DSM*-type diagnostic categories and symptom scale-based approaches to psychopathology, the latter are sometimes referred to as being "empirical" or "emprically derived" (see, e.g., Achenbach, 1985). The implication seems to be that diagnostic categories are *not* empirically derived. Because science is substantially an empirical enterprise, this is tantamount to suggesting that such categories are unscientific. The *Oxford English Dictionary* defines the relevant uses of the term empirical as follows: "Of a physician: that bases his methods of practice on the results of observation and experiment, not on scientific theory; Pertaining to or derived from experience." Note that empirical does not exclude but is not restricted to meaning "derived by principal components analysis with varimax rotation" (to summarize the basic scale-based approach). The group consensus methods used to develop current child psy-

chiatric nosologies like the *DSM-IV* are firmly based on clinical observation and current research, and are, therefore, empirical. For instance, the substantial changes made in the diagnostic criteria for oppositional disorder and the anxiety disorders in childhood and adolescence in *DSM-IV* were based upon a range of research observations, including field trials set up specifically to examine the effects of a variety of possible changes to the criteria. The point here is not that the resulting changes were necessarily correct, or led to the identification of definitively distinct disorders, but that empirical methods are now equally characteristic of the development of categorical nosologies and dimensional approaches for developmental psychopathology. Of course, it remains a problem to decide *which* empirical approach will best advance understanding of a given question.

Quantitative versus what?

In comparing assessment approaches, Achenbach (1985) also contrasts the use of quantitative measures with categorical diagnoses, going on to explain that by quantitative measures he means checklist scores as opposed to *DSM* diagnoses. While his critique of the lack of definition of items in the *DSM-III-R* categories has a great deal of merit, the more general undertone identifying science with quantification is being used implicitly to devalue categorical approaches. Many real quantities are genuinely binary or polychotomous and not continuous: for instance, one either dies or one does not; one is either homozygous or heterozygous (e.g., for phenylketonuria or Huntingdon disease). The argument should be about which metric is appropriate and whether the measure used is adequate to the task of placing individuals in proper relation to one another on that metric.

The Construction of Scales and Categories

The role of expert opinion

An often repeated argument in favor of dimensional measurement is that real (numerically quantified) associations between phenomena are the basis of scale score based syndrome descriptions, whereas categorical nosologies are dependent upon expert opinion. There are indeed differences between the dimensional and categorical approaches along these lines, but they are not as extreme as some would have us believe. In the development of a symptom scale, only a limited number of items are ever included in the item pool for analysis. Who chooses these items? The scale developer does, of course, who supposedly deserves the title of "expert." Sometimes the scale developer will poll others to assist in the definition of scale content, but those others will usually be clinicians (just as in the case of categorical diagnosis; see, e.g., Achenbach, 1966).

Expert decisions also enter the process in the analysis stage. A recurring theme in the measurement of psychopathology is whether to include or exclude those rare but characteristic symptoms of a disorder in the item pool, a decision that is often coupled to the decision as to whether the focus is on measurement of clinical or general population samples. Without special adaptation of the instrument, and particularly in general population samples, such items can often appear to degrade the measurement performance. As a consequence of such preliminary analysis, the initial item pool of the CBCL was winnowed down to exclude items that were rarely reported by parents as being positive. The decision to exclude such items obviously has a bearing on what the final item content of each factor observed will be.

The choice of analytical technique can also have an effect on the content of the dimensions resulting from a dimensional measure. The apparent need to reject rare items is commonly exaggerated by the use of ordinary factor analysis, a circumstance in which the use of formal item response models is clearly more appropriate. Many general checklist developers (Conners, 1997; Quay, 1977; Verhulst & Achenbach, 1995) used principal components analysis with varimax rotations to derive factor structures to provide internal validation. What would the results have been had they decided to use maximum likelihood factorization, oblique instead of orthogonal rotations, different rules for factor retention, or different factor loading criteria to decide which items would count toward final factor scores?

The point here is not that the dimensional measures we have are defective, but that their contents are not the result of simply "finding out" the structure of things in the real world. At every level, the things that are "discovered" are defined and constrained by their developers. Moreover, once discovered, they became reified, constraining subsequent thought and observation. Of course, exactly the same is true of categorical nosologies. Diagnostic interviews tend to focus on measuring only the phenomena mentioned in the current diagnostic criteria (and tend to be modified if the criteria change). Thus, the diagnosis, once defined, becomes reified because noncriterial symptomatology is no longer measured. For instance, the ways in which the category of depression has been implemented in the *DSM* system is inimical to demonstrating possible differences between child and adult manifestations of depression. On the other hand, the use of clinician and research experts to revisit and refine official diagnostic criteria means that a process is in place to implement warranted changes. The fact that clinicians are also involved in these reviews offers a particular opportunity for refining criteria in the light of extensive clinical experience, without the need to wait while new instrumentation is developed. This is far from being a perfect system, but it has proved quite capable of avoiding ossification. Indeed, a common complaint is that the American Psychiatric Association changes the DSM criteria too often.

*Common measurement practices
and assumptions*

Cairns and Green (1979) outlined a number of assumptions underlying the use of rating scales, which, it turns out, also underlie the use of diagnostic criteria. First, consider the *DSM-IV* diagnosis of oppositional defiant disorder. Eight symptoms are to be considered, and four must be present in order for the diagnosis to be given. The second criterion is "often argues with adults." It would seem that the clinician (or computer diagnostic algorithm) must make several judgments in order to determine whether this criterion is met: (a) Does the child manifest the behavior "arguing with adults?" (b) How often does the child manifest that behavior? (c) Is that frequency great enough to be called "often?" The second of these questions involves a dimension, and the third, the imposition of a "cut-point" on that dimension. All the criteria for oppositional disorder involve the same basic format. That is, all of them require the diagnostician to jump back and forth between categorical judgments (such as "does the child argue with adults—yes or no") and dimensional judgments (such as "how often"). Once all the criterion symptoms have been assessed, the number of positives must be counted; if their sum is four or more, then the diagnosis is given. Once again, a dimension (number of symptoms) is being constructed and then reduced to a category by means of a cut-point.

Now, consider item 3 of the symptom section of the CBCL, "argues a lot." This time it is the parent who must make the categorical decision "does my child argue?" Next she must consider how often the child argues (dimensional) and then decide whether that is "a lot" (categorical). The final stage involves a 3-point choice deciding whether the result of the earlier deliberations should result in a final answer of *not true*, *somewhat or sometimes true*, or *very true*. This last involves a shift back into dimensional mode, with the minimum number of levels to avoid being a categorical decision. We have been hard put to come up with any examples of symptoms that do not involve this sort of back and forth.

Second, it must be assumed that the informant shares with the diagnostician or scale developer an understanding of exactly which behaviors of the child represent the attribute of interest. However, it is obvious to any clinician that it often requires hard work to find out what you want to know because nonclinicians do not all use the same psychopathological terms in the same way. It is also obvious to anyone who teaches clinicians that they do not all share the same definition of every symptom. Neither the *DSM-IV* nor any checklist that we know of provides definitions of symptom items. Consider CBCL item 5, "behaves like opposite sex." One can hardly expect that everyone has the same notion of what "behaving like the opposite sex" entails. Exactly the same problem arises with the criteria for *DSM-IV* gender identity disorder. We

doubt that any two clinicians will agree on exactly what constitutes "intense desire to participate in the stereotypical games and pastimes of the other sex." However, interviewer-based interviews have gone some way toward providing (operational and/or conceptual) definitions for interviewers and clinicians in an attempt to improve standardization at the symptom level (Angold & Fisher, 1999).

Third, the informant must be able to extract the relevant behaviors or states from the stream of everyday life and determine how often they occur. We would also add that this must be done in relation to the relevant time frame (e.g., the past 6 months for the CBCL and a variety of frames for *DSM-IV* diagnoses).

Fourth, the informant or diagnostician must then reduce the information already extracted to the appropriate metric for the final coding (e.g., *not true*, *somewhat or sometimes true*, *very true*, or *often true* on the CBCL or *symptom present/absent* for *DSM-IV*). Different parents judge the frequencies necessary to fall into such categories very differently. It is also worth noting that there is very little information about what constitutes normative behavior as far as most symptoms are concerned. Until recently (Angold & Costello, 1996), for instance, there have been, as far as we know, no data on how often oppositional disorder symptoms occur in the general population. In other words, the decision as to where in the frequency distribution to set the cut-point for "often argues with adults" has necessarily been left to the vagaries of individual guesswork. It would seem, therefore, that the measurement processes that are used to obtain categorical and dimensional characterisations of psychopathology share rather more in common than the proponents of each would have us believe.

Does it Matter?

Intervention

In certain circumstances, decisions must be made about intervention, and for clinical treatment these decisions are invariably categorical. For instance, before treating a child with stimulants, it is necessary to determine whether that child has symptoms of sufficient intensity to warrant such treatment. The *DSM-IV* category of attention-deficit/hyperactivity disorder (ADHD) defines a group of children who are likely to benefit from such treatment. However, it is not the case that someone with a minimal amount of ADHD symptomatology will benefit from a minimal amount of stimulant medication. Rather, the decision to prescribe stimulants should institute a full trial of stimulants in reasonable doses. It does not matter for the purposes of our argument *how* the decision to provide treatment is made. It could be argued that such a decision should be based on the results of a well-known questionnaire (such as the Conners scale in the case of ADHD) or even on neuropsychological testing, without recourse to the *DSM-IV* criteria. But whatever assessment method is used, some cutoff point will have to be used to determine whether to institute treatment. Thus, no matter how dimensional the approach used for assessment, at the point at which a decision to treat or not to treat is made, all the assessment information must be reduced to a cateogical statement. It is usual to call the categorical statement a "diagnosis."

This view reflects the clinical perspective. Were we to adopt a community health perspective, then interventions need not necessarily be targeted at only those currently with the disorder. A dimensional view would suggest that health benefits can be obtained by reducing a subject's score, wherever they are on the distribution of scores, or that at least a downward shift in the mean would also deliver a reduction in the prevalence of the pathological upper tail. From such a perspective quite a different set of interventions become eligible for consideration (Offord, Kraemer, Kazdin, Jensen, & Harrington, 1998), although few of them would involve mass pharmacotherapy. Of course, community health interventions are also possible for disorders viewed as categorical, but these commonly involve targeting effort through the use of screening. Thus, the conceptualization and measurement of psychopathology as either dimensional or categorical may have both intended theoretical implications for and unintended force of habit associations with clinical practice and public health policy.

Communication

Having an agreed system of measurement is essential for both scientific advance and for providing a communication bridge between laboratory and clinical settings (Sonuga–Barke, 1998). However, the choice between categories or dimensions for psychiatric outcomes tends also to influence how risk and protective factors are measured and which specific tools for analysis and interpretation are used. Categorical outcomes tend to be associated with categorical predictors and with methods of analysis like logistic regression and log-linear models that report effects in terms of odds ratios. Dimensional outcomes are commonly associated with dimensional predictors and analyzed using conventional analysis of variance and regression that report effects in terms of mean differences, sums of squares, partial correlations, and proportion of explained variance (r^2). Although there are notable exceptions, to a considerable extent, psychiatry does not have its own training schemes in research methodology. Instead, the traditional contributing disciplines of psychology and epidemiology present independent methodological frameworks for dimensional and for categorical outcomes. Moreover, statistical texts traditionally place methods for dimensional and categorical data in different chapters with little or no attempt at integration. As a consequence, although we may be able to undertake and interpret analyses within each measurement tradition, how many of us have any feel for how the effects described in one tradition map onto effects described in the other? We suspect our skills and knowledge in this respect are very poor.

Consider the case in which a psychologically trained researcher regresses a normally distributed risk on a normally distributed outcome while our medically trained researcher imposes cut-points on both of these continuous measures, cross-tabulating the resulting binary risk and binary outcome in order to estimate an odds ratio. Figure 1 shows the results of a set of simulations of the relationship of the psychologist's r^2 value to the medic's odds ratio for different choices of cut-point. We see that for any one set of cut-points, a sim-

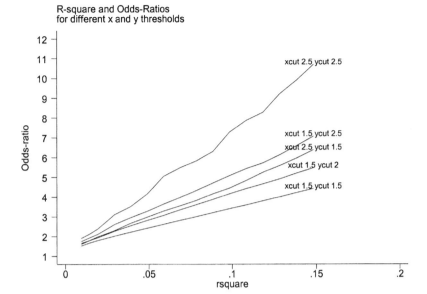

Figure 1. The relationship between dimensional and categorical effect estimates.

ple linear relationship prevails between the medic's odds ratio and the psychologist's r^2. For example, setting both cut-points at 1.5 *SD* identifies 6.7% as exposed to the risk and 6.7% as exhibiting the outcome, and the estimated odds ratio turns out to be about 35 times the r^2 value. Unfortunately, different choices of cut-point for either the risk measure or the outcome measure lead to different linear relationships. Cut-points of 2 and 2.5 *SD* identify 2.3 and 0.6% of the continuous distribution to be in the positive category, respectively. Raise the cut-point of either risk exposure or outcome to 2.5 *SD* (or raise both of them to 2 *SD*) and the odds ratio becomes about 50 times the r^2 value. Raise both cut-points to 2.5 *SD* to examine how extreme risk exposure is related to extreme outcome, and the estimated odds ratio will be more than 80 times the r^2 value of the underlying continuous measures. This figure tells us that to translate the reports of effects from the language of categories to the language of dimensions; although it maybe feasible in simple cases, is not entirely straightforward and is likely to be difficult for more complex problems.

There are some particular models and settings in which natural relationships arise. Where we have exposure to risk measured on a continuous scale, the case-control methodology leads us to expect that the cases will have a higher mean exposure than controls. Where the individual exposure measures are normally distributed around their respective group means and they have a common variance, then there is a little known but the simple relationship in which the difference in means divided by the within group variance turns out to be equal to the log-odds ratio for the effect of the risk measure on outcome (Pickles & Clayton, 2002). This equivalence is valuable not only conceptually but also practically for power calculations and more advanced modeling.

The so-called normal liability model also provides a framework that is helpful for communicating in the language of both perspectives. As in our simulations above, a categorical outcome can be viewed as having been obtained by placing a threshold on a potentially continuously scored outcome. However, in the normal liability model the analysis is explicitly based on the assumption of the normality (conditional on predictors). This leads to the estimation of effects on the probit scale, rather than on the logistic (log-odds ratio) scale of traditional epidemiology. The advantage is that, subject to the usual vagaries of sampling error and the correctness of the normality and linearity assumptions of the model, the estimated effect of some predictor that we might obtain from a probit model of the categorical outcome is the same as the regression coefficient from a linear regression analysis of the dimensional outcome. It also provides a single framework within which simultaneous analysis of categorical and dimensional outcomes can be undertaken and for the application of latent variable models to such data (e.g., Muthén & Muthén, 2001). It would seem, therefore, that studies could be more easily compared and understood were we to use and report results from such probit and regression based models rather than using logistic regression.

Unfortunately, although the probit design offers advantages with respect to comparability for the categorical–dimensional issue, it has disadvantages when it comes to comparability over sample design. Sample selection has been crucial to scientific advance in epidemiology, with heavy oversampling of cases in case-control designs and heavy oversampling of the risk exposed in high-risk designs being key elements of many powerful studies. As a measure of effect, the odds ratio is the only measure that is unaffected by the use of one or other of these designs and gives (within sampling error) the same estimate as if a simple random sample of a general population cohort had been used. Systematic review across an immense range of studies is therefore possible. By contrast, effect estimates on the probit scale do not share this invariance property and will vary with the design of the study. The relative sizes of coefficients (comparing one risk to another) and their significance will typically be very similar, whether using either probit or logistic, but only for a quite limited range of outcome rate is there a simple relationship between the absolute size of the coefficients (the log-odds coefficient being about 3 times the probit estimate within that range,

Maddala, 1983). Outside of this range, translation becomes more difficult.

This problem of translating from the language of categories to the language of dimensions is an important one, and it makes productive multidisciplinary research more difficult to achieve. Within research groups it suggests that we should be willing to run parallel analyses where we can. In research dissemination it suggests that, at the very least, we should provide additional pieces of information to enable results to be translated from one perspective to the other, and we may need to communicate key results in both languages. This would require authors and editors to adopt a more flexible use of journal space (article text, footnotes, appendices, and supporting web-based material). For methodologists it suggests that we should be doing more not only in providing integrated training but also in conducting more pragmatic research to chart in more detail areas of equivalence and difference and elaborate measures of effect and impact more generally (Kraemer et al., 1999).

Metatheoretical considerations

Sonuga–Barke (1998) has made much of the metatheoretical implications of adopting a categorical or a dimensional approach. He argues that the dimensional view is more open to environmental explanations of pathology, notably psychosocial explanations. By contrast a categorical view lends itself to within individual explanations, notably neurobiological explanations. We suspect that this association between measurement approach and type of explanation is just a historical accident resulting from the coincidental timing of interest in diagnostic categories and biological psychiatry, on the one hand, and guild issues of psychologist versus psychiatrist, on the other. As far as we are concerned there is nothing intrinsic to categories or dimensions that predisposes to explanations involving either nature or nurture. Nonetheless, we would agree that there are features about categorical or dimensional measurement that make them more or less suitable for operationalizing particular types of theory.

The categorical view lends itself to explorations of interactions and more fully multivariate analyses, such as log-linear models and developments thereof. Those wishing to operationalize interactionist theory (Magnusson, 1988a, 1988b), have found this much easier to do within a categorical framework, using techniques such as configural frequency analysis (von Eye, 1990). Indeed, in some circles, the dimensional approach has become almost synonymous with "variable-based analysis," a pejorative term now used by those who prefer a categorical "person-based analysis." However, the source measures for such analyses need not be categorical but can be made categorical through the use of cluster analysis (e.g., Bergman, 2001). Moreover, some variable-based models such as random effects growth-curve models can capture and display some of the key features of the interactionist view, notably individual differences (see Pickles, 1989); and structural equation models are slowly becoming more elaborate, with mixture models (Muthen & Muthen, 2000), nonparametric discrete class factors (Rabe–Hesketh, Pickles, & Skrondal, 2002), multiplicative random effects (Pickles et al., 1996, 1998), and interactions and nonlinear effects (Schumacker & Marcoulides, 1998) now all being possible. Analyses that reflect the interests of interactionists are, therefore, becoming possible in a dimensional framework. However, much remains to be done both conceptually and in improving software implementations.

Categorical and dimensional views also lend themselves to the consideration of rather different types of developmental mechanisms. For instance, a substantial body of psychological theory has regarded development as progression through a series of stages (e.g., Kohlberg, 1976; Piaget, 1932, on moral development). The supposition of a stage, in fact, provides a model with a remarkable range of capacities. First elaborated in the context of cancer development these have also been described in the context of developmental psychopathology (Pickles, 1993). A key supposition of such theories is that each stage is qualitatively distinct from the one before and from the one that follows. Stage progression may then provide an opportunity for developmental changes in etiology, with one set of risk and protective factors influencing progress from stage A to stage B, whereas another set is important in the progression from stage B to stage C. The manner in which the effects of risk and protective factors combine to increase or decrease the rate of the final outcome will depend upon the transitions they impact upon. If the factors operate on the same stage transition, the null expectation is that they represent different "causes" or "pathways" and thus are likely to have effects that combine in an additive fashion. By contrast, factors that act on stage transitions at different points in the sequence can be expected to have effects that combine multiplicatively: the effect of the first factor increases the potential pool of subjects available on which the second factor can operate. Thus, how the effects of factors combine is potentially informative as to the structure of stages. Positing fewer or more stages also influences the expected age distribution at which the final developmental stage would be reached, and even the forms of pathology that we might entertain, for example, suggesting forms of pathology consistent with halted, delayed, or premature progression. It is also possible to operationalize stages as latent classes, which are either not directly or only partially observable (Macready & Drayton, 1994).

In a similar fashion, developmental pathways provide a means of linking potentially theoretically distinct steps into a chain of simple transitions. Such pathways have considerable intuitive appeal; and, when combined with bifurcating graphical displays, they are capable of conveying valuable information with respect to both the absolute and relative impacts of risk factors. In Figure 2 (adapted from Hill et al., 2001), the path thicknesses allow a comparison of both the relative and the absolute frequencies and the co-occurrence of recalled child sexual abuse and neglectful parenting and their association with gaining supportive adult love relationships. The position and angles of the paths shows the individual and joint impacts of the factors on depression during adulthood, including the effect modification exhibited by the protective impact of a supportive adult love relationship being restricted to those experiencing neglectful parenting, not childhood sexual abuse. This simple diagram is thus ca-

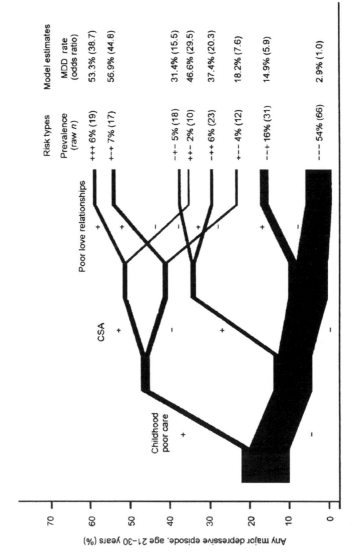

Figure 2. A graphical display of categorically defined developmental pathways (Hill et al., 2001).

pable of displaying complex multivariate relationships linked to clearly articulated theory. We know of no way of constructing a comparable diagram where the risks are treated as continuous variables.

This is not to say that mechanisms cannot be analyzed and displayed using models and methods based on dimensions. However, perhaps unlike physicists, we do not seem to have developed our intuitive grasp of such models very far. Formal dynamic models for continuous variables are typically very much more demanding of mathematics and require graphical display that can seem substantially more abstract than those described above. If we are willing to make wide-ranging linearity assumptions, then path diagrams from the structural equation modeling tradition can provide highly effective and parsimonious representations of complex multivariate problems. However, the difficulties in examining interactions and nonlinearities and the lack of highlighting of individual differences are substantial limitations of such methods. The language of categories seems to have a simplicity of vocabulary and grammar that is more sympathetic to our developmental theories. However, we should not allow this to prevent us from continuing to consider alternative models based on dimensions and improving our fluency with the language of continuous variables suitable for their description.

Relevant Forms of Evidence for Categories or Dimensions

Bimodality

Can we tell from the data we collect whether the scientific reality is one of dimensions or categories? Some phenomena relevant to psychopathology are self-evidently categorical or so nearly so as to be reasonably regarded as being categorical under most circumstances: sex comes to mind as an example. A phenomenon might also be so dramatically bimodally distributed that it makes little sense to treat it in any way but categorically, except in studies that concentrate specifically on the rare individuals who fall between the two modes.

Are we able to reveal categories more generally from the scores on a "dimensional" scale? The often cited bump at the lower end of the otherwise normal IQ distribution is an indication of the presence of a group of individuals with a range of disorders affecting IQ that are rarely found in the rest of the IQ range. A number of attempts to detect points of rarity and humps in symptom distributions have been made. That these have mostly been unsuccessful is exactly what the statistical theory on the monotonic transformation of continuous distributions would have led us to expect, because this makes clear that any continuous distribution, however bimodal, can be mapped into a unimodal one without disturbing the rank order of subjects. Only if we have other theory and evidence that justifies the particular level of measurement scale used and thus rules out the use of such a transformation can bimodality be used as evidence of a category. In fact, distributions of symptom counts in both children and adults appear, besides the discretization arising from consideration of a finite pool of symptoms, to be resolutely continuous.

Skewed distributions

Can we at least say that pathology is the tail of a skewed rather than a normal distribution? The form of any distribution of psychopathology will depend on the way in which psychopathology is measured. If one includes items in one's symptom scale that have varying prevalence (one from another) and reflect varying degrees of normality and abnormality, then it is easy enough to generate a roughly normally distributed curve. However, most of what clinicians would regard as being symptoms are simply absent in most people, with the result that general population symptom scores from interviewer-based interviews and many questionnaire item totals are heavily skewed to the right (i.e., most people have zero or very low scores). Such item total distributions should not be analyzed using standard normal theory regression's but they can be analyzed directly by the use of transformations, robust parameter covariance estimation, or an appropriate choice of generalized linear model based on Poisson, gamma, or inverse power distributions. An alternative approach is to adopt an explicit measurement model in which the items are considered as measuring some underlying liability or propensity but are also subject to the impact of other factors, loosely referred to as measurement error. In their seminal work on psychometric scale construction, Lord and Novick (1968) showed that highly skewed item totals are a natural consequence of the use of low prevalence items even when the true liability distribution is normal. Using antisocial behavior and depression items from the National Longitudinal Study of Adolescent Health and the National Longitudinal Survey of Youth, van den Oord, Pickles, and Waldman (2003) compared the fit of models that assumed normal and skewed liability distributions. They found little evidence to reject the assumption of a normal liability distribution.

Latent classes and nonparametric maximum likelihood

Does the foregoing evidence demonstrate that psychopathology is, in fact, continuous and possibly normally distributed? This is not necessarily so. Just because a distribution is continuous does not mean that the phenomenon underlying it is not categorical. Suppose for a moment that there really were a brain disease called depression and you either have it or do not. Suppose also that at some point in the future some aspects of the mechanism of this disease will be discovered so that an accurate diagnostic test will be available; but, for now, we have to rely on asking a lot of questions about phenomena that are related to the real disease but also have a range of other causes. Let us also assume that the disease is not very common (say it affects 4% of the population) but some of the other causes of individual "depressive" symptoms (e.g., primary sleep disorders, anxiety disorders, bereavement, physical illnesses) are as common or more common. Let us also take into account that our available questioning techniques are imperfect measures, even at the symptom level. In other words, we face measurement error at both the symptom and diagnostic levels. What would we expect the distribution of "depres-

sive" symptoms to look like? The result would be a distribution in which many people had a few symptoms and a few had many symptoms, with no sharp cutoff between the two. Our "real" depressives would be concentrated in the upper tail of the distribution, but because of the imperfections of our question-based assessment approach, some would be in the lower body of the distribution. Thus, even if we were measuring the correct symptoms, we could expect that our purely categorical disease would be hidden within a continuous symptom distribution. Can we recover such "hidden" latent classes?

Eaves et al. (1993) illustrated a model-based approach to this problem by identifying latent classes underlying the profiles of item scores over eight different items on antisocial behavior from the Rutter A-scale using children from the VTSABD (Eaves et al., 1993). Not surprisingly, a model in which all children were assumed to share a single common response profile arising from a single liability class was both implausible and fit badly. Postulating that the population was made up of a mixture of two classes of children, each with a distinct profile, fit the data much better; but postulating a mixture of three classes produced a still better fit; these are shown in Figure 3. What is striking about the profiles of the three-class solution is that they never cross. The classes are essentially ordered along a single dimension of increased liability that applies to all items (hence all the represented facets of behavior) and thus probably just reflects severity. Did this mean there were classes of severity and this was evidence for the existence of corresponding "real" categorical types of children?

The answer is "probably not." In numerical computation, a technique called Gaussian quadrature is one of the standard methods of representing a normal distribution. In this approach we replace the smoothly varying density over an infinite range of possible values by a limited number of spikes at a set of specific values, and each spike is assigned a probability weight. When used as a liability distribution, a few spikes perform like a smooth normal distribution to a surprising degree of accuracy, although for some problems a lot

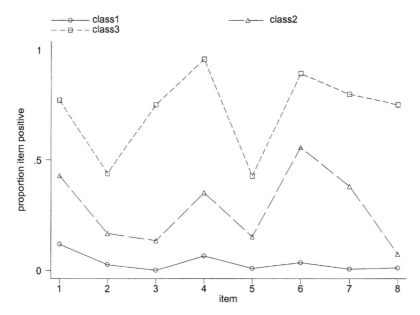

Figure 3. Item profiles for estimated latent classes from the Virginia Twin Study of Adolescent Behavioral Development (Eaves et al., 1993), Rutter A-scale items: 1 = *temper,* 2 = *steals,* 3 = *destroys,* 4 = *fights,* 5 = *not liked,* 6 = *disobeys,* 7 = *lies,* 8 = *bullies.*

of spikes may be necessary. The spikes are, mathematically speaking, identical to a set of ordered latent classes with fixed relative locations and size. If we thought of them as latent classes, then we would be assuming that the population was actually made up of classes, one corresponding to each spike. However, when we use them in Gaussian quadrature, there is no expectation that individuals "belong" to one or other of these spikes; rather, we are assuming that the population is actually normally and continuously distributed, but we are *approximating* that distribution by these spikes. Indeed, the expected score (posterior mean) of an individual on the dimension is an average (weighted by the posterior probability of belonging to each spike) of all the possible spike locations. When we plot the distribution of individual liability estimates that derive from such a model, we obtain a smooth distribution that lies between the two extreme spikes.

An intriguing extension of this approach, which corresponds exactly to ordered latent classes, is to let the location and sizes of the spikes be free parameters. Both theoretical and empirical work in statistics (e.g., Laird, 1978; Lindsay, Clogg, & Grego, 1991) has shown that the nonparametric estimator of the underlying distribution, essentially the best fitting distribution, is just such a set of discrete classes of this kind, *even when the underlying distribution is continuous.* Thus, even were children actually smoothly distributed over a continuous scale of liability, a representation in terms of a mixture of ordered categories would fit the data better than the model in which we used the correct smooth distribution! Moreover, this maximally fitting latent class representation is achieved with a remarkably small number of categories (often no more than three or four, the number depending mainly on the number of items used in the scale or profile). If one tries to fit more than this number of classes (spikes), then maximum likelihood estimation will indicate that extra class as being redundant by either assigning a zero probability weight to one of the classes (spikes) or positioning one class in the same position as another. One consequence of all this is that results showing an ordered set of classes, such as those we have reported so far from the Eaves et al. (1993) analysis, cannot be taken as evidence for the existence of distinct "types" of children, but they may simply be the best way to statistically represent a smooth distribution.

On postulating a fourth category, Eaves et al. (1993) found that the former third category was split into two, one of children who stole and one of children who did not. On the face of it, this is more convincing evidence of distinct types of children because it is not merely a distinction in terms of severity. In practice there are reasons to doubt this, too. First, this subtyping may be reflecting not discrete categories but the fact that the children are smoothly distributed over two dimensions, the second now being a stealing dimension. (We know that the argument of the previous paragraph also applies to multidimensional data; see Davies & Pickles, 1987.) Second, the improvement in model fit from three to four latent classes, although significant, was modest. Third, classes distinguished by the complete absence of one item can result from the use of too small a sample size, and one must be very cautious about the interpretation of class profile differences under these circumstances. Kendler et al. (1998) applied similar methods to adult psychosis, identifying six classes with somewhat different symptom profiles. Caution is clearly recommended before interpreting such findings as proving a particular taxonomy or even excluding dimensional underpinnings.

Trajectories, timing, and events

Particularly in the area of antisocial behavior, researchers have become enthusiastic about a variant of this latent class approach, one in which the classes define developmental trajectories and the classification is based on a set of measures over time rather than over a single cross-section (Nagin & Land, 1993). The data required for such analyses consist of symptom or behavioral profiles obtained over a series of occasions. Previous work and theoretical considerations have led to an expecta-

tion of finding three groups: one with early-onset and persistent disorder, one adolescense limited group, and one nonantisocial group (Moffitt, 1993). In practice, however, results have been mixed; it is becoming clear that the specific groupings that are identified are dependent on the data that are chosen or available for analysis. For example, if the window of observation is extended beyond early adulthood, then additional desistance and late-onset classes can be identified. The approach does provide a sound framework within which to compare models that impose alternative restrictions on the number or form of classes, but as in all such tests there is an assumption that the overall class of models being considered includes one that is correct. Moreover, the approach does not explicitly consider dimensional alternatives that could yield equally well fitting models, nor that some of the models may be close approximations to a nonparametric maximum likelihood representation, one that we have seen is quite neutral on the category or dimension question.

As we have just seen, among the distinguishing features of trajectories are differences in age of onset and desistance. Methods of analysis specific to the timing of events have been developed, in the form of survival and event history models (Allison, 1984; Cox, 1972), and differences in age of onset have been used to distinguish qualitatively different forms of pathology, as when early onset dementia was linked to APO-E4 (reviewed in Ritchie & Dupuy, 1999). Event history methods typically presuppose that a categorical phenomenon exists with an onset occurring in a sharply localized period of time. However, much psychopathology is not of this kind. There may be early-onset prodromal symptoms, or symptom severity may increment progressively over time. Whether we can consider a developmental onset as an event may depend on our study design. For example, at age 6, very few girls are biologically competent to become pregnant, but by age 16 most are. Thus, in a comparison of 6- and 16-year-olds, pubertal status has a strongly bimodal distribution and some sort of transitional "event" (i.e., puberty) has apparently occurred. However, if one were studying just 11-year-old girls, a wide range of pubertal statuses would be observed and this condition might best be regarded as being dimensionally distributed. When viewed over the longer period, pubertal development could be treated as an event and its timing analyzed using survival analysis methods. Even when restricted to the teenage years, some aspects of pubertal development such as menarche remain more event-like, but others, such as breast development are often better approached using growth curves. Pickles et al. (1996, 1998) contrasted these two types of event onset as "hard" and "soft"; they showed that, although they seemed to be under the control of a common set of genes, when gathered by means of retrospective report, these two types of events suffered different forms of measurement error (Huttenlocher, Hedges, & Prochaska, 1988). Hard events suffered heteroscedastic measurement error (random error that increases with time since the event), but soft events were prone to telescoping (systematic bias in which the reported time is moved toward the time at which the report was elicited). Overall, therefore, interest in timing and age of onset favors the presumption of a categorical phenomenon but does not exclude underlying dimensional variation. Nonetheless, the researcher may need to remain sensitive to the possibly differing measurement issues that arise with hard and soft events.

Nonlinearity

If the distribution of the indicators of the pathology alone cannot help, perhaps we should expand the scope of potential evidence by looking for some sort of validator. What can the relationship of pathology to some other variable tell us about the nature of that pathology? Simple linear logistic regressions provide estimates of effects that average across the whole sample ranges of the predictor variables, whereas ordinary correlations and linear regressions estimate average relationships across the ranges of both the predictors and the outcome variable. It is also the case that a computer statistical package will fit a linear model of this sort if asked of it, even if any relationship is shared by only part of the range of the predictor variable. Without deliberate effort, the routine use of these standard statistical techniques rarely bring such discontinuities to the researcher's attention, but they may be important indicators of the presence of categorical states.

An essential feature of the categorical disease entity model (at least as it is implemented in the *DSM-IV*) is that the categories should be associated with functional impairment (Wakefield, 1992, 1997). Pickles et al. (2001), again using the VTSABD, examined how symptom related impairment increased with the number of symptoms. For conduct disorder, oppositional defiant disorder, and depression, there was a smooth linear relationship. There was no evidence of any discontinuity or jump in impairment associated with the *DSM-III-R* symptom cutoffs, or any other plausible symptom cutoff. Impairment increased with severity, but disorder per se added nothing more. Had it been found that symptoms at or above the threshold were associated with a more marked increase in impairment than those below the threshold, then could this have been taken as evidence of a discrete pathology? Again, the answer is "not necessarily." As with inference from the shape of the symptom distribution itself, consideration still has to be given to whether a transformation of the impairment scale was appropriate and whether applying such a transformation would have eliminated the evidence for nonlinearity.

Risk to other relatives has also been used as a potential validator of a category. Using the Twins Early Development Study, Dale et al. (1998) applied the DeFries and Fulker (1985) regression method to assess differential heritability of language problems: whether heritability increased or decreased as the severity of problems experienced by the proband increased. In a general population sample of UK twins, they found that language skills at age 2 were predominantly influenced by environmental factors but that genetic factors appeared to be of greater importance for the most severely delayed. This provided some support for the distinctiveness of severe language problems. However, here, the results of the DeFries–Fulker method can also be quite sensitive to the choice of transformation applied to the phenotypic measure.

Maximizing within category association

The previous section hints that the kind of evidence that could be persuasive of the existence of categories involves showing that different categories possess distinctive patterns of association (Meehl, 1992). Meehl (Meehl, 1995; Waller & Meehl, 1998) formalizes this approach into the maximum covariance (MAXCOV) criterion. This requires that we consider at least three variables, say x, y, and z. A priori considerations suggest that one of these, say x, is thought to be an indicator of a binary categorical variable rather than a measure of some underlying dimensional score. If correct, then we would expect those in one category to have lower values and those in the other category to have higher values of x. Moreover, on the supposition that categories are internally homogeneous, we would expect that if we considered each category separately, there would be a rather modest covariance between y and z, whereas if we took a mix of subjects from both categories, we would observe a more substantial $y-z$ covariance. For example, x could be a symptom score and y and z could be two measures of risk, say parental neglect and problems with peers. Within the disorder group we might expect both risk factors to be raised, whereas in the normal group we would expect both to be low, resulting in low within group covariances. Only when the groups are mixed do we see that the two risk factors covary together.

Meehl formalizes this into a criterion. The $y-z$ covariance is calculated for sets of subjects defined by a range or window of values of x. This is repeated several times, moving the window across the distribution of x. Plotted (with suitable smoothing) against the midvalue of each window, the $y-z$ covariance will oscillate randomly if there is no category underlying x, but it will increase to a maximum and then decrease if a category underlies x, the MAXCOV being that obtained from the window position in which subjects from each category are equally represented. The plot thus allows both the categorical nature and the prevalence of the categories to be identified.

Do we see such patterns in real samples? Waller, Putnam, and Carlson (1996) applied the MAXCOV criterion (and other related methods) to data from a case-normal control study of dissociative identity disorder and found strong evidence for a categorically distinct pattern of association among a subset of the symptoms of the Dissociative Experiences Scale (Bernstein–Carlson & Putnam, 1986). In this application one cannot help feeling, however, that the selection of subjects from the extremes that is a consequence of the case-normal control design is likely to favor taxon hunters. However, perhaps more importantly, we should question the underlying model. First, the expectation of no within category association is an assumption and there would seem to be many circumstances where our scientific theory might suggest categories that are distinguished, not by having a common lack of association between y and z, but by them having distinctively different patterns of association, say, being positively associated in one category and not, or even negatively, associated in the other. For example, in a study of the symptomatology shown by relatives of autistic probands, Pickles et al. (2001) found that the proportion of affected relatives appeared to increase with the severity of autism shown by the proband, but only among probands with "useful speech." This raised the possibility that speech was a marker for etiologically distinct forms of autism. Second, the categoric nature of x clearly depends upon the choice of y and z. What do we conclude if we apply the MAXCOV approach with variables x, y, and z and find evidence for categories underlying x, but then apply the same approach to x, u, and v and find evidence for x being continuous?

Dimensional or Categorical Nature Versus Dimensional and Categorical Properties: Depression in the Great Smoky Mountains Study

The question above is resolved when we recognize that we never directly observe our objects of interest but instead observe their properties. Different properties do not need to conform to a single conceptual model of the pathology.

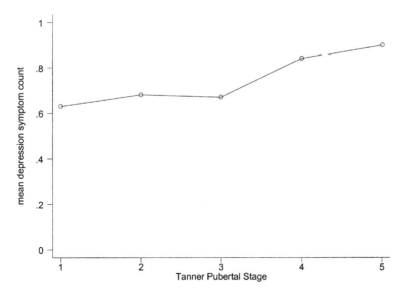

Figure 4. The mean *DSM-IV* depression symptom count by pubertal stage for girls from the Great Smoky Mountains Study.

We illustrate this point with data from the Great Smoky Mountains Study. We examine first the relationship between puberty and depression in girls. We began this line of research in an attempt to clarify the timing and causes of the emergence of the female preponderance of depression observed in adults, and have concluded that the most potent factor appears to be increasing levels of sex steroid hormones acting through a mechanism unrelated to effects on secondary sex characteristics (Angold, Costello, & Worthman, 1998, 1999; Angold & Worthman, 1993). Here we present some additional analyses of this topic designed to illustrate some of the analytical issues we have discussed thus far.

First, we note that *DSM-IV* depression and dysthymia symptom counts were "continuously" (but certainly not normally) distributed, with no obvious points of rarity or bulges in the distribution. As shown in Figure 4, the count also increased with Tanner stage, but this increase was not linear on the Tanner scale. The counts were very similar at Stages 1, 2, or 3 but higher at stages 4 and 5. If we ignore this and simply fit a linear regression model, we find no significant relationship be-

tween the Tanner stage and the number of depressive symptoms ($p = .3$).

However, if one divides the Tanner stage into two categories formed by grouping stage 3 or below versus stage 4 and above, the significance of the effect *increases* ($p = .07$). Taking this analysis a step further, we can examine the outcome variable (depressive symptom count) in a similar way. However, it turns out that the relationship between pubertal stage and symptom count is *not uniform across the range of symptom counts*. Figure 5 shows that there is no relationship between pubertal stage and the probability of having just one symptom. All of the effect of puberty on symptoms is carried by those with two or more symptoms, odds ratio (OR) = 1.7; 95% confidence interval (CI) 1.2–2.5, $p = .008$. Thus, it turns out that we are dealing with a relationship that is most parsimoniously described as categorical, even though both the predictor and outcome variables were measured on dimensional scales.

It is well known that if a genuinely dimensional relationship exists between two phenomena, then modeling it as a categorical relationship is wasteful of information (and

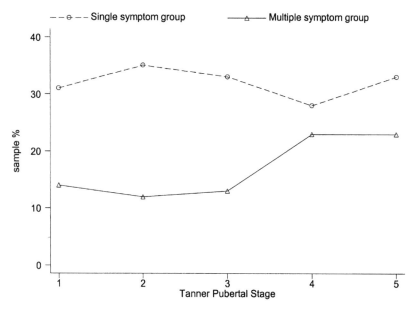

Figure 5. Sample proportions with one or more *DSM-IV* symptoms of depression by pubertal stage for girls, from the Great Smoky Mountains Study.

therefore power). Thus, if a continuous relationship exists across the range of two variables, then performing a median split on each and testing the relationship using a 2 × 2 contingency table will underestimate the size of the relationship. However, it seems to be less appreciated that the same is true if one imposes a continuous metric on a categorical relationship.

We next turn to examine the relationship of the count of depressive symptoms to a risk index defined by a summary scale of 26 social, family, and life event risk factors for psychopathology. Here we observe a quite different pattern. In this case, we see, in Figure 6, what looks like a genuinely dimensional relationship. No cut-point on the predictor risk factor scale or the depression scale produced a larger test statistic for the association between these two variables than the linear association of the two (means ratio from Poisson regression = 1.14; 95% CI = 1.10–1.19; $p < .0001$). What we see is that the "same psychopathology" may apparently behave both categorically and dimensionally in relation to different risk factors.

Conclusions

It is perhaps unsurprising that psychopathologists continue to debate the issues surrounding the use of categorical and dimensional perspectives. Their workplaces and research centers are dominated by medical doctors, who draw on a long tradition of discrete medical diagnoses and therapeutic interventions, and by psychologists, who are part of a long tradition of population measurement and continuous scale score construction. It is hard to emphasize just how profound are the consequences of these contrasting perspectives for the cultures of these two disciplines.

There is a strong desire for our chosen taxonomy to be "right." Meehl approvingly quotes the aphorism from Plato, that we should "cut nature at its joints" and points to the fact that we have gophers and chipmunks but we do not have "gophmunks." We cannot add, mix,

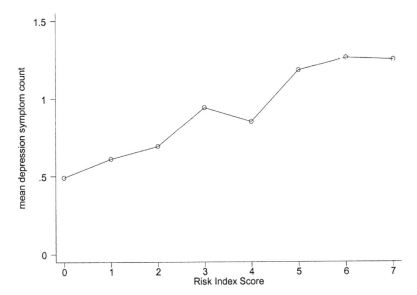

Figure 6. The mean *DSM-IV* depression symptom count by risk index score for girls from the Great Smoky Mountains Study.

and average these qualitatively distinct species as we could were the distinctions between them quantitative. While it should be emphasized that Meehl does not argue that there are not also important dimensions of variation, there is nonetheless the sense that, once a qualitative facet has been found, the objects or phenomena are therefore categorical in nature. Before drawing such a conclusion, it is worth noting that species boundaries are by no means so distinct and in the process of evolution gophmunks might very well appear! After all, the whole notion of evolution first required acceptance of the mutability of species. More importantly, we believe that the species analogy places the focus of attention on some abstract state of nature of the object of study, rather than on the properties that it exhibits. It is through these properties that we largely define objects of study, the properties are many and it is they that are also commonly of direct scientific and clinical interest. Crucially, our argument is that these varied properties need not be consistent with a single state of nature. Rather than the analogy with

species, we prefer an analogy with high school theories of the duality of light. When it comes to understanding refraction, a conception of light as behaving as a continuous wave turns out to be helpful, whereas particulate behavior is more helpful conceptually for understanding reflection and energy transfer. In the same way, to understand depression, we find circumstances where it behaves as a dimension and circumstances where it behaves as a more discrete phenomenon. Thus, while we accept the absence of gophmunks, we can envisage purposes, such as making Brunswick Stew, where we are merely concerned with weight, and the difference between a small gopher and a large chipmunk counts for nothing (except among those who believe that only squirrel should appear in Brunswick Stew). The important issue is not whether depression is categorical or dimensional in any general sense, but how its relationships with etiological, outcome, and other factors are manifested. If we are to answer those questions properly, then we need to keep an open mind about the shapes of the associational curves. In other words, we need to adopt a truly empirical approach that is unblinkered by either categorical or dimensional prejudices.

There are a number of consequences of holding this view. First, we should strive against the metatheoretical implications of a choice that results in us unconsciously selecting whole superstructures of thought and practice when we choose to use categories or dimensions. Second, although there may well be circumstances in which one perspective is clearly more parsimonious, these are probably comparatively rare and proving the empirical advantage of one or the other is nontrivial, and may not often be worth the trouble. Thus, we will typically find that we need to entertain both conceptions simultaneously, exploring analyses and elaborating theories that are not exclusively in one tradition or the other. Third, we should exploit the advantages of each perspective as and when it is opportune. Those advantages could relate to the ease of operationalizing a theory, ease of measurement, ease of analysis, or merely ease of communicating the results. However, in so doing, we need to remain cautious and to avoid both over interpretation and implying that alternative conceptions have been empirically excluded, when they have not. Fourth, as methodologists we should also be working to develop a more fluid set of tools to assist in analysis and communication in this bilingual world.

References

Achenbach, T. M. (1966). The classification of children's psychiatric symptoms: A factor-analytic study. *Psychological Monographs, 80,* 1–37.

Achenbach, T. M. (1985). *Assessment and taxonomy of child and adolescent psychopathology.* Beverly Hills, CA: Sage.

Achenbach, T. M. (1991a). *Child Behavior Checklist: Teacher's Report Form.* Burlington, VT: University of Vermont, Center for Children, Youth, and Families.

Achenbach, T. M. (1991b). The derivation of taxonomic constructs: A necessary stage in the development of developmental psychopathology. In D. Cicchetti & S. Toth (Eds.), *Rochester symposium on developmental psychopathology: Vol. 3. Models and integrations.* Rochester, NY: University of Rochester Press.

Achenbach, T. M. (1991c). *Manual for the Child Behavior Checklist 4–18 and 1991 profile.* Burlington, VT: University of Vermont, Department of Psychiatry.

Achenbach, T. M. (1992). *Manual for the Child Behavior Checklist/2–3.* Burlington, VT: University of Vermont, Department of Psychiatry.

Achenbach, T. M., Conners, C. K., Quay, H. C., Verhulst, F. C., & Howell, C. T. (1989). Replication of empirically derived syndromes as a basis for taxonomy of child/adolescent psychopathology. *Journal of Abnormal Child Psychology, 17,* 299–323.

Achenbach, T. M., & Edelbrock, C. S. (1978). The classification of child psychopathology: A review and analysis of empirical efforts. *Psychological Review, 85,* 1275–1301.

Achenbach, T. M., & Edelbrock, C. (1991). *Child Behavior Checklist: Youth Self-Report.* Burlington, VT: University of Vermont, Center for Children, Youth, and Families.

Achenbach, T. M., & Rescorla, L. A. (2000). *Manual for the ASEBA Preschool Forms and Profiles: An integrated system of multi-informant assessment.* Burlington, VT: University of Vermont, Department of Psychiatry.

Allison, P. D. (1984) *Event history analysis. Regression for longitudinal event data.* Newbury Park, CA: Sage.

American Psychiatric Association. (1952). *Diagnostic and statistical manual of mental disorders* (1st ed.). Washington, DC: American Psychiatric Association.

American Psychiatric Association. (1968). *Diagnostic and statistical manual of mental disorders* (2nd ed.). Washington, DC: American Psychiatric Press.

American Psychiatric Association. (1980). *Diagnostic and statistical manual of mental disorders* (3rd ed.). Washington, DC: American Psychiatric Press.

American Psychiatric Association. (1994). *Diagnostic and statistical manual of mental disorders* (4th ed.). Washington, DC: American Psychiatric Press.

Angold, A., & Costello, E. J. (1996). Toward establishing an empirical basis for the diagnosis of Oppositional Defiant disorder. *Journal of the American Academy of Child and Adolescent Psychiatry, 35,* 1205–1212.

Angold, A., Costello, E. J., & Worthman, C. M. (1998). Puberty and depression: The roles of age, pubertal status, and pubertal timing. *Psychological Medicine, 28,* 51–61.

Angold, A., Costello, E. J., & Worthman, C. M. (1999). Pubertal changes in hormone levels and depression in girls. *Psychological Medicine, 29,* 1043–1053.

Angold, A., & Fisher, P. W. (1999). Interviewer-based interviews. In D. Shaffer, C. Lucas, & J. Richters (Eds.), *Diagnostic assessment in child and adolescent psychopathology* (pp. 34–64). New York: Guilford Press.

Angold, A., & Worthman, C. W. (1993). Puberty onset of gender differences in rates of depression: A developmental, epidemiologic and neuroendocrine perspective. *Journal of Affective Disorders, 29,* 145–158.

Berger, M., Yule, W., & Rutter, M. (1975). Attainment and adjustment in two geographical areas II. The prevalence of specific reading retardation. *British Journal of Psychiatry, 126,* 510–519.

Bergman, L. R. (2001) A person approach in research on adolescence: Some methodological challenges. *Journal of Adolescent Research 16,* 28–53.

Bernstein–Carlson, E. B., & Putnam, F.W. (1986). Development, reliability, and validity of a dissociation scale. *Journal of Nervous and Mental Disease, 174,* 727–735.

Categories and dimensions 549

Blashfield, R. K. (1982). Feighner et al., invisible colleges, and the Matthew effect. *Schizophrenia Bulletin, 8,* 1–12.

Cairns, R. B., & Green, J. A. (1979). How to assess personality and social patterns: Ratings or observations? In R. B. Cairns (Ed.), The analysis of social interaction: Methods, issues and illustrations. Hillsdale, NJ: Erlbaum.

Conners, C. K. (1997). *Conners' Rating Scales Revised: Instruments for use with children and adolescents.* North Tonawanda, NY: Multi-Health Systems.

Costello, E. J., Angold, A., Burns, B. J., Stangl, D. K., Tweed, D. L., Erkanli, A., & Worthman, C. M. (1996). The Great Smoky Mountains Study of Youth. Goals, design, methods, and the prevalence of *DSM-III-R* disorders. *Archives of General Psychiatry, 53,* 1129–1136.

Cox, D. R. (1972). Regression models and life-tables (with discussion). *Journal of the Royal Statistical Society B, 74,* 187–200.

Crijnen, A., Achenbach, T. M., & Verhulst, F. C. (1997). Comparisons of problems reported by parents of children in 12 cultures: Total problems, externalizing, and internalizing. *Journal of the American Academy of Child and Adolescent Psychiatry, 36,* 1269–1277.

Cullen, K. J., & Boundy, C. A. P. (1966). The prevalence of behavior disorders in the children of 1000 Western Australian families. *Medical Journal of Australia, 2,* 805–808.

Cummings, J. D. (1944). The incidence of emotional symptoms in school children. *British Journal of Educational Psychology, 14,* 151–161.

Dale, P. S., Simonoff, E., Bishop, D. V. M., Eley, T. C., Oliver, B., Price, P.S., Purcell, S., Stevenson, J., & Plomin, R. (1998). Genetic involvement in language delay in 2 year-old children. *Nature Neuroscience, 1,* 324–328.

Davies, R. B., & Pickles, A. R. (1987). A joint trip-timing/store-type choice model for grocery shopping including feedback, inventory effects and non-parametric control for omitted variables. *Transportation Research, 21,* 345–361.

DeFries, J. C., & Fulker, D. W. (1985). Multiple regression analysis of twin data. *Behavior Genetics, 15,* 467–473.

Eaves, L. J., Silberg, J. L., Hewitt, J. K., Rutter, M., Meyer, M., Neale, M., & Pickles, A. (1993). Analyzing twin resemblance in multisymptom data: Genetic application of latent class models for symptoms of conduct disorder in juvenile boys. *Behavior Genetics, 23,* 5–19.

Gould, M. S., Wunsch-Hitzig, R., & Dohrenwend, B. (1981). Estimating the prevalence of child psychopathology. *Journal of the American Academy of Child Psychiatry, 20,* 462–476.

Graham, P., & Rutter, M. (1973). Psychiatric disorders in the young adolescent: A follow-up study. *Proceedings of the Royal Society of Medicine, 6,* 1226–1229.

Griffiths, W. (1952). *Behavior difficulties of children as perceived and judged by parents, teachers, and children themselves.* Minneapolis, MN: The University of Minnesota Press.

Haggerty, M. E. (1925). The incidence of undesirable behavior in public school children. *Journal of Educational Research, 12,* 102–122.

Hill, J., Pickles, A., Burnside, E., Byatt, M., Rollinson, L., Davis, R., & Harvey, K. (2001). Child sexual abuse, poor parental care and adult depression: Evidence for different mechanisms. *British Journal of Psychiatry, 179,* 110–115.

Huttenlocher, J., Hedges, L., & Prochaska, V. (1988). Hierarchical organisation in ordered domains: Estimating dates of events. *Psychological Review, 95,* 471–484.

Kendall, M. (1991). The major functional psychoses: Are they independent entities or part of a continuum? Philosophical and conceptual issues underlying the debate. In A. Kerr & H. McLelland (Eds.), *Concepts of mental disorder: A continuing debate* (pp. 1–16). London: Gaskell.

Kendler, K., Karkowski, L., & Walsh, D. (1998). The structure of psychosis: Latent class analysis of probands from the Roscommon Family Study. *Archives of General Psychiatry 55,* 492–499.

Kohlberg, L. (1976). Moral stages and moralization. In T. Lickona (Ed.), *Moral development and behavior* (pp. 31–53). New York: Holt Rinehart & Winston.

Kraemer, H. C., Kazdin, A. E., Offord, D. R., Kessler, R. C., Jensen, P. S., & Kupfer, D. J. (1999). Measuring the potency of risk factors for clinical or policy significance. *Psychological Methods, 4,* 257–271.

Laird, N. M. (1978). Non-parametric maximum likelihood estimation of a mixing distribution. *Journal of the American Statistical Association, 73,* 805–811.

Lapouse, R. (1966). The epidemiology of behavior disorders in children. *American Journal of Disfunctional Children, 111,* 594–599.

Lapouse, R. L., & Monk, M. A. (1958). An epidemiologic study of behavior characteristics in children. *American Journal of Public Health, 48,* 1134–1144.

Lapouse, R. L., & Monk, M. A. (1964). Behavior deviations in a representative sample of children: Variation by sex, age, race, social class and family size. *American Journal of Orthopsychiatry, 34,* 436–446.

Lindsay, B. G., Clogg, C. C., & Grego, J. (1991). Semiparametric estimation in the Rasch model and related exponential models, including a simple latent class model for item analysis. *Journal of the American Statistical Association, 86,* 96–107.

Long, A. (1941). Parents' reports of undesirable behavior in children. *Child Development, 12,* 43–62.

Lord, F. M., & Novick, M. R. (1968). *Statistical theories of mental test scores.* Reading, MA: Addison–Wesley.

Macready, G. B., & Dayton, C. M. (1994). Latent class models for longitudinal assessment of trait acquisition. In A. von Eye & C. C. Clogg (Eds.), *Latent variable analysis* (pp. 245–273). Thousand Oaks, CA: Sage.

Maddala, G. (1983). *Limited dependent and qualitative variables in econometrics.* New York: Cambridge University Press.

Magnusson, D. (1988a). Methodological and research strategical considerations of an interactional perspective. In D. Magnusson (Ed.), *Paths through life: Vol. 1. Individual development from an interactional perspective: A longitudinal study* (pp. 62–82). Hillsdale, NJ: Erlbaum.

Magnusson, D. (1988b). A theoretical framework: The interactional perspective. In D. Magnusson (Ed.), *Paths through life: Vol. 1. Individual development from an interactional perspective: A longitudinal study* (pp. 15–43). Hillsdale, NJ: Erlbaum.

McFie, B. S. (1934). Behavior and personality difficulties in school children. *British Journal of Educational Psychology, 4,* 34.

Meehl, P. E. (1992). Factors, and taxa, traits and types,

difference of degree and differences of kind. *Journal of Personality, 60,* 117–174.

Meehl, P. E. (1995). Bootstrap taxometrics: Solving the classification problem in psychpathology. *American Psychologist, 50,* 266–275.

Moffitt, T. E. (1993). Adolescence-limited and life-course-persistent-offending: A complementary pair of developmental theories. In T. P. Thornberry (Ed.), *Developmental theories of crime and delinquency* (pp. 11–55). New Brunswick, NJ: Transaction.

Muthen, B., & Muthen, L. (2000). Integrating person-centred and variable-centred analyses: Growth mixture modeling with latent trajectory classes. *Alcoholism: Clinical and Experimental Research, 24,* 882–891.

Muthén, L. K., & Muthén, B. (2001). *Mplus User's Guide.* Los Angeles, CA: Muthén & Muthén.

Nagin, D. S., & Land, K. C. (1993). Age, criminal careers and population heterogeneity: Specification and estimation of a non-parametric mixed Poisson model. *Criminology, 31,* 327–362.

Offord, D. R., Kraemer, H. C., Kazdin, A. E., Jensen, P. S., & Harrington, R. (1998). Lowering the burden of suffering from child-psychiatric disorder: Trade-offs among clinical, targeted, and universal interventions. *Journal of the American Academy of Child and Adolescent Psychiatry, 37,* 686–694.

Olson, W. C. (1930). *Problem tendencies in children.* Minneapolis, MN: University of Minnesota Press.

Piaget, J. (1932). *The moral judgment of the child.* New York: Harcourt, Brace & Company.

Pickles A. R. (1989). Statistical modelling of longitudinal data. In M. Rutter (Ed.), *The power of longitudinal data: Studies of risk and protective factors for psychosocial disorder* (pp. 62–76). Cambridge: Cambridge University Press.

Pickles, A. (1993). Stages, precursors and causes in development. In D. F. Hay & A. Angold (Eds.), *Precursors and causes in development and psychopathology* (pp. 23–50). Chichester, UK: Wiley.

Pickles, A., & Clayton, D. G. (2002). *Log-odds estimates for mis-measured exposures using normal theory random effects models.* Unpublished manuscript, University of Manchester.

Pickles, A., Pickering, K., Simonoff, E., Meyer, J., Silberg, J. & Maes, H. (1998). Genetic "clocks" and "soft" events: A twin model for pubertal development and other recalled sequences of developmental milestones. *Behavior Genetics, 28,* 243–253.

Pickles, A., Pickering, K., & Taylor, C. (1996). Reconciling recalled dates of developmental milestones, events and transitions: A mixed GLM with random mean and variance functions. *Journal of the Royal Statistical Society* Series A, *159,* 225–234.

Pickles, A., Rowe, R., Simonoff, E., Foley, D., Rutter, M. N., & Silberg, J. (2001). Child psychiatric symptoms and psycho-social impairment: Relationship and prognostic significance. *British Journal of Psychiatry, 179,* 230–235.

Quay, H. C. (1977). Measuring dimensions of deviant behavior: The Behavior Problem Checklist. *Journal of Abnormal Child Psychology, 5,* 277–287.

Rabe–Hesketh, S., Pickles, A., & Skrondal, A. (2002). *Correcting for covariate measurement error in logistic regression using a nonparametric maximum likelihood estimation.* Manuscript submitted for publication.

Ritchie, K., & Dupuy, A. M. (1999) . The current status

of APO E4 as a risk factor for Alzheimer's disease: An epidemiological perspective. *International Journal of Geriatric Psychiatry, 14,* 695–700.

Rutter, M. (1965). Classification and categorization in child psychiatry. *Journal of Child Psychology and Psychiatry, 6,* 71–83.

Rutter, M. (1976). Research report: Isle of Wight studies 1964–1974. *Psychological Medicine, 6,* 313–332.

Rutter, M., Graham, P., Chadwick, O. F. D., & Yule, W. (1976). Adolescent turmoil: Fact or fiction? *Journal of Child Psychology and Psychiatry, 17,* 35–56.

Rutter, M., Lebovici, S., Eisenberg, L., Sneznevskij, A. V., Sadoun, R., Brooke, E., & Lin, T. Y. (1969). A tri-axial classification of mental disorders in childhood: An international study. *Journal of Child Psychology and Psychiatry, 10,* 41–61.

Rutter, M., & Shaffer, D. (1980). *DSM-III*: A step forward or back in terms of the classification of child psychiatric disorders? *Journal of the American Academy of Child Psychiatry, 19,* 371–394.

Rutter, M., Tizard, J., & Whitmore, K. (1970). *Education, health, and behaviour.* London: Longman.

Rutter, M., Yule, B., Morton, J., & Bagley, C. (1975). Children of West Indian immigrants III: Home circumstances and family patterns. *Journal of Child Psychology and Psychiatry, 16,* 105–123.

Rutter, M., Yule, B., Quinton, D., Rowlands, O., Yule, W., & Berger, M. (1974). Attainment and adjustment in two geographical areas III. Some factors accounting for area differences. *British Journal of Psychiatry, 125,* 520–533.

Rutter, M., Yule, W., Berger, M., Yule, B., Morton, J., & Bagley, C. (1974). Children of West Indian immigrants: I. Rates of behavioural deviance and of psychiatric disorder. *Journal of Child Psychology and Psychiatry, 15,* 241–262.

Rutter, M. L., Shaffer, D., & Sturge, C. (1979). *A guide to a multi-axial classification scheme for psychiatric disorders in childhood and adolescence.* London: Frowde & Co. Ltd.

Schumacker, R. E., & Marcoulides, G. A. (1998). *Interaction and nonlinear effects in structural equation modeling.* Mahwah, NJ: Erlbaum.

Shaffer, D., Fisher, P. W., & Lucas, C. P. (1999). Respondent-based interviews. In D. Shaffer, C. P. Lucas, & J. E. Richters (Eds.), *Diagnostic assessment in child and adolescent psychopathology* (pp. 3–33). New York: Guilford Press.

Sonuga–Barke, E. J. S. (1998). Categorical models of childhood disorder: A conceptual and empirical analysis. *Journal of Child Psychology and Psychiatry, 39,* 115–133.

Srole, L., Langner, T. S., Mitchell, S. T., Opler, M. K., & Rennie, T. A. C. (1962). *Mental health in the metropolis: The Midtown Study.* New York: McGraw-Hill.

Taylor, E. (1994). Similarities and differences in *DSM-IV* and *ICD-10* diagnostic criteria. *Child and Adolescent Psychiatric Clinics of North America, 3,* 209–226.

Van den Oord, E., Pickles, A., & Waldman, I. (2003). Normal variation and abnormality: An empirical study of the liability distributions underlying depression and delinquency. *Journal of Child Psychology and Psychiatry, 44,* 180–192.

Verhulst, F. C., & Achenbach, T. M. (1995). Empirically based assessment and taxonomy of psychopathology: Cross-cultural applications. A Review. *European Child and Adolescent Psychiatry, 4,* 61–76.

von Eye, A. (1990). *Introduction to configural frequency*

Categories and dimensions 551

analysis: *The search for types and anti-types in cross-classifications.* Cambridge: Cambridge University Press.

Wakefield, J. C. (1992). Disorder as harmful dysfunction: A conceptual critique of *DSM III R*'s definition of mental disorder. *Psychological Review, 99,* 232–247.

Wakefield, J. C. (1997). When is development disordered? Developmental psychopathology and the harmful dysfunction analysis of mental disorders. *Development and Psychopathology, 9,* 269–290.

Waller, N. G., & Meehl, P. E. (1998). *Multivariate taxometric procedures. Distinguishing types from continua.* Thousand Oaks, CA: Sage.

Waller, N. G., Putnam, F. W., & Carlson, E. (1996). Types of dissociation and dissociative types: A taxonometric analysis of the Dissociative Experiences Scale. *Psychological Methods, 3,* 300–321.

Wilson, M. (1993). *DSM-II* and the transformation of American psychiatry: A history. *American Journal of Psychiatry, 150,* 399–410.

World Health Organization (1993). *ICD-10 Classification of mental and behavioural disorders: Diagnostic criteria for research.* Geneva: World Health Organization.

World Health Organization (1994). *ICD-10 Classification of mental and behavioural disorders; Clinical descriptions and diagnostic guidelines.* Geneva: World Health Organization.

Wickman, E. K. (1928). *Children's behavior and teachers' attitudes.* New York: Commonwealth Fund.

Young–Masten, I. (1938). Behavior problems of elementary school children: A descriptive and comparative study. *Genetic Psychology Monographs, 20,* 123–180.

Yourman, J. (1932). Children identified by their teachers as problems. *Journal of Educational Sociology, 5,* 334–343.

Yule, W., Berger, M., Rutter, M., & Yule, B. (1975). Children of West Indian immigrants: II. Intellectual performance and reading attainment. *Journal of Child Psychology and Psychiatry, 16,* 1–17.

[20]

The British Child and Adolescent Mental Health Survey 1999: The Prevalence of *DSM-IV* Disorders

TAMSIN FORD, M.R.C.PSYCH., ROBERT GOODMAN, F.R.C.PSYCH., AND HOWARD MELTZER, PH.D.

ABSTRACT

Objective: To describe the prevalence of *DSM-IV* disorders and comorbidity in a large population-based sample of British children and adolescents. **Method:** Using a one-phase design, 10,438 children were assessed using the Development and Well-Being Assessment (DAWBA), a structured interview with verbatim reports reviewed by clinicians so that information from parents, teachers, and children was combined in a manner that emulated the clinical process. The authors' analysis examined comorbidity and the influence of teacher reports. **Results:** The overall prevalence of *DSM-IV* disorders was 9.5% (95% confidence interval 8.8–10.1%), but 2.1% of children were assigned "not otherwise specified" rather than operationalized diagnoses. After adjusting for the presence of a third disorder, there was no longer significant comorbidity between anxiety and conduct disorder or attention-deficit/hyperactivity disorder (ADHD), or between depression and oppositional defiant disorder. A comparison of the disorders in children with and without teacher reports suggested that the prevalence of conduct disorders and ADHD would be underestimated in the absence of teacher information. **Conclusions:** Roughly 1 in 10 children have at least one *DSM-IV* disorder, involving a level of distress or social impairment likely to warrant treatment. Comorbidity reported between some childhood diagnoses may be due to the association of both disorders with a third. Diagnoses of conduct disorder and ADHD may be missed if information is not sought from teachers about children's functioning in school. *J. Am. Acad. Child Adolesc. Psychiatry,* 2003, 42(10):1203–1211. **Key Words:** epidemiology, prevalence.

Childhood psychiatric disorder can prevent a young person from reaching his or her full potential by disrupting normal development. Prevention, detection, and treatment of these problems are important not only to relieve current distress but also to improve adult functioning and prevent the perpetuation of disadvantage into the next generation. Effective service planning depends initially on accurate estimates of the prevalence of disorder in the population.

However, several major methodological problem areas make it hard to provide accurate prevalence estimates, which include the combination of informants' reports, the loss of precision in two-phase surveys, comorbidity, the inability of fully structured interviews to deal with threshold cases, and respondent confusion. In this article we present the prevalence estimates from a large, national, population-based survey in Britain that used validated measures and emulated the clinical process in the method of combining informant reports. Although the prevalence of *ICD-10* disorders has been published in an official report by the British Office for National Statistics, which carried out the study (Meltzer et al., 2000), this is the first time that the prevalence of *DSM-IV* disorders has been documented.

Accepted April 29, 2003.

Dr. Goodman is Professor of Brain and Behavioral Medicine and Dr. Ford is a clinical training fellow in the Department of Child and Adolescent Psychiatry at the Institute of Psychiatry, King's College London. Dr. Meltzer is a principal social researcher at the Office for National Statistics.

The British Department of Health funded the original survey and Dr. Ford completed the work while on a Wellcome Trust Fellowship.

Correspondence to Dr. Ford, PO85, Department of Child and Adolescent Psychiatry, Institute of Psychiatry, Denmark Hill, London SE58AF, England; e-mail: t.ford@iop.kcl.ac.uk.

0890-8567/03/4210–1203©2003 by the American Academy of Child and Adolescent Psychiatry.

DOI: 10.1097/01.chi.0000081820.25107.ae

METHOD

Participants

In Great Britain (England, Wales, and Scotland, but not Northern Ireland), "child benefit" is a universal state benefit payable for each child in the family, and it has an extremely high uptake. The child benefit register was used to develop a sampling frame of postal sectors from England, Wales, and Scotland that, after excluding families with no recorded ZIP code or subject to current revision of their record, was estimated to represent 90% of all British children (Meltzer et al., 2000). Four hundred seventy-five postal sectors (out of the 9,000 covering Great Britain) were sampled with a probability related to size of the sector, and stratified by regional health authority and socioeconomic group. Children were listed within each sector by age within gender.

Thirty children aged 5 to 15 were systematically sampled within each postal sector (total 14,250), of whom 5.5% (790) were ineligible, and 6.5% (931) families opted out before their details were passed to the investigators. Most (629) ineligible families had moved and could not be traced, but other reasons for exclusion at this stage were that the child was in foster care, had died, or was outside the age criterion. Information was collected on 10,438 (83%) of the 12,529 eligible children, comprising 10,405 (99.7%) parent interviews, 4115 (90.9%) interviews of 11- to 15-year-olds, and 8382 (80.3%) teacher reports. Interviewers were unable to contact 2% of eligible families, and 15% refused to participate.

Forty-nine percent of participating children came from families where the principal wage earner had a manual job, and in just under a quarter (24%) the weekly household income was less than $300, while 23% had a mother with no educational qualifications. Fifty percent of participating children were boys, and fewer older children participated (44% aged 11–15). Twenty-two percent were from single-parent families, and 11% were from reconstituted families. The ethnicity of participating children is described below.

Measures

The Development and Well-Being Assessment (DAWBA) was developed for this survey. It consists of a structured interview administered by lay interviewers who also recorded verbatim accounts of any reported problems (Goodman et al., 2000). A team of child and adolescent psychiatrists reviewed both the verbatim accounts and the answers to structured questions about symptoms and their impact (i.e., resultant distress and social impairment) before assigning diagnoses according to *DSM-IV* criteria (American Psychiatric Association, 1994). Previous studies have generated three main lines of evidence for the validity of the DAWBA, both in English and in Portuguese translation. First, independent DAWBA reassessments of children attending mental health clinics have generated substantial agreement between the clinic diagnosis and the DAWBA diagnosis (Fleitlich-Bilyk, 2002; Goodman et al., 2000). Second, there are striking differences between rates of diagnosis in clinic and community samples (Fleitlich-Bilyk, 2002; Goodman et al., 2000). Finally, within community samples, subjects with and without diagnosed disorders differ markedly in external characteristics and prognosis (Goodman et al., 2000, 2002).

As part of the DAWBA process, clinical raters use the verbatim reports to check that respondents have understood what they had been asked, to assign "not otherwise specified" (NOS) diagnoses, and to decide whose account to prioritize when there is disagreement between different informants. No one category of informant is automatically prioritized: details in the transcripts that corroborate symptom reports are used to determine the weight given to each informant. The aim is to emulate the clinical process as closely as possible, because rigid rules for combining information from different informants can be problematic. In the present study, all clinical ratings were made by two clinical raters: a fully qualified child and adolescent psychiatrist (T.F.) with 3 years of postgraduate basic psychiatric training followed by 3 years of training in child and adolescent psychiatry, and a trainee child and adolescent psychiatrist who had completed 3 years of basic psychiatry training that had included 6 months' experience of child and adolescent psychiatry. Both raters were trained and supervised by a senior child and adolescent psychiatrist (R.G.). Except for the reliability exercise

discussed below, all "hard-to-call" diagnoses were discussed until a consensus was reached. Having just two clinical raters and regular consensus meetings with a supervisor made it easier to maintain diagnostic consistency.

The κ statistic for chance-corrected agreement between the two clinical raters who independently rated 500 children was 0.86 for any disorder (SE 0.04), 0.57 for internalizing disorders (SE 0.11), and 0.98 for externalizing disorders (SE 0.02). The test–retest reliability of the DAWBA was not assessed since, as discussed in more detail elsewhere (Goodman et al., 2000), readministration after a short interval would have been difficult to interpret due to the effects of attenuation or respondent fatigue, while readministration after a longer interval would have confounded test–retest unreliability with genuine remission or deterioration.

Children were assigned a diagnosis only if their symptoms were causing significant distress or social impairment. For each problem area, informants were asked if the difficulties caused the child distress or interfered with family life, peer relationships, leisure activities, or learning on a 4-point scale: "not at all," "a little," "a medium amount," and "a great deal." The diagnostic threshold was set at "a medium amount" of distress or impairment according to at least one informant.

The questions in the structured part of the DAWBA interview were closely related to *DSM-IV* and *ICD-10* (World Health Organization, 1993) diagnostic criteria and focused on current rather than life-time problems to obtain prevalence estimates that were relevant to service planning. The DAWBA interview was administered to all parents and to all children aged 11 or over; a shortened version of the DAWBA was mailed to the child's teacher. As children are thought to be poor informants about attention-deficit/hyperactivity disorder (ADHD) (Bird et al., 1991), they were asked only whether their teacher and family had complained about hyperactivity and poor attention, and whether they thought that they had problems in this area. In other respects the parent, child, and teacher interview schedules were as similar as possible. Children under the age of 11 were not interviewed as previous studies suggested that the information obtained would be unreliable (Fallon and Schwab-Stone, 1994; Schwab-Stone et al., 1996). Further information on the DAWBA is available from *http://www.dawba.com*, including on-line and downloadable versions of the measures and demonstrations of the clinical rating process.

For our analyses of the relative contribution of teacher reports to overall diagnoses, we supplemented the clinical review diagnoses described above with parent-based diagnoses. A computer algorithm assigned the parent-based diagnoses when symptoms and impact criteria for operationalized *DSM-IV* criteria were met according to parental answers to structured questions. These parent-based diagnoses did not draw on information from teachers or youth, did not incorporate any element of clinical judgment, and were not used in our detailed analyses of prevalence or comorbidity.

Data Analysis

The sample was weighted according to non-response by region, age, and sex with a correction factor that returned the weighted sample to its original size. We used the Statistics/Data Analysis Program (STATA 6) survey program, which uses Taylor series linearization methods to adjust for sampling weights and clustering within strata and primary sampling units (postal sectors) in the calculation of test statistics and standard errors (Stata Corp., 1997).

We examined associations with age, gender, and ethnicity with the prevalence of different *DSM-IV* disorders using χ^2 and χ^2 for trend. We used logistic regression to determine the odds of comorbidity between any two of the five major types of disorder (anxiety,

ADHD, depression, oppositional defiant, and conduct disorders) while adjusting for the others.

RESULTS

Prevalence of Childhood Psychiatric Disorder

At least one *DSM-IV* diagnosis was present in 983 children, representing a weighted prevalence of 9.5% (95% confidence interval [CI] 8.8–10.1%). A fifth of these children (2.1%) had nonoperationalized or "not otherwise specified" diagnoses (anxiety NOS, depression NOS, or disruptive disorder NOS) that failed to meet current *DSM-IV* criteria but were causing the child significant impairment or distress.

Table 1 presents the prevalence of individual diagnoses and diagnostic groupings by age and gender. Nonoperationalized disorders were significantly more common among boys and older children. Most of the age and gender effects were in the expected direction: for instance, all the disruptive disorders were significantly more frequent in boys, as were pervasive developmental disorders, while eating disorders were more common in girls. Similarly, the prevalence of conduct and depressive disorders, along with certain anxiety disorders, increases with age. The prevalence of traumatic incidents reported by parents increased with age from 8.7% in 5- to 10-year-olds to 12.6% in 11- to 15-year-olds (χ^2 = 40.0, p = .001), accounting for some of the increase in posttraumatic stress disorder with age. In general, the increase in the prevalence of disorder with age was gradual and did not have a sudden step at age 11 when child assessments began, suggesting that the age-related increase was not simply attributable to the presence of an additional informant from the age of 11.

Ethnic minorities represented 8.7% of the sample, which was representative of the British population according to the 1991 census. Relatively small numbers in each minority group made it difficult to detect and interpret associations between ethnic group and disorder. Ethnicity (white 91.3%, Asian 4.2%, African-Caribbean 2.4%, other 2.1%) had no detectable associations with most *DSM-IV* disorders, with the exception that Asian children (Indian, Pakistani, Bangladeshi, and Chinese) had a lower prevalence of oppositional defiant disorder (p = .02) and perhaps ADHD (p = .06).

Comorbidity

Of the children with any *DSM-IV* diagnosis, 222 (22%) had two, 49 (5%) had three, 17 (2%) had four,

and 4 (0.4%) had five disorders. Figure 1 illustrates the comorbidity between anxiety disorders, depressive disorders, and disruptive disorders. Children with depression were most likely to have a comorbid diagnosis (66%), while children with a disruptive disorder were least likely to do so (21%). Just over a quarter of those with anxiety disorders (27%) had comorbid depression or disruptive disorder, but children who had an anxiety disorder also often had more than one anxiety diagnosis. Of the 391 children with any anxiety disorder, 57 (15%) had two, 15 (4%) had three, and 2 (0.5%) had four anxiety disorders. Separation anxiety disorder and generalized anxiety disorder occurred together most often (15 cases), while separation anxiety disorder also tended to be comorbid with specific (12) and social (12) phobias. All the other anxiety disorders co-occurred in fewer than 10 instances.

As comorbidity between ADHD and another disruptive disorder was also very common, this is illustrated in a separate diagram (Fig. 2). Figure 2 reflects the fact that *DSM-IV* stipulates that oppositional defiant and conduct disorders should be treated as separate diagnoses, and thus comorbidity between them cannot occur in this system. Over half the children with ADHD had a comorbid behavior disorder, while approximately a quarter of children with either conduct disorder (27%) or oppositional defiant disorder (26%) also merited a diagnosis of ADHD.

At a univariate level, children with anxiety, depression, ADHD, or conduct or oppositional disorder all had significantly increased odds of having another major type of disorder. Figure 3 demonstrates the strength of the adjusted associations between the five main categories of disorder. After adjusting for the presence of other disorders, there was no longer a significant association between ADHD and either anxiety (odds ratio 0.8, 95% CI 0.5–1.8) or depression (odds ratio 1.3, 95% CI 0.6–3.1), between anxiety and conduct disorder (odds ratio 1.8, 95% CI 0.9–3.7), or between depression and oppositional defiant disorder (odds ratio 1.8, 95% CI 0.8–4.4).

Contribution of Teacher-Reported Information

While parents and 11- to 15-year-olds nearly all provided information, about a fifth of teachers did not, enabling us to examine the contribution of teacher reports to the clinician review process. We examined the ratio of clinician review diagnoses (based on all available information) to parent-based diagnoses (based solely on parental responses to structured questions). If

TABLE 1

Percentage (Standard Errors) of Children with *DSM-IV* Disorders in the British Child and Mental Health Survey in 1999 (BCAMHS 99)

DSM-IV Disorder	Gender (*n*)		Age in years (*n*)				Total
	Male (5,212)	Female (5,226)	5–7 (2,964)	8–10 (2,949)	11–12 (1,901)	13–15 (2,624)	(10,438)
Any psychatric diagnosis	11.56	7.41***	7.79	8.60	9.59	12.19***	9.48
	(0.05)	(0.04)	(0.05)	(0.05)	(0.07)	(0.07)	(0.33)
Anxiety disorders							
Any anxiety disorder	3.50	4.04	3.19	3.05	3.95	5.04***	3.77
	(0.25)	(0.27)	(0.31)	(0.34)	(0.45)	(0.47)	(0.19)
Separation anxiety disorder	1.19	1.14	1.48	1.09	1.11	0.97	1.17
	(0.14)	(0.15)	(0.22)	(0.21)	(0.24)	(0.19)	(0.10)
Specific phobia	0.90	1.07	1.17	0.97	1.16	0.68	1.00
	(0.13)	(0.14)	(0.19)	(0.19)	(0.25)	(0.16)	(0.10)
Social phobia	0.36	0.29	0.33	0.24	0.37	0.38	0.32
	(0.01)	(0.01)	(0.01)	(0.01)	(0.14)	(0.11)	(0.05)
Posttraumatic stress disorder	0.11	0.18	0.03	0	0.35	0.27**	0.14
	(0.04)	(0.06)	(0.03)		(0.01)	(0.01)	(0.04)
OCD	0.26	0.24	0.03	0.14	0.21	0.63***	0.25
	(0.08)	(0.07)	(0.03)	(0.07)	(0.10)	(0.17)	(0.05)
General anxiety disorder	0.57	0.73	0.16	0.57	0.74	0.18***	0.65
	(0.01)	(0.01)	(0.07)	(0.13)	(0.20)	(0.22)	(0.08)
Panic disorder	0.17	0.11	0	0	0.10	0.47***	0.14
	(0.06)	(0.05)			(0.07)	(0.14)	(0.04)
Agoraphobia	0.06	0.09	0	0	0.06	0.22*	0.07
	(0.03)	(0.04)			(0.05)	(0.09)	(0.02)
Anxiety NOS	0.84	1.02	0.48	0.67	0.87	1.73***	0.93
	(0.13)	(0.13)	(0.13)	(0.14)	(0.22)	(0.25)	(0.90)
Depressive disorders							
Any depressive disorder	0.87	0.97	0.14	0.34	0.71	2.53***	0.92
	(0.14)	(0.14)	(0.09)	(0.11)	(0.20)	(0.32)	(0.10)
Major depressive disorder	0.65	0.72	0.14	0.27	0.44	1.87***	0.68
	(0.11)	(0.13)	(0.09)	(0.09)	(0.14)	(0.28)	(0.09)
Depression NOS	0.22	0.25	0	0.07	0.26	0.66***	0.24
	(0.07)	(0.07)		(0.05)	(0.11)	(0.15)	(0.05)
Disruptive disorders							
Any disruptive disorder	8.50	3.31***	5.00	5.88	5.85	7.04**	5.90
	(0.39)	(0.25)	(0.38)	(0.41)	(0.53)	(0.52)	(0.23)
Any ADHD	3.62	0.85***	1.90	2.49	2.57	2.10	2.23
	(0.26)	(0.13)	(0.24)	(0.28)	(0.36)	(0.31)	(0.15)
ADHD combined	2.34	0.48***	1.51	1.50	1.56	1.11	1.41
	(0.20)	(0.09)	(0.21)	(0.21)	(0.26)	(0.21)	(0.11)
ADHD inattentive	1.00	0.33***	0.20	0.88	0.67	0.93**	0.67
	(0.14)	(0.08)	(0.08)	(0.17)	(0.18)	(0.20)	(0.09)
ADHD hyperactive	0.28	0.04**	0.18	0.10	0.34	0.08	0.16
	(0.07)	(0.04)	(0.08)	(0.06)	(0.13)	(0.06)	(0.39)
Oppositional defiant disorder	3.24	1.39***	2.65	2.80	2.31	1.43**	2.31
	(0.25)	(0.16)	(0.30)	(0.30)	(0.35)	(0.23)	(0.14)
Conduct disorder	2.13	0.81***	0.59	0.78	1.25	3.31***	1.47
	(0.22)	(0.12)	(0.13)	(0.17)	(0.38)	(0.38)	(0.13)
Disruptive disorder NOS	1.42	0.68*	0.71	0.88	1.19	1.50	1.05
	(0.18)	(0.12)	(0.15)	(0.17)	(0.24)	(0.24)	(0.10)

—Continued

TABLE 1
Continued

	Gender (*n*)		Age in years (*n*)				
DSM-IV Disorder	Male (5,212)	Female (5,226)	5–7 (2,964)	8–10 (2,949)	11–12 (1,901)	13 15 (2,624)	Total (10,438)
Less common disorders							
PDD	**0.47**	**0.09****	0.40	0.31	0.09	0.24	0.29
	(0.09)	(0.04)	(0.11)	(0.11)	(0.06)	(0.10)	(0.05)
Eating disorders	**0.04**	**0.19***	0	0	0.15	**0.34****	0.12
	(0.03)	(0.06)			(0.09)	(0.11)	(0.03)
Tic disorders	0.09	0.04	0.03	0.07	0.12	0.07	0.07
	(0.04)	(0.03)	(0.03)	(0.05)	(0.09)	(0.05)	(0.03)
"Not otherwise specified" disorders							
NOS disorders	**2.40**	**1.80***	**1.16**	**1.58**	**2.17**	**3.61*****	2.09
	(0.24)	(0.18)	(0.21)	(0.24)	(0.35)	(0.38)	(0.20)

Note: Figures in **bold type** reflect statistically significant differences between gender or age bands, *p < .05 but *p* > .01; **p < .01 but *p* > .001; ***p < .001. OCD = obsessive-compulsive disorder; NOS = not otherwise specified; ADHD = attention-deficit/hyperactivity disorder; PDD = pervasive developmental disorders.

teacher reports were irrelevant to the clinician review process, then the ratio of clinician review to parent-based diagnoses should have been the same for subjects with teacher data (*n* = 8,382) and the subjects without (*n* = 2,056). As Table 2 shows, this was the case for emotional disorders, whereas information from teachers did increase the ratio of clinician review to parent-based diagnoses for disruptive disorders. This is evidence that teacher reports often persuaded the clinical raters to make diagnoses of disruptive disorders that they would not have made on the basis of parent reports and, for 11- to 15-year-olds, self-report.

Table 3 extrapolates from the ratios presented in Table 2 to estimate the clinician review prevalence of disorders if teacher information had been available not on 80% of the sample, but on 100% or 0%. To obtain these estimates, the rates of parent-based diagnoses for the entire sample were multiplied by the ratios given in

Table 2 for subjects who did have teacher data (for the 100% estimate) and who lacked teacher data (for the 0% estimate). Emotional disorders are not presented in Table 3 since the evidence from Table 2 suggests that the clinician review prevalence of emotional disorders would be the same with or without teacher information.

DISCUSSION

Prevalence of Childhood Psychiatric Disorders

The British Child and Mental Health Survey in 1999 (BCAMHS 99) was completed in one phase, so that all parents, most teachers, and the great majority of 11- to 15-year-olds contributed information that was

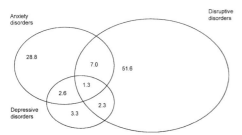

Fig. 1 Comorbidity (%) among the 983 children with a psychiatric disorder.

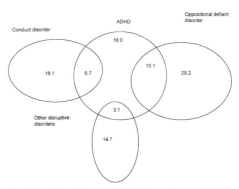

Fig. 2 Comorbidity (%) among the 612 children with externalizing disorders. ADHD = attention-deficit/hyperactivity disorder.

1207

FORD ET AL.

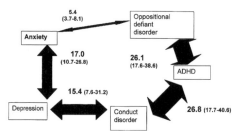

Fig. 3 Adjusted odds ratios (and 95% confidence intervals) for comorbid *DSM-IV* disorders. ADHD = attention-deficit/hyperactivity disorder.

TABLE 3
Estimated Prevalence of *DSM-IV* Disorder in Relation to Teacher Reports

Disorder	Estimated Prevalence of Disorder (%)	
	No Teacher Information on Any Subject	Teacher Information on All Subjects
ADHD	1.4	2.4
ODD/CD	3.1	5.4
Any psychiatric diagnosis	8.0	9.8

Note: ADHD = attention-deficit/hyperactivity disorder; ODD/CD = oppositional defiant and conduct disorder combined.

used to decide whether the child had a disorder. This approach avoided the loss of precision that may occur with a two-phase design deploying a screening measure before a more in-depth diagnostic assessment. The advantages of a highly structured interview that can be administered by interviewers without formal psychiatric training was combined with the advantages of a clinician review to increase the clinical relevance of diagnoses and to combine information from informants in a manner that emulates clinical practice. Data collection involved about 300 lay interviewers in the field but only two clinical raters and one supervisor back at base, thereby reducing costs and increasing diagnostic consistency. This made it economically feasible to obtain detailed interview measures on >10,000 subjects and still use clinicians for the diagnostic rating.

The comparison of prevalence studies of childhood psychiatric disorder is problematic due to the wide variation in sampling, measures, diagnostic criteria, and methods of combining informants reports, in addition to differences in age range and the types of disorders

TABLE 2
Ratio of Clinician-Rated to Parent-Based Disorders in Children With and Without a Teacher Report

	Ratio of Clinician/Parent Disorders Without Teacher Data (*n* = 2,056)	Ratio of Clinician/Parent Disorders With Teacher Data (*n* = 8,382)	Significance of the Difference in Ratio
Emotional disorders	1.11 (104/94)	1.08 (342/317)	0.88
ODD/CD	1.18 (85/72)	2.02 (417/206)	0.003
ADHD	0.76 (28/37)	1.28 (204/159)	0.05
Any disorder	1.19 (184/155)	1.47 (799/544)	0.08

Note: ODD/CD = oppositional defiant and conduct disorder combined; ADHD = attention-deficit/hyperactivity disorder.

studied. Given these methodological problems, it is not surprising that a recent review of 52 studies in 20 countries conducted over 40 years demonstrated a range in estimated prevalence from 1% to 51% (Roberts, 1998), though it is worth noting that the median prevalence was 12% for prepubescent school-age children and 15% among adolescents. Canino et al. (1995) pointed out that early studies provided lower prevalence estimates of child psychiatric disorder than surveys published in the 1980s and 1990s, suggesting the possibility of a secular trend in addition to methodological differences.

The overall prevalence of psychiatric disorder in BCAMHS 99 of 9.5% (95% CI 8.8–10.1%) was at the lower end of the range reported by other studies, for which there are several possible explanations. The absence of teacher information on 20% of subjects depressed the prevalence by about 0.4%. More importantly, since the survey was intended to inform service planning, the diagnostic procedure incorporated impact criteria that were designed to detect disorders that resulted in significant interference in the child's life and merited clinical intervention. Several studies have demonstrated that the inclusion of impact criteria decreases prevalence estimates, with studies insisting on at least moderate impairment reporting rates of 4.4% to 18.7% (Anderson et al., 1987; Bird et al., 1988; Costello et al., 1996; Esser et al., 1990; Fombonne, 1994; Gomez-Beneyeto et al., 1994; Shaffer et al., 1996; Simonoff et al., 1997; Verhulst et al., 1997; Vikan, 1985). When considering the relationship between diagnosis and contact with services, Costello et al. (1993) estimated that approximately 1 child in 10 had both a disorder and impairment, which accords very closely to the prevalence found in BCAMHS 99. Our survey is also one of few epidemiological surveys using *DSM-IV*, whose emphasis on significant distress or impairment, in contrast to earlier editions, reduced the prevalence of anxiety and tic disorders in particular (Simonoff et al., 1997).

Another reason for the relatively low prevalence in the BCAMHS is that the age range only extended to 15, while several other studies have included 16- and 17-year-olds (Bird et al., 1988; Goodman et al., 1998; Kashani et al., 1987; Lewinsohn et al., 1993; Offord et al., 1987; Sanford et al., 1992; Shaffer et al., 1996; Simonoff et al., 1997; Verhulst et al., 1997). Several investigators have demonstrated an increase with age in the prevalence of childhood psychiatric disorder in general (McGee et al., 1990; Simonoff et al., 1997) or of certain disorders such as depression and conduct disorder in particular (Bird et al., 1988 Breton et al., 1999; Gomez-Beneyeto et al., 1994; Offord et al., 1987; Rutter et al., 1976). A relatively young sample might therefore be expected to have a lower overall prevalence. The low prevalence of disorders that commonly have their onset in adolescence, such as depression (0.92%), panic disorder (0.14%), obsessive-compulsive disorder (0.25%), and eating disorders (0.12%), supports this argument. Finally, the range of disorders studied will obviously influence the overall prevalence, and the BCAMHS 99 excluded elimination, somatization, and substance abuse disorders. Recent surveys reported the prevalence of elimination, somatization, and substance abuse disorders to be 1.2% to 11%, 2%, and 0.1% to 5.5% (Bird et al., 1988; Costello et al., 1996; Fergusson et al., 1993; Gomez-Beneyeto et al., 1994; Kashani et al., 1987; Shaffer et al., 1996; Verhulst et al., 1997).

"Not Otherwise Specified" Disorders

A fifth of the children with a psychiatric disorder had nonoperationalized or "not otherwise specified" disorders. All of the children with "not otherwise specified" disorders met our impairment criteria but either had too few symptoms to meet diagnostic criteria or had symptoms from several *DSM-IV* categories but an insufficient number to meet one particular diagnosis. Other studies have also found that a substantial number of children with impairment do not easily fit current classification systems (Angold et al., 1999a; Goodman et al., 1996). As these children may warrant clinical intervention, it would be foolish to omit them from epidemiological studies purely because current diagnostic criteria do not recognize them. Indeed, these partial and mixed syndromes are important to identify and study to improve the classification system. Using

clinical judgment to review symptom and impairment scores in the light of verbatim reports about areas of difficulty permits the recognition of nonoperationalized disorders without undermining reliability and validity (Goodman et al., 1996).

Comorbidity

Over the past decade, the study of comorbidity has assumed greater importance in the hope that a better understanding of the ways in which disorders combine will inform both developmental psychopathology and classification systems (Angold et al., 1999b). The comorbidity rate of 29% in BCAMHS 99 compares with reported rates of 25% to 89% in other recent epidemiological surveys (Bird et al., 1988; Costello et al., 1996; Goodman et al., 1998; Kashani et al., 1987; McGee et al., 1990; Simonoff et al., 1997; Verhulst et al., 1997). The strict impact criteria that resulted in a relatively low prevalence for the BCAMHS 99 survey may also account for the relatively low comorbidity rate.

Most investigators have examined comorbidity between pairs of diagnoses without controlling for indirect associations between disorders occurring because both are related to a third disorder. Angold et al. (unpublished) controlled for the presence of more than two disorders and found that the associations between anxiety and conduct disorder and between depression and ADHD disappeared, findings replicated in this British sample. The similarity between our findings and those of Angold et al. is particularly striking since we used a different analytic strategy. Whereas Angold et al. found an association between oppositional defiant disorder and depression, we found an association between conduct disorder and depression. This discrepancy may be due to the fact that we followed the *DSM-IV* rule that a diagnosis of conduct disorder takes precedence over a diagnosis of oppositional defiant disorder, whereas Angold et al. allowed both diagnoses to be made on the same child. Following *DSM-IV* rules means that children with oppositional defiant disorder tend to be younger and therefore at lower risk of depression. Overall, there is an emerging consensus that comorbidity is selective, being particularly evident between anxiety and depression, between ADHD and behavior disorders, and between depression and at least some behavior disorders.

Importance of Teacher Reports

Although many large epidemiological surveys have not sought information from teachers (Costello et al.,

FORD ET AL.

1996; Esser et al., 1990; Fergusson et al., 1993; Kashani et al., 1987; McGee et al., 1990; Shaffer et al., 1996), our findings suggest that this potentially results in an underestimate of the prevalence of ADHD and behavior disorders. Teachers may be the only informants for school-based disorders, and as *DSM-IV* requires impairment due to ADHD symptoms to be present in at least two settings, it can be very difficult to be certain about these diagnoses in the absence of information from school. A strength of BCAMHS 99 is that the questions asked of teachers were closely related to *DSM-IV* criteria, following in the tradition of the clinical assessment used in the Ontario Child Health Survey (Boyle et al., 1987). Other surveys have used symptom checklists such as the Rutter B scale (Anderson et al., 1987; Fombonne, 1994; Rutter et al., 1976) and the Teacher Report Form (Offord et al., 1987; Verhulst et al., 1997), which may not be so easily tied to diagnostic criteria.

Clinical Implications

Although principally an epidemiological study, our findings emphasize the importance of liaison with teachers, particularly when considering a diagnosis of ADHD, oppositional defiant disorder, or conduct disorder. Similarly, the study underlines the importance of considering comorbid diagnoses, especially among the emotional disorders or the disruptive disorders. Our findings also suggest that it is important to look for depression among children with conduct disorder.

Limitations

The sampling frame was estimated not to cover 10% of British children due to inaccuracies in the child benefit register. The prevalence of childhood psychiatric disorder may well differ between these children, together with the families who opted out or refused to participate. People of low socioeconomic status and those living in urban environments are both less likely to participate in research and to have higher rates of psychiatric illness (Cox et al., 1977; Market Research Society, 1981). Thus we weighted our estimates for non-response according to age, gender, and region. The survey's response rate of 83% compares favorably with the range of 71% to 92% and a median of 78% reported for other epidemiological surveys (Bird et al., 1988; Breton et al., 1999; Costello et al., 1996; Esser et al., 1990; Fergusson et al., 1993; Fombonne, 1994; Gomez-Beneyeto et al., 1994; Goodman et al., 1998;

Kashani et al., 1987; McGee et al., 1990; Sanford et al., 1992; Vikan, 1985). The combination of a structured interview and clinician review of the transcripts seemed to work well, but the advantages and limitations of this sort of approach will be more evident when results of a planned head-to-head comparison of the DAWBA with standard structured and semistructured assessments are available.

Conclusions

The BCAMHS 99 assessed 10,438 children in a one-phase design with up to three informants per child, using a structured interview. Clinicians reviewed the symptoms and impairment scores together with the transcripts about problem areas for all the children. The total prevalence of childhood psychiatric disorder among this large, nationally representative sample of British children was 9.5%. There was comorbidity between anxiety and depression, ADHD and behavior disorders, and depression and conduct disorder, even when the presence of a third disorder was controlled. Our methodology suggests that future morbidity surveys need to consider the influence of teacher reports on the prevalence of ADHD and behavior disorders.

REFERENCES

American Psychiatric Association (1994), *Diagnostic and Statistical Manual of Mental Disorders, 4th edition (DSM-IV)*. Washington, DC: American Psychiatric Association

Anderson JC, William S, McGee R, Silva A (1987), *DSM-III* disorders in preadolescent children. *Arch Gen Psychiatry* 44:69–76

Angold A, Costello EJ, Farmer EZ, Burns BJ, Erkanli A (1999a), Impaired but undiagnosed. *J Am Acad Child Adolesc Psychiatry* 38:129–137

Angold A, Costello EJ, Erkanli A (1999b), Comorbidity. *J Child Psychol Psychiatry* 40:57–87

Boyle MH, Offord DR, Hafmann HG et al. (1987), Ontario Health Survey 1. Methodology. *Arch Gen Psychiatry* 44:826–831

Bird HR, Canino G, Rubio-Stipec M et al. (1988), Estimates of the prevalence of childhood maladjustment in a community survey in Puerto Rico. *Arch Gen Psychiatry* 45:1120–1126

Bird HR, Gould MS, Staghezza B (1991), Aggregating data from multiple informants in child psychiatry epidemiological research. *J Am Acad Child Adolesc Psychiatry* 31:78–85

Breton JJ, Bergeron L, Valla JP et al. (1999), Quebec Child Mental Health Survey: prevalence of *DSM-III-R* mental health disorders. *J Child Psychol Psychiatry* 40:375–384

Canino G, Bird R, Rubio-Stupec M, Bravo M (1995), Child psychiatric epidemiology: what have we learned and what we need to learn. *Int J Methods Psychiatr Res* 5:79–92

Costello E, Angold A, Burns B et al. (1996), The Great Smoky Mountain Study of Youth: goals, designs, methods, and the prevalence of *DSM-III-R* disorders. *Arch Gen Psychiatry* 53:1129–1136

Costello EJ, Burns BJ, Angold A, Leaf P (1993), How can epidemiology improve mental health services for children and adolescents? *J Am Acad Child Adolesc Psychiatry* 32:1106–1113

Cox A, Rutter M, Yule B, Quinton D (1977), Bias resulting from missing information some epidemiological findings. *Br J Prev Soc Med* 31:131–136

Esser G, Schmidt H, Woerner W (1990), Epidemiology and course of psychiatric disorders in school age children: results of a longitudinal study. *J Child Psychol Psychiatry* 31:243–263

Fallon T, Schwab-Stone M (1994), Determinants of reliability in psychiatric survey of children aged 6-12. *J Child Psychol Psychiatry* 35:1391–1408

Fergusson DM, Horwood J, Lynskey MT (1993), Prevalence and comorbidity of *DSM-III-R* diagnoses in a birth cohort of 15 year olds. *J Am Acad Child Adolesc Psychiatry* 32:1127–1134

Fleitlich-Bilyk BW (2002), *The Prevalence of Psychiatric Disorders in 7-14 Year Olds in the South East of Brazil*. PhD thesis, Institute of Psychiatry, London. Available from Professor Robert Goodman, PO85 Department of Child and Adolescent Psychiatry, Institute of Psychiatry, De Crespigny Park, London SE5 8AZ, England

Fombonne E (1994), The Chartres Study 1: prevalence of psychiatric disorders among French school-aged children. *Br J Psychiatry* 164:69–79

Gomez-Beneyto M, Bonet A, Catala MA et al. (1994), Prevalence of mental disorders among children in Valencia, Spain. *Acta Psychiatr Scand* 89:352–357

Goodman R, Yude C, Richards H, Taylor E (1996), Rating child psychiatric caseness from detailed case histories. *J Child Psychol Psychiatry* 37:369–379

Goodman R, Ford T, Richards H et al. (2000), The Development and Well-being Assessment: description and initial validation of an integrated assessment of child and adolescent psychopathology. *J Child Psychol Psychiatry* 41:645–657

Goodman R, Ford T, Meltzer H (2002), Mental health problems of children in the community: 18 month follow up. *Br Med J* 324:1496–1497

Goodman SH, Hoven CW, Narrow WE et al. (1998), Measurement of risk factors for mental disorders and competence in a psychiatric epidemiologic community survey: the National Institute of Mental Health Methods for the Epidemiology of Child and Adolescent Mental Disorders (MECA) study. *Soc Psychiatry Psychiatr Epidemiol* 33:162–173

Kashani JH, Niels CB, Hoeper EW et al. (1987), Psychiatric disorders in a community sample of adolescents. *Am J Psychiatry* 144:584–589

Lewinsohn PM, Hops H, Roberts RE et al. (1993), Adolescent psychopathology, 1: prevalence and incidence of depression and other *DSM-III-R* disorders in high school students. *J Abnormal Psychol* 102:133–144

Market Research Society (1981), Report of the second working party on respondent co-operation: 1977–1980. *J Market Res Soc* 23:3–25

McGee R, Feehan M, Williams S et al. (1990), *DSM-III* disorders in a large sample of adolescents. *J Am Acad Child Adolesc Psychiatry* 29:611–619

Meltzer H, Garward R, Goodman R, Ford T (2000), *Mental Health of Children and Adolescents in Great Britain*. London: The Stationery Office

Offord DR, Boyle MH, Szatmari P et al. (1987), Ontario Child Health Survey II: six-month prevalence of disorder and rates of service utilisation. *Arch Gen Psychiatry* 44:832–836

Roberts R (1998), Prevalence of psychopathology among children and adolescents. *Am J Psychiatry* 155:715–725

Rutter M, Tizard J, Yule W et al. (1976), Isle of Wight Studies, 1964–74. *Psychol Med* 6:313–332

Sanford MN, Offord DR, Boyle MH et al. (1992), Ontario Health Study: social and school impairments. *J Am Acad Child Adolesc Psychiatry* 31:60–67

Schwab-Stone ME, Shaffer D, Dulcan MK et al. (1996), Criterion validity of the NIMH Diagnostic Interview Schedule for Children Version 2.3 (DISC 2.3). *J Am Acad Child Adolesc Psychiatry* 35:878–888

Shaffer D, Fisher P, Dulcan MK et al. (1996), The NIMH Diagnostic Interview Schedule for Children Version 2.3 (DISC-2.3): description, acceptability, prevalence rates and performance in the MECA study. *J Am Acad Child Adolesc Psychiatry* 35:865–877

Simonoff E, Pickles A, Meyer J et al. (1997), The Virginia Twin Study of adolescent behavioural development; influences of age, sex and impairment on rates of disorder. *Arch Gen Psychiatry* 54:801–808

Stata Corporation (1997), *STATA Reference Manual, Release 6, Volume 4, Su-Z*. College Station, TX: Stata Press, pp 15–99

Verhulst FC, van der Ende J, Kasius MC (1997), The prevalence of *DSM-III-R* diagnoses in a national sample of Dutch adolescents. *Arch Gen Psychiatry* 54:326–329

Vikan A (1985), Psychiatric epidemiology in a sample of 1,510 10-year old children 1: prevalence. *J Child Psychol Psychiatry* 26:55–75

World Health Organization (1993), *The ICD-10 Classification of Mental and Behavioural Disorders: Diagnostic Criteria for Research*. Geneva: World Health Organization

[21]

Psychiatric disorder among British children looked after by local authorities: comparison with children living in private households

TAMSIN FORD, PANOS VOSTANIS, HOWARD MELTZER and ROBERT GOODMAN

Background Children looked after by local authorities are at higher risk of poor psychosocial outcomes than children living in private households, but nationally representative and random samples of the two groups of children have not previously been compared.

Aims To find explanations for the increased prevalence of psychiatric disorder in children looked after by local authorities.

Method We examined socio-demographic characteristics and psychopathology by type of placement among children looked after in Britain by local authorities (n=1453), and compared these children with deprived and non-deprived children living in private households (n=10 428).

Results Children looked after by local authorities had higher levels of psychopathology, educational difficulties and neurodevelopmental disorders, and 'looked after' status was independently associated with nearly all types of psychiatric disorder after adjusting for these educational and physical factors. The prevalence of psychiatric disorder was particularly high among those living in residential care and with many recent changes of placement.

Conclusions Our findings indicate a need for greater support of this vulnerable group of children.

Declaration of interest None.

Children and young people who have been looked after by the local authority are at increased risk of poor outcome in terms of child and adult mental health, educational attainment, employment and criminality, yet studies from North America and Europe suggest that they often lack access to appropriate services (Rosenfeld *et al*, 1997; Geen *et al*, 2005; Viner & Taylor, 2005; Browne *et al*, 2006). Despite their high risk, children looked after by local authorities are often excluded from epidemiological studies owing to their high mobility and difficulties surrounding parental responsibility and informed consent (Rosenfeld *et al*, 1997). Understanding how the distribution of potential risk factors in children who are looked after compares with those in children living in private households may provide important clues about aetiology that can be used in targeting interventions (Jenkins, 2001). To our knowledge this is the largest epidemiological study of looked after children, and is unusual in using a random sample and including young people from the full range of placements. We examined the relationships of care-related variables and other correlates to psychiatric disorder and compared children looked after by UK local authorities with children living in private households to look for explanations for the increased prevalence of childhood psychiatric disorder.

METHOD

Samples

We combined data from three surveys of looked after British children and one survey of British children in private households; all these surveys were nationally representative and used the same instruments to assess psychopathology and some of its correlates (Meltzer *et al*, 2000, 2003, 2004*a*,*b*).

Children looked after by local authorities

Random samples of children (aged 5–17 years) looked after by local authorities were selected from the relevant databases in England, Scotland and Wales (Fig. 1). A contact person in each administrative area was sent child summary forms for each child selected from that area. After obtaining whatever consent the local authority deemed necessary, the contact person was responsible for ensuring that the child's social worker completed the information on the child summary forms and for returning the completed forms to the Office for National Statistics.

Similar proportions of children from each country were deemed ineligible, and response rates among eligible children were very high. As previous analysis demonstrated that the prevalence rates of psychiatric disorders were not significantly different between the three countries (Meltzer *et al*, 2004*a*,*b*), and we were not trying to establish an accurate measurement of prevalence but were primarily interested in the association of disorder with correlates, we have combined data from all three surveys without weights. Analyses comparing the children looked after by local authorities with children living in private households excluded looked after children aged 16–17 years (n=290) to fit with the age range in the private household survey.

Private household sample

The child benefit register was used as the sampling frame for England, Wales and Scotland, and 14 250 children were sampled by postal sector. Information was collected on 10 438 (83%) of the 12 529 eligible children, aged 5–15 years 5.5% (790) were ineligible and 6.5% of families (931) opted out (Meltzer *et al*, 2000).

Measures

We used the Development and Well-Being Assessment (DAWBA; Goodman *et al*, 2000) to assess psychiatric disorder in all four surveys. This structured interview was administered by lay interviewers to the parents or carers of all children, and also to the children themselves if they were at least 11 years old, and the interviewers also recorded detailed verbatim descriptions of any problem areas. An abbreviated version was sent to the child's teacher. A small team of experienced clinicians used the information provided by all the informants, combining information as they would in the clinic, to make diagnoses according to ICD–10 criteria (World Health Organization, 1993). In the validation study, the DAWBA provided excellent

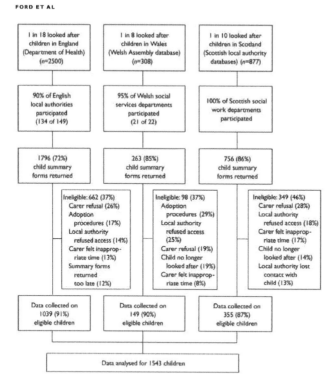

Fig. I Diagram illustrating the sample selection and response rate from the surveys of children looked after by local authorities in England, Wales and Scotland, listing the five main reasons for ineligibility in each country.

worked or worked in unskilled occupations. We tested differences between the three groups using logistic regression to adjust for age and gender, because the children looked after by local authorities were significantly older and more likely to be boys (see Table 2) and the prevalence of childhood psychiatric disorder varied by both these characteristics (Meltzer *et al*, 2000, 2003). As psychological adjustment is more than the presence or absence of a psychiatric disorder, we used the bandings for the carer-completed SDQ to identify particularly well-adjusted children on the basis of scores within the normal range for all of the sub-scales. Finally, we explored the relationship between potential correlates of psychiatric disorder among children looked after by local authorities and the private household survey using logistic regression and used general linear modelling to examine the fit of the data to multiplicative and additive models.

RESULTS

Children looked after by local authorities

Children looked after by local authorities from different types of placement differed significantly in relation to socio-demographic characteristics (Table 1), with a higher proportion of boys in residential care, and of girls and children from Black and minority ethnic groups living independently. Black and minority ethnic children and children from England and Wales were the least likely to be living with their natural parents. Younger children tended to live with kinship carers (mean age 10.5 years 95% CI 9.9–11.0), foster carers (11.8 years, 95% CI 11.5–12.0) or their natural parents (11.2 years, 95% CI 10.7–11.7), whereas adolescents were more likely to be living in residential settings (13.6 years, 95% CI 13.3–13.9) or independently (16.6 years, 95% CI 16.4–16.8); $F=55.4$, $P<0.001$. Placement type also varied by care history, with children who entered the care system in adolescence and more recently most likely to be living in residential care or independently, in contrast to children who were taken into care at a very early age or had been in care for several years, who were more likely to be living in a family placement.

There were also significant differences in the prevalence of psychiatric disorder according to the type of placement, with high

discrimination between community and clinical samples (Goodman *et al*, 2000). Within the community sample, children with DAWBA diagnoses differed markedly from those without such a diagnosis in external characteristics and prognosis, whereas there were high levels of agreement between the DAWBA and case notes among the clinical sample (Kendall's tau $b=0.47$–0.70).

Parents, teachers and children aged 11 years or over also completed the Strengths and Difficulties Questionnaire (SDQ; Goodman, 2001) a well-validated measure of common childhood psychopathology comprising the following scales: total difficulties, emotional symptoms, conduct problems, hyperactivity, peer problems, prosocial behaviour and impact. Parents or carers were asked whether their child suffered from a list of conditions, and the derived variable 'neurodevelopmental disorder' included children reported to have cerebral palsy, epilepsy, muscle disease or

weakness, or coordination problems. Teachers provided data on attainment, an estimate of mental age and reported whether the child had a Statement of Special Educational Needs. Social workers and carers of the children looked after by local authorities provided data on the child's care history.

Analysis

The analysis was conducted using Stata 8 and the Statistical Package for the Social Sciences (SPSS) version 12.01 for Windows. We tested differences in socio-demographic characteristics, diagnosis and placement history according to type of placement using chi-squared tests for categorical variables and one-way analysis of variance for continuous variables, in the whole population of children looked after by local authorities ($n=1543$). We classified children living in private households as disadvantaged if their parents had either never

Table I Socio-demographic characteristics, care history and psychiatric disorder in British children (age 5–17 years) looked after by local authorities, according to type of placement

Characteristic (number of children with data)	Percentage of children in placement					Percentage of all children looked after by local authorities (n=1543)	P[1]
	Foster care (n=839)	Living with natural parents (n=206)	Kinship care (n=168)	Residential care (n=279)	Living independently (n=51)		
Gender (n=1543)							
Male	57.4	56.3	45.8	65.9	51.0	57.4	0.001
Female	42.6	43.7	54.2	34.1	49.0	42.6	
Country (n=1543)							
England	74.0	52.9	54.8	63.8	76.5	67.3	<0.001
Scotland	15.9	38.8	29.8	29.4	19.6	23.0	
Wales	10.1	8.3	15.5	6.8	3.9	9.7	
Ethnic group[2] (n=1529)							
White	89.5	96.6	92.9	90.7	80.4	90.7	0.008
Black	5.4	1.5	3.6	4.3	5.9	4.5	
Other	5.1	1.9	3.6	5.0	13.7	4.8	
Age when first looked after (n=1260)							
<5	31.2	32.7	38.8	16.5	7.9	29.0	<0.001
5–10	49.6	41.5	47.5	43.6	13.2	46.2	
11–15	18.6	25.8	13.7	39.0	68.4	24.0	
16–17	0.7	0	0	0.9	10.5	0.9	
Years in current placement (n=1411)							
<1	31.7	37.3	25.6	50.9	100	35.3	<0.001
1–1.9	22.6	22.2	15.5	24.0	0	22.0	
2–3.9	22.6	23.8	25.6	17.9	0	22.1	
⩾4	23.2	16.7	33.3	7.2	0	20.6	
Placement changes last year (n=1417)							
0	28.1	25.0	30.9	16.3	12.5	25.5	<0.001
1	47.4	50.0	57.9	39.3	32.5	47.0	
2	17.3	18.3	7.2	25.0	25.0	17.9	
⩾3	7.2	6.7	3.9	19.4	30.0	9.6	
Psychiatric disorder[3] (n=1543)							
Yes	38.6	48.1	31.5	71.0	49.0	45.3	<0.001
No	61.4	51.9	68.5	29.0	51.0	54.7	
Emotional disorder (n=1543)							
Yes	9.7	18.0	7.7	18.6	17.6	12.4	<0.001
No	90.3	82.0	92.3	81.4	82.4	87.6	
Conduct disorder (n=1543)							
Yes	32.3	35.9	26.8	61.3	39.2	37.7	<0.001
No	67.7	64.1	73.2	38.7	60.8	62.3	
Hyperkinetic disorder (n=1543)							
Yes	8.5	9.2	6.0	10.0	2.0	8.4	0.26
No	91.5	90.8	94.0	90.0	98.0	91.6	

1. Chi-squared test.
2. Only 12 children were Asian, so this group was assigned to the 'other' category.
3. Psychiatric diagnoses were available for all children looked after by local authorities.

rates of emotional and conduct disorder among children in residential placements or living independently. Hyperkinetic disorder showed a similar trend and the failure to detect a significant association may relate to lack of power and/or the older age of children living in this setting, who would be less likely to have these symptoms. Children with psychiatric disorder entered the care system later (mean age 7.7 years, 95% CI 6.7–7.3, v. 7.0 years, 95% CI 7.3–8.0; $F=8.6$, $P=0.003$), reported more changes in placement within the past 12 months (1.4 changes, 95% CI 1.3–1.5, in those with a psychiatric disorder v. 1.0 changes, 95% CI 0.9–1.1, in those without, $F=39.4$, $P<0.001$), and had lived for less time in their current placement (2.4 years,

95% CI 2.3–2.6 *v.* 3.0 years, 95% CI 2.8–3.1, F=30.4, P<0.003). However, missing data about all three care-related variables varied systematically with the type of placement, in that children living with their natural parents or independently were particularly likely to have missing data (age first looked after χ^2=10.4, d.f.=4, P=0.03; changes of placement within the past year χ^2=879, d.f.=4, P<0.001; duration of current placement χ^2=27.0, d.f.=4, P<0.001). Children with psychiatric disorder were also overrepresented among those

with missing data (χ^2=8.9, d.f.=1, P=0.003).

Comparison of the two groups

Children looked after by local authorities had a higher prevalence of educational and neurodevelopmental difficulties than the disadvantaged and non-disadvantaged children living in private households (Table 2). After adjusting for age and gender, the prevalence of most psychiatric disorders was also significantly higher, whether the

comparison group was all children from private households or just the most disadvantaged children from private households. For most disorders, the highest prevalence was for the children looked after by local authorities and the lowest prevalence was for the non-disadvantaged children from the private households; disadvantaged children from private households generally had intermediate rates.

The proportion of children without a psychiatric disorder who were particularly well adjusted in terms of scoring in the

Table 2 Comparison of children looked after by local authorities with children living in private households

	OR (95% CI)[1]	Prevalence (%)		
		Children looked after by local authorities (*n*=1253)	Disadvantaged private household sample (*n*=761)	Remaining children from the private household sample (*n*=9677)
Socio-demographic variables				
Male		57.1***²,³	45.9*³	50.3
Older (11–15 *v.* 5–10)		59.0***²,³	41.9	43.5
White (*v.* Black or minority ethnic)		91.6	89.8	91.5
Neurodevelopmental disorder		12.8***²,³	4.5	3.3
Statement of special educational needs		23.0***²,³	4.5**³	2.9
Carer report of learning difficulties		36.9***²,³	12.2***³	8.3
Literacy or numeracy problems		34.3***²,³	20.4***³	10.4
Mental age 60% or less of chronological age		10.7***²,³	1.5	1.3
ICD–10 psychiatric diagnosis				
At least one diagnosis	4.92 (4.13–5.85)	46.4***²,³	14.6***³	8.5
Any anxiety disorder	2.09 (1.58–2.76)	11.1***²,³	5.5**³	3.6
Separation anxiety	1.92 (1.05–3.51)	2.0***³	1.7**³	0.7
Specific phobia		1.1	1.1	1.0
Social phobia		0.7	0.5	0.3
Panic disorder		0	0.1	0.1
Post-traumatic stress disorder	11.76 (4.98–27.76)	1.9*²,***³	0.5*³	0.1
Obsessive–compulsive disorder		0.2	0.5	0.2
Generalised anxiety disorder	1.61 (0.78–3.32)	1.9***³	0.9	0.6
Other anxiety disorder	2.86 (1.86–4.39)	4.4**²,***³	1.4	1.2
Depression	2.28 (1.34–3.88)	3.4*²,***³	1.2	0.9
Hyperkinesis	3.90 (2.80–5.42)	8.7**²,³	1.3	1.1
Any behavioural disorder	7.53 (6.21–9.14)	38.9***²,³	9.7***³	4.3
Oppositional defiant	3.60 (1.50–2.66)	12.2***²,³	4.5***³	2.4
Conduct disorder[4]	9.34 (7.26–12.03)	26.7***²,³	5.3***³	1.9
Autistic-spectrum disorder	1.38 (0.68–2.81)	2.6**²,***³	0.1	0.3
Other disorders[5]	1.22 (0.33–4.33)	0.6*²	0.8**³	0.2

1. Adjusted odds ratios for looked after status in relation to living in a private household for disorders with significant differences in prevalence between the two samples, with 95% confidence intervals.
2. Significantly different from disadvantaged children living in private households, using logistic regression to adjust for age and gender.
3. Significantly different from non-disadvantaged children living in private households, using logistic regression to adjust for age and gender using logistic regression.
4. Includes socialised conduct disorder, unsocialised conduct disorder, conduct disorder confined to the family context, or other conduct disorder; but does not include oppositional defiant disorder.
5. Includes tic disorders, eating disorders, stereotypic movement disorders and selective mutism.
*P<0.05, **P<0.01, ***P<0.001.

normal range on all six SDQ sub-scales was 9% (58 of 670) among the looked-after sample as opposed to 41% (265 of 649) among the disadvantaged children and 53% (4619 of 8733) among the rest of the private household sample ($\chi^2=506$, d.f.=2, $P<0.001$).

Complete data on correlates were available for multivariate analysis on 72% of children, but children with a psychiatric disorder ($\chi^2=14.6$, d.f.=1, $P<0.001$) and children who were looked after ($\chi^2=32.7$, d.f.=1, $P<0.001$) were more likely to have missing data on correlates. The odds ratios in Table 2 indicate that looked after status was an independent correlate of all the psychiatric disorders that were more common in this group with the exception of autistic-spectrum disorders and generalised anxiety disorder, even after adjusting for other potential correlates. Looked after status had the strongest association with disorders in which environmental factors are believed to have a leading role, such as post-traumatic stress disorder and conduct disorder. Literacy and numeracy problems were correlates of all disorders except depression among children who were looked after, whereas global learning disability was related only to pervasive developmental disorders and generalised anxiety disorder (more details of this analysis are available from the authors). The relationship of age and gender varied with the different types of psychiatric disorder in the looked after children, as one would predict from epidemiological findings in children living in private households. Thus, older children were more likely to have generalised and other anxiety disorders, post-traumatic stress disorder, depression and conduct disorder, whereas younger children were more likely to have oppositional defiant disorder, hyperkinetic disorder and separation anxiety disorder. Girls were more likely to have post-traumatic stress disorder; boys were more likely to be diagnosed with hyperkinetic disorder, and conduct or oppositional defiant disorder.

Table 3 shows how the influence of looked after status interacted with other correlates in relation to the presence of psychiatric disorder. Looked after status interacted with learning difficulties in an additive way, with learning difficulties resulting in a similar percentage increase in the prevalence of psychiatric disorder in children who were and were not looked after. In contrast, looked after status interacted with gender and age in a

Table 3. Comparison of the impact of four risk factors on rates of psychiatric disorder in children looked after by local authorities and children in private households.

	Prevalence of any ICD–10 psychiatric diagnosis		Interaction	
	Looked after	Private household	Additive model	Multiplicative model
Gender				
Male, %	53.7	10.7		
Female, %	36.6	7.1		
Difference (male — female), %	17.1	3.6	$P<0.001$	
Odds ratio (male:female) (95% CI)	2.01 (1.60–2.52)	1.56 (1.36–1.79)		$P=0.07$
Age				
11–15 years, %	50.1	10.5		
5–10 years, %	41.1	7.6		
Difference (older — younger), %	9.0	2.9	$P=0.0001$	
Odds ratio (older:younger) (95%CI)	1.43 (1.15–1.81)	1.42 (1.24–1.63)		$P=0.9$
Neurodevelopmental difficulties				
Yes, %	58.4	31.8		
No, %	41.6	8.1		
Difference (yes — no), %	16.8	23.7	$P=0.002$	
Odds ratio (yes:no) (95% CI)	1.74 (1.25–2.44)	5.29 (4.18–6.70)		$P<0.001$
Carer-reported learning difficulties				
Yes, %	61.7	29.2		
No, %	37.4	7.1		
Difference (yes–no), %	24.3	22.1	$P=0.3$	
Odds ratio (yes:no) (95% CI)	2.69 (2.12–3.41)	5.41 (4.58–6.39)		$P<0.001$

multiplicative way, with similar odds ratios in children who were and were not looked after. The findings for neurodevelopmental difficulties were intermediate, with an interaction that was more than additive but less than multiplicative.

DISCUSSION

Our study suggests that British children who are looked after by the local authority have a higher prevalence of both psychosocial adversity and psychiatric disorder than the most socio-economically disadvantaged children living in private households, and that care-related variables are strongly related to mental health. The prevalence estimates from the surveys that provided data for this paper ranged from 45% to 49%, falling in the middle of the range of previous estimates of 17% to 89% from other studies conducted in Britain, America and Canada (Wolkind & Rutter, 1973; Stein et al, 1994; McCann et al, 1996; Quinton et al, 1998; Dimigen et al, 1999; Leslie et al, 2000, 2005; dosReis et al,

2001; Farmer et al, 2001; Garland et al, 2001; Meltzer et al, 2003, 2004a,b; Blower et al, 2004; Mount et al, 2004; Rodrigues, 2004; Costello et al, 2005). Some of the variation among the prevalence rates for children looked after by local authorities can be attributed to differences in the date, duration and size of the studies; the measures of psychopathology used; and the age and placement of the children studied. Since psychological adjustment is more than the absence of a psychiatric disorder, it is important to note that even after excluding children with a psychiatric disorder, fewer than one in ten children looked after by local authorities demonstrated particularly good psychological adjustment, compared with around one in two children living in private households. Whether judged categorically or dimensionally, our study showed that children looked after by local authorities had significantly poorer mental health than the most disadvantaged children outside the care system.

Our study also replicates and extends the findings of three North American groups that have compared children in the public care system with disadvantaged children living in private households, all of which reported higher rates of psychopathology in the children looked after in public care (Stein *et al*, 1996; dosReis *et al*, 2001; Farmer *et al*, 2001). Stein *et al* (1996) compared children fostered by the Children's Aid Society with a clinical and a general population sample in Canada. The same correlates (socio-economic deprivation, parental criminality and male gender) predicted psychopathology regardless of group membership. Both our findings and those of Stein *et al* suggest that by the time children are in the care system they have experienced high levels of psychosocial adversity, which provides an explanation for the raised prevalence of some psychiatric disorders. dos Reis *et al* (2001) reported higher rates of mental health service use among children on Medicaid because they were in foster care (62%), compared with groups receiving Medicaid because of physical or psychological disability (29%) or poverty (4%). Fostered children had higher rates of attention-deficit hyperactivity disorder (ADHD), depression and adjustment disorders compared with the other groups. Differences in the types of psychiatric disorders prevalent in different groups of children in that study and in our study provide potential clues about aetiology. Developmental difficulties such as autism and ADHD may be more prevalent among children looked after by local authorities owing to the failure of services to provide adequate support to families trying to cope with these very demanding children. The increment in psychosocial adversity may partially explain the parallel increment in the more environmentally mediated disorders (post-traumatic stress disorder, depression, anxiety and conduct disorder) among the disadvantaged and looked after groups compared with the more advantaged children living in private households. Our findings suggest that age, gender and learning disability act in a similar manner in both populations, with age and gender multiplying the prevalence and learning disability increasing it by a fixed proportion. If these patterns of interaction are replicated by further studies, they may offer clues to psychopathological mechanisms; for example, additive effects may reflect causal pathways in parallel, whereas multiplicative effects may reflect causal pathways in series.

Strengths and limitations

The strengths of this study include data drawn from large population-based samples that used the same methodology and measures administered by the same team of researchers to nationally representative groups of children who were and were not looked after. The sample of children who were looked after included children living in all kinds of placement types, rather than just focusing on foster care, as found in other studies (Stein *et al*, 1996; Phillips, 1997; Quinton *et al*, 1998; Leslie *et al*, 2000; Farmer *et al*, 2001), and did not include children in contact with social services for other reasons (Garland *et al*, 2001; Burns *et al*, 2004).

Unfortunately there were few shared potential correlates between the children looked after by local authorities and those living with private households, limiting our comparison. Such lack of access to historical information is one of the common difficulties of working with and studying children looked after by local authorities, and also makes it difficult to draw conclusions about how far looked after status contributes directly to poor mental health. Children looked after by local authorities had higher levels of educational disadvantage than deprived children living in private households, so the relationship of looked after status to psychiatric disorder might be due to confounding by other aspects of social adversity that we were not able to control for. The fact that children living in residential care were more likely both to have a psychiatric disorder and to have had multiple placements within the past year indicates the problem of studying these factors in cross-sectional studies. Are children with psychiatric disorders more likely than other children to suffer multiple breakdowns in placement and end up in residential placements, or do multiple placements and/or communal living precipitate psychiatric disorder? Although psychological difficulties may be the result of placement instability, it is not unusual for children who are looked after to be referred to mental health services with an undetected psychiatric disorder (Rubin *et al*, 2004). We suspect that both processes are at work, but prospective longitudinal studies are needed to assess their individual impact. In addition, both the care-related variables and educational disadvantage may be markers of abuse, trauma or attachment difficulties that might explain both

the increased prevalence of psychiatric disorder and the poor educational attainment and care history in these children.

Between a third and a half of the original random samples were deemed ineligible, meaning that despite a high response rate respondents might not be representative of children looked after by local authorities. Children undergoing adoption or returned to their parents might be expected to have a lower prevalence of psychiatric disorder, whereas local authority or carer refusal to grant access may be an indicator of poor mental health, making it difficult to estimate how our findings might be influenced by our difficulty in accessing the children looked after by local authorities. Missing data on care-related variables for the looked after children varied systematically by the type of placement, with more missing data on young people living independently or with their natural parents, making the results less reliable in these groups. The disproportionate loss of data on possible correlates among looked after children with psychiatric disorders reduced our power to detect positive associations, but we can be confident of the associations that we have detected. Despite these limitations, our study is one of the largest and most systematic studies of children looked after by local authorities carried out to date.

Clinical and policy implications

Concerns about the unmet needs and poor outcomes of children in the care system in America led to the development of 'treatment foster care' and the increased use of kinship care (Rosenfeld *et al*, 1997; Chamberlain, 2003). Similar initiatives in Iceland, Norway, Slovenia and the UK aim to minimise the number of children in institutional care, but alternatives to institutional care are underutilised in much of the rest of Europe (Browne *et al*, 2006). In Britain, children looked after by local authorities are recognised by the children's National Service Framework (Department of Health, 2004) and *Every Child Matters* (Chief Secretary to the Treasury, 2003) as a group who are particularly vulnerable to psychological difficulties and are often denied access to services, leading to the development of dedicated mental health teams.

Our findings underline the need for services to ensure that the emotional and behavioural difficulties of children looked after by local authorities are understood by professionals working with these children. In some cases, the diagnosis of a psychiatric disorder may provide access to evidence-based treatments and reduce the chance of a placement breaking down. In other cases it might be more appropriate to focus on changing the care or educational environment rather than labelling affected children as psychiatrically disordered. Specialist mental health services need to support other professionals working in this area to minimise the impact of being looked after and to allow a greater proportion of these children to fulfil their potential as adults. This study shows that residential social workers are dealing with many children with serious psychiatric disorders, and yet many have little training or support for the identification and management of these difficulties. Evaluations of treatment foster care suggest that foster carers and social workers could also benefit from this kind of input (Chamberlain, 2003). Given the high levels of educational disadvantage among children looked after by local authorities, and given that carer-reported learning difficulties were frequently an independent predictor of psychiatric disorder, professionals working with this population should try to ensure that these children are provided with suitable school placements and adequate additional support where necessary.

Future research

Our findings suggest that fewer than one in ten of the children looked after by local authorities had positively good mental health and that their substantially increased prevalence of psychiatric disorder was at least partially explained because they had also experienced particularly high levels of psychosocial and educational adversity. However, there was also a strong association between psychiatric disorder and care-related variables. Longitudinal studies of the mental health of children looked after by local authorities are required to tease apart the causal relationship of care-related variables, early physical and psychosocial adversity, and constitutional factors in the child.

TAMSIN FORD, PhD, Institute of Psychiatry, King's College London, PANOS VOSTANIS, MD, Department of Health Sciences, Leicester University, HOWARD MELTZER, PhD, ROBERT GOODMAN, PhD, Institute of Psychiatry, King's College London, London, UK

Correspondence: Dr Tamsin Ford, Box 085, Department of Child and Adolescent Psychiatry, Institute of Psychiatry, De Crespigny Park, London SE5 8AF, UK. Email: t.ford@iop.kcl.ac.uk

(First received 4 April 2006, final revision 13 September 2006, accepted 7 November 2006)

REFERENCES

Blower, A., Addo, A., Hodgson, J., et al (2004) Mental health of children looked after by local authorities: a needs assessment. *Clinical Child Psychology and Psychiatry,* **9**, 117–129.

Browne, K., Hamilton-Giachritsis, C., Johnson, R., et al (2006) Overuse of institutional care for children in Europe. *BMJ,* **322**, 485–487.

Burns, B. J., Phillips, S. D., Wagner, H. R., et al (2004) Mental health need and access to mental health services by youths involved with child welfare: a national survey. *Journal of the American Academy of Child and Adolescent Psychiatry,* **43**, 960–970.

Chamberlain, P. (2003) The Oregon multidimensional treatment foster care model: features, outcomes, and progress in dissemination. *Cognitive and Behavioral Practice,* **10**, 303–312.

Chief Secretary to the Treasury (2003) *Every Child Matters.* TSO (The Stationery Office).

Costello, E. J., Egger, H. & Angold, A. (2005) 10-year research update review: the epidemiology of child and adolescent psychiatric disorders: I. Methods and public health burden. *Journal of the American Academy of Child and Adolescent Psychiatry,* **44**, 972–986.

Department of Health (2004) *National Service Framework for Children, Young People and Maternity Services: The Mental Health and Psychological Well-being of Children and Young People.* TSO (The Stationery Office).

Dimigen, G., Del Priore, C., Butler, S., et al (1999) Psychiatric disorder among children at time of entering local authority care: questionnaire survey. *BMJ,* **319**, 675.

dosReis, S., Zito, J. M., Safer, D., et al (2001) Mental health services for youths in foster care and disabled youths. *American Journal of Public Health,* **91**, 1094–1099.

Farmer, E. M. Z., Burns, B. J., Chapman, M. V., et al (2001) Use of mental health services by youth in contact with social services. *Social Service Review,* **75**, 605–624.

Garland, A. F., Hough, R. L., McCabe, K. M., et al (2001) Prevalence of psychiatric disorders in youths across five sectors of care. *Journal of the American Academy of Child and Adolescent Psychiatry,* **40**, 409–418.

Geen, R., Sommers, A. & Cohen, M. (2005) *Medicaid Spending of Foster Children.* Child Welfare Program Brief No 2. Urban Institute; (http://www.urban.org/uploadedPDF/311221_medicaid_spending.pdf).

Goodman, R. (2001) Psychometric properties of the Strengths and Difficulties Questionnaire (SDQ). *Journal of the American Academy of Child and Adolescent Psychiatry,* **40**, 1337–1345.

Goodman, R., Ford, T., Richards, H., et al (2000) The Development and Well-Being Assessment: description and initial validation of an integrated assessment of child and adolescent psychopathology. *Journal of Child Psychology and Psychiatry,* **41**, 645–657.

Jenkins, R. (2001) Making epidemiology useful: the contribution of epidemiology to government policy. *Acta Psychiatrica Scandinavica,* **103**, 2–14.

Leslie, L. K., Landsverk, J., Loftstrom, R. E., et al (2000) Children in foster care: factors influencing outpatient mental health service use. *Child Abuse and Neglect,* **24**, 465–476.

Leslie, L. K., Gordon, J. N., Meneken, L., et al (2005) The physical, developmental and mental health needs of young children in child welfare by initial placement type. *Developmental and Behavioral Pediatrics,* **26**, 177–185.

McCann, J., James, A., Wilson, S., et al (1996) Prevalence of psychiatric disorders in young people in the care system. *BMJ,* **313**, 1529–1530.

Meltzer, M., Gatward, R., Goodman, R., et al (2000) *Mental Health of Children and Adolescents in Great Britain.* TSO (The Stationery Office).

Meltzer, M., Gatward, R., Corbin, T., et al (2003) *The Mental Health of Young People Looked After by Local Authorities in England.* TSO (The Stationery Office).

Meltzer, H., Lader, D., Corbin, T., et al (2004a) *The Mental Health of Young People Looked After in Scotland.* TSO (The Stationery Office).

Meltzer, H., Lader, D., Corbin, T., et al (2004b) *The Mental Health of Young People Looked After in Wales.* TSO (The Stationery Office).

Mount, J., Lister, A. & Bennun, I. (2004) Identifying the mental health needs of looked after young people. *Clinical Child Psychology and Psychiatry,* **9**, 363–382.

Phillips, J. (1997) Meeting the psychiatric needs of children in foster care. *Psychiatric Bulletin,* **21**, 609–611.

Quinton, D., Rushton, A., Dance, C., et al (1998) *Joining New Families: A Study of Adoption and Fostering in Middle Childhood.* Wiley.

Rodrigues, V. C. (2004) Health of children looked after by the local authorities. *Public Health,* **118**, 370–376.

Rosenfeld, A. A., Pilowsky, D. J., Fine, P., et al (1997) Foster care: an update. *Journal of the American Academy of Child and Adolescent Psychiatry,* **36**, 448–457.

Rubin, D. M., Alessandrini, E. A., Feudtner, C., et al (2004) Placement stability and mental health costs for children in foster care. *Pediatrics,* **113**, 1336–1341.

Stein, E., Rae-Grant, N., Ackland, S., et al (1994) Psychiatric disorders of children 'in care': methodology and demographic correlates. *Canadian Journal of Psychiatry,* **39**, 341–347.

Stein, E., Evans, B., Mazumber, R., et al (1996) The mental health of children in foster care: a comparison with community and clinical samples. *Canadian Journal of Psychiatry,* **41**, 385–391.

Viner, R. M. & Taylor, B. (2005) Adult health and social outcomes of children who have been in public care: population-based study. *Pediatrics,* **115**, 894–899.

Wolkind, S. & Rutter, M. (1973) Children who have been 'in care' — an epidemiological study. *Journal of Child Psychology and Psychiatry,* **14**, 97–105.

World Health Organization (1993) *The ICD–10 Classification of Mental and Behavioural Disorders; Diagnostic Criteria for Research.* WHO.

[22]

Comorbidity

Adrian Angold, E. Jane Costello, and Alaattin Erkanli

Duke University Medical Center, Durham, U.S.A.

We review recent research on the prevalence, causes, and effects of diagnostic comorbidity among the most common groups of child and adolescent psychiatric disorders; anxiety disorders, depressive disorders, attention deficit hyperactivity disorders, oppositional defiant and conduct disorders, and substance abuse. A meta-analysis of representative general population studies provides estimates of the strength of associations between pairs of disorders with narrower confidence intervals than have previously been available. Current evidence convincingly eliminates methodological factors as a major cause of comorbidity. We review the implications of comorbidity for understanding the development of psychopathology and for nosology.

Keywords: Diagnosis, comorbidity, child, adolescent, nosology.

Abbreviations: ADHD: attention deficit hyperactivity disorder; BPD: bipolar disorder; CD: conduct disorder; CI: confidence intervals; ECA: Epidemiologic Catchment Area Study; GAD: generalized anxiety disorder; MDD: major depressive disorder; OAD: overanxious disorder; ODD: oppositional disorders; OR: odds ratios; SAD: separation anxiety disorder.

Introduction

The first quantitative descriptions of general population comorbidity between classes of child and adolescent psychiatric disorders assessed with structured diagnostics appeared only in 1987 (J. C. Anderson, Williams, McGee, & Silva, 1987; Kashani et al., 1987), but since then the number of publications that pay explicit attention to comorbidity has increased exponentially. As a crude index of interest in comorbidity, we conducted a PsycINFO search on the stem "comorb" appearing in the title or abstract fields in citations containing the stems "child" or "adolesc" in any field. No citations appeared for the years before 1986, but in the following years the numbers of citations were: 1986—1, 1987—3, 1988—9, 1989—23, 1990—33, 1991—37, 1992—62, 1993—89, 1994—92, 1995—134, 1996—157, 1997—143. Even this is an underestimate of the increase in attention in comorbidity, first because the PsycINFO database is distinctly patchy in its coverage of the relevant material, and second because it is now commonplace for authors of papers on individual disorders without a special focus on comorbidity to enumerate the rates of other diagnoses in their samples, and to consider the possible impact of comorbidity on their findings. Ten years ago neither of these practices was common. A similar increase in interest in comorbidity is evident in the adult psychiatric literature. It is no accident that in the U.S.A. the most recent national epidemiological study of psychiatric disorders was called the National Comorbidity Survey (Kessler, 1994; Kessler et al., 1994). Indeed, Kendall and Clarkin (1992, p. 833) regard the study of comorbidity as the "premier challenge facing mental health professionals in the 1990s".

As late as 1991, Caron and Rutter (1991), using data from Anderson's work on the Dunedin Longitudinal Study (J. C. Anderson et al., 1987), showed that comorbidity between disorders occurred much more frequently than could be accounted for by the rate of occurrence of the individual disorders in the general population; that is the levels of comorbidity typically seen in the population resulted from *covariation* between disorders (Lilienfeld, Waldman, & Israel, 1994). This is not to say that earlier clinicians and researchers were unaware of the existence of comorbidity. Nothing could be further from the truth; witness the venerable category "mixed disorder of conduct and emotions" in the Tenth Revision of the *International classification of diseases* (ICD-10); or the vast parent questionnaire literature, which showed many years ago that there was substantial overlap among the various factors extracted from large normative samples of children; or work in the 1960s on school phobia showing that depressive symptoms were very common in children with this anxiety disorder (Hersov, 1960a, b). Rather, what has changed is the way in which comorbidity is treated. The purpose of the ICD-10 category of mixed disorder of conduct and emotions was to allow symptomatically mixed states to be allocated a *single* diagnosis. On the other hand, proponents of the factor analytic approach to syndrome definition (e.g. Achenbach, 1966; Arnold & Smeltzer, 1974) developed the idea that patterns of psychopathology were a matter

Requests for reprints to: Adrian Angold, MRCPsych, Developmental Epidemiology Program, DUMC Box 3454, Durham, NC 27710, U.S.A.

of continuous variation along a series of scales, which could, in turn, be grouped together to yield overall levels of psychopathology. From this perspective, comorbidity was seen as an indication of the failure of categorical diagnosis to describe appropriately separable syndromes on the one hand, and an artefact of the failure to recognize the covariation between naturally occurring scalar syndromes on the other.

More recently, the study of comorbidity has begun to emerge as an important task in itself, with the recognition that understanding how comorbidity arises may inform our understanding of the development of psychopathology. In effect, rather than being seen simply as a bothersome problem to be ignored, or an embarrassment to categorical diagnosis, or something to be defined away by the use of combined diagnostic categories, comorbidity has emerged as an opportunity for understanding better the development of psychopathology, and as a potential tool for improving nosology. A number of review articles (see, for example Abikoff & Klein, 1992; Achenbach, 1990, 1995; Angold & Costello, 1993; Caron & Rutter, 1991; Hinshaw, Lahey, & Hart, 1993; Kendall, Kortlander, Chansky, & Brady, 1992; D. N. Klein & Riso, 1993; Loeber & Keenan, 1994; Nottelmann & Jensen, 1995; Rutter, 1997) have detailed the importance of taking comorbidity into account for understanding the etiology, course, and treatment of psychiatric disorders, so we will not repeat their arguments. Several of these contributions have also included long lists of possible explanations for comorbidity, and our aim here is to examine research that has addressed the methodological and substantive issues raised by these lists. We shall begin by attempting to clarify some terminology, then move on to a review and meta-analysis of the evidence for associations between the most common child and adolescent psychiatric disorders. The third part of the paper consists of evidence which indicates that comorbidity is not simply a methodological problem. The penultimate and longest section consists of a series of explorations of research findings on pairs of comorbid diagnoses intended to illustrate ways in which comorbidity has been treated in attempts to understand the causes of psychopathology and to refine nosology. Finally, we offer some recommendations for future research on comorbidity. As we pursue this agenda, we shall consider only the most common disorders of children and adolescents—attention deficit hyperactivity disorders (ADHD), oppositional disorders (ODD), conduct disorders (CD), depressive disorders, anxiety disorders, and substance use and abuse. There are two reasons for this. First, only for these disorders is there clear evidence from general population studies that comorbidity is not an artefact of referral. Second, we cannot think of a disorder in which comorbidity has not been reported, and our aim here is to review approaches to understanding comorbidity, rather than to list every paper that has ever reported rates of comorbidity.

Some Terminology

In this section we consider some terms that we think are helpful in talking about comorbidity, and another term that we think is unhelpful.

Disorder and Disease Comorbidity

In many branches of medicine, interest in comorbidity centers on the co-occurrence of two (or more) different *diseases*; for instance, comorbidity between carcinoma of the bronchus and chronic bronchitis. In such cases each individual disease is well established in its own right. Both carcinoma of the bronchus and chronic bronchitis are relatively well defined as clinical entities, their etiologies and pathophysiologies are known to be quite different, and they are treated quite differently. In child and adolescent psychiatry our disease categories are much less well established. We deal mostly with *disorders*, that is, behavioral and psychological syndromes that are deviant from some standard of normality (Angold, 1988). This is an important distinction, because comorbidity between disorders may imply that there is a problem with the classification system, rather than any meaningful association between underlying diseases indexed by that classification. The fact that we are not dealing with clearly validated disease entities does not, however, mean that there is no point studying psychiatric comorbidity. Indeed, the opposite is the case, since understanding the presence of comorbidity between psychiatric conditions offers a means of correcting and validating psychiatric nosology. The key point is that the study of comorbidity does not depend upon the existence of well-validated disease entities, but may actually be particularly informative in the case of poorly validated disorders. If diseases represent the "well-validated" subset of disorders, then the set of explanations of disorder comorbidity is a *superset* of the set of possible explanations of disease comorbidity.

Homotypic vs. Heterotypic Comorbidity

Developmental psychopathologists are used to the concepts of homotypic and heterotypic continuity. The first refers to continuity of some phenomenon over time in a form that changes relatively little. For instance, the fact that depressed adolescents are more likely than nondepressed adolescents to be depressed in adulthood points to a degree of homotypic continuity in depression. Heterotypic continuity, on the other hand, refers to a continuous process that generates manifestations of *different* forms over time. Thus, the finding from the Dunedin Longitudinal Study (McGee, Feehan, Williams, & Anderson, 1992) that disruptive behaviour disorders in girls predicted emotional disorders several years later is evidence for heterotypic continuity between disruptive and emotional disorders in girls. By analogy, studies of comorbidity may be seen as being of two types: (1) those that examine comorbidity between disorders within a diagnostic grouping (such as the co-occurrence of major depression and dysthymia), and (2) those that deal with comorbidity between disorders from different diagnostic groupings (such as depression and conduct disorder). We propose to call the first studies of *homotypic comorbidity* and the second studies of *heterotypic comorbidity*. Just as there is no hard and fast rule about just how similar states have to be over time to be called examples of homotypic continuity, so there can be no rigid distinction between homotypic and heterotypic comorbidity. Nonetheless, the distinction is useful because the implications of these two types of comorbidity tend to be rather different, and they are rarely addressed in the same paper.

Familial Comorbidity

Comorbidity occurs not only within individuals; it also occurs within families. For instance, relatives of children with ADHD have higher rates of antisocial personality disorder, hysteria, alcoholism and substance dependence, and unipolar depression (Biederman et al., 1992; Biederman, Faraone, Keenan, Knee, & Tsuang, 1990; Cantwell, 1972; McCormick, 1995; Morrison, 1980). The children of depressed parents clearly have elevated rates of depression compared to the children of the non-depressed, but they are also at higher risk of having anxiety and disruptive behavior disorders (Beardslee et al., 1996; Beidel & Turner, 1997; Decina et al., 1983; Gershon et al., 1985; Grigoroiu-Serbanescu et al., 1991; Grigoroiu-Serbanescu, Christodorescu, Totoescu, & Jipescu, 1991; Hammen, 1992; Hammen et al., 1987; D. W. Klein & Depue, 1985; Last, Hersen, Kazdin, Francis, & Grubb, 1987; Lewinsohn, Hops, Roberts, Seeley, & Andrews, 1993; J. M. McClellan, Rubert, Reichler, & Sylvester, 1990; Merikangas, Prusoff, & Weissman, 1988; Moreau, Weissman, & Warner, 1990; Morrison & Stewart, 1971; Nurnberger et al., 1988; Orvaschel, 1990; Orvaschel, Walsh-Allis, Ye, & Walsh, 1988; Sylvester, Hyde, & Reichler, 1988; Turner, Beidel, & Costello, 1987; Warner, Mufson, & Weissman, 1995; Weissman, Fendrich, Warner, & Wickramaratne, 1992; Welner, Welner, McCrary, & Leonard, 1977). Children of parents with "pure" anxiety disorders have been found to have little but anxiety disorders, whereas those with depressed or mixed anxious-depressed parents have a much wider range of disorders (Beidel & Turner, 1997). Whether these effects are attributable to genes or environments or both, consideration of comorbidity has proved to be very important for family genetic studies of psychopathology. As we shall see below, family genetic methods provide some powerful tools for unraveling the meaning of patterns of comorbidity observed in individuals. However, it should not be supposed that shared risk necessarily implies that what were thought to be two disorders are in reality one. The often quoted example of the various disease risks associated with smoking serves here (e.g. Rutter, 1994). No-one wants to claim that chronic bronchitis and myocardial infarction are the same disease, though both occur much more frequently in smokers. But, to pursue the analogy a little further, what about atherosclerotic stroke and myocardial infarction? In this case, there are many similarities in pathogenesis, but the affected organ varies. We could argue that these are alternative manifestations of the same disease, but from the perspective of differential diagnosis in the emergency room, it is more helpful to be thinking about "diseases of the brain" when a stroke patient comes in, and "diseases of the heart" when the patient complains of crushing central chest pain. Certainly the treatment of the two conditions will differ in many ways. The point here is that "diseases" are not obvious "natural" categories in any branch of medicine (D. N. Klein & Riso, 1993), and that boundary problems abound in

relation to medical disease, just as they do in mental disease. Rather, diseases (or disorders) are groupings of phenomena established over time by their utility for describing and organizing those phenomena and responses to them. Furthermore, comorbidity between entirely "unrelated" physical diseases is very common, especially in older adults. We are now used to data reporting *lifetime* rates of psychiatric comorbidity. How many of us have *not* had at least two different sorts of physical disease in our lives? In old age, simultaneous comorbidity is also the norm, as any family practitioner know. For instance, most 90-year-old men with osteo-arthritis will also have prostate cancer. So there is nothing particularly special about comorbidity among psychiatric disorders in this respect.

If we were to find that some pair of disorders, say depression and anxiety, was associated with identical risk factors, brain correlates, relapse rates, and treatment responses, insofar as it was in our power to measure them, perhaps it would be right to call them instances of the same disorder. But that would still leave unanswered the important question of why some people present with this disorder in the form of a major depression, whereas others never have such an episode. It is hard to believe that the phenomenological differences between depressed and anxious people are generated by some purely random process, and even if they were, we would still want to know where the "randomizer" was and how it worked. Thus, even if many, or even all, examples of "comorbidity" turn out to be alternative expressions of some unitary underlying psychopathological process or processes, the phenomenon currently called "comorbidity" will still need explaining.

Concurrent vs. Successive Comorbidity

One problem with the term "comorbidity" is that it has been used to include a multitude of different temporal relationships amongst disorders. Whereas some child and adolescent studies have considered disorders co-occurring over a relatively short span of time, others have reported rates of co-occurrence over 6 months, 1 year, 3 years, or the individual's lifetime to date. Clearly such different time spans will allow very different types of temporal relationships between comorbid disorders. For instance, comorbidity between current disorders at the time of assessment means that both must be present at the same time. Although their times of onset and offset may not be coterminous, during some period they must have been present concurrently. We propose to label such co-occurrence *concurrent comorbidity*. The two disorders "run together", perhaps not only in time but in phenomenology.

When considering reports of lifetime comorbidity, the disorders in question may never have been present simultaneously, but may have occurred widely separated in time. When two disorders do not overlap in time, we suggest that the term *successive comorbidity* could be used. At least it would be helpful to know more about the degree to which comorbidity represents the occurrence of multiple disorders in succession as opposed to multiple disorders occurring at the same points in time. Data from the Oregon Adolescent Depression Project (Rohde,

Lewinsohn, & Seeley, 1991) indicate that current (and, therefore, necessarily *con*current) and lifetime co-morbidity rates can be very different. For instance, they found that the odds ratio (OR) for current comorbidity between unipolar depression and any other diagnosis was 9.6; that for lifetime comorbidity was only 2.8. This implies that adolescents who had formerly been de-pressed, but were not currently depressed, were unlikely also to have had other disorders. However, studies of rates of concurrent comorbidity in younger children do not support this implication (see Table 3). This suggests that lifetime recall probably underestimates comorbidity rates quite substantially. One obvious problem here is that estimates of lifetime comorbidity rely upon indi-viduals remembering the symptoms of two separate disorders. The only way to avoid this apparent problem is to measure concurrent and successive comorbidity *pro-spectively* in longitudinal studies.

Primary vs. Secondary Disorders

The distinction between primary and secondary de-pressions was introduced by Woodruff, Murphy, and Herjanic (1967), and has been taken up by some child and adolescent researchers (G. A. Carlson & Cantwell, 1979, 1980; R. C. Friedman, Hurt, Clarkin, & Corn, 1983; Geller, Chestnut, Miller, Price, & Yates, 1985; Puig-Antich, 1982). A primary affective disorder is one occurring in a person who has not had a preceding nonaffective psychiatric illness. A secondary affective disorder is one occurring in a patient who has had a preexisting, diagnosable, nonaffective, psychiatric illness. However, we find that this is a confusing terminological distinction because it diverges from the meanings of primary and secondary in medicine in general and reduces the complex issue of relationships over time to a di-chotomy. In the rest of medicine, a secondary condition is *caused* by a primary condition. For instance, renal failure secondary to a myocardial infarction generally results from hypoperfusion of the kidneys caused by a cata-strophic drop in blood pressure following the infarction. No-one would think of calling a heart attack secondary to chicken pox just because the latter occurred first. The issue of whether a later-occurring psychiatric disorder is caused by an earlier disorder is one we shall take up later, but so far none of the common psychiatric co-morbidities has been shown to result from one disorder causing another. The second problem with the primary/secondary distinction is that it is a poor representation of the complex questions concerning timing that are key to developmental psychopathology. We seek to identify characteristic pathological processes that operate over developmental time, and just finding out which disorder occurred first hardly does justice to this quest (although it may be a start).

The Uses of General Population Surveys and Clinical Studies in Research on Comorbidity

In this section we consider the pros and cons of using clinical and community-based samples to provide in-formation about comorbidity. Many of studies of co-morbidity in clinical samples have been published re-cently, making it imperative that we clearly understand the limitations of clinical samples for this purpose. The problem, of course, is that clinical samples are anything but representative of individuals with the disorder in the general population. Individuals presenting to specialty treatment settings have more severe symptomatology, are more impaired, and come from families that feel more burdened by their children's problems, than are indiv-iduals with psychiatric disorders who do not present for treatment (see, e.g., Angold, Messer, et al., 1998). In the Great Smoky Mountains Study, a community study of children's mental health service use, we found that comorbid individuals were more than twice as likely to be receiving psychiatric services as individuals with only a single diagnosis (Costello et al., 1996).

This means that clinical studies are of no use for providing unbiased prevalence or incidence rates of comorbidity, or unbiased estimates of risk factors for comorbidity. The only exception to this rule occurs when most individuals with a disorder can be expected to present for treatment. So, for instance, a local or regional autism treatment program might have among its patients a reasonably representative sample of autistic people, but even where there is no referral bias whatsoever, clinical samples will produce *incorrect* estimates of the strength of the association between disorders. We point this out because some studies of clinical samples have reported that there was no greater association than expected by chance between particular pairs of disorder, and these results have then been quoted by others and contrasted with other studies where a significant association was found. Consider a neater world than ours, where there were just three disorders, A, B, and C, each of which occurred in 10% of the population. A always occurs alone. Half of those with B also have C, and half of those with C have B. If we were to take a general population sample of 100 people, we would expect to see the relationship between B and C appearing as in Table 1. From this table we can compute a joint odds ratio describing the strength of the relationship between B and C. It yields an OR value of 17. With a sample of 100, this is a highly significant effect ($p = .0003$).

Now suppose that we have a perfect clinical system

Table 1

Hypothetical Co-distribution of B and C in 100 Children in the General Population

	C absent	C present
B absent	85	5
B present	5	5

Table 2

Resulting Co-distribution of B and C in 100 Children in the Perfect Clinic

	C absent	C present
B absent	40	20
B present	20	20

that identifies all individuals with a disorder and leaves out everyone without a disorder. In other words, there is no referral bias whatsoever. Given the population base rates, we expect 40% of clinic patients to have nothing but A, and 60% to have B or C or both. Let us now take a clinic sample of 100 children and look at the relationship between B and C; it will be as shown in Table 2. Notice that in Table 2 we have exactly *correct* estimates of the *proportions* of individuals with B who also have C and vice versa, because there is no Berkson's bias or referral bias. However, when we compute the joint OR, it is only 2 and this is "not significant" ($p = .1$). Even in this perfect world an attempt to estimate the strength or "statistical significance" of associations between disorders from clinical populations is misleading. We have, therefore, not considered clinic-based studies in our discussion of the strengths of associations between disorders.

Given this unavoidable situation, what use are clinical samples for the study of comorbidity? The answer is that they are very useful when their limitations are appreciated:

(1) When the target groups to which one wishes to generalize one's results are other clinical samples, then clinical research may provide more useful information than will general population studies. For instance, the clinical literature on comorbidity of depression with other diagnoses has indicated that, in clinical settings, when an individual presents with CD it is important to make a careful assessment of the possibility that the individual is also suffering from depression (Puig-Antich, 1982).

(2) When a disorder is rare, there may be no epidemiological studies of sufficient scale to inform us about its associations with other disorders. In these circumstances, clinical studies may provide the only available data on associations with other disorders. For instance, there is a dearth of diagnostic general population studies of comorbidity in obsessive-compulsive disorder or the eating disorders. The clinical data, however, indicate that these are conditions associated with considerable diagnostic comorbidity, and thereby point to the need for general population studies to address this issue in relation to their etiologies and development. Even when a disorder is relatively common, there may simply be no general population data published on its associations with other disorders. None of the recent diagnostic general population studies has, for instance, reported rates of comorbidity with enuresis. Here clinical studies provide an important laboratory for the development of hypotheses about the nature of individual disorders and the associations between disorders.

However, one must remain aware that in clinic samples apparent correlates of disorder may actually be correlates of *referral* rather than true associations with the disorder itself. An example is the association between ADHD and mania. Farone et al. (1997b) have said that the "co-occurrence of attention deficit hyperactivity disorder (ADHD) and bipolar disorder (BPD) is not a rare event. Clinical studies of children and adolescents show that rates of ADHD range from 57% to 98% in bipolar patients (Borchardt & Berstein, 1995; Geller, Sun, Zimmerman, Frazier, & Williams, 1995; West, McElroy, Strakowski, Keck, & McConville, 1995; West et al., 1996; Wozniak et al., 1995) and rates of BPD range from 11% to 22% in ADHD patients (Biederman, Faraone, & Mick, 1996; Butler, Arredondo, & McCloskey, 1995)". In his commentary on the Faraone et al. paper, Werry (1997) points out that "we do not want to see a massive overdiagnosis of ADHD as BPD, nor as comorbid disorders" (see also J. McClellan, 1998). If we take as the proposed rate of BPD in ADHD the mean of the two available estimates, we have a rate of 16.5%. If we take the general population rate of DSM ADHD to be 5%, then we would expect the rate of comorbid mania and ADHD in the general population to be 0.825%. The National Comorbidity Survey (Kessler et al., 1994) gives the lifetime prevalence of mania as 1.6%. If these clinical rates are correct, then over half of the lifetime cases of disorders involving mania have already had their onsets by late childhood, in association with ADHD. Of course, this is not impossible, but it would mean that the estimates of lifetime rates of BPD, estimated in the Oregon Adolescent Depression Project at two time points 1 year apart, for older adolescents, of 0.58% and 0.72%, were underestimates of the total lifetime prevalence of BPD by late adolescence. It would also suggest that all or nearly all cases of BPD would have had ADHD, whereas only 11% did so (Lewinsohn, Klein, & Seeley, 1995). As we have seen, even the clinical studies of juvenile BPD do not support this contention. In the Great Smoky Mountains Study (Costello et al., 1996), only 6 children or adolescents out of 1420 were observed to have been in a manic or hypomanic episode during the 3 months preceding any 1 of 4 annual interviews (a weighted population prevalence rate of 0.41%), whereas 92 (weighted 3.4%) met criteria for ADHD in at least one wave. Only one subject had both a manic episode and met criteria for ADHD, giving weighted population estimates of 0.9% for the rate of mania in those with ADHD (vs. 0.39% in those without ADHD), and a rate of 7% for ADHD in those with mania (vs. 3% in those without mania). Neither of these studies proves that there is no association between ADHD and BPD; indeed, given the ubiquity of comorbidity amongst other diagnoses, it would be surprising if there were not. They do, however, seriously challenge the notion that "co-occurrence of attention deficit hyperactivity disorder (ADHD) and bipolar disorder (BPD) is not a rare event". Both studies indicate that the co-occurrence of these disorders in the general population is a *very rare* event. On the other hand it is easy to see how their co-occurrence would be very likely to result in referral to specialist services at a major center with a particular interest in such problems. The point here is not to condemn clinical studies of rates of comorbidity, but to sound a warning about their interpretation. In following up this question, Faraone and his colleagues (Faraone et al., 1997b) have produced evidence from a family study that comorbid ADHD and BPD may indeed be familially distinct from other forms of ADHD. It may be rare, but at present it appears that it does exist. As we have already said, in the absence of epidemiologic data, such clinical studies can be an important stimulus to research.

(3) When one is concerned with identifying potential risk factors, case-control designs are often appropriately employed. Cases of a particular disorder may be identified from clinical samples and compared with "normal" controls and/or cases of other disorders and/or cases of mixed disorders. Some very informative work about the implications or comorbidity (see below) has been done in this way. As always, the concern is the degree to which the findings from such studies generalize to the whole universe of cases of the disorders in question. One must recognize that clinical research of this sort may be quite misleading. The classic example is given by Berkson (1946), who showed that the supposed association between gall bladder disease and diabetes, which had led some to undertake cholecystectomies for the treatment of diabetes, was the spurious statistical result of the independent disease-specific probabilities for treatment (note that Berkson's bias does *not* refer either to "selection bias" or to situations in which comorbidity results in a probability of treatment for comorbid cases that is higher than expected on the basis of the individual disease-specific probabilities for treatment). On the other hand, it would be foolish to ignore the results of clinical research on comorbidity on the grounds that the results are almost certain to suffer from unknown effects of sampling bias. The proper response is to recognize the problems and move on to research designs that overcome them. Indeed, in a number of areas, the clinical studies of comorbidity have pushed well ahead of the general population data, and epidemiologists need to be refocused from documenting rates of association between disorders on to considering the implications of those associations for etiology and development.

(4) Very little developmental epidemiological work has been done on the implications of comorbidity for the development and outcomes of psychiatric disorders. With the same caveats as already mentioned, a group of interesting clinical studies is the source for most of the work in this important area. Diagnostic, longitudinal, general population studies large enough to allow the identification of effects of the presence of one disorder upon another are expensive and time-consuming to conduct, difficult to keep funded, and very thin on the ground. It is to be hoped that those that do exist will be used to address some of the comorbidity issues raised by the rapidly expanding clinical literature.

The Contribution of "Empirically Derived Syndromes" to the Study of Comorbidity

Before moving on to a review of the literature on comorbidity based on the DSM in its various recent revisions (American Psychiatric Association, 1980, 1987, 1994), we briefly consider two other lines of research, one using symptom scales, and the other the ICD (World Health Organization, 1993) taxonomy.

A very large body of literature based on parent questionnaires has established at least seven highly replicable factor-analytically derived syndromes that can be applied to boys and girls of all ages. The most frequently used version identifies seven syndromes found in both genders (aggressive, anxious/depressed, attention problems, delinquent, schizoid, somatic complaints, and withdrawn), and two gender-specific syndromes labeled socially inept (boys) and mean (girls) (Achenbach, Conners, Quay, Verhulst, & Howell, 1989). These "narrow-band syndromes" can be grouped statistically into two "broad-band syndromes" labeled "internalizing" and "externalizing", which correspond broadly to what have long been called emotional and behavioral disorders. It is also well established that the internalizing and externalizing syndromes are correlated with one another (Garnefski & Diekstra, 1997; McConaughy & Achenbach, 1994). In other words, there is unassailable evidence of "comorbidity" between statistically derived syndromes.

Looking within syndromes, we also see that they often do not conform to the structure of individual diagnoses in the ICD or DSM systems. For instance, the aggressive syndrome includes "ADHD" items like talking too much and impulsivity, and mood-related items like sulking, irritability, and changeable mood; the anxious/depressed syndrome includes, as its name suggests, a mixture of depressive and anxiety symptoms; the delinquent syndrome includes use of alcohol and drugs; the withdrawn syndrome includes depressed mood and anxiety symptoms like shyness and self-consciousness. Thus, within syndromes we see that the statistical structure of symptomatology implies what, from a diagnostic perspective, is called comorbidity. Whether one looks across or within statistically derived psychopathological syndromes, there are structural relationships indicating that such syndromes are not statistically independent of one another and that the content of individual syndromes consists of mixtures of different "types" of symptoms. All this was clearly established before the child and adolescent diagnostic literature began to pay much serious research attention to comorbidity as a topic for investigation.

The Contribution of ICD-based Studies

The Isle of Wight and associated epidemiological studies (Graham & Rutter, 1973; Rutter, Tizard, & Whitmore, 1970), which pioneered the use of structured psychiatric interviewing in epidemiological studies of child psychopathology, used a taxonomy based on the ICD; one that differed from DSM-III in several ways. Most important for our discussion here is the use of a specific "mixed disorder" category for children defined by the presence of both conduct disorder and emotional or neurotic disorders. Mixed disorder was the third most common diagnosis in this population when the children were first interviewed at age 10 to 11 years (Rutter & Graham, 1966) and also when the children were re-interviewed at age 14–15 years (Graham & Rutter, 1973). Mixed disorder was diagnosed 14 times more often than would be expected from the prevalence of the separate disorders at age 10–11, and 8 times more often at age 14–15. In a similar study carried out in an inner-London borough, all disorders were diagnosed more frequently than on the Isle of Wight, while mixed disorders were three times more common than expected by chance.

Similar findings were reported from a partial replication of the Isle of Wight study carried out in Mannheim, Germany, on 1486 children born in 1970. Mixed disorders were nine times more common than expected by chance at age 8, and four times more common at age 13, when they were the third most common diagnosis (Esser, Schmidt, & Woerner, 1990; Laucht & Schmidt, 1987). Vikan (1985), using the Isle of Wight interview and the ICD classification with 1510 Norwegian children, also reported that mixed disorders were the third most prevalent diagnosis; more frequent than the prevalence of either conduct or neurotic disorders alone would predict. Fombonne's French study (1994) gives numbers of children with mixed disorders of conduct and emotions suggesting that comorbidity occurred much more frequently than chance would predict, but because of sampling stratification and the need to use weights for computing prevalence and co-occurrence statistics, this cannot be confirmed from the reported data.

Thus, long before the advent of the DSM-III, comorbidity was recognized as being so much a feature of child and adolescent psychopathology that it was not regarded as "comorbidity" in the sense of an association between disorders, but as the basis for a particular class of disorders.

Rates of Diagnostic Comorbidity from General Population Surveys Using the DSM

In this section we review the literature on comorbidity generated by the use of the DSM, in its three most recent editions.

Table 3 lists recent community studies that have used standardized psychiatric interviews with parents and children to generate diagnoses according to the DSM-III, DSM-III-R, or DSM-IV and have reported rates of comorbidity between disorders in such a way as to permit us to determine the joint OR for the pairs of disorders or types of disorder. We concentrate on four types of disorder: depressive disorders, anxiety disorders, ADHD, and ODD and CD—all but two studies provided only figures for combined ODD/CD. Most studies did not provide data on substance abuse disorders, so these are omitted. One paper on comorbidity from the Oregon Adolescent Depression Project (Lewinsohn et al., 1993) reported lifetime comorbidity rates for a combined diagnostic group including ADHD, ODD, and CD, and so those results have not been reported in the table;

rather, we have used the current diagnostic data reported in Rohde et al. (1991), where CD and ODD were combined, apparently without ADHD, which they do not consider at all. Here obsessive-compulsive disorders were included in the anxiety disorders group, but since these were very uncommon compared with other anxiety disorders (Lewinsohn et al., 1993), we did not allow this difference from other studies to preclude anxiety comorbidity data from this study from inclusion in Table 3. The report from the Virginia Twin Study of Adolescent Behavioral Development (Simonoff et al., 1997) also presented some problems for this analysis. First, raw data on comorbidity rates were only presented for a subset of the combinations considered here. Though OR and confidence intervals (CI) for a wider range of combinations are provided, these also did not consider groupings of diagnoses that parallel those in most other studies. Data on CD and ODD were reported separately and we selected the more prevalent of the two disorders (CD) to represent this grouping. Similarly, separation anxiety disorder, overanxious disorder, simple phobia, agoraphobia, and social phobia were all reported separately. Again we chose the most prevalent (overanxious disorder) to represent the anxiety disorders. In all cases relating to this study we considered rates of comorbidity for diagnoses associated with impairment (separate figures for diagnoses without impairment were also reported by these authors).

The two pioneering papers in this literature (Anderson et al., 1987; Kashani et al., 1987) employed the very helpful practice of presenting their comorbidity data in the form of Venn diagrams, with the numbers of individuals in each pure or comorbid group. The publications associated with the Dunedin study have continued the practice. The critical issue here is not the diagram (although it is a convenient and comprehensible way to present data that otherwise require a relatively complex contingency table), but the provision of all the information pertinent to calculating correlational statistics and their CI. Formal tests of whether comorbidity exceeds the level expected by chance are rare in the published literature. Bird and his colleagues computed the phi agreement statistic (the equivalent of the Pearson correlation coefficient for a 2-by-2 table). Caron and Rutter (1991) showed that the association of disorders was much higher than that expected by chance for the 11-year-olds from the Dunedin Study. Drs Hector Bird and Patricia Cohen kindly computed associational statistics from their datasets for inclusion in our 1985 review of depressive comorbidity (Angold & Costello, 1993), and those figures have been included here, and the contributions from the Virginia Twin Study (Simonoff et al., 1997) and the Christchurch Health and Development Study (Fergusson, Horwood, & Lynskey, 1993a) provided CI around OR for comorbidity. We computed all the other ORs and CI in the table from data provided in the relevant papers. Since several studies have reported separately on comorbidity from different waves of data collection, we broke out data from the Great Smoky Mountains Study by wave, although elsewhere comorbidity in this study has been reported across waves (Angold, Erkanli, Egger, & Costello, 1998). We strongly recommend that papers on comorbidity include all the

Table 3

Rates of Diagnosis and Comorbidity in General Population Studies

Study (DSM)	N	Age	Time frame	Pop. rate of a (%)	b (%)	Rate of a in b (%)	not b (%)	Rate of b in a (%)	not a (%)	OR	CI	p
a = ADHD, b = CD/ODD												
1 (III)	792	11	1 yr	6.7	9.1	34.7	4.4	47.2	7.1	11.6	6.3–21.5	***
2 (III)	943	15	1 yr	2.1	9.0	4.7	1.9	20.0	8.8	2.6	0.9–8.0	***
5 (III)	278	7–11	6 mo	2.3	9.8	13.0	1.2	54.6	8.7	12.6	3.6–44.1	***
6 (IIIR)	278	12–18	6 mo	12.2	13.9	41.0	7.5	46.9	9.4	8.6	3.8–48.7	***
11 (III)	222	9–16	6 mo	10.0	10.5	35.7	—	93.0	—	phi = .47	—	***
12 (IIIR)	1015	9–13	3 mo	1.9	5.2	11.8	1.3	33.3	4.7	10.2	4.5–22.3	***
13 (IV)	970	10–14	3 mo	1.0	4.8	7.5	0.69	35.5	4.5	11.7	4.9–28.2	***
14 (IV)	928	11–15	3 mo	0.9	3.3	5.8	0.7	22.1	3.1	8.7	2.0–37.9	**
15 (IV)	820	12–16	3 mo	0.6	2.9	3.1	0.6	13.9	3.6	5.6	0.7–44.6	n.s.
16 (IIIR)	323	9–13	3 mo	1.3	6.6	4.8	1.0	25.0	6.3	4.9	0.5–49.6	n.s.
17 (IV)	317	10–14	3 mo	1.3	8.3	7.7	0.7	50.0	7.7	11.9	1.6–88.4	*
18 (IV)	304	11–15	3 mo	1.0	5.0	13.3	0.35	67.0	4.4	43.7	3.7–513	**
19 (IV)	289	12–16	3 mo	0.4	4.2	8.3	0.0	100.0	3.9	—	—	—
20 (IIIR)	986	15	6 mo	4.8	10.8	—	—	—	—	26.8	13.7–52.4	*
21 (IIIR)	2762	8–16	3 mo	1.4	4.3	—	—	—	—	3.2	0.9–8.7	n.s.
a = ADHD, b = Depression												
1 (III)	792	11	1 yr	6.7	1.8	57.1	6.5	15.1	0.91	19.3	6.4–58.2	***
2 (III)	943	15	1 yr	2.1	4.2	2.5	2.1	5.0	4.2	1.2	0.2–9.1	n.s.
5 (III)	278	7–11	1 yr	2.3	1.6	13.5	2.2	9.1	1.4	7.1	0.7–72.9	n.s.
6 (IIIR)	278	12–18	6 mo	12.2	4.2	25.2	11.6	8.7	3.6	2.6	0.8–8.3	n.s.
7 (IIIR)	776	9–18	1 yr	12.0	3.4	46.2	10.8	12.9	2.1	7.1	3.7–16.5	***
8 (IIIR)	776	11–20	1 yr	7.6	2.8	22.7	7.2	8.5	2.3	3.8	1.3–10.9	**
11 (III)	222	9–16	6 mo	10.0	8.0	13.0	—	44.5	—	37.1	—	**
12 (IIIR)	1015	9–13	3 mo	1.9	1.5	15.5	1.6	12.8	1.3	11.1	3.6–33.3	***
13 (IV)	970	10–14	3 mo	1.0	3.0	2.4	1.0	7.2	3.0	2.5	0.5–11.7	n.s.
14 (IV)	928	11–15	3 mo	0.9	3.2	3.5	0.8	13.2	3.1	7.7	1.0–22.5	n.s.
15 (IV)	820	12–16	3 mo	0.6	2.7	0.0	0.7	0.0	2.7	—	—	—
16 (IIIR)	323	9–13	3 mo	1.3	0.31	0.0	1.3	0.0	0.32	—	—	—
17 (IV)	317	10–14	3 mo	1.3	1.6	40.0	0.7	50.0	1.0	102.0	10.6–987	***
18 (IV)	304	11–15	3 mo	1.0	4.3	7.7	0.7	33.3	4.0	11.9	1.0–140	*
19 (IV)	289	12–16	3 mo	0.4	1.8	0.0	0.4	0.0	1.8	—	—	—
20 (IIIR)	986	15	6 mo	4.8	6.6	—	—	—	—	4.5	2.1–9.6	*
21 (IIIR)	2762	8–16	3 mo	1.4	1.2	—	—	—	—	1.7	0.0–10.4	n.s.
a = ADHD, b = Anxiety												
1 (III)	792	11	1 yr	6.7	7.4	23.7	6.0	26.4	6.8	4.9	2.5–9.7	***
2 (III)	943	15	1 yr	2.1	10.7	4.0	1.9	20.0	10.5	2.1	0.7–6.5	n.s.
5 (III)	278	7–11	1 yr	2.3	15.4	5.5	1.8	36.4	14.9	3.3	1.0–11.7	n.s.
6 (IIIR)	278	12–18	6 mo	12.2	14.4	21.1	10.7	25.0	13.0	2.2	1.0–5.1	n.s.
11 (III)	222	9–16	6 mo	10.0	—	22.0	—	50.8	—	phi = .16	—	*
12 (IIIR)	1015	9–13	3 mo	1.9	5.5	4.3	1.7	12.8	5.3	2.6	1.0–6.7	*
13 (IV)	970	10–14	3 mo	1.02	3.7	4.7	0.9	17.2	3.6	5.6	1.9–16.2	**
14 (IV)	928	11–15	3 mo	0.9	2.8	5.3	0.7	17.2	2.7	7.4	1.7–33.3	**
15 (IV)	820	12–16	3 mo	0.6	1.0	0.0	0.6	0.0	1.0	—	—	—
16 (IIIR)	323	9–13	3 mo	1.3	5.3	0.0	1.3	0.0	5.4	—	—	—
17 (IV)	317	10–14	3 mo	1.3	3.8	0.0	1.3	0.0	3.9	—	—	—
18 (IV)	304	11–15	3 mo	1.0	2.0	16.7	0.7	33.3	1.7	29.2	2.3–377	**
19 (IV)	289	12–16	3 mo	0.4	3.9	0.0	0.4	0.0	3.9	—	—	—
20 (IIIR)	986	15	6 mo	4.8	12.8	—	—	—	—	1.0	0.4–2.5	n.s.
21 (IIIR)	2762	8–16	3 mo	1.4	4.4	—	—	—	—	2.6	0.5–8.6	n.s.
a = CD/ODD, b = Depression												
1 (III)	792	11	1 yr	9.1	1.8	78.6	8.7	15.3	0.47	38.3	10.4–141	***
2 (III)	943	15	1 yr	9.0	4.2	32.5	8.0	15.3	3.15	5.6	2.7–11.2	***
3 (III)	930	18	1 yr	5.5	18.0	7.2	5.1	23.5	17.6	1.4	0.7–2.8	n.s.
4 (III)	150	14–16	1 yr	14.7	8.0	83.3	8.7	45.9	1.6	52.5	10.3–268	***
5 (III)	278	7–11	1 yr	9.8	1.6	13.5	9.7	2.2	1.5	1.5	0.2–14.3	n.s.
6 (IIIR)	278	12–18	6 mo	13.9	4.2	67.7	11.6	20.4	1.6	15.9	4.4–58.0	***
7 (IIIR)	776	9–18	1 yr	7.1	3.4	23.7	6.6	10.9	2.8	4.3	1.6–11.5	*
8 (IIIR)	776	11–20	1 yr	5.8	2.8	22.7	5.3	11.1	2.3	5.2	1.9–13.9	*
9 (IIIR)	1710	14–18	curr	1.8	2.9	8.0	1.6	12.9	2.7	5.3	1.8–15.7	**
11 (III)	222	9–16	6 mo	10.5	8.0	55.8	—	45.4	—	18.4	6.1–55.3	***
12 (IIIR)	1015	9–13	3 mo	5.2	1.5	28.9	4.8	8.4	1.1	8.0	2.8–22.6	***
13 (IV)	970	10–14	3 mo	4.9	3.1	25.7	4.3	16.0	2.4	7.8	2.6–23.1	***
14 (IV)	928	11–15	3 mo	3.4	3.2	42.9	2.0	41.4	1.9	36.2	11.1–118	***
15 (IV)	820	12–16	3 mo	2.9	2.7	4.4	2.9	4.0	2.6	1.6	0.4–6.5	n.s.
16 (IIIR)	323	9–13	3 mo	6.5	0.31	0.0	6.5	0.0	0.33	—	—	—
17 (IV)	317	10–14	3 mo	8.2	1.6	60.0	7.4	11.5	0.7	18.8	3.0–118	**

COMORBIDITY 65

Table 3 (*cont.*)

Study (DSM)	N	Age	Time frame	Pop. rate of		Rate of a in		Rate of b in		OR	CI	p
				a (%)	b (%)	b (%)	not b (%)	a (%)	not a (%)			
18 (IV)	304	11–15	3 mo	5.3	4.3	38.5	3.8	31.3	2.8	15.9	4.5–56.6	***
19 (IV)	289	12–16	3 mo	4.2	1.7	0.0	4.2	0.0	1.8	—	—	
20 (IIIR)	986	15	6 mo	10.8	6.6	—	—	—	—	3.4	1.9–6.3	*
21 (IIIR)	2762	8–16	3 mo	4.3	1.2	—	—	—	—	11.2	4.6–25.6	*
a = CD/ODD, b = Anxiety												
1 (III)	792	11	1 yr	9.1	7.4	32.2	8.1	26.4	6.3	5.4	2.9–9.9	***
2 (III)	943	15	1 yr	9.0	10.7	7.1	9.4	7.1	11.1	0.61	0.3–1.4	n.s.
3 (IIIR)	930	18	1 yr	5.5	19.7	7.1	5.1	25.5	19.3	1.4	0.7–2.7	n.s.
4 (III)	150	14–16	1 yr	14.7	8.7	69.2	9.5	40.9	3.1	21.5	5.8–79.5	***
5 (III)	278	7–11	1 yr	9.8	15.4	19.4	8.0	30.7	13.8	2.8	1.3–6.12	**
6 (IIIR)	278	12–18	6 mo	13.9	14.4	20.8	12.8	21.6	13.3	1.8	0.8–3.9	n.s.
11 (III)	222	9–16	1 yr	—	—	62.4	—	55.3	—	phi = .14	—	*
12 (III)	1015	9–13	3 mo	5.2	5.5	18.3	4.4	19.2	4.7	4.81	2.1–10.9	***
13 (IV)	970	10–14	3 mo	4.9	3.8	13.0	4.6	9.9	3.4	3.1	1.4–6.9	**
14 (IV)	928	11–15	3 mo	3.4	2.8	7.9	3.2	6.6	2.7	2.6	0.9–7.7	n.s.
15 (IV)	820	12–16	3 mo	2.9	1.0	16.2	2.8	5.5	0.9	6.8	1.6–29.6	**
16 (IIIR)	323	9–13	3 mo	6.5	5.3	5.9	6.5	4.8	5.3	0.89	0.11–7.1	n.s.
17 (IV)	317	10–14	3 mo	8.2	3.8	33.3	7.2	15.4	2.8	6.4	1.8–23.0	**
18 (IV)	304	11–15	3 mo	5.3	2.0	33.3	4.7	12.5	1.4	10.1	1.7–60.2	*
19 (IV)	289	12–16	3 mo	4.2	3.8	27.3	3.2	25.0	2.9	11.2	2.5–49.4	**
20 (IIIR)	986	15	6 mo	10.8	12.8	—	—	—	—	3.2	1.8–5.5	*
21 (IIIR)	2762	8–16	3 mo	4.3	4.4	—	—	—	—	3.7	1.9–6.8	*
a = Depression, b = Anxiety												
1 (III)	792	11	1 yr	1.8	7.4	17.0	0.61	71.4	7.0	33.1	10.0–109	***
2 (III)	943	15	1 yr	4.2	10.7	12.9	3.2	32.5	9.8	4.5	2.2–9.0	***
3 (IIIR)	930	18	1 yr	18.0	19.7	45.9	11.1	50.3	13.0	6.8	4.7–9.8	***
4 (III)	150	14–16	1 yr	8.0	8.7	69.2	2.2	75.0	2.9	100.5	19.5–520	***
5 (III)	278	7–11	1 yr	1.6	15.4	4.4	1.1	43.3	15.0	4.3	0.6–31.0	n.s.
6 (IIIR)	278	12–18	6 mo	4.2	14.4	12.3	2.8	42.4	13.2	4.9	1.5–15.6	**
7 (IIIR)	776	9–18	1 yr	3.4	19.6	7.2	2.5	42.3	18.8	3.2	1.4–7.6	**
8 (IIIR)	776	11–20	1 yr	2.8	10.4	11.1	2.1	40.9	9.5	6.6	2.7–16.2	***
9 (IIIR)	1710	14–18	curr	2.9	3.2	16.7	18.0	18.0	2.7	7.9	3.6–17.2	***
10 (III)	1170	15–18	life	20.4	8.8	48.7	17.6	21.0	5.7	4.4	3.1–6.3	***
11 (III)	222	9–16	6 mo	8.0	6.6	50.0	5.2	38.9	3.6	16.0	4.6–55.3	***
12 (III)	1015	9–13	3 mo	1.5	5.5	8.01	1.1	28.6	5.09	7.5	2.6–21.7	***
13 (IV)	970	10–14	3 mo	3.1	3.8	17.0	2.5	20.9	3.2	7.9	2.2–28.5	**
14 (IV)	928	11–15	3 mo	3.2	2.8	23.7	2.6	20.7	2.2	11.5	3.2–40.6	***
15 (IV)	820	12–16	3 mo	2.7	1.0	58.5	2.1	21.5	0.42	65.2	12.5–341	***
16 (IIIR)	323	9–13	3 mo	0.31	5.3	0.0	0.33	0.0	5.3	—	—	
17 (IV)	317	10–14	3 mo	1.6	3.8	16.7	1.0	40.0	3.2	20.1	3.0–134	**
18 (IV)	304	11–15	3 mo	4.3	2.0	33.3	3.7	15.4	1.4	13.0	2.2–79.0	**
19 (IV)	289	12–16	3 mo	1.7	3.8	18.2	1.1	40.0	3.2	20.4	3.0–137	**
20 (IIIR)	986	15	6 mo	6.6	12.8	—	—	—	—	4.6	2.6–8.0	*
21 (IIIR)	2762	8–16	3 mo	1.2	4.4	—	—	—	—	24.5	10.8–55.9	*

$*p < .05; **p < .01; ***p < .001$.
Study 1. (Anderson et al., 1987).
Study 2. (McGee et al., 1990) A follow-up of Study 1.
Study 3. (Feehan, McGee, Raja, & Williams, 1994) A follow-up of Studies 1 and 2.
Study 4. (Kashani et al., 1987).
Study 5. (Costello et al., 1988).
Study 6. Costello, unpublished DISC DSM-IIIR diagnoses from a 5-year follow-up of Study 5.
Study 7. (Velez, Johnson, & Cohen, 1989).
Study 8. (Velez et al., 1989) A follow-up of Study 7.
Study 9. (Rohde et al., 1991).
Study 10. (Lewinsohn et al., 1993).
Study 11. (Bird, Gould, & Staghezza, 1993).
Study 12–15. (Angold, Costello, et al., 1998) Four annual waves of data collection.
Study 16–19. (Costello, Farmer, Angold, Burns, & Erkanli, 1997) Four annual waves of data collection.
Study 20. (Fergusson et al., 1993a). p values reported only as > or < .05.
Study 21. (Simonoff et al., 1997). p values reported only as > or < .05.

data necessary to reconstruct the multi-way contingency table that will allow others to compute any and all relevant correlational statistics. For studies that involved complex sampling designs requiring weighted analyses, the weighted percentages for the cells from each pairwise comparison are informative, as are the OR and 95% CI around the OR. Of course, other statistics may well be appropriate for particular purposes, but adoption of this basic set would greatly facilitate comparisons across studies in future.

A Meta-analysis of General Population Estimates of the Strengths of Associations between Disorders

One notable aspect of Table 3 is the wide CI around the estimates of the degree of association (OR) between disorders. Since instances of specific types of disorder are relatively uncommon in the general population, estimates of the probabilities of co-occurrences between disorders are based on small numbers of subjects in the comorbid cell, with the result that estimates based on any individual cross-sectional study or wave of a longitudinal study of the sizes found in child psychiatric epidemiology are of relatively low reliability (i.e. they have wide CI). Meta-analysis provides a means of combining information from multiple studies to produce an overall estimate of parameters of interest. Since a reasonable number of general population estimates of comorbidity rates were available in a form that allowed us to compute 95% CI around the OR for associations between disorders, we undertook the task of using all this information to come up with a single estimate of the strength of association between each pair of disorders.

Statistical Considerations

In combining results from several studies, an important issue is the assessment of variability between the study effects. If this variability is not large, then a weighted average of the individual study effects suffices to produce a reliable estimate of the overall effects, with the weights being equal to the reciprocals of the estimated variances of the individual study effects. If, however, there is evidence of heterogeneity among the individual study estimates, then failure to account for it will produce an estimate of the effect with a standard error substantially smaller than it should be.

We began, therefore, by performing chi-square tests of heterogeneity for each of the OR (using the log odds ratios) we planned to compute. The estimates for three of the comparisons (CD/ODD–depression, CD/ODD–anxiety, depression–anxiety) revealed heterogeneity, while those for the other three (ADHD–anxiety, ADHD–CD/ODD, and ADHD–depression) did not. To conduct meta-analyses for the three homogeneous pairs, we used the standard fixed effect model, which assumes that each study effect is estimating a common unknown study effect (i.e. the common mean). The resulting estimate of the common mean is the usual weighted (i.e. pooled) estimate with weights being equal to the inverse of the variances of the estimated log-odds ratios. For the heterogenous cases, we assumed that each study effect is estimating its own unknown effect, which, in turn, is assumed to be a random sample from the population of all study effects, having an unknown common mean and unknown variance. These parameters can be estimated using a hierarchical Bayesian approach. For the required computations, we used the BUGS package. We used empirical uniform prior distributions for the common mean and variance, with upper and lower bounds respectively taken to be slightly less than and greater than the values provided in each dataset. We also used other priors for

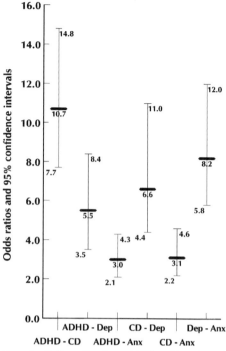

Figure 1.   Median odds ratios and 95% confidence intervals from the meta-analysis of community sample based studies of comorbidity.

sensitivity analyses, but the overall estimates were not very sensitive to variations in the priors.

Results

The resulting median OR (thick central black bars), and their 95% CI (the thin lines extending above and below the black bars) are shown in Fig. 1. As expected, the 95% CI are now sufficiently narrow that we can be confident that all the OR are *not* the same, although there are highly significant associations between all pairs of disorders. When the OR for one pairing falls outside the 95% CI for another pairing we can say that the association between one pair and another pair is significantly different in strength (at the .05 level). The most obvious difference is that the association between CD/ODD and anxiety disorders is weaker than that between CD and depression. The relationship between ADHD and anxiety is also lower than that between ADHD and depression. This is important because it argues against the existence of a unitary association between "internalizing" and "externalizing" disorders. The other interesting point is that depression is almost as strongly related to CD/ODD as it is to anxiety.

Causes of Comorbidity

It is established that comorbidity is a real and unavoidable characteristic of the common childhood and adolescent psychiatric disorders, but how does this come about? What are the mechanisms that generate comorbidity? We should begin by saying that this question cannot be answered at present for any pair of disorders, but that there is a growing body of evidence relevant to understanding the causes of comorbidity. We have divided these contributions into four groups; (1) those that address the possibility that comorbidity may be the result of one or more methodological artefacts, (2) explanations in terms of problems with current official psychiatric nosologies, (3) evidence that certain diagnostic pairings are merely the statistical product of "real" relationships between both of that pair and a third disorder, and (4) explanations involving substantive causes for comorbidity. For each of the substantive explanations, we present a "case study" consisting of the evidence relating to that explanation for a particular type of comorbidity. Each of these "case studies" was selected either because the explanatory mechanism seemed particularly pertinent to that type of comorbidity, or because the literature relating to that type of comorbidity has tended to concentrate on that explanatory mechanism.

Is Comorbidity a Methodological Artefact?

Several authors have discussed the possibility that apparent comorbidity is simply an artefact, rather than a real psychopathological phenomenon (see, for instance, Angold & Costello, 1992, 1993; Caron & Rutter, 1991). The possibilities here include effects of referral bias, rater expectancy, or halo effects, and effects of current information collection strategies, such as the use of multiple informants.

Comorbidity in clinical samples is not just an effect of referral bias. The data we have presented establish beyond a reasonable doubt that the comorbidity seen in clinical samples is not simply the result of Berkson's or clinical referral biases, but represents a psychopathological phenomenon in relation to DSM-III, DSM-III-R, and DSM-IV diagnoses. The data from general population scale score studies discussed above also indicate that this relationship is present at all levels of severity of symptomatology.

Comorbidity is not just an effect of rater expectancies (halo effects) or information collection strategies. When clinicians conduct assessments unaided by structured procedures, it has been shown in many branches of medicine that they adopt idiosyncratic decision procedures and are subject to many information-collection and decision-making biases, some of which could result in the appearance of comorbidity. However, the use of structured assessments for research purposes, and the demonstration that comorbidity is seen with self-report questionnaires from children, parent-report questionnaires about children, respondent-based interviews, and interviewer-based interviews conducted with both parents and children, rule out clinician bias or interviewer expectancies as possible explanations of the observed rates of comorbidity.

Comorbidity is not a result of the use of multiple informants. Imagine a child who cried every day on leaving for school, and reported that this was because she was afraid of leaving the house. A parent could misinterpret this symptom of separation anxiety as being a manifestation of depressed mood and report it as such. Using the usual multiple-reporter combinatorial rule (that a symptom counts as being present if reported by either the parent or the child), a situation like this could result in the same symptom appearing as both separation anxiety and depressed mood. Although this may sometimes occur, it cannot be the explanation for most comorbidity, for four reasons. First, adult studies, which usually employ only a single informant, find high rates of comorbidity—rates that are similar to those described in childhood. Second, Lewinsohn's study of adolescents, which employed only self-reports, documents rates of comorbidity that are similar to those derived from multi-reporter studies (Lewinsohn, Klein, et al., 1995; Lewinsohn, Rohde, Seeley, & Hops, 1991; Rohde et al., 1991; Rohde, Lewinsohn, & Seeley, 1996). Third, Jensen et al.'s (1995) work on children of the military found, using only parent reports, that the mean number of diagnoses per child in those with a diagnosis was 1.3, compared with 1.4 for child-only reports, and 1.4 for combined reports. Fourth, the parent-report scale score literature discussed above shows that there are correlations between factors, and the content of the factors is such as to indicate that there are links between what diagnosticians call "different disorders".

Comorbidity is not the result of single behaviors resulting in the coding of multiple symptoms. Another possible cause of comorbidity is that different aspects of a single behavioral or emotional state may result in coding as multiple symptoms given the definitions incorporated into current interview schedules and questionnaires. For instance, if a child "often leaves seat in classroom or in other situations in which remaining seated is expected", that symptom counts towards the diagnosis of ADHD. However, if the child is told to sit still and fails to do so, it would not be unnatural for a parent or teacher to report that the child "often actively defies or refuses to comply with adults' requests or rules", thus the single behavioral problem also serves as the basis for a positive coding on a symptom of ODD. It is also easy to see how the frustration felt in the face of the frequent repetition of such a scenario between an adult and a child could lead to arguments resulting in the child being described as "often losing temper", "often arguing with adults", "often touchy or easily annoyed by others", and "often angry and resentful". Now the child has sufficient symptoms to meet criteria for ODD provided that he or she is also impaired. Is it helpful to classify the child as suffering from two disorders—ADHD and ODD—or would it be better to regard that individual as having ADHD with resultant impairment of relationships with adults? Clearly, the latter makes more sense in relation to this example, but our technology for discriminating between "independent" ODD and "dependent" ODD is not well advanced. At least the designation of comorbidity signals that not all ADHD children have major problems of the ODD sort, and provides an index of when such additional problems are present. It may well be that in time we will find that it is better to regard some of what we now call "symptoms of a second disorder" as impairments resulting from an underlying disorder, with the result, perhaps, that ODD in those with ADHD would be seen as a "complication" rather than a separate diagnosis. On the other hand, this mechanism could not explain comorbidity between CD and depression, or CD and ADHD, or anxiety and depression, so this methodological problem also fails to offer a possible general explanation for comorbidity.

In summary, comorbidity is not the product of any likely methodological problem or bias.

Is Comorbidity an Artefact of Current Diagnostic Systems?

Having rejected the possibility that comorbidity is solely the spurious product of methodological problems, we turn our attention to the possibility that the diagnostic systems we use might result in comorbidity between supposed "disorders", when the underlying disorders themselves are unrelated. Here we consider possible effects of the inclusion of nonspecific symptoms in the definitions of multiple diagnostic categories, and then go on to discuss the idea that our whole categorical diagnostic system may be fundamentally flawed.

"Nonspecific symptoms" as an explanation for heterotypic comorbidity. Several authors have pointed out that comorbidity could be generated by the fact that individual "nonspecific" symptoms are shared by disparate diagnoses (e.g. Caron & Rutter, 1991), with the result that a certain amount of overlap is built into the diagnostic system. This raises the question of the degree to which the current DSM and ICD nosologies really suffer from this problem. All that needs to be done to examine this possibility is to look at the criteria for different disorders to determine the degree of overlap. When one does so, this possibility fades for some pairs of diagnoses. The criteria for CD do not overlap at all with those for depressive disorders, anxiety disorders, or ADHD, but there is no doubt that CD is often comorbid with all three, so overlapping symptom lists cannot be the explanation in this case. On the other hand, irritability is common in depressive episodes and several symptoms of ODD could result from irritability (e.g. often loses temper). The DSM-III-R and DSM-IV criteria require that the ODD symptoms should not occur exclusively during a mood disorder, but this sort of criterion is very difficult to implement in practice, especially with disorders of long duration, when it may be difficult to remember what the child's behavior was like before the mood disorder arose. This difficulty is exacerbated by the fact that it may not be clear just when the mood disorder should be regarded as having begun or ended. Sleep disturbances are included in the criteria both for depressive disorders and anxiety disorders, as are concentration difficulties and fatigue. Thus, a child who had had these three symptoms for a year, and who also manifested both depressed mood and anxiety or worry, would thereby meet DSM-IV criteria for both dysthymic disorder and generalized anxiety disorder. Indeed, after only 2 weeks of symptoms such a child could also meet criteria for the new DSM-IV experimental category of minor depression. Three diagnoses from a total of five symptoms! Before we conclude that this explains comorbidity, we should remember that such work as has been done on this question indicates that there is also comorbidity between the non-overlapping symptoms of such syndromes, again suggesting that comorbidity is not just an artefact of our flawed diagnostic system. Two studies have looked at whether comorbidity remains when overlapping symptoms are removed from the criteria for the diagnosis for two disorders. Milberger and colleagues (Milberger, Biederman, Faraone, Murphy, & Tsuang, 1995) examined comorbidity with ADHD by removing symptoms that overlapped with the criteria for depression or generalized anxiety and reallocating diagnoses according to two different methods. The great majority of individuals maintained their comorbid diagnoses even when the overlapping symptoms were taken out of consideration. Biederman and colleagues (Biederman, Faraone, Mick, & Lelon, 1995), using the same approach, found that eliminating overlapping symptoms failed to eliminate comorbidity between depression and ADHD or ODD. It seems safe to conclude, therefore, that comorbidity is not *just* an artefact of overlapping diagnostic criteria.

One reaction to this might be to suggest that we should remove the offending criteria in order to produce better demarcated categories. However, this solution will result in *atypical* symptoms becoming the diagnostic criteria for the major disorders. Both depressed and anxious individuals really do suffer from sleep disturbances and fatigue, and they have difficulty in concentrating. If we consider only the criteria not shared between disorders we will end up ignoring many key symptoms. Neither is this how we would behave in any other branch of medicine. We would hardly deny the right of the symptoms of chest pain, breathlessness, and cough to be considered in the diagnosis of both myocardial infarction and pneumonia. To ignore them and rely on nonshared symptoms would be a disaster. This example, of course, points to where the real problem lies. The issue is not the inclusion of similar symptoms in different diagnoses, but the paucity of research on the *differential characteristics* of those symptoms in different disorders. When the patient describes crushing central chest pain, radiating down the left arm to the elbow, with breathlessness and cough exacerbated by lying flat, we can be pretty sure that pneumonia is not the problem. But we know very little abut the specifics of the "nonspecific" symptoms in psychiatry. There are now many studies large enough to allow examination of the ways in which, for example, the sleep disturbances of anxious and depressed patients differ. For instance, Angold found that mild insomnia (occurring on fewer than 12 nights in 3 months) was strongly associated with anxiety disorders, and less strongly associated with depression, but that severe insomnia (most nights over 3 months) was significantly associated only with depression. Thus, severe insomnia was evidence of depression, but not of anxiety (Angold, 1996). There is a real need for more work detailing the qualitative and quantitative aspects of individual symptoms in relation to different diagnoses, and we believe that such an approach could go a long way toward cleaning up the boundaries between diagnoses. However, there is no reason to suppose that it will make comorbidity go away.

Comorbidity as evidence that the official diagnostic system is fundamentally flawed at the conceptual level. Some of the most radical critiques of diagnostic "medical" models of psychopathology have used the fact of comorbidity as a plank in the argument that diagnostic approaches simply impose arbitrary cutpoints on a series of dimensional phenomena. Comorbidity arises because diagnosticians insist on assigning naturally linked sets of phenomena to different classes of disorder. For instance, the "depression" dimension that repeatedly emerges from general population questionnaire studies of psychopathology always contains a mixture of what, from a diagnostic perspective, would be called depressive and anxiety symptoms (Achenbach et al., 1989). The problem became acute with DSM-III, when diagnostic criteria were developed for a much greater number of "specific" diagnoses for children and adolescents than had previously existed. Indeed, whole new disorders were invented: for instance, conduct disorder was split into oppositional defiant disorder and conduct disorder (it remains a single category in ICD-10). Doubts about whether this proliferation of categories in DSM-III was going to be helpful were expressed by some proponents of the diagnostic approach at the time (Rutter & Shaffer, 1980), and there is surely no doubt that the criteria for individual diagnoses ran far ahead of the research supporting them—witness the very substantial changes that have continued to appear with each revision of the DSM. In spite of all these problems, however, the recent diagnostic literature has been helpful in two ways. First, it has shown that associations between symptoms of different types occur at the extremes of the distributions of psychopathology, and not just at the level of factor scores in relation to mild symptomatology, which could be interpreted as not being measures of serious clinical disorders. In other words, we can be sure that what the diagnostically inclined call comorbidity is a feature of behavioral and emotional problems across the entire range of severity. This is important because many severe manifestations of disturbance are not included in the scales upon which "empirical" syndromes have been based, as a result of the fact that they occur too rarely in the general population to be suitable for inclusion in classical factor analyses. The clinical literature on comorbidity has also indicated that comorbidity is an issue for a range of relatively uncommon syndromes, such as post-traumatic stress disorder, eating disorders, or bipolar disorders, which are not identified in generic general population questionnaire studies.

Whether one sees comorbidity as diagnostic misrepresentation of naturally linked phenomena, or overlap between more-or-less well-defined natural categories, the issue for future research is the same: to explore why symptoms group together in the ways that they do, and why there is overlap between syndromes, whether defined by diagnostic criteria or factor scores. In phenomenological terms, for instance, depressed mood and anxiety are not the same thing; why then do they so often occur together? On the other hand, why is it that some individuals with depressed mood are not anxious? These questions can be cast in factor terms by asking why some

individuals with a high depression factor have mostly "depressive" symptoms, while others have mostly "anxiety" symptoms, and still others have a mixture of both? On the other hand, we can ask why do some individuals who meet diagnostic criteria for a depressive disorder also meet criteria for an anxiety disorder, while others do not? One possible answer to both questions is that "depression" and "anxiety" are simply alternative manifestations of the same underlying diathesis and that the diagnostic criteria are carving nature anywhere but at the joints. However, it is also possible that the links are due to correlations between separate sets of causes for anxiety and depressive disorders. Some genetic studies of adults suggest that depression and anxiety have a similar genetic basis, but that environmental factors determine whether this is expressed as depression or anxiety (Kendler, Heath, Martin, & Eaves, 1987), whereas other studies have indicated that different sorts of life events are related to depression and anxiety (Brown, Harris, & Eales, 1993).

It would not be surprising if some aspects of comorbidity do arise because our diagnostic criteria have not drawn the appropriate boundaries between disorders (see the discussion of examples of the causes of homotypic comorbidity below). That is one reason for doing research on comorbidity. As Achenbach (1990) has pointed out, both categorical and quantitative models offer complementary approaches to the issue of nosology.

"Epiphenomenal" Comorbidity

The standard approach to quantifying comorbidity has been to look at the pairwise concordances among diagnoses. As we have seen, there is no doubt that this approach has shown that the common conditions occur together much more frequently than can be explained by chance associations. When three conditions are all associated with one another, it is possible that one of the pairwise associations is nothing other than the mathematical product of the other two. We will refer to this possibility as *epiphenomenal comorbidity* (Angold, Erkanli, Egger, & Costello, 1998). To present a concrete example, we have shown that there are significant associations between depressive and anxiety disorders, depressive and conduct disorders, and anxiety and conduct disorders (see Fig. 1). Perhaps the last of these associations could be explained simply by the second—anxiety disorders are only seen more often in those with CD because people with CD are more likely to be depressed, and this depressed group includes a substantial number of individuals who also have an anxiety disorder. The Great Smoky Mountains Study provided a large enough sample to test for this possibility, by controlling each pairwise comparison for the effects of other comorbidities. The results support this epiphenomenal explanation for the relationship between depression and ADHD (via anxiety and CD), and for the relationship between CD and anxiety (via depression) and ODD and anxiety (via ADHD). For instance, the OR for the association between anxiety and ODD fell from 3.0 to a nonsignificant 0.56 when other comorbidities were controlled for. In other words, there was no independent relationship between ODD and anxiety disorders. On the other hand, there were independent associations of CD with ODD, CD and ODD with depression and ADHD, and ADHD and depression with anxiety. The apparent pairwise covariation of ADHD with depression, and CD and ODD with anxiety, was explained by comorbidity between other pairs of disorders; it was an epiphenomenon of the relationships between other pairs of disorders. These results need to be replicated, but they do suggest that some simplification of the problem of comorbidity may be at hand—we may have to explain only a subset of the possible pairings of disorders. We should note that this does not mean that those who *do* have both depression and ADHD do not have "real" depression or ADHD (see, e.g., Biederman, Mick, & Faraone, 1998). It simply means that, in the absence of comorbid anxiety, CD, or ODD, depressed individuals are no more likely to have ADHD than children who are psychiatrically well.

This review of methodological and nosological explanations for comorbidity leads us to the conclusion that one of the major achievements of research on comorbidity over the last decade has been its demonstration that we are dealing with a real phenomenon. We still cannot be sure to what extent comorbidity implies that we should change our diagnostic categories, but it has certainly led to much more work being done to examine the psychometric properties of those categories and to modify them on the basis of information generated by research than has been the case in the past. The challenge now lies in explaining how comorbidity comes to be so common. So we turn our attention to what is known about the substantive causes of comorbidity. Among the many possible causes of comorbidity (Angold & Costello, 1993; Caron & Rutter, 1991; D. N. Klein & Riso, 1993), the type of explanation most commonly investigated has varied according to the group of diagnoses being studied. We have, therefore, presented research on the causes of comorbidity between or within groups of diagnoses as case studies of particular explanatory possibilities. We do not imply that for each pair only the explanations discussed in relation to that pair are relevant; clearly, each possible explanation could be examined in every case.

Causes of Homotypic Comorbidity

Homotypic comorbidity has been most studied in relation to the anxiety disorders, CD/ODD, and the depressive disorders (particularly unipolar depression and dysthymia). We examine three key potential causes of homotypic comorbidity; (1) invalidity of individual diagnostic categories (anxiety disorders), (2) that current diagnostic boundaries may obscure developmental continuities at the symptom level (CD/ODD), and (3) that homotypic comorbidity over time may be a marker for underlying homotypic *continuity* of a single disease process (dysthymia/depression). It will be seen that (2) and (3) are restatements of the same idea in slightly different terms, reflecting differences in the ways in which comorbidity has been approached in these two diagnostic areas.

Homotypic comorbidity in anxiety disorders—evidence for the invalidity of current diagnostic categories? Of the common disorders, anxiety disorders have received much less research attention than the disruptive behavior disorders and depression, and uncertainties about the classification of these disorders is probably greater than in relation to any other major category of child and adolescent disorder. DSM-III introduced three "new" diagnoses for children: separation anxiety disorder (SAD), overanxious disorder (OAD), and avoidant disorder. These have no parallel in the classification of adult disorders. Only SAD has survived into DSM-IV, and that survival can be attributed to the fact that the category was solidly based on longstanding clinical research on "school phobia" (e.g. Hersov, 1960a, b) and a vast literature on separation responses in children. Avoidant disorder was little more than a category for shyness, and has now been folded back into social phobia. OAD was an attempt to provide a category for the commonly seen generally worried or anxious child, at a time when no-one knew whether such children would or would not meet adult criteria for generalized anxiety disorder. DSM-III-R specified the criteria for OAD in greater detail (although there had been little research on the topic), but again produced a category that drew substantial criticism. R. G. Klein, Tancer, and Werry (1994) in their report to the DSM-IV work group on anxiety disorders, noted that what little research had been done on the phenomenology of OAD pointed to "a lack of syndromal specificity for several items in the criteria and to their limited face validity because of their overlap with the clinical criteria of other anxiety disorders". Their recommendation was that OAD be retained, but "modified to remove the considerable clinical overlap with the other anxiety disorders".

These conclusions appear to be well supported by the research evidence. Kashani and Orvaschel's general population study found that of children with OAD, 55% met criteria for a second anxiety diagnosis, compared with 42% of children with SAD (Kashani & Orvaschel, 1990), whereas in the Dunedin Longitudinal Study, only 15% of those with an anxiety diagnosis met criteria for two or more anxiety diagnoses (McGee et al., 1990). Last, Strauss, and Francis (1987) found that 45% of children with OAD had no other anxiety diagnosis in an anxiety clinic sample, compared with 56% of children with SAD—hardly a significant difference given the small numbers involved. In an earlier paper, which appears to have been based on a substantially overlapping sample, this group reported that OAD was associated with much greater comorbidity with other anxiety disorders than was SAD, but even here only "more than half" of the OAD group had a second anxiety disorder diagnosis (Last, Hersen, Kazdin, Finkelstein, & Strauss, 1987). It has also been found that children with OAD and SAD can be discriminated in terms of the types of worries they report (Last, Hersen, Kazdin, Finkelstein, et al., 1987), that children presenting to clinics with OAD are older, but of higher socioeconomic status than those presenting with SAD (Last, Hersen, Kazdin, Finkelstein, et al., 1987; Last, Perrin, Hersen, & Kazdin, 1992), and that panic disorder is more common in the families of OAD children than it is in the families of children with SAD

(Last, Hersen, Kazdin, Orvaschel, & Perrin, 1991). In other words, there is evidence that OAD and other anxiety diagnoses are not just measures of a single unitary construct. We do not mean to suggest that homotypic comorbidity amongst the anxiety disorders is not a significant issue; there is no doubt that it is, both cross-sectionally and even more so when lifetime diagnosis is considered (Beidel, Fink, & Turner, 1996; Biederman et al., 1997; Bradley & Hood, 1993; Clark, Smith, Neighbors, Skerlec, & Randall, 1994; Francis, Last, & Strauss, 1992; Hirshfeld et al., 1992; Keller, Lavori, Wunder, et al., 1992; Last et al., 1992). The question is what to do about such issues.

The DSM-IV solution was to abolish OAD and substitute a special subset of generalized anxiety disorder (GAD) for children and adolescents, requiring only one symptom apart from worrying or anxiety from a list that overlaps greatly with the symptoms of depression or dysthymia (restlessness, fatigability, difficulty concentrating, irritability, and sleep disturbance). It is hard to see how this will reduce homotypic comorbidity among the anxiety disorders, and it could actually increase heterotypic comorbidity. Indeed, the reported levels of comorbidity amongst all the anxiety diagnoses could equally have been used as evidence for the abolition of each individual disorder, and all the current categories would have ended up collapsed into one. Even more damagingly, if the level of homotypic comorbidity displayed by OAD is sufficient for it to be removed as a diagnosis, then all of the diagnostic distinctions currently made in child and adolescent psychiatry would be liable to abolition because, as we have seen, rates of some types of heterotypic comorbidity are as high as those associated with the homotypic comorbidity of OAD. Lest this seem to be an argument in favor of abolishing diagnosis and adopting a purely dimensional approach to psychopathology, we must remember that the effort to define syndromes using factor analysis, or to base typologies of children on cluster analyses of factor scores, would be equally undermined by the correlations between factors (see e.g. McConaughy & Achenbach, 1994; Verhulst & van der Ende, 1993). We would end up where we were 30 years ago, with nothing but generic measures of "disturbance". A start had been made on differentiating OAD from the generic mass of anxiety symptoms, but given the fact that the "replacement" diagnosis of a special childhood form of GAD is defined quite differently from OAD, that task will now have to begin again with GAD. As the two following examples will demonstrate, research in this area would likely benefit from a more developmental approach than has hitherto usually been adopted.

Homotypic comorbidity in conduct and oppositional defiant disorders—does diagnosis obscure developmental progressions at the symptom level? The diagnostic criteria for antisocial personality disorder require that conduct problems should have been present in adolescence, and the DSM-IV diagnosis of CD precludes that of ODD, whereas in ICD-10 the two diagnoses are treated as a single category. All of these diagnostic rules recognize the well-established fact that there is a developmental pathway from oppositional problems in childhood through adolescent conduct disorder to anti-

social personality disorder (Fergusson, Lynskey, & Horwood, 1996a; Loeber, Green, Keenan, & Lahey, 1995; Loeber, Green, Lahey, Christ, & Frick, 1992; L. N. Robins, 1974). It is also well established that this pathway grows narrower with time—there are more oppositional children than there are CD adolescents than there are adults with antisocial personality disorder. Here is an unusual situation in which "comorbidity" is either *required* (the relationship between CD and antisocial personality disorder) or *forbidden* (the relationship between CD and ODD) at different points in the developmental trajectory of the disorder. If we confine ourselves to childhood and adolescence, and thereby to the relationship between ODD and CD, we find that the small literature comparing the correlates of these two disorders finds them to be similar in terms of socio-economic status, family history, and impairment, but that the relationships of these factors with CD are stronger (Faraone, Biederman, Keenan, & Tsuang, 1991; Frick et al., 1992; Rey, Bashir, & Schwartz, 1988). There seems to be good evidence then that ODD is often a developmental precursor of CD, which could be regarded as being a later and more severe manifestation of a process that earlier appeared as oppositionality. Under this assumption, it is a serious problem that the organization of the diagnostic criteria for ODD and CD creates a disjunction between the two. Many ODD behaviors become less common between childhood and adolescence (Campbell, 1990; Loeber, Lahey, & Thomas, 1991), whereas many CD behaviors (especially covert behaviors) become more common (Farrington, 1986; Farrington, Loeber, & Elliott, 1990; Le Blanc & Fréchette, 1989; Loeber, 1988). Given that the criteria for ODD and CD do not overlap in content, this means that it is possible for an individual who has previously met criteria for ODD, and who will later meet criteria for CD, to meet criteria for neither at an intermediate stage, despite having, say, three ODD symptoms and two CD symptoms at that point—a total of five relevant symptoms when ODD requires only four symptoms and CD only three. Considerations of this sort, combined with work on symptom aggregation and a willingness to consider symptoms that are not included in the DSM definitions of ODD and CD, led Loeber and his colleagues (Loeber, Keenan, Lahey, Green, & Thomas, 1993; Russo, Loeber, Lahey, & Keenan, 1994) to suggest that these diagnoses be replaced by three categories ordered both in time and severity, which they called "modified oppositional disorder", "intermediate CD", and "advanced CD".

In many ways it would be attractive to accept this position, or something very like it, but we also have to remember that questionnaire studies consistently find that oppositional-type behaviors and CD-type behaviors load on different factors (Achenbach, Connors, Quay, Verhulst, & Howell, 1989; Frick et al., in press); that a number of individuals begin to manifest notable CD behaviors in adolescence, without a previous history of antisocial behavior (Loeber, 1988; Moffitt, 1990; Moffitt, Caspi, Dickson, Silva, & Stanton, 1996); and that this group probably has better adult outcomes than the early-onset group. There is also evidence that the transition from having ODD plus fewer than three CD symptoms to having at least three symptoms of CD is associated with a sharp increase in police contacts and school suspensions (Lahey et al., 1990), which suggests that it may be more useful to regard ODD and CD as being different conditions. Our aim here is not to take a stand on what the answer should be, but rather to point out some features of the work done in this regard that could serve as a model for other areas. First, the notion of development has been taken seriously, and a good deal of attention has been paid to the relative timing of onsets and offsets of *individual symptoms*. Second, the diagnostic categories have been subjected to serious scrutiny, and various alternatives *based on empirical research* have been experimented with. Third, methods usually associated with the questionnaire approach to psychopathology, like factor analysis of individual items, have sometimes been applied to the distinction between ODD and CD, with interesting results. For instance, Frick et al. (1991) found that bullying (a symptom of CD) consistently loaded on an ODD factor, whereas fighting and lying (again both CD symptoms) loaded equally on both the ODD and CD factors. Another report from the same study (Loeber et al., 1995) found that physical fighting was the single symptom of all the symptoms of CD that best predicted the onset of full CD. This suggests that bullying may be misplaced in the diagnostic criteria, whereas fighting and lying may belong in *both* sets of criteria, if they are to be kept separate. Overall, the work in this area can be seen as having treated the diagnostic criteria as "hypotheses" to be examined and tested. In our present state of knowledge this would appear to be the right attitude to take to all diagnoses in child and adolescent psychiatry.

Homotypic comorbidity between major depression and dysthymia—a marker of homotypic continuity? A second area in which the study of homotypic comorbidity has moved beyond rates of comorbidity to studying comorbidity longitudinally concerns the affective disorders. Some adult studies have suggested that major depression, dysthymia, and the simultaneous comorbidity of the two represent either nothing more than separate phases or manifestations of the same disorder (e.g. Keller, Lavori, Mueller, et al., 1992; Keller, Shapiro, Lavori, & Wolfe, 1982a, b; D. F. Klein, 1990), or points on a continuum of severity of depressive conditions (Angst & Dobler-Mikola, 1984; Angst, Dobler-Mikola, & Binder, 1984). Several studies have identified differences between children with dysthymia, major depression, and double depression in symptomatology, impairment, heterotypic comorbidity, and rates of suicidality (Asarnow & Ben-Meir, 1994; Ferro, Carlson, Grayson, & Klein, 1994; Fine, Moretti, Haley, & Marriage, 1985; Ryan et al., 1987; Shain, King, Naylor, & Alessi, 1991), but even these can be interpreted as indicating that "major depression may be the driving force behind the expression of depressive symptomatology, regardless of whether the child is acutely or chronically depressed" (Ferro et al., 1994).

Longitudinal studies of children have, on the whole, given a similar impression (see e.g. Kovacs et al., 1984), but Kovacs' 12-year clinical follow-up of children with major depressive episodes and dysthymia resulted in a rather more differentiated conclusion. By the 12-year follow-up (Kovacs, 1996), no less than 76% of children

whose first depression was dysthymic disorder had a subsequent major depressive disorder and 13% had a bipolar disorder. Of those whose first episode was a major depressive episode, 48% later met criteria for dysthymia and 15% had bipolar disorders. These writers go on to emphasize that childhood dysthymia in their sample *did not* persist into adulthood itself, but exerted its influence on later risk for affective disorder through major depressive episodes. They now regard childhood-onset dysthymic disorder as an "early marker of recurrent affective illness". Here we see the fruits of careful long-term follow-up of diagnostically well-characterized samples for clarifying comorbidity issues. However, Kovacs and her colleagues suggest that we should maintain the distinction between early-onset dysthymic disorder (with somewhat modified diagnostic criteria) and major depressive disorder (MDD), because the former had an earlier age of onset (see also Ferro et al., 1994), a subset of early dysthymics did not develop MDD, dysthymia was associated with shorter disorder-free periods than MDD without dysthymia, and first-episode dysthymia and MDD carried different levels of risk for later affective and substance use disorders. There are interesting parallels here with Lewinsohn and colleagues' work on older adolescents (Lewinsohn et al., 1991). They found that lifetime comorbidity between MDD and dysthymia was twice as high in their adolescent general population sample as in an adult sample, and that dysthymia nearly always preceded MDD when both occurred. However, MDD was vastly more common than dysthymia in adolescents.

Here again, we see that attention to timing yields important findings. We also see that research under the heading of "comorbidity" has stimulated exploration of the *development of patterns of symptomatology*. At present there seems to be more to be gained, as Kovacs and her colleagues have indicated, by exploring the implications of the "separate" diagnoses of dysthymia and major depression, and their co-occurrence, than in collapsing them into a single diagnosis. Such studies could lead eventually to the lumping together of dysthymia and major depression, or to further splitting of these diagnostic categories (perhaps "double depression", as comorbidity between MDD and dysthymia is sometimes called, should be a separate diagnosis). Ignoring these indications that there are developmental differences between depression and dysthymia, however, would be counterproductive. We need longitudinal, general population samples of sufficient size to allow comparisons among individuals with MDD, dysthymia, and both disorders.

Causes of Heterotypic Comorbidity

Heterotypic comorbidity involves comorbidity of diagnoses from different diagnostic groupings (for instance depression and CD). Here we consider the following possible causes for comorbidity; (1) that it is nothing more than a marker for the severity of a relatively undifferentiated mass of symptoms upon which arbitrary diagnostic cutpoints have been imposed; (2) that one disorder may be nothing more than a particular manifestation of another disorder; (3) that it may be caused by the other disorder; (4) that the two disorders may share certain causes, while differing etiologically in some other ways; and (5) that comorbidity may be a marker for specific subtypes of disorder. We then go on to emphasize the importance of timing in the study of comorbidity.

Heterotypic comorbidity as a marker of severity. Comorbidity has often been associated with increased levels of symptomatology within each of the disorders making up the comorbid group, and with increased levels of impairment in functioning. Comorbid conditions have also been associated with higher levels of psychosocial adversity. For instance, individuals with both ADHD and ODD or CD have higher levels of CD/ODD symptoms than children with "pure" CD (Hinshaw et al., 1993; Kuhne, Schachar, & Tannock, 1997; Offord, Sullivan, Allen, & Abrams, 1979; Walker, Lahey, Hynd, & Frame, 1987), greater levels of parental psychopathology, conflictual interactions with parents, peer rejection, school problems, and psychosocial adversity (Abikoff & Klein, 1992; C. L. Carlson, Tamm, & Gaub, 1997; Fletcher, Fisher, Barkley, & Smallish, 1996; C. Johnston & Pelham, 1986; Kuhne et al., 1997; Lahey et al., 1988; Milich & Dodge, 1984; Reeves, Werry, Elkind, & Zametkin,1987; Schachar & Wachsmuth, 1990), and worse outcomes than those with either ADHD or conduct problems alone (see Barkley, 1990; Lyons, Serbin, & Marchessault, 1988; Satterfield & Schell, 1997; Taylor, Chadwick, Heptinstall, & Danckaerts, 1996, for a review).

Similar indications of the malignancy of comorbidity have been reported for the associations of ADHD with depression or anxiety disorders (Jensen, Shervette, Xenakis, & Richters, 1993), though other data suggest that comorbidity between ADHD and internalizing disorders may not necessarily be indicative of more severe ADHD (August, Realmuto, MacDonald, Nugent, & Crosby, 1996; Pliszka, 1992). The indications are that depression has little effect on the course of CD (Capaldi, 1992; Zoccolillo, 1992), though there are suggestions that CD may be associated with more severe concurrent depressions (Marriage, Fine, Moretti, & Haley, 1986; Noam, Paget, Valiant, Borst, & Bartok, 1994; Rudolph, Hammen, & Burge, 1994), but perhaps with less risk that depression will continue into adulthood (Harrington, Fudge, Rutter, Pickles, & Hill, 1991). On the other hand, the combination of CD and depression is strongly associated with suicide, especially when combined with alcohol use (Andrews & Lewinsohn, 1992; Brent, Kolko, Allan, & Brown, 1990; Brent, Kolko, et al., 1993; Brent et al., 1988; Brent, Perper, et al., 1993; Lewinsohn, Rohde, & Seeley, 1994; Martunnen, Aro, Henriksson, & Lönnqvist, 1991; Rohde et al., 1991; Shaffer, 1993; Shaffer & Fisher, 1981).

CD with an anxiety disorder has been associated with less impairment (Walker et al., 1991), and perhaps lower rates of aggression and violent crime (Hinshaw et al., 1993), at least in younger children, and with higher levels of evening salivary cortisol than those found in either CD or anxiety alone (McBurnett et al., 1991). On the other hand, several studies of shyness and social withdrawal indicate that these features have negative implications for children with conduct problems (see Loeber & Keenan,

1994, for a review). Both anxiety and depression may also be more severe when they occur together (Last, Perrin, Hersen, & Kazdin, 1996).

It is hard to draw any hard and fast conclusions from this confusing literature, but it cannot be said to support the notion that comorbidity is simply a marker for overall severity of the component disorders. Rather it points to complex relationships among disorders over time, and in the case of suicide, to the particularly negative effects of depression and conduct disorder.

Comorbidity between conduct disorders and depressive disorders—are the latter simply part of the former, does CD cause depression, or do CD and depression have common or correlated causes? Zoccolillo's (1992) thoughtful review of the relationships between conduct disorder and depressive and emotional disorders across the life span concluded that, in our present state of knowledge, separate disorders should be diagnosed when conditions comorbid with CD are observed, and it firmly rejected the ICD-10 category of depressive conduct disorder. In considering the very limited evidence on a variety of explanations for CD comorbidity, he concluded that the best solution might be to regard CD as a "disorder of multiple dysfunction", with depression or anxiety representing dysfunctions in affect regulation and CD presumably being a form of social dysregulation. Given the evidence cited, it seems that this conclusion is only meant to apply to life-course persistent conduct problems. His key lines of evidence were: (1) the more severe the antisocial behavior, the greater the likelihood of comorbidity with non-antisocial disorders; (2) CD only predicts *adult* affective disturbance in individuals who have persistent antisocial behavior in adulthood; and (3) CD is associated with earlier onset of affective disturbances, at around the same time as the first CD symptoms appear. A good deal of additional work is needed to provide convincing evidence on each of these topics, but they also admit an alternative explanation—that CD causes affective disorders. Aggressive and CD children often interpret the social actions of others as being hostile (Quiggle, Garber, Panak, & Dodge, 1992), have problems in all sorts of social relationships, do poorly at school, get into serious trouble with the authorities, and are often told that they are bad. The literatures on life events, chronic difficulties and hassles, and cognitive styles in depression suggest that these correlates of CD could cause depression (see Capaldi, 1992, for a version of this model). This suggests the hypothesis that individuals with CD who had lower rates of difficulties arising from their CD behavior would manifest less depression. If specific predictors of the appearance of depression in CD (other than just the severity of CD itself) could be identified, and some or all of those predictors were effects of CD, then it would be reasonable to regard CD as causing depression. If depression were simply a manifestation of the diathesis underlying CD, no such specific risk factors should be identified because CD itself is the risk. An alternative approach was employed by Fergusson and his colleagues (Fergusson, Lynskey, & Horwood, 1996b). They fit structural equation models to their general population data to test the contrasting hypotheses that the relationship between CD and depression was either the result of correlations among the risk factors for the two disorders or the result of reciprocal causation. They found no support for the idea that either disorder caused the other, but noted that a substantial amount of the covariation between them could be explained by their having common or correlated risk factors. This elegant study underscores the usefulness of having measures of comorbidity on individuals at more than one point in time, and suggests an analytic approach that could be replicated with data from several of the general population studies listed in Table 3.

The work of Cohen and her colleagues (Cohen, Brook, Cohen, Velez, & Garcia, 1990) illustrates an alternative approach involving direct statistical comparisons among the relationships of risk factors measured in childhood with internalizing, externalizing, and substance abuse problems measured 8 years later. This study found that certain risk factors were "common" to more than one problem outcome. For instance, parental mental illness and remarriage were associated with both internalizing and externalizing problems. Other factors appeared to be relatively "specific" to only one sort of problem. For instance, residential instability was protective against substance abuse, but had no significant effect on either internalizing or externalizing problems. Family social isolation was related only to internalizing problems. The key strengths of this study are that it involves simultaneous examination of the effects of multiple risk factors on multiple outcomes measured at multiple points in time. Many statistical approaches to complex longitudinal data are now available, and, although it is often difficult to decide exactly how to implement the effects of comorbidity in such models, this general approach is one that deserves to be much more widely implemented.

Heterotypic comorbidity as a means of subtyping disorders—the case of ADHD. It has often been suggested that comorbidity may provide a means of subtyping disorders, and this possibility has been taken up in ICD-10 by the inclusion of diagnoses like hyperkinetic conduct disorder. The process began with clinical studies documenting high rates of comorbidity in clinical populations of children with ADHD, which led investigators to suggest that there might be meaningful differences in the nature of comorbid and non-comorbid disorders (e.g. Biederman, Newcorn, & Sprich, 1991; Jensen, Martin, & Cantwell, 1997; Munir, Biederman, & Knee, 1987; Schachar & Logan, 1990). The evidence discussed above, that ADHD comorbid with conduct problems had particularly malignant outcomes, strengthened the case (Taylor, 1994). More recently, family studies have lent further weight to the argument. These provide strong evidence that antisocial, substance abuse, and depressive disorders are more common in the parents of children with combined ADHD and CD/ODD than in parents of children with "pure" ADHD, but not unassailable evidence that hyperkinetic conduct disorder is a familially distinct subtype (see Faraone, Biederman, Jetton, & Tsuang, 1997). Results from the Virginia Twin Study of Adolescent Behavioral Development also suggest a common genetic component underlying hyperkinetic disorder and CD in younger boys (Silberg, Meyer, et al., 1996; Silberg, Rutter, et al., 1996), but weaker genetic liability for non-comorbid antisocial behavior. On the other hand,

some longitudinal data have not supported the subtype hypothesis (e.g. Taylor et al., 1996), and the literatures on pharmacotherapy and neuropsychological tests in ADHD indicate that the presence of conduct problems has little effect on the response of ADHD symptoms to medications or neuropsychological performance (Abikoff & Klein, 1992; Schachar & Rannock, 1995; Seidman et al., 1995). At least some of the data can also be seen to support the idea that ADHD and antisocial behavior reflect "different phases of the manifestation of the same underlying liability" (Rutter, 1997); in other words, heterotypic continuity in a unitary underlying disease.

This chain of work from cross-sectional observations of high rates of comorbidity to longitudinal outcome studies and family genetic approaches provides a good model of how progress can be made in understanding the implications of comorbidity. For instance, there is evidence that rates of both depressive and anxiety disorders are higher in the relatives of children with ADHD (Biederman et al., 1990; Biederman, Faraone, Keenan, & Tsuang, 1991; Perrin & Last, 1996). We can also expect ever-finer tuning of questions concerning comorbidity, since there is already evidence that the different subtypes of ADHD are associated with different patterns of comorbidity; in particular, that emotional disorders may be more strongly associated with non-hyperactive attention deficit disorder, whereas the combined subtype is more strongly associated with CD (see Eiraldi, Power, & Nezu, 1997, for a discussion of these findings and comments on the possible effects of changes in the subtyping of ADHD introduced in DSM-IV). Some are already moving towards subtyping the comorbid subtypes; witness Biederman and colleagues' (Biederman, Faraone, Milberger, et al., 1996) work suggesting that in ADHD there are two subtypes of ODD comorbidity with different correlates, course, and outcomes—one that is prodromal to CD and one that rarely progresses to CD. In contrast, we also have to remember that it may be relatively hard to find "pure" disorders, so we can also interpret the relationship between ADHD and ODD as failing to support the existence of meaningful distinctions between them (Paternite, Loney, & Roberts, 1995). However, the use of clinical samples to determine whether there are "pure" types of frequently comorbid disorders is particular problematic, because clinical presentation is associated with comorbidity (Angold, Messer, et al., 1998).

Combined Subtypes—Implications for Research on "Criteria Sets and Axes Provided for Further Study"

The two "combined" conditions for which there is most research support in child and adolescent psychiatry are hyperkinetic CD and depressive CD. However, it is interesting to note that the data typically adduced in favor of these two categories differ. Depressive CD is supported by arguments that the psychosocial and genetic correlates and outcomes of the combined category are more like those of CD than they are like those of depression—hence depressive CD is basically a form of CD. In essence, the combined form is *not* distinct from

CD (Esser et al., 1990; Harrington et al., 1991; Renouf, Kovacs, & Mukerji, 1997; Steinhausen & Reitzle, 1996). Coupled with this is evidence that the depressions in depressive CD *are* distinct from other depressions, though there is also evidence that they may not be so distinct as all that (J. E. Fleming, Boyle, & Offord, 1993; Kovacs, Paulauskas, Gatsonis, & Richards, 1988). On the other hand the evidence in favor of considering a separate subtype of hyperkinetic CD (or perhaps it would be better called conduct disordered ADHD) is that this condition is distinct *both* from other forms of ADHD *and* from other forms of CD.

In this field, we have a fairly noncontroversial approach to deciding whether conditions are separate, which relies on demonstrating *differences* between putative disorders at multiple levels (Cantwell, 1995; E. Robins & Guze, 1970; Rutter, 1978). According to this approach, lack of differentiation between pure CD and depressive CD is evidence that depressive CD is not a separate condition from CD, as Steinhausen and Reitzle (1996) have pointed out. But in the case of hyperkinetic CD, the argument is that both the ADHD and the CD components are different in the combined disorder. By the logic that allows a new subcategory to be created when only one of the components is different in the combined form compared with the pure form, a situation in which both components are different should surely be regarded as having identified a separate disorder. The danger here is that we could end up with an even greater proliferation of disorders than we already have, let alone of subcategories. If only one component of the combined disorder needs to be different from its uncombined form, we also face a possible proliferation of subcategories, because there are so many possible combinations of even a few disorders—and they all occur. One wonders, for instance, whether individuals with CD and ADHD and depression are not dissimilar in some ways from "pure" hyperkinetic CD. If any one of the three components were to be shown to have different correlates, then we would have a new subtype, presumably called "depressive hyperkinetic conduct disorder". Now such subtypes may exist, but with comorbidity being such a ubiquitous and poorly understood phenomenon, we imagine few would want to take this route. Similarly, psychometric evidence that the relationship between aggression and depression is a specific case of a broad-band association between internalizing and externalizing disorders (Weiss & Catron, 1994) leads us to expect that we would have to produce a similar group of subtypes for those with disruptive disorders and anxiety.

We suggest that *disorders* defined by comorbidity should be different from the pure forms of *both* their components. By this rule, the data on comorbid ADHD and CD is evidence for establishing a separate *diagnosis* based on comorbidity. This working hypothesis would be consistent with Zoccolillo's "disorder of multiple dysfunction" (Zoccolillo, 1992).

What about situations where one subcomponent only has been shown to differ from its "pure" form? There we have a valid *subtype* of *that* individual disorder. At first sight it may seem that this will create a confusing number of subcategories, but there are some important advantages to this solution. Let us suppose for a moment that

further research reveals that most depressions associated with CD were nonfamilial disorders that did not continue into adulthood, as current evidence suggests may be the case (Harrington et al., 1991). Let us also suppose (although the evidence is not yet available on this) that these did not respond to medications known to work in non-comorbid depressions. Let us also suppose that the typical non-comorbid depression was a highly familial disorder with a higher probability of continuation into adulthood and a good response to medication. In this hypothetical scenario we have good evidence that these two sorts of depression are meaningfully different. Let us also suppose that, say, pathological guilt and feelings of worthlessness are uncommon in the comorbid subtype compared with the non-comorbid subtype. We know that depression is relatively common in the general population, so some individuals with CD would actually be expected to have depressions of the *non*-comorbid type. If one were to see a child with CD who had a strong family history of depression, in a depressive episode involving pathological guilt and feelings of worthlessness, it would be appropriate to offer antidepressant medication, because that individual had a form of depression that resembled non-CD depression. This approach focuses attention on the place where the differences between the comorbid and the non-comorbid forms lie, whereas subtyping the CD focuses attention on the place where there are no differences. It may also avoid the possibility that we will need to create subcategories of depressive ODD and depressive ADHD, since if it were found that individuals with these disorders had depressions that were like those in CD, it would be necessary only to rename the comorbid depressive subtype to reflect its relations with all of the disruptive behavior disorders. The third potential advantage of subtyping the disorder where the differences lie stems from the fact that *most* depressions are comorbid with another disorder or disorders. If we find that the manifestations and correlates of depression are typically somewhat different in relation to each of the different disorders with which it co-occurs, we could end up effectively abolishing the diagnosis of depression if we treated each of these as a subtype of another disorder. In fact we would be back to the situation that pertained before the 1970s, when everyone recognized that depressive symptoms occurred in children, but no-one was given the diagnosis because these symptoms were seen as "reactions" to other underlying processes. In the face of growing evidence that there are effective treatments for depression, even when it is comorbid with other disorders, this would seem to be a serious mistake. If, on the other hand, we recognized subtypes of depression that differed in some, or all, of their correlates and outcomes, we would, at least, have a coherent description of depressive conditions available from the nosology.

An example for the future: Mixed anxiety-depressive disorder. Having set out this position, let us now turn to what is likely to emerge as a new line of comorbidity research over the next few years. Mixed anxiety-depressive disorder, one of the criteria sets "provided for further study" by DSM-IV, can be expected to spawn some work on this topic, if only because any study that included assessments of the regular DSM-III-R or DSM-IV anxiety and depressive disorders is likely to be able to generate diagnoses according to these experimental criteria. In the absence of any published research to date, we can nonetheless predict some findings from what we already know about the relationship between depression and anxiety. There is bound to be a big overlap between this disorder and GAD because so many of the symptoms overlap, and GAD requires only one symptom in addition to anxiety or worrying. Second, we can expect it to be quite common, so long as the exclusion criteria are ignored, as they usually have been in comorbidity research. But can we expect it to be differentiable from other depression or anxiety categories? First, it seems likely to be potentially useful as a residual category for individuals who are impaired but do not meet criteria for another diagnosis. The problem in this situation is that research algorithms do not diagnose the various not otherwise specified (NOS) categories provided by DSM-IV for these individuals (Angold, Costello, Farmer, Burns, & Erkanli, in press), so having a residual diagnosis with a specified set of criteria may be a help. On the other hand, we already have multiple overlapping diagnoses in the anxiety disorders, so do we really need another one? As we have already indicated, the answer to this lies in being able to differentiate between individuals with mixed symptoms and those with "pure" symptoms, and there are some indications in the current literature that there are differences between mixed and "pure" anxiety and depressive disorders. For instance, Kelvin, Goodyer, and Altham (1996) found that high emotionality on a temperament measure was associated with comorbidity between depression and anxiety, and particularly with the association between separation anxiety and dysthymia. Goodyer, Herbert, Secher, and Pearson (1997) found that depression at 36-week follow-up was predicted by severity of depression at presentation and comorbidity with obsessive-compulsive disorder. In another study, he and his colleagues (Herbert et al., 1996) found that comorbid panic or phobic disorders were associated with the *absence* of high evening cortisol in MDD. Lewinsohn, Rohde, et al. (1995) found that comorbidity with depression had a very substantial negative impact on the outcome of anxiety disorders. Williamson et al. (1995) found that comorbid anxiety *reduced* the rate of nonaffective diagnoses in relatives of depressed adolescents. On the other hand, Kovacs et al. (1989) and Alpert, Maddocks, Rosenbaum, and Fava (1994) reported that anxiety preceded depression in about two thirds of cases where they occurred together (see also Giaconia et al., 1994) and often persisted after the depression had remitted, but had no effect on the course of either MDD or dysthymia. Stark, Kaslow, and Laurent (1993) could not distinguish between anxious, depressed, and anxious-depressed individuals on the basis of several scale scores (but their samples were small). There seems to be enough evidence here to suggest that mixed disorders may constitute either a subtype of depression or anxiety or even perhaps a separate diagnosis. We suggest that the decision depends upon which comorbid components differ from their "pure" counterparts.

The Importance of Timing in Comorbidity Research: Substance Abuse—Timing of Onset or Comorbidity as Predictors of Adult Outcomes?

Another area where a key issue in the relationship between disorders turns on developmental timing concerns substance abuse and other psychiatric disorders. Many retrospective studies have noted the link between reported early onset of drug use and later persistence or problem use (Andreasson, Allebeck, Brandt, & Romelsjo, 1992; Kandel, Davies, Karus, & Yamaguchi, 1986; Kaplan, Martin, Johnson, & Robbins, 1986; Mills & Noyes, 1984; L. N. Robins & Murphy, 1967; L. N. Robins & Przybeck, 1985; L. N. Robins & Ratcliff, 1980; Welte & Barnes, 1985; Yamaguchi & Kandel, 1984). Anthony and Petronis (1995), for example, made elegant use of the Epidemiologic Catchment Area Study (ECA) data to show that risk of adult drug problems was linearly related to age at onset, being twice as high in adults reporting first use before age 13 as in those with first use after age 17. The time from first use to problem use was around 4 years, irrespective of age at first use. Although prospective data are generally to be preferred, there is a shortage of prospective studies with a sufficiently long timespan to compare adult outcomes of early vs. late onset of use in adolescence (Kandel, 1978). Remarkably, we could find no prospective study testing Anthony and Petronis's retrospective finding of a linear relationship between age at onset and probability of adult problem drug use. Most of the prospective studies simply compare later drug use of early users with early nonusers, but still point to the negative impact of early use for later problem use (Anderson, Bergman, & Magnusson, 1989; Boyle et al., 1992; Stein, Newcomb, & Bentler, 1987; Van Kammen, Loeber, & Stouthamer-Loeber, 1991; Windle, 1990; Zucker & Gomberg, 1986). Fleming and colleagues (J. P. Fleming, Kellam, & Brown, 1982) found that early-onset drug use predicted intensity of use at age 16–17; "The strongest contrast in frequency of use is between those teenagers who first used the substances after age 15 and those who initiated use prior to age 15". The small but intensive New York Longitudinal Study (Tubman, Vicary, von Eye, & Lerner, 1990) suggested that early-onset drug use (13–15 years) carried a worse adult prognosis than later-onset drug use (16–19). Overall, there is a strong support for the idea that early onset of substance use is associated with a worse substance abuse prognosis in adulthood.

Numerous questionnaire and diagnostic studies have demonstrated associations between adolescent drug and alcohol use and various forms of psychopathology, including low self-esteem, depression scale scores, antisocial behavior, rebelliousness, aggressiveness, crime, delinquency, truancy and poor school performance, CD, anxiety disorders, depressive disorders, suicide, and ADHD (see, e.g., Beals et al., 1997; Brent et al., 1986; Bukstein, Glancy, & Kaminer, 1992; Clayton, 1989; Deykin, Buka, & Zeena, 1992; Deykin, Levy, & Wells, 1987; Fergusson et al., 1993a; Greenbaum, Prange, Friedman, & Silver, 1991; Hovens, Cantwell, & Kiriakos, 1994; Jessor & Jessor, 1977; L. D. Johnston, O'Malley, & Eveland, 1978a; Kaminer, Tarter, Bukstein, & Kabene, 1992; Kandel et al., 1986; Kandel, Kessler, & Margulies,

1978; Kandel, Single, & Kessler, 1976; Kaplan, 1980; King et al., 1996; Kleinman, Wish, Deren, & Rainone, 1986; Neighbors, Kempton, & Forehand, 1992; Paton & Kandel, 1978; Paton, Kessler, & Kandel, 1977; Smith & Fogg, 1979; Stowell & Estroff, 1992; Wingard, Huba, & Bentler, 1979). In fact, many studies of antisocial behavior still include early drug use as one among a range of possible symptoms (e.g. Elliott, Huizinga, & Ageton, 1984; Farrell & Taylor, 1994; Farrington, 1983; Hammersley, Forsyth, & Lavelle, 1990; Moffitt, 1993), although it is treated in DSM-IV as an *associated* symptom. Children who *later* become problem drinkers or drug users have been found to have high rates of school dropout and poor achievement, rebelliousness, antisocial behavior, aggressive behavior, delinquency, and family problems (Anderson et al., 1989; Barnes, 1984; Barnes & Welte, 1986; Boyle & Offord, 1991; Cairns & Cairns, 1994; G. A. Carlson, Bromet, & Jandorf, 1998; Chilcoat & Anthony, 1996; Fergusson et al., 1993a; Greenbaum et al., 1991; Jessor et al., 1980; Jessor, Graves, Hanson, & Jessor, 1968; L. D. Johnston et al., 1978b; Jones, 1968; Kandel et al., 1978; Kaplan, 1980; Kleinman et al., 1986; Kleinman, Wish, Deren, Rainone, & Morehouse, 1988; Knop, Goodwin, Teasdale, Mikkelsen, & Schulsinger, 1984; Knop, Teasdale, Schulsinger, & Goodwin, 1985; J. McCord, McCord, & Thurber, 1962; W. McCord & McCord, 1960; Monnelly, Hartl, & Elderkin, 1983; Orive & Gerard, 1980; Ricks & Berry, 1970; L. N. Robins, 1974; L. N. Robins & Murphy, 1967; L. N. Robins & Wish, 1977; Rydelius, 1981; Santo, Hooper, Friedman, & Conner, 1980; Schuckit, 1982; Vaillant & Milofsky, 1982; Windle & Barnes, 1988; Zucker & Barron, 1973; Zucker & DeVoe, 1975).

Studies of temporal ordering have generally found that onset of other psychiatric disorders precedes that of problem alcohol and drug use (Boyle et al., 1992; Ellickson & Hays, 1991; Elliott, Huizinga, & Menard, 1988; Gittelman, Mannuzza, Shenker, & Bonagura, 1985; Rohde et al., 1996; Van Kammen & Loeber, 1994), but this may be because it takes longer to reach DSM-level drug abuse or dependence than to manifest other disorders. Loeber (1988, pp. 94–95) summarizes the evidence in relation to delinquency thus: "Across different delinquent types of offenders, about twice as many initiate drug use after their delinquent involvement compared with initiating delinquency after drug use." However, one would expect that the trajectory of antisocial behavior would be interwoven with the trajectory of drug involvement (A. S. Friedman, Utada, Glickman, & Morrissey, 1987). Brook, Cohen, and Brook's (1998) work provides a nice example here. Across the period from middle adolescence to early adulthood, they found no evidence that depressive disorders, anxiety disorders, or CD had any influence on later drug use once adolescents had started to use drugs. On the other hand, drug use was related to the development of later depressive disorders. As the authors of this study pointed out, their findings do not contradict the idea that *earlier* psychiatric problems (such as CD in late childhood or early adolescence) are associated with later substance abuse. Indeed, their own earlier work showed pathways from various childhood personality characteristics and aggression to later substance use, mediated by depressive

symptoms and unconventionality (Brook, Whiteman, Balka, & Cohen, 1997; Brook, Whiteman, Cohen, Shapiro, & Balka, 1995; Brook, Whiteman, Finch, & Cohen, 1995; Brook, Whiteman, Finch, & Cohen, 1996). General developmental principles (Costello & Angold, 1996) teach us that relationships among disorders may change over time as patterns of reciprocal influence between the causes and effects of different forms of psychopathology become established.

Almost all this research has been on boys only, and we need more work on girls, especially since what has been done suggests that drug use may follow depression or anxiety in girls, but that this order is reversed in boys (Rohde et al., 1996). In passing, we should also note that studies showing that ADHD is probably associated with an increased risk of substance abuse have also found this association to be mediated through the high rates of CD that occur in ADHD, rather than being a direct effect of ADHD itself (Fergusson, Lynskey, & Horwood, 1993b; Gittelman et al., 1985; Loney, 1988). Here we see that it is sometimes necessary to consider three-way comorbidities over time.

Robins, using data from two follow-up studies and from the ECA, states (L. N. Robins & McEvoy, 1990, p. 196),

> Abuse is extremely rare for those free of (early) conduct problems, no matter how early substance use began. At every other level of conduct problems, however, the earlier that use begins, the greater is the likelihood of substance abuse.... For those first using substances before age 20, the number of conduct problems was an even better predictor of substance abuse than was age of onset (before or after age 15). Among those beginning substance use before age 15 with seven or more conduct problems, more than half developed substance abuse; with only one conduct problem, only 5% did so. When first use occurred between ages 15 and 19, there is still a large effect from number of conduct problems, but the control for age of first use somewhat reduced their impact.

Despite the mass of literature reviewed above, we can find no direct, prospective test of this important conclusion. Also, the implications for intervention drawn by Robins are open to question when she argues that her findings support a "Just say later" prevention strategy, to delay onset of drug use to beyond age 15 or 19 (Robins & McEvoy, 1990, p. 203). The data we have presented could also be seen as indicating that it is conduct problem comorbidity that predicts later drug abuse, not age of initiation of use itself, and that the apparent effect of age at initiation results from earlier initiation of substance use by individuals with conduct problems (and perhaps other psychiatric disorders). These contrasting hypotheses are directly testable, though we are aware of no prospective study that has tested them.

Conclusions

The last 10 years have seen comorbidity established as unquestionably "real", and attitudes have swung towards regarding comorbidity as an opportunity for better understanding of the development of psychopathology. The result has been a good deal of research aimed at improving diagnostic boundaries, and describing the course and correlates of comorbid and "pure" disorders.

As we have already said, in no case can we be sure that we understand the substantive causes of comorbidity between any pair of diagnoses. However, we can be sure that substantive causes need to be sought, because none of the possible methodological explanations for comorbidity holds water for all pairs of diagnoses. We can also reject the notion that all child psychopathology constitutes an undifferentiated mass upon which diagnostic conventions impose meaningless categorical boundaries, though the various individual anxiety diagnoses are so poorly validated in childhood that homotypic comorbidity amongst them is probably partly explained by inappropriate diagnostic boundary placement. On the other hand, nonspecific symptoms in the criterion sets for disorders do not explain comorbidity between disorders sharing those symptoms. Even if we reject categorical diagnosis, we still have to explain why there are correlations among different dimensions of psychopathology derived from factor analysis, while a single factor does not suffice to explain covariation among symptoms. There is little evidence that any one disorder directly causes any other disorder, but it is likely that some homotypic comorbid patterns (depression with dysthymia and ODD with CD) represent developmental sequences of unitary underlying developmental psychopathologic processes (at least in some individuals). There is enough evidence to support continuing research on the idea that certain patterns of heterotypic comorbidity (particulary hyperkinetic CD, depressive CD, and anxious depression) represent separate subtypes or even diagnoses from their component diagnoses (though this is by no means proven). On the other hand, comorbidity of CD or ODD with anxiety, and ADHD with depression, may simply be epiphenomenal. Different disorders appear to share some risk factors in common, but there are also risk factors that are specific to particular disorders, so the presence of shared risk factors is likely to be an important component in the causation of comorbidity.

At many points in our discussion, the topic of timing has come up, and we need to remember that this is a key component for understanding comorbidity. Most studies of the subject in both childhood and adulthood have relied either on a single wave of cross-sectional data, or relied on recall of disorders over the whole life course. Both of these approaches involve a "snapshot" at a particular point in time, and are incapable of providing descriptions of the interplay of shared and specific risk factors over time and their effects on diagnostic status, again over time. Now there is a need to shift beyond documenting rates of comorbidity to studying correlates and implications of comorbidity over time in the hope of identifying likely etiological mechanisms. One obvious conclusion is that community-based longitudinal diagnostic studies will be needed. These studies will have to be large enough to separate out the specific and nonspecific effects of a range of risk factors across a range of diagnoses. A start has been made in this area, but we have a long way to go. Family genetic approaches are already

making a big contribution, and twin studies that focus on comorbidity will also be productive (Rutter, 1997). Very little attention has yet been paid to age or gender effects on comorbidity, and the psychobiology of "pure" and comorbid conditions has hardly begun to be addressed. There are still a lot of conceptual confusions and conflicts to be sorted out if we are to have a set of coherent explanations of comorbidity and nosological responses to them, but there is also a much better appreciation of what the problems are, and of the need to use multiple approaches to overcoming them. If things move as fast over the next 10 years as they have over the last 10, comorbidity may have ceased to be a problem by the time this journal commissions another research review.

References

Abikoff, H., & Klein, R. G. (1992). Attention-deficit hyperactivity and conduct disorder: Comorbidity and implications for treatment. *Journal of Consulting and Clinical Psychology, 60*, 881–892.

Achenbach, T. M. (1966). The classification of children's psychiatric symptoms: A factor-analytic study. *Psychological Monographs, 80*, 1–37.

Achenbach, T. M. (1990). "Comorbidity" in child and adolescent psychiatry: Categorical and quantitative perspectives. *Journal of Child and Adolescent Psychopharmacology, 1*, 271–278.

Achenbach, T. M. (1995). Diagnosis, assessment, and comorbidity in psychosocial treatment research. *Journal of Abnormal Child Psychology, 23*, 45–65.

Achenbach, T. M., Conners, C. K., Quay, H. C., Verhulst, F. C., & Howell, C. T. (1989). Replication of empirically derived syndromes as a basis for taxonomy of child/adolescent psychopathology. *Journal of Abnormal Child Psychology, 17*, 299–323.

Alpert, J. E., Maddocks, A., Rosenbaum, J. F., & Fava, M. (1994). Childhood psychopathology retrospectively assessed among adults with early onset major depression. *Journal of Affective Disorders, 31*, 165–171.

American Psychiatric Association. (1980). *Diagnostic and statistical manual of mental disorders* (3rd ed., DSM-III). Washington, DC: American Psychiatric Press.

American Psychiatric Association. (1987). *Diagnostic and statistical manual of mental disorders* (3rd ed. revised, DSM-III-R). Washington, DC: American Psychiatric Press.

American Psychiatric Association. (1994). *Diagnostic and statistical manual of mental disorders* (4th ed., DSM-IV). Washington, DC: American Psychiatric Press.

Anderson, J. C., Williams, S., McGee, R., & Silva, P. A. (1987). DSM-III disorders in preadolescent children: Prevalence in a large sample from the general population. *Archives of General Psychiatry, 44*, 69–77.

Anderson, T., Bergman, L. R., & Magnusson, D. (1989). Patterns of adjustment problems and alcohol abuse in early adulthood: A prospective longitudinal study. *Development and Psychopathology, 1*, 119–131.

Andreasson, S., Allebeck, P., Brandt, L., & Romelsjo, A. (1992). Antecedents and covariates of high alcohol consumption in young men. *Alcoholism, Clinical and Experimental Research, 16*, 708–713.

Andrews, J. A., & Lewinsohn, P. M. (1992). Suicidal attempts among older adolescents: Prevalence and co-occurrence with psychiatric disorders. *Journal of the American Academy of Child and Adolescent Psychiatry, 31*, 655–662.

Angold, A. (1988). Childhood and adolescent depression I: Epidemiological and aetiological aspects. *British Journal of Psychiatry, 152*, 601–617.

Angold, A. (1996). *Effects of puberty on eating and sleeping: Implications for depression.* Invited presentation at National Institute of Mental Health Workshop: "Neurobiology of Adolescent Depression: Sleep-Arousal Regulation and Related Developmental Changes", Rockville, MD.

Angold, A., & Costello, E. J. (1992). Comorbidity in children and adolescents with depression. In M. Lewis & D. P. Cantwell (Eds.), *Child and adolescent psychiatric clinics of North America: Mood disorders* (pp. 1–21). Philadelphia, PA: W. B. Saunders Company.

Angold, A., & Costello, E. J. (1993). Depressive comorbidity in children and adolescents: Empirical, theoretical, and methodological issues. *American Journal of Psychiatry, 150,* 1779–1791.

Angold, A., Costello, E. J., Farmer, E. M. Z., Burns, B. J., & Erkanli, A. (in press). Impaired but undiagnosed. *Journal of the American Academy of Child and Adolescent Psychiatry.*

Angold, A., Erkanli, A., Egger, H. M., & Costello, E. J. (1998). *Comorbidity real and "epiphenomenal" in the Great Smoky Mountains Study.* Manuscript submitted for publication.

Angold, A., Messer, S. C., Stangl, D., Farmer, E. M. Z., Costello, E. J., & Burns, B. J. (1998). Perceived parental burden and service use for child and adolescent psychiatric disorders. *American Journal of Public Health, 88,* 75–80.

Angst, J., & Dobler-Mikola, A. (1984). The Zurich Study: II. The continuum from normal to pathological depressive mood swings. *European Archives of Psychiatry and Neurological Sciences, 234,* 21–29.

Angst, J., Dobler-Mikola, A., & Binder, J. (1984). The Zurich study—A prospective epidemiological study of depressive, neurotic and psychosomatic syndromes. I. Problem, methodology. *European Archives of Psychiatry and Neurological Sciences, 234,* 13–20.

Anthony, J. C., & Petronis, K. R. (1995). Early-onset drug use and risk of later drug problems. *Drug and Alcohol Dependence, 40,* 9–15.

Arnold, E., & Smeltzer, D. J. (1974). Behavior checklist factor analysis for children and adolescents. *Archives of General Psychiatry, 30,* 799–804.

Asarnow, J. R., & Ben-Meir, S. (1994). Children with schizophrenia spectrum and depressive disorders: A comparative study of premorbid adjustment, onset pattern and severity of impairment. *Journal of Child Psychology and Psychiatry, 29,* 477–488.

August, G. J., Realmuto, G. M., MacDonald, A. W., Nugent, S. M., & Crosby, R. (1996). Prevalence of ADHD and comorbid disorders among elementary school children screened for disruptive behavior. *Journal of Abnormal Child Psychology, 24,* 571–595.

Barkley, R. A. (1990). The adolescent outcome of hyperactive children diagnosed by research criteria: I. An 8-year prospective follow-up study. *Journal of the American Academy of Child and Adolescent Psychiatry, 29,* 546–557.

Barnes, G. M. (1984). Adolescent alcohol abuse and other problem behaviors: Their relationships and common parental influences. *Journal of Youth and Adolescence, 13,* 329–348.

Barnes, G. M., & Welte, J. W. (1986). Patterns and predictors of alcohol use among 7–12th grade students in New York State. *Journal of Studies on Alcohol, 47,* 53–62.

Beals, J., Piasecki, J., Nelson, S., Jones, M., Keane, E., Dauphinais, P., Shirt, R. R., Sack, W. H., & Manson, S. M. (1997). Psychiatric disorder among American Indian adolescents: Prevalence in northern plains youth. *Journal of the American Academy of Child and Adolescent Psychiatry, 36,* 1252–1259.

Beardslee, W. R., Keller, M. B., Seifer, R., Lavori, P. W., Staley, J., Podorefsky, D., & Shera, D. (1996). Prediction of adolescent affective disorder: Effects of prior parental affective disorders and child psychopathology. *Journal of the American Academy of Child and Adolescent Psychiatry, 35,* 279–288.

Beidel, D., Fink, C. M., & Turner, S. M. (1996). Stability of anxious symptomatology in children. *Journal of Abnormal Child Psychology, 24,* 257–269.

Beidel, D., & Turner, S. M. (1997). At risk for anxiety: I. Psychopathology in the offspring of anxious parents. *Journal of the American Academy of Child and Adolescent Psychiatry, 36,* 918–924.

Berkson, J. (1946). Limitations of the application of fourfold table analysis to hospital data. *Biometrics Bulletin, 2,* 47–52.

Biederman, J., Faraone, S., Mick, E., & Lelon, E. (1995). Psychiatric comorbidity among referred juveniles with major depression: Fact or artefact? *Journal of the American Academy of Child and Adolescent Psychiatry, 34,* 579–590.

Biederman, J., Faraone, S. V., Keenan, K., Benjamin, J., Krifcher, B., Moore, C., Sprich, S., Ugaglia, K., Jellinek, M. S., Steingard, R., Spencer, T., Norman, D., Kolodny, R., Kraus, I., Perrin, J., Keller, M. B., & Tsuang, M. T. (1992). Further evidence for family-genetic risk factors in Attention Deficit Hyperactivity Disorder: Patterns of comorbidity in probands and relatives in psychiatrically and pediatrically referred samples. *Archives of General Psychiatry,* 728–738.

Biederman, J., Faraone, S. V., Keenan, K., Knee, D., & Tsuang, M. T. (1990). Family-genetic and psychosocial risk factors in DSM-III attention deficit disorder. *Journal of the American Academy of Child and Adolescent Psychiatry, 29,* 526–533.

Biederman, J., Faraone, S. V., Keenan, K., & Tsuang, M. T. (1991). Evidence of familial association between attention deficit disorder and major affective disorders. *Archives of General Psychiatry, 48,* 633–642.

Biederman, J., Faraone, S. V., Marrs, A., Moore, P., Garcia, J., Ablon, S., Mick, E., Gershon, J., & Kearns, M. E. (1997). Panic disorder and agoraphobia in consecutively referred children and adolescents. *Journal of the American Academy of Child and Adolescent Psychiatry, 36,* 214–223.

Biederman, J., Faraone, S. V., & Mick, E. (1996). Attention deficit hyperactivity disorder and juvenile mania? An overlooked comorbidity? *Journal of the American Academy of Child and Adolescent Psychiatry, 35,* 997–1008.

Biederman, J., Faraone, S. V., Milberger, S., Jetton, J. G., Chen, L., Mick, E., Greene, R. W., & Russell, R. L. (1996). Is childhood oppositional defiant disorder a precursor to adolescent conduct disorder? Findings from a four-year follow-up study of children with ADHD. *Journal of the American Academy of Child and Adolescent Psychiatry, 35,* 1193–1204.

Biederman, J., Mick, E., & Faraone, S. V. (1998). Depression in attention deficit hyperactivity disorder (ADHD) children: "True" depression or demoralization? *Journal of Affective Disorders, 47,* 113–122.

Biederman, J., Newcorn, J., & Sprich, S. (1991). Comorbidity of attention deficit hyperactivity disorder with conduct, depressive, anxiety, and other disorders. *American Journal of Psychiatry, 148,* 564–577.

Bird, H. R., Gould, M. S., & Staghezza, B. M. (1993). Patterns of diagnostic comorbidity in a community sample of children aged 9 through 16 years. *Journal of the American Academy of Child and Adolescent Psychiatry, 32,* 361–368.

Borchardt, C. M., & Bernstein, G. A. (1995). Comorbid disorders in hospitalized bipolar adolescents compared with unipolar depressed adolescents. *Child Psychiatry and Human Development, 26,* 11–18.

Boyle, M. H., & Offord, D. R. (1991). Psychiatric disorder and substance use in adolescence. *Canadian Journal of Psychiatry, 36,* 699–705.

Boyle, M. H., Offord, D. R., Racine, Y. A., Szatmari, P., Fleming, J. E., & Links, P. S. (1992). Predicting substance use in late adolescence: Results from the Ontario Child Health Study follow-up. *American Journal of Psychiatry, 149*, 761–767.

Bradley, S. J., & Hood, J. (1993). Psychiatrically referred adolescents with panic attacks: Presenting symptoms, stressors, and comorbidity. *Journal of the American Academy of Child and Adolescent Psychiatry, 32*, 826–829.

Brent, D. A., Kalas, R., Edelbrock, C., Costello, A. J., Dulcan, M. K., & Conover, N. (1986). Psychopathology and its relationship to suicidal ideation in childhood and adolescence. *Journal of the American Academy of Child and Adolescent Psychiatry, 25*, 666–673.

Brent, D. A., Kolko, D. J., Allan, M. J., & Brown, R. V. (1990). Suicidality in affectively disordered adolescent inpatients. *Journal of the American Academy of Child and Adolescent Psychiatry, 29*, 586–593.

Brent, D. A., Kolko, D. J., Wartella, M. E., Boylan, M. B., Moritz, G., Baugher, M., & Zelenak, J. P. (1993). Adolescent psychiatric inpatients' risk of suicide attempt at 6-month follow-up. *Journal of the American Academy of Child and Adolescent Psychiatry, 32*, 95–105.

Brent, D. A., Perper, J. A., Goldstein, C. E., Kolko, D. J., Allan, M. J., Allman, C. J., & Zelenak, J. P. (1988). Risk factors for adolescent suicide. A comparison of adolescent suicide victims with suicidal inpatients. *Archives of General Psychiatry, 45*, 581–588.

Brent, D. A., Perper, J. A., Moritz, G., Allman, C., Friend, A., Roth, C., Schweers, J., Balach, L., & Baugher, M. (1993). Psychiatric risk factors for adolescent suicide: A case-control study. *Journal of the Academy of Child and Adolescent Psychiatry, 32*, 521–529.

Brook, J. S., Cohen, P., & Brook, D. W. (1998). Longitudinal study of co-occurring psychiatric disorders and substance use. *Journal of the American Academy of Child and Adolescent Psychiatry, 37*, 322–330.

Brook, J. S., Whiteman, M., Balka, E. B., & Cohen, P. (1997). Drug use and delinquency: Shared and unshared risk factors in African American and Puerto Rican adolescents. *Journal of Genetic Psychology, 158*, 25–39.

Brook, J. S., Whiteman, M., Cohen, P., Shapiro, J., & Balka, E. (1995). Longitudinally predicting late adolescent and young adult drug use: Childhood and adolescent precursors. *Journal of the American Academy of Child and Adolescent Psychiatry, 34*, 1230–1238.

Brook, J. S., Whiteman, M., Finch, S., & Cohen, P. (1995). Aggression, intrapsychic distress, and drug use. Antecedent and intervening processes. *Journal of the American Academy of Child and Adolescent Psychiatry, 34*, 1076–1084.

Brook, J. S., Whiteman, M., Finch, S. J., & Cohen, P. (1996). Young adult drug use and delinquency: Childhood antecedents and adolescent mediators. *Journal of the American Academy of Child and Adolescent Psychiatry, 35*, 1584–1592.

Brown, G. W., Harris, T. O., & Eales, M. J., (1993). Aetiology of anxiety and depressive disorders in an inner-city population: II. Comorbidity and adversity. *Psychological Medicine, 23*, 155–165.

Bukstein, O. G., Glancy, L. J., & Kaminer, Y. (1992). Patterns of affective comorbidity in a clinical population of dually diagnosed adolescent substance abusers. *Journal of the American Academy of Child and Adolescent Psychiatry, 31*, 1041–1045.

Butler, S. F., Arredondo, D. E., & McCloskey, V. (1995). Affective comorbidity in children and adolescents with attention deficit hyperactivity disorder. *Annals of Clinical Psychiatry, 7*, 51–55.

Cairns, R. B., & Cairns, B. D. (1994). Lost and found: I. Recovery of subjects in longitudinal research. In R. B. Cairns

& B. D. Cairns (Eds.), *Lifelines and risks: Pathways of youth in our time.* New York: Cambridge University Press.

Campbell, S. B. (1990). *Behavior problems in preschool children: Developmental and clinical issues.* New York: Guilford Press.

Cantwell, D. P. (1972). Psychiatric illness in the families of hyperactive children. *Archives of General Psychiatry, 27*, 414–423.

Cantwell, D. P. C. (1995). Child psychiatry: Introduction and overview. In H. I. Kaplan & B. J. Sadock (Eds.), *Comprehensive textbook of psychiatry* (pp. 2151–2154). Baltimore, MD: Williams & Wilkins.

Capaldi, D. M. (1992). Co-occurrence of conduct problems and depressive symptoms in early adolescent boys: II. A 2-year follow-up at grade 8. *Development and Psychopathology, 4*, 125–144.

Carlson, C. L., Tamm, L., & Gaub, M. (1997). Gender differences in children with ADHD, ODD, and co-occurring ADHD/ODD identified in a school population. *Journal of the American Academy of Child and Adolescent Psychiatry, 36*, 1706–1714.

Carlson, G. A., Bromet, E. J., & Jandorf, L. (1998). Conduct disorder and mania: What does it mean to adults? *Journal of Affective Disorders, 48*, 199–205.

Carlson, G. A., & Cantwell, D. P. (1979). A survey of depressive symptoms in a child and adolescent psychiatric population: Interview data. *Journal of the American Academy of Child and Adolescent Psychiatry, 18*, 587–599.

Carlson, G. A., & Cantwell, D. P. (1980). Unmasking masked depression in children and adolescents. *American Journal of Psychiatry, 137*, 445–449.

Caron, C., & Rutter, M. (1991). Comorbidity in child psychopathology: Concepts, issues and research strategies. *Journal of Child Psychology and Psychiatry, 32*, 1063–1080.

Chilcoat, H. D., & Anthony, J. C. (1996). Impact of parents monitoring on initiation of drug use through late childhood. *Journal of the American Academy of Child and Adolescent Psychiatry, 35*, 91–100.

Clark, D. B., Smith, M. G., Neighbors, B. D., Skerlec, L. M., & Randall, R. (1994). Anxiety disorders in adolescence: Characteristics, prevalence, and comorbidities. *Clinical Psychology Review, 14*, 113–137.

Clayton, R. R. (1989). Transitions in drug use: Risk and protective factors. In M. Glantz & R. Pickens (Eds.), *Vulnerability to drug abuse* (pp. 15–51). Washington, DC: American Psychological Association.

Cohen, P., Brook, J. S., Cohen, J., Velez, N., & Garcia, M. (1990). Common and uncommon pathways to adolescent psychopathology and problem behavior. In L. N. Robins (Ed.), *Straight and devious pathways from childhood to adulthood* (pp. 242–258). New York: Cambridge University Press.

Costello, E. J., & Angold, A. (1996). Developmental psychopathology. In R. B. Cairns, G. H. Elder, & E. J. Costello (Eds.), *Developmental science* (pp. 23–56). New York: Cambridge University Press.

Costello, E. J., Angold, A., Burns, B. J., Stangl, D. K., Tweed, D. L., Erkanli, A., & Worthman, C. M. (1996). The Great Smoky Mountains Study of Youth: Goals, designs, methods, and the prevalence of DSM-III-R disorders. *Archives of General Psychiatry, 53*, 1129–1136.

Costello, E. J., Costello, A. J., Edelbrock, C., Burns, B. J., Dulcan, M. K., Brent, D., & Janiszewski, S. (1988). Psychiatric disorders in pediatric primary care: Prevalence and risk factors. *Archives of General Psychiatry, 45*, 1107–1116.

Costello, E. J., Farmer, E., Angold, A., Burns, B., & Erkanli, A. (1997). Psychiatric disorders among American Indian and white youth in Appalachia: The Great Smoky Mountains study. *American Journal of Public Health, 87*, 827–832.

Decina, P., Kestenbaum, C., Farber, S., Kron, L., Gargan, M.,

Sackheim, H., & Fieve, R. (1983). Clinical and psychological assessment of children of bipolar probands. *American Journal of Psychiatry, 140,* 548–553.

Deykin, E. Y., Buka, S. L., & Zeena, T. H. (1992). Depressive illness among chemically dependent adolescents. *American Journal of Psychiatry, 149,* 1341–1347.

Deykin, E. Y., Levy, J. C., & Wells, V. (1987). Adolescent depression, alcohol and drug abuse. *American Journal of Psychiatry, 77,* 178–181.

Eiraldi, R. B., Power, T. J., & Nezu, C. M. (1997). Patterns of comorbidity associated with subtypes of attention-deficit/ hyperactivity disorder among 6–12-year-old children. *Journal of the American Academy of Child and Adolescent Psychiatry, 36,* 503–514.

Ellickson, P. L., & Hays, R. D. (1991). Antecedents of drinking among young adolescents with different alcohol use histories. *Journal of Studies on Alcohol, 52,* 398–408.

Elliott, D. S., Huizinga, D., & Ageton, S. S. (1984). *Explaining delinquency and drug use.* Beverly Hills, CA: Sage Publications.

Elliott, D. S., Huizinga, D., & Menard, S. (1988). *Multiple problem youth: Delinquency, substance use and mental health problems.* New York: Springer-Verlag Publishing.

Esser, G., Schmidt, M. H., & Woerner, W. (1990). Epidemiology and course of psychiatric disorders in school-age children—results of a longitudinal study. *Journal of Child Psychology and Psychiatry, 31,* 243–263.

Faraone, S. V., Biederman, J., Jetton, J. G., & Tsuang, M. T. (1997). Attention deficit disorder and conduct disorder. Longitudinal evidence for a familial subtype. *Psychological Medicine, 27,* 291–300.

Faraone, S. V., Biederman, J., Keenan, K., & Tsuang, M. T. (1991). Separation of DSM-III attention deficit disorder and conduct disorder: Evidence from a family-genetic study of American child psychiatric patients. *Psychological Medicine, 21,* 109–121.

Faraone, S. V., Biederman, J., Mennin, D., Wozniak, J., & Spencer, T. (1997). Attention-deficit hyperactivity disorder with bipolar disorder: A familial subtype? *Journal of the American Academy of Child and Adolescent Psychiatry, 36,* 1378–1387.

Farrell, M., & Taylor, E. (1994). Drug and alcohol use and misuse. In M. Rutter, E. Taylor, & L. Hersov (Eds.), *Child and adolescent psychiatry: Modern approaches* (pp. 529–545). Oxford: Blackwell Scientific Publications.

Farrington, D. P. (1983). Offending from 10 to 25 years of age. In K. T. VanDusen & S. A. Mednick (Eds.), *Prospective studies of crime and delinquency* (pp. 17–37). Boston, MA: Kluwer-Nijhoff.

Farrington, D. P. (1986). Age and crime. *Crime and Justice: An Annual Review of Research, 7,* 29–90.

Farrington, D. P., Loeber, R., & Elliott, D. S. (1990). Advancing knowledge about the onset of delinquency and crime. In B. B. Lahey & A. E. Kazdin (Eds.), *Advances in clinical child psychology* (pp. 283–342). New York: Plenum Press.

Feehan, M., McGee, R., Raja, S. N., & Williams, S. M. (1994). DSM-III-R disorders in New Zealand 18-year-olds. *Australian and New Zealand Journal of Psychiatry, 28,* 87–99.

Fergusson, D. M., Horwood, L. J., & Lynskey, M. T. (1993a). Prevalence and comorbidity of DSM-III-R diagnoses in a birth cohort of 15-year-olds. *Journal of the American Academy of Child and Adolescent Psychiatry, 32,* 1127–1134.

Fergusson, D. M., Lynskey, M. T., & Horwood, L. J. (1993b). Conduct problems and attention deficit behaviour in middle childhood and cannabis use by age 15. *Australian and New Zealand Journal of Psychiatry, 27,* 673–682.

Fergusson, D. M., Lynskey, M. T., & Horwood, L. J. (1996a). Factors associated with continuity and change in disruptive behavior patterns between childhood and adolescence. *Journal of Abnormal Child Psychology, 24,* 533–553.

Fergusson, D. M., Lynskey, M. T., & Horwood, L. J. (1996b). Origins of comorbidity between conduct and affective disorders. *Journal of the American Academy of Child and Adolescent Psychiatry, 35,* 451–460.

Ferro, T., Carlson, G. A., Grayson, P., & Klein, D. N. (1994). Depressive disorders: Distinctions in children. *Journal of the American Academy of Child and Adolescent Psychiatry, 33,* 664–670.

Fine, S., Moretti, M., Haley, G., & Marriage, K. (1985). Affective disorders in children and adolescents: The dysthymic disorder dilemma. *Canadian Journal of Psychiatry, 30,* 173–177.

Fleming, J. E., Boyle, M. H., & Offord, D. R. (1993). The outcome of adolescent depression in the Ontario child health study follow-up. *Journal of the American Academy of Child and Adolescent Psychiatry, 32,* 28–33.

Fleming, J. P., Kellam, S. G., & Brown, C. H. (1982). Early predictors of age at first use of alcohol, marijuana, and cigarettes. *Drug and Alcohol Dependence, 9,* 285–303.

Fletcher, K. E., Fisher, M., Barkley, R. A., & Smallish, L. (1996). A sequential analysis of the mother-adolescent interactions of ADHD, ADHD/ODD, and normal teenagers during neutral and conflict discussions. *Journal of Abnormal Child Psychology, 24,* 271–297.

Fombonne, E. (1994). The Chartres Study: I. Prevalence of psychiatric disorders among French school-aged children. *British Journal of Psychiatry, 164,* 69–79.

Francis, G., Last, C. G., & Strauss, C. C. (1992). Avoidant disorder and social phobia in children and adolescents. *Journal of the American Academy of Child and Adolescent Psychiatry, 31,* 1086–1089.

Frick, P. J., Lahey, B. B., Loeber, R., Stouthamer-Loeber, M., Christ, M. A. G., & Hanson, K. (1992). Familial risk factors to oppositional defiant disorder and conduct disorder: Parental psychopathology and maternal parenting. *Journal of Consulting and Clinical Psychology, 60,* 49–55.

Frick, P. J., Lahey, B. B., Loeber, R., Stouthamer-Loeber, M., Green, S., Hart, E. L., & Christ, A. G. (1991). Oppositional defiant disorder and conduct disorder in boys: Patterns of behavioral covariation. *Journal of Clinical Child Psychology, 20,* 202–208.

Frick, P. J., Lahey, B. B., Loeber, R., Tannenbaum, L., Van Horn, Y., Christ, M. A. G., Hart, E. A., & Hanson, K. (in press). Oppositional defiant disorder and conduct disorder: A meta-analytic review of factor analyses and cross-validation in a clinic sample. *Clinical Psychology Review.*

Friedman, A. S., Utada, A. T., Glickman, N. W., & Morrissey, M. R. (1987). Psychopathology as an antecedent to, and as a "consequence of", substance use in adolescence. *Drug Education, 17,* 233–244.

Friedman, R. C., Hurt, S. W., Clarkin, J. F., & Corn, R. (1983). Primary and secondary affective disorders in adolescents and young adults. *Acta Psychiatrica Scandinavica, 67,* 226–235.

Garnefski, N., & Diekstra, R. F. W. (1997). "Comorbidity" of behavioral, emotional, and cognitive problems in adolescence. *Journal of Youth and Adolescence, 26,* 321–338.

Geller, B., Chestnut, E. C., Miller, M. D., Price, D. T., & Yates, E. (1985). Preliminary data on DSM-III associated features of major depressive disorder in children and adolescents. *American Journal of Psychiatry, 142,* 643–644.

Geller, B., Sun, K., Zimmerman, B., Frazier, J., & Williams, M. (1995). Complex and rapid-cycling in bipolar children and adolescents: A preliminary study. *Journal of Affective Disorders, 34,* 259–268.

Gershon, E. S., McKnew, D., Cytryn, L., Hamovit, J., Schreiber, J., Hibbs, E., & Pelligrini, D. (1985). Diagnoses in school-age children of bipolar affective disorder patients and normal controls. *Journal of Affective Disorders, 8*, 283–291.

Giaconia, R. M., Reinherz, H. Z., Silverman, A. B., Pakiz, B., Frost, A. K., & Cohen, E. (1994). Ages of onset of psychiatric disorders in a community population of older adolescents. *Journal of the American Academy of Child and Adolescent Psychiatry, 33*, 706–717.

Gittelman, R., Mannuzza, S., Shenker, R., & Bonagura, N. (1985). Hyperactive boys almost grown up: I. Psychiatric status. *Archives of General Psychiatry, 42*, 937–947.

Goodyer, I. M., Herbert, J., Secher, S. M., & Pearson, J. (1997). Short-term outcome of major depression: I. Comorbidity and severity at presentation as predictors of persistent disorder. *Journal of the American Academy of Child and Adolescent Psychiatry, 36*, 179–187.

Graham, P., & Rutter, M. (1973). Psychiatric disorders in the young adolescent: A follow-up study. In *Proceedings of the Royal Society of Medicine, 6*, 1226–1229.

Greenbaum, P. E., Prange, M. E., Friedman, R. M., & Silver, S. E. (1991). Substance abuse prevalence and comorbidity with other psychiatric disorders among adolescents with severe emotional disturbances. *Journal of the American Academy of Child and Adolescent Psychiatry, 30*, 575–583.

Grigoroiu-Serbanescu, M., Christodorescu, D., Magureanu, S., Jupescu, I., Totoescu, A., Marinescu, E., Ardelean, V., & Popa, S. (1991). Adolescent offspring of endogenous unipolar depressive parents and of normal parents. *Journal of Affective Disorder, 21*, 185–198.

Grigoroiu-Serbanescu, M., Christodorescu, D., Totoescu, A., & Jipescu, I. (1991). Depressive disorders and depressive personality traits in offspring aged 10–17 of bipolar and of normal parents. *Journal of Youth and Adolescence, 20*, 135–148.

Hammen, C. (1992). The family-environmental context of depression: A perspective on children's risk. In D. Cicchetti & S. L. Toth (Eds.), *Developmental perspectives on depression—Rochester Symposium on Developmental Psychopathology* (pp. 251–281). Rochester, NY: University of Rochester Press.

Hammen, C., Gordon, D., Burge, D., Adrian, C., Jaenicke, C., & Hiroto, D. (1987). Maternal affective disorders, illness and stress: Risk for children's psychopathology. *American Journal of Psychiatry, 144*, 736–741.

Hammersley, R., Forsyth, A., & Lavelle, T. (1990). The criminality of new drug users in Glasgow. *British Journal of Addictions, 85*, 1583–1594.

Harrington, R., Fudge, H., Rutter, M., Pickles, A., & Hill, J. (1991). Adult outcomes of childhood and adolescent depression: II. Links with antisocial disorders. *Journal of the American Academy of Child and Adolescent Psychiatry, 30*, 434–439.

Herbert, J., Goodyer, I. M., Altham, P. M. E., Pearson, J., Secher, S. M., & Shiers, H. M. (1996). Adrenal secretion and major depression in 8- to 16-year-olds: II. Influence of comorbidity at presentation. *Psychological Medicine, 26*, 257–263.

Hersov, L. A. (1960a). Persistent non-attendance at school. *Journal of Child Psychology and Psychiatry, 1*, 130–136.

Hersov, L. A. (1960b). Refusal to go to school. *Journal of Child Psychology and Psychiatry, 1*, 137–145.

Hinshaw, S. P., Lahey, B. B., & Hart, E. L. (1993). Issues of taxonomy and comorbidity in the development of conduct disorder. Special Issue: Toward a development perspective on conduct disorder. *Development and Psychopathology, 5*, 31–49.

Hirshfeld, D. R., Rosenbaum, J. F., Biederman, J., Bolduc, E. A., Faraone, S. V., Snidman, N. S., Reznick, J. S., & Kagan, J. (1992). Stable behavioral inhibition and its association with anxiety disorder. *Journal of the American Academy of Child and Adolescent Psychiatry, 31*, 103–111.

Hovens, J. G. F. M., Cantwell, D. P., & Kiriakos, L. (1994). Psychiatric comorbidity in hospitalized adolescent substance abusers. *Journal of the Academy of Child and Adolescent Psychiatry, 33*, 476–483.

Jensen, P. S., Martin, D., & Cantwell, D. P. (1997). Comorbidity in ADHD: Implications for research practice, and DSM-V. *Journal of the American Academy of Child and Adolescent Psychiatry, 36*, 1065–1079.

Jensen, P. S., Shervette, R. E., Xenakis, S. N., & Richters, J. (1993). Anxiety and depressive disorders in attention deficit disorder with hyperactivity: New findings. *American Journal of Psychiatry, 150*, 1203–1209.

Jensen, P. S., Watanabe, H. K., Richters, J. E., Cortes, R., Roper, M., & Liu, S. (1995). Prevalence of mental disorder in military children and adolescents: Findings from a two-stage community survey. *Journal of the American Academy of Child and Adolescent Psychiatry, 34*, 1514–1524.

Jessor, R., Chase, J. A., Donovan, J. E., Graves, T., Hanson, R., Jessor, S. S., & Jessor, S. P. (1980). Psychosocial correlates of marijuana use and problem drinking in a national sample of adolescents. *American Journal of Public Health, 70*, 604–613.

Jessor, R., Graves, T., Hanson, R., & Jessor, S. (1968). *Society, personality, and deviant behavior*. New York: Holt, Rinehart & Winston.

Jessor, R., & Jessor, S. L. (1977). *Problem behavior and psychosocial development—A longitudinal study of youth*. New York: Academic Press.

Johnston, C., & Pelham, W. E. (1986). Teacher ratings predict parent ratings of aggression at 3-year follow-up in boys with attention deficit disorder with hyperactivity. *Journal of Consulting and Clinical Psychology, 54*, 571–572.

Johnston, L. D., O'Malley, P., & Eveland, L. (1978a). Drugs and delinquency: A search for causal connections. In D. B. Kandel (Ed.), *Longitudinal research on drug use: Empirical findings and methodological issues* (pp. 132–156). Washington, DC: Hemisphere-Wiley.

Johnston, L. D., O'Malley, P. M., & Eveland, L. K. (1978b). Drugs and delinquency: A search for causal connections. In D. B. Kandel (Ed.) *Longitudinal research on drug use: Empirical findings and methodological issues* (pp. 137–156). Washington, DC: Hemisphere Publishing Corporation.

Jones, M. C. (1968). Personality correlates and antecedents of drinking patterns in adult males. *Journal of Consulting and Clinical Psychology, 1*, 2–12.

Kaminer, Y., Tarter, R. E., Bukstein, O. G., & Kabene, M. (1992). Comparison of treatment completers and noncompleters among dually diagnosed substance abusing adolescents. *Journal of the American Academy of Child and Adolescent Psychiatry, 31*, 1046–1049.

Kandel, D. B. (1978). Convergences in prospective longitudinal surveys of drug use in normal populations. In D. B. Kandel (Ed.), *Longitudinal research on drug use: Empirical findings and methodological issues* (pp. 3–38). Washington, DC: Hemisphere Publishing Corporation.

Kandel, D. B., Davies, M., Karus, D., & Yamuguchi, K. (1986). The consequences in young adulthood of adolescent drug involvement. *Archives of General Psychiatry, 43*, 746–754.

Kandel, D. B., Kessler, R. C., & Margulies, R. Z. (1978). Antecedents of adolescent initiation into stages of drug use. *Journal of Youth and Adolescence, 7*, 13–40.

Kandel, D. B., Single, E., & Kessler, R. C. (1976). The epidemiology of drug use among New York State high school students. Distribution, trends and change in rates of use. *American Journal of Public Health, 66*, 43–53.

Kaplan, H. B. (1980). *Deviant behavior in defense of self*. New York: Academic Press.

Kaplan, H. J., Martin, S. S., Johnson, R. J., & Robbins, C. A. (1986). Escalation of marijuana use: Application of a general theory of deviant behavior. *Journal of Health and Social Behavior, 27,* 44–61.

Kashani, J. H., Beck, N. C., Hoeper, E. W., Fallahi, C., Corcoran, C. M., Mcallister, J. A., Rosenberg, T. K., & Reid, J. C. (1987). Psychiatric disorders in a community sample of adolescents. *American Journal of Psychiatry, 144,* 584–589.

Kashani, J. H., & Orvaschel, H. (1990). A community study of anxiety in children and adolescents. *American Journal of Psychiatry, 147,* 313–318.

Keller, M. B., Lavori, P. W., Mueller, T. I., Endicott, J., Coryell, W., Hirschfeld, R. M. A., & Shhea, T. (1992). Time to recovery, chronicity, and levels of psychopathology in major depression: A 5-year prospective follow-up of 431 subjects. *Archives of General Psychiatry, 49,* 809–816.

Keller, M. B., Lavori, P. W., Wunder, J., Beardslee, W. R., Schwartz, C. E., & Roth, J. (1992). Chronic course of anxiety disorders in children and adolescents. *Journal of the American Academy of Child and Adolescent Psychiatry, 31,* 595–599.

Keller, M. B., Shapiro, R. W., Lavori, P. W., & Wolfe, N. (1982a). Recovery in major depressive disorder analysis with the life table and regression models. *Archives of General Psychiatry, 39,* 905–910.

Keller, M. B., Shapiro, R. W., Lavori, P. W., & Wolfe, N. (1982b). Relapse in major depressive disorder: Analysis with the life table. *Archives of General Psychiatry, 39,* 911–915.

Kelvin, R. G., Goodyer, I. M., & Altham, P. M. E. (1996). Temperament and psychopathology amongst siblings of probands with depressive and anxiety disorders. *Journal of Child Psychology and Psychiatry, 37,* 543–550.

Kendall, P. C., & Clarkin, J. F. (1992). Introduction to Special Section: Comorbidity and treatment implications. *Journal of Clinical and Consulting Psychology, 60,* 833–834.

Kendall, P. C., Kortlander, E., Chansky, T. E., & Brady, E. U. (1992). Comorbidity of anxiety and depression in youth: Treatment implications. *Journal of Consulting and Clinical Psychology, 60,* 869–880.

Kendler, K. S., Heath, A. C., Martin, N. G., & Eaves, L. J. (1987). Symptoms of anxiety and symptoms of depression. Same genes, different environments? *Archives of General Psychiatry, 122,* 451–457.

Kessler, R. C. (1994). The National Comorbidity Survey of the United States. *International Review of Psychiatry, 6,* 365–376.

Kessler, R. C., McGonagle, K. A., Zhao, S., Nelson, C. B., Hughes, M., Eshleman, S., Wittchen, H. U., & Kendler, K. S. (1994). Lifetime and 12-month prevalence of DSM-III-R psychiatric disorders in the United States: Results from the National Comorbidity Study. *Archives of General Psychiatry, 51,* 8–19.

King, C. A., Ghaziuddin, N., McGovern, L., Brand, E., Hill, E., & Naylor, M. (1996). Predictors of comorbid alcohol and substance abuse in depressed adolescents. *Journal of the American Academy of Child and Adolescent Psychiatry, 35,* 743–751.

Klein, D. F. (1990). Symptom criteria and family history in major depression. *American Journal of Psychiatry, 147,* 850–854.

Klein, D. N., & Riso, L. P. (1993). Psychiatric disorders: Problems of boundaries and comorbidity. In C. G. Costello (Ed.), *Basic issues in psychopathology* (pp. 19–66). New York: Guilford Press.

Klein, D. W., & Depue, R. A. (1985). Obsessional personality traits and risk for bipolar affective disorder: An offspring study. *Journal of Abnormal Psychology, 84,* 291–297.

Klein, R. G., Tancer, N. K., & Werry, J. S. (1994). Anxiety disorders of childhood or adolescence. In T. A. Widiger,

A. J. Frances, H. A. Pincus, R. Ross, M. B. First, & W. Davis (Eds.), *DSM-IV sourcebook* (pp. 221–239). Washington, DC: American Psychiatric Association.

Kleinman, P. H., Wish, E. D., Deren, S., & Rainone, G. (1986). Multiple drug use: A symptomatic behavior. *Journal of Psychoactive Drugs, 18,* 77–86.

Kleinman, P. H., Wish, E. D., Deren, S., Rainone, G., & Morehouse, E. (1988). Daily marijuana use and problem behaviors among adolescents. *International Journal of the Addictions, 23,* 87–107.

Knop, J., Goodwin, D. W., Teasdale, T. W., Mikkelsen, U., & Schulsinger, F. (1984). Longitudinal research, methods, and uses in behavioral sciences. In D. W. Goodwin, K. T. Van Dusen, & S. A. Mednick (Eds.), *Longitudinal research in alcoholism* (pp. 107–124). Boston, MA: Kluwer Academic Publishers.

Knop, J., Teasdale, T. W., Schulsinger, F., & Goodwin, D. W. (1985). A prospective study of young men at risk for alcoholism: School behavior and achievement. *Journal of Studies on Alcohol, 46,* 273–278.

Kovacs, M. (1996). Presentation and course of major depressive disorder during childhood and later years of the life span. *Journal of the American Academy of Child and Adolescent Psychiatry, 35,* 705–715.

Kovacs, M., Feinberg, T. L., Crouse-Novak, M. A., Paulauskas, S. L., Pollock, M., & Finklestein, R. (1984). Depressive disorders in childhood: II. A longitudinal study of the risk for a subsequent major depression. *Archives of General Psychiatry, 41,* 643–649.

Kovacs, M., Gatsonis, C., Paulauskas, S. L., & Richards, C. (1989). Depressive disorders in childhood: IV. A longitudinal study of comorbidity with and risk for anxiety disorders. *Archives of General Psychiatry, 46,* 776–782.

Kovacs, M., Paulauskas, S., Gatsonis, C., & Richards, C. (1988). Depressive disorders in childhood: III. A longitudinal study of comorbidity with and risk for conduct disorders. *Journal of Affective Disorders, 15,* 205–217.

Kuhne, M., Schachar, R., & Tannock, R. (1997). Impact of comorbid oppositional or conduct problems on attention-deficit hyperactivity disorder. *Journal of the American Academy of Child and Adolescent Psychiatry, 36,* 1715–1725.

Lahey, B. B., Loeber, R., Stouthamer-Loeber, M., Christ, M. A. G., Green, S., Russo, M. F., Frick, P. J., & Dulcan, M. (1990). Comparison of DSM-III and DSM-III-R diagnoses for prepubertal children: Changes in prevalence and validity. *Journal of the American Academy of Child and Adolescent Psychiatry, 29,* 620–626.

Lahey, B. B., Piacentini, J. C., McBurnett, K., Stone, P., Hartdagen, S., & Hynd, G. (1988). Psychopathology in the parents of children with conduct disorder and hyperactivity. *Journal of the American Academy of Child and Adolescent Psychiatry, 27,* 163–170.

Last, C. G., Hersen, M., Kazdin, A. E., Finkelstein, R., & Strauss, C. C. (1987). Comparison of DSM-III separation anxiety and overanxious disorders: Demographic characteristics and patterns of comorbidity. *Journal of the American Academy of Child and Adolescent Psychiatry, 26,* 527–531.

Last, C. G., Hersen, M., Kazdin, A. E., Francis, G., & Grubb, H. J. (1987). Psychiatric illness in the mothers of anxious children. *American Journal of Psychiatry, 144,* 1580–1583.

Last, C. G., Hersen, M., Kazdin, A., Orvaschel, H., & Perrin, S. (1991). Anxiety disorders in children and their families. *Archives of General Psychiatry, 48,* 928–934.

Last, C. G., Perrin, S., Hersen, M., & Kazdin, A. (1992). DSM-III-R anxiety disorders in children: Sociodemographic and clinical characteristics. *Journal of the American Academy of Child and Adolescent Psychiatry, 31,* 1070–1076.

Last, C. G., Perrin, S., Hersen, M., & Kazdin, A. E. (1996). A prospective study of childhood anxiety disorders. *Journal of the American Academy of Child and Adolescent Psychiatry, 35,* 1502–1510.

Last, C. G., Strauss, C. C., & Francis, G. (1987). Comorbidity among childhood anxiety disorders. *Journal of Nervous and Mental Disease, 175,* 726–730.

Laucht, M., & Schmidt, M. H. (1987). Psychiatric disorders at the age of 13: Results and problems of a long-term study. In B. Cooper (Ed.), *Psychiatric epidemiology: Progress and prospects* (pp. 212–224). London: Croom Helm.

Le Blanc, M., & Fréchette, M. (1989). *Male criminal activity from childhood through youth: Multilevel and developmental perspectives.* New York: Springer-Verlag.

Lewinsohn, P. M., Hops, H., Roberts, R. E., Seeley, J. R., & Andrews, J. A. (1993). Adolescent psychopathology: I. Prevalence and incidence of depression and other DSM-III-R disorders in high school students. *Journal of Abnormal Psychology, 102,* 133–144.

Lewinsohn, P. M., Klein, D. N., & Seeley, J. R. (1995). Bipolar disorders in a community sample of older adolescents: Prevalence, phenomenology, comorbidity, and course. *Journal of the American Academy of Child and Adolescent Psychiatry, 34,* 454–463.

Lewinsohn, P. M., Rohde, P., & Seeley, J. R. (1994). Psychosocial risk factors for future adolescent suicide attempts. *Journal of Consulting and Clinical Psychology, 62,* 297–305.

Lewinsohn, P. M., Rohde, P., & Seeley, J. R. (1995). Adolescent psychopathology: III. The clinical consequences of comorbidity. *Journal of the American Academy of Child and Adolescent Psychiatry, 34,* 510–519.

Lewinsohn, P. M., Rohde, P., Seeley, J. R., & Hops, H. (1991). Comorbidity of unipolar depression: I. Major depression with dysthymia. *Journal of Abnormal Psychology, 100,* 205–213.

Lilienfeld, S. O., Waldman, I. D., & Israel, A. C. (1994). A critical examination of the use of the term and concept of comorbidity in psychopathology research. *Clinical Psychology—Science and Practice, 1,* 71–83.

Loeber, R. (1988). Natural histories of conduct problems, delinquency, and associated substance use: Evidence for developmental progressions. In B. B. Lahey & A. E. Kazdin (Eds.), *Advances in clinical child psychology* (pp. 73–125). New York: Plenum Press.

Loeber, R., Green, S., Keenan, K., & Lahey, B. B. (1995). Which boys will fare worse? Early predictors of the onset of conduct disorder in a six-year longitudinal study. *Journal of the American Academy of Child and Adolescent Psychiatry, 34,* 499–509.

Loeber, R., Green, S. M., Lahey, B. B., Christ, M. A. G., & Frick, P. J. (1992). Developmental sequences in the age of onset of disruptive child behaviors. *Journal of Child and Family Studies, 1,* 21–41.

Loeber, R., & Keenan, K. (1994). Interaction between conduct disorder and its comorbid conditions: Effects of age and gender. *Clinical Psychology Review, 14,* 497–523.

Loeber, R., Keenan, K., Lahey, B. B., Green, S. M., & Thomas, C. (1993). Evidence for developmentally based diagnoses of oppositional defiant disorder and conduct disorder. *Journal of Abnormal Child Psychology, 21,* 377–410.

Loeber, R., Lahey, B. B., & Thomas, C. (1991). Diagnostic conundrum of oppositional defiant disorder and conduct disorder. *Journal of Abnormal Psychology, 100,* 379–390.

Loney, J. (1988). *Adolescent drug abuse: Analyses of treatment research.* Rockville, MD: National Institute on Drug Abuse Office of Science.

Lyons, J., Serbin, L. A., & Marchessault, K. (1988). The social behavior of peer-identified aggressive, withdrawn, and aggressive/withdrawn children. *Journal of Abnormal Child Psychology, 16,* 539–552.

Marriage, K., Fine, S., Moretti, M., & Haley, G. (1986). Relationship between depression and conduct disorder in children and adolescents. *Journal of the American Academy of Child Psychiatry, 25,* 687–691.

Martunnen, M. J., Aro, H. M., Henriksson, M. M., & Lönnqvist, J. K. (1991). Mental disorders in adolescent suicide: DSM-III-R axes I and II diagnoses in suicides among 13- to 19-year-olds in Finland. *Archives of General Psychiatry, 48,* 834–839.

McBurnett, K., Lahey, B. B., Frick, P. J., Risch, C., Loeber, R., Hart, E. L., Christ, M. A. G., & Hanson, K. S. (1991). Anxiety, inhibition, and conduct disorder in children. II. Relation to salivary cortisol. *Journal of the American Academy of Child and Adolescent Psychiatry, 30,* 192–196.

McClellan, J. (1998). Mania in young children. *Journal of the American Academy of Child and Adolescent Psychiatry, 37,* 346–347.

McClellan, J. M., Rubert, M. P., Reichler, R. J., & Sylvester, C. E. (1990). Attention deficit disorder in children at risk for anxiety and depression. *Journal of the American Academy of Child and Adolescent Psychiatry, 29,* 534–539.

McConaughy, S. H., & Achenbach, T. M. (1994). Comorbidity of empirically based syndromes in matched general population and clinical samples. *Journal of Child Psychology and Psychiatry, 35,* 1141–1157.

McCord, J., McCord, W., & Thurber, E. (1962). Some effects of paternal absence in male children. *Journal of Abnormal and Social Psychology, 64,* 361–369.

McCord, W., & McCord, J. (1960). *Origins of alcoholism.* Stanford, CA: Stanford University Press.

McCormick, L. H. (1995). Depression in mothers of children with attention deficit hyperactivity disorder. *Family Medicine, 27,* 176–179.

McGee, R., Feehan, M., Williams, S., & Anderson, J. (1992). DSM-III disorders from age 11 to age 15 years. *Journal of the American Academy of Child and Adolescent Psychiatry, 31,* 51–59.

McGee, R., Feehan, M., Williams, S., Partridge, F., Silva, P. A., & Kelly, J. (1990). DSM-III disorders in a large sample of adolescents. *Journal of the American Academy of Child and Adolescent Psychiatry, 29,* 611–619.

Merikangas, K. R., Prusoff, B. A., & Weissman, M. M. (1988). Parental concordance for affective disorders: Psychopathology in offspring. *Journal of Affective Disorders, 15,* 279–290.

Milberger, S., Biederman, J., Faraone, S. V., Murphy, J., & Tsuang, M. T. (1995). Attention deficit hyperactivity disorder and comorbid disorders: Issues of overlapping symptoms. *American Journal of Psychiatry, 152,* 1793–1799.

Milich, R., & Dodge, K. A. (1984). Social information processing in child psychiatric populations. *Journal of Abnormal Child Psychology, 12,* 471–490.

Mills, C. J., & Noyes, H. L. (1984). Patterns and correlates of initial and subsequent drug use among adolescents. *Journal of Consulting and Clinical Psychology, 52,* 231–243.

Moffitt, T. E. (1990). Juvenile delinquency and attention deficit disorder: Boys' developmental trajectories from age 3 to age 15. *Child Development, 61,* 893–910.

Moffitt, T. E. (1993). Adolescence-limited and life-course-persistent antisocial behavior: A developmental taxonomy. *Psychological Review, 100,* 674–701.

Moffitt, T. E., Caspi, A., Dickson, N., Silva, P., & Stanton, W. (1996). Childhood-onset versus adolescent-onset antisocial conduct problems in males: Natural history from ages 3 to 18 years. *Development and Psychopathology, 8,* 399–424.

Monnelly, E. P., Hartl, E. M., & Elderkin, R. (1983). Constitutional factors predictive of alcoholism in a follow-up of delinquent boys. *Journal of Studies on Alcoholism, 43,* 888–909.

Moreau, D. L., Weissman, M., & Warner, V. (1990). Panic disorder in children at high risk for depression. *Annual Progress in Child Psychiatry and Child Development, 146,* 363–367.

Morrison, J. L. (1980). Adult psychiatric disorder in parents of hyperactive children. *American Journal of Psychiatry, 137,* 825–827.

Morrison, J. L., & Stewart, M. A. (1971). A family study of the hyperactive child syndrome. *Biological Psychiatry, 3,* 189–195.

Munir, K., Biederman, J., & Knee, D. (1987). Psychiatric comorbidity in patients with attention deficit disorder: A controlled study. *Journal of the American Academy of Child and Adolescent Psychiatry, 26,* 844–848.

Neighbors, B., Kempton, T., & Forehand, R. (1992). Co-occurrence of substance abuse with conduct, anxiety, and depression disorders in juvenile delinquents. *Additive Behaviors, 17,* 379–386.

Noam, G. G., Paget, K., Valiant, G., Borst, S., & Bartok, J. (1994). Conduct and affective disorders in developmental perspective: A systematic study of adolescent psychopathology. *Development and Psychopathology, 6,* 519–532.

Nottelmann, E. D., & Jensen, P. S. (1995). Comorbidity of disorders in children and adolescents: Developmental perspectives. In T. H. Ollendick & R. J. Prinz (Eds.), *Advances in clinical child psychology: Vol. 17* (pp. 109–155). New York: Plenum Press.

Nurnberger, J. I., Hamovit, J., Hibbs, E., Pellegrini, D., Guroff, J. J., Maxwell, M. E., Smith, A., & Gershon, E. S. (1988). A high-risk study of primary affective disorder: Selection of subjects, initial assessment, and 1-to 2-year follow-up. In D. L. Dunner, E. S. Gershon, & J. E. Barrett (Eds.), *Relatives at risk for mental disorder* (pp. 161–177). New York: Raven Press.

Offord, D. R., Sullivan, K., Allen, N., & Abrams, N. (1979). Delinquency and hyperactivity. *Journal of Nervous and Mental Disorders, 167,* 734–741.

Orive, R. M., & Gerard, H. B. (1980). Personality, attitudinal and social correlates of drug use. *International Journal of the Addictions, 15,* 869–881.

Orvaschel, H. (1990). Early onset psychiatric disorder in high risk children and increased familial morbidity. *Journal of the American Academy of Child and Adolescent Psychiatry, 29,* 184–188.

Orvaschel, H., Walsh-Allis, G., Ye, W., & Walsh, G. T. (1988). Psychopathology in children of parents with recurrent depression. *Journal of Abnormal Child Psychology, 16,* 17–28.

Paternite, C. E., Loney, J., & Roberts, M. A. (1995). External validation of oppositional disorder and attention deficit disorder with hyperactivity. *Journal of Abnormal Child Psychology, 23,* 453–471.

Paton, S., & Kandel, D. (1978). Psychological factors and adolescent illicit drug use: Ethnicity and sex differences. *Adolescence, 13,* 187–200.

Paton, S., Kessler, R., & Kandel, D. (1977). Depressive mood and adolescent illicit drug use: A longitudinal analysis. *Journal of Genetic Psychology, 131,* 267–289.

Perrin, S., & Last, C. G. (1996). Relationship between ADHD and anxiety in boys: Result from a family study. *Journal of the American Academy of Child and Adolescent Psychiatry, 35,* 988–996.

Pliszka, S. R. (1992). Comorbidity of attention-deficit hyperactivity disorder and overanxious disorder. *Journal of the American Academy of Child and Adolescent Psychiatry, 31,* 197–203.

Puig-Antich, J. (1982). Major depression and conduct disorder in prepuberty. *Journal of the American Academy of Child Psychiatry, 21,* 118–128.

Quiggle, N. L., Garber, J., Panak, W. F., & Dodge, K. A. (1992). Social information processing in aggressive and depressed children. *Child Development, 63,* 1305–1320.

Reeves, J. C., Werry, J. S., Elkind, G. S., & Zametkin, A. (1987). Attention deficit, conduct, oppositional and anxiety disorders in children: II. Clinical characteristics. *Journal of the American Academy of Child and Adolescent Psychiatry, 26,* 144–155.

Renouf, A. G., Kovacs, M., & Mukerji, P. (1997). Relationship of depressive, conduct, and comorbid disorders and social functioning in childhood. *Journal of the American Academy of Child and Adolescent Psychiatry, 36,* 998–1004.

Rey, J. M., Bashir, M. R., & Schwartz, M. (1988). Oppositional disorder: Fact or fiction? *Journal of the American Academy of Child and Adolescent Psychiatry, 27,* 157–162.

Ricks, D., & Berry, J. C. (1970). Family and symptom patterns that precede schizophrenia. In M. Roff & D. F. Ricks (Eds.), *Life history research in psychopathology* (pp. 31–50). Minneapolis, MN: University of Minnesota Press.

Robins, E., & Guze, S. B. (1970). Establishment of diagnostic validity in psychiatric illness: Its application to schizophrenia. *American Journal of Psychiatry, 126,* 107–111.

Robins, L. N. (1974). *Deviant children grown up.* Huntington, NY: Krieger.

Robins, L. N., & McEvoy, L. (1990). Conduct problems as predictors of substance abuse. In L. N. Robins & M. Rutter (Eds.), *Straight and devious pathways from childhood to adulthood* (pp. 182–204). Cambridge: Cambridge University Press.

Robins, L. N., & Murphy, G. E. (1967). Drug use in a normal population of young negro men. *American Journal of Public Health and the Nations Health, 57,* 1580–1596.

Robins, L. N., & Przybeck, T. R. (1985). *Age of onset of drug use as a factor in drug and other disorders.* Rockville, MD: National Institute of Drug Abuse Research.

Robins, L. N., & Ratcliff, K. S. (1980). Childhood conduct disorders and later arrest. In L. N. Robins, P. J. Clayton, & J. K. Wing (Eds.), *The social consequences of psychiatric illness* (pp. 248–263). New York: Brunner/Mazel.

Robins, L. N., & Wish, E. (1977). Childhood deviance as a developmental process. A study of 223 urban black men from birth to 18. *Social Forces, 56,* 448–473.

Rohde, P., Lewinsohn, P. M., & Seeley, J. R. (1991). Comorbidity of unipolar depression: II. Comorbidity with other mental disorders in adolescents and adults. *Journal of Abnormal Psychology, 100,* 214–222.

Rohde, P., Lewinsohn, P. M., & Seeley, J. R. (1996). Psychiatric comorbidity in problematic alcohol use in high school students. *Journal of the American Academy of Child and Adolescent Psychiatry, 35,* 101–109.

Rudolph, K. D., Hammen, C., & Burge, D. (1994). Interpersonal functioning and depressive symptoms in childhood: Addressing the issues of specificity and comorbidity. *Journal of Abnormal Child Psychology, 22,* 355–371.

Russo, M. F., Loeber, R., Lahey, B. B., & Keenan, K. (1994). Oppositional defiant and conduct disorders: Validation of the DSM-III-R and an alternative diagnostic option. *Journal of Clinical Child Psychology, 23,* 56–68.

Rutter, M. (1978). Diagnostic validity in child psychiatry. *Advances in Biological Psychiatry, 2,* 2–22.

Rutter, M. (1994). Comorbidity: Meanings and mechanisms. *Clinical Psychology—Science and Practice, 1,* 100–103.

Rutter, M. (1997). Comorbidity: Concepts, claims and choices. *Criminal Behavior and Mental Health, 7,* 265–285.

Rutter, M., & Graham, P. (1966). Psychiatric disorder in 10- and 11-year-old children. *Proceedings of the Royal Society of Medicine, 59,* 382–387.

Rutter, M., & Shaffer, D. (1980). DSM-III: A step forward or back in terms of the classification of child psychiatric disorders? *Journal of the American Academy of Child Psychiatry, 19*, 371–394.

Rutter, M., Tizard, J., & Whitmore, K. (1970). *Education, health, and behaviour.* London: Longman.

Ryan, N., Puig-Antich, J., Ambrosini, P. J., Rabinovich, H., Robinson, D., Nelson, B., Iyengar, S., & Twomey, J. (1987). The clinical picture of major depression in children and adolescents. *Archives of General Psychiatry, 44*, 854–861.

Rydelius, P. A. (1981). Children of alcoholic fathers, their social adjustment and health status over 20 years. *Personality and Social Psychiatry Journal, 286*, 1–89.

Santo, Y., Hooper, H. E., Friedman, A. S., & Conner, W. (1980). Criminal behavior of adolescent nonheroin polydrug abusers in drug treatment programs. *Contemporary Drug Problems, Fall, 301*–325.

Satterfield, J. H., & Schell, A. (1997). A perspective study of hyperactive boys with conduct problems and normal boys: Adolescent and adult criminality. *Journal of the American Academy of Child and Adolescent Psychiatry, 36*, 1726–1735.

Schachar, R., & Logan, G. D. (1990). Impulsivity and inhibitory control in development and psychopathology. *Developmental Psychopathology, 26*, 1–11.

Schachar, R., & Rannock, R. (1995). Test of four hypotheses for the comorbidity of attention-deficit hyperactivity disorder and conduct disorder. *Journal of the American Academy of Child and Adolescent Psychiatry, 34*, 639–648.

Schachar, R., & Wachsmuth, R. (1990). Hyperactivity and parental psychopathology. *Journal of Child Psychology and Psychiatry, 31*, 381–392.

Schuckit, M. A. (1982). A study of young men with alcoholic close relatives. *American Journal of Psychiatry, 139*, 791–794.

Seidman, L. J., Biederman, J., Faraone, S. V., Milberger, S., Norman, D., Seiverd, K., Benedict, K., Guite, J., Mick, E., & Kiely, K. (1995). Effects of family history and comorbidity on the neuropsychological performance of children with ADHD: Preliminary findings. *Journal of the American Academy of Child and Adolescent Psychiatry, 34*, 1015–1024.

Shaffer, D. (1993). Suicide: Risk factors and the public health. *American Journal of Public Health, 83*, 171–172.

Shaffer, D., & Fisher, P. W. (1981). The epidemiology of suicide in children and young adolescents. *Journal of the American Academy of Child Psychiatry, 20*, 545–565.

Shain, B. N., King, C. A., Naylor, M., & Alessi, N. E. (1991). Chronic depression and hospital course in adolescents. *Journal of the American Academy of Child and Adolescent Psychiatry, 30*, 428–433.

Silberg, J., Meyer, J., Pickles, A., Simonoff, E., Eaves, L., Hewitt, J., Maes, H., & Rutter, M. (1996). Heterogeneity among juvenile antisocial behaviours: Findings from the Virginia Twin Study of Adolescent Behavioural Development (VTSABD). *Genetics of Criminal and Antisocial Behaviour: Ciba Foundation Symposium, 194*, 76–92.

Silberg, J. L., Rutter, M. L., Meyer, J. M., Maes, H. H., Hewitt, J. K., Simonoff, E., Pickles, A. R., Loeber, R., & Eaves, L. J. (1996). Genetic and environmental influences on the covariation between hyperactivity and conduct disturbances in juvenile twins. *Journal of Child Psychology and Psychiatry, 37*, 803–816.

Simonoff, E., Pickles, A., Meyer, J. M., Silberg, J. L., Maes, H. H., Loeber, R., Rutter, M., Hewitt, J. K., & Eaves, L. J. (1997). The Virginia Twin Study of Adolescent Behavioral Development: Influences of age, sex and impairment on rates of disorder. *Archives of General Psychiatry, 54*, 801–808.

Smith, G. N., & Fogg, C. P. (1979). *Research in community and mental health: An annual compilation of research.* Greenwich, CT: JAI Press.

Stark, K. D., Kaslow, N. J., & Laurent, J. (1993). The assessment of depression in children: Are we assessing depression or the broad-band construct of negative affectivity? *Journal of Emotional and Behavioral Disorders, 1*, 149–154.

Stein, J. A., Newcomb, M. D., & Bentler, P. M. (1987). An 8-year study of multiple influences on drug use and drug use consequences. *Journal of Personality and Social Psychology, 53*, 1094–1105.

Steinhausen, H.-C., & Reitzle, M. (1996). The validity of mixed disorders of conduct and emotions in children and adolescents: A research note. *Journal of Child Psychology and Psychiatry, 37*, 339–343.

Stowell, R. J. A., & Estroff, T. W. (1992). Psychiatric disorders in substance-abusing adolescent inpatients: A pilot study. *Journal of the American Academy of Child and Adolescent Psychiatry, 31*, 1036–1040.

Sylvester, C. E., Hyde, T. S., & Reichler, R. J. (1988). Clinical psychopathology among children of adults with panic disorder. In D. L. Dunner, E. S. Gershon, & J. E. Barrett (Eds.), *Relatives at risk for mental disorder* (pp. 87–99). New York: Raven Press.

Taylor, E. (1994). Similarities and differences in DSM-IV and ICD-10 diagnostic criteria. *Child and Adolescent Psychiatric Clinics of North America, 3*, 209–226.

Taylor, E., Chadwick, O., Heptinstall, E., & Danckaerts, M. (1996). Hyperactivity and conduct problems as risk factors for adolescent development. *Journal of the American Academy of Child and Adolescent Psychiatry, 35*, 1213–1226.

Tubman, J. G., Vicary, J. R., von Eye, A., & Lerner, J. V. (1990). Longitudinal substance use and adult adjustment. *Journal of Substance Abuse, 2*, 317–334.

Turner, S. M., Beidel, D. C., & Costello, A. (1987). Psychopathology in the offspring of anxiety disorders patients. *Journal of Consulting and Clinical Psychology, 55*, 229–235.

Vaillant, G. E., & Milofsky, E. S. (1982). The etiology of alcoholism: A prospective viewpoint. *American Psychologist, 37*, 294–503.

Van Kammen, W. B., & Loeber, R. (1994). Are fluctuations in delinquent activities related to the onset and offset in juvenile illegal drug use and drug dealing? *Journal of Drug Issues, 24*, 9–24.

Van Kammen, W. B., Loeber, R., & Stouthamer-Loeber, M. (1991). Substance use and its relationship to conduct problems and delinquency in young boys. *Journal of Youth and Adolescence, 20*, 399–413.

Velez, C. N., Johnson, J., & Cohen, P. (1989). A longitudinal analysis of selected risk factors of childhood psychopathology. *Journal of the American Academy of Child and Adolescent Psychiatry, 28*, 861–864.

Verhulst, F. C., & van der Ende, J. (1993). "Comorbidity" in an epidemiological sample: A longitudinal perspective. *Journal of Child Psychology and Psychiatry, 34*, 767–783.

Vikan, A. (1985). Psychiatric epidemiology in a sample of 1510 10-year-old children: I. Prevalence. *Journal of Child Psychology and Psychiatry, 26*, 55–75.

Walker, J. L., Lahey, B. B., Hynd, G. W., & Frame, C. L. (1987). Comparison of specific patterns of antisocial behavior in children with conduct disorder with or without co-existing hyperactivity. *Journal of Consulting and Clinical Psychology, 55*, 910–913.

Walker, J. L., Lahey, B. B., Russo, M. F., Frick, P. J., Christ, M. A. G., McBurnett, K., Loeber, R., Stouthamer-Loeber, M., & Green, S. M. (1991). Anxiety, inhibition, and conduct disorder in children: I. Relations to social impairment. *Journal of the American Academy of Child and Adolescent Psychiatry, 30*, 187–191.

Warner, V., Mufson, L., & Weissman, M. M. (1995). Offspring at high and low risk for depression and anxiety: Mechanisms of psychiatric disorder. *Journal of the American Academy of Child and Adolescent Psychiatry, 34*, 786–797.

Weiss, B., & Catron, T. (1994). Specificity of the comorbidity of aggression and depression in children. *Journal of Abnormal Child Psychology, 22,* 389–401.

Weissman, M. M., Fendrich, M., Warner, V., & Wickramaratne, P. (1992). Incidence of psychiatric disorder in offspring at high and low risk for depression. *Journal of the American Academy of Child and Adolescent Psychiatry, 31,* 640–648.

Welner, Z., Welner, A., McCrary, M. D., & Leonard, M. A. (1977). Psychopathology in children of inpatients with depression. *Journal of Nervous and Mental Disorders, 164,* 408–413.

Welte, J. W., & Barnes, G. M. (1985). Alcohol: The gateway to other drug use among secondary-school students. *Journal of Youth and Adolescence, 14,* 487–498.

Werry, J. S. (1997). Discussion of: "Attention-deficit hyperactivity disorder with bipolar disorder: A familial subtype?". *Journal of the American Academy of Child and Adolescent Psychiatry, 36,* 1388–1390.

West, S. A., McElroy, S. L., Strakowski, S. M., Keck, P. E., & McConville, B. J. (1995). Attention deficit hyperactivity disorder in adolescent mania. *American Journal of Psychiatry, 152,* 271–273.

West, S. A., Strakowski, S. M., Sax, K. W., McElroy, S. L., Keck, P. E., & McConville, B. J. (1996). Phenomenology and comorbidity of adolescents hospitalized for the treatment of acute mania. *Biological Psychiatry, 39,* 458–460.

Williamson, D. E., Ryan, N. D., Birmaher, B., Dahl, R. E., Kaufman, J., Rao, U., & Puig-Antich, J. (1995). A case-control family history study of depression in adolescents. *Journal of the American Academy of Child and Adolescent Psychiatry, 34,* 1596–1607.

Windle, M. (1990). A longitudinal study of antisocial behaviors in early adolescence as predictors of late adolescent substance use: Gender and ethnic group differences. *Journal of Abnormal Psychology, 99,* 86–91.

Windle, M., & Barnes, G. M. (1988). Similarities and differences in correlates of alcohol consumption and problem behaviors among male and female adolescents. *International Journal of the Addictions, 23,* 707–728.

Wingard, J. A., Huba, C. G., & Bentler, P. M. (1979). The relationship of personality structure to patterns of adolescent substance use. *Multivariate Behavior Research, 14,* 131–143.

Woodruff, R. A., Murphy, G. E., & Herjanic, M. (1967). The natural history of affective disorders: I. Symptoms of 72 patients at the time of index hospital admission. *Journal of Psychiatric Research, 5,* 255–263.

World Health Organization. (1993). *The ICD-10 classification of mental and behavioural disorders: Diagnostic criteria for research.* Geneva: World Health Organization.

Wozniak, J., Biederman, J., Kiely, K., Ablon, J. S., Faraone, S. V., Mundy, E., & Mennin, D. (1995). Mania-like symptoms suggestive of childhood-onset bipolar disorder in clinically referred children. *Journal of the American Academy of Child and Adolescent Psychiatry, 34,* 867–876.

Yamaguchi, K., & Kandel, D. B. (1984). Patterns of drug use from adolescence to young adulthood: II. Sequences of progression. *American Journal of Public Health, 74,* 668–672.

Zoccolillo, M. (1992). Co-occurrence of conduct disorder and its adult outcomes with depressive and anxiety disorders. A review. *Journal of the American Academy of Child and Adolescent Psychiatry, 31,* 547–556.

Zucker, R., & Barron, F. (Eds.). (1973). *Research on alcoholism I: Clinical problems and special populations.* Washington, DC: U.S. Government Printing Office.

Zucker, R., & DeVoe, C. (1975). *Life history research in psychopathology.* Minneapolis, MN: University of Minnesota Press.

Zucker, R., & Gomberg, E. S. L. (1986). Etiology of alcoholism reconsidered: The case for biopsychosocial process. *American Psychologist, 41,* 783–793.

Manuscript accepted 21 September 1998

[23]

Time trends in adolescent mental health

Stephan Collishaw,[1] Barbara Maughan,[1] Robert Goodman,[2] and Andrew Pickles[3]

[1]MRC Social, Genetic, and Developmental Psychiatry Centre, Institute of Psychiatry, King's College London, UK; [2]Department of Child and Adolescent Psychiatry, Institute of Psychiatry, London, UK; [3]School of Epidemiology and Health Science, and Centre for Census and Survey Research, University of Manchester, UK

Background: Existing evidence points to a substantial rise in psychosocial disorders affecting young people over the past 50 years (Rutter & Smith, 1995). However, there are major methodological challenges in providing conclusive answers about secular changes in disorder. Comparisons of rates of disorder at different time points are often affected by changes in diagnostic criteria, differences in assessment methods, and changes in official reporting practices. Few studies have examined this issue using the same instruments at each time point. **Methods:** The current study assessed the extent to which conduct, hyperactive and emotional problems have become more common over a 25-year period in three general population samples of UK adolescents. The samples used in this study were the adolescent sweeps of the National Child Development Study and the 1970 Birth Cohort Study, and the 1999 British Child and Adolescent Mental Health Survey. Comparable questionnaires were completed by parents of 15–16-year-olds at each time point (1974, 1986, and 1999). **Results and conclusions:** Results showed a substantial increase in adolescent conduct problems over the 25-year study period that has affected males and females, all social classes and all family types. There was also evidence for a recent rise in emotional problems, but mixed evidence in relation to rates of hyperactive behaviour. Further analyses using longitudinal data from the first two cohorts showed that long-term outcomes for adolescents with conduct problems were closely similar. This provided evidence that observed trends were unaffected by possible changes in reporting thresholds. **Keywords:** Time trends, adolescence, mental health, birth cohorts, UK. **Abbreviations:** NCDS: National Child Development Study; BCS70: 1970 British Cohort Study; B-CAMHS99: British Child and Adolescent Mental Health Study 1999; SDQ: Strengths and Difficulties Questionnaire; POR: proportional odds ratio; OR: odds ratio.

A commonly held belief is that young people today are more badly behaved and more troubled by emotional difficulties than those in the past. Studies testing this assumption have examined time trends in reported prevalence rates of disorder, official record data for suicide and crime, and lifetime rates of disorder reported retrospectively by individuals in different birth cohorts. In general, all of these sources point to rising rates of conduct problems, depression, and suicide in nearly all developed countries since the Second World War (Rutter & Smith, 1995; Fombonne, 1998). However, methodological limitations make it difficult to provide conclusive answers. The comparison of rates of disorder assessed at different time points is complicated by changing diagnostic criteria, differences in assessment methods, and variations in official reporting practices. In contrast, studies using equivalent methods of assessment have often been limited by their retrospective nature. Very few studies have provided contemporaneous assessments using the same measures at each time point. The aim of the current study is to capitalise on comparable measures available from three large-scale British cohorts to test the extent of historical trends in adolescent mental health in the UK.

Probably the greatest interest in the possibility of secular trends in psychopathology came from the Epidemiological Catchment Area study, where lifetime rates of mental disorders were examined by age

of respondent in a large-scale cross-sectional survey of the adult population of the US (Robins & Regier, 1991). If different birth cohorts were at equal risk for disorder, lifetime rates of disorders would be expected to increase with the age of respondents due to the increasing length of their at-risk periods. Instead, however, there were steep declines with age in the lifetime prevalence of depression, other affective disorders, and retrospectively reported conduct symptoms, suggesting that successive birth cohorts were at increasing risk of mental disorders (see also Lewinsohn, Rohde, Seeley, & Fischer, 1993; Kessler, McGonagle, Swartz, Blazer, & Nelson, 1993; Cross-National Collaborative Group, 1992). However, three potential artefacts should be considered. First, older people may be less willing to admit to mental health problems than younger people. Second, age is confounded with length of recall period, and younger people may provide more accurate estimates of episodes of disorder. Finally, samples are necessarily biased by only including survivors.

Official statistics provide a second source of data on time trends. Crime statistics demonstrate a steep rise in recorded crime over the second half of the 20th century, affecting most types of crime and most developed countries (Rutter, Giller, & Hagell, 1998; Fombonne, 1998). Similarly, rates of recorded suicides have increased in the US and in European countries (Fombonne, 1998; JAMA, 1995; Shaffer, 1988), particularly among young males (Diekstra,

Kienhorst, & de Wilde, 1995). However, the interpretation of official record data is complicated by changes in the reporting and definition of particular outcomes. For example, changing social and legal norms influence the recording of suicide on death certificates. Similarly, variations in recorded crime may arise due to changes in recording and enforcement practice.

In principle, epidemiological studies of child and adolescent psychopathology could also be informative on time trends, as such studies have been conducted for over 40 years. In practice, changes in diagnostic criteria, and wide variations in approaches to the assessment of disorder, make it extremely difficult to interpret differences between studies in terms of historical trends alone (Roberts, Attkisson, & Rosenblatt, 1998). Parent and teacher rating scales offer a more promising basis for assessing historical trends, because a relatively small number of instruments, with well-established psychometric properties, have been consistently used over many years.

A number of studies have now examined historical changes in rates of emotional and behavioural problems using the same instruments at each time point (Achenbach, Dumenci, & Rescorla, 2003; De Jong, 1997; East & Campbell, 1999; Rahim & Cederblad, 1984; Verhulst, van der Ende, & Rietbergen, 1997; West & Sweeting, 2003). Findings from different countries have produced somewhat different results, indicating the likelihood of culture-specific trends (see also Smith & Rutter, 1995). Rahim and Cederblad (1984) found increased rates of parent-rated behaviour problems between 1965 and 1980 in Khartoum, Sudan. In the US, Achenbach et al. (2003) examined changes in the prevalence of parent-rated behaviour problems over a 23-year period (1976, 1989, 1999) in non-referred samples of children. Problem scores increased between 1976 and 1989, and then dropped in the most recent cohort. In the Netherlands, by contrast, there appears to have been little change between 1983 and 1993 in the prevalence of common childhood mental health problems (Verhulst et al., 1997; De Jong, 1997).

So far as we are aware, only two studies of this kind have examined time trends in adolescent mental health in UK samples. West and Sweeting (2003) compared levels of 'psychological distress' using the General Health Questionnaire completed by adolescents in Scotland in 1987 and 1999. They found increased rates of worry and distress among girls, but not among boys, and attributed these patterns to an increase in educational expectations. Comparisons of self-reported crime, assessed with repeated questions in the Youth Lifestyle Surveys, point to increased law-breaking by UK adolescents (both males and females) between 1992 and 1999 (East & Campbell, 1999).

It should be noted that even comparisons of rates of disorder collected using the same instruments

cannot rule out the possibility of reporting artefacts. Parent, teacher and self-ratings of behavioural and emotional problems may all be affected by the 'topicality' of particular disorders, and by changes in social norms. For example, parents may be more concerned about disorders that have received a greater amount of recent media coverage, and may therefore more readily label particular behaviours in these terms than they did in the past. Similarly, overt expressions of emotional difficulties (e.g., talking about depressive feelings, crying) may be reported more commonly among males than in the past, because such expressions are now seen as more socially acceptable. Even in studies using exactly the same measures it is hard to rule out the possibility of reporting artefacts of this kind. One possible solution is to examine links between measures of disorder and later associated outcomes. If later outcomes are as strongly associated with a particular disorder in successive cohorts, then this provides strong evidence that any increase in the rate of the disorder is not due to a change in reporting thresholds (Robins, 2001).

Against this background, our study had two main aims. First, it examined whether there have been increases in parent-rated emotional and behavioural problems over the last 25 years of the 20th century in the UK using data from three national samples. Second, it addressed whether any observed changes in parent-rated behaviour reflect real changes in child behaviour, or changes in reporting thresholds. The possibility of reporter effects was tested by examining associations with later outcomes, using longitudinal data available for two of the three samples.

Methods

Samples and design

Three studies were used in this investigation – the National Child Development Study (NCDS; Fogelman, 1983), the 1970 British Cohort study (BCS70; Butler & Golding, 1986), and the 1999 British Child and Adolescent Mental Health Survey (B-CAMHS99; Meltzer, Gatward, Goodman, & Ford, 2000). NCDS and BCS70 are ongoing, prospective studies of all children born in the UK in one week in 1958 (3–9 March) and 1970 (5–11 April) respectively. Parent ratings of behavioural problems were taken from the 16-year-old follow-up stages (i.e., 1974 in NCDS and 1986 in BCS70). Complete data at birth and in adolescence were available for 10,499 study members (5371 boys and 5128 girls) in NCDS and for 7293 study members (3533 boys and 3760 girls) in BCS70. Adult outcome data were available on reduced *N*s (7404 for NCDS and 5620 for BCS70). B-CAMHS99 examined the mental health of a representative sample of over 10,000 5–15-year-olds living in private households in the UK in 1999. Full details of the sampling strategy are provided by Meltzer et al. (2000). We focused on data collected on the 868 15-year-olds (439 boys and 429 girls) included in the sample. All three studies included roughly similar proportions of boys and girls, and included young people from the full spectrum of socio-economic backgrounds. As expected from well-documented socio-demographic trends (Hess, 1995; Office for National Statistics, 2000; Ferri, Bynner, & Wadsworth, 2003), lone parent and reconstituted families were more common in the more recent cohorts. In addition, the proportion of children from ethnic minority backgrounds included in the samples also increased, from 1.7% in NCDS to 2.7% in BCS70 and 9.3% in B-CAMHS99. This difference arose in part due to demographic trends, but also because the study samples for the first two cohorts were restricted to those born in the UK, whilst the third cohort included in-migrants post-birth.

Measures

Behaviour ratings at 15/16 years. Parents in NCDS and BCS70 answered questions taken from the Rutter A scale (Rutter, Tizard, & Whitmore, 1970; Elander & Rutter, 1996), whilst parents in B-CAMHS99 completed the Strengths and Difficulties Questionnaire (SDQ; Goodman, 1997). Questionnaire items assessed behavioural and emotional problems on 3-point scales (typically: '0 – not true; 1 – somewhat true; 2 – certainly true'). The questionnaire used in NCDS was almost identical to the conventional form of the Rutter A scale. BCS70 included 18 questions selected from the Rutter questionnaire, with only minor changes in the wording of occasional questions (e.g., 'Does she have any...' changed to 'Is there any...'). B-CAMHS99 used the SDQ in its standard format. The Rutter A scale formed the basis for the development of the SDQ, and the items considered here were worded in closely comparable ways on each questionnaire.

The following individual items were examined: fighting, bullying, stealing, lying, disobedience, fidgeting, restlessness, inattention, misery, worries, fearful of new situations. These items were selected because factor analyses showed that they loaded strongly and specifically onto one of three factors of interest: conduct, hyperactive and emotional problems. Occasional missing data were imputed using hotdeck imputation, substituting values from randomly drawn subjects closely matched on remaining items. Individual items were combined into five subscales: a 4-point aggressive conduct scale (fighting, bullying), a 6-point non-aggressive conduct scale (stealing, lying, disobedience), a 10-point overall conduct scale (sum of aggressive and non-aggressive scales), a 6-point hyperactive problems scale (fidgeting, restlessness, inattention), and a 6-point emotional scale (misery, worries, fearful of new situations). Alpha reliabilities were calculated separately for each scale and each cohort, and ranged from .55 (emotional problems, NCDS) to .75 (conduct problems, BCS70). In addition, data from a calibration study (see below) were used to test the relationships between the measures of hyperactive, emotional and conduct problems used here and standard SDQ subscale measures of each type of problem. Correlations were .79 for hyperactive problems, .84 for emotional problems and .86 for conduct problems. To assess cohort effects in rates of more marked conduct, emotional and hyperactive problems, scale scores were

dichotomised. To do this the three datasets were pooled, and cut-points on each scale were taken as closely as possible to the 90th percentile on all three samples combined (3 points or more for each of the conduct, hyperactive and emotional problem scales).

Despite the similarity of the Rutter scale and the SDQ, we were keen to ensure that measures of behaviour at all three time points were directly comparable. A calibration study was undertaken in which parents of additional samples of adolescents completed both the Rutter A scale and the SDQ. Participants were recruited from four secondary schools ($N = 219$), from a sample of adolescents referred for psychiatric problems ($N = 78$), and a control sample ($N = 87$). The school samples were drawn from non-selective state schools in outer London, included 57% boys, and ranged in age from 14 to 17 years (mean age = 15.2 years). The clinic sample and matched controls lived in greater London, included 48% boys, and ranged in age from 11 to 16 years (mean age = 13.2 years). The order in which parents completed the questionnaires was counterbalanced.

The calibration sample was used to impute Rutter questionnaire individual item scores, scale totals, and dichotomous problem scores for B-CAMHS99 study members on the basis of their SDQ scores. All imputation was undertaken separately for girls and boys. For each Rutter-based measure, the calibration sample was used to fit ordinal logistic regression models to predict each target Rutter measure from several SDQ measures. The chosen SDQ measures consisted of any closely matching items, relevant subscale scores and the overall SDQ scale score, except when these showed levels of association below $p = .1$. While the ordinary 'fitted value' from such a model may in some sense be the best predicted value for a particular individual, this value reflects neither the true variability in the population (fitted values have less variation than observed values) nor our level of uncertainty in that value. Multiple imputation (Rubin, 1987; Schafer, 1997) overcomes these problems. To reflect this uncertainty and variability, we first sampled values for the estimated coefficients from our ordinal logistic regressions by draws from their estimated covariance matrix. We then used these sampled coefficients to predict the probability of each feasible response value for each individual. For each individual, one of these response values was then picked with probability equal to this estimated response probability. These three steps were repeated 20 times to produce 20 B-CAMHS99 datasets, each with potentially different imputed Rutter measures. When taken together, these 20 datasets properly reflect both the behavioural variation as reported by the SDQ, as well as any remaining imprecision in how this would be reflected in Rutter A-scale-based measures. For proper statistical inference these datasets must be analysed jointly, as described later.

Socio-demographic information at age 15/16. Information from parental interviews was used to provide indicators of family type (both natural parents, one parent, reconstituted family/other), family size (only child, two or three children, four or more children), and housing tenure (owner-occupier vs. other). Family social class was assigned according to Registrar General classification (Office of Population Censuses and Surveys, 1993). Furthermore, a variable was derived identifying those belonging to ethnic minority groups.

Information from NCDS and BCS70 at birth. Information collected from parents of NCDS and BCS70 study members shortly after birth was used to explore sample attrition in these two studies by age 16. Factors of interest included gender, birth weight, maternal age, and maternal smoking in pregnancy (after 4 months). Socio-demographic indicators included marital status of the child's parents, maternal education beyond the minimum school-leaving age; region (London and South East vs. other for NCDS; London vs. other for BCS70) and father's social class.

Adult outcomes for NCDS and BCS70 study members. Follow-up data from interviews carried out with study members in NCDS at age 33, and BCS70 at age 29/30, were used to validate reports of adolescent conduct problems. Comparable dichotomous indicators were derived for poor occupational outcomes (unemployed at follow-up; ever dismissed from a job) and other indicators of socio-economic difficulties (receipt by study member or partner of income-linked state benefits; ever homeless). Indicators of relationship and parenting problems were included (three or more cohabitations/marriages of one month or more since age 16; 19 years or younger at birth of first child). Finally, measures of self-reported health, current smoking, drinking problems, and help-seeking for mental health problems were examined. Participants rated their current health on a four-point scale (poor or fair compared against good or excellent), which has been reported to be a reliable and valid index of ill health (Manor, Matthews, & Power, 2001). The CAGE questionnaire (lifetime version) provides a brief screen for problem drinking (Mayfield, McLeod, & Hall, 1974). Scores of two or more are a good indicator of alcohol problems in community samples (King, 1986). Study members reported whether or not they had sought help from a GP, hospital doctor or specialist for any adult mental health problems in the previous ten years in NCDS, and since the age of 16 in BCS70. Previous research has highlighted the increased risk for multiple co-occurring problems across a range of domains of adult functioning for children with conduct problems (Maughan & Rutter, 2001). We therefore constructed an overall index of adult difficulties through a count of these adult problems, with a score of four or more providing a measure of marked problems in adult functioning. Though there were no comparable indicators of adolescent or adult criminality across the three studies, study members in BCS70 were asked to report any police arrests and court convictions by age 30 years.

Analysis strategy

Response and attrition. The longitudinal nature of NCDS and BCS70 allowed an assessment of the pattern of attrition at age 16 by comparing the characteristics of responders and non-responders using data collected at

birth. Data on predictors of non-response measured at birth were available for 16,812 cases in NCDS and 16,237 cases in BCS70. Of these, 10,499 (62%) in NCDS and 7293 (45%) in BCS70 also had complete data in adolescence. Multivariate analyses demonstrated that response in both studies was higher for girls, for children of married parents, for higher socio-economic groups, and that it varied by region and was positively related to birth weight. In BCS70, response was also related positively to maternal age, maternal education and maternal non-smoking in pregnancy. Weights were estimated separately for each cohort using predicted values derived from logistic regression analyses of these predictors on age 16 response, and scaled back to preserve the *N* with actual data. The top 1% weights were trimmed to the next highest value to reduce the impact of extreme outliers. As the appendix shows, the weights adequately corrected known biases associated with response. The standard weights devised for B-CAMHS99 were used to address unequal probability of selection and non-response bias, particularly according to region, gender and age (see Meltzer et al., 2000 for details).

Response rates in adulthood for NCDS and BCS70 were good, considering the length of the follow-up period (71% of those included at age 16 for NCDS and 77% for BCS70). Response was predicted by gender, and by age 16 conduct scale score, family type, social class and housing tenure. A second set of weights was estimated to account for these potential biases, using an equivalent approach to that described above. These weights were combined with the age 16 weights, so that the data sets remained as representative as possible of the samples originally recruited at birth.

Analyses. The analyses were structured as follows. First, to evaluate evidence for secular change in emotional and behavioural problems, the distributions of scores on the conduct, hyperactive and emotional problem scales were compared across the three studies. Rates of more marked problems in each domain were also examined. Then, the overlaps between conduct problems, hyperactive behaviour and emotional difficulties were examined, and analyses of time trends were repeated controlling for co-occurring difficulties. For conduct scores, additional analyses examined time-trends by socio-demographic group, and considered aggressive and non-aggressive scale scores separately. A final section assessed the contribution of possible reporter effects by testing whether adolescent conduct problems in 1974 and 1986 were equally predictive of outcomes some 15 years later.

All analyses included response/sample weights, and were conducted in Stata (StataCorp, 2002). Proportional-odds ordinal logistic regression was used to test the effect of cohort on conduct, hyperactive and emotional scale scores, and for analyses of the three-level individual items. Results are described in terms of proportional odds ratios (POR) and 95% confidence intervals [CI]. A POR can be interpreted as the increase in the odds of crossing any particular threshold on the outcome scale, given a single unit increase in the predictor (cohort). Logistic regressions were used for analyses of binary outcomes (i.e., rates of high scores in each domain), with effects of cohort described in terms of odds ratios (OR) and 95% confidence intervals

1354   Stephan Collishaw et al.

[CI]. Odds ratios were also used to describe the impact of conduct problems on adult outcomes for NCDS and BCS70. If time trends in rates of conduct problems are not due to reporter effects, then no changes in risk for later outcomes would be expected. Tests of interactions between cohort and conduct problems in logistic regression models formally assessed changes in the strength of associations with adult outcomes over time. Special techniques for the joint analysis of datasets derived by multiple imputation have been developed (Rubin, 1987), and shown to have good statistical properties. Analyses involving all three cohorts were undertaken using the hotdeck procedure (Mander & Clayton, 1999) to allow the joint analysis of datasets derived by multiple imputation. This procedure runs a given analysis on each of the datasets in turn. The results are combined, taking account of statistical uncertainty as estimated by each analysis (the reported standard errors), and of imputation uncertainty as reflected in variation of findings between datasets (between dataset variation in parameter estimates).

Two points need to be borne in mind in interpreting the findings. First, given the large size of the first two cohorts, even quite small variations may yield highly significant results in statistical terms for comparisons of NCDS and BCS70. Second, the conservative approach to the comparability of the SDQ and Rutter-A scale and the lower sample N for B-CAMHS99 resulted in a reduction in power for analyses involving B-CAMHS99. This means that marginally significant differences may reflect quite substantial changes in levels of difficulties over time. It is therefore important that proportional odds ratios and odds ratios are considered alongside quoted significance levels and confidence intervals.

Results

I. *Trends in adolescent behavioural and emotional problems: 1974–1999*

Conduct problems.

Trends in total conduct scale scores. As shown in Figure 1, there was evidence for a substantial increase in adolescent conduct problems between 1974 and 1999 for both genders. Ordinal logistic regression analyses showed a significant effect of cohort on conduct scale scores for boys (POR = 1.33 [95% CI = 1.20–1.47], *p* < .001) and for girls (POR = 1.31 [95% CI = 1.18–1.45], *p* < .001). There

was no significant interaction between cohort and gender (*p* > .7) – as shown in Figure 1 there appear to have been parallel increases in conduct problems for both genders. Overall, scores increased from 1974 to 1986 (POR = 1.29 [95% CI = 1.21–1.37], *p* < .001), and again between 1986 and 1999 (POR = 1.42 [95% CI = 1.12–1.80], *p* = .001).

Trends in rates of high conduct problem scores. Proportions of each cohort scoring above cut-points used to identify more severe problems in the conduct, hyperactive and emotional domains are shown in Table 1. In relation to conduct problems, the effect of cohort was substantial. Over the 25-year period of the study the proportion of adolescent boys and girls with conduct problems on this definition more than doubled.

Hyperactive problems.

Trends in hyperactive problem scale scores. Mean hyperactive problem scale scores are shown for each of the three samples and separately by gender in Figure 2. Ordinal logistic regression analyses showed no significant linear effects of cohort on hyperactive problem scale scores for boys (POR = 1.00 [95% CI = .90–1.11]) or for girls (POR = 1.09 [95% CI = .96–1.23]).

Table 1 Proportions with conduct, hyperactive and emotional problems by gender and cohort

	1974 %	1986 %	1999 %	C2 vs. C1 OR [95% CI]	C3 vs. C2 OR [95% CI]
Conduct problems					
Boys	7.6	12.1	16.7	1.67 [1.4–1.9]	1.44 [.9–2.3]
Girls	6.0	8.6	13.1	1.47 [1.2–1.7]	1.59 [.95–2.7]
Total	6.8	10.4	14.9	1.58 [1.4–1.8]	1.50 [1.1–2.0]
Hyperactive problems					
Boys	11.1	8.3	16.9	.73 [.6–.9]	2.22 [1.4–3.5]
Girls	6.6	5.7	7.1	.86 [.7–1.04]	1.25 [.7–2.3]
Total	8.9	7.1	12.0	.78 [.7–.9]	1.79 [1.3–2.5]
Emotional problems					
Boys	7.8	7.8	13.3	.99 [.8–1.2]	1.79 [.96–3.4]
Girls	12.8	13.4	20.4	1.05 [.9–1.2]	1.64 [.9–3.0]
Total	10.2	10.5	16.9	1.03 [.9–1.1]	1.72 [1.1–2.7]

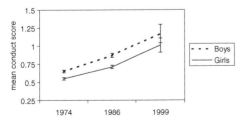

Figure 1 Conduct problems by gender: 1974–1999. Mean scale scores and standard errors shown

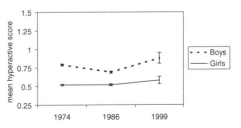

Figure 2 Hyperactive behaviour by gender: 1974–1999. Mean scale scores and standard errors shown

Trends in rates of high hyperactive problem scores.
Rates of more severe hyperactive problems are
shown in Table 1. High hyperactive problem scores
for boys decreased between 1974 and 1986
($p = .001$), and then increased between 1986 and
1999 ($p = .001$). There were no significant changes
in high hyperactive problem scores for girls between
1974 and 1986 ($p = .11$) or between 1986 and 1999
($p = .4$).

Emotional problems.

Trends in emotional problem scale scores. Mean
scores on the emotional problem scale are shown by
cohort and gender in Figure 3. Ordinal logistic
regressions confirmed that there had been little or no
change in emotional scale scores between 1974 and
1986 for either gender (boys: POR = 1.08 [95%
CI = .99–1.17], $p = .07$; girls: POR = 1.04 [95%
CI = .96–1.13], $p = .32$), followed by upward trends
between 1986 and 1999 (boys: POR = 1.42 [95%
CI = .89–2.28], $p = .09$; girls: POR = 1.50 [95%
CI = .93–2.42], $p = .06$).

Trends in rates of high emotional problem scores.
There were no changes in rates of categorically defined emotional problems between 1974 and 1986,
followed by substantial increases in high emotional
problem scores between 1986 and 1999 (see Table 1).

*Overlaps between conduct, hyperactive, and emo-
tional problems.* The analyses so far have shown
that conduct problems increased substantially between 1974 and 1999. Emotional problems also increased, but only between 1986 and 1999. Finally,
evidence in relation to trends in hyperactive behaviours was less clear-cut. Figure 4 shows that there
was a significant overlap between each type of
problem. Adolescents with hyperactive problems had
odds ranging from 5.6 to 12.7 of having comorbid
conduct problems. Those with emotional problems
had odds of between 2.9 and 4.8 of having comorbid
conduct problems. Finally, children with hyperactive
problems had odds ranging from 3.4 to 4.6 of having
comorbid emotional problems. There was a significant interaction between cohort and hyperactive
problems ($p = .02$) and a marginal interaction

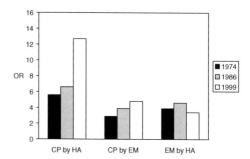

Figure 4 Odds ratios describing comorbidity between
problem subtypes by cohort. Conduct problems (CP),
Emotional problems (EM) and Hyperactive problems
(HA)

between cohort and emotional problems ($p = .07$) in
predicting odds of conduct problems. These results
suggest that levels of co-occurrence between conduct
problems and other difficulties have increased over
time. The interaction between hyperactive problems
and cohort in the prediction of emotional problems
was not significant ($p > .7$).

*Independence of cohort effects on emotional and
behavioural problems.* Given the strong overlaps
between problem types, we went on to explore how
far observed time-trends were independent, or
whether trends in one type of difficulty mediated
effects on others. Main effects of cohort on each type
of problem were tested again, but this time adding
controls for co-occurring problems. Ordinal logistic
regression analyses of scale scores continued to
show a large increase over time in conduct scores not
attenuated by controls for concurrent difficulties
(POR = 1.34 [95% CI = 1.23–1.46], $p < .001$). Once
other difficulties are accounted for, the increase in
emotional problem scores between 1986 and 1999
also continued to be marginally significant
(POR = 1.36 [95% CI = .96–1.94, $p = .05$]. Analyses
of hyperactivity scores for boys continued to show a
significant decrease between 1974 and 1986
(POR = .84 [95% CI = .77–.92], $p < .001$). No other
effects were significant.

II. Generality of time trends in conduct problems

Given that the most consistent time trends appeared
to affect levels of conduct problems, additional
analyses examined whether these trends varied by
socio-demographic indicators, and whether trends
differed for different types of conduct problems.

*Trends in conduct problems by socio-demographic
indicators.* Table 2 shows mean conduct scores in
the three studies broken down by a range of socio-
demographic indicators. There were substantial

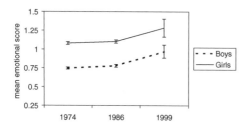

Figure 3 Emotional problems by gender: 1974–1999.
Mean scale scores and standard errors shown

Table 2 Time trends in conduct problems by socio-demographic group

	1974 mean score	1986 mean score	1999 mean score	p[1]
Family type				
Two natural parents	.55	.69	.92	<.001
Single parent	.82	1.16	1.37	.001
Reconstituted	1.03	1.14	1.38	.07
Family size				
Only child	.38	.69	.93	<.001
2 or 3 children	.54	.74	1.14	<.001
4+ children	.95	1.29	1.61	<.001
Family social class				
I	.30	.55	.51	.02
II	.41	.58	.89	<.001
IIINM	.46	.67	1.14	<.001
IIIM	.65	.85	1.23	<.001
IV	.70	.98	1.29	<.001
V	.97	1.11	1.75	.01
Other, not known	.98	1.63	1.76	.01
Home owner				
No	.76	1.12	1.59	<.001
Yes	.44	.68	.88	<.001

[1] Significance of linear trends as estimated using ordinal logistic regressions (z-test).

Table 3 Conduct problems. Item prevalence by cohort

Item[1] (rating)	1974 %	1986 %	1999 %	p[2]
Fighting				
somewhat true	10.4	9.9	12.8	.67
certainly true	1.7	1.3	3.1	
Bullying				
somewhat true	4.8	6.2	5.7	.01
certainly true	.8	.9	1.3	
Stealing				
somewhat true	3.0	6.3	7.3	<.001
certainly true	.3	1.4	.7	
Lying				
somewhat true	11.4	14.7	19.8	<.001
certainly true	1.3	1.7	3.6	
Disobedience				
somewhat true	17.5	24.4	25.8	<.001
certainly true	2.5	3.6	6.1	

[1] Items rated on three-point scales (for the SDQ: not true; somewhat true; certainly true).
[2] Significance of linear trends as estimated using ordinal logistic regressions (z-test).

increases in conduct scores over successive cohorts for all family types, and all social groups. There were no significant interactions between cohort and family size, family social class, or tenure. A marginal interaction between cohort and family type (*p* = .03) indicated greater increases in conduct scores for children in single parent families.

Given the differences in the ethnic composition of the three studies, additional analyses examined rates of conduct problems separately for white and non-white study members. The results showed a linear increase in conduct problems for those classified as white, and a peak in parent-reported problems in 1986 for non-whites. In the final cohort – the only one with sizable proportions of ethnic minorities – there was no difference in levels of parent-reported conduct problems between white and non-white study members.

Trends in individual conduct problem items. The pattern of results for individual conduct problem items (see Table 3) showed that the greatest increases with time were found for stealing, lying and disobedience. Analyses of aggressive and non-aggressive conduct scale scores showed a marginal increase in aggressive problems for boys (POR = 1.16 [95% CI = .99–1.35], *p* = .04), but no time trends in aggression scores for girls (POR = .94 [95% CI = .82–1.07], *p* > .2). In contrast, there were substantial increases in non-aggressive problems over time for both boys (POR = 1.38 [95% CI = 1.24–1.53], *p* < .001), and girls (POR = 1.47 [95% CI = 1.31–1.66], *p* < .001).

III. *Adult outcomes of conduct problems*

Links between conduct problems and later criminality. Whilst directly comparable indicators of study members' criminal involvement were not available for the three studies, follow-up self-report data of police arrests and court convictions in BCS70 appeared to corroborate and validate parent ratings of conduct problems. Thirty-seven percent of adolescents with high parent-rated conduct problem scores reported a police arrest by age 30, compared with 15% of those without marked conduct problems, OR = 3.51 [95% CI = 2.8–4.3]. Similarly, 28% of BCS70 study members with high conduct problem scores reported a court conviction by age 30, compared with 11% of those without marked conduct problems, OR = 3.18 [95% CI = 2.5–4.0].

Outcomes of conduct problems: comparison of NCDS and BCS70. The final series of analyses was designed to explore whether observed results reflected reporter effects or real changes in the prevalence of behaviour problems over time, by testing for changes in associations with later outcomes. Longitudinal data from NCDS and BCS70 allowed tests of the prediction of a variety of adult outcomes. Analyses focused on conduct problems, as these showed the most consistent time trends. If time trends reflect changes in parents' reporting rather than real changes in adolescent behaviour, then reduced associations with known outcomes of conduct problems would be expected. In contrast, associations that remained stable over time would provide further evidence that there has been a real rise in the level of teenage conduct problems.

Rates of a variety of adult outcomes (assessed at age 33 for NCDS and at age 29/30 for BCS70) are shown separately for those with and without high

Table 4 Adult outcomes for adolescents with conduct problems

| | NCDS – age 33, year 1991 | | | BCS70 – age 29/30, year 1999 | | | |
| | Conduct problems | | | Conduct problems | | | |
	No $N^2 = 6979$ %	Yes $N = 425$ %	OR [95% CI]	No $N = 5142$ %	Yes $N = 478$ %	OR [95% CI]	Interaction[1] (p)
Occupation							
Unemployed	3.7	10.7	3.12 [2.2–4.4]	2.5	5.8	2.40 [1.5–3.9]	.39
Sacked	2.8	5.2	1.86 [1.2–3.0]	3.3	6.8	2.13 [1.4–3.3]	.68
Other SES							
Benefits	12.7	28.0	2.67 [2.1–3.4]	12.8	28.1	2.67 [2.1–3.4]	.99
Homelessness	3.8	6.3	1.72 [1.1–2.6]	4.8	14.5	3.40 [2.5–4.7]	.01
Relationships and children							
3+ cohabitations	3.4	6.7	2.06 [1.3–3.2]	2.2	5.0	2.38 [1.5–3.8]	.66
Teenage parent	6.9	16.4	2.64 [2.0–3.5]	4.6	11.8	2.74 [2.0–3.8]	.86
Health							
Poor health	13.0	19.8	1.64 [1.3–2.1]	14.2	20.7	1.58 [1.2–2.0]	.84
Alcohol problems	11.9	19.5	1.79 [1.4–2.3]	14.2	18.3	1.35 [1.0–1.8]	.14
Smoking	31.2	59.7	3.27 [2.7–4.0]	32.2	59.3	3.07 [2.5–3.8]	.66
Help-seeking	21.4	33.7	1.87 [1.5–2.3]	23.6	31.0	1.46 [1.2–1.8]	.11
Total problems							
4 or more	5.4	17.2	3.61 [2.7–4.8]	5.7	18.2	3.69 [2.8–4.9]	.92

[1]Test of interaction between conduct problems and cohort in prediction of adult outcomes.
[2]Unweighted Ns.

adolescent conduct problem scores in Table 4. High conduct scores were strongly associated with poorer adult functioning across a variety of domains for both cohorts. Tests of interactions between cohort and conduct problems were only significant in one instance – high levels of adolescent conduct problems were more strongly associated with adult homelessness ($p = .01$) in the second cohort than in the first. In addition, there were marginally reduced associations with adult alcohol problems ($p = .14$) and help-seeking for mental health problems ($p = .11$) for the second cohort. As shown in Table 4, adolescents with high conduct problem scores had equally high risks in both cohorts of multiple poor outcomes (four or more indicators of difficulties in adulthood).

These findings are also relevant for examining the longer-term implications of increases in adolescent conduct problems. A recalculation of the data in terms of population attributable risk fractions showed that the proportions of the risk for poor adult outcome associated with high conduct scores increased between NCDS and BCS70 for many of the indicators studied. Attributable risk fractions increased from 7% to 11% for sackings, from 8% to 11% for dependence on benefits, from 3% to 17% for homelessness, from 9% to 15% for teenage parenthood and from 6% to 8% for smoking. The mean attributable risk fraction linked with high conduct scores rose from 6.2% for NCDS to 9.6% for BCS70. In relation to the indicator of poor functioning across multiple domains, the population attributable fraction associated with conduct problems rose from 13% for NCDS to 19% for BCS70.

Discussion

Overview

This study set out to assess whether adolescent emotional and behavioural problems have become more common in the UK, by comparing parent ratings collected from general population samples in 1974, 1986 and 1999. Conduct scores increased markedly for both genders, for all family types, and across all social class categories over this 25-year period. Overall, each successive cohort had increased odds of high conduct problems of around 1.5. Time trends appeared more marked for non-aggressive conduct problems than for aggressive problems. Hyperactive problem scores for boys decreased between 1974 and 1986, and then increased again by 1999; for girls hyperactivity scores remained stable throughout the study period. Rates of emotional problems remained stable between 1974 and 1986, and then increased between 1986 and 1999, both for males and females. Analyses that accounted for the overlap between conduct problems, emotional difficulties, and hyperactive behaviour confirmed a strong independent effect of cohort on the rate of conduct problems.

Further analyses examined the impact of conduct problems on long-term outcomes for the first two cohorts. The findings here are important for several reasons. Methodologically, a comparison of the predictive power of conduct problems to later outcomes provides an important test of the validity of the observed time trends (Robins, 2001). If adolescent conduct problems have increased over time, as suggested by parental reports, then the long-term prediction to later adult difficulties should have remained the same. In contrast, if apparent time trends arose due to reporting artefacts, more 'false negative' cases would be identified in more recent cohorts, resulting in decreased levels of association with negative adult outcomes over time. From a policy perspective, the results are also important, as to our knowledge this is the first study to use longitudinal data to document the long-term implications of secular changes in adolescent mental health.

Individuals with high conduct problem scores in both studies had a poorer prognosis for a range of psychosocial outcomes. Conduct problems had an important impact on study members' occupational records and on their socio-economic status (increased unemployment, more job dismissals, greater dependence on state benefits and increased homelessness). Individuals with conduct problems also had less stable partnerships and were more likely to have children at an early age. Finally, conduct problems were associated with poor self-rated health, smoking, problem drinking and help-seeking for mental health problems. On the whole, the impact of conduct problems in later life appeared not to differ by cohort, indicating that observed time trends in rates of conduct problems are unlikely to reflect reporter bias.

Strengths and limitations

As outlined in the introduction, this study has a number of strengths for assessing time trends in adolescent mental health. The most central of these is the availability of closely comparable assessments of common emotional and behavioural problems experienced by young people in three large nationally representative UK samples spanning 25 years. The second major strength was the longitudinal nature of NCDS and BCS70, allowing an assessment of reporter effects, and an assessment of the likely long-term implications of time trends in adolescent mental health. It is equally important, however, to acknowledge several limitations. In spite of the similarity of the measures of behaviour used in each cohort, the questionnaires were not identical. We used data from a calibration study to ensure comparability of the Rutter A scale and the Strengths and Difficulties Questionnaire. Furthermore, the analytical approach modelled, as accurately as possible, uncertainty in estimates for calibrated scores. However, this conservative approach meant that estimates of levels of difficulties in 1999 were less precise than those for 1974 and 1986. Whilst we found clear evidence for a consistent rise in conduct problems over the whole study period, future studies will need to address the extent of the recent rise in emotional problems, and whether this is a transitory phenomenon or the beginning of a longer-term trend.

A second limitation was the reliance on parental reports of adolescent problems. Ideally, it would

have been preferable to confirm the present findings with data collected from multiple informants. Note, however, that studies of time trends in the US have shown comparable results for analyses of parent, teacher and youth self-reports (Achenbach, Dumenci, & Rescorla, 2002; Achenbach et al., 2003).

Third, the marked changes in the proportions of adolescents from ethnic minority groups included in the three studies mean that we were unable to determine whether the trends we detected in white adolescents have also been mirrored among teenagers of specific minority groups. In these nationally based samples, time trends in conduct problems were largely independent of ethnic group status, and levels of conduct problems in the most recent sample (the only one with a sizable proportion of minority group participants) did not differ between white and non-white adolescents. In a similar way, results from the Health Survey for England showed only minor variations in SDQ scores by ethnic group (Nazroo, Becher, Kelly, & McMunn, 2001). We must await further data from more recent cohorts to assess these issues in more detail.

Time trends in conduct problems

The findings showed an increase in conduct problems between 1974 and 1999, consistent with findings from the Youth Lifestyle Surveys showing increases in self-report offending for 14–17-year-olds between 1992 and 1999 (East & Campbell, 1999). The adult longitudinal outcome data for NCDS and BCS70 suggest that these results reflect real changes in behaviour. They also raise important questions about the long-term implications for affected individuals, and for society as a whole, of these rising rates of adolescent conduct problems.

A number of authors have argued that conduct disturbances are heterogeneous, and that there is an important distinction between conduct problems involving physical aggression, and other types of conduct problems (e.g., Achenbach, Conners, Quay, Verhulst, & Howell, 1989; Maughan, Pickles, Rowe, Costello, & Angold, 2000). For example, Maughan et al. (2000) reported that the overlap between developmental trajectory classes for aggressive and non-aggressive subtypes is limited, and that both types of problem independently predict police contacts and arrests. The demonstration of a dissociation in time trends for non-aggressive and aggressive conduct problems is consistent with a conceptual distinction between these two behavioural subtypes.

Time trends in emotional problems

Emotional problems appear to have increased between 1986 and 1999, but not between 1974 and 1986. Reduced power for analyses involving the third cohort meant that apparently sizeable differences between rates of emotional problems in 1999 and the previous two cohorts were only marginally significant. Nevertheless, adolescents in 1999 had estimated odds of a high emotional problem score that were 1.7 times greater than in 1986. West and Sweeting (2003) also found an increase in self-reports of psychological distress between 1987 and 1999 among 15-year-olds in studies conducted in Scotland. However, the findings of their study differed in that this trend was only apparent for girls. Further data on more recent cohorts are needed to clarify the precise nature of time trends affecting rates of emotional problems.

Time trends in hyperactive problems

Data on time trends in rates of hyperactivity are considerably more sparse than for other disorders, in part because reliable retrospective measures of hyperactivity have only recently been developed, and in part because of changes over time in the definition of hyperkinetic disorder (Prosser & McArdle, 1996). Repeated cross-sectional surveys using teacher and parent reports thus provide the only source of evidence on this issue to date. The present study provides the first evidence on time trends in the UK. There was some evidence for change over time in scores for boys, whilst scores for girls remained stable over all three studies. Overall, however, trends in hyperactive problems were less clear-cut than for other types of adolescent difficulty. Once again, future data points would be helpful in clarifying possible trends. In addition, because hyperactive behaviours may be less salient indicators of psychopathology in the teens than at younger ages, studies of time trends in hyperactivity in younger children would be especially valuable.

Time trends in patterns of comorbidity

A further issue of interest is whether there have been changes in the extent to which different types of problem co-occur. It is well known that childhood disorders often occur together (Caron & Rutter, 1991; Angold, Costello, & Erkanli, 1999), and this comorbidity is related to differences in expression and prognosis for particular disorders (Angold et al., 1999). Roberts et al. (1998) have suggested that very little is known about the prevalence of different patterns of comorbidity in epidemiological samples. In the present study, the largest overlap was observed between conduct and hyperactive problems in all three cohorts. Furthermore, there were smaller (though still substantial) levels of co-occurrence between emotional and conduct problems and between emotional and hyperactive problems in all three samples. Our findings also suggest that there has been an increase in the levels of comorbidity between conduct problems and other difficulties.

Implications

The results have important practical and theoretical implications. As we have seen, rising rates of conduct problems have had long-term consequences for individuals' occupational and socio-economic outcomes, for relationships and parenting, and for adult physical and mental health. In addition, time trends in conduct problems raise important questions about their implications for UK society as a whole. For the adult difficulties examined in this study, the proportion of risk associated with conduct problems rose substantially between cohort 1 and cohort 2. For example, in NCDS 13% of the risk for markedly poor adult functioning (difficulties on four or more outcomes) was attributable to the group with conduct problems. This figure rose to 19% in BCS70 as the number of children with conduct problems increased. These findings complement previous research, showing that conduct problems are associated with a formidable long-term economic cost to society (Scott, Knapp, Henderson, & Maughan, 2001). There is an urgent need to identify the underlying reasons for the increase in conduct problems over recent years, and to explore how best to intervene at both individual and societal levels to address this problem. In a similar way, a rise in adolescent emotional difficulties is likely to have long-term consequences, both with respect to the prevalence of adult affective and anxiety disorders (e.g., Fombonne, Wostear, Cooper, Harrington, & Rutter, 2001; Lewinsohn, Rohde, Klein, & Seeley, 1999), and also more broadly for a range of psychosocial outcomes (Fergusson & Woodward, 2002).

Understanding time trends in adolescent mental health

It is beyond the scope of this paper to explore explanatory factors in detail, though we hope to do this in subsequent reports. At this stage, however, a number of general issues can be highlighted. First, evidence on secular change in the prevalence of psychosocial disorders provides strong support for the role of environmental influences on psychosocial development. It is most unlikely that changes in the gene pool alone could explain short-term time trends in rates of disorder (Rutter, 2001). Second, an examination of broader societal trends affecting the lives of children and adolescents seems likely to provide important clues as to possible reasons for trends in mental health.

Recent decades have seen considerable change in the social and family contexts in which children grow up in many Western societies. Changes in the nature of the family include rising divorce rates, a greater number of cohabiting couples, and increasing numbers of single parent and step families. Other changes include increasing numbers of dual-earner households and children looked after in day-care facilities

1360   Stephan Collishaw et al.

of variable quality. Given that many of these factors are known to be associated with adolescent conduct problems (Hill & Maughan, 2001), it is certainly plausible that these changes have contributed to rising rates of adolescent difficulties. If – as is often argued – family influences affect children's adjustment through more proximal processes such as parenting practices or the quality of parental relationships (Hill, 2002), then it follows that changes in family context are only likely to explain time trends in conduct problems if there have been concomitant changes in intra-family dynamics of this kind. Further research is needed to explore these possibilities.

Other societal changes relate to material resources. On the whole, these have improved at the same time as mental health problems have worsened. However, whilst absolute levels of material resources may have improved for later-born cohorts, socio-economic inequalities also appear to have increased (Ferri et al., 2003), and it is possible that this has contributed to time trends in adolescent mental health problems. Furthermore, Schoon et al. (2002) and Ferri et al. (2003) have argued that many contextual factors, including ones related to socio-economic deprivation and inequality, have become relatively more important in their impact on child development over time. One important lesson appears to be that simple comparisons of time trends in mental health problems and time trends in possible contextual influences may be misleading. Changes in the prevalence of risk factors may be off-set by changes in the impact and correlates of risk factors.

In addition to general changes in family structure and socio-economic conditions, there have also been numerous other changes in adolescents' lifestyles, experiences and expectations. Rutter and Smith (1995) point to an increase in the availability of drugs, a lengthening of the adolescent time period, a greater freedom for adolescents to make their own decisions about sexuality and love relationships, and a greater emphasis on educational attainment. Specific evidence on which if any of these changes contribute to time trends in adolescent adjustment problems is limited. One exception is the study by West and Sweeting (2003) who examined the impact of educational stressors on levels of psychological distress over a 12-year time period among 15-year-olds in the West of Scotland. They found that personal worries (e.g., about appearance) had a constant impact on psychological distress over time. In contrast, worries about school performance increased among girls, and this in turn contributed to an increase in their levels of distress over the course of the study.

Although we were not able to explore these issues in detail here, our present results do provide some hints as to the nature of the mechanisms that are likely to be involved. As we have seen, conduct problems increased over time for young people in each and every family type and socio-economic grouping, as well as for boys and for girls. These uniform effects

suggest that specific socio-demographic trends such as rising divorce rates cannot by themselves fully explain time trends in adolescent adjustment. Instead, one possibility is that relatively broad societal changes (e.g., in the media, youth culture or social cohesion) are affecting adolescent mental health. As Rutter (1995) noted, studies of change over time (like cross-cultural comparisons) are particularly valuable in highlighting explanatory factors of this kind that may be hidden by their relative lack of variation within a particular population. A second possibility is that there has been a 'snowballing' effect. Relatively modest changes in rates of adolescent conduct problems in one 'generation' may create a feedback loop, increasing the exposure to certain environmental risks – a greater likelihood of belonging to a deviant peer group, for example, or changes in youth culture and the media catering for changing adolescent needs and tastes. Such contextual effects may then in turn further increase the risks for conduct problems in the next 'generation' of adolescents (see Dickens & Flynn, 2001 for a discussion of social multiplier effects of this kind).

Conclusions

The results of this study show that there have been important trends in adolescents' behavioural and emotional problems over the last 25 years of the 20th century in the UK. Conduct problems became significantly more common over the whole study period, and there were increases in emotional problems between 1986 and 1999. Increasing rates of conduct problems were found for males and females, for young people in all social groups, and for all family types. The similarity of the associations with long-term outcomes for successive cohorts makes it unlikely that the results are due to reporting artefacts.

Acknowledgements

We are grateful to the Nuffield Foundation for grant 00.27 to Barbara Maughan, Robert Goodman and Stephan Collishaw in support of this work. We are also grateful to schools and parents who helped with the calibration exercise, to the UK Data Archive for providing access to data from the National Child Development Study and the 1970 British Cohort Study, and to Howard Meltzer at the Office of National Statistics for providing access to data from the 1999 British Child and Adolescent Mental Health Survey.

Correspondence to

Stephan Collishaw, MRC Social, Genetic, and Developmental Psychiatry Centre, Box Number PO46, Institute of Psychiatry, 16 De Crespigny Park, London SE5 8AF, UK; Tel: 020 7848 0487; Email: s.collishaw@iop.kcl.ac.uk

References

Achenbach, T.M., Conners, C.K., Quay, H.C., Verhulst, F.C., & Howell, C.T. (1989). Replication of empirically derived syndromes as a basis for taxonomy of child/adolescent psychopathology. *Journal of Abnormal Child Psychology, 17*, 299–323.

Achenbach, T.M., Dumenci, L., & Rescorla, L.A. (2002). Ten-year comparisons of problems and competencies for national samples of youth: Self, parent and teacher reports. *Journal of Emotional and Behavioral Disorders, 10*, 194–203.

Achenbach, T.M., Dumenci, L., & Rescorla, L.A. (2003). Are American children's problems still getting worse? A 23-year comparison. *Journal of Abnormal Child Psychology, 31*, 1–11.

Angold, A., Costello, E.J., & Erkanli, A. (1999). Comorbidity. *Journal of Child Psychology and Psychiatry, 40*, 57–87.

Butler, N., & Golding, J. (1986). *From birth to five: A study of health and behaviour of Britain's 5-year-olds.* Oxford: Pergamon Press.

Caron, C., & Rutter, M. (1991). Comorbidity in child psychopathology – concepts, issues and research strategies. *Journal of Child Psychology and Psychiatry, 32*, 1063–1080.

Cross-National Collaborative Group. (1992). The changing rate of major depression. *Journal of the American Medical Association, 268*, 3098–3105.

Dickens, W.T., & Flynn, J.R. (2001). Heritability estimates versus large environmental effects: The IQ paradox resolved. *Psychological Review, 108*, 346–369.

Diekstra, R.F.W., Kienhorst, C.W.M., & de Wilde, E.J. (1995). Suicide and suicidal behaviour among adolescents. In M. Rutter & D.J. Smith (Eds.), *Psychosocial disorders in young people: Time trends and their causes* (pp. 686–782). Chichester: John Wiley & Sons.

East, K., & Campbell, S. (1999). Aspects of crime. *Young offenders 1999.* Home Office Internet publication. Retrieved 14 March 2003 from http://www.homeoffice.gov.uk/rds/youthjustice1.html.

Elander, J., & Rutter, M. (1996). Use and development of the Rutter parents' and teachers' scales. *International Journal of Methods in Psychiatric Research, 6*, 63–78.

Fergusson, D.M., & Woodward, L.J. (2002). Mental health, educational, and social role outcomes of adolescents with depression. *Archives of General Psychiatry, 59*, 225–231.

Ferri, E., Bynner, J., & Wadsworth, M. (2003). *Changing Britain. Changing lives. Three generations at the turn of the century.* London: Institute of Education Publications.

Fogelman, K. (1983). *Growing up in Great Britain.* London: MacMillan.

Fombonne, E. (1998). Increased rates of psychosocial disorders in youth. *European Archives of Psychiatry and Clinical Neuroscience, 248*, 14–21.

Fombonne, E., Wostear, G., Cooper, V., Harrington, R., & Rutter, M. (2001). The Maudsley long-term follow-up of child and adolescent depression. I. Psychiatric outcomes in adulthood. *British Journal of Psychiatry, 179*, 210–217.

Goodman, R. (1997). The Strengths and Difficulties Questionnaire: A research note. *Journal of Child Psychology and Psychiatry, 38*, 581–586.

Hess, L.E. (1995). Changing family patterns in Western Europe: Opportunity and risk factors for adolescent development. In M. Rutter & D.J. Smith (Eds.), *Psychosocial disorders in young people: Time trends and their causes* (pp. 104–193). Chichester: John Wiley & Sons.

Hill, J. (2002). Biological, psychological and social processes in the conduct disorders. *Journal of Child Psychology and Psychiatry, 43*, 133–164.

Hill, J., & Maughan B. (2001). *Conduct disorders in childhood and adolescence* (pp. 507–552). Cambridge: Cambridge University Press.

JAMA. (1995). Suicide among children, adolescents, and young adults: United States, 1980–1992 (editorial). *Journal of the American Medical Association, 274*, 451–452.

De Jong, P.F. (1997). Short-term trends in Dutch children's attention problems. *European Child and Adolescent Psychiatry, 6*, 73–80.

Kessler, R.C., McGonagle, K.A., Swartz, M., Blazer, D.G., & Nelson, C.B. (1993). Sex and depression in the National Comorbidity Survey. I. Lifetime prevalence, chronicity and recurrence. *Journal of Affective Disorders, 29*, 85–96.

King, M. (1986). At risk drinking among general practice attenders: Validation of the CAGE questionnaire. *Psychological Medicine, 16*, 213–217.

Lewinsohn, P.M., Rohde, P., Klein, D.N., & Seeley, J.R. (1999). Natural course of adolescent major depressive disorder: I. Continuity into young adulthood. *Journal of the American Academy of Child and Adolescent Psychiatry, 38*, 56–63.

Lewinsohn, P.M., Rohde, P., Seeley, J.R., & Fischer, S.A. (1993). Age-cohort changes in the lifetime occurrence of depression and other mental disorders. *Journal of Abnormal Psychology, 102*, 110–120.

Mander, A., & Clayton, D. (1999). HOTDECK: Stata module to impute missing values using the hotdeck method. Statistical Software Components S36690 (rev. 12 September 2002). Boston, MA: Boston College, Department of Economics.

Manor, O., Matthews, S., & Power, C. (2001). Self-rated health and longstanding illness: Inter-relationships with morbidity in early adulthood. *International Journal of Epidemiology, 30*, 600–607.

Maughan, B., Pickles, A., Rowe, R., Costello, E.J., & Angold, A. (2000). Developmental trajectories of aggressive and non-aggressive conduct problems. *Journal of Quantitative Criminology, 16*, 199–221.

Maughan, B., & Rutter, M. (2001). Antisocial children grown up. In J. Hill & B. Maughan (Eds.), *Conduct disorders in childhood and adolescence* (pp. 507–552). Cambridge: Cambridge University Press.

Mayfield, D., McLeod, G., & Hall, P. (1974). The CAGE questionnaire. Validation of a new alcohol screening instrument. *American Journal of Psychiatry, 131*, 1121–1123.

Meltzer, H., Gatward, R., Goodman, R., & Ford, T. (2000). *The mental health of children and adolescents in Great Britain: Summary report.* London: The Stationery Office.

1362 Stephan Collishaw et al.

Nazroo, J., Becher, H., Kelly, Y., & McMunn, A. (2001). Children's health. In B. Erens, P. Primatesta, & G. Prior (Eds.), *Health Survey for England: The health of minority ethnic groups '99. Vol. 1: Findings.* London. The Stationeration Office.

Office for National Statistics. (2000). *Population Trends, 102.* London: The Stationery Office.

Office of Population Censuses and Surveys. (1993). *Standard occupational classification.* London: The Stationery Office.

Prosser, J., & McArdle, P. (1996). The changing mental health of children and adolescents: Evidence for a deterioration? *Psychological Medicine, 26,* 715–725.

Rahim, S.I.A., & Cederblad, M. (1984). Effects of rapid urbanisation on child behaviour and health in a part of Khartoum, Sudan. *Journal of Child Psychology and Psychiatry, 25,* 629–641.

Roberts, R.E., Attkisson, C.C., & Rosenblatt, A. (1998). Prevalence of psychopathology among children and adolescents. *American Journal of Psychiatry, 155,* 715–725.

Robins, L.N. (2001). Making sense of the increasing prevalence of conduct disorder. In J. Green & W. Yule (Eds.), *Research and innovation on the road to modern child psychiatry. Vol. 1. Festschrift for Professor Sir Michael Rutter* (pp. 115–128). Glasgow: Gaskell.

Robins, L.N., & Regier, D.A. (1991). *Psychiatric disorders in America: The Epidemiologic Catchment Area Study.* New York: The Free Press.

Rubin, D.B. (1987). *Multiple imputation for nonresponse in surveys.* New York: John Wiley and Sons.

Rutter, M. (1995). Causal concepts and their testing. In M. Rutter & D.J. Smith (Eds.), *Psychosocial disorders in young people: Time trends and their causes.* (pp. 7–34). Chichester: John Wiley & Sons.

Rutter, M. (2001). Psychosocial adversity and child psychopathology. In J. Green & W. Yule (Eds.), *Research and innovation on the road to modern child psychiatry. Vol. 1. Festschrift for Professor Sir Michael Rutter* (pp. 129–152). Glasgow: Gaskell.

Rutter, M., Giller, H., & Hagell, A. (1998). *Antisocial behavior by young people.* Cambridge: Cambridge University Press.

Rutter, M., & Smith, D.J. (1995). *Psychosocial disorders in young people: Time trends and their causes.* Chichester: John Wiley & Sons.

Rutter, M., Tizard, J., & Whitmore, K. (1970). *Education, health and behaviour.* London: Longman.

Schafer, J.L. (1997). *Analysis of incomplete multivariate data.* London: Chapman & Hall.

Schoon, I., Bynner, J., Joshi, H., Parsons, S., Wiggins, R.D., & Sacker, A. (2002). The influence of context, timing, and duration of risk experiences for the passage from childhood to midadulthood. *Child Development, 73,* 1486–1504.

Scott, S., Knapp, M., Henderson, J., & Maughan, B. (2001). Financial cost of social exclusion: Follow up study of antisocial children into adulthood. *British Medical Journal, 323,* 191–194.

Shaffer, D. (1988). The epidemiology of teen suicide: An examination of risk factors. *Journal of Clinical Psychiatry, 49,* 36–41.

Smith, D.J., & Rutter, M. (1995). Time trends in psychosocial disorders of youth. In M. Rutter & D.J. Smith (Eds.), *Psychosocial disorders in young people: Time trends and their causes (pp. 763–781).* Chichester: John Wiley & Sons.

StataCorp. (2002). Stata Statistical Software: Release 7.0. College Station, Texas: Stata.

Verhulst, F.C., van der Ende, J., & Rietbergen, A. (1997). Ten-year time trends of psychopathology in Dutch children and adolescents: No evidence for strong trends. *Acta Psychiatrica Scandinavica, 96,* 7–13.

West, P., & Sweeting, H. (2003). Fifteen, female and stressed: Changing patterns of psychological distress over time. *Journal of Child Psychology and Psychiatry, 44,* 399–411.

Manuscript accepted 26 January 2004

Appendix Response biases in NCDS and BCS70 in relation to characteristics at birth. Efficacy of weights in correcting these biases

	NCDS			BCS70		
		Complete data at 16			Complete data at 16	
	Birth	Unweighted	Weighted	Birth	Unweighted	Weighted
N =	16,812	10,499	10,499	16,237	7293	7293
Male (%)	51.6	51.2	51.7	51.7	48.4	51.5
Birth weight (kg, mean)	3.27	3.30	3.27	3.27	3.32	3.28
Maternal age (years, mean)	27.45	27.42	27.44	25.90	25.93	25.89
Mother smoked in pregnancy (%)	33.6	33.0	33.5	41.4	38.6	41.7
Parents unmarried (%)	4.0	3.3	4.0	7.4	4.8	7.2
Mother did not stay at school (%)	74.9	74.9	74.9	65.4	62.1	65.6
Father's social class (%)						
I, II	16.8	16.7	16.9	15.9	17.9	16.0
IIINM	9.3	9.6	9.3	11.2	13.5	11.3
IIIM	49.0	49.1	49.0	44.3	44.0	44.4
IV, V	21.1	21.5	22.0	20.8	18.9	20.6
Other	.3	.3	.3	3.0	2.7	3.0
No father figure	3.4	2.7	3.4	4.8	3.0	4.6
Region						
London & SE (cohort 1) (%)	19.8	17.6	19.8			
London (cohort 2) (%)				12.7	8.5	12.6

[24]

Twenty-year trends in emotional and behavioral problems in Dutch children in a changing society

Tick NT, van der Ende J, Verhulst FC. Twenty-year trends in emotional and behavioral problems in Dutch children in a changing society.

Objective: Research into changes in the prevalence of children's psychiatric diagnoses has indicated an increase in recent decades. However, methodological problems may have influenced results. This study compared children's emotional and behavioral problem levels across three population samples from different time points across 20 years, assessed with identical methodologies.
Method: We compared Child Behavior Checklists and Teacher's Report Forms across three population samples of 6- to 16-year olds, assessed in 1983, 1993, and 2003.
Results: We found evidence for small increases in the mean population levels of parent-reported problems, and in the percentages of children with serious problems. These changes concerned mostly internalizing problems. Teacher reports showed less changes. Decreases in scores were found on several areas of competence. Changes were the strongest between 1993 and 2003.
Conclusion: We found evidence for small increases in Dutch children's problems. Further developments must be monitored, as this trend may continue and have serious societal consequences.

N. T. Tick, J. van der Ende, F. C. Verhulst

Department of Child and Adolescent Psychiatry, Erasmus MC - Sophia Children's Hospital, Rotterdam, the Netherlands

Key words: child; adolescent; emotional disturbance; behavioral symptoms; trends

Jan van der Ende, Erasmus MC - Sophia Children's Hospital, Department of Child and Adolescent Psychiatry, PO Box 2060, 3000 CB, Rotterdam, the Netherlands.
E-mail: jan.vanderende@erasmusmc.nl

Accepted for publication June 21, 2007

Significant outcomes

- There have been small increases in the levels of Dutch children's parent-reported emotional and behavioral problems between 1983 and 2003, which concern mostly internalizing problems.
- Teacher reports showed only a very small secular increase with regard to children's attention problems.
- The proportion of children who experience serious emotional and behavioral problems and may be in need of help has increased between 1983 and 2003.

Limitations

- The three samples had different response rates (85.1% in 1983, 81.9% in 1993, and 74.8% in 2003).
- As only Dutch-speaking parents participated in this study, the generalizability of the results is limited to the Dutch-speaking population.
- The classification system to determine the socioeconomic status for the 2003 sample was different from the other two samples.

Introduction

In recent years, western societies have experienced several societal changes that may have had their impact on children's wellbeing. For example, divorce rates have risen, and an increasing proportion of children are living in single-parent families (1). Information about secular trends in children's emotional and behavioral problems can tell us if there are empirical grounds for concern about children's wellbeing. Such information is also of importance for forecasting service needs in the population and, subsequently, in developing an effective health service policy.

Time trend research has shown that children's mental health problems have increased over recent decades (2–4). Treatment data and patient records have suggested increases in the number of children diagnosed with Attention-Deficit/Hyperactivity Disorder (5–7). Also, epidemiological studies have suggested an increase in the prevalence of autism (8–11), and studies on depression have found higher lifetime prevalences in younger birth cohorts, suggesting an earlier age of onset and a secular increase in the prevalence of this disorder (12, 13). Furthermore, increasingly more children were admitted to outpatient clinics or were hospitalized for a mental illness, and there is also increasing use of psychotropic medication among children (14–17). Concurrently, crime rates have risen over the last half of the 20th century (18), and suicide rates have increased over recent decades (19).

Many of these findings, however, are hampered by methodological problems. Results of studies on psychiatric diagnoses are often influenced by changes in diagnostic criteria over time or by a better recognition of diagnoses by clinicians, resulting from an increased knowledge of the relevant symptoms (4, 9, 12). In addition, determining the lifetime prevalence of a psychiatric diagnosis can be influenced by recall problems (20). Furthermore, trends in medication use or hospitalization and treatment data do not necessarily reflect secular changes in psychiatric problems, as these trends are influenced by the availability of medication, prescription practices, availability of hospital beds and societal attitudes toward treatment. Moreover, crime and suicide statistics are influenced by registration practices that can be subject to change over time. For instance, behavior not leading to a criminal conviction is not registered, which leaves many cases unnoticed.

A more direct way to investigate secular changes in children's emotional and behavioral problems is to compare general population samples from different time periods that are assessed with identical measures, generating comparable data that have not been influenced by variations in method (4). Only few such studies have been conducted so far, with varying results. No clear changes were seen among Dutch children's emotional and behavioral problems between 1983 and 1993 (21). British adolescents' emotional and behavioral problems were found to have increased during 1974–1999 (22). A Finnish study found

evidence that boys' problems decreased during 1989–1999, whereas girls' problems increased (23). American children's emotional and behavioral problems were shown to have increased during 1976–1989, but they decreased during 1989–1999 (24). Most of these studies had some limitations, however, as they investigated only a 10-year period (21, 23), had only data on two time points available (21, 23), focused on a limited age range (22, 23), or obtained data from only one informant (22).

Aims of the study

Given the sparse number of studies that compared identical assessments from population samples from different time periods, and given the limitations of most of the studies that have been conducted, we investigated the 20-year secular changes during 1983–2003 in Dutch children's emotional and behavioral problems and competences in the general population. We compared parent reports and teacher reports on Dutch children's emotional and behavioral problems and competences that were obtained in 1983, 1993 and 2003. We also investigated whether possible time trends differed for boys and girls or for different age groups.

Material and methods

Participants

For this study, we used three population samples one assessed in 1983, one assessed in 1993 and one assessed in 2003. Written informed consent was obtained from the parents of the subjects after explaining the study to them. Moreover, a Medical Ethics Committee approved all studies. The age range differed for the three samples. To enable comparison between these samples, we used only parent reports for 6- to 16-year olds and teacher reports for 6- to 12-year olds.

1983 Sample

For the 1983 sample, 2600 children were randomly selected from municipal registers in the province of Zuid-Holland. Two municipalities declined to participate and five parents did not consent to provide demographic information on their child, leaving 2517 parents to be contacted. Of the 2447 four- to sixteen-year-old children whose parents were reached, 14 children were excluded from participation; parents of eight children did not speak Dutch, and for six children no eligible parent was available because these children were institutionalized or were living in a foster home. Data collection took place between February 1983 and May 1983. Of the eligible parents, 2076 (85.1%) completed the Child Behavior Checklist (CBCL). Teacher's Report Forms (TRFs) were obtained for 1067 (83.8%) of the 1273 four to twelve-year olds whose parents gave their written permission [for a detailed description of the sample and procedure, see Verhulst et al. (25)]. The present study included 1735 six- to sixteen-year olds with valid CBCLs and 902 six- to twelve-year olds with valid TRFs. In line with Achenbach and Rescorla (26), a questionnaire was considered valid when no more than eight items were left unanswered.

1993 Sample

The 1993 sample originally consisted of 2917 randomly selected 4- to 18-year olds living in the Netherlands. Data collection took place between April 1993 and June 1993. Forty-eight children were excluded from the sample—34 children because their parents did not speak Dutch and 14 children because of physical or intellectual disability. Of the 2719 parents who could be reached, 2227 parents completed the CBCL (81.9%). TRFs were obtained for 1720 (82.8%) of the 2078 four- to eighteen-year olds whose parents gave their written permission (95%) [for a detailed description of the sample and procedure, see Verhulst et al. (27)].

Whereas both the 1983 and 2003 samples were drawn from the province of Zuid-Holland, the 1993 sample was a national sample. We therefore performed ANCOVA, with age, gender, socioeconomic status (SES) and ethnicity as covariates, to examine if there were significant differences in mean scale scores on the CBCL and TRF scales between children from the 1993 sample living in Zuid-Holland and children from the 1993 sample living elsewhere in the Netherlands. No significant differences were found ($P < 0.05$, two-tailed). We therefore decided to use the entire 1993 sample. We included 1715 six- to sixteen-year olds with valid CBCLs and 897 six- to twelve-year olds with valid TRFs.

2003 Sample

For the 2003 sample, 2567 six- to eighteen-year olds were randomly selected from municipal registers of 35 municipalities in the Dutch province of Zuid-Holland. Parents were sent letters, explaining the survey. Within a couple of weeks, parents were contacted by telephone or at home, and were asked

to participate in the study. Data collection took place between December 2003 and April 2005. Of the 2567 children, we were able to contact the parents of 2536 children. We excluded 250 children from the sample; 191 whose parents did not speak the Dutch language, 31 who had physical or mental disability, 22 who departed from the study area and six for whom no person could complete the questionnaire, because of their living conditions. Of the remaining 2286 eligible respondents, 1710 (74.8%) parents participated. Children of the responding vs. the non-responding parents did not differ with regard to sex ($\chi^2 = 1.6$, df $= 1$, $P > 0.05$). Subsequently, 786 (87.2%) parents of the 901 six- to twelve-year-old children attending school gave written consent to send the TRF to the child's teacher. Completed TRFs were obtained for 719 (91.5%) children. The present study included 1417 six- to sixteen-year olds with valid CBCLs, and 719 six- to twelve-year olds with valid TRFs.

As Table 1 indicates, the 2003 sample consisted of fewer children with low SES than the 1983 and the 1993 sample. When comparing the SES distribution of the 2003 sample with the general SES distribution in the province of Zuid-Holland in 2003 (28), the low SES group appears to be somewhat underrepresented, probably as a result of exclusion and attrition. In 2003, significantly more people with non-Dutch ethnicity participated

Table 1. Demographics

Sample	1983 ($n = 1735$)	1993 ($n = 1715$)	2003 ($n = 1417$)
Gender			
Male	49.0	50.6	49.8
Female	51.0	49.4	50.2
Age (years)			
6–11	55.8	56.1	53.9
12–16	44.2	43.9	46.1
SES*			
Low	33.8	27.4	23.7
Middle	32.3	38.9	40.6
High	33.9	33.8	35.7
Ethnicity†			
Dutch	96.9	91.2	78.3
Non-Dutch	3.1	8.8	21.7
Informant‡			
Mother	88.3	95.5	94.9
Other	11.7	4.5	5.1

Values are expressed in percentage. SES, socioeconomic status.
*Significantly different SES distribution (more low SES participants) in 1983 than in 1993 ($\chi^2 = 22.0$, df $= 2$, $P < 0.001$) or in 2003 ($\chi^2 = 42.7$, df $= 2$, $P < 0.001$).
†Significantly more non-Dutch participants in 1993 than in 1983 ($\chi^2 = 50.0$, df $= 1$, $P < 0.001$), and significantly more non-Dutch participants in 2003 than in 1983 ($\chi^2 = 265.9$, df $= 1$, $P < 0.001$) or in 1993 ($\chi^2 = 102.4$, df $= 1$, $P < 0.001$).
‡Significantly more mothers completed the Child Behavior Checklist in 1993 ($\chi^2 = 60.1$, df $= 1$, $P < 0.001$) and in 2003 ($\chi^2 = 42.9$, df $= 1$, $P < 0.001$) than in 1983.

than in 1983 or in 1993, which represents a societal development that has taken place over recent decades (28). In 1983, the CBCL was completed by a significantly smaller proportion of mothers than in 1993 or in 2003.

Measures

Emotional and behavioral problems

The CBCL and TRF are instruments of the Achenbach System of Empirically Based Assessment (ASEBA). These interrelated questionnaires have good validity and reliability (26). The CBCL and TRF contain both problem items and competence items. The problem items are scored on a 3-point scale, with responses: 0 = not true, 1 = somewhat or sometimes true, 2 = very true or often true. On the CBCL, parents were asked to rate the child's problems over the preceding 6 months. On the TRF, teachers were asked to rate the child's problems over the preceding 2 months. The problem items on these questionnaires are scored on eight empirically based syndromes that were derived by factor analyses and are similar across the CBCL and TRF: Anxious/Depressed, Withdrawn/Depressed, Somatic Complaints, Social Problems, Thought Problems, Attention Problems, Rule-Breaking Behavior and Aggressive Behavior (26). The first three syndromes are also scored on a broadband scale designated as Internalizing, while the last two syndromes are scored on a broadband scale designated as Externalizing. All items can be summed to compute a Total Problems score. The CBCL competence items can be clustered in the following subscales: Activity, Social, School competence, and Total Competence. The TRF competence items can be clustered in an Academic Performance and an Adaptive Functioning scale. Because the ASEBA questionnaires were revised in 2001, we used only the items that were on both pre-2001 and 2001 editions. We therefore excluded six CBCL and three TRF problem items.

Demographic variables

The total sample was divided into four age groups: i) 6–8 years, ii) 9–11 years (9–12 years for the TRF), iii) 12–14 years, iv) 15–18 years. For the 1983 sample and the 1993 sample, SES was scored according to a six-step scale of parental occupation (29) and subsequently divided into three SES levels (1 and 2 = low SES, 3 and 4 = middle SES, 5 and 6 = high SES). For the 2003 sample, we used a five-step Standard Classification of Occupations (30).

We made a classification that was comparable to the 1983 and 1993 classification: low SES (unemployed, elementary and lower occupations), middle SES (secondary occupations), and high SES (higher and scientific occupations). Ethnicity was classified as Dutch or non-Dutch. Children with at least one parent born outside of the Netherlands were classified as non-Dutch. For our CBCL analyses, the variable informant was classified as mother or other, including fathers and other informants.

Statistical analyses

For the CBCL, we performed 3 (year) $\times$ 2 (gender) $\times$ 4 (age group) ANCOVA on the syndrome scales, the broadband scales, the Total Problems scale, and the competence scales in order to test for differences in the mean scale scores ($P < 0.05$, two-tailed). To investigate how the population means have changed, regardless of the changes in societal distribution, we used SES, ethnicity and informant as covariates. For the TRF we performed 3 $\times$ 2$\times$2 ANCOVA on the same scales, with SES and ethnicity as covariates. We report estimated scale means for the three assessment years, which are predicted means that account for differences among the other variables in the specified model. We also report percentages of explained variance that indicate effect sizes for the significant effects of year and interactions of year by age or year by gender. An effect size of 1–5.9% is small, an effect size of 6–13.8% is medium and an effect size exceeding 13.8% is large (31). To investigate whether the percentage of children scoring in the deviant range of the scales differed between 1983, 1993 and 2003, we first calculated cut-off scores on the CBCL and TRF problem scales for gender and age (6–11 and 12–18 for the CBCL; 6–12 for the TRF) separately, thereby creating four different CBCL norm groups and two TRF norm groups. In line with Achenbach and Rescorla (26), children having a Total Problems, Internalizing or Externalizing score in the 84th percentile of the norm group or higher were classified as having deviant problems. With regard to the syndrome scales, children scoring in the 93rd percentile or higher were classified as having deviant problems. We performed logistic regressions to calculate percentages that were adjusted for the effects of SES and ethnicity. To judge the magnitude of the effects of the differences, we used the effect size h, as proposed by Cohen (31) to judge differences between proportions.

To investigate whether the comorbidity distribution differed for the three samples, and to combine data from the two informants, we computed a variable that indicated whether the child scored deviant on either the internalizing scale, the externalizing scale or on both. Children were classified as scoring deviant when at least one of the two informants scored him or her as deviant. We performed χ^2d analyses to examine whether this distribution differed for the three samples. As we used both teacher reports and parent reports, this analysis could only be performed on the 6- to 12-year olds.

Results

Time trends in parent reports

Scores on 10 out of 11 scales showed significant effects of year, indicating that there were significant differences between means in 1983, 1993, and 2003 (Table 2). Five scales showed a consistent increase between 1983 and 2003. Three scales increased only significantly between 1993 and 2003, whereas one scale, Withdrawn/Depressed, decreased between 1983 and 1993, and increased between 1993 and 2003. However, changes on only three of the scales had at least a small effect size (31). These were: Anxious/Depressed, Somatic Problems, and Internalizing.

Significant interaction effects of year by age group were found for five scales (data not shown): Withdrawn/Depressed, Rule Breaking Behavior, Aggressive Behavior, Externalizing, and Total Problems. These interactions indicated that between 1983 and 1993, scores increased for the 12- to 16-year olds, whereas scores decreased for

the 6- to 11-year olds. Between 1993 and 2003, scores increased for all age groups. However, none of these interaction effects reached the size of a small effect (31). There were no significant interaction effects of year by gender.

Significant effects of SES for all scales indicated higher problem scores in low SES children. However, on only three scales these effects reached the size of a small effect: Rule-Breaking Behavior, Externalizing, and Total Problems. Five scales showed significant effects of ethnicity, indicating higher problem scores for non-Dutch children. However, none of these reached the size of a small effect.

Time trends in teacher reports

A significant effect of year was found for only one TRF scale, indicating that Attention Problems scores were significantly higher in 2003 than in 1983 and 1993 (Table 2). However, this change did not reach the size of a small effect according to Cohen (31). Results showed no significant interaction effects of year by age group or year by gender in the TRF reports (data not shown).

Significant effects of SES for 10 of the 11 scales indicated higher problem scores in low SES children. For only three scales (Total Problems, Social Problems, and Attention Problems) these effects reached the size of a small effect. Effects of ethnicity were significant for eight scales and indicated higher problem scores for non-Dutch children. However, only the effect of ethnicity on the Rule-Breaking Behavior scale reached the size of a small effect.

Table 2. CBCL (Child Behavior Checklist)- and Teacher's Report Form (TRF)-estimated means and percentages of explained variance for significant effects of year resulting from ANCOVA ($P < 0.05$, two-tailed)

	CBCL				TRF			
	1983	1993	2003	%*	1983	1993	2003	%*
Syndrome scales								
Anxious/Depressed	2.3	2.6	3.2	1.3 $^{3>2>1}$	2.9	3.1	3.0	–
Withdrawn/Depressed	1.7	1.5	1.8	0.4 $^{3>2,3>1,1>2}$	1.8	1.7	1.6	–
Somatic Complaints	1.0	1.2	1.5	1.2 $^{3>2>1}$	0.4	0.4	0.5	–
Social Problems	2.1	2.0	2.3	0.2 $^{3>2,3>1}$	1.8	1.9	1.8	–
Thought Problems	1.5	1.8	2.0	0.9 $^{3>2>1}$	0.5	0.6	0.6	–
Attention Problems	2.6	2.5	2.8	0.2 $^{3>2>2}$	7.2	7.6	8.6	0.5 $^{3>1,3>2}$
Rule-Breaking Behavior	1.2	1.3	1.5	0.5 $^{3>2>1}$	0.8	0.8	0.9	–
Aggressive Behavior	4.7	4.4	4.7	–	3.2	2.9	3.3	–
Broadband scales								
Internalizing	5.0	5.4	6.5	1.3 $^{3>2>1}$	5.1	5.3	5.1	–
Externalizing	5.8	5.7	6.2	0.1 $^{3>2}$	3.9	3.7	4.1	–
Total Problems	19.9	20.2	23.5	0.9 $^{3>1,3>2}$	19.2	19.6	20.9	–

*3 > 1 indicates mean score in 2003 significantly higher than mean score in 1983; 3 > 2 indicates mean score in 2003 significantly higher than mean score in 1993; 2 > 1 indicates mean score in 1993 higher than mean score in 1983.

Table 3. Estimated percentages of children scoring in the deviant range of the CBCL (Child Behavior Checklist) and Teacher's Report Form (TRF) scales

	CBCL*			TRF*		
	1983	1993	2003	1983	1993	2003
Syndrome scales						
Anxious/Depressed	7.1 ab	9.3 bc	14.4 ac	8.0	8.5	8.3
Withdrawn/Depressed	11.1	10.9	12.8	12.3	12.0	10.8
Somatic Complaints	9.0 a	10.8 c	16.6 ac	9.8	11.0	12.4
Social Problems	9.8 a	9.5 c	12.3 ac	8.8	10.2	9.6
Thought Problems	8.0 ab	11.2 b	12.2 a	12.8	13.5	13.7
Attention Problems	10.9 b	8.8 b	10.9	6.9 a	6.5 c	10.1 ac
Rule-Breaking Behavior	10.9 a	9.8 c	14.1 ac	12.3 a	13.3	15.9 a
Aggressive Behavior	10.1 a	7.2 a	9.2	8.4	7.0	8.5
Broadband scales						
Externalizing	18.4	17.7 c	20.9 c	20.4	18.6 c	23.2 c
Internalizing	16.5 a	18.0 c	26.8 ac	16.3	18.1	17.6
Total Problems	16.3 a	14.3 c	22.0 ac	15.4	17.0	19.0

*Identical lower-case letters indicate that logistic regressions have shown significant differences between these percentages in different years (*P* < 0.05).

Children scoring in the deviant range

Logistic regressions that were used to calculate percentages of deviant scoring children showed a significant effect of year for 10 out of 11 CBCL scales, indicating that there were significant differences between the proportions of deviant-scoring children in 1983, 1993, and 2003 (Table 3). The percentage of deviant scorers increased continuously between 1983 and 2003 for the Anxious/Depressed scale. For most scales, logistic regression results indicated that the percentages increased significantly between 1993 and 2003, and not between 1983 and 1993. For the Thought Problems scale, however, the increase took place between 1983 and 1993. Decreases during 1983–1993 were seen for the Attention Problems scale and the Aggressive Behavior scale. However, only three of the changes reached the size of a small effect (31). These were the changes between 1983 and 2003 in the proportions of deviant-scoring children on the Anxious/Depressed, the Somatic Complaints and the Internalizing scale (data not shown).

For the TRF, significant increases between 1993 and 2003 were seen in proportions of deviant scorers on the Attention Problems scale and the Externalizing scale (Table 3). For the Rule-Breaking Behavior scale, percentages increased between 1983 and 2003. None of these changes reached the size of a small effect (31).

Competence scores

As Table 4 indicates, we found several significant changes for the competence scales. Scores on the CBCL Activity and Total Competence scale increased between 1983 and 2003, but decreased

Table 4. Estimated means and percentages of explained variance for effects on competence scales of the CBCL (Child Behavior Checklist) and Teacher's Report Forms (TRF), resulting from ANCOVA (*P* < 0.05, two-tailed)

	Means*			
	1983	1993	2003	Year
Competence scores: CBCL				
Activity	6.9 a	8.2 a	7.5 a	4.6
Social	7.7 a	7.8 b	8.3 ab	1.1
School Competence	4.9 a	4.9 b	4.6 ab	2.0
Total Competence	19.5 a	21.0 a	20.4 a	2.3
Competence scores: TRF				
Academic Performance	3.4 ab	3.7 b	3.6 a	3.2
Adaptive Functioning	17.6 a	18.6 ab	17.7 b	1.0

*Identical lower-case letters indicate significant differences between these means (*P* < 0.05).

again between 1993 and 2003, as did the TRF Adaptive Functioning scale score. The CBCL Social score increased between 1993 and 2003, whereas the CBCL School Competence score decreased between 1993 and 2003. The score on the TRF Academic Performance scale increased significantly between 1983 and 1993, but did not change between 1993 and 2003.

Comorbidity

Results indicated that when both teacher and parent reports were considered, there were changes in the distribution of the children who had either no deviant score, only a deviant internalizing score, only a deviant externalizing score or had both internalizing and externalizing deviant scores (Table 5). In 2003 there were more children with internalizing problems or with both internalizing and internalizing problems than in 1993 or 1983. When only the children with deviant scores were

479

Table 5. Percentages of children with deviant scores according to parents or teachers

	% of deviant-scoring children		
	1983*	1993†	2003*†
None	54.2	55.2	47.5
Deviant internalizing only	14.0	15.8	19.2
Deviant externalizing only	16.0	16.9	15.0
Deviant internalizing and externalizing	15.8	12.1	18.3

*The 1983 distribution differs significantly from the 2003 distribution (χ^2 = 11.8, df = 3, P < 0.01).

†The 1993 distribution differs significantly from the 2003 distribution (χ^2 = 18.6, df = 3, P < 0.001).

included in the analyses, the 2003 distribution differed significantly from the 1993 distribution (χ^2 = 9.2, df = 2, P = 0.01), with more children with internalizing problems or with a combination of problems.

Discussion

We investigated 20-year time trends in parent- and teacher-reported emotional and behavioral problems among Dutch children. We found several small increases between 1983 and 2003, mainly regarding parent-reported internalizing problem scores and in the proportion of children scoring in the deviant range of several problem scales. For several competencies, mean scale scores decreased, mostly between 1993 and 2003. We found no clear evidence for gender- or age-specific trends.

We found an increase in several parent-reported internalizing problems, mostly Anxious/Depressed and Somatic Problems, over the 20-year period of investigation. Scores significantly increased between 1993 and 2003. The percentages of deviant scoring children also increased significantly for these scales. No such developments were seen on the teacher reports.

These findings are partially in line with the findings of Collishaw et al. (22), who found that parent-reported emotional problems increased among British adolescents, and with the findings of Santalahti et al. (32), who found that parent-reported somatic problems increased among Finnish children. However, teacher- and parent-reported emotional problems of these Finnish children did not increase. Although Achenbach et al. (24) found an increase in parent-reported internalizing problems of American children between 1976 and 1989, this increase was followed by a decrease between 1989 and 1999, which contradicts our findings. In a recent meta-analysis, Costello et al. (33) found no evidence for an increase in child and adolescent

depression since the 1970s. Hence, findings from different population studies on secular increases in internalizing problems vary.

With regard to externalizing problems, no increases in the parent and teacher reports reached the size of a small effect. However, the percentages of children scoring deviant on the Rule-Breaking Behavior scale increased significantly for both parents and teachers. Teacher reports also showed an increase between 1983 and 2003 in the proportion of children with deviant externalizing scores. Our findings are less strong than the clear increase in parent-reported conduct problems in British 15- and 16-year olds' conduct problems between 1974 and 1999, which was found by Collishaw et al. (22). However, Sourander et al. (23) found no increases in such problems among Finnish children. Achenbach et al. (24, 32) found an increase in American children's externalizing problems between 1976 and 1989, but this was followed by a decrease between 1989 and 1999, which is not in line with our findings.

Teacher reports indicated a small increase in Attention Problems and an increase in deviant scoring children on this scale. No clear changes in hyperactive problems were found among British adolescents (22). Sourander et al. (23) found a small decrease in teacher-reported hyperactive problems of Finnish boys, while girls' problems increased. Achenbach found a decrease in attention problems during the 1990s among American children according to their parents and teachers. Our findings also indicate a small increase in parent-reported Thought Problems between 1983 and 1993. No such development was seen among American children (24, 34).

Children with both serious internalizing and externalizing problems, according to either parents or teachers, were more prevalent among the children with problems in 2003 than in 1993 or 1983. This indicates that not only has the number of children with serious internalizing problems increased, but also the number of children that are having serious problems on both the emotional and behavioral area, which is a worrisome development.

Most competencies increased between 1983 and 1993, but decreased again between 1993 and 2003. The increase in Dutch children's problems, which mostly took place between 1993 and 2003, seems to be accompanied by a decrease in several competencies. Achenbach et al. (24) also investigated secular changes in competencies, but their results indicated a decrease between 1976 and 1989, and an increase between 1989 and 1999 in American children's competencies.

The comparison with findings from population studies that were conducted in other countries highlight intercultural and inter-informant differences. A cross-cultural comparison reveals a complex picture. Although earlier studies have described increases in the prevalence and treatment of psychiatric diagnoses (5–13), the studies comparing population samples, using a more direct methodology, could not confirm such clear changes. Given the variety of results, one may wonder whether such secular changes can be compared cross-culturally. However, many developments that change the environment of children, and that therefore are thought to affect such secular changes, are taking place throughout the Western world (e.g. changing societal distribution, economic growth, changing family structures, increased employment of mothers, changing leisure activities). The fact that the different population studies cannot be compared exactly given the use of different instruments, different informants, different age ranges, and different time periods, may have affected the differences between the results to some extent.

Differences in results appear also between informants. Our results have shown the strongest changes in the parent reports and weaker changes in teacher reports. Differences between informants are seen in other time trend studies as well (23, 24, 34, 35). It is widely acknowledged that multiple informants are needed to obtain a comprehensive view on children's behavior (36), because discrepancies are often found among informants (37, 38). These discrepancies present challenges as to interpretation, considering that no informant qualifies as the 'gold standard.' Children's problems at school may show different trends than at home. Informants' frames of reference may change over time as well, which could contribute to differences in time trends across different informants. Given these complexities, it is important to look at the overall picture. Hence, although parent reports showed clearer changes than teacher reports, we found evidence that children's emotional and behavioral problems increased over the period 1983–2003.

Our study enabled us to investigate the presence of time trends, but it did not enable us to explain such secular changes. Explaining time trends is difficult, considering that as time passes, many developments take place on a more proximal and a more distal level. Moreover, as some societal developments are often thought to have a negative effect on children's wellbeing (rising divorce rates and changing family structures, changing leisure activities of families, political tension), other developments may have positive effects on children's wellbeing (economical growth has created opportunities for children; prevention and intervention projects focus at children with problems). A first step toward understanding the effects of such developments is to investigate the presence of secular changes, by conducting methodologically valid studies.

Although we have tried to determine the importance of the effects by commenting on the effect sizes, it can be argued that the change itself is more important than the effect size, considering its possible public health implications. On the one hand, all effects of the increases we found were very small, so it is difficult to consider our data firm evidence that children are doing worse. On the other hand, considering the subject under investigation, the small increases we found may have worrisome consequences. Small increases may lead to a marked increase in individuals with problem scores at the high end of the distribution and who may be in need of mental health care. We indeed found a small, but significant increase in the proportion of children scoring in the deviant range of the scales. As these children will marry and bear their own children, who are at higher risk for problems given their parental psychopathology, effects of small changes may compound to have serious consequences at a societal level. It is also important to bear in mind that our findings span a relatively brief time interval. Our study showed that over a 20-year period more changes could be identified than over a 10-year period. Further studies are needed to monitor further developments, cross-cultural differences and explanatory mechanisms. These studies need to focus on changes in service use as well. If data on secular changes in problems are combined with data on changes service use, this elucidates how the number of children that experience an unmet need develops over time, which is sufficient information for developing an effective health service policy.

This study has several limitations. The most important limitation was that the 2003 sample differed from the 1983 and the 1993 samples in several ways. First, the response rate of the 2003 sample was lower than that of the 1983 and 1993 sample, which could have affected the results. When comparing the 2003 low SES distribution to the general SES distribution in Zuid-Holland (28), the low SES group appears to be underrepresented. This probably has influenced the difference in SES distribution between the two samples, and contradicts the appeared effect that in 2003 there were less 'poor' children living in the province of Zuid-Holland. The fact that different classification systems were used to determine SES in the two samples may also have contributed to the differences in SES distribution. If there would have been less attrition and exclusion in the low SES group, we suspect that trends would have been somewhat stronger, as probably the low SES children with most problems did not participate.

Another limitation of our study was that 7.2% of the children selected for the 2003 sample were not assessed, because their parents could not speak Dutch. Most were low SES Turkish and Moroccan immigrants. A consequence of excluding a substantial proportion of children, because their parents did not speak Dutch is that our findings can only be generalized to the Dutch-speaking part of the population. As studies in the Netherlands have shown some evidence that these children have higher problems than Dutch children, although evidence is somewhat mixed (39–41), and as we have found some significant effects of ethnicity in this study, we might have excluded a specific, more problematic group. Including ethnicity as a covariate may not be sufficient to control for the effects of the increase in non-Dutch children. We therefore rerun our analyses on the Dutch children only. These analyses revealed similar results.

The development that society is becoming increasingly multicultural may have an effect on the mean population problem levels of children, especially as effects of ethnicity indicated non-Dutch children to have higher problem levels. It can be argued that we were not able to gain insight into such effects, as we controlled for ethnicity. We therefore repeated our analyses without including ethnicity as a covariate. However, these analyses revealed similar results.

Another limitation is that we have conducted tests for many outcomes, which increases the odds of finding significant results. To evaluate the importance of the significant effects, we have taken into account effect size as well. Also, we only used data on teachers and parents, and not self-reports, which may especially be important with regard to internalizing problems in adolescence.

In conclusion, although problem levels in society showed only small increases, we found evidence that the proportion of children with serious problems, especially internalizing problems, have increased between 1983 and 2003. Furthermore, according to teacher reports, attention problems among children are increasing, which may have consequences for children's scholar functioning. As the small effects we found may have larger societal consequences, mental health services, as well as the school system, should be prepared and equipped to deal with a possible rise in children and adolescents with problems, and there is a need for adequate programs on prevention and intervention.

Acknowledgements

This study was supported by grant SSWO 960 from the Sophia Foundation of Medical Research. We thank Thomas M. Achenbach for his valuable comments and suggestions.

References

1. HESS LE. Changing family patterns in Western Europe: opportunity and risk factors for adolescent development. In: RUTTER M, SMITH DJ, eds. Psychosocial disorders in young people, time trends and their causes. Chichester: Wiley, 1995:104–193.
2. RUTTER M, SMITH DJ. Psychosocial disorders in young people. Time trends and their causes. Chichester: Whiley, 1995.
3. FOMBONNE E. Increased rates of psychosocial disorders in youth. Eur Arch Psychiatry Clin Neurosci 1998;**248**:14–21.
4. MAUGHAN B, IERVOLINO AC, COLLISHAW S. Time trends in child and adolescent mental disorders. Curr Opin Psychiatry 2005;**18**:381–385.
5. TOH S. Datapoints: trends in ADHD and stimulant use among children, 1993–2003. Psychiatr Serv 2006;**57**:1091.
6. ROBISON LM, SKAER TL, SCLAR DA, GALIN RS. Is attention deficit hyperactivity disorder increasing among girls? CNS Drugs 2002;**16**:129–137.
7. OLFSON M, GAMEROFF MJ, MARCUS SC, JENSEN PS. National trends in the treatment of attention deficit hyperactivity disorder. Am J Psychiatry 2003;**160**:1071–1077.
8. GURNEY JG, FRITZ MS, NESS KK, SIEVERS P, NEWSCHAFFER CJ, SHAPIRO EG. Analysis of prevalence trends of autism spectrum disorder in Minnesota. Arch Pediatr Adolesc Med 2003;**157**:622–627.
9. FOMBONNE E. Is there an epidemic of autism? Pediatrics 2001;**107**:411–412.
10. CROEN LA, GRETHER JK, HOOGSTRATE J, SELVIN S. The changing prevalence of autism in California. J Autism Dev Disord 2002;**32**:207–215.
11. WEBB EV, LOBO S, HERVAS A, SCOURFIELD J, FRASER WI. The changing prevalence of autistic disorder in a Welsh health district. Dev Med Child Neurol 1997;**39**:150–152.
12. FOMBONNE E. Depressive disorders; time trends and possible explanatory mechanisms. In: RUTTER M, SMITH DJ, eds. Psychosocial disorders in young people, time trends and their causes. Wiley, 1995: 544–615.
13. FOMBONNE E. Increased rates of depression: update of epidemiological findings and analytical problems. Acta Psychiatr Scand 1994;**90**:145–156.
14. MA J, LEE KV, STAFFORD RS. Depression treatment during outpatient visits by U.S. children and adolescents. J Adolesc Health 2005;**37**:434–442.
15. KANTER RK, MORAN JR. Recent trends in pediatric hospitalization in New York state. J Pediatr 2006;**148**:637–641.
16. OLFSON M, BLANCO C, LIU L, MORENO C, LAJE G. National trends in the outpatient treatment of children and adolescents with antipsychotic drugs. Arch Gen Psychiatry 2006; **63**:679–685.
17. ZITO JM, SAFER DJ, DOSREIS S et al. Rising prevalence of antidepressants among US youths. Pediatrics 2002; **109**:721–727.

18. SMITH DJ. Youth crime and conduct disorders: trends, patterns and causal explanations. In: RUTTER M, SMITH DJ, eds. Psychosocial disorders in young people, time trends and their causes. Chichester: Wiley, 1995:389–489.

19. RUTZ EM, WASSERMAN D. Trends in adolescent suicide mortality in the WHO European Region. Eur Child Adolesc Psychiatry 2004;**13**:321–331.

20. GIUFFRA LA, RISCH N. Diminished recall and the cohort effect of major depression: a simulation study. Psychol Med 1994;**24**:375–383.

21. VERHULST FC, VAN DER ENDE J, RIETBERGEN A. Ten-year time trends of psychopathology in Dutch children and adolescents: no evidence for strong trends. Acta Psychiatr Scand 1997;**96**:7–13.

22. COLLISHAW S, MAUGHAN B, GOODMAN R, PICKLES A. Time trends in adolescent mental health. J Child Psychol Psychiatry 2004;**45**:1350–1362.

23. SOURANDER A, SANTALAHTI P, HAAVISTO A, PIHA J, IKAHEIMO K, HELENIUS H. Have there been changes in children's psychiatric symptoms and mental health service use? A 10-year comparison from Finland. J Am Acad Child Adolesc Psychiatry 2004;**43**:1134–1145.

24. ACHENBACH TM, DUMENCI L, RESCORLA LA. Are American children's problems still getting worse? A 23-year comparison. J Abnorm Child Psychol 2003;**31**:1–11.

25. VERHULST FC, AKKERHUIS GW, ALTHAUS M. Mental health in Dutch children: (I). A cross-cultural comparison. Acta Psychiatr Scand Suppl 1985;**323**:1–108.

26. ACHENBACH TM, RESCORLA LA. Manual for the ASEBA school-age forms and profiles. Burlington, VT: University of Vermont Research Center for Children, Youth & Families, 2001.

27. VERHULST FC, VAN DER ENDE J, FERDINAND RF, KASIUS MC. The prevalence of DSM-III-R diagnoses in a national sample of Dutch adolescents. Arch Gen Psychiatry 1997;**54**:329–336.

28. CBS. Statline Databank; Central Bureau of Statistics [WWW document]. http://www.cbs.nl/nl-NL/default.htm [accessed on 20 December 2006].

29. VAN WESTERLAAK JM, KROPMAN JA, COLLARIS JWM. Beroepenklapper (Index of occupations). Nijmegen, the Netherlands: Instituut voor toegepaste sociologie, 1975.

30. CBS. Standard classification of occupations. Heerlen/Voorburg: Central Bureau of Statistics, 2001.

31. COHEN J. Statistical power analysis for the behavioural sciences, 2nd edn. Hillsdale, New Jersey: Lawrence Erlbaum Associates, 1998.

32. SANTALAHTI P, AROMAA M, SOURANDER A, HELENIUS H, PIHA J. Have there been changes in children's psychosomatic symptoms? A 10-year comparison from Finland. Pediatrics 2005;**115**:e434–e442.

33. COSTELLO EJ, ERKANLI A, ANGOLD A. Is there an epidemic of child or adolescent depression? J Child Psychol Psychiatry 2006;**47**:1263–1271.

34. ACHENBACH TM, DUMENCI L, RESCORLA LA. Is American student behavior getting worse? Teacher ratings over an 18-year period. School Psych Rev 2002;**31**:428–442.

35. ACHENBACH TM, DUMENCI L, RESCORLA LA. Ten-year comparisons of problems and competencies for national samples of youth: self, parent and teacher reports. J Emotion Behav Disord 2002;**10**:194–203.

36. FERDINAND RF, VAN DER ENDE J, VERHULST FC. Parent-adolescent disagreement regarding psychopathology in adolescents from the general population as a risk factor for adverse outcome. J Abnorm Psychol 2004;**113**:198–206.

37. VAN DER ENDE J. Multiple informants: multiple views. In: KOOT HM, CRIJNEN AA, FERDINAND RF, eds. Child psychiatric epidemiology: accomplishments and future directions. Assen: Van Gorcum, 1999:39–52.

38. DE LOS REYES A, KAZDIN AE. Informant discrepancies in the assessment of childhood psychopathology: a critical review, theoretical framework, and recommendations for further study. Psychol Bull 2005;**131**:483–509.

39. BENGI ARSLAN L, VERHULST FC, EROL N. Understanding childhood (problem) behaviors from a cultural perspective: comparison of problem behaviors and competencies in Turkish immigrant, Turkish and Dutch children. Soc Psychiatry Psychiatr Epidemiol 1997;**32**:477–484.

40. JANSSEN MMM, VERHULST FC, BENGI ARSLAN L, EROL N, SALTER CJ, CRIJNEN AAM. Comparison of self-reported emotional and behavioral problems in Turkish immigrant, Dutch and Turkish adolescents. Soc Psychiatry Psychiatr Epidemiol 2004;**39**:133–140.

41. STEVENS GWJM, PELS T, BENGI ARSLAN L, VERHULST FC, VOLLEBERGH WAM, CRIJNEN AAM. Parent, teacher and self-reported problem behavior in the Netherlands: comparing Moroccan immigrant with Dutch and with Turkish immigrant children and adolescents. Soc Psychiatry Psychiatr Epidemiol 2003;**38**:576–585.

[25]

Are American Children's Problems Still Getting Worse?
A 23-Year Comparison

Thomas M. Achenbach,[1,3] Levent Dumenci,[1] and Leslie A. Rescorla[2]

Received July 19, 2002; revision received September 24, 2002; accepted September 24, 2002

Child Behavior Checklists were completed in home interviews by parents of 7–16-year-olds in 1976, 1989, and 1999. Competence scores decreased from 1976 to 1989, but increased in 1999. Problem scores increased from 1976 to 1989 and decreased in 1999 but remained higher than in 1976. Items, empirically based scales, and *DSM*-oriented scales showed similar patterns for demographically similar nonreferred samples assessed in 1976, 1989, and 1999 and for national samples that included referred children assessed in 1989 and 1999. For the 114 problem items that were common to the 1976, 1989, and 1999 assessments, the Q correlation was .98 between the mean scores on the 114 items in 1976 versus 1989 and was .94 between the mean scores on the 114 items in 1976 vs. 1999. This indicated very high stability in the rank ordering of item scores across intervals up to 23 years. For all children, the 1-year prevalence rate for mental health services use was 13.2% in 1989 versus 12.8% in 1999. For children with deviant Total Problems scores, the 1989 prevalence for service use was 30.5 versus 26.6% in 1999. Neither difference was statistically significant.

KEY WORDS: epidemiology; secular changes; Child Behavior Checklist; behavior problems; mental health services.

From the clinical perspective, children's behavioral and emotional problems are viewed at the level of individual characteristics of the children, their families, and their immediate environments. From the epidemiological perspective, by contrast, children's problems are viewed at the level of prevalence rates in populations. Data on prevalence rates provide an essential basis for estimating service needs. However, differences in prevalence rates are also valuable for the light they may shed on etiological and protective factors. Even though many individual factors determine which children manifest each problem, the overall prevalence of particular problems may vary between groups and between times within populations.

In reviewing 52 epidemiological studies of child and adolescent disorders, Roberts, Attkisson, and Rosenblatt (1998) found tremendous variation in prevalence rates, ranging from 1 to 50%. Because the studies used such different methods of case ascertainment and case definition, it was difficult to draw rigorous conclusions about changes in prevalence rates in particular populations. In fact, none of the studies applied the same methods to large samples from the same populations over substantial intervals.

To identify possible changes in prevalence rates in the absence of rigorous epidemiological comparisons, Rutter and Smith (1995) reviewed various kinds of findings related to deviant behavior occurring at different points in time. They concluded that adolescent conduct disorders, substance abuse, depression, and suicide had increased over the preceding 50 years in developed countries. In reviewing the Rutter and Smith book, Fergusson (1996) hypothesized that increasingly diverse childrearing conditions, values, stresses, and advantages might cause not only more disorders, but also more cases of especially good adjustment. Increases in reported disorders might thus incorrectly imply that all children's adjustment is worsening, whereas the proportion of well-adjusted children might increase as well. Apparent changes in rates of disorders might also reflect changes in diagnostic criteria, mental health services, and record keeping, such as

[1]Department of Psychiatry, University of Vermont, Burlington, Vermont.
[2]Department of Psychology, Bryn Mawr College, Bryn Mawr, Pennsylvania.
[3]Address all correspondence to Thomas M. Achenbach, Department of Psychiatry, University of Vermont, 1 South Prospect Street, Burlington, Vermont 05401-3456; e-mail: thomas.achenbach@uvm.edu.

whether youthful suicides are accurately reported on death certificates (Males, 1991).

To measure changes in problems, similar standardized procedures are needed to assess representative samples of populations at different points in time. As an example, the *Monitoring the Future* study has used anonymous questionnaires to assess drug use in national samples of American adolescents annually since 1975 (Johnston, O'Malley, & Bachman, 2001). The findings suggest that variations in drug use are specific to the introduction, reputation, and availability of particular drugs. The prevalence of drug use may thus not be an accurate indicator of other problems.

To track a broader spectrum of problems, plus adaptive behaviors, two studies have compared Child Behavior Checklist (CBCL) and Teacher's Report Form (TRF) scores for randomly selected children over substantial intervals. In one study, Achenbach and Howell (1993) found small but significant decreases in American children's competence scores (effect sizes [ES] 1 to 5%), plus increases in problem scores (ES 1 to 4%) from 1976 to 1989. TRF scores showed parallel changes from 1981 to 1989 (ES 1 to 2%). In the second study, Dutch children's CBCLs and TRFs showed no significant changes in Total Problems scores from 1983 to 1993, but did show significant, though small, decreases in competencies and increases in problems on some scales (ES 1%; Verhulst, van der Ende, & Rietbergen, 1997).

Both studies analyzed competence and problem scores in population samples, rather than diagnoses or official records, such as death certificates. The decreased competence and increased problem scores may argue against Fergusson's (1996) hypothesis that increases in disorders may mask increased variation, which also includes better adjustment for portions of the population. However, additional standardized assessments of population samples are needed to measure changes in children's functioning. Population samples are also needed to measure changes in the proportions of American children receiving mental health services, as the United States has no standardized national measures (Indicators of Children's Wellbeing, 2002).

To determine whether American children's functioning continued to worsen, the present study was designed to test changes in competencies and problems reported by parents of American children from 1976 to 1999. In particular, we tested whether significant trends toward declining competence scores and increasing problem scores found from 1976 to 1989 continued 10 years later and whether scores were significantly associated with age, gender, socioeconomic status (SES), and ethnicity. The study was also designed to test changes in the proportions of children obtaining deviant scores and in the proportions of children

receiving mental health services. In addition, because the Columbine High School shootings occurred during our 1999 survey, we tested effects of the resulting publicity on parent-reported competencies and problems.

METHOD

Data Collection

Home interview surveys in 1976, 1989, and 1999 obtained parents' responses to the CBCL, which has extensive reliability and validity data and has been used in thousands of studies from 50 countries (Bérubé & Achenbach, 2003). All 20 CBCL competence items had counterparts in 1976, 1989, and 1999 that remained in the same sequential order and were scored in the same way on *Activities*, *Social*, *School*, and *Total Competence* scales. Of the 120 CBCL problem items, we analyzed the 114 that were common to the 1976, 1989, and 1999 assessments. The 114 items that were used for all three assessments remained in the same sequential order. The six items that were added in 1999 were placed in the sequential locations previously occupied by the six items that were deleted.

We scored the 1976, 1989, and 1999 data on the following eight syndromes that were derived from new factor analyses of parent, teacher, and self-ratings: *Anxious/Depressed, Withdrawn/Depressed, Somatic Complaints, Social Problems, Thought Problems, Attention Problems, Rule-Breaking Behavior*, and *Aggressive Behavior*. (Achenbach and Rescorla, 2001, detail the syndromes and the six changed problem items that were omitted from the present study.) The 2001 syndromes correlate highly with previous versions (Achenbach, 1991), but "Withdrawn/Depressed" was previously called "Withdrawn," whereas "Rule-Breaking Behavior" was previously called "Delinquent Behavior." Anxious/Depressed, Withdrawn/Depressed, and Somatic Complaints comprise an *Internalizing* grouping, whereas Rule-Breaking Behavior and Aggressive Behavior comprise an *Externalizing* grouping. All 114 problem items common to the 1976, 1989, and 1999 assessments were summed to provide a *Total Problems* score.

The 1976, 1989, and 1999 problem items were also scored on new DSM-oriented scales, which were constructed by having child psychiatrists and psychologists from 16 cultures identify CBCL items that are very consistent with diagnostic categories of the *DSM-IV* (American Psychiatric Association [APA], 1994). The scales are designated as *Affective Problems, Anxiety Problems, Somatic Problems, Attention Deficit/Hyperactivity Problems, Oppositional Defiant Problems*, and *Conduct Problems*. Both the *DSM*-oriented and the empirically based scales were normed on nonreferred children drawn from the 1999 national sample described in this paper (Achenbach and Rescorla, 2001, provide details of the nonreferred normative samples).

In 1976, 1989, and 1999, we used the following procedure to maximize response rates, standardization, and accuracy: After a parent or surrogate agreed to be interviewed, the home interviewer handed the respondent the CBCL. Reading aloud from a second CBCL, the interviewer entered the respondent's answers. This procedure approximated self-administration conditions by enabling respondents to see all items, while preventing embarrassment and errors among respondents who could not complete forms independently.

Samples

In all samples, one child per household was randomly selected, excluding children with mental retardation or major physical disabilities and those with no English-speaking parent figure.

1976 Sample

The initial 1976 sample included ages 4 through 16. In the District of Columbia, Maryland, and Virginia, blocks were randomly selected within census tracts stratified to approximate a normal distribution of SES and the 80% White/20% African American distribution characterizing the clinical sample with which comparisons were made (Achenbach & Edelbrock, 1981). Children were omitted if their parents responded affirmatively to questions about whether the children had been evaluated or treated during the previous year by a guidance clinic, other mental health agency, psychiatrist, or psychologist. Of the 1,752 eligible children identified in the survey, CBCLs were completed for 1,442 (82.3%). From these, 50 nonreferred children of each gender at each age from 4 to 16 were selected to form a normative sample. However, as explained later, the present analyses used 1976 data only for ages 7–16 to correspond to the 1989 and 1999 samples.

1989 Sample

In 1986, a home interview survey was conducted by Temple University's Institute for Survey Research (ISR). ISR used its 100-site sampling frame of the 48 contiguous states to select a sample that was representative of American 4–16-year-olds with respect to SES, ethnicity,

region, and urbanization (Achenbach, Howell, Quay, and Conners, 1991, provide details). In 1989, home interviewers again visited the parents who had participated in the 1986 survey. Parents received $15 for completing the CBCL and a half-hour interview. In 1989, CBCLs were completed for 2,466 (90.2%) of the 2,734 children who had been assessed in 1986. As explained later, the present analyses used data for the children who were 7–16 years old in 1989.

1999 Sample

In 1999, ISR assessed a new national probability sample using the same sampling frame and interview procedures as in 1989, except that the 1999 sample spanned ages 1½–90 years. Developmentally appropriate procedures, instruments, and informants were used for each age group of child and adult participants. Parents of the children received $10 for completing the CBCL and a brief interview. CBCL forms were completed for 1,641 (93.0%) of the 1,765 identified eligible 7–16-year-olds.

After completing the CBCL, 1989 and 1999 parents were asked: "In the past 12 months, has (child) received any mental health services from a mental health professional, such as a psychiatrist, psychologist, social worker, therapist, counselor, or any other mental health professional?" Based on follow-up questions, answers were coded positive only if they referred to nonprimary care specialists, which included school psychologists if they provided service for mental health problems.

Demographically Similar Nonreferred Samples

To maximize comparability across the 23 years from 1976 to 1999, we used the 1976 and 1989 samples ($N = $ 670 each) of White and African American nonreferred 7–16-year-olds previously described by Achenbach and Howell (1993). We then selected 670 nonreferred White and African American 7–16-year-olds from the 1999 national survey who could be matched as closely as possible to the 1976 and 1989 children for gender, age, ethnicity, and SES. The restriction to White and African American ethnicity was necessary because the 1976 sample included too few children of other ethnic groups for analysis. The age restriction was necessary because the 1976 sample spanned ages 4–16, whereas the 1989 sample spanned ages 7–18. Ages 7–16 were thus common to both samples. As summarized in Table I, children from all three samples were matched precisely for gender, and as closely as possible for age, for ethnicity, and for SES. SES was scored for parents' occupations according to Hollingshead's (1957, 1975) scales. If remunerative occupations were reported

Table I. Description of Samples

	Nonreferred samples			Complete samples	
Variable	1976 ($N = 670$)	1989 ($N = 670$)	1999 ($N = 670$)	1989 ($N = 1,885$)	1999 ($N = 1,641$)
Gender					
Female	52	52	52	50	47
Male	48	48	48	50	53
Age (years)					
7–8	22	22	20	20	17
9–10	20	20	20	20	17
11–12	20	20	22	20	24
13–14	20	20	20	21	21
15–16	18	18	18	19	20
Socioeconomic status (SES)[a]					
Lower	34	38	37	20	16
Middle	29	27	29	45	52
Upper	37	35	35	35	33
Ethnicity[b]					
African American	18	22	24	16	19
White	82	78	76	73	61
Other	—	—	—	11	20
Informants[c]					
Mother	82	83	76	82	72
Father	14	13	22	15	22
Other	4	4	2	3	6

Note. Values are percentages.

[a]Based on Hollingshead (1957, 1975) occupational scores; 1999 complete sample had a significantly larger proportion of middle SES than 1989, $\chi_2^2 = 15.9$, $p < .001$.

[b]1999 complete sample had a significantly smaller proportion of Whites than 1989, $\chi_2^2 = 65.8$, $p < .001$.

[c]1999 samples had significantly ($p < .001$) smaller proportions of mothers than earlier samples: $\chi_4^2 = 28.4$ for demographically similar samples; and $\chi_2^2 = 51.5$ for complete samples.

for both parents, the higher status occupation was used to score SES. (Achenbach and Howell, 1993, provide details of calibration between the 1957 and 1975 Hollingshead occupational scores and the groupings of occupational scores into lower, middle, and upper SES levels.) Because age, ethnic, and SES differences in the samples from 1976 to 1999 precluded exact matching, we controlled the small differences on these variables by blocking age in 2-year intervals and by covarying ethnicity and SES. Although imperfect, matching was desirable to provide continuity with data back to 1976 and with the previous 1976 versus 1989 comparisons (Achenbach & Howell, 1993).

1989 and 1999 National Samples Including Referred Children

We also compared the complete 1989 versus 1999 national samples ($N = 1,885$ and $1,641$, respectively, for ages 7–16). For the 10 years from 1989 to 1999, these comparisons tested whether competence and problem scores changed in representative samples that included referred children and ethnicities in addition to white and

African American. The 1976 sample was not included in these comparisons because it was a regional sample that excluded referred children and was ethnically less diverse.

Statistics

We used MANCOVAs and ANCOVAs to test differences between 1976, 1989, and 1999 scores, with gender and age as additional main effects. To control for and measure effects of SES, ethnicity, and respondent (mother vs. other), we included these as covariates. Similar analyses were used to compare scores before versus after the Columbine shootings. We used chi square tests to test differences in the proportion of children categorized as scoring in the normal versus combined borderline and clinical ranges and in the proportion receiving mental health services. Pearson correlations were used to test the stability of item rankings from one year to another.

Because the large samples afforded high statistical power to detect small ES (percentage of variance accounted for; Cohen, 1988), we report only effects significant at

$p \leq .01$ by two-tailed tests, unless otherwise noted. To indicate possible chance effects, we superscript the n smallest significant effects, where n is the number expected by chance in each set of N analyses, using $p < .01$ protection levels (Sakoda, Cohen, & Beall, 1954).

RESULTS

1976 vs. 1989 vs. 1999 Demographically Similar Nonreferred Samples

Separate 3 (1976 vs. 1989 vs. 1999) $\times$ 2 (gender) $\times$ 5 (ages 7–8, 9–10, 11–12, 13–14, 15–16) MANCOVAs were performed on each of the following: 114 problem items that were common to the three assessments; 20 compe-

tence items; 3 competence scales; 8 syndromes; 6 DSM-oriented scales; and the Internalizing and Externalizing groupings. Separate ANCOVAs were performed on Total Competence and Total Problems scores. Covariates were SES, White versus African American ethnicity, and respondent (mother vs. other).

Table II shows significant effects of year for all 21 scales, with the largest being 3% ES on Activities and Total Problems. Although the effects were small by Cohen's (1988) criteria, the patterns were quite consistent, with scores being least favorable on 19 (90%) out of 21 scales in 1989 (binomial $p < .01$). As Fig. 1 shows, mean Total Competence scores were higher in 1976 and 1999 than in 1989 (25.1 and 25.3 vs. 24.2, $p < .01$). Total Problems scores were lowest in 1976 (mean = 18.0), intermediate in 1999 (mean = 21.4), and highest in 1989

Table II. Percentage of Variance Accounted for by Significant ($p \leq 0.01$) Effects of Year (1976 vs. 1989 vs. 1999) and Demographics on Child Behavior Checklist Scales

Scale	Year[a]	Gender[b]	Age[c]	SES[d]	Ethnicity[e]
Competence scales					
Activities	3	—	—	3	2
Social	1[f]	—	2[O]	4	2
School	1[f]	3[F]	1[Y]	4	1
Total Competence	2	—	—	6	3
Syndrome scales					
Anxious/Depressed	2	—	1[Y,f]	—	<1[f]
Withdrawn/Depressed	2	—	2[O]	—	—
Somatic Complaints	1	—	—	1[f]	—
Social Problems	1	—	2[Y]	1	—
Thought Problems	2	<1[M,f]	2[Y]	1[f]	—
Attention Problems	2	2[M]	—	1	—
Rule-Breaking Behavior	1	2[M]	—	1	—
Aggressive Behavior	2	1[M]	1[Y]	1	—
DSM-oriented scales					
Affective Problems	1	—	—	—	—
Anxiety Problems	2	—	1[Y,f]	—	—
Somatic Problems	1	—	—	1[f]	—
Attention Deficit/Hyperactivity	1	1[M]	2[Y]	1	—
Oppositional Defiant Problems	2	1[M]	1[Y]	—	—
Conduct Problems	1	2[M]	—	1	<1[f]
Broad problem scales					
Internalizing	2	—	—	—	—
Externalizing	2	1[M]	—	1	—
Total Problems	3	<1[M,f]	1[Y,f]	1	—

Note. Numbers in the table indicate the percentage of variance accounted for by each independent variable and covariate, where the effect was significant at $p \leq .01$. Significant effects of interactions and informant (mother vs. other) were fewer than expected by chance.

[a] On competence scales, 1989 was lowest, except on School, where 1989 and 1999 were equal. On problem scales, 1989 was highest, except on Thought Problems, where 1989 = 1.6 vs. 1.7 for 1999 (*ns*).

[b] F = females higher; M = males higher.

[c] O = older higher; Y = younger higher.

[d] Significant SES effects indicated higher competence and lower problem scores for upper SES.

[e] Significant ethnicity effects indicated higher competence and lower problem scores for Whites.

[f] *ns* when corrected for number of analyses.

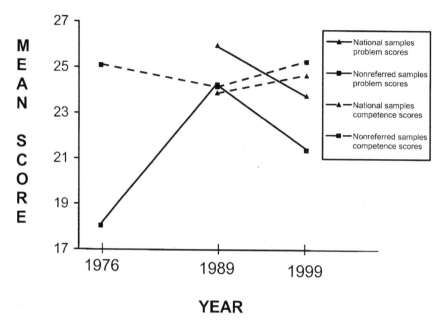

Fig. 1. Mean total competence and problem scores by year. Competence scores are represented by broken lines; problem scores are represented by solid lines. Demographically similar nonreferred samples are represented by squares; complete national samples are represented by triangles.

(mean = 24.3; all differences $p < .01$). In terms of standard deviation units, the difference between 1976 versus 1989 = .39 SD; 1976 versus 1999 = .22 SD; and 1989 versus 1999 = .18 SD.

Nine (45%) of the 20 competence items showed significant effects of year, with 1989 being lowest on 4 and tied with 1999 for lowest on 2. Forty-eight (42%) of the 114 problem items showed significant effects of year, with 1989 being highest on 32 (67%) of the 48 (binomial $p < .05$) and tied with 1999 for highest on 2.

1989 vs. 1999 National Samples

The 1976–1989–1999 comparisons reported above involved demographically similar samples of nonreferred children because (a) the 1976 sample excluded referred children; (b) we wished to control for demographic changes in the population; and (c) we wished to extend the previous comparisons of the 1976 versus 1989 samples to a demographically similar 1999 sample. But would similar conclusions be supported by nationally representative samples that included referred children? To find out, we

compared our entire 1989 versus 1999 national samples that included referred children and reflected demographic changes. As Table 1 shows, the inclusion of all 7–16-year-olds from the national samples resulted in significantly larger proportions of nonwhite and middle SES participants ($p < .001$ by chi squares) in 1999 than 1989. The proportion of informants who were mothers was also lowest in 1999 ($p < .001$ by chi squares for demographically similar and complete samples).

To compare the 1989 versus 1999 national samples, we performed 2 (1989 vs. 1999) × 2 (gender) × 5 (ages 7–8, 9–10, 11–12, 13–14, 15–16) MANCOVAs and ANCOVAs, with the same demographic covariates as in the 1976–1989–1999 comparisons. However, by including additional ethnicities, we were able to add a covariate for children who were neither White nor African American. To determine whether the covariates affected the results, we performed similar analyses without covariates. Because the significant effects on all scale scores and most item scores were the same, we report results with covariates, which more closely paralleled our comparisons of the 1976, 1989, and 1999 samples.

All significant changes in scale scores reflected higher competence (ES 1–3%) and lower problem scores (ES < 1 to 1%) in 1999 than 1989, with one exception: DSM-oriented Oppositional Defiant Problems scores increased from 1989 to 1999 (ES 1%). The 8 (38%) out of 21 scales having significantly more favorable scores in 1999 were Activities, Total Competence, Withdrawn/Depressed, Social Problems, Aggressive Behavior, Internalizing, Externalizing, and Total Problems. As Fig. 1 shows, the differences between the 1989 and 1999 national samples (represented by triangles) paralleled the differences between the 1989 and 1999 demographically similar nonreferred samples (represented by squares). However, as would be expected from inclusion of referred children, the mean problem scores were somewhat higher (1989 = 26.0, 1999 = 23.9) and the competence scores were lower (1989 = 23.9, 1999 = 24.7) in the national samples than in the nonreferred samples.

Among the items that showed significant changes from 1989 to 1999, 8 (40%) of the 20 competence items were significantly lower in 1989, whereas 4 (20%) were significantly lower in 1999; 21 (18%) of the 114 problem items were significantly higher in 1989, whereas only 5 (4%) were significantly higher in 1999 (binomial $p < .01$).

Categorical Analyses

To test changes in the prevalence of deviant scores, we used 2×2 chi square tests to compare the proportions of the entire 1989 versus 1999 national samples scoring in the normal versus the combined borderline and clinical ranges. The cutpoints for the combined borderline and clinical ranges were based on the lowest 7% of scores in the nonreferred normative sample on the Activities, Social, and School scales; the highest 7% of scores in the nonreferred normative sample on the syndrome and DSM-oriented scales; the lowest 16% in the nonreferred normative sample on the Total Competence scale; and the highest 16% in the nonreferred normative sample on the Internalizing, Externalizing, and Total Problems scales. Details of cutpoints are provided by Achenbach and Rescorla, 2001.

Significantly fewer 1999 children than 1989 children obtained deviant scores on 6 (29%) of the 21 scales, including the Activities, Total Competence, Internalizing, Externalizing, Total Problems, and DSM-oriented Conduct Problems scales. Although Conduct Problems was the only DSM-oriented scale to show a significant change in scores categorized as deviant in 1989 versus 1999, the absolute prevalence rates for deviant scores on the

Table III. Percentage of Deviant Scores on DSM-Oriented Scales in Complete 1989 and 1999 National Samples

| | Percentage of deviant scores[a] | |
Scale	1989	1999
Affective Problems[b]	9.4	8.6
Anxiety Problems	9.5	10.4
Somatic Problems	9.3	7.9
Attention Deficit/ Hyperactivity Problems[c]	2.2	3.5
Oppositional Defiant Problems	10.8	9.3
Conduct Problems[d]	9.2	6.8[e]

[a]Deviant scores include those that were in the combined borderline and clinical ranges defined as being ≥93rd percentile ($T \geq 65$) of nonreferred normative samples of each gender (Achenbach & Rescorla, 2001).
[b]Percentage of deviant scores in both years was reduced by omission of Item 5 (There is very little that he/she enjoys), because it was not included in 1989 assessment.
[c]Percentage of deviant scores in both years was reduced by omission of Items 4 (Fails to finish things he/she starts) and 78 (Inattentive or easily distracted), because they were not included in 1989 assessment.
[d]Percentage of deviant scores in both years was reduced by omission of Item 28 (Breaks rules at home, school, or elsewhere), because it was not included in 1989 assessment.
[e]Deviant scores for Conduct Problems were significantly less prevalent in 1999 than 1989, $\chi^2 = 7.18$, $p = .007$. After Bonferroni correction, $p = .042$.

DSM-oriented scales may be of interest and are shown in Table III. As indicated in the footnotes to Table III, the percentage of deviant scores in both years was reduced by omission of items that changed from 1989 to 1999 on the following scales: Affective Problems, Attention Deficit/Hyperactivity Problems, and Conduct Problems.

For the entire 1989 versus 1999 national samples, the percentage of children receiving mental health services in the 12 months preceding the CBCL did not differ significantly (13.2% in 1989 vs. 12.8% in 1999, $p = .75$). Nor did the percentage receiving mental health services differ for children having deviant Total Problems scores (30.5% in 1989 vs. 26.6% in 1999, $p = .26$).

Stability of Item Ranks

To test the stability of problem item rankings, we computed Pearson r between the mean scores obtained by a sample on each item and the mean item scores for other samples. For example, we computed the mean 1976 score on each of the 114 problem items to form one set of 114 scores. We then computed the mean 1989 score on each of the 114 problem items to form a second set of 114 scores. To test the stability of item rankings from

1976 to 1989, we used the formula for Pearson *r* to obtain the correlation between the set of 114 mean item scores in 1976 and the set of 114 mean item scores in 1989. (The correlation between the two sets of item scores can be viewed as a *Q* correlation, because it expressed the association between two sets of scores for numerous variables, rather than an *R* correlation, which would express the association between two variables measured in numerous individuals.) For demographically similar samples, the *r* was .98 between 1976 and 1989 scores, .94 between 1976 and 1999, and .97 between 1989 and 1999. For competence items, *r* was .99 between 1976 and 1989, .97 between 1976 and 1999, and .98 between 1989 and 1999.

To identify problem items that showed the biggest changes from one demographically similar sample to another, we ranked the item means from 1 (highest mean) to 114 in each demographically similar sample. Seven out of 114 items (6%) showed significant ($p < .01$) increases of ≥ 15 ranks from 1976 to later years. The percentage of change in the mean score for each of these seven items is shown in Table IV. For example, Item 11's rank rose from 46 in 1976 to 31 in 1999. Its mean increased from .15 to .26 (+73%).

The biggest change in mean scores was the increase of 242% from a mean of .04 in 1976 to a mean of .10 in 1999 for the open-ended item 113 (Other Problems), which reflected parents' increased tendency to report more problems that were not listed on the CBCL. However, even the 1999 mean was only .10 on a 0–1–2 scale. Other items

Table IV. Items That Rose ≥ 15 Ranks From One Matched Sample to Another

	Rank		
Item[a]	1976	1989	1999
11. Too dependent	46 (+73%[c])	41	31
39. Bad companions	75 (+118%[b]) (+162%[c])	60	47
58. Picks body parts	61 (+130%[c])	48	37
61. Poor school work	50 (+100%[b])	35	36
102. Underactive	83 (+117%[c])	69	68
109. Whining	56 (+117%[b]) (+175%[c])	37	23
113. Other problems	92 (+242%[c])	88	73

Note. The numbers in the columns headed 1976, 1989, and 1999 are the items' ranks in those years. The item with the highest mean score was ranked 1. Percentages in parentheses indicate significant ($p < .01$) changes in mean scores when items whose wording did not change rose ≥ 15 ranks. No items showed significant decreases of ≥ 15 ranks.
[a]Items are listed with the number that they have on the CBCL and summaries of their content.
[b]Percent change in mean score to 1989.
[c]Percent change in mean score to 1999.

that rose ≥ 15 ranks and $\geq 150\%$ in mean scores included 39 (Hangs around with others who get in trouble), rising 118% from 1976 to 1989 and 162% from 1976 to 1999 (mean = .07, .15, .18); and 109 (Whining), rising 117% from 1976 to 1989 and 175% from 1976 to 1999 (.12, .26, .33). There were no significant decreases of ≥ 15 ranks.

Columbine Shootings

The Columbine shootings occurred on 4/20/99. To assess the effects of the resulting publicity, we compared CBCL scores obtained in our 1999 national sample by 529 children from 2/3/99 through 4/19/99 with scores obtained by 377 children from 4/21/99 through 7/31/99, using MANCOVAs and ANCOVAs like those described earlier. No significant effects were found: Mean Total Problems scores were 24.4 before versus 24.2 after Columbine.

DISCUSSION

Are American children's problems still getting worse? When analyzed in multiple ways, parents' responses to the CBCL in 1976, 1989, and 1999 consistently gave the following answer: Changes in item and scale scores from 1976 to 1989 reflected increasing problems and decreasing competencies, but these trends were reversed from 1989 to 1999. When we compared quantitative scores for demographically similar nonreferred children across 1976, 1989, and 1999, all 21 competence and problem scales showed significant effects of year. The 1989 sample obtained the lowest competence scores and the highest problem scores on 19 of the 21 scales.

When the entire 1989 and 1999 national samples were quantitatively compared, eight scale scores showed significant improvements, whereas only the DSM-oriented Oppositional Defiant Problems scale indicated more problems in 1999. Individual items bore out the scale score findings, with most significant differences reflecting lower competence scores and higher problem scores in 1989 than 1999. Although less sensitive than quantitative comparisons, all six significant categorical comparisons reflected declines in the prevalence of deviant scores from 1989 to 1999.

Did the 1999 problem scores return to the 1976 levels? As shown by the solid line in Fig. 1 for the demographically similar samples, the 1999 Total Problems mean of 21.4 was about midway between the means for 1976 (18.0) and 1989 (24.3). As shown by the broken line in Fig. 1 for the demographically similar samples, the 1999 Total Competence mean of 25.3 was nonsignificantly higher than the 1976 mean of 25.1, and both were significantly higher than the 1989 mean of 24 2. The competence and problem scores were not merely mirror images of each other, as indicated by the following low concurrent correlations between them: $-.20$ in 1976, $-.16$ in 1989, and $-.31$ in 1999 (all $p < .01$). (Note that the concurrent correlations were negative in each year, because high competence scores were associated with relatively low problem scores.)

Mental Health Services

Because detailed service data were not obtained in 1976 and referred children were excluded from that sample, we compared mental health service rates only for the entire 1989 versus 1999 national samples. In answering the interview question about whether their child had been seen by mental health professionals in the preceding 12 months, 13.2% of parents said "yes" in 1989 versus 12.8% in 1999, a nonsignificant difference ($p = .75$). For children who had deviant Total Problems scores, 30.5% of parents reported services in 1989 versus 26.6% in 1999, also a nonsignificant difference ($p = .26$). The prevalence rates of mental health services thus did not change significantly from 1989 to 1999, either for the entire national samples or for children with deviant CBCL Total Problems scores.

Demographic Differences

Interactions of assessment year with gender and age did not exceed chance expectations, nor did informant effects tested as covariates. The overall patterns of 1976, 1989, and 1999 scores were thus not affected by the children's gender or age, nor by whether informants were mothers or others. Across 1976, 1989, and 1999, some mean scale scores did differ significantly by gender, age, SES, and ethnicity, as shown in Table II. On the problem scales, effects of ethnicity did not exceed chance expectations, whereas SES effects did not exceed 1% ES. The larger effects of SES and ethnicity on the competence scales reflected the commonly found tendency for such scores to be lower for lower SES and minority groups.

Stability and Change in Item Ranks

Correlations between mean item scores indicated very high stability from 1976 to 1989 and 1999, and from 1989 to 1999, ranging from .94 to .98 for problem items and .97 to .99 for competence items. Despite overall increases in scores from 1976 to 1989 and decreases from

1989 to 1999, there was thus great consistency in the items that parents scored highest, intermediate, and lowest across 23 years. Nevertheless, as shown in Table IV, the following items rose the most in rank order and mean scores: Items 39 (Hangs around with others who get in trouble); 109 (Whining); and 113. (Other problems).

The most worrisome increase was for Item 39, which reflects rising concerns about children's peers, despite decreases in most other 1999 problem scores. Most cross-cultural comparisons have not revealed especially high scores for American children on Item 39 (Achenbach et al., 1990; Achenbach, Hensley, Phares, & Grayson, 1990; Achenbach, Verhulst, Baron, & Akkerhuis, 1987; Stanger, Fombonne, & Achenbach, 1994; Weisz et al., 1987). Besides our own, the only other published test of secular trends in CBCL problem scores also revealed a significant rise from 1983 to 1993 on Item 39 for Dutch children (Verhulst et al., 1997).

The rise in scores on Item 109 (Whining) may reflect a continuing intensification of particular childrearing dynamics. Although it could also reflect a change in parent's perceptions of what constitutes whining, this item was one of the five that showed significant increases of ≥ 15 ranks in teachers' ratings over an 18-year period (Achenbach, Dumenci, & Rescorla, 2002a). Although other cross-cultural comparisons have not revealed elevated scores for whining among American children, the biggest difference between American and Jamaican children's problems reflected higher American scores on Item 109 (Lambert, Knight, Taylor, & Achenbach, 1994).

Perspectives on Secular Trends

Parents' responses to the CBCL indicate that American children's functioning is not steadily worsening. According to quantitative and categorical analyses of diverse competence and problem scores, parents' reports revealed significant improvements from 1989 to 1999, which followed significant worsening from 1976 to 1989. Although the present data reflect parents' perceptions, teacher reports and self-reports have indicated similar secular trends (Achenbach et al., 2002a,b). There is thus consistency in reports by three important types of informants regarding children's functioning. Causation is hard to test, but it can be speculated that childrearing conditions were enhanced by better economic conditions, lower unemployment, and less crime during the 1990s than the 1980s.

The closest parallel to the present study is the *Monitoring the Future* study (Johnston et al., 2001) of drug use reported by national samples of American students since 1975. Ups and downs in use of particular drugs have primarily reflected market factors specific to those drugs, rather than changes in overall levels of problems. With respect to psychopathology, there is a paucity of standardized national data for any single point in time, much less for comparisons at different points in time (Indictors of Children's Wellbeing, 2002). Various sources suggest a point-prevalence rate of about 20% for child mental disorders (Manteuffel, Stephens, & Santiago, 2002). This approximates the 21.9% of our complete 1999 national sample having Total Problems scores in the combined borderline and clinical ranges. In the absence of a national system for collecting standardized data on children receiving mental health services, our findings of 13.2% receiving services in 1989 and 12.8% in 1999 are probably good benchmarks that indicate remarkable stability over a decade. In one of the few comparable studies, early 1990s samples from three eastern urban areas yielded a 9.1% rate, but this excluded inpatient, residential, and school services (Leaf et al., 1996).

Rutter and Smith's (1995) conclusions that adolescent disorders increased over the preceding 50 years reflect the pathological extremes of problems. By contrast, Fergusson's (1996) hypothesis that increasing social diversity might promote more cases of good adjustment, as well as more disorders, encourages examination of entire distributions of functioning rather than just the pathological extremes. Consistent with Fergusson's hypothesis, standard deviations of Total Problems scores increased across the 1976, 1989, and 1999 demographically similar samples (15.1, 16.3, 16.9) and across the 1989 and 1999 national samples (18.2, 19.0). The increases were significant by Levene's test for 1976 versus 1989 ($p = .036$) and 1976 versus 1999 ($p < .01$) but not 1989 versus 1999. Despite the conventional wisdom that kids are getting worse, broad distributions of functioning must be assessed to detect improvement as well as worsening.

Can dramatic events affect parents' reports of children's problems? We found no significant differences between CBCL scores obtained in the months preceding versus following the Columbine shootings, with mean Total Problems scores being 24.4 versus 24.2. This suggests that parents' reports of their children's behavior are not significantly affected by publicity about youthful deviance.

Limitations

Comprehensive assessment of children typically requires data from teachers and the children themselves, as well as from parents. Our 23-year comparison was limited to parent data, because only parent data were obtained in 1976. Furthermore, the 1976 sample was drawn only

from Washington, DC, Maryland, and Virginia. However, teachers' reports for 1981–82 samples from Nebraska, Tennessee, and Pennsylvania and for our 1989 and 1999 national samples also revealed significant increases in problems in 1989 and decreases in 1999. In addition, youths' self-reports revealed small decreases in problems from our 1989 to our 1999 national samples (Achenbach, Dumenci, & Rescorla, 2002a,b).

Epidemiological data are sometimes weighted to compensate for high attrition, for over- or undersampling of particular groups, and for other deviations from representativeness. Although the original report of our 1976 sample used weighting (Achenbach & Edelbrock, 1981), our 1989 and 1999 national probability sampling designs and high completion rates obviated any likely benefits of weighting.

Clinical Implications

Clinical services aim to help individuals. Yet, to evaluate individuals' needs for services, clinicians need norms to identify deviance from developmentally appropriate functioning. Like standardized ability tests, standardized and normed procedures can help clinicians identify deviance from prevailing levels of behavioral/emotional problems and competencies.

To be valid, norms must be based on large, representative samples of relevant populations and must be periodically updated. We found that parents reported significantly fewer problems and more competencies in 1999 than 1989. The 1999 competence scores were similar to 1976 scores but 1999 problem scores were higher than 1976 problem scores. The findings were similar for empirically based syndromes and for DSM-oriented scales that comprise problems identified by psychiatrists and psychologists from 16 cultures as being very consistent with DSM categories.

To facilitate clinical applications, data from the 1999 national sample are incorporated into normed profiles for hand scoring and computer scoring both the empirically based syndromes and DSM-oriented scales (Achenbach & Rescorla, 2001). Secular changes may also need to be considered in diagnostic criteria. For example, the steady increase from 1976 to 1999 in scores for *Hangs around with others who get in trouble* may be relevant to future criteria for the Adolescent Onset Type of Conduct Disorder (APA, 1994).

Steady increases in scores for *Whining* according to both parent and teacher reports may reflect trends in child-rearing dynamics. Although whining may not seem clinically important, ANCOVAs have shown that this item

Are Children's Problems Getting Worse? 11

was significantly associated with referral for mental health services according to both parent ratings (ES = 6%) and teacher ratings (ES = 5%; Achenbach & Rescorla, 2001). The ES of 6 and 5% indicated large enough elevations in scores for whining among referred children to suggest that it deserves clinical attention.

ACKNOWLEDGMENTS

This work was supported by NIMH Grant MH40305 and the Research Center for Children, Youth, and Families. We are grateful to David Fergusson, Robert Krueger, Stephanie McConaughy, and Frank Verhulst for their helpful comments on drafts of this paper.

REFERENCES

Achenbach, T. M. (1991). *Manual for the Child Behavior Checklist/4-18 and 1991 Profile.* Burlington, VT: University of Vermont Department of Psychiatry.

Achenbach, T. M., Bird, H. R., Canino, G. J., Phares, V., Gould, M., & Rubio-Stipec, M. (1990). Epidemiological comparisons of Puerto Rican and U.S. mainland children: Parent, teacher, and self reports. *Journal of the American Academy of Child and Adolescent Psychiatry, 29,* 84–93.

Achenbach, T. M., Dumenci, L., & Rescorla, L. A. (2002a). Is American student behavior getting worse? Teacher ratings over an 18-year period. *School Psychology Review, 31,* 428–442.

Achenbach, T. M., Dumenci, L., & Rescorla, L. A. (2002b). Ten-year comparisons of problems and competencies for national samples of youth: Self, parent, and teacher reports. *Journal of Emotional and Behavioral Disorders, 10,* 194–203.

Achenbach, T. M., & Edelbrock, C. (1981). Behavioral problems and competencies reported by parents of normal and disturbed children aged four to sixteen. *Monographs of the Society for Research in Child Development, 46* (Serial No. 188).

Achenbach, T. M., Hensley, V. R., Phares, V., & Grayson, D. (1990). Problems and competencies reported by parents of Australian and American children. *Journal of Child Psychology and Psychiatry, 31,* 265–286.

Achenbach, T. M., & Howell, C. T. (1993). Are American children's problems getting worse? A 13-year comparison. *Journal of the American Academy of Child and Adolescent Psychiatry, 32,* 1145–1154.

Achenbach, T. M., Howell, C. T., Quay, H. C., & Conners, C. K. (1991). National survey of problems and competencies among 4- to 16-year-olds: Parents' reports for normative and clinical samples. *Monographs of the Society for Research in Child Development, 56* (Serial No. 225).

Achenbach, T. M., & Rescorla, L. A. (2001). *Manual for the ASEBA School-Age Forms and Profiles.* Burlington, VT: University of Vermont Research Center for Children, Youth, and Families.

Achenbach, T. M., Verhulst, F. C., Baron, G. D., & Akkerhuis, G. W. (1987). Epidemiological comparisons of American and Dutch children: I. Behavioral/emotional problems and competencies reported by parents for ages 4 to 16. *Journal of the American Academy of Child and Adolescent Psychiatry, 26,* 317–325.

American Psychiatric Association. (1994). *Diagnostic and statistical manual of mental disorders* (4th ed.). Washington, DC: American Psychiatric Association.

Bérubé, R. L., & Achenbach, T. M. (2003). *Bibliography of published studies using the Achenbach System of Empirically Based Assessment (ASEBA): 2003 edition.* Burlington, VT: University of Vermont Research Center for Children, Youth, and Families.

Cohen, J. (1988). *Statistical power analysis for the behavioral sciences* (2nd ed.). New York: Academic Press.

Fergusson, D. M. (1996). Critical notice. *Journal of Child Psychology and Psychiatry, 37,* 485–487.

Hollingshead, A. B. (1957). *Two factor index of social position.* Unpublished paper, Yale University Department of Sociology, New Haven, CT.

Hollingshead, A. B. (1975). *Four factor index of social status.* Unpublished paper, Yale University Department of Sociology, New Haven, CT.

Indicators of Children's Wellbeing. (2002). http://childStats.gov

Johnston, L. D., O'Malley, P. M., & Bachman, J. G. (2001). *Monitoring the future.* Bethesda, MD: National Institute on Drug Abuse.

Lambert, M. C., Knight, F., Taylor, R., & Achenbach, T. M. (1994). Epidemiology of behavioral and emotional problems among children of Jamaica and the United States: Parent reports for ages 6–11. *Journal of Abnormal Child Psychology, 22,* 113–128.

Leaf, P. J., Alegria, M., Cohen, P., Goodman, S. H., Horwitz, S. M., Hoven, C. W., Narrow, W. E., Vaden-Kierman, M., & Regier, D. A. (1996). Mental health service use in the community and schools: Results from the Four-Community MECA Study. *Journal of the American Academy of Child and Adolescent Psychiatry, 35,* 889–897.

Males, M. (1991). Teen suicide and changing cause-of-death certification, 1953–1987. *Suicide and Life-Threatening Behavior, 21,* 245–259.

Manteuffel, B., Stephens, R. L., & Santiago, R. (2002). Overview of the National Evaluation of the Comprehensive Community Mental Health Services for Children and Their Families Program and summary of current findings. *Child Services: Social Policy, Research, and Practice, 5,* 3–20.

Roberts, R. E., Attkisson, C., & Rosenblatt, A. (1998). Prevalence of psychopathology among children and adolescents. *American Journal of Psychiatry, 55,* 715–725.

Rutter, M., & Smith, D. J. (Eds.). (1995). *Psychosocial disorders in young people: Time, trends, and their causes.* Chichester: Wiley.

Sakoda, J. M., Cohen, B. H., & Beall, G. (1954). Test of significance for a series of statistical tests. *Psychological Bulletin, 51,* 172–175.

Stanger, C., Fombonne, E., & Achenbach, T. M. (1994). Epidemiological comparisons of American and French children: Parent reports of problems and competencies for ages 6–11. *European Child and Adolescent Psychiatry, 3,* 16–29.

Verhulst, F. C., van der Ende, J. R. A., & Rietbergen, A. (1997). Ten-year time trends of psychopathology in Dutch children and adolescents: No evidence for strong trends. *Acta Psychiatrica Scandinavica, 96,* 7–13.

Weisz, J. R., Suwanlert, S., Chaiyasit, W., Weiss, B., Achenbach, T. M., & Walter, B. R. (1987). Epidemiology of behavioral and emotional problems among Thai and American children: Parent reports for ages 6–11. *Journal of the American Academy of Child and Adolescent Psychiatry, 26,* 890–897.

Name Index

Abelson, R. 214
Achenbach, T.M. xxi, 321, 342, 357, 358, 361, 365–75
Adams, B.N. 166
Ainsworth, Leonard 7, 9
Ainsworth, Mary D. Salter xii, xxii, 5–13
Alexander, Karl L. xviii, 185–98
Allport, G.W. 211
Alpert, J.E. 316
Altham, P.M.E. 328
Anderson, J.C. 309
Angold, Adrian xix, xxi, xxii, 233–47, 249–66,
    267–89, 297, 309–39
Anthony, J.C. 328
Astone, N.M. 157
Attkisson, C. 365
Axford, Nick xi

Baker, Jessica H. xvi, 93–104
Baron, R. 171
Bates, J.E. 204, 215
Bauman, M.L. 258
Bayley, Nancy 45
Bell, R.Q. 84
Bell, S.M. 10
Belsky, J. 146
Berkson, J. 314, 319
Berliner, David 194
Biederman, J. 320
Bird, Hector 315
Black, J.E. 18
Blatz, William E. 6–7
Block, J. 204–5
Block, J.H. 205
Bolger, K.E. 168
Bouchard, T. 90
Bowlby, John xii, xxii, 5–13, 128, 139
Bradley, Robert H. xviii, 155–83, 160, 162, 165,
    166, 170
Bremner, J. Douglas xvii, 117–25
Bretherton, I. 10
Brody, G.H. 143, 168
Bronfenbrenner, Urie xiv, 163
Brook, D.W. 329
Brook, J.S. 329
Brooks-Gunn, J. 165, 172, 173, 174
Brown, G.W. 11

Burton, L.M. 50
Buss, Emily xi

Cairns, R.B. 270
Caldwell, B.M. 165
Canino, G. 296
Caron, C. 309
Caspi, Avshalom xviii, xxi, 199–229, 259
Cederblad, M. 342
Champagne, Frances A. xvi, 105–10
Chess, S. 200
Chomsky, N. 82
Ciccheti, D. 250
Clark, L.A. 214
Clarkin, J.F. 309
Clausen, John 45, 53
Cloninger, C.R. 201
Cohen, J. 358, 359, 369
Cohen, Patricia 315, 326, 329
Coleman, J.S. 156
Collishaw, S. 251, 341–53, 361
Compas, B.E. 172
Conger, R.D. 143, 161
Corwyn, Robert F. xviii, 155–83
Corzine, J. 162
Costello, E. Jane xix, xx, xxiii, 249–66, 251–68,
    309–39, 361
Courtney, Mark xi
Crick, N.R. 209
Croft, C. 26
Curley, James P. xvi, 105–10

Darwin, Charles 12
Dawkins, R. 94
DeFries, J.C. 281
DeGarmo, D.S. 160
Dodge, K.A. 209
Dolan, A.B. 88
Dos Reis, S. 306
Dumaret, A.C. 25
Dumenci, Levant 365–75
Duncan, G.J. 173
Duyme, M. 25

Earls, F. 174
Earls, Tony 233

Eaton, W.O. 204
Eaves, L.J. 278, 280
Eder, R. 228
Egger, Helen 233–47
Eisenberg, N. 206
Elder, Glen H. Jr xiii, 45, 143
Elkins, I.J. 101
Ennett, S.T. 174
Entwisle, D.R. 157, 174, 185–98
Erikson, Erik 7
Erkanli, Alaattin 309–39
Escalona, S.C. 84
Evans, G.W. 165
Eysenck, H.J. 207

Faraone, S.V. 314
Fava, M. 328
Fergusson, D.M. 325, 365, 366, 374
Ferri, E. 351
Fleming, J.P. 328
Fodor, J. 82
Foley, Debra L. 249–66, 251
Fombonne, E. 252, 315
Ford, Tamsin xx, 291–9, 301–7
Foster, E.M. 242, 243
Freud, Anna 6
Freud, Sigmund 6, 117
Frick, P.J. 324
Fulker, D.W. 283

Garbarino, J. 174
Garber, J. 250
Garmezy, N. 172, 250
Gately, T. 174
Gesell, A. 82
Glueck, Eleanor 52, 66
Glueck, Sheldon 52, 66
Goldsmith, H.H. 227, 228
Goodman, E. 159
Goodman, Robert 291–9, 301–7, 341–53
Goodyer, I.M. 328
Gottlieb, G. 81, 83
Graziano, W.G. 206
Green, J.A. 270
Greenberg, M.T. 174
Greenough, W.T. 18
Grissmer, David W. 194
Guo, G. 165
Gurvits, T.G. 121

Haeckel, Ernst 34
Hareven, Tamara 48
Harlow, Harry 8, 106

Harris, K.M. 165
Harris, T. 11
Hart, B. 160
Hauser, Robert M. 194
Heinicke, Christoph 8
Herbert, J. 328
Herjanic, M. 312
Hertzman, C. 159
Heyns, Barbara 185
Hinde, Robert 8
Hodges, J. 27
Hoff-Ginsberg, E. 160
Hollingshead, A.B. 367
Holmbeck, Grayson N. 138
Holzer, C.E. 241
Howell, C.T. 366, 367
Hubel, D.H. 19
Huxley, Julian 7
Hviid, A. 258

Ilg, F.L. 82

Jaffee, S.R. 76, 251
Jencks, C. 173
Jensen, P.S. 319
Jones, Harold 45
Jones, Mary 45

Kagan, J. 18
Kamin, L.J. 88
Kaoukji, Dwan
Kaplow, J.B. 256
Kashani, J.H. 310
Kaslow, N.J. 328
Keating, D.P. 112
Kelvin, R.G. 328
Kendall, P.C. 309
Kendler, Kenneth S. xvi, 93–104, 280
Kennedy, W. 159
Kenny, D. 171
Kessler, R.C. 251, 252
Klebanov, P.K. 174
Klein, Melanie 8
Klein, R.G. 322
Klerman, L.V. 163
Klopfer, Bruno 7
Kohn, M.L. 160
Kovacs, M. 324, 328
Kraepelin, E. 117
Krantz, J.Z. 88

Lahey, B. 253
Laub, J. 66

Laurent, J. 328
Leventhal, T. 172, 173, 174
Lewinsohn, P.M. 253–4, 255, 319, 324, 328
Little, Michael xi–xxiv
Loeber, R. 323, 329
Lord, F.M. 278
Lorenz, Konrad 7
Lytton, H. 84, 90

M'Jid, Najat xi
McCall, R.B. 86
McCartney, Kathleen xv, 81–92, 102
Maccoby, E.E. 84
McEwen, Bruce 118
Macfarlane, Jean 45, 53
MacLean, Mavis xi
McLoyd, V.C. 166, 168
McNally, R.J. 121
Maddocks, A. 328
Madsen, K.M. 258
Main, Mary 12
Marjoribanks, K. 160
Marshall, W.A. 33
Martin, C.A. 114
Masten, Ann S. xvii, 133–53
Matheny, A.P. 88
Maughan, Barbara xi–xxiv, 127–31, 341–53
Mayer, S. 173
Mead, Margaret 7
Meaney, Michael 74
Meehl, P.E. 267, 282, 284, 285
Meltzer, Howard 291–9, 301–7
Menaghan, E.G. 160
Mendel, Gregor 74
Mercer, Edith 7
Mercy, J.A. 159–60
Milberger, S. 320
Mineka, S. 214
Modell, J. 48
Moffitt, T.E. 253
Mortorell, R. 163
Mpofu, E. 160
Murphy, G.E. 312

Nelson, K.B. 258
Neugarten, Bernice 49
Novick, M.R. 282

O, Anna 117
O'Connor, Thomas G. 17–30, 76
Olfson, M. 242
Olson, Linda Steffel 185–98
Ortega, S.T. 162

Orvaschel, H. 322
Osofsky, J.D. 173

Parcel, T.L. 160
Parkes, Colin Murray 11
Patton, George C. xiii, 33–42, 237
Paus, T. 111
Pearson, J. 328
Petronis, K.R. 328
Piaget, Jean 7, 82, 83
Pickles, Andrew xix, 27, 267–89, 341–53
Plato, 284
Plomin, R. 83–4, 90, 94
Pollitt, E. 163
Posner, M.I. 205
Power, C. 159

Quinton, D. 65

Rahim, S.I.A. 342
Reitzle, M. 327
Rescorla, Leslie A. 357, 358, 365–75
Riser-Danner, L. 227
Risley, T.R. 160
Roberts, R.E. 350, 365
Robertson, James 6, 7, 8
Robins, L. 251, 329
Rohde, P. 315, 328
Rosenbaum, J.F. 328
Rosenblatt, A. 365
Rothbart, M.K. 201, 202, 204, 205, 215
Roy, P. 27
Rutter, Michael xii, xiii, xv, xxii, 17–30, 59–70, 73–9, 131, 250, 251, 259, 268, 278, 309, 351, 365, 374

Sampson, R. 66
Santalahti, P. 361
Sapolsky, Robert 118
Sass, K.J. 120
Scarr, Sandra xv, 81–92, 102, 159–60
Schooler, C. 160
Schoon, I. 351
Secher, S.M. 328
Seeman, T.E. 171
Shaffer, Anne xvii, 133–53
Sheline, Y. 121
Shin, L.M. 121
Shiner, Rebecca xviii, 199–229
Smith, D.J. 131, 351, 365, 374
Smith, J.R. 160
Smith, R.S. xviii, 217
Snidman, N. 260

Sonuga-Barke, E.J.S. 274
Sourander, A. 361
Spitz, R.A. 139
Sroufe, Alan 12,
Sroufe, L.A. 250
Stark, K.D. 328
Stayton, D.J. 10
Steelman, L.C. 159–60
Stein, B.D. 242
Stein, E. 306
Stein, M.B. 121
Steinberg, Laurence xvii, 111–6
Steinhaussen, H.C. 327
Stolz, Lois 52
Sung, M. 255
Susser, Ezra 261
Susser, Mervin 261
Sweeting, H. 350, 351

Tancer, N.K. 322
Tanner, J.M. 33
Taylor, S.E. 171
Terman, Lewis 46, 47, 50, 52, 53
Thoburn, June xi
Thomas, A. 200
Thomas, C.R. 241
Thompson, C. 256
Tick, N.T. xxi, 355–64
Tizard, B. 27
Tomkiewicz, S. 25
Treiber, R. 159
Tremblay, R.E. 250–1

Valenzuela, M. 164
Van den Boom, D.C. 145
Van den Brink, W. 214
Van den Oord, E. 278

Van der Ende, J. 355–64
Van de Vijver, F.J.R. 160
Vega, W. 251
Verheul, R. 214
Verhulst, F.C. 355–64
Vikan, A. 315
Viner, Russell xiii, 33–42
Von Bertalanffy, Ludwig 7
Vostanis, Panos 301–7

Waddington, C.H. 85
Wakefield, A.J. 257
Walberg, H.J. 160
Waldman, I. 278
Wallace, C.S. 18
Watson, D. 214
Weinberg, R.A. 86, 88, 159–60
Weisz, John 242
Werner, E.E. xviii, 217
Werry, J.S. 322
West, P. 350, 351
Whitaker, A.G. 256
White, K.R. 160
Widiger, T.A. 214
Wiesel, T.N. 19
Williamson, D.E. 328
Wills, T.A. 169
Wilson, M. 268
Wilson, R.S. 88,
Wilson, W.J. 173
Wittig, Barbara 9, 10
Wolkind, S.N. 27
Woodruff, R.A. 312

Young, G. 174

Zoccolillo, M. 325, 327